Visual Basic 2005 Cookbook™

Other resources from O'Reilly

Related titles
ASP.NET 2.0 Cookbook™
Programming Atlas
Programming .NET
  Components
Programming ASP.NET
Programming Visual Basic
  2005

VB.NET Language Pocket
  Reference
Visual Basic 2005 in a
  Nutshell
Visual Basic 2005 Jumpstart
Visual Basic 2005:
  A Developer's Notebook™
Visual Studio Hacks™

oreilly.com
oreilly.com is more than a complete catalog of O'Reilly books. You'll also find links to news, events, articles, weblogs, sample chapters, and code examples.

oreillynet.com is the essential portal for developers interested in open and emerging technologies, including new platforms, programming languages, and operating systems.

Conferences
O'Reilly brings diverse innovators together to nurture the ideas that spark revolutionary industries. We specialize in documenting the latest tools and systems, translating the innovator's knowledge into useful skills for those in the trenches. Visit *conferences.oreilly.com* for our upcoming events.

Safari Bookshelf (*safari.oreilly.com*) is the premier online reference library for programmers and IT professionals. Conduct searches across more than 1,000 books. Subscribers can zero in on answers to time-critical questions in a matter of seconds. Read the books on your Bookshelf from cover to cover or simply flip to the page you need. Try it today for free.

Visual Basic 2005 Cookbook™

Tim Patrick and John Clark Craig

O'REILLY®

Beijing · Cambridge · Farnham · Köln · Paris · Sebastopol · Taipei · Tokyo

Visual Basic 2005 Cookbook™
by Tim Patrick and John Clark Craig

Copyright © 2006 O'Reilly Media, Inc. All rights reserved.
Printed in the United States of America.

Published by O'Reilly Media, Inc., 1005 Gravenstein Highway North, Sebastopol, CA 95472.

O'Reilly books may be purchased for educational, business, or sales promotional use. Online editions are also available for most titles (*safari.oreilly.com*). For more information, contact our corporate/institutional sales department: (800) 998-9938 or *corporate@oreilly.com*.

Editor: John Osborn	**Indexer:** John Bickelhaupt
Production Editor: Colleen Gorman	**Cover Designer:** Karen Montgomery
Copyeditor: Rachel Wheeler	**Interior Designer:** David Futato
Proofreader: Mary Anne Mayo	**Illustrators:** Robert Romano and Jessamyn Read

Printing History:

September 2006: First Edition.

 This book uses RepKover™, a durable and flexible lay-flat binding.

ISBN-10: 0-596-10177-5
ISBN-13: 978-0-596-10177-0

[M]

In loving memory of Jeanie Craig (1950–2005).
Jeanie... Thank you for sharing your life, your
spirit, and your love. Our dreams go on, and our
love is eternal.

—John Craig

To my parents, Don and Darla, who both know
how to cook.

—Tim Patrick

Table of Contents

Preface . . . . **xvii**

1. Visual Basic Programming **1**
  1.1 Creating a Windows Forms Application   1
  1.2 Creating a Console Application   10
  1.3 Creating an ASP.NET Web Forms Application   13

2. The Development Environment **21**
  2.1 Discovering and Using a Code Snippet   21
  2.2 Creating a New Snippet   23
  2.3 Sharing Snippets   26
  2.4 Adding Snippet Files to Visual Studio   26
  2.5 Getting an Application's Version Number   27
  2.6 Letting Visual Studio Automatically Update an Application's
       Version Number   28
  2.7 Setting the Startup Form for an Application   29
  2.8 Setting the Startup to a Sub Main Procedure   30
  2.9 Getting an Application's Command Line   31
  2.10 Testing an Application's Command Line   33
  2.11 Obfuscating an Application   33
  2.12 Determining if an Application Is Running in the Visual Studio
       Environment   36
  2.13 Accessing Environment Variables   36
  2.14 Accessing the Registry   37
  2.15 Getting System Information   40
  2.16 Getting the User's Name   44

3. Application Organization **45**

    3.1 Creating a Code Module   45

    3.2 Creating a Class   47

    3.3 Creating a Structure   50

    3.4 Creating Other Item Types   52

    3.5 Creating Object Instances   56

    3.6 Initializing a Class Instance with Data   57

    3.7 Releasing an Instance's Resources   59

    3.8 Using Namespaces   61

    3.9 Splitting a Class Across Multiple Files   63

    3.10 Creating a Form Based on Another Form   64

    3.11 Passing and Returning Structures and Other Objects   65

    3.12 Creating and Using an Enumeration   66

    3.13 Converting Between Numeric and String Enumeration Values   68

    3.14 Creating a Method That Accepts Different Sets of Arguments   69

    3.15 Using Standard Operators for Nonstandard Purposes   70

    3.16 Enforcing Strong Data Typing in an Otherwise Weakly Typed
Collection   73

4. Forms, Controls, and Other Useful Objects **77**

    4.1 Creating and Adding Controls at Runtime   77

    4.2 Iterating Through All Controls on a Form   79

    4.3 Sharing Event-Handler Logic Among Many Controls   81

    4.4 Working with Timers   82

    4.5 Determining if a Control Can Take the Focus   83

    4.6 Programmatically Clicking a Button   84

    4.7 Drawing a Control   84

    4.8 Making a Form the Top-Most Form   87

    4.9 Indicating the Accept and Cancel Buttons on a Form   87

    4.10 Remembering a Form's Position Between Uses   88

    4.11 Attaching a Control to the Edge of a Form   90

    4.12 Moving or Resizing Controls as a Form Resizes   92

    4.13 Limiting the Sizing of a Form   95

    4.14 Centering a Form   96

    4.15 Creating and Moving a Borderless Form   96

    4.16 Creating a Fading Form   98

    4.17 Creating a Nonrectangular Form   99

    4.18 Changing Menus at Runtime   101

    4.19 Creating Shortcut Menus   104

5. Strings **107**

   5.1 Using a StringBuilder   107

5.1	Using a StringBuilder	107
5.2	Creating a String of N Identical Characters	109
5.3	Creating a String by Repeating a String N Times	111
5.4	Obfuscating a String	112
5.5	Converting Binary Data to a Hexadecimal String	113
5.6	Extracting Substrings from Larger Strings	115
5.7	Converting a String's Case	116
5.8	Comparing Strings with Case Sensitivity	118
5.9	Comparing Strings Without Case Sensitivity	119
5.10	Converting Strings to and from Character Arrays	120
5.11	Converting Strings to and from Byte Arrays	121
5.12	Tallying Characters	122
5.13	Counting Words	124
5.14	Removing Extra Whitespace	125
5.15	Using the Correct End-of-Line Characters	126
5.16	Replacing Substrings	128
5.17	Inserting a Character or String	129
5.18	Inserting a Line	130
5.19	Double-Spacing a String	133
5.20	Formatting Numbers into Strings	134
5.21	Trimming Sets of Characters from a String	136
5.22	Identifying and Validating Types of Data in a String	137
5.23	Converting Strings Between Encoding Systems	139
5.24	Determining a Character's Type	141
5.25	Parsing Strings	143
5.26	Concatenating Strings	144
5.27	Speeding Up String Manipulation	146
5.28	Counting Occurrences of a Substring	148
5.29	Padding a String for Exact Length and Alignment	150
5.30	Converting Tabs to Spaces	151
5.31	Reversing a String	153
5.32	Shuffling a String	154
5.33	Using a Simple String Encryption	155
5.34	Converting a String to Morse Code	158
5.35	Adding Strings to an Application's Resources	159
5.36	Converting Any Data to a String	161
5.37	Using Regular Expressions to Extract All Numbers	162

5.38 Getting a Count of Regular Expression Matches 164
5.39 Getting the Nth Regular Expression Match 165
5.40 Compiling Regular Expressions for Speed 166
5.41 Using Regular Expressions to Validate Data 168
5.42 Using Regular Expressions to Count Characters, Words, or Lines 169
5.43 Converting a String to and from Base64 170
5.44 Splitting a String 172
5.45 Creating a String of Space Characters 173

6. Numbers and Math **175**
6.1 Using Compact Operator Notation 175
6.2 Choosing Integers of the Right Size and Type for the Job 178
6.3 Using Unsigned Integers 180
6.4 Swapping Two Integers Without Using a Third 181
6.5 Using Single- and Double-Precision Variables 183
6.6 Using Decimal Variables for Maximum Precision 184
6.7 Converting Between Number Types 185
6.8 Rounding Numbers Accurately 188
6.9 Declaring Loop Counters Within Loops 189
6.10 Converting Between Radians and Degrees 190
6.11 Limiting Angles to a Range 191
6.12 Creating Double-Precision Point Variables 193
6.13 Converting Between Rectangular and Polar Coordinates 195
6.14 Creating Three-Dimensional Variables 197
6.15 Converting Between Rectangular, Spherical, and Cylindrical
       Coordinates 198
6.16 Working with Complex Numbers 201
6.17 Solving Right Triangles 204
6.18 Solving Any Triangle 208
6.19 Determining if a String Contains a Valid Number 215
6.20 Converting Numbers to Integers 216
6.21 Calculating π to Thousands of Digits 218
6.22 Getting a Number's Prime Factors 222
6.23 Using Recursion to Calculate Factorials 224
6.24 Manipulating Bits with Bitwise Operators 225
6.25 Storing and Retrieving Bits in a BitArray 227
6.26 Enhancing the Random Number Generator 230
6.27 Generating Random Integers in a Range 234
6.28 Generating Random Real Numbers in a Range 236

6.29   Generating Normal-Distribution Random Numbers   237

6.30   Generating Exponential-Distribution Random Numbers   239

6.31   Creating a Matrix   240

6.32   Inverting a Matrix   241

6.33   Calculating the Determinant of a Matrix   243

6.34   Solving Simultaneous Equations   245

6.35   Listing of the MatrixHelper Class   247

7.   Dates and Times **255**

7.1   Getting the System Date and Time   255

7.2   Accessing the System's Time Zone   257

7.3   Using System Ticks   258

7.4   Timing Application Activities   260

7.5   Calculating Elapsed Time Using Ticks   261

7.6   Calculating Elapsed Time with the Stopwatch   262

7.7   Extracting Year, Month, and Day Numbers from a Date Value   263

7.8   Extracting Hour, Minute, and Second Numbers from a Date Value   264

7.9   Creating a Date or Time Value from Its Parts   266

7.10   Formatting Dates and Times   267

7.11   Parsing and Validating Dates and Times   270

7.12   Adding to Dates and Times   271

7.13   Subtracting from Dates and Times   273

7.14   Determining the Number of Days Between Two Dates   274

7.15   Determining the Day of the Week for a Date   276

7.16   Determining the Day of the Year for a Date   277

7.17   Determining the Number of Days in a Month   277

7.18   Using Controls to Enter or Select a Date   278

7.19   Calculating the Phase of the Moon   281

7.20   Creating a Calendar   282

7.21   Checking for Leap Years   284

7.22   Dates and Times in ISO 8601 Formats   284

8.   Arrays and Collections **286**

8.1   Filling an Array While Declaring It   286

8.2   Sorting Array Elements   287

8.3   Reversing an Array   290

8.4   Inserting into an Array   292

8.5   Shuffling an Array   294

8.6   Swapping Two Array Values   295

8.7 Resizing Arrays Without Losing Existing Values   297
8.8 Quickly Copying Part of an Array into Another   298
8.9 Writing a Comma-Separated-Values File from a String Array   301
8.10 Reading a Comma-Separated-Values File into a String Array   302
8.11 Using a Multivalue Array Instead of a Two-Dimensional Array   304
8.12 Converting Between Delimited Strings and Arrays   306
8.13 Formatting an Array as a Single String   307
8.14 Iterating Through Array Elements   309
8.15 Passing Arrays to Methods   310
8.16 Returning Arrays from Functions   312
8.17 Creating a Collection   313
8.18 Inserting an Item into a Collection   315
8.19 Deleting a Collection Item   316
8.20 Iterating Through a Collection   317

9. Graphics **319**
9.1 Creating Graphics Objects   319
9.2 Drawing on Controls for Special Effects   322
9.3 Letting the User Select a Color   326
9.4 Working with Coordinate Systems (Pixels, Inches, Centimeters)   328
9.5 Creating a Bitmap   332
9.6 Setting a Background Color   335
9.7 Drawing Lines, Ellipses, and Rectangles   336
9.8 Drawing Lines One Pixel Wide Regardless of Scaling   340
9.9 Forcing a Form or Control to Redraw   342
9.10 Using Transparency   345
9.11 Scaling with Transforms   347
9.12 Using an Outline Path   350
9.13 Using Gradients for Smooth Color Changes   352
9.14 Drawing Bezier Splines   355
9.15 Drawing Cardinal Splines   357
9.16 Limiting Display Updates to Specific Regions   359
9.17 Drawing Text   361
9.18 Rotating Text to Any Angle   366
9.19 Mirroring Text on the Canvas   367
9.20 Getting the Height and Width of a Graphic String   370
9.21 Drawing Text with Outlines and Drop Shadows   373
9.22 Calculating a Nice Axis   375
9.23 Drawing a Simple Chart   377

9.24 Creating Odd-Shaped Forms and Controls 381

9.25 Using the RGB, HSB (HSV), and HSL Color Schemes 383

9.26 Creating a Rubber-Band Rectangular Selection 387

9.27 Animating with Transparency 393

9.28 Substitutions for Obsolete Visual Basic 6.0 Features 395

10. Multimedia **399**

10.1 Playing an Audio File 399

10.2 Displaying Image Files 401

10.3 Playing a Video File 403

10.4 Making Your Computer Beep 403

10.5 Creating an Animation Using Multiple Images 405

10.6 Creating an Animation by Generating Multiple Bitmaps 408

10.7 Creating an Animation by Drawing at Runtime 411

10.8 Creating Animated Sprites 412

10.9 Resizing and Compressing JPEG Files 417

10.10 Getting JPEG Extended Information 421

10.11 Creating Thumbnails 424

10.12 Displaying Images While Controlling Stretching and Sizing 424

10.13 Scrolling Images 429

10.14 Merging Two or More Images 431

10.15 Using Resource Images 434

10.16 Capturing an Image of the Screen 435

10.17 Getting Display Dimensions 439

10.18 Speeding Up Image Processing 441

10.19 Converting an Image to Grayscale 445

10.20 Performing Edge Detection on an Image 448

10.21 Full Listing of the LockImage Class 451

11. Printing **457**

11.1 Enumerating Printers 457

11.2 Sending "Raw" Data to a Printer 458

11.3 Get Details About the Default Printer 461

11.4 Creating a Print Preview 462

11.5 Prompting for Printed Page Settings 464

11.6 Drawing Text and Graphics to a Printer 466

11.7 Determining the Print Destination 468

11.8 Creating Graph Paper 470

12. Files and File Systems **473**

   12.1 Enumerating Drives   473

   12.2 Determining if a Directory Exists   475

   12.3 Creating a New Directory   477

   12.4 Copying Directories   478

   12.5 Moving Directories   480

   12.6 Renaming Directories   481

   12.7 Parsing File and Directory Paths   483

   12.8 Searching Iteratively Through Directories and Subdirectories   484

   12.9 Finding Directories and Files Using Wildcards   487

   12.10 Determining if a File Exists   490

   12.11 Getting and Setting File Attributes   491

   12.12 Accessing Special User and Windows Directories   493

   12.13 Determining the Space on a Drive   498

   12.14 Browsing for a Directory   500

   12.15 Getting File Information   502

   12.16 Using File-Access Methods   504

   12.17 Reading and Writing Files as Strings   508

   12.18 Reading and Writing Binary Files   510

   12.19 Copying or Moving a File   511

   12.20 Sending a File to the Recycle Bin   513

   12.21 Creating a Temporary File   514

   12.22 Calculating a Checksum for a File   515

   12.23 Comparing Two Files for Equality   518

   12.24 Locking a File During Access   519

   12.25 Reading from a File at a Specific Position   520

   12.26 Reading and Writing Objects in a File   521

   12.27 Creating a Comma-Separated-Values File   524

13. Databases **526**

   13.1 Connecting to a Data Provider   526

   13.2 Issuing SQL Commands   529

   13.3 Retrieving Results from a Database Query   530

   13.4 Using SQL Parameters   532

   13.5 Using Stored Procedures   534

   13.6 Using Transactions   536

   13.7 Storing the Results of a Query in Memory   537

   13.8 Creating In-Memory Data Tables Manually   541

13.9   Writing In-Memory Data Tables to an XML File   542

13.10   Reading an XML File into In-Memory Data Tables   544

14.   Special Programming Techniques **545**

14.1   Preventing Multiple Instances of a Running Application   545

14.2   Creating a Simple User Control   548

14.3   Describing User Control Properties   552

14.4   Starting Other Applications by EXE, Document, or URL   554

14.5   Waiting for Applications to Finish   556

14.6   List All Running Processes   557

14.7   Terminating a Running Process   558

14.8   Pausing Execution of a Program   560

14.9   Control Applications by Simulating Keystrokes   561

14.10   Watching for File and Directory Changes   565

14.11   Creating an Icon in the System Tray   568

14.12   Accessing the Clipboard   569

14.13   Adding Tooltips to Controls   573

14.14   Dragging and Dropping Files to a ListBox   574

14.15   Dragging and Dropping Between ListBox Controls   576

14.16   Disposing of Objects Appropriately   580

14.17   Fine-Tuning Garbage Collection   582

14.18   Moving the (Mouse) Cursor   584

14.19   Intercepting All Key Presses on a Form   585

14.20   Accessing the Registry   586

14.21   Running Procedures in Threads   592

14.22   Reading XML into a TreeView   596

14.23   Creating an XML Document   599

14.24   Validating an XML Document   604

14.25   Using Generic Collections   605

14.26   Creating a Screensaver   607

14.27   Localizing the Controls on a Form   613

14.28   Adding Pop-up Help to Controls   616

14.29   Maintaining User-Specific Settings Between Uses of an Application   617

14.30   Verifying a Credit Card Number   619

14.31   Capturing a Console Application's Output   621

14.32   Reading an Assembly's Details   624

14.33   Performing Serial I/O   627

14.34   Rebooting the System   629

15. Exceptions **633**

    15.1 Catching an Exception   633

    15.2 Throwing an Exception   635

    15.3 Catching Unhandled Exceptions   636

    15.4 Displaying Exception Information   639

    15.5 Creating New Exception Types   640

    15.6 Ignoring Exceptions in a Block of Code   642

16. Cryptography and Compression **644**

    16.1 Generating a Hash   644

    16.2 Encrypting and Decrypting a String   646

    16.3 Encrypting and Decrypting a File   650

    16.4 Prompting for a Username and Password   653

    16.5 Handling Passwords Securely   655

    16.6 Compressing and Decompressing a String   656

    16.7 Compressing and Decompressing a File   658

    16.8 Generating Cryptographically Secure Random Numbers   662

    16.9 Complete Listing of the Crypto.vb Module   663

    16.10 Complete Listing of the Compress.vb Module   668

17. Web Development **671**

    17.1 Displaying Web Pages on a Form   671

    17.2 Accessing Content Within an HTML Document   675

    17.3 Getting All Links from a Web Page   676

    17.4 Get the Local Computer's IP Address   679

    17.5 Resolving a Host Name or IP Address for Another Computer   680

    17.6 Pinging an IP Address   681

    17.7 Using FTP to Download Files   682

    17.8 Calling a Web Service   684

    17.9 Sending Email Using SMTP   687

    17.10 Getting POP3 Emails   689

    17.11 Sending a Message to Another Computer   696

    17.12 Adding Hyperlinks to a (Desktop) Form   697

Index **699**

Preface

Most of us learn to cook at an early age, starting with peanut butter and jelly sand-wiches and quickly progressing to macaroni and cheese. But very few people make it to the advanced cooking stage, whipping up new culinary creations in the blink of an eye and dazzling all who taste the literal fruits of our labor. And for most of us, that's OK. We don't expect any more than the ordinary, the mundane, on our daily plates.

But in the programming world, things are different. Users expect the moon when it comes to software quality, and if you can't deliver something more than just the mundane, you're sure to get an earful. Visual Basic 2005 is a good tool for writing great programs, but it is also very good at letting people write ordinary software. Ordinary cooking usually only results in ordinary food, but ordinary programming can lead to something much worse: bugs. So how can you take your programming to the "master chef" level?

For those of you who have limited creative talent in the kitchen, and even for experts who are just looking to try something new, there are cookbooks galore at your local bookstore and smiling chefs each Saturday morning on your local PBS station. For Visual Basic programmers, locating a similar type of cookbook of "programming rec-ipes" has been somewhat difficult—until now. The book you are now holding, *Visual Basic 2005 Cookbook*, is the recipe book you have been looking for. It's chock full of tasty software development tidbits that you can try right now in your kitchen—that is, at your computer.

The recipes in this cookbook will introduce you to a wide range of Visual Basic 2005 programming topics, from simple string and number manipulation to advanced top-ics involving animations and matrix transformations. Some of the recipes may not be to your taste, but many of them will be just what you need. Perhaps you're in the middle of a meaty project, and you aren't sure how to copy an existing directory from one place to another. A quick look at Recipe 12.4, "Copying Directories," will provide the missing ingredients and keep your whole project from boiling over. Or maybe you are trying to format some content for the printer, and you want to draw a text string at a 27.3-degree angle. If so, you are likely hungry for what's in Recipe 9.18, "Rotating Text to any Angle."

In the world of cooking, regular practice brings noticeable improvements in the quality of your food. It is our belief that regular programming practice using the recipes in this book will bring similar improvements in your software development life. Bon appétit!

Who This Book Is For

Visual Basic 2005 Cookbook includes a large variety of recipes, and it was written to meet the needs of a wide range of software developers, from the novice programmer trying out new code to the professional full-time developer. No matter what your level of expertise, you will benefit from the recipes found in each chapter. But even the simplest recipes assume a minimum understanding of Visual Basic and .NET programming concepts. If you are a first-time programmer still learning the basics of loop constructs and conditions, you might want to spend a little more time with a good tutorial book such as *Programming Visual Basic 2005* by Jesse Liberty (O'Reilly) before you dive into the recipes found in these pages.

This book was written with two purposes in mind. The first was a desire to help readers expand their understanding of general and specific programming concepts and algorithms. As you read and study the recipes in this book, you should become more fluent not just in the Visual Basic language, but in the mindset that is required to develop high-quality and stable code. The book's second purpose was to help professional programmers (and also recreational programmers) become more productive by providing a collection of software answers to the questions that may stump them from time to time. If either of these purposes resonates with you and your programming needs, this book is definitely for you.

How This Book Is Organized

Visual Basic 2005 Cookbook is primarily a reference book. Each recipe is organized as a problem/solution pair: you have a problem, you locate a recipe that concerns your problem, and then you obtain the solution through the code and discussion included with the recipe. If you are the adventurous type, you can read through the book from cover to cover, and we will applaud you all the way. For most readers, the skim-and-look-up method will probably work better. The ample index pages should help you find the recipe you need quickly.

The recipes in the book are organized into general programming topic areas, by chapter. The following miniature table of contents quickly summarizes what you'll find in each chapter:

Chapter 1, *Visual Basic Programming*

This chapter introduces you to the three main types of projects you will develop using Visual Basic: desktop applications, console applications, and web (ASP.NET) applications.

Chapter 2, *The Development Environment*

This chapter shows you how to use some of the newer features of Visual Studio and introduces the new Visual Basic 2005 My namespace feature. It also discusses development issues concerning general system resources such as the registry and the clipboard.

Chapter 3, *Application Organization*

The recipes in this chapter cover the core programming concepts found in classes, structures, and modules, including method usage and operator overloading.

Chapter 4, *Forms, Controls, and Other Useful Objects*

As the chapter title implies, the recipes found here deal with Windows Forms (desktop) applications, with a strong emphasis on using the various controls available for building them.

Chapter 5, *Strings*

This chapter includes dozens of recipes that focus on strings and string manipulation. A few recipes focus on regular expression processing.

Chapter 6, *Numbers and Math*

The .NET Framework, and by extension Visual Basic, includes several data types that each manipulate different sizes and ranges of numbers. This chapter's recipes show you ways to interact with those data types and values. For those who miss their high school math classes, there are several recipes that deal with more advanced math topics, including geometry and linear algebra.

Chapter 7, *Dates and Times*

The recipes in this chapter demonstrate how to use and manipulate date and time values and the components from which they are built. Timing and time ranges are also covered.

Chapter 8, *Arrays and Collections*

Storing individual data values is fine, but sometimes you need to store a whole bunch of similar values as a group. This chapter shows you how to do just that by demonstrating various features of arrays and collections. Generics, new to Visual Basic 2005, play a prominent role in this chapter.

Chapter 9, *Graphics*

This chapter discusses the graphics features included with .NET, focusing on the many GDI+ graphic objects that let you draw complex shapes and text on almost any display surface.

Chapter 10, *Multimedia*

Moving pictures and sounds are the core of this chapter. The recipes found here will help you bring action to otherwise static forms and applications.

Chapter 11, *Printing*

Printing in .NET depends on GDI+ and its drawing engine. While some of the recipes in Chapter 9 will be useful for general printing, you'll find recipes dealing with other printing-specific topics, such as print preview support and the incorporation of user-specified page settings, in this chapter.

Chapter 12, *Files and File Systems*

This chapter focuses on the interaction between software and the data stored in disk files. Also covered are the different methods you can use to access and manage the file systems and directories where such files reside.

Chapter 13, *Databases*

Most Visual Basic applications communicate with one or more database systems. This chapter's recipes demonstrate different methods you can use in your applications to join databases and users through the medium of your custom software.

Chapter 14, *Special Programming Techniques*

If you didn't find it in another chapter, it's here. This somewhat large chapter covers topics that didn't fit neatly into other chapters. But in our opinion, it includes some of the most interesting and tasty recipes in the entire book.

Chapter 15, *Exceptions*

Error processing is the focus of this chapter. Its recipes deal specifically with exceptions and error management in your Visual Basic applications.

Chapter 16, *Cryptography and Compression*

Shh—some of the recipes in this chapter are secret. But it's all right for you to read them and use them to protect and ensure the integrity of the data managed by your application.

Chapter 17, *Web Development*

Most of the recipes in this book can be used in desktop or web-based applications, but there are a few special topics that are unique to ASP.NET applications. They appear in this chapter.

Most of the book's recipes include source code you can use in your own applications. Some of the code samples are rather long, and typing them in while reading this book would be a chore. That's why we've made the source code for most recipes available as a separate download from the O'Reilly Media web site. To access the code, locate this book's web page at *http://www.oreilly.com/catalog/vb2005ckbk/*.

What You Need to Use This Book

The recipes included in this book were designed specifically for use with Visual Basic 2005 or later. While some of the more general recipes will work with earlier versions of Visual Basic .NET, many other recipes will generate compile-time or runtime errors if you attempt to use them with earlier versions.

If you do not yet own a copy of Visual Studio 2005, and you aren't sure if you are ready to make the financial investment to obtain it, you can use the free version of the development environment, Microsoft Visual Basic 2005 Express Edition. Although this version does not include all of the features included with the Standard, Professional, and Enterprise editions of the product, you will be able to use most of the recipes in this book with it.

Microsoft Visual Basic 2005 Express Edition can build only desktop applications. If you are looking for a no-cost tool for ASP.NET application development, try the Microsoft Visual Web Developer 2005 Express Edition.

Both Express Edition tools are available from Microsoft's MSDN web site at *http://msdn.microsoft.com/express/*.

The recipes in this book were all developed using Visual Studio 2005 Professional Edition.

Conventions Used in This Book

The following typographical conventions are used in this book:

Plain text
> Indicates menu titles, menu options, menu buttons, and keyboard accelerators (such as Alt and Ctrl).

Italic
> Indicates new terms, URLs, email addresses, filenames, file extensions, pathnames, and directories.

`Constant width`
> Indicates commands, options, switches, variables, attributes, keys, functions, types, classes, namespaces, methods, modules, properties, parameters, values, objects, statements, keywords, events, event handlers, XML tags, HTML tags, macros, the contents of files, or the output from commands.

`Constant width bold`
> Shows commands or other text that should be typed literally by the user; also used for emphasis within code.

`Constant width italic`
> Shows text that should be replaced with user-supplied values.

This icon signifies a tip, suggestion, or general note.

This icon indicates a warning or caution.

Using Code Examples

This book is here to help you get your job done. In general, you may use the code in this book in your programs and documentation. You do not need to contact us for permission unless you're reproducing a significant portion of the code. For example, writing a program that uses several chunks of code from this book does not require permission. Selling or distributing a CD-ROM of examples from O'Reilly books *does* require permission. Answering a question by citing this book and quoting example code does not require permission. Incorporating a significant amount of example code from this book into your product's documentation *does* require permission.

We appreciate, but do not require, attribution. An attribution usually includes the title, author, publisher, and ISBN. For example: "*Visual Basic 2005 Cookbook* by Tim Patrick and John Clark Craig. Copyright 2006 O'Reilly Media, Inc., 978-0-596-10177-0."

If you feel your use of code examples falls outside fair use or the permission given above, feel free to contact us at *permissions@oreilly.com*.

Comments and Questions

Please address comments and questions concerning this book to the publisher:

> O'Reilly Media, Inc.
> 1005 Gravenstein Highway North
> Sebastopol, CA 95472
> (800) 998-9938 (in the United States or Canada)
> (707) 829-0515 (international or local)
> (707) 829-0104 (fax)

We have a web page for this book that lists errata, examples, and any additional information. You can access this page at:

> *http://www.oreilly.com/catalog/vb2005ckbk/*

To comment or ask technical questions about this book, send email to:

> *bookquestions@oreilly.com*

For more information about our books, conferences, Resource Centers, and the O'Reilly Network, see our web site at:

http://www.oreilly.com

Safari® Enabled

 When you see a Safari Enabled icon on the cover of your favorite technology book, that means the book is available online through the O'Reilly Network Safari Bookshelf.

Safari offers a solution that's better than e-books. It's a virtual library that lets you easily search thousands of top tech books, cut and paste code samples, download chapters, and find quick answers when you need the most accurate, current information. Try it for free at *http://safari.oreilly.com*.

Acknowledgments

For those of you who plan on writing a computer book some day, we wholeheartedly recommend O'Reilly Media for your publishing consideration. It produces great books—including this one—year after year, books that regularly meet the computing needs of readers. And here is why: the people who work at O'Reilly aren't just book publishers, they are technology lovers. They actually understand and try out the code included in their books.

The authors wish to especially thank John Osborn and Ralph Davis for their constant editorial devotion and dedication to this book, from the first glimmer of interest during the "idea phase," to the final push to get every word just where it needed to be. Also essential were Caitrin McCollough and the dozens of other technically adept people who had their fingers in this project.

Jay Schmelzer and Steve Saunders provided regular and valuable feedback on all technical aspects of the book. If you find any problem with any of the code in this book, it was probably something we added in after they had a chance to review each chapter.

From Tim Patrick

Once again my family has been incredibly patient with me as I spent time playing with the computer. You would think that there would be a limit on how many times a person can hear me say "Just one more paragraph," and still love me. But they do.

My beautiful wife Maki is certainly the best wife anyone could find, and I sometimes feel sad for all of the other husbands who have to settle for less than what I have. And when I also take into account my son Spencer, who is just becoming a fourth grader as I write this, I truly know that I am one blessed man. It is a miracle of God that such joy comes through the two people I get to be with each and every day.

Although I see her much less often, my agent Claudette Moore is also a treasure. She lets me call her and talk about boring paperwork and new book ideas that I should get to work on later today. Thank you again for being part of the fun of writing.

Thanks to John Craig, John Osborn, Ralph Davis, and the team at O'Reilly for trusting me with a portion of this book's content. As everyone in the computer industry already knew, O'Reilly Media is a top-notch group producing great technical resources.

From John Clark Craig

This has been a bittersweet year of transition for me, starting with the unexpected death of Jeanie, my wonderful wife of 34 years, soon after the first few chapters were authored. Jeanie was always supportive of my book writing, and she was very excited about this one. I know she still is.

My family and friends have been a steadfast source of joy, inspiration, and support throughout this year. Dakotah and Makayla are the best grandkids a guy could ever hope for, and all my parents, siblings, and in-laws have been there for me when I needed them most.

My fiancée EJ Thornton has been an absolute angel, and a bright guiding light in my life for the past few months. Thank you EJ for bringing a renewal of meaning and purpose to my life, and thank you Jeanie for blessing us and for bringing us together!

I owe a huge debt of gratitude to Tim Patrick for jumping in with his tremendous talent to help create this book, to Ralph Davis for his great editorial skills and emotional support (Ralph's wife passed away recently, too), to John Osborn for his nearly infinite patience, understanding, and guidance on this project, and to everyone else involved at O'Reilly.

Finally, I want to thank Microsoft for creating an excellent set of programming tools for today's software development needs. In particular, the recent decision to make Visual Basic 2005 Express "free forever" to the public was a smart win/win decision for us all.

CHAPTER 1

Visual Basic Programming

1.0   Introduction

When Visual Basic 1.0 was introduced in the early 1990s, it greatly simplified Windows application development. Visual Basic 2005 continues the tradition by providing a programmer-friendly environment in which you can write powerful desktop, web-based, and mobile applications quickly and easily.

In this introductory chapter you'll see just how easy it is to write a variety of applications by developing a simple application in three Visual Basic–supported flavors: a desktop application ("Windows Forms"), a console application, and a web-based application ("Web Forms" via ASP.NET).

The three recipes in this chapter are meant to be read as a set. The first recipe, which focuses on Windows Forms, includes additional background information concerning the logic of the application developed in all three recipes. Be sure to read this recipe first.

1.1   Creating a Windows Forms Application

Problem

You want to develop a Windows Forms application that converts between the Fahrenheit, Celsius, and kelvin temperature systems.

Solution

Sample code folder: Chapter 01\Forms Version

Create a Windows Forms application, and add the appropriate controls and logic.

Discussion

Start Visual Studio 2005, and then create a new project. The Start Page includes a link to do this, or you can use the File → New Project menu command. The New Project dialog appears, as shown in Figure 1-1.

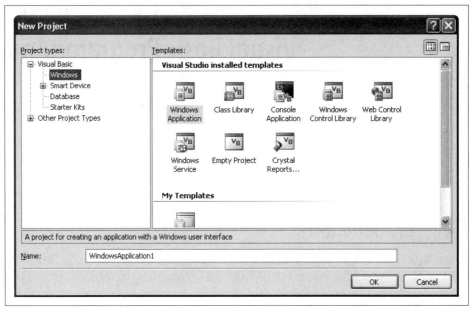

Figure 1-1. Visual Studio's New Project dialog

Each template listed in this dialog starts with the most basic and empty Visual Basic project and adds just enough source code and configuration settings to get you started on the selected application type. You could choose the Blank Solution template and work your way up to the functionality provided through the Windows Application template, but that's more than we need to accomplish right now.

Select Visual Basic (or the Windows entry under Visual Basic) in the "Project types" field and Windows Application in the Templates field, enter the name of your project in the Name field (let's call ours "FormConvertTemp"), and click the OK button.

As Visual Studio works behind the scenes to configure the initial project features, let's take a few minutes to review some high school science. The three temperature systems in this program—Fahrenheit, Celsius, and kelvin—are often used to measure heat in the various scientific disciplines:

- In the Celsius (or Centigrade) scale, water freezes at 0°C and reaches its boiling point at 100°C. This makes it a pretty simple measurement system, at least where water is concerned. Celsius is used as the common temperature measurement system in most countries.

- The Fahrenheit system uses the environment of its founder, Gabriel Fahrenheit, as its basis for measurement. 0°F, at the lower end of the 0-to-100 scale, is rumored to be the coldest temperature that Fahrenheit measured near his home one winter. The 100°F mark is based on his own body temperature. This system, used in America and a few other locations, is especially convenient if you are a German scientist with a slight fever.

- The kelvin system uses the same scale size as the Celsius system, but places 0K at *absolute zero*, the theoretical temperature at which all super-quantum molecular activity ceases. 0K is equivalent to –273.15°C, and all other temperatures on the kelvin scale are converted to Celsius through a simple adjustment of that same 273.15° value. Kelvin is one of the seven base SI (*Système International d'Unités*) units of measure and is used in scientific work.

The ability to convert between the different systems is important, not only for international relations, but also for health considerations ("Mom, I'm too sick to go to school today; I have a temperature of 310.15K!").

By now, Visual Studio should have completed its work and presented you with the initial project form (Figure 1-2).

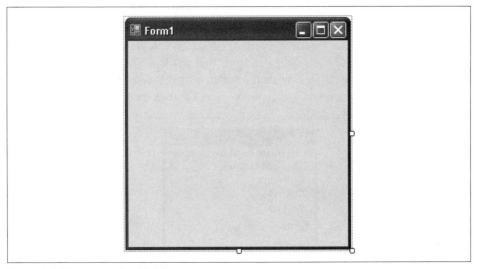

Figure 1-2. Your project's initial form

The form you see represents the initial main form of your application. It is part of a *project*, a collection of files usually tied to a single *target*, such as an application, a dynamic-link library, or some other output. In Windows Forms projects, the target is an executable file (with an EXE file extension) that contains a compiled .NET application. All of the files in your project are listed in the Solution Explorer, one of the standard tool windows in Visual Studio (Figure 1-3).

The top edge of the Solution Explorer includes a set of toolbar buttons that help you "explore the solution." The most interesting of these buttons is the second from left, the Show All Files button. Clicking this button toggles the view of files included in your project. Most of the files included in your application are hidden from view by

Figure 1-3. The Visual Studio Solution Explorer

default. Visual Studio does an amazing amount of work behind the scenes, and most of this work is stored in hidden project files. Most of these files contain code automatically generated by Visual Studio as you design your program. A few of these files, such as *ApplicationEvents.vb*, do contain code that you can update manually, but most of your development time will focus on the files that are always displayed.

The main area of the form is its design *surface*, on which you place (or "draw") *controls*. The Toolbox (Figure 1-4) contains the controls that you can add to your form; it's just one of the many "tool windows" available within Visual Studio. If it's not already displayed, open the Toolbox now through the View → Toolbox menu command.

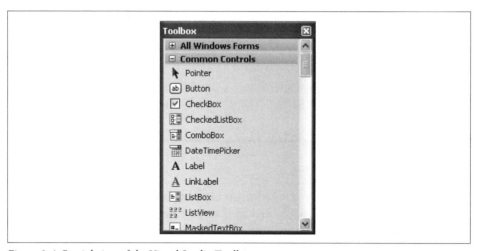

Figure 1-4. Partial view of the Visual Studio Toolbox

The selection of controls included in the Toolbox varies based on the active project and window. Beyond the default controls, several third parties offer enhanced controls for use in your projects. Once installed, these controls also appear in the Toolbox.

Each form or control has a default configuration, as determined by the developer of the control. You can alter this configuration by changing the active form's or control's properties through the Properties window (Figure 1-5). If it is not already in view, display the Properties window with the View → Properties Window menu command.

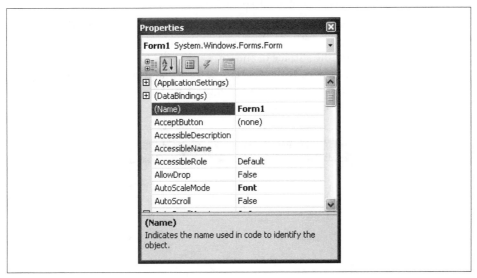

Figure 1-5. Partial view of the Properties window

The properties for the active item are pretty easy to adjust: select the form or control you want to modify, select a property in the Properties window based on the property name in the left column, and use the mouse or keyboard to modify its value in the right column. Some properties can be expanded into distinct sub-properties using the plus sign (+) to the left of the property name. And while most properties accept simple text values, others have mouse-friendly drop-down editors.

Before adding controls to our form, let's configure the properties of the form itself. Using the Properties window, set the form's properties as shown in Table 1-1. This table lists only those properties that deviate from their default settings.

Table 1-1. Application form property changes

Property name	New setting
(Name)	ConvertForm
FormBorderStyle	FixedSingle
MaximizeBox	False
MinimizeBox	False
StartPosition	CenterScreen
Text	Convert Temperatures

Now let's add the controls to the form. This project will use seven controls:

- Three RadioButton controls to select the source temperature system
- Three TextBox controls for entering and displaying temperatures
- One Button control to initiate the conversion

Use the Toolbox to select and add controls to the form. Add a control either by double-clicking on the control in the Toolbox or by selecting the control in the Toolbox and then "drawing" it on the surface of the form using the mouse. Go ahead and add the three RadioButton controls, three TextBox controls, and one Button control, and arrange them so that your form resembles Figure 1-6. You may also want to resize the form to visually fit the contained controls.

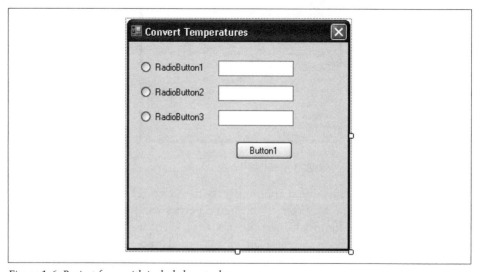

Figure 1-6. Project form with included controls

Some of the properties in these controls also need to be adjusted. Use the values in Table 1-2 to guide you through the property updates.

Table 1-2. Custom property settings for each control

Control	Property name	New setting
RadioButton1	(Name)	SourceFahrenheit
	Checked	True
	Text	&Fahrenheit
RadioButton2	(Name)	SourceCelsius
	Text	&Celsius
RadioButton3	(Name)	SourceKelvin
	Text	&kelvin
TextBox1	(Name)	ValueFahrenheit

Table 1-2. Custom property settings for each control (continued)

Control	Property name	New setting
TextBox2	(Name)	ValueCelsius
TextBox3	(Name)	ValueKelvin
Button	(Name)	ConvertTemperature
	Text	Convert

The "&" character added to some of the properties sets the keyboard shortcut for that control so that the user can activate it with the Alt+*key* keyboard sequence.

There are two more tasks to perform on the form itself before we start writing code, both destined to make the form easier to use. The first is to allow the Enter or Return key to act like a click on the ConvertTemperature button. This is done by setting one of the form's properties: AcceptButton. Setting this property to the name of a valid control—in this case, the ConvertTemperature button control—enables this keyboard action. Go ahead and set the form's AcceptButton property now.

The second user-friendly update involves setting the "tab order" of the controls on the form. The Tab key allows the user to move from one form control to another, but the movement may look somewhat random to the user unless you specifically declare the order. To set the tab order, first make sure that the form—and not one of its contained controls—is the active object in the designer window. Then select the View → Tab Order menu command. A small number appears next to each control. To readjust the tab order, click the controls in the order you want them to appear (Figure 1-7). You can also set the tab order by altering the TabIndex property of each control, but the mouse method is generally quicker.

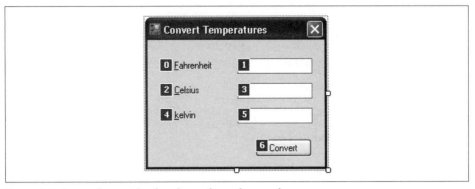

Figure 1-7. Project form with tab order set for each control

When you are finished, select the View → Tab Order menu command once more (or press the Escape key) to return to standard editing.

Now it's time to program! All of the code for this application will appear in the ConvertTemperature button's Click event procedure, which you can access by double-clicking on the ConvertTemperature button itself. Visual Studio switches to a code editor with the following event procedure template ready to use:

```
Public Class ConvertForm
    Private Sub ConvertTemperature_Click( _
        ByVal sender As System.Object, _
        ByVal e As System.EventArgs) _
        Handles ConvertTemperature.Click

    End Sub
End Class
```

Add the following code to the Click event procedure body. It determines the source temperature type, checks for valid input, and then performs the conversion:

```
' ----- Convert between Fahrenheit, Celsius, and kelvin.
On Error Resume Next

If (SourceFahrenheit.Checked = True) Then
    ' ----- Convert from Fahrenheit to other types.
    If (IsNumeric(ValueFahrenheit.Text) = True) Then
        ' ----- F->C, F->K.
        ValueCelsius.Text = _
            (Val(ValueFahrenheit.Text) - 32) / 1.8
        ValueKelvin.Text = _
            ((Val(ValueFahrenheit.Text) - 32) / 1.8) + 273.15
    Else
        ' ----- Invalid data.
        ValueCelsius.Text = "Error"
        ValueKelvin.Text = "Error"
    End If
ElseIf (SourceCelsius.Checked = True) Then
    ' ----- Convert from Celsius to other types.
    If (IsNumeric(ValueCelsius.Text) = True) Then
        ' ----- C->F, C->K.
        ValueFahrenheit.Text = _
            (Val(ValueCelsius.Text) * 1.8) + 32
        ValueKelvin.Text = Val(ValueCelsius.Text) + 273.15
    Else
        ' ----- Invalid data.
        ValueFahrenheit.Text = "Error"
        ValueKelvin.Text = "Error"
    End If
Else
    ' ----- Convert from kelvin to other types.
    If (IsNumeric(ValueKelvin.Text) = True) Then
        ' ----- K->F, K->C.
        ValueFahrenheit.Text = _
            ((Val(ValueKelvin.Text) - 273.15) * 1.8) + 32
        ValueCelsius.Text = Val(ValueKelvin.Text) - 273.15
```

```
        Else
            ' ----- Invalid data.
            ValueFahrenheit.Text = "Error"
            ValueCelsius.Text = "Error"
        End If
    End If
```

The program is now ready to use in all weather conditions.

Although this program is pure .NET through and through, the only .NET code we witnessed was through the event handler. The call to the ConvertTemperature_Click event happens indirectly in the code; there is no line of source code, at least in your code, that makes a direct call to the event handler.

When the user clicks on the ConvertTemperature button, the low-level device driver for the mouse inserts mouse-down and mouse-up events into the global Windows input-processing queue. The device driver doesn't know anything about the various windows displayed on-screen or about .NET; it reports only that a mouse event occurred at a specific X and Y position on the screen. The Windows operating system uses this location to determine which window or control was clicked. Once that's determined, it sends relevant messages to the message queue of the application that owns the clicked window. The application notifies the clicked control that the user has, in fact, clicked that control. Finally, the code within the .NET control issues a RaiseEvent statement, which triggers a call to the ConvertTemperature_Click event handler.

That's a lot of steps between your finger and the event handler. Fortunately, you don't have to handle all of those steps yourself. The relevant logic already exists in Windows and in .NET; you just have to write the event handler and connect it to the specific event through the handler's Handles keyword (which Visual Basic 2005 generates for you):

```
    Private Sub ConvertTemperature_Click( _
        ByVal sender As System.Object, _
        ByVal e As System.EventArgs) _
        Handles ConvertTemperature.Click
```

The rest of the code in the application is composed of standard logic and calculations that you might find in code from any programming language: If conditional statements, assignment statements, and expression processing with operators such as the multiplication operator (*).

See Also

The other recipes in this chapter demonstrate how to implement the same program, using different types of interfaces.

1.2 Creating a Console Application

Problem

You want to develop a Console application that converts between the Fahrenheit, Celsius, and kelvin temperature systems.

Solution

Sample code folder: Chapter 01\Console Version

Create a Windows Console application, and add logic to perform all the calculations based on the user's input. First, read through Recipe 1.1 for background information on using Visual Studio and on converting between the various temperature systems.

Discussion

Start Visual Studio 2005, and then use the File → New Project menu command to create a new project. Select the Windows project type, and then select the Console Application template. Click OK to create the new project. Since a console application doesn't have a special user interface, Visual Studio simply displays the default code block for the new project:

```
Module Module1
    Sub Main( )

    End Sub
End Module
```

There are a few different ways to rename the module. If you only want to change the name in the code, just replace the word "Module1" with something like "Convert-Temperature":

```
Module ConvertTemperature
```

Unfortunately, this requires you to make a change to the project's properties. Before the change, Visual Studio planned to start the program from the Sub Main routine in the Module1 module. But since you changed the name, there is no longer a Module1 for Visual Studio to use.

To modify the properties, select the Project → ConsoleApplication1 Properties menu command, or double-click on the My Project item in the Solution Explorer panel. When the Project Properties window appears, the Application tab in that window should already be active. To change the starting code for the program, select "ConvertTemperature" from the "Startup object" field. Then close the Project Properties window, and return to the code.

If you want to avoid all of this unpleasantness, rename the module's filename instead of its name in the code. To do this, right-click the *Module1.vb* file in the Solution

Explorer, choose the Rename command from the shortcut menu that appears, and give it a new name such as *ConvertTemperature.vb*. (Don't forget the *.vb* extension.) Visual Studio will change the module name as well and fix up all the other loose connections.

All of the conversion code will go in the Sub Main routine:

```vb
Module ConvertTemperature
    Sub Main( )
        ' ----- The program starts here.
        Dim userInput As String
        Dim sourceType As String

        On Error Resume Next

        ' ----- Display general instructions.
        Console.WriteLine("Instructions:" & vbCrLf & _
            "To convert temperature, enter a starting " & _
            "temperature, followed" & vbCrLf & _
            "by one of the following letters:" & vbCrLf & _
            "  F = Fahrenheit" & vbCrLf & _
            "  C = Celsius" & vbCrLf & _
            "  K = kelvin" & vbCrLf & _
            "Enter a blank line to exit." & vbCrLf)

        ' ----- The program continues until the user
        '       enters a blank line.
        Do While True
            ' ----- Prompt the user.
            Console.WriteLine("Enter a source temperature.")
            Console.Write("> ")
            userInput = Console.ReadLine( )

            ' ----- A blank line exits the application.
            If (Trim(userInput) = "") Then Exit Do

            ' ----- Determine the source type.
            userInput = UCase(userInput)
            If (InStr(userInput, "F") > 0) Then
                ' ----- Start with Fahrenheit.
                sourceType = "F"
                userInput = Replace(userInput, "F", "")
            ElseIf (InStr(userInput, "C") > 0) Then
                ' ----- Start with Celsius.
                sourceType = "C"
                userInput = Replace(userInput, "C", "")
            ElseIf (InStr(userInput, "K") > 0) Then
                ' ----- Start with kelvin.
                sourceType = "K"
                userInput = Replace(userInput, "K", "")
            Else
                ' ----- Invalid entry.
                Console.WriteLine("Invalid input: " & _
```

```
                userInput & vbCrLf)
            Continue Do
        End If

        ' ----- Check for a valid temperature.
        userInput = Trim(userInput)
        If (IsNumeric(userInput) = False) Then
            Console.WriteLine("Invalid number: " & _
                userInput & vbCrLf)
            Continue Do
        End If

        ' ----- Time to convert.
        If (sourceType = "F") Then
            ' ----- Convert from Fahrenheit to other types.
            Console.WriteLine(" Fahrenheit: " & userInput)
            Console.WriteLine(" Celsius:    " & _
                (Val(userInput) - 32) / 1.8)
            Console.WriteLine(" kelvin:     " & _
                ((Val(userInput) - 32) / 1.8) + 273.15)
        ElseIf (sourceType = "C") Then
            ' ----- Convert from Celsius to other types.
            Console.WriteLine(" Fahrenheit: " & _
                (Val(userInput) * 1.8) + 32)
            Console.WriteLine(" Celsius:    " & userInput)
            Console.WriteLine(" kelvin:     " & _
                Val(userInput) + 273.15)
        Else
            ' ----- Convert from kelvin to other types.
            Console.WriteLine(" Fahrenheit: " & _
                ((Val(userInput) - 273.15) * 1.8) + 32)
            Console.WriteLine(" Celsius:    " & _
                Val(userInput) - 273.15)
            Console.WriteLine(" kelvin:     " & userInput)
        End If
    Loop
    End
    End Sub
End Module
```

Running the program opens up a command window. You will immediately be prompted to enter a source temperature. The program continues to convert values until it detects a blank line for input. Here is a typical short session:

```
Instructions:
To convert temperature, enter a starting temperature, followed
by one of the following letters:
  F = Fahrenheit
  C = Celsius
  K = kelvin
Enter a blank line to exit.

Enter a source temperature.
> 37c
```

```
    Fahrenheit: 98.6
    Celsius:    37
    kelvin:     310.15
Enter a source temperature.
>
```

Console applications bring back memories of those pre-Windows days when the 80-by-24-character console display was the primary user interface mechanism on the IBM PC platform. Text input and output, and maybe some simple character-based graphics and color, were all the visual glitz that a programmer could use.

Console applications in .NET use that same basic text-presentation system as their primary interface, but they also include the full power of the .NET libraries. For the actual user interaction, the Console object takes center stage. It includes features that let you display text on the console (Write( ), WriteLine( )), retrieve user input (Read( ), ReadKey( ), ReadLine( )), and manipulate the console window in other useful ways.

The temperature conversion program uses the Console object and some basic temperature formulas within its core processing loop. First, it gets a line of input from the user and stores it as a string:

```
userInput = Console.ReadLine( )
```

The input must be a valid number, plus the letter F, C, or K. The letter can appear anywhere in the number: 37C is the same as C37 is the same as 3C7. Once the program has extracted the numeric temperature and its source system, it performs the conversion; it then outputs the results using the Console.WriteLine( ) method.

See Also

The recipes in this chapter should be read together to gain a full understanding of general .NET application development concepts.

1.3   Creating an ASP.NET Web Forms Application

Problem

You want to develop a Web Forms application in ASP.NET that converts between the Fahrenheit, Celsius, and kelvin temperature systems.

Solution

Sample code folder: Chapter 01\Web Version

Create a new Web Forms application, and use ASP.NET development tools and coding methods to craft your application. First, read through Recipe 1.1 for background information on using Visual Studio and on converting between the various temperature systems.

Discussion

Start Visual Studio 2005, and then create a new web site (not a "New Project"). You can use either the Create Web Site link on the Start Page or the File → New Web Site menu command. The New Web Site dialog appears, as shown in Figure 1-8.

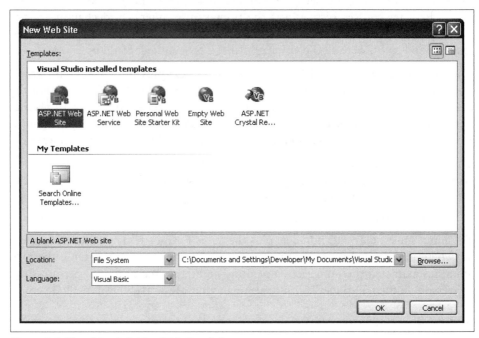

Figure 1-8. Visual Studio's New Web Site dialog

Make sure that ASP.NET Web Site is selected in the list of templates, choose File System for the location type, enter the new directory name (or just use the default, although we're going to use "WebConvertTemp" as the final directory component), naturally select Visual Basic as the programming language, and then click the OK button.

Visual Studio does a little work and then presents you with a blank page. This is a web page document on which you will place your various web display elements. By default, it acts like a word processing document, in which added elements flow left to right, top to bottom. You can opt to place elements at specific locations, but we'll stick with the default placement mode for this program.

If it's not already in view, display the Toolbox through the View → Toolbox menu command. No doubt you've already seen the Toolbox used in Windows Forms applications. The tools displayed now are similar, although they are for specific use by ASP.NET applications only.

As with Windows Forms applications, Visual Studio presents the user interface to you, secretly writing the code behind the scenes. The generated code in Windows Forms is all Visual Basic code; you can write an entire Windows Forms application in Notepad using only Visual Basic statements. ASP.NET applications use Visual Basic for core logic and "code behind" event handlers, but the user interface is defined through an HTML/XML mix. You can modify this HTML yourself (click on the Source button at the bottom of the web page window to see the HTML generated so far) and have the changes reflected in the user interface.

For this project, let's take things easy and simply use the Toolbox to add display elements. Make sure you are in Design view (instead of HTML Markup/Source view). Type the following text into the web page document, and then press Enter:

```
Convert Temperature
```

Add the following usage text below this, and press Enter again:

```
Select the source temperature system, enter the value,
and then click the Convert button.
```

The text is somewhat plain, so let's do a little formatting. Highlight the word "Convert" in the usage text, and press the Control-B key combination to make the text bold, just as you would in most word processors.

I think the title line would also look better as a heading. Switch into HTML mode by clicking on the Source button at the bottom of the page or selecting the View → Markup menu command. You should see the following HTML code, or something pretty close to it:

```
<%@ Page Language="VB" AutoEventWireup="false"
CodeFile="Default.aspx.vb" Inherits="_Default" %>

<!DOCTYPE html PUBLIC "-//W3C//DTD XHTML 1.0 Transitional//EN"
  "http://www.w3.org/TR/xhtml1/DTD/xhtml1-transitional.dtd">

<html xmlns="http://www.w3.org/1999/xhtml" >
<head runat="server">
    <title>Untitled Page</title>
</head>
<body>
    <form id="form1" runat="server">
    <div>
        Convert Temperature<br />
        Select the source temperature system, enter the value,
        and then click the <strong>Convert</strong>
        button.<br />

    </div>
    </form>
</body>
</html>
```

If you've written HTML in the past, this should mostly look familiar. Modify the "Convert Temperature" line to include <h1> (heading level #1) tags around the text, removing the <br> tag:

```
<h1>Convert Temperature</h1>
```

Return to the user interface designer by clicking on the Design button at the bottom of the page or using the View → Designer menu command.

Next, we need to add a selector for the three different temperature systems. To add an instance of the RadioButtonList control to the end of the web page, click at the bottom of the web page and then double-click on the RadioButtonList item in the Toolbox. A default single-item list appears. This list includes a "task pane," as shown in Figure 1-9 (Visual Studio includes such "smart tags" and task panes for many user interface elements). Click on the Edit Items link in this pop up.

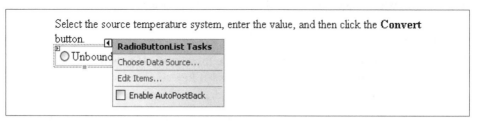

Figure 1-9. Convenient features for user interface elements

Use the ListItem Collection Editor that appears to add each temperature system. Table 1-3 contains the data you need to enter your selections. When you are done, close the ListItem Collection Editor window.

Table 1-3. Radio button list items

Member	Text	Value
0	Fahrenheit	F
1	Celsius	C
2	kelvin	K

Since we'll be interacting with this radio button list in code, we need to give it a meaningful name. In the Properties window, set the (ID) property to "SourceType."

Back in the web page designer, start a new line with the text "From Temperature:" and follow it with a TextBox control from the Toolbox. Name the control (that is, set its (ID) field to) "SourceValue."

On yet another line, add a Button control, name it "ConvertNow," and set its Text property to "Convert." A click on this button is destined to generate the converted temperatures.

That's it for the data-entry portion, though we still need a place to display the results. We'll use a simple table presentation. First, set off the results visibly by adding a Horizontal Rule control. This is actually a standard HTML element, so you'll find it in the HTML section of the Toolbox. After that, add a title that reads "Temperature Results" (add the <h1> tags if you wish).

Now add a table through the Layout → Insert Table menu command. When the Insert Table form (Figure 1-10) prompts you for a table size, specify three rows and two columns, and then click OK. When the table appears, enter the names of the three temperature systems in the left-most cells: Fahrenheit, Celsius, and kelvin.

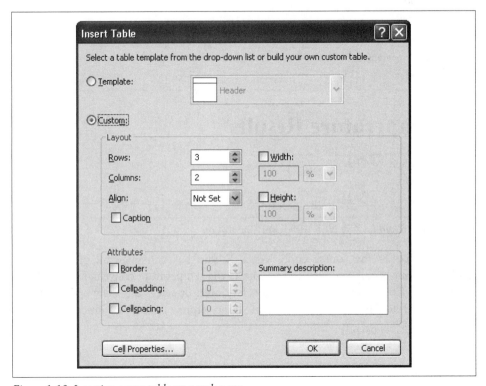

Figure 1-10. Inserting a new table on a web page

ASP.NET table cells can include names, and we will use such names to update the right-most cells with converted temperature data. As you click in each right-column cell, the Properties window displays the details for each related <td> element. Update the (ID) property of each cell to use the following cell names, from top to bottom: "ResultFahrenheit," "ResultCelsius," and "ResultKelvin."

Let's make one final change to the presentation. In Visual Studio's Properties window, select DOCUMENT from the list of objects at the top of the panel. Modify the Title property, which currently contains "Untitled Page," to read "Convert Temperature" instead. This is the title that appears in the browser's titlebar when running the application.

That's it for the user interface design. You should now have a web-page display similar to Figure 1-11.

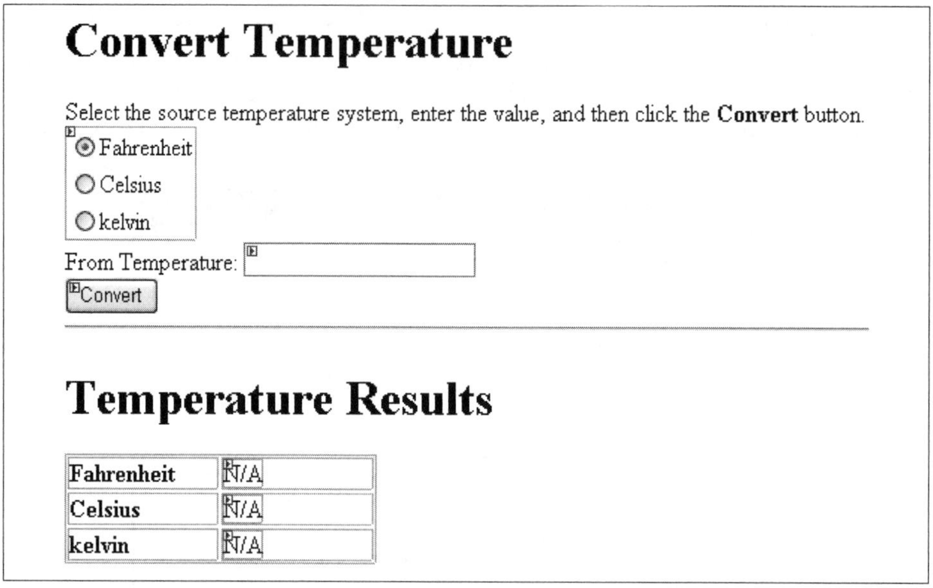

Figure 1-11. A beautiful ASP.NET Web Forms application

Let's move on to the source code. Visual Studio has generated all of the HTML markup on our behalf, but we need to supply the temperature conversion logic. Click on the View Code button in the Solution Explorer, or select the View → Code menu command. Although it's not much, Visual Studio wrote a little bit of this code, too:

```
Partial Class _Default
    Inherits System.Web.UI.Page

End Class
```

The only code we need to add is the event handler for the Convert button that performs the actual conversion. Add this code to the project. You can double-click on the Convert button in the designer to have Visual Studio add the event handler template:

```
Protected Sub ConvertNow_Click(ByVal sender As Object, _
    ByVal e As System.EventArgs) Handles ConvertNow.Click
    ' ----- The conversion occurs here.
    Dim origValue As Double

    If (IsNumeric(SourceValue.Text) = True) Then
        ' ----- The user supplied a number. Convert it.
        origValue = CDbl(SourceValue.Text)
        If (SourceType.SelectedValue = "F") Then
```

```
      ' ----- From Fahrenheit.
      ResultFahrenheit.Text = CStr(origValue)
      ResultCelsius.Text = CStr((origValue - 32) / 1.8)
      ResultKelvin.Text = CStr(((origValue - 32) / 1.8) + _
         273.15)
   ElseIf (SourceType.SelectedValue = "C") Then
      ' ----- From Celsius.
      ResultFahrenheit.Text = CStr((origValue * 1.8) + 32)
      ResultCelsius.Text = CStr(origValue)
      ResultKelvin.Text = CStr(origValue + 273.15)
   Else
      ' ----- From kelvin.
      ResultFahrenheit.Text = CStr(((origValue - 273.15) * _
         1.8) + 32)
      ResultCelsius.Text = CStr(origValue - 273.15)
      ResultKelvin.Text = CStr(origValue)
   End If
Else
   ' ----- Unknown source value.
   ResultFahrenheit.Text = "???"
   ResultCelsius.Text = "???"
   ResultKelvin.Text = "???"
End If
End Sub
```

If you've already read the other recipes in this chapter, this code should look some-what familiar. It simply applies the standard temperature-conversion formulas to the source number based on the type of source temperature selected, then puts the results in the output display fields.

 When you run this recipe, it properly converts temperatures but only when you click on the Convert button directly. If you're like us, you want to reduce the number of keystrokes and mouse clicks you need to use in any program. The program doesn't convert properly if you simply hit the Enter key from the source temperature field, SourceValue. ASP.NET has a way to change this behavior. Add this event handler to your application to enable conversion via the Enter key (or add the RegisterHiddenField( ) statement to your Page_Load event if you already have that handler).

```
Protected Sub Page_Load(ByVal sender As Object, _
   ByVal e As System.EventArgs) Handles Me.Load
   ClientScript.RegisterHiddenField("__EVENTTARGET", _
      "ConvertNow")
End Sub
```

It's hard to read, but there are two underscore characters before "EVENTTARGET."

The code you use to develop ASP.NET applications is not exactly the same as the code you use for desktop applications, but it's close. Event handlers in ASP.NET look like event handlers in Windows Forms applications, although the timing of the events is a little different. Functions that exist for calculation purposes only and that have no direct interaction with the user or the user interface may be moved freely between Windows Forms and Web Forms applications, but some of the code is very much tied to the ASP.NET programming model. Still, that's what you would expect given that half of a Web Forms application's user-interface code is written in HTML instead of Visual Basic.

The HTML code that is included is a little nonstandard. Take a look at the HTML markup associated with the application (select View → Markup when the designer is in view). Although there are the standard <body> and <table> tags throughout the page, there are also some tags that begin with asp:, as in <asp:RadioButtonList>. Each tag represents a Web Forms Server Control and is directly tied to a .NET Framework–coded class (a class you can instantiate and manipulate just like any other .NET class). The RadioButtonList class, for instance, is found in the System.Web.UI.WebControls namespace, along with most of the other ASP.NET-specific controls.

When ASP.NET processes a web page with these embedded web controls, the control class emits standard HTML code in place of the <asp:RadioButtonList> tag set.

Fortunately, you don't need to know how the internals of these classes work or exactly what kind of HTML they emit. You can simply add the controls to your web page using drag-and-drop, and interact with each control through its events and properties. And that's what we did here. We added a couple of controls to a form, adjusted their properties, and then responded to a single event. These actions resulted in a complete web-based application. ASP.NET even adjusts the emitted HTML for the user based on the flavor of the browser being used.

See Also

The recipes in this chapter should be read together to gain a full understanding of general .NET application development concepts.

The Development Environment

2.0   Introduction

Did you know that the Visual Basic 2005 compiler is available to you free of charge? You can download the .NET Framework with all included compilers directly from Microsoft's web site, and start using it immediately to develop and distribute your own .NET applications, all without shelling out a single penny.

Well, there are a few caveats. The main one is that you will have to use a tool such as Notepad to write all of your source code. And you will need to hand-type the statements that start the compilation process through the Windows Command Prompt. But other than that, it's a piece of cake. And it's still free.

If you're not that bold, you should probably fork over a little cash to obtain Visual Studio, the programming environment of choice for .NET application development. Although it's not free, you definitely get what you pay for. (Actually, Visual Basic 2005 Express Edition is free, so you get even more than you pay for.) Visual Studio is stuffed with features and support tools and visual designers and behind-the-scenes automatic code generation wizards, all of which let you concentrate on developing great code without having to worry about the picky details of setting up the compiler and deployment options.

This chapter discusses some of the snazzy features included with Visual Studio 2005. As with all the chapters in this book, we have concentrated on Visual Studio 2005 Professional Edition. However, most, if not all, recipes in this book should work with any edition of Visual Studio.

2.1   Discovering and Using a Code Snippet

Problem

You know that Visual Studio came with a bunch of prewritten "snippets" that you can use in your applications, but you don't know where to find them in the vast Visual Studio menu system.

Solution

Code snippets are among the IntelliSense features included with Visual Studio. To find and insert a snippet, use the different snippet-related menus and keyboard sequences.

Discussion

To insert a code snippet into your source code, right-click at the desired location with the mouse, choose Insert Snippet from the shortcut menu (Figure 2-1), and navigate to the snippet you want to use.

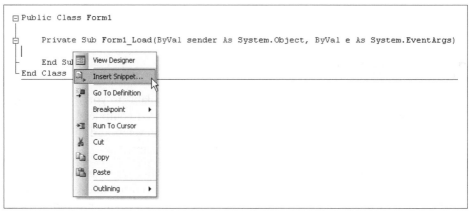

Figure 2-1. Inserting a snippet with the mouse

An even faster method is to type a question mark (?) anywhere in the source code and then press the Tab key. The more formal location of this same command within the Visual Studio menu system is at Edit → IntelliSense → Insert Snippet. If you are in any way mouse-phobic when developing source code, you can use the default Visual Basic keyboard shortcut of Control-K followed by Control-X to get to the snippet picker.

Using any of these methods to access snippets presents the top-level set of snippet folders, as shown in Figure 2-2.

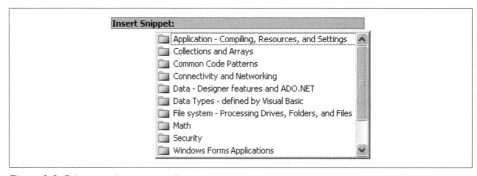

Figure 2-2. Primary snippet categories

To negotiate the hierarchy, use the mouse or arrow keys to select a folder or item in the pop-up list, or type a partial list name followed by the Enter key. Selecting a snippet folder updates the list with the items and subfolders in that selected folder. For example, in Figure 2-2, selecting "Math" with the mouse or typing "Math" from the keyboard followed by the Enter key, will open the "Math" snippet folder and display any folders or items contained within that folder. Selecting an item inserts the chosen snippet.

Each snippet contains a useful block of prewritten code, but many also include some intelligence. Some snippets include "fill in the blank" templates that provide areas for you to supply your custom values. For instance, the Data Types—defined by Visual Basic → Convert a Number to a Hexadecimal String snippet includes a field for the source value, moving the insertion point to that field immediately upon pasting the snippet in the code:

```
Dim hexString As String = Hex(48)
```

Some snippets place multiple lines of source code in the code editor, sometimes with multiple replacement fields. The Common Code Patterns → Types → Define a Structure snippet defines this multiline structure:

```
Structure MyStructure
    Public ValueOne As Integer
    Public ValueTwo As Boolean
End Structure
```

Some snippets add code to various places in your source-code file and may make other updates to your project. The Security → Encrypt a String snippet not only adds code to the active procedure but also adds Imports statements to the top of the source-code file if references to the namespaces it uses are not already there.

Snippets are somewhat location-dependent. Most are written to be used inside a subroutine, function, or property accessor, while a few are designed for placement outside of routines or classes. If you insert a snippet at the top of a source-code file, outside of any class context, it will be riddled with errors.

Snippets are actually specially formatted XML files, with attributes containing the special insertion rules for each snippet.

See Also

Recipes 2.2, 2.3, and 2.4 provide additional information on code snippets.

2.2   Creating a New Snippet

Problem

You've written an especially useful block of source code, and you want to save it as a code snippet for use in other applications.

Solution

To save a block of code as a snippet for reuse, use the Code Snippet Editor for Visual Basic 2005 to create and store the snippet, or hand-code the required XML file yourself and place it in an appropriate directory.

Discussion

To add a new snippet to the set of available snippets in your Visual Studio environment, fire up the Snippet Editor, and right-click on the folder where you want the snippet to appear, then select Add New Snippet from the shortcut menu. (An Add New Folder option lets you adjust the available folders. You can also create subordinate folders to a reasonable depth.) Type or paste your code into the blank pane of the Editor tab, using the Replacements tab to add any replaceable parameters. Click the Save icon near the top of the Snippet Editor to store your results. The new snippet will be available immediately within Visual Studio.

> The Snippet Editor is a community-developed application available to you as a free download. You can contribute features to it yourself if you are so inclined. It's part of the "GotDotNet" Community, located at *http://www.gotdotnet.com*, in its "Workspaces" area.
>
> It's also possible to code snippets yourself, using the markup specified by the Microsoft XML snippet schema. However, doing so is not for the faint of heart, and with few exceptions, the Snippet Editor is more than adequate.

Figure 2-3 shows the "Convert a Number to a Hexadecimal String" snippet used earlier, as presented in the Snippet Editor.

You are probably dying to see the actual XML that makes up a code snippet, so here is the XML for that snippet:

```xml
<?xml version="1.0" encoding="UTF-8"?>
<CodeSnippets xmlns=
  "http://schemas.microsoft.com/VisualStudio/2005/CodeSnippet">
  <CodeSnippet Format="1.0.0">
    <Header>
      <Title>Convert a Number to a Hexadecimal String</Title>
      <Author>Microsoft Corporation</Author>
      <Description>Returns the hexadecimal
        representation of an integer.</Description>
      <Shortcut>typeHex</Shortcut>
    </Header>
    <Snippet>
      <Imports>
        <Import>
          <Namespace>System</Namespace>
        </Import>
        <Import>
```

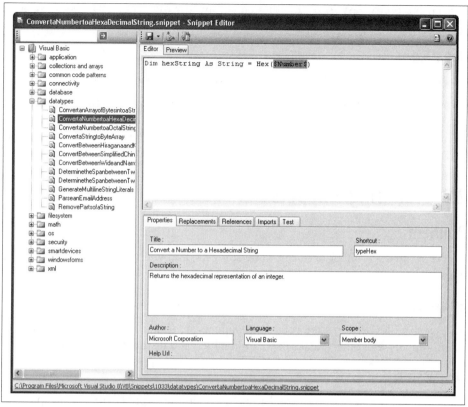

Figure 2-3. The Snippet Editor

```
        <Namespace>Microsoft.VisualBasic</Namespace>
      </Import>
    </Imports>
    <Declarations>
      <Literal>
        <ID>Number</ID>
        <Type />
        <ToolTip>Replace with an integer.</ToolTip>
        <Default>48</Default>
        <Function />
      </Literal>
    </Declarations>
    <Code Language="VB" Kind="method body">
      <![CDATA[Dim hexString As String = Hex($Number$)]]>
    </Code>
  </Snippet>
  </CodeSnippet>
</CodeSnippets>
```

You can find this particular block of snippet code at *C:\Program Files\Microsoft Visual Studio 8\VB\Snippets\1033\datatypes\ConvertaNumbertoaHexaDecimalString.*

snippet. It's pretty easy to read, although a pain to write. That's why we have software applications like the Snippet Editor.

See Also

Recipes 2.1, 2.3, and 2.4 provide additional information on code snippets.

If you really feel that you must write your own snippets and use all the advanced features available within the XML schema, Microsoft's MSDN Library has full documentation on using and designing snippets. Link to *http://msdn.microsoft.com*, and search for "snippet."

2.3   Sharing Snippets

Problem

You've created a number of terrific code snippets, and you would like to share them with others.

Solution

The *.snippet* files used to store your code snippets are simple disk-based XML files. To share snippets with others, make copies of the files, and distribute them as needed.

Discussion

The code snippet technology included in Visual Studio is pretty basic. It simply presents a list of code snippet files found in directories you specify. As long as snippet files appear in directories referenced by Visual Studio, those snippets are available for use.

On your system, you can probably find all the Microsoft-supplied snippets in the *C:\Program Files\Microsoft Visual Studio 8\VB\Snippets\1033* folder.

See Also

Recipes 2.1, 2.2, and 2.4 provide additional information on code snippets.

2.4   Adding Snippet Files to Visual Studio

Problem

Someone else has chosen to share snippet files with you, and you're ready to use them.

Solution

Upon receiving one or more snippet files, you can integrate them into your own copy of Visual Studio using the Code Snippets Manager.

Discussion

The Code Snippets Manager is accessed through Visual Studio's Tools → Code Snippets Manager menu command. The Add button on the form lets you add an entire directory of snippets to Visual Studio, while the Import button adds a single snippet file.

The quality of the code snippets you receive from others may be limited by the skill and trustworthiness of their developers. *Caveat emptor.*

See Also

Recipes 2.1, 2.2, and 2.3 provide additional information on code snippets.

2.5   Getting an Application's Version Number

Problem

You would like to display the version number of your application on its "About" form.

Solution

Sample code folder: Chapter 02\VersionNumbers

Use the `My.Application.Info.Version` object to access the version number of the application, and store the result in a `Label` control.

Discussion

Visual Basic stores an application's version number as a four-part "dot"-delimited value, such as:

```
1.2.3.4
```

The four components represent the *major*, *minor*, *build*, and *revision* numbers, respectively. They are made available through an instance of the `System.Version` class obtained from the `My.Application.Info.Version` object. You can use the members of this class to display version information when needed. The following code assumes your form has a label named `VersionNumber`:

```
Public Class Form1
    Private Sub Form1_Load(ByVal sender As System.Object, _
        ByVal e As System.EventArgs) Handles MyBase.Load
        With My.Application.Info.Version
            VersionNumber.Text = "Version " & .Major & _
                "." & .Minor & " (Build " & .Build & "." & _
                .Revision & ")"
        End With
    End Sub
End Class
```

Figure 2-4 displays the typical output for a version value set to 1.2.3.4.

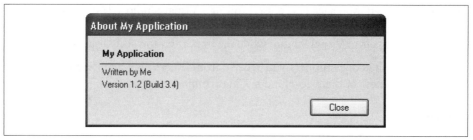

Figure 2-4. Displaying an application version number

If you aren't concerned about the display format of the version number, have the Version object format itself:

```
VersionNumber.Text = My.Application.Info.Version.ToString( )
```

Each .NET assembly has a four-part version number, defined as an assembly attribute in the project's source code. In a typical Visual Basic 2005 application, this attribute is stored in the *AssemblyInfo.vb* file, which appears only when you have Show All Files enabled in Visual Studio's Solution Explorer panel. If you open this file, you will quickly find the line that sets the version number:

```
<Assembly: AssemblyVersion("1.0.0.0")>
```

Altering the four-part number in the string modifies the assembly's version number. Visual Studio also provides a way to set this through a property form. From the Project Properties window, select the Application tab, and then click the Assembly Information button. The version number is set through the four fields named Assembly Version.

See Also

Recipe 2.6 adds some automation to the version number process.

2.6 Letting Visual Studio Automatically Update an Application's Version Number

Problem

You want to ensure that the version number changes at least a little each time you build the application, but repeatedly updating the version number by hand is a hassle.

Solution

Let Visual Basic update the build and revision components of the version number for you. Instead of supplying digits for these components, use an asterisk for the build component:

```
<Assembly: AssemblyVersion("1.2.*")>
```

If you want to control the build number but have Visual Basic generate the revision number, include the digits for the build component and use an asterisk for the revision component:

```
<Assembly: AssemblyVersion("1.2.3.*")>
```

Discussion

Visual Basic will auto-generate build and revision numbers for you if you supply an asterisk in place of actual digits. When auto-generating the build number, Visual Basic uses the number of days since January 1, 2000. When auto-generating the revision number, Visual Basic uses the number of seconds elapsed since midnight of the current day, divided by two. This value starts over at zero each midnight.

Although Visual Basic will update the build and revision numbers for you, you must supply the major and minor version numbers.

2.7 Setting the Startup Form for an Application

Problem

You want to indicate which of the several Windows Forms your application uses is the "main" form, the focal point of the application.

Solution

The application's main form is set through the Project Properties window. From that window, select the Application tab, and then use the "Startup form" field to select the form to use for the main form.

Discussion

You can start up your Visual Basic application using the Windows Forms Application Framework, or without it. The "Enable application framework" field on the Application tab of the Project Properties window enables or disables this feature. When it's enabled, Visual Basic controls the startup process associated with your selected startup form. The Application Framework fires events during the startup process that you can use to include your own custom code. To access these events, click the View Application Events button on the Application panel of the Project Properties window.

If you disable the Application Framework, you have more control over the startup process. All Visual Basic applications begin by running a shared method named Main( ), which will appear somewhere in your application's source code. You can use the "Startup form" field on the Application tab to tell Visual Basic to use the Main( ) method included with a specific form's code. If you do not supply such a method, Visual Basic will implicitly add one to the startup form, using code that looks something like this:

```
Public Shared Sub Main( )
    Application.Run(My.Forms.Form1)
End Sub
```

You may add such a method to your startup form and include additional code as needed.

2.8   Setting the Startup to a Sub Main Procedure

Problem

You decide, after all, that you want to run your own startup code and display the main form after doing some initial nonform processing.

Solution

Sample code folder: Chapter 02\SubMainStartup

Add a Main( ) method to a module in your application, and use that as the startup code. You will need to display forms on your own.

Discussion

Add a module to your project, and then add the Main( ) method with at least the following code:

```
Module Module1
    Public Sub Main( )
        ' ----- Add startup code here, then...
        Application.Run(My.Forms.Form1)
        ' ...passing the startup form as the argument.
    End Sub
End Module
```

Next, mark this Main( ) method as the startup code for your application, via the Application tab of the Project Properties window. Disable the Windows Forms Application Framework by clearing the "Enable application framework" field. Then set the "Startup form" field on that same tab to "Sub Main."

As discussed in the previous recipe, all applications begin from some shared method named Main( ). You can supply your own Main( ) method, and it doesn't need to be part of a form. Adding it to a module with your own initialization code gives you the most control over the application's startup process.

The `Application.Run( )` method runs the primary message loop for your application, a standard part of all Windows desktop programs. Pass an instance of your startup form as an argument; Visual Basic will display this form and keep the program running until the user closes this form.

Because you must disable the Application Framework to use a custom `Main( )` method, some of the convenience and usability features included with the Framework will not be enabled by default. For instance, you will have to manually display and hide any "splash" form that appears during the initialization phase of your application.

See Also

See Recipe 2.7 for additional discussion about startup procedures in Visual Basic applications.

2.9   Getting an Application's Command Line

Problem

You've designed your program to support optional command-line arguments, and you want to process them.

Solution

There are a few different ways to examine and process the command-line options supplied to your program. The first and easiest of the methods involves the Visual Basic `Command( )` function, part of the `Microsoft.VisualBasic` namespace. This function returns the entire set of command-line options as a `String`. For instance, if the user enters the following command:

```
MyApp.exe /option1 /option2 filename.txt
```

the `Command( )` function returns:

```
/option1 /option2 filename.txt
```

The application name and extension are always removed from the string; `Command( )` returns only the options, not the program name.

Because `Command( )` returns a single string with the entire command-line option text, the responsibility for parsing each option from the string rests on your shoulders. However, Visual Basic also supplies a pre-parsed version of the options through the `My.Application.CommandLineArgs` collection. Each zero-based argument in the collection includes one of the original space-delimited options as entered by the user. Thus, using the example command line from just a few paragraphs ago, the following method call:

```
MsgBox(My.Application.CommandLineArgs(1))
```

displays `/option2`, because the collection is zero-based.

Discussion

Many applications support optional command-line arguments, generally to alter the initial view of the application on startup. Normally such arguments are entered through the Windows command prompt, *cmd.exe*. For example, the *Notepad.exe* program accepts a single command-line argument, a filename to open immediately:

```
Notepad.exe c:\temp\DataFile.txt
```

Windows does provide some support for command-line option usage. If you create a shortcut to an application, the Target field in the shortcut's properties (accessed by right-clicking on the shortcut icon and selecting Properties) will accept command-line arguments after the executable name.

If you use the Windows File Explorer to drag and drop a file onto an application (EXE) icon, Windows starts the application, adding the dropped file's name as a command-line argument.

No matter which method you use to add command-line arguments to your application, they are received through the Command( ) and My.Application.CommandLineArgs features of Visual Basic.

There is one exception to this general rule. Visual Basic applications can be configured as "single-instance" applications by selecting the "Make single instance application" field on the Application tab of the Project Properties window. If a user tries to start a second instance of a single-instance application when an instance is already running, the second instance will not run. Instead, a special event triggers in the first instance, informing the program that the user wants to start a new instance. It is up to the program to determine how to handle such requests. The Command( ) and CommandLineArgs features indicate only the options for the initial instance of a single-instance program; command-line arguments for subsequent instances are processed as part of the arguments to the special additional-instance event.

To use this special StartupNextInstance event:

1. Access the Application tab of the Project Properties window.
2. Click on the View Application Events button on that tab to display the source code from the *ApplicationEvents.vb* file.
3. Select "(MyApplication Events)" from the Class Name list that is above and to the left of the code window.
4. Select "StartupNextInstance" from the Method Name list just to the right of the Class Name list.

The following code fragment appears:

```
Private Sub MyApplication_StartupNextInstance( _
      ByVal sender As Object, ByVal e As _
      Microsoft.VisualBasic.ApplicationServices. _
```

```
StartupNextInstanceEventArgs) _
Handles Me.StartupNextInstance
```

```
End Sub
```

The e argument includes a `CommandLine` collection member that works just like the `My.Application.CommandLineArgs` collection but is specific to the new instance requested by the user.

2.10   Testing an Application's Command Line

Problem

You have written an application that supports various custom command-line arguments, and you'd like to test the argument-parsing code from within the development environment.

Solution

Use the "Command line arguments" field in the Project Properties window to enter or modify the temporary testing command-line arguments.

Discussion

You can test this code by setting a temporary command-line argument string for use in your program:

1. Access the Debug tab of the Project Properties window.

2. Type your temporary command line in the "Command line arguments" field.

This temporary argument string is used only when running programs within the Visual Studio development environment.

2.11   Obfuscating an Application

Problem

You've written a pretty cool application, and you'd like to sell it to customers. But you also know that the Intermediate Language (IL) code generated by the Visual Basic compiler can easily be read and turned back into reasonable source code by ne'er-do-wells intent on reaping ill-gotten rewards from your hard effort.

Solution

Use an obfuscator to alter the compiled application, making futile any attempt to reverse-engineer the application back into understandable source code. There are several third-party obfuscators on the market that target .NET-compiled applications.

These programs work with any compiled .NET application, whether they were written in Visual Basic, C#, or some other .NET-enabled language.

Visual Studio 2005 also includes an obfuscator you can use with your own applications. It's called Dotfuscator Community Edition, and although it comes with Visual Studio, it's actually developed by a separate company named PreEmptive Solutions.

It's pretty easy to perform a basic obfuscation using Dotfuscator. First, make sure you have built your application to an EXE executable (or DLL, if relevant). From Visual Studio, select the Tools → Dotfuscator Community Edition menu command. Once you get past some advertising, you will be prompted to create a new project. This is not a Visual Studio project, but a Dotfuscator project. A new project appears via the main Dotfuscator form, as shown in Figure 2-5.

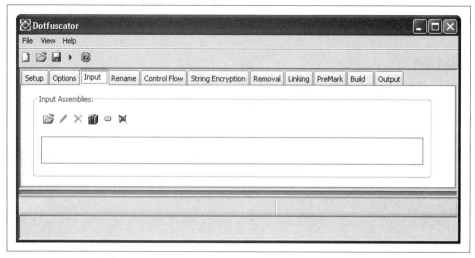

Figure 2-5. A new Dotfuscator project

On the Input tab, use the left-most icon (the Open Folder icon) to locate your EXE assembly. Use the other tabs to fine-tune the obfuscation, if desired. Then use the File → Build menu command to generate an obfuscated version of the project. You'll be prompted to save the settings for this project. Once generated, the obfuscated version of the project appears in a directory named *Dotfuscated* in the same directory where you saved the settings.

Discussion

We obfuscated a simple Windows Forms application that contained (1) a mostly empty form, (2) a static label on that form, and (3) a Click event handler for the label that just displays a message box. We used Microsoft's *IL Disassembler* (*ildasm.exe*, one of the tools included with the .NET Framework SDK installed with Visual Studio) to view the internals of the "before" (Figure 2-6) and "after" (Figure 2-7) assemblies.

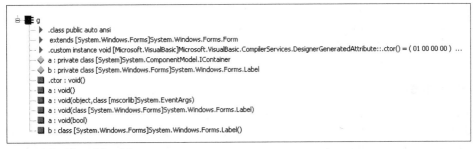

```
⊟ ■ WindowsApplication1.Form1
    ├ ▶ .class public auto ansi
    ├ ▶ extends [System.Windows.Forms]System.Windows.Forms.Form
    ├ ▶ .custom instance void [Microsoft.VisualBasic]Microsoft.VisualBasic.CompilerServices.DesignerGeneratedAttribute::.ctor() = ( 01 00 00 00 ) ...
    ├ ◇ _Label1 : private class [System.Windows.Forms]System.Windows.Forms.Label
    ├ ◇ components : private class [System]System.ComponentModel.IContainer
    ├ ■ .ctor : void()
    ├ ■ Dispose : void(bool)
    ├ ■ InitializeComponent : void()
    ├ ■ Label1_Click : void(object,class [mscorlib]System.EventArgs)
    ├ ■ get_Label1 : class [System.Windows.Forms]System.Windows.Forms.Label()
    ├ ■ set_Label1 : void(class [System.Windows.Forms]System.Windows.Forms.Label)
    └ ▲ Label1 : instance class [System.Windows.Forms]System.Windows.Forms.Label()
```

Figure 2-6. Before obfuscation

```
⊟ ■ g
    ├ ▶ .class public auto ansi
    ├ ▶ extends [System.Windows.Forms]System.Windows.Forms.Form
    ├ ▶ .custom instance void [Microsoft.VisualBasic]Microsoft.VisualBasic.CompilerServices.DesignerGeneratedAttribute::.ctor() = ( 01 00 00 00 ) ...
    ├ ◇ a : private class [System]System.ComponentModel.IContainer
    ├ ◇ b : private class [System.Windows.Forms]System.Windows.Forms.Label
    ├ ■ .ctor : void()
    ├ ■ a : void()
    ├ ■ a : void(object,class [mscorlib]System.EventArgs)
    ├ ■ a : void(class [System.Windows.Forms]System.Windows.Forms.Label)
    ├ ■ a : void(bool)
    └ ■ b : class [System.Windows.Forms]System.Windows.Forms.Label()
```

Figure 2-7. After obfuscation

Clearly, the obfuscation process did make some changes, but in a simple program like this, it's not too difficult to see what it did. It's interesting that the old set_Label1 property component was renamed to a, but the related get_Label1 was renamed b; that's obfuscation in action. Local variables and even embedded strings go through some of the same scrambling procedures. The goal is to scramble the code enough to keep it safe from prying eyes but keep it stable enough to work exactly as it did before obfuscation.

Dotfuscator Community Edition contains basic obfuscation functionality. If you want something more stringent, you will have to upgrade to one of PreEmptive's more advanced versions (for a fee) or find another obfuscation product from a different vendor. Be aware that obfuscation is not for all applications, at least according to the warning label on the Dotfuscator product. It implies that the product is safe to use as long as your application:

> is not designed or intended for use in, or on applications intended for use in on-line control of aircraft, air traffic, aircraft navigation or aircraft communications; or in medical, biological, pharmaceutical, or other life-dependent applications; or in the design, construction, operation or maintenance of any nuclear facility.

See Also

Some of the recipes in Chapter 16 will help you obfuscate—that is, encrypt—the data used by your application.

2.12 Determining if an Application Is Running in the Visual Studio Environment

Problem

Your application needs to respond one way if it is running in the Visual Studio development environment and another way if it is running as a standalone application. For instance, you might want to issue a Stop statement on errors when in the debugging environment but log the errors to a file when running as a standalone application.

Solution

There are a few different ways to determine the running environment of your application, but the simplest is to examine the System.Diagnostics.Debugger.IsAttached flag. If this property is True, your application is running in the development environment.

Discussion

The IsAttached property indicates True whenever your application is running in a debugger that properly sets the underlying value of this flag. That means that if the flag is True, the program may be running in some environment other than Visual Studio. But if your program is running in some nonVisual Studio debugger, there are probably bigger issues of concern.

2.13 Accessing Environment Variables

Problem

Your program relies on data stored in DOS-style environment variables, and you're ready to retrieve some of those values.

Solution

Use the My.Application.GetEnvironmentVariable( ) method to retrieve specific environment variable values.

Discussion

Microsoft's MS-DOS operating system predated Windows, and when Windows was first released, it needed to use and support many of the existing MS-DOS features. One such feature involved *environment variables*, a collection of name/value pairs that served as a set of global constants programs could read and use. For instance, the PATH variable stored a list of directories Windows used to locate programs. Other applications could read the PATH variable for their own use.

To retrieve the PATH environment variable from Visual Basic, use this statement:

```
Dim thePath As String = _
    My.Application.GetEnvironmentVariable("PATH")
```

An error occurs if you supply a variable name that does not exist. If it does exist, the method returns just the value of the variable, not its name.

Visual Basic also includes a built-in Environ() function that provides similar functionality:

```
Dim thePath As String = Environ("PATH")
```

If the supplied variable name cannot be found, Environ() returns an empty string without raising an error.

Environ() also retrieves environment variables by numeric position. The following code scans through the set of environment variables until it hits a blank result, indicating the end of the set of variables:

```
Dim counter As Integer
Dim fullVariable As String
Dim namePart As String
Dim valuePart As String
Dim equalsPosition As Integer

For counter = 1 To 255
    fullVariable = Environ(counter)
    If (fullVariable = "") Then Exit For
    equalsPosition = InStr(fullVariable, "=")
    If (equalsPosition > 0) Then
        namePart = Left(fullVariable, equalsPosition - 1)
        valuePart = Mid(fullVariable, equalsPosition + 1)
        ' ----- Use these values as needed.
    End If
Next counter
```

See Also

For additional information on environment variables, see the online help included with Microsoft Windows. On Windows XP, access help from the Start button (Start → Help), and search for "environment variables."

2.14 Accessing the Registry

Problem

Although you have been warned that accessing the registry can lead to system instability, you need to store and retrieve values in one or more of the registry hives.

Solution

Use the registry features in the My.Computer.Registry object to read, write, and otherwise manipulate registry information.

Discussion

The My.Computer.Registry object includes the following members:

ClassesRoot *field*
> Returns a RegistryKey object that refers to the HKEY_CLASSES_ROOT top-level key of the registry.

CurrentConfig *field*
> Returns a RegistryKey object that refers to the HKEY_CURRENT_CONFIG top-level key of the registry.

CurrentUser *field*
> Returns a RegistryKey object that refers to the HKEY_CURRENT_USER top-level key of the registry.

DynData *field*
> Returns a RegistryKey object that refers to the HKEY_DYN_DATA top-level key of the registry.

GetValue( ) *method*
> Retrieves the data associated with a specific key and value somewhere in the registry.

LocalMachine *field*
> Returns a RegistryKey object that refers to the HKEY_LOCAL_MACHINE top-level key of the registry.

PerformanceData *field*
> Returns a RegistryKey object that refers to the HKEY_PERFORMANCE_DATA top-level key of the registry.

SetValue( ) *method*
> Adds or updates the data associated with a specific key and value somewhere in the registry.

Users *field*
> Returns a RegistryKey object that refers to the HKEY_USERS top-level key of the registry.

Most of the Registry members return a RegistryKey object, a generic object that can refer to any key within the registry. This object also has many useful members. Some members let you manipulate the keys that appear just below the one represented by the RegistryKey object:

- CreateSubKey( ) method
- DeleteSubKey( ) method

- `DeleteSubKeyTree( )` method
- `GetSubKeyNames( )` method
- `OpenSubKey( )` method
- `SubKeyCount` property

Other members focus on the values tied to the active key:

- `DeleteValue( )` method
- `GetValue( )` method
- `GetValueKind( )` method
- `GetValueNames( )` method
- `SetValue( )` method
- `ValueCount` property

Using any of the registry-related members is simple. For instance, you can display the `\\HKEY_CURRENT_USER\Environment\TEMP` value (Environment is a key, TEMP is a value) using the following statement:

```
MsgBox(My.Computer.Registry.GetValue( _
    "HKEY_CURRENT_USER\Environment", "TEMP", ""))
```

On our system, this statement displays the following result:

```
C:\Documents and Settings\Administrator\Local Settings\Temp
```

But if you use the RegEdit application to view that same value, you see something a little different:

```
%USERPROFILE%\Local Settings\Temp
```

The `GetValue( )` method performs some basic environment variable substitution on the stored registry value before returning it back to you. To get the unexpanded version, you need to go through one of the exposed `RegistryKey` objects:

```
Dim envKey As Microsoft.Win32.RegistryKey = _
    My.Computer.Registry.CurrentUser.OpenSubKey( _
    "Environment", False)
MsgBox(envKey.GetValue("TEMP", "", _
    Microsoft.Win32.RegistryValueOptions. _
    DoNotExpandEnvironmentNames))
envKey.Close( )
```

The `DoNotExpandEnvironmentNames` flag prompts the `GetValue( )` method to return the original unexpanded version of the value.

The Windows registry combines a machine- and user-specific hierarchical database of text, numeric, and binary values for use by both the operating system and applications installed on the local system. The hierarchy is akin to the directory/file structure used in the Windows file system, in which *keys* parallel directories, and *values* are similar to files. However, the registry is much more limited in what it can store at each hierarchy level.

Keys are named branches, all starting from a limited set of top-level keys known as *hives*. Each key can include any number of subkeys, plus zero or more values. Each value can store basic data values or can simply exist without data. Each key has a *default value* that includes no specific name. Figure 2-8 shows some of the components of the registry as viewed through the RegEdit application included with Windows.

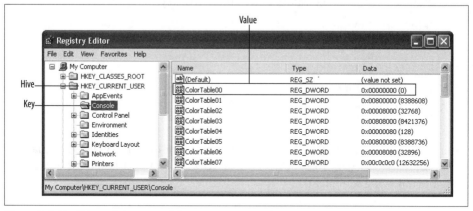

Figure 2-8. RegEdit and the parts of the registry

Users needing access to the registry must be authorized through Windows. Normally, a user has full read/write access to all hives associated with the active user account, plus at least read access to most of the system hives. However, an administrator can place restrictions on portions of the registry, so error handling is recommended when using the various registry features of .NET.

The focus on the Windows registry has changed over the years. Originally, it was designed to support the Object Linking and Embedding (OLE) features of Windows and to provide central access to common system settings. For a while, Microsoft encouraged software developers to use the registry for application-specific settings as well. Unfortunately, this led to "registry bloat" that in some cases reduced overall application and system performance. Microsoft now recommends that applications store system-wide and user-specific settings in separate configuration files in the standard file system. With .NET's limited dependence on OLE/ActiveX components, even Microsoft is getting in on the separate-configuration-file act.

2.15 Getting System Information

Problem

You've heard that .NET provides powerful access to the most essential features of Windows, but the Framework Class Library is huge, and you're not sure where to find the total amount of memory installed on the local system. How can you get system-specific information quickly and easily?

Solution

Use the various objects and members of Visual Basic's My namespace. Microsoft introduced this new feature in the 2005 release of the language.

Discussion

The My namespace was added to Visual Basic to help restore some of the simplicity and accessibility of Visual Basic that was lost in its transition to .NET.

For example, to determine the amount of installed memory on the local system, use the following statement:

```
Dim installedMemory As Long = _
    My.Computer.Info.TotalPhysicalMemory
```

Another useful source of system settings is the `System.Windows.Forms.SystemInformation` object, which has dozens of informative members.

The My hierarchy makes an incredible number of features available in one easy-to-access place. Table 2-1 includes a small sampling of the information you can obtain from the My namespace.

Table 2-1. A sampling of My features

If you need to access this information...	...use this My namespace member
The command-line arguments used to start the program	`My.Application.CommandLineArgs`
The application version number	`My.Application.Info.Version`
The set of all forms currently open	`My.Application.OpenForms`
Features to read and write clipboard data	`My.Computer.Clipboard`
The current value of the system timer	`My.Computer.Clock.TickCount`
The current directory recognized by the application	`My.Computer.FileSystem.CurrentDirectory`
The location of the user's "My Documents" directory	`My.Computer.FileSystem.SpecialDirectories.MyDocuments`
The directory used to store the user's temporary files	`My.Computer.FileSystem.SpecialDirectories.Temp`
The version of the operating system	`My.Computer.Info.OSVersion`
Total installed memory	`My.Computer.Info.TotalPhysicalMemory`
Whether the user's mouse has a scroll wheel installed	`My.Computer.Mouse.WheelExists`
The assigned name of the computer	`My.Computer.Name`
Whether access to Internet or the local network is enabled	`My.Computer.Network.IsAvailable`
The assigned name of the current Windows user	`My.User.Name`

The My namespace collects some of the most useful and (sometimes) complex areas of the .NET Framework Class Libraries and makes them available in a simpler and more ordered format. The My keyword, a new 2005 feature specific to Visual Basic, is at the top of a hierarchy of features that are organized much like .NET namespaces. Each major object node within the hierarchy implements various properties and methods that are relevant to the specific object. In most cases, each method or property can be found somewhere else in the large set of .NET classes, although it may take several source code steps to obtain the information you need from that distant member.

The following list of objects summarizes the features exposed through the My hierarchy:

My.Application
> Provides access to application- and instance-specific settings, such as command-line arguments, and in-effect regional and language settings.

My.Application.Info
> Reports details about the active executing assembly, including its title and version number.

My.Application.Log
> Provides access to trace recording and logging features for desktop and console applications (not ASP.NET).

My.Computer
> Exposes information pertaining to the computer running the application. Most of the members of this object are other subordinate objects with their own methods and properties.

My.Computer.Audio
> Enables you to play system and file-based sounds.

My.Computer.Clipboard
> Provides access to features that let you place data on the system clipboard and retrieve data back from that same clipboard in a variety of common and custom data formats.

My.Computer.Clock
> Provides access to the current system time in a standard or local format.

My.Computer.FileSystem
> Provides access to various features that let you manage files and directories on local and remote file systems and that manipulate path strings.

My.Computer.FileSystem.SpecialDirectories
> Reports locations of the various special directories, such as the "My Documents" directory.

My.Computer.Info
> Reveals information about the local operating system and memory usage.

My.Computer.Keyboard
> Reports the current state of the keyboard.

`My.Computer.Mouse`

Reports various properties of the installed mouse.

`My.Computer.Network`

Reports availability of the network connection on the current workstation, and provides features that let you transfer data over that network.

`My.Computer.Ports`

Provides access to the system serial ports.

`My.Computer.Registry`

Provides features that let you manage the keys and values within the Windows registry.

`My.Forms`

Provides access to all forms defined in the active Windows Forms application.

`My.Log`

Provides access to trace recording and logging features for ASP.NET applications only.

`My.Request`

Replicates the Active Server Pages "Request" object within an ASP.NET application.

`My.Resources`

Provides access to application-specific resources, including string, graphic, and binary resource data.

`My.Response`

Replicates the Active Server Pages "Response" object within an ASP.NET application.

`My.Settings`

Provides access to system- and user-focused configuration settings used by the application and automatically stored in application-specific XML configuration files.

`My.User`

Contains authentication and identity details gathered about the current user, either through Windows authentication or some other authentication scheme.

`My.WebServices`

Contains a collection of all XML web services known to the active application. This object is not available in ASP.NET applications; it is only used by Windows Forms, console, and other non-web application types.

See Also

For a full reference of the objects and members included in the My hierarchy, see *Visual Basic 2005 in a Nutshell* by Tim Patrick, Steven Roman, Ron Petrusha, and Paul Lomaxone, one of O'Reilly's reference works focused on the Visual Basic language.

All members of the My namespace hierarchy are fully documented in the MSDN documentation included with Visual Studio.

2.16 Getting the User's Name

Problem

You need to obtain the name of the current Windows user.

Solution

Use the My.User.Name property to get the domain and login ID of the current user.

Discussion

The My.User.Name property returns a string containing the current user ID and related domain name in the format "domain/user." If the user is part of a workgroup instead of a domain, the domain portion may be replaced by the local machine name. Applications written using ASP.NET do not have access to the same type of user information as desktop applications because Web Forms programs run in the context of a special web-application user.

If your application uses an authentication system other than the default Windows security scheme, My.User.Name may return information about the current user in a different format.

If you don't like the merged "domain/user" format, you can get the individual components from other areas within the .NET object hierarchy. These three properties will probably get you what you need:

- System.Environment.MachineName
- System.Environment.UserDomainName
- System.Environment.UserName

If you are interested in identifying the registered owner of the local workstation, you can find that information in the system portion of the registry. The key is:

    \\HKEY_LOCAL_MACHINE\SOFTWARE\Microsoft\Windows\CurrentVersion

The RegisteredOrganization and RegisteredOwner values within that key supply the values that you often see when installing new software on your system.

See Also

Recipe 2.15 provides additional resources for gathering system- and user-specific details from .NET.

Application Organization

3.0 Introduction

This chapter shows you how some of the object-oriented programming (OOP) features in Visual Basic 2005 are used to build Visual Basic applications. These features include class constructors, namespaces, and support for overloading. While you will spend most of your coding life writing the basic logic of your functions, properties, and Sub procedures, you wouldn't be able to do it without the basic container systems introduced here.

3.1 Creating a Code Module

Problem

You would like to add some general methods and fields that are accessible to your entire application.

Solution

Add a code module—a construct that is similar to a class, but uses the Module keyword instead of Class—to your application.

Discussion

Visual Basic includes three major code and value containers: classes, structures, and modules. All three types are based on the core definition of a class, but there are times when you'll want to choose one over another. Modules are useful for storing functions, subroutines, constants, and variable fields that are considered "global" to your entire application. In pre-.NET versions of Visual Basic, most nonform-specific code was stored in a similar "module file" (with a ".bas" file extension). Modules in .NET provide some of that same functionality but in an object-oriented context.

If you've already created a new project or opened an existing project in Visual Studio, you can add a new module through the Project → Add Module menu command. The Add New Item dialog (Figure 3-1) should already have the Module template selected. Simply give it a useful name in the Name field, then click the Add button.

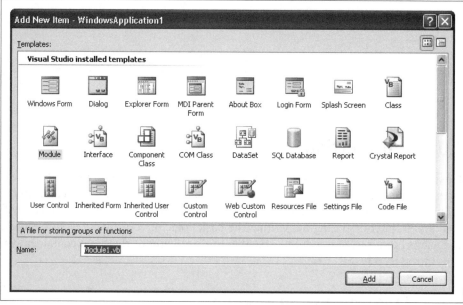

Figure 3-1. Visual Studio's Add New Item dialog

Visual Studio presents you with the code for this new template:

```
Module Module1

End Module
```

You can start adding members to the module immediately. Supported members include Sub procedures, functions, properties, events, delegates, classes, structures, and enumerations. Before coding each member, decide the access you want to grant and prefix the definition with the appropriate access keyword (Public, Shared, or Friend). For instance, the following block of code adds a function to the module Module1 and assigns the function Public access:

```
Module Module1
    Public Function DoubleIt(ByVal origValue As Integer) _
          As Integer
       Return origValue * 2
    End Function
End Module
```

Modules specify their own access levels, using the Public or Friend keywords; the default is Friend. All members of a module act as if they are marked with the Shared keyword. That is, you can use any member of a module without creating an instance of the module itself. And that's a good thing because Visual Basic will not allow you to create an instance of a module.

You aren't required to create separate source-code files for new modules (or for classes or structures, which are discussed in later recipes), although you should. Having a one-to-one correspondence between modules (or classes or structures) and source-code files makes things easier to manage. Still, you may need to double up constructs in a single source-code file. If you already have a file with a class defined, you can include a module definition in the same file, outside the class:

```
Class SomeClass
    ' ----- Class members go here.
End Class
Module SomeModule
    ' ----- Module members go here.
End Module
```

If you try to do this in a form class file for a desktop application project, the Visual Studio Form Designer looks only at the first class in the file. If you insert a module (or a structure or another class) before the form-derived class in the file, Visual Studio can't display the form.

All members of a module are shared and can be used immediately throughout the application. You can limit a member to just the code within the module by using the Private access-level keyword with that member:

```
Module Module1
    Private Sub InModuleUseOnly( )
    End Sub
End Module
```

This is commonly done with so-called helper methods that can be accessed only by other, more prominent methods in the same module.

See Also

Recipes 3.2 and 3.3 introduce classes and structures, the two other major type constructs in Visual Basic.

3.2   Creating a Class

Problem

You need to add a new class to your Visual Basic application.

Solution

To add a new project class to your application, select the Project → Add Class menu command, and complete the Add New Item dialog.

Discussion

The Add New Item dialog, shown in Figure 3-2, prompts you by selecting the Class template.

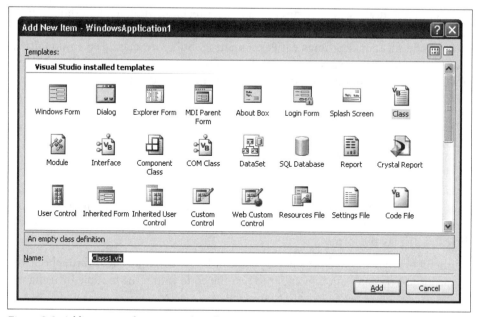

Figure 3-2. Adding a new class in Visual Studio

Give your class a new name, and then click the Add button. Visual Basic displays your newly added class in a code editor window. For example, providing "Class1.vb" for the new class filename adds the class source-code file and displays the following empty class template:

```
Public Class Class1

End Class
```

Of the various object types included with Visual Basic (classes, structures, and modules), classes have the most flexibility and the least restrictions on use. You can add pretty much any supported member type, including Sub procedures, functions, fields, constants, enumerations, events, delegates, other classes and structures, and properties. Here is a simple class that uses many of those features:

```
Public Class Employee
    ' ----- Basic employee information fields.
    Public LastName As String
    Public FirstName As String
    Public HireDate As Date
    Public JobType As EmployeeJobType
    Private CurrentSalary As Decimal
```

```
' ----- Supplies values to the JobType public field.
Public Enum EmployeeJobType
   CLevel
   Manager
   NonManager
   Contractor
End Enum

' ----- Used by the SalaryChanged event arguments.
Public Class SalaryChangedEventArgs
   Inherits System.EventArgs
   Public OldSalary As Decimal
   Public NewSalary As Decimal
End Class

' ----- Argument signature for the SalaryChanged event.
Public Delegate Sub SalaryChangedDelegate( _
   ByVal sender As Object, _
   ByVal e As SalaryChangedEventArgs)

' ----- Issued when private CurrentSalary field changes.
Public Event SalaryChanged As SalaryChangedDelegate

Public Function GetFullName() As String
   ' ----- Return a nicely formatted name.
   Return FirstName & " " & LastName
End Function

Public Sub GiveRaise(ByVal percentIncrease As Decimal)
   ' ----- To raise 10%, set percentIncrease to 0.10.
   Dim changeDetail As New SalaryChangedEventArgs

   ' ----- Record the new salary, keeping track
   '       of the change.
   changeDetail.OldSalary = CurrentSalary
   CurrentSalary += (CurrentSalary * percentIncrease)
   changeDetail.NewSalary = CurrentSalary

   ' ----- Inform anyone who may be interested.
   RaiseEvent SalaryChanged(Me, changeDetail)
End Sub

Public Property Salary() As Decimal
   Get
      ' ----- Report the current salary level.
      Return CurrentSalary
   End Get
   Set(ByVal value As Decimal)
      ' ----- Update the private CurrentSalary field.
      Dim changeDetail As New SalaryChangedEventArgs

      ' ----- Ignore negative salaries.
      If (value < 0@) Then Exit Property
```

```
        ' ----- Record the new salary, keeping track
        '       of the change.
        changeDetail.OldSalary = CurrentSalary
        CurrentSalary = value
        changeDetail.NewSalary = value

        ' ----- Inform anyone who may be interested.
        RaiseEvent SalaryChanged(Me, changeDetail)
      End Set
    End Property
  End Class
```

One source-code file may include multiple classes, structures, and modules:

```
Class Class1
   ' ----- First class members go here.
End Class
Class Class2
   ' ----- Second class members go here.
End Class
```

If you attempt this in a form class file, the Visual Studio Form Designer looks only at the first class in the file. If you insert a class (or structure or module) before the form-derived class in the file, Visual Studio can't display the form.

Classes are the basic building blocks of Visual Basic applications. The two other major types—structures and modules—are variations of the basic class type, with certain restrictions that make them useful in certain cases.

The code for a class usually appears in a source-code file all its own, although you can divide a class into multiple files (see Recipe 3.9). You can also store multiple classes in a single source-code file, but this can quickly clutter your code.

See Also

Recipes 3.1 and 3.3 introduce modules and structures, the two other major type constructs in Visual Basic.

3.3 Creating a Structure

Problem

You would like to add a new structure to your Visual Basic application.

Solution

Visual Studio does not include an Add Structure menu command, or even a structure-focused template available via the Project → Add New Item menu command. If you want to include a structure in a file all its own, use the Project → Add New Item menu command, and select the Code File template in the Add New Item dialog, as

shown in Figure 3-3. You can also simply type a new structure construct in any existing source-code file.

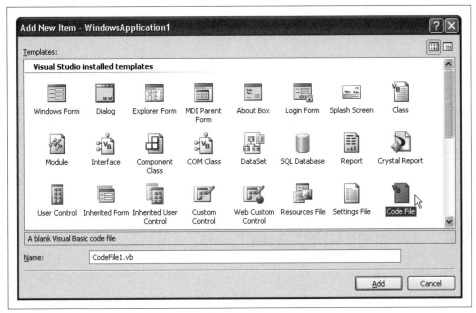

Figure 3-3. Adding a new structure in Visual Studio

Discussion

The syntax for a structure is very similar to that of a class:

```
Structure Structure1

End Structure
```

Add members to your structure just as you would in a class. Since structures cannot
be used to derive other structures, some keywords that support derived classes (such
as the `Protected` and `MustOverride` keywords) cannot be used.

Structures must have at least one public instance member or event definition.

The .NET Framework defines two categories of types: *reference types* and *value
types*. Value types contain basic data at the memory location assigned for a specific
instance. If you looked at the memory location assigned to an `Integer` value type
instance, you would find the `Integer` value that the program last assigned to that
variable.

Reference types store their data indirectly. The memory location assigned to a reference type contains another memory address that identifies the true storage area of
the data. (This is similar to the pointer used in programming languages such as C.)

In Visual Basic, classes define reference types, while structures define value types. All classes and structures ultimately derive from the common System.Object class, but value types go through the related System.ValueType class on the way to System.Object.

Because structures store their data directly, they are sometimes faster to use (by the CPU) than classes, and their data can be stored on the application stack. Classes always require one or more trips to main memory. However, structures do have some limitations not placed on classes. Structures cannot be used as bases for other structures, nor can a structure derive from other structures or classes. Also, structures do not support *destructors*, which are special methods included in classes that perform final cleanup of resources whenever a class instance is being destroyed.

See Also

Recipes 3.1 and 3.2 introduce modules and classes, the two other major type constructs in Visual Basic.

3.4 Creating Other Item Types

Problem

Are there any other types of files or items I can add to a Visual Basic project?

Solution

The Add New Item dialog, accessed through the Project → Add New Item menu command, includes a large selection of template choices. Select the one that meets your needs. Some templates use a different default file extension than the standard *.vb* extension.

Discussion

Here are the Visual Basic–specific template choices installed by default with Visual Studio 2005 Professional Edition:

Windows Form
> Adds a blank Windows form, derived from System.Windows.Forms.Form.

Dialog
> Adds a new Windows "dialog-style" form to your project, derived from System. Windows.Forms.Form. The form includes basic OK and Cancel buttons and is configured for typical dialog presentation.

Explorer Form
> Adds a new Windows form to your project that has the basic look and functionality of the Windows File Explorer (*explorer.exe*). The main area of the form combines TreeView and ListView controls that provide an interface to the file system.

MDI Parent Form

If you are designing a Multi Document Interface (MDI) application, this form represents the parent that will include the various child "document" forms.

About Box

Adds a new "About" form to your project. This is a standard Windows form, predesigned to look like a typical About form. It automatically fills in application-specific details such as the version number. You must add the code elsewhere in your project to display this form.

Login Form

Adds a new "Login" form to your project. This form includes the "look and feel" of a login form only; you must supply authentication code on your own.

Splash Screen

Adds a new "Splash Screen" form to your project. This form appears as your application performs basic initialization during startup.

Class

Adds a new class file to your project, containing an empty class definition named according to the filename you provide.

Module

Adds a new module file to your project, containing an empty module definition named according to the filename you provide.

Interface

Adds a new interface file to your project, containing an empty interface definition named according to the filename you provide. By custom, interface names always begin with a capital letter "I."

Component Class

Adds a new "component" to your project, derived from `System.ComponentModel.Component`. The .NET component model provides basic interaction services for classes defined as components. All Windows Forms controls are components.

COM Class

Adds a new class file to your project that exposes COM interface features. This is done via the `ComClassAttribute` attribute. All exposed interfaces have to be marshaled across the managed .NET boundary, although .NET performs most of the difficult work for you.

Data Set

Adds a new data set to your project with an *.xsd* file extension. These data sets provide a visual design experience to underlying data stores, such as databases. You can include queried data from several data sources.

SQL Database

Adds a new SQL Server database file with an *.mdf* file extension. This file is managed by SQL Server, and you must have that product installed to use this item type.

Report

Visual Studio includes its own banded report writer that you can use to create data reports. This item adds a new report with an *.rdlc* file extension. The report designer interacts with data sources defined in your application.

Crystal Report

Crystal Reports is a third-party banded reporting tool included with Visual Studio. This item adds a new Crystal Report to your application with an ".rpt" file extension. Enhanced versions of the Crystal Reports product are available from its vendor, Business Objects. (Crystal Reports has passed through several ownership changes since its initial version. Business Objects is the owner as of this writing.)

User Control

Adds a new user control file to your application, derived from System.Windows. Forms.UserControl. User controls contain full user interaction functionality, similar to the controls already included in the Visual Studio Toolbox. You can build your control from other controls in the Toolbox or from scratch by managing all input and display needs.

Inherited Form

Adds a new form based on another form already found in your project. When selected, Visual Studio displays the Inheritance Picker dialog with a list of all forms in your project. Visual Studio must be able to create an instance of each potential form. Therefore, you must have built your project at least once, including the form to be inherited. Also, the Inheritance Picker will exclude any form marked as MustInherit. You can manually create inherited forms using the Inherits keyword.

Inherited User Control

Adds a new user control based on another user control already found in your project. When selected, Visual Studio displays the Inheritance Picker dialog with a list of all user controls in your project. Visual Studio must be able to create an instance of each potential user control. Therefore, you must have built your project at least once, including the user control to be inherited. Also, the Inheritance Picker will exclude any user control marked as MustInherit. You can manually create inherited controls using the Inherits keyword.

Custom Control

Creates a new user control but with more emphasis on controls that will contain no existing subordinate controls. You will manage the full display of the control yourself.

Web Custom Control

Creates a new web control for use in ASP.NET applications that's similar to the controls supplied with the Web Forms package. You are responsible for all HTML rendering code.

Resources File

Adds a new resource file to your project, with an *.resx* file extension. New Windows Forms projects already include a project-focused resource file.

Settings File

Adds a ".settings" file to your application that stores application- or user-specific settings. Windows Forms applications already include both kinds of settings support.

Code File

Adds a blank code file to your project. The file will be completely empty, waiting for you to add a class, module, structure, or other content.

Class Diagram

Adds a new class diagram file with a *.cd* file extension. Class diagrams let you define classes, structures, interfaces, and other basic types using a visual designer interface. Visual Studio manages the other files in your application as you make changes to the class diagram.

XML File

Adds a new XML (Extensible Markup Language) file with an *.xml* file extension. Visual Studio includes basic IntelliSense support for editing XML files.

XML Schema

Adds a new XSD (XML Schema Definition) file with an *.xsd* file extension. XSD files can be used to validate XML data.

XSLT File

Adds a new XSLT (Extensible Stylesheet Language Transformation) file with an *.xslt* file extension. XSLT files are used to transform XML data into another format (either XML or any other format).

Text File

Adds a blank text file to your project with a *.txt* file extension. You can add any text to this file that you wish.

HTML Page

Adds a new HTML file with an *.htm* file extension. Visual Studio includes extended support for editing web pages.

Bitmap File

Adds a new bitmap file with a *.bmp* file extension that you can edit directly in Visual Studio.

Cursor File

Adds a new icon file with a *.cur* file extension that you can edit directly in Visual Studio.

Icon File

Adds a new icon file with an *.ico* file extension that you can edit directly in Visual Studio.

Application Configuration File

Adds a new *.config* settings file to your application. This file is often used to configure an application from .NET's point of view. To store application- and user-specific usage settings, consider a settings file instead.

Transactional Component

Adds a new transactional component that manages the lifetime of some data, resource, or activity. These components inherit from the System. EnterpriseServices.ServicedComponent class and exist mainly to interact within COM+ environments.

Installer Class

Adds an installer class you can use to create custom installation scenarios for .NET applications. For typical .NET applications, you should consider creating a standard deployment project instead.

Windows Service

Adds a class that supports the creation of a Windows Service. Services have no direct user interface, so you should not add this template to a Windows Forms application.

If you use one of the other Visual Studio editions, such as the Express Edition, the list of available templates may differ. If you have installed third-party products that enhance Visual Studio, you may see additional templates related to those products.

The My Templates section of the Add New Item dialog includes custom file templates that you have added yourself, primarily through the Export Template Wizard available through the File → Export Template menu command.

See Also

This recipe does not discuss the types of items you can add to an ASP.NET web project. See the recipes in Chapter 17 for additional information on creating web projects.

3.5 Creating Object Instances

Problem

You need to create an instance of a class or structure.

Solution

Use the New keyword to create a new class or structure instance.

Discussion

There are three basic places you use the New keyword:

- When you declare a new instance of a type. The Dim statement offers a few different variations when using the New keyword. Both of the following examples create a new instance of a project-specific Employee class. Other than the minor syntax differences, the two lines are functionally identical:

```
Dim someEmployee As New Employee
Dim someEmployee As Employee = New Employee
```

- When you assign new instances to existing variables. Once you have a variable defined, you can assign it an instance using New:

```
Dim someEmployee As Employee
someEmployee = New Employee
```

- In-line, whenever you need an instance that you don't capture in a variable. Sometimes you simply need a class to exist only within a statement, perhaps as an argument to another function. This is quite common when working with GDI+ graphic elements, such as pens. The following code block draws a line on a form during its Paint event. It creates a new Pen object that disappears once the call to DrawLine( ) ends:

```
Private Sub Form1_Paint(ByVal sender As Object, _
      ByVal e As System.Windows.Forms.PaintEventArgs) _
      Handles Me.Paint
   e.Graphics.DrawLine(New Pen(Color.Red), 0, 0, 100, 100)
End Sub
```

All three uses of New can be intermixed within the same block of code, and you can choose what best fits the needs and logic of the code block.

See Also

The New keyword is also used in a different context to create class constructors. See Recipe 3.6 for additional details.

3.6   Initializing a Class Instance with Data

Problem

You want to ensure that some of the fields of a class are initialized before any of the exposed members of the class are used.

Solution

Add one or more custom constructors to your class.

Discussion

Constructors are Sub procedures named New:

```
Public Sub New( )

End Sub
```

A constructor with no arguments implements the *default constructor*. This is the constructor that is called anytime a new instance of the class is requested without additional initialization:

```
Dim someEmployee As New Employee
```

'*Custom constructors* include one or more arguments. This sample accepts an initial employee name and assigns it to the public Name field:

```
Class Employee
    Public Name As String = "Unknown"

    Public Sub New(ByVal fullName As String)
        If (Trim(fullName) <> "") Then Name = fullName
    End Sub
End Class
```

One feature of classes is *overloaded methods*, which use the special Overloads keyword. This feature lets you use the same method name more than once in the same class, but have each method accept a different set of arguments. (See Recipe 3.14 for more information.) Constructors can also be overloaded, but they don't require the Overloads keyword:

```
Class Employee
    Public Name As String = "Unknown"
    Public Salary As Decimal = 0@

    Public Sub New(ByVal fullName As String)
        If (Trim(fullName) <> "") Then Name = fullName
    End Sub

    Public Sub New(ByVal fullName As String, _
            ByVal startingSalary As Decimal)
        If (Trim(fullName) <> "") Then Name = fullName
        If (startingSalary >= 0@) Then Salary = startingSalary
    End Sub
End Class
```

Visual Basic calls the appropriate constructor based on the argument signature:

```
' ----- Uses the one-argument constructor.
Dim someEmployee As New Employee("John Smith")
' ----- Uses the two-argument constructor.
Dim someEmployee As New Employee("John Smith", 50000@)
```

As an alternative way of doing the same thing, this sample class could have used an optional argument on a single constructor:

```
Class Employee
    Public Name As String = "Unknown"
    Public Salary As Decimal = 0@

    Public Sub New(ByVal fullName As String, _
            Optional ByVal startingSalary As Decimal = 0@)
```

```
          If (Trim(fullName) <> "") Then Name = fullName
          If (startingSalary >= 0@) Then Salary = startingSalary
      End Sub
   End Class
```

If you don't supply a default constructor but do supply constructors with arguments, any use of the class requires constructor arguments. If you want the arguments to be optional, either use the `Optional` keyword or include a default constructor with no arguments.

All classes must have a constructor, even classes that perform no specific initialization. Consider this empty class:

```
   Class Employee

   End Class
```

Although you don't see a specific constructor, a default constructor is there, supplied on your behalf by the Visual Basic compiler. Any constructor you supply, default or with arguments, replaces the one added by Visual Basic.

All classes (except `System.Object`) derive from some other class. The default constructor for the base class is called implicitly from a derived class's constructor. Derived classes can also use a specific base-class constructor by calling it directly:

```
   Class Manager
      Inherits Employee

      Public Sub New( )
         MyBase.New("Unnamed New Employee")
      End Sub
   End Class
```

You can create instances of either classes or structures in your code. Modules cannot be instantiated, and therefore they do not use constructors.

See Also

Recipe 3.7 discusses destructors, which handle the end of an instance's lifetime instead of its beginning.

3.7   Releasing an Instance's Resources

Problem

Your class instance allocates resources during its lifetime, and you want to ensure that those resources are freed when the object is destroyed.

Solution

Add a `Finalize( )` method to your class that includes any cleanup code you need to run before .NET destroys the class instance. `Finalize( )` is a method included in the `System.Object` base class. To use it in your code, you must override it:

```
Protected Overrides Sub Finalize( )
```

Because a base class from which you derive may need to perform its own cleanup, you should always call its `Finalize( )` method:

```
Protected Overrides Sub Finalize( )
    ' ----- Perform my cleanup, then...
    MyBase.Finalize( )
End Sub
```

Discussion

.NET includes a process, known as *garbage collection*, which automatically releases all memory associated with a class instance. However, it doesn't know what processing is required to release any acquired external resources, such as database connections. Therefore, you must provide that logic in a special method, implemented through an override of the `Finalize( )` method. This special method is known as the class's *destructor*.

The garbage collector in .NET runs as needed, so there is no guarantee that your `Finalize( )` method will be called at the moment you release all references to an instance. It may be called one second, ten seconds, or ten minutes later, possibly long after your application has stopped running. If you need resources to be released in a timelier manner, combine the destructor with the `IDisposable` interface. This interface defines features that help release resources on a schedule you determine. More specifically, resources are released whenever the related `Dispose( )` method is called on your instance. (You could simply include your own custom `FreeResources( )` method in your class, but using `IDisposable` allows Visual Basic to get more involved in the cleanup process.)

To enable `IDisposable` in your class, add an `Implements` statement at the top of the class:

```
Class ResourceUsingClass
    Implements IDisposable
End Class
```

When you add that `Implements` line to your class, Visual Studio automatically adds a template of features:

```
Class ResourceUsingClass
    Implements IDisposable

    ' To detect redundant calls
    Private disposedValue As Boolean = False
```

```
    ' IDisposable
    Protected Overridable Sub Dispose( _
        ByVal disposing As Boolean)
      If Not Me.disposedValue Then
        If disposing Then
          ' TODO: free unmanaged resources when
          '       explicitly called
        End If

        ' TODO: free shared unmanaged resources
      End If
      Me.disposedValue = True
    End Sub

#Region " IDisposable Support "
    ' This code added by Visual Basic to correctly
    ' implement the disposable pattern.
    Public Sub Dispose() Implements IDisposable.Dispose
        ' Do not change this code. Put cleanup code in
        ' Dispose(ByVal disposing As Boolean) above.
        Dispose(True)
        GC.SuppressFinalize(Me)
    End Sub
#End Region

End Class
```

Fill in the "TODO" parts of the code with your resource-freeing logic.

When using the IDisposable interface, you should still implement the Finalize( ) destructor just in case someone forgets to call Dispose( ). Maintain a flag in your class that indicates whether resources have been properly freed or not. The disposedValue variable that Visual Studio generated serves this purpose.

Some Visual Basic features call Dispose( ) automatically when working with IDisposable-enabled objects. The Visual Basic Using statement exists to destroy objects when they are no longer needed, and it calls Dispose( ) automatically:

```
Using externalResources As New ResourceUsingClass
    ' ----- Work with the externalResources instance here.
End Using
' ----- At this point, externalResources.Dispose has been
'       called automatically by the End Using statement.
```

See Also

Recipe 3.6 discusses constructors, the opposite of destructors.

3.8   Using Namespaces

Problem

You want to place your classes within a specific .NET namespace.

Solution

Use the `Namespace` statement together with the default namespace identified in a project's properties.

Discussion

Every Visual Basic application resides within a default namespace, what we'll call the "absolute namespace position" for your application. Visual Studio automatically sets this to a top-level namespace with the same name as your project. For instance, if you just accept the default "WindowsApplication1" name for a new Windows Forms application, the namespace is also named `WindowsApplication1`. Since it's a top-level namespace, it resides at the same hierarchy position as the `System` namespace.

To alter the namespace for your project, open the Project Properties window, and change the "Root namespace" field on the Application tab. You can change it to use an existing namespace, such as `System.Windows.Forms`, but then you must take care to avoid naming conflicts with your classes.

When generating a full .NET application (EXE), your choice of namespace is not too problematic because that namespace exists only within the view of your program and its lifetime. Two applications using the `WindowsApplication1` namespace will not conflict with each other. However, if you generate a .NET library (DLL) for general distribution to others outside your organization, you should select a namespace that will avoid conflicts with others. Microsoft recommends that you use a combination of your company name and the product name, as they did with the `Microsoft.VisualBasic` namespace.

Beyond the absolute namespace position, you can place your classes and other types in a "relative namespace position" within the larger default absolute namespace. When you add a class (or other type) to your project, it appears in the absolute namespace position:

```
Class Class1

End Class
```

If your project uses `WindowsApplication1` as its absolute namespace, this class appears as `WindowsApplication1.Class1`. In relative positioning, you can insert a new namespace between the absolute position and the class:

```
Namespace CoolClasses
    Class Class1

    End Class
End Namespace
```

Now, `Class1` is fully referenced as `WindowsApplication1.CoolClasses.Class1`.

The `Namespace` keyword may include multiple namespace components (separated by periods), and you can nest them as well:

```
Namespace CoolClasses
    Namespace SomewhatCool.BarelyCool
        Class Class1

        End Class
    End Namespace
End Namespace
```

This `Class1` lives at `WindowsApplication1.CoolClasses.SomewhatCool.BarelyCool`.

3.9   Splitting a Class Across Multiple Files

Problem

You have a class that is simply too much to manage reasonably in a single source-code file, and you would like to split it up.

Solution

Use the `Partial` keyword on a class to enable splitting the implementation of that class across multiple physical source files:

```
Partial Class Class1

End Class
```

Discussion

Visual Basic now includes a *partial class* feature that Visual Studio uses to separate automatically generated code from nongenerated code. This feature is available to use in your own classes. Before Visual Basic 2005, if you tried to split a class by using the `Class` statement multiple times on the same class name, the program would not compile. But now you can break up your class into separate sections:

```
Class Class1
    ' ----- Some class members are defined here.
End Class
Partial Class Class1
    ' ----- More class members are defined here.
End Class
```

The key is the word `Partial`. Adding the keyword `Partial` to at least one of the class components tells the Visual Basic compiler to collect all the parts and put them together before it builds the compiled version of your program, even if those parts exist in different files.

You do not need to include Partial on every part of the class, just on one of the parts. Also, if your class inherits from another class or implements an interface, you need to include only the Inherits or Implements keyword in one of the class portions.

All class parts must exist in the context of the same namespace. If you create different class definitions with the same name but in different namespaces, they will be distinct and unrelated classes.

3.10   Creating a Form Based on Another Form

Problem

You've created a basic form, and you would like to use it to create other forms that extend the functionality of the basic form.

Solution

Create an inheritance relationship between the original form (the "base" class) and the form with the extended features (the "inherited" class). There are a few different ways to accomplish this, but the easiest is to let Visual Studio establish the inheritance relationship for you through the Inheritance Picker dialog.

Discussion

Use the Project → Add Windows Form menu command to add the new form to a new or existing Windows Forms project. When the Add New Item dialog appears, select Inherited Form from the list of templates, type your new form's filename in the Name field, and then click the Add button. As long as there are other forms defined in your application, you will see the Inheritance Picker dialog (Figure 3-4).

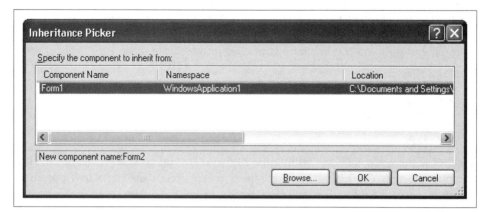

Figure 3-4. Visual Studio's Inheritance Picker dialog

To establish the inheritance relationship, select the base form from the list of available forms, and then click the OK button. Visual Studio will add a new form that is derived from the selected base form.

All forms added to your Windows Forms project use inheritance. By default, new forms derive from `System.Windows.Forms.Form`, but you can indicate another base form from your own project. If you look in the "designer" file associated with the form, you will see the following statements in standard forms:

```
Partial Class Form2
    Inherits System.Windows.Forms.Form
```

When you alter the base class through the Inheritance Picker, these statements change to reflect the selected base form:

```
Partial Class Form2
    Inherits WindowsApplication1.Form1
```

(A form's designer file is hidden by default. Click on the Show All Files button in the Solution Explorer, and then expand the branch for a form to see its designer file.)

You can manually establish the inheritance relationship by modifying the `Inherits` statement yourself to include the correct base class.

Visual Studio must be able to create an instance of the base form before it can show you the derived form through the Form Designer (or even list the form in the Inheritance Picker). This requires that a compiled version of that base form exists. Before using the Inheritance Picker to establish form relationships, build your project using the Build → Build WindowsApplication1 (or similar) menu command.

See Also

Although it's not covered in a separate recipe in this chapter, creating inherited user controls follows the same process. Select Inherited User Control in the Add New Item dialog's template list to establish such a relationship.

3.11 Passing and Returning Structures and Other Objects

Problem

You need to pass complex data types to a function, or return an equally complex type.

Solution

Just pass the data. Complex data in .NET is really no different from simple data in how it is passed to or returned from functions.

Discussion

Arrays are probably the most cumbersome, only because you have to add two extra characters in the function definition. The following function definition accepts an Integer array and returns a related String array:

```
Public Function ConvertIntArrayToString( _
    ByVal origArray() As Integer) As String()
    ' ----- Take a basic Integer array, and return a
    '       String equivalent.
    Dim newArray(UBound(origArray)) As String

    For counter As Integer = 0 To UBound(origArray)
        newArray(counter) = CStr(origArray(counter))
    Next counter

    Return newArray
End Function
```

In some non-.NET languages—including earlier versions of Visual Basic—it is not always obvious how you pass complex data types, such as complete arrays, into and out of functions. In .NET, it's a snap. All complex data types—instances of structures and classes—are simple variables that can be passed freely through arguments or return values. An array is a standard reference type, even if it contains value type elements.

3.12   Creating and Using an Enumeration

Problem

You want to add a set of related constants to your project and establish variables based on that set of constants.

Solution

Add an enumeration to your namespace, class, or other type using the Enum statement. Then use the name of the enumeration just as you would any other .NET integral data type.

Discussion

Enum lets you build a list of related integer values:

```
Enum StorageMedia
    Floppy
    CD
    DVD
    FlashRAM
    Paper
End Enum
```

In this enumeration, all elements are of type Integer, with values ranging from 0 (Floppy) to 4 (Paper). You can select a different type through an As clause, and you can indicate specific numeric values:

```
Enum StorageMedia As Short
    Floppy = 100
    CD
    DVD
    FlashRAM
    Paper = 500
End Enum
```

After you've created your enumeration, refer to individual members by combining the enumeration name and the member name:

```
storageType = StorageMedia.FlashRAM
```

Creating variables of an enumeration type is just as simple:

```
Dim storageType As StorageMedia
```

Although storageType might act like a Short or Integer (as defined through the underlying Enum statement), it is truly a variable of type StorageMedia, a new data type all its own.

Without enumerations, the only way to create a related set of integer values is to define multiple constants and trust yourself to use them as a set. Enumerations bundle like elements, making it easier to keep track of the relationships. Visual Studio also picks up on this relationship, using enumerations to enhance IntelliSense, as shown in Figure 3-5.

Figure 3-5. Using IntelliSense with enumerations

Although enumeration variables are typed to the specific Enum, Visual Basic allows you to assign any numeric values (limited to the underlying type of the Enum) to those variables. For instance, Visual Basic doesn't stop you from assigning the value 700 to the storageType variable, even though none of the StorageMedia enumeration members have a value of 700.

3.13   Converting Between Numeric and String Enumeration Values

Problem

While you intend to use an enumeration through its members and their numeric equivalents, you also need to be able to get the string name of an enumeration member and convert it back to numeric form from that string.

Solution

Use the string conversion features of the System.Enum class and its derived enumerations to manipulate the members through strings.

Discussion

Moving from a numeric member to string form is simple, and you've probably already done something similar for other types. Let's reuse the enumeration from Recipe 3.12:

```
Enum StorageMedia
   Floppy
   CD
   DVD
   FlashRAM
   Paper
End Enum
```

If you've created an enumeration variable:

```
Dim storageType As StorageMedia = StorageMedia.FlashRAM
```

you can convert its value to string form using the ToString( ) member:

```
Dim stringForm As String = storageType.ToString( )
MsgBox(stringForm)  ' Displays "FlashRAM"
```

Converting back from a string is just slightly more indirect. Use the System.Enum class's Parse( ) method to restore a string back to its original numeric value:

```
storageType = System.Enum.Parse(GetType(StorageMedia), "DVD")
MsgBox(CInt(storageType))     ' Displays 2
MsgBox(storageType.ToString)  ' Displays "DVD"
```

Visual Basic compiles the full name of each enumeration member into the target application. You can take advantage of these stored names to shuttle enumeration values between their integer and string forms.

If you pass an invalid string to the Parse( ) method, an error will occur, so keep an eye on that enumerated data.

3.14 Creating a Method That Accepts Different Sets of Arguments

Problem

You have a great function that generates its results based on one type of data, but you'd like to reuse that function with other data types or argument signatures.

Solution

Use method overloading to provide different versions of the same method.

Discussion

You may sometimes write applications that communicate with Oracle databases. Supplying dates to Oracle SQL statements is frequently done using Oracle's TO_DATE function. When building SQL statements in my .NET application, you can prepare a Date variable for use in Oracle by first wrapping it in a TO_DATE function. There are other times when all you have is a date in a user-entered string format, and you need to prepare that date for use by Oracle. To support both original date and string data values, you can use an overloaded Oracle preparation function:

```
Public Overloads Function ToOracleDate( _
      ByVal origDate As Date) As String
   Return "TO_DATE('" & Format(origDate, "MM/dd/yyyy") & _
      "', 'MM/DD/YYYY')"
End Function

Public Overloads Function ToOracleDate( _
      ByVal origDate As String) As String
   If (Trim(origDate) = "") Then
      Return "NULL"
   Else
      Return ToOracleDate(CDate(origDate))
   End If
End Function
```

The Overloads keyword informs Visual Basic that you are trying to overload a single function name with two different argument signature variations. In this example, the string version calls the date version for some of its processing. This sharing of processing logic can help keep your code simple even when using multiple overloads.

The .NET Framework makes extensive use of method overloading, including overloads of some Visual Basic features. The InStr( ) function, which locates a smaller string within a larger one, uses overloading to support the interesting syntax it inherited from Visual Basic 1.0. The basic syntax uses two strings, the one being searched and the one being sought:

```
Public Function InStr(ByVal String1 As String, _
   ByVal String2 As String) As Integer
```

The second variation inserts an Integer starting position as the first argument:

```
Public Function InStr(ByVal Start As Integer, _
    ByVal String1 As String, ByVal String2 As String) As Integer
```

Since Visual Basic does not support optional arguments anywhere but at the end of an argument list, this function uses overloading to support the argument variety.

Overloading is different from *overriding*. Overriding occurs only in inheritance relationships, when a function in a derived class alters or replaces the logic for an identical function in a base class. Overridden functions must have the same argument signature in both the base and derived classes.

There are no fixed limits on the number of overloads you can use in a single method. And while constructors (Sub New procedures) also use a form of overloading, they do not require the Overloads keyword.

See Also

See Recipe 3.6 for information on overloading using class constructors.

3.15 Using Standard Operators for Nonstandard Purposes

Problem

The basic Visual Basic operators, such as the addition operator (+), seem so useful that you would like to use them for your own custom classes.

Solution

Use *operator overloading*, a new feature in Visual Basic 2005, to allow your own classes to interact with each other through the standard Visual Basic operators.

Discussion

Operator overloading extends method overloading to include the standard Visual Basic operators. In a way, it treats operators such as +, *, and Or as method names. Consider a class that manages scientific specimens:

```
Class Specimen
```

If your application supports the idea of combining two specimens, resulting in a merged yet single larger specimen, it would be great to be able to use the addition operator to merge two distinct specimens into a single combined specimen:

```
Dim part1 As New Specimen
Dim part2 As New Specimen
Dim combinedParts As Specimen
'...later...
combinedParts = part1 + part2
```

To add support for addition to this class, overload the + operator by adding an Operator definition to the class:

```
Public Shared Operator +(ByVal firstPart As Specimen, _
    ByVal secondPart As Specimen) As Specimen
  Dim mergedSpecimen As New Specimen

  ' ----- Add logic to merge the two parts, then...
  Return mergedSpecimen
End Operator
```

You can include different input or output types in the overloaded function, as long as at least one input or output matches the class in which the overload appears:

```
Public Shared Operator +(ByVal singlePage As Page, _
    ByVal sourceBook As Book) As Book
  ' ----- Adds a page to a book.

End Operator
```

All overloaded operators must include the Shared keyword in the definition.

For unary operators, such as the Not operator, only a single argument is sent to the overloaded function. Table 3-1 lists the overloadable operators.

Table 3-1. Overloadable operators

Operator	Description
+ (Unary)	*Unary plus* operator, as in the expression "+5." Unary plus is seldom used in standard Visual Basic programming, but you can use it for your own classes. `Shared Operator +(ByVal arg1 As Type) As Type`
- (Unary)	*Unary negation* operator, as in "-5." `Shared Operator -(ByVal arg1 As Type) As Type`

+	*Addition* operator, used to "add" items together.
	
	`Shared Operator +(ByVal arg1 As Type, _`
	`    ByVal arg2 As Type) As Type`

-	*Subtraction operator*, used to "subtract" one item from another.
	
	`Shared Operator -(ByVal arg1 As Type, _`
	`    ByVal arg2 As Type) As Type`

*	*Multiplication* operator.
	
	`Shared Operator *(ByVal arg1 As Type, _`
	`    ByVal arg2 As Type) As Type`

/	*Division* operator.
	
	`Shared Operator /(ByVal arg1 As Type, _`
	`    ByVal arg2 As Type) As Type`

\	*Integer division* operator.
	
	`Shared Operator \(ByVal arg1 As Type, _`
	`    ByVal arg2 As Type) As Type`

Mod	*Modulo* operator.
	
	`Shared Operator Mod(ByVal arg1 As Type, _`
	`    ByVal arg2 As Type) As Type`

Table 3-1. Overloadable operators (continued)

Operator	Description
&	*Concatenation* operator. ```Shared Operator &(ByVal arg1 As Type, _` ` ByVal arg2 As Type) As Type```
^	*Exponentiation* operator. ```Shared Operator ^(ByVal arg1 As Type, _` ` ByVal arg2 As Type) As Type```
<<	*Shift left* operator. Since the operand to the right of the standard operator is always an Integer, the second argument passed to the overload is also an Integer. ```Shared Operator <<(ByVal arg1 As Type, _` ` ByVal arg2 As Integer) As Type```
>>	*Shift right* operator. Since the operand to the right of the standard operator is always an Integer, the second argument passed to the overload is also an Integer. ```Shared Operator >>(ByVal arg1 As Type, _` ` ByVal arg2 As Integer) As Type```
=	*Equal to* comparison operator, for use in If and similar statements. You must also overload the related <> (not equal to) operator. ```Shared Operator =(ByVal arg1 As Type, _` ` ByVal arg2 As Type) As Boolean```
<	*Less than* comparison operator, for use in If and similar statements. You must also overload the related > (greater than) operator. ```Shared Operator <(ByVal arg1 As Type, _` ` ByVal arg2 As Type) As Boolean```
>	*Greater than* comparison operator, for use in If and similar statements. You must also overload the related < (less than) operator. ```Shared Operator >(ByVal arg1 As Type, _` ` ByVal arg2 As Type) As Boolean```
<=	*Less than or equal to* comparison operator, for use in If and similar statements. You must also overload the related >= (greater than or equal to) operator. ```Shared Operator <=(ByVal arg1 As Type, _` ` ByVal arg2 As Type) As Boolean```
>=	*Greater than or equal to* comparison operator, for use in If and similar statements. You must also overload the related <= (less than or equal to) operator. ```Shared Operator >=(ByVal arg1 As Type, _` ` ByVal arg2 As Type) As Boolean```
<>	*Not equal to* comparison operator, for use in If and similar statements. You must also overload the related = (equal to) operator. ```Shared Operator <>(ByVal arg1 As Type, _` ` ByVal arg2 As Type) As Boolean```
Not	*Bitwise negation* operator. ```Shared Operator Not(ByVal arg1 As Type) As Type```
IsTrue	Used to support overloading of the OrElse operator. You must also overload the related IsFalse operator, and you will probably want to overload Or as well. ```Shared Operator IsTrue(ByVal arg1 As Type) _` ` As Boolean```

Table 3-1. Overloadable operators (continued)

Operator	Description
IsFalse	Used to support overloading of the AndAlso operator. You must also overload the related IsTrue operator, and you will probably want to overload And as well. ``` Shared Operator IsFalse(ByVal arg1 As Type) _ As Boolean ```
And	*Bitwise conjunction* operator. ``` Shared Operator And(ByVal arg1 As Type, _ ByVal arg2 As Type) As Type ```
Or	*Bitwise disjunction* operator. ``` Shared Operator Or(ByVal arg1 As Type, _ ByVal arg2 As Type) As Type ```
Xor	*Bitwise exclusion* operator. ``` Shared Operator Xor(ByVal arg1 As Type, _ ByVal arg2 As Type) As Type ```
Like	*Pattern comparison* operator. The second operator is always a pattern string. ``` Shared Operator Like(ByVal arg1 As Type, _ ByVal arg2 As String) As Boolean ```
CType	*Type conversion* operator, for converting between different core and custom data types. Visual Basic supports two types of conversions: *narrowing* and *widening*. In narrowing conversions there is a chance that the source data will not fit in the target data type, as when converting a Long to an Integer. Conversions in the other direction are widening, and these never result in data loss. You must specify the type of conversion using the Narrowing or Widening keyword. ``` Shared [Narrowing	Widening] Operator _ CType(ByVal sourceData As Type) As Type ```

You can overload overloaded operators. That is, you can include multiple overloads for, say, the addition (+) operator in a single class, as long as the argument signatures differ.

While operator overloading can make your code more straightforward, it can also add a level of confusion, since you will be using operators in a way that is not part of the standard language usage. Where there is the possibility of confusion, add meaningful comments to the code to guide the reader through the rough spots.

See Also

Recipe 3.14 discusses standard method overloading.

3.16 Enforcing Strong Data Typing in an Otherwise Weakly Typed Collection

Problem

You have created a generic collection class that is quite useful and will support data of any class or type. You want to ensure that data types are never mixed within a single instance of the collection. That is, if a collection contains String values, you never want Integer values added to that same collection.

Solution

Use *generics* to restrict the types of data interactions a class may have.

Discussion

Generics allow you to make substitutions of generic data-type placeholders with actual data types. Consider this simple class:

```
Class MultiShow
   Public DisplayValue As String
   Public InterValue As String
   Public Sub ShowDouble( )
      ' ----- Display two copies of the value.
      MsgBox(DisplayValue & InterValue & DisplayValue)
   End Sub
   Public Sub ShowTriple( )
      ' ----- Display three copies of the value.
      MsgBox(DisplayValue & InterValue & DisplayValue & _
         InterValue & DisplayValue)
   End Sub
End Class
```

This class facilitates the display of some stored string value. But what if you wanted to display Integer data? You would have to rewrite the class, redefining DisplayValue and InterValue as Integer types. And that wouldn't help you much if you then wanted to use Date values. You could replace String with Object, but this approach would not help you if you needed to ensure that DisplayValue and InterValue were the same data type.

Generics allow you to treat a class in a generic manner where data types are concerned. Adding generics to our MultiShow class results in the following code:

```
Class MultiShow(Of T)
   Public DisplayValue As T
   Public InterValue As T
   Public Sub ShowDouble( )
      ' ----- Display two copies of the value.
      MsgBox( _
         DisplayValue.ToString() & InterValue.ToString() ) & _
         DisplayValue.ToString())
   End Sub
   Public Sub ShowTriple( )
      ' ----- Display three copies of the value.
      MsgBox( _
         DisplayValue.ToString() & InterValue.ToString() & _
         DisplayValue.ToString() & InterValue.ToString() & _
         DisplayValue.ToString())
   End Sub
End Class
```

The Of T clause enables generics on the class. T acts like a placeholder (you don't have to use T; you can give the placeholder any name you want) for a data type used somewhere in the class. In this example, we used T twice to set the data types for the public fields:

```
Public DisplayValue As T
Public InterValue As T
```

To use this class, include an Of *datatype* clause in your reference declaration:

```
Dim dataShow As New MultiShow(Of String)
```

In the dataShow instance, String is used anywhere T appears in the class definition. It's as if Visual Basic generated a String-specific version of the MultiShow class for you. To generate an Integer version, just update the declaration:

```
Dim dataShow As New MultiShow(Of Integer)
```

Each instance variation of a generic class you define is truly a distinct data type. You cannot pass data freely between instances of MultiShow(Of Integer) and MultiShow(Of String) without conversion, just as you cannot pass data between Date and Integer data types without conversion.

You can include multiple data-type placeholders by separating them with commas:

```
Class MultiShow(Of T1, T2)
    Public DisplayValue As T1
    Public InterValue As T2
```

Now you can provide either identical or distinct data types for T1 and T2:

```
Dim dataShowUnited As New MultiShow(Of String, String)
Dim dataShowDivided As New MultiShow(Of String, Integer)
```

In addition to simple data-type placeholders, you can include restrictions on each placeholder to limit the types of data used by the class. You can design a generic class that will limit the data-type substitution to just the Form class or any class derived from Form:

```
Class FunForms(Of T As System.Windows.Forms.Form)

End Class
```

Interface-specific limits work as well:

```
Class ThrowAways(Of T As System.IDisposable)

End Class
```

If you want to create new instances of T (whatever it is) within your class, use the As New restriction in the generic definition:

```
Class EntryManager(Of T As New)
    Public Function BuildNewEntry( ) As T
        ' ----- Create a new object.
        Dim result As New T
```

```
        ...
        Return result
    End Function
End Class
```

This works only if the data type replacing T includes a default constructor (that is, a constructor with no arguments).

Each data-type placeholder in the generic definition can include multiple constraints, all surrounded with curly braces:

```
Class FunForms(Of T As {System.Windows.Forms.Form, New})

End Class
```

The list of multiple restrictions can include multiple interfaces if needed, but only one standard class (such as System.Windows.Forms.Form) is permitted per placeholder.

Generics are useful when defining collection classes. Adding a generic restriction to a collection ensures that objects of only a single type can be added to the collection, a restriction that may be useful in some cases. For example, a Collection(Of String) allows only String values to be added to the collection.

See Also

Chapter 14 includes recipes that show you how to use specific generic collection classes.

Forms, Controls, and Other Useful Objects

4.0   Introduction

If you are writing a desktop application, you are dealing with forms and controls. Since its first release, Visual Basic has made the dream of drag-and-drop programming possible: just add some controls to a form, press F5, and go.

While this method works, it allows you to design only the most rudimentary applications. Most programs require gobs of code for each on-screen control. Fortunately, .NET simplifies a lot of the plumbing associated with complex controls, so you can just focus on the logic that responds directly to a user action. This chapter shows you how to take advantage of the control features included with .NET's Windows Forms library.

4.1   Creating and Adding Controls at Runtime

Problem

You need to add one or more controls to a form dynamically at runtime. You used to do something similar to this in Visual Basic 6.0 using control arrays, but those do not exist in Visual Basic 2005.

Solution

Sample code folder: Chapter 04\DynamicControls

You can add any control to a form at runtime just by creating an instance of it. Your code can define the initial properties, such as the location of the control on the form, at runtime. You can also connect events for these runtime controls to event handlers, although the handler methods must exist at design time. (Technically, it's possible to write a method at runtime, but such programming is beyond the scope of this book and is generally frowned upon.)

Discussion

To test this method of dynamically creating controls, start by creating a new Windows Forms application and add the following source code to Form1's code template:

```
Private Sub ShowTheTime(ByVal sender As System.Object, _
      ByVal e As System.EventArgs)
   ' ----- Display the time in the text box, if it exists.
   Dim theTextBox As TextBox

   ' ----- Locate and update the text control.
   theTextBox = Me.Controls("TimeTextBox")
   If (theTextBox IsNot Nothing) Then
      theTextBox.Text = Now.ToLongTimeString()
   End If
End Sub

Private Sub Form1_Load(ByVal sender As Object, _
      ByVal e As System.EventArgs) Handles Me.Load
   ' ----- Add controls at runtime.
   Dim dynamicText As TextBox = Nothing
   Dim dynamicButton As Button

   ' ----- Dynamically add a text box control to the form.
   dynamicText = New Windows.Forms.TextBox
   dynamicText.Name = "TimeTextBox"
   dynamicText.Location = New System.Drawing.Point(8, 8)
   dynamicText.Size = New System.Drawing.Size(232, 20)
   dynamicText.TabIndex = 0
   Me.Controls.Add(dynamicText)

   ' ----- Dynamically add a button control to the form.
   dynamicButton = New Windows.Forms.Button
   dynamicButton.Location = New System.Drawing.Point(144, 32)
   dynamicButton.Size = New System.Drawing.Size(99, 23)
   dynamicButton.Text = "Get Time"
   dynamicButton.UseVisualStyleBackColor = True
   dynamicButton.TabIndex = 1
   Me.Controls.Add(dynamicButton)

   ' ----- Connect the button to an event handler.
   AddHandler dynamicButton.Click, AddressOf ShowTheTime
End Sub
```

When you run the program, you will see two controls—a TextBox control and a Button control—magically appear on the previously empty form. Clicking the button calls the prewritten event handler, which inserts the current time into the text box, as shown in Figure 4-1.

In Visual Basic 6.0, if you wanted to add a control to a form at runtime it was necessary to create a design-time control just like it, and create a dynamic copy of it at runtime. This was due, in part, to the special design-time method used to record form controls. If you opened up the *.frm* file for a Visual Basic 6.0 form, you would see non–Visual Basic code at the top of the file that defined the controls and the form itself.

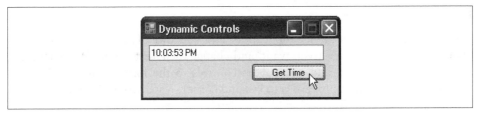

Figure 4-1. Dynamically generated controls on a form

In Visual Basic 2005, all form controls, and even the form itself, exist through standard object creation. When `Form1` appears on the screen in a running program, it's because somewhere in your program there is code that creates a new instance of `Form1` and calls its `Show` method:

```
(New Form1).Show
```

Although you add controls to your form using the Visual Studio Form Designer, Visual Studio actually generates runtime code for you that dynamically creates the controls and adds them to the form. All this code is generally hidden in the form's *designer file*. To view this file, select the Project → Show All Files menu command, and expand the branch for one of your forms in the Solution Explorer panel. By default, `Form1`'s designer file is named *Form1.Designer.vb*.

To create the source code for this project, we added a `TextBox` and a `Button` control to the form and then opened the designer code file. We then copied selected lines from that file and made slight adjustments before pasting that code into the form's `Load` event handler. Finally, we deleted the design-time controls from the form.

See Also

Recipes 4.2 and 4.3 also discuss features that are replacements for Visual Basic 6.0 control arrays.

4.2   Iterating Through All Controls on a Form

Problem

You need to make updates to some or all controls on a form at runtime, and all in a common way. You aren't excited about copying and pasting the same lines over and over again to make the changes to every instance of the same control type.

Solution

Sample code folder: Chapter 04\IteratingControls

The form maintains a collection of all controls on the form. Iterate through this collection, and make your changes as you pass by each item.

Discussion

Create a new Windows Forms application, and add three Label controls to Form1. Name the controls whatever you want, and change their Text properties to anything you want as well. Next, add two Button controls to the form, named ActRed and ActNormal. Set their Text properties to Red and Normal, respectively. Then add the following source code to the form's code template:

```
Private Sub ActRed_Click(ByVal sender As System.Object, _
      ByVal e As System.EventArgs) Handles ActRed.Click
   ' ----- Set the background of all labels to red.
   UpdateAllLabels(Color.Red)
End Sub

Private Sub ActNormal_Click(ByVal sender As System.Object, _
      ByVal e As System.EventArgs) Handles ActNormal.Click
   ' ----- Set the background of all labels to the
   '       standard color.
   UpdateAllLabels(SystemColors.Control)
End Sub

Private Sub UpdateAllLabels(ByVal withColor As Drawing.Color)
   ' ----- Scan all controls, looking for labels.
   For Each scanControls As Control In Me.Controls
      If (TypeOf scanControls Is Label) Then
         scanControls.BackColor = withColor
      End If
   Next scanControls
End Sub
```

When you run the code and click on each button, the background color of the three labels changes as indicated by the clicked button. Figure 4-2 shows a sample use of this code.

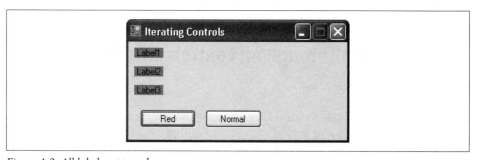

Figure 4-2. All labels set to red

All of a form's controls appear in a collection accessed through the form's Controls property. Because it is a standard collection, you can iterate through it using the For Each statement, or any other technique that accesses elements of a collection. You can also reference controls by string name:

```
Dim firstButton = Me.Controls("ActRed")
```

Although controls of all types are added to the Controls collection, you can still determine their derived data types using the TypeOf statement, as is done in this recipe's sample code. This can help you limit updates to a certain type of control in the collection.

See Also

Recipes 4.1 and 4.3 also discuss features that are replacements for Visual Basic 6.0 control arrays.

4.3   Sharing Event-Handler Logic Among Many Controls

Problem

You have many controls that should use identical event-handler logic for some of their events. You don't want to rewrite the logic for each control. You accomplished this in Visual Basic 6.0 using control arrays, but they no longer exist in Visual Basic 2005.

Solution

Sample code folder: Chapter 04\SharingControlLogic

You can use a single .NET method as the event handler for any number of control events on the form, as long as those events share a common set of event arguments.

Discussion

Visual Basic 6.0 included a feature called *control arrays* that allowed developers to share a single event-handler procedure among multiple controls. The controls in the array had to be of the same type and share a common name. They differed only by the values of their numeric Index properties. Each event handler also included an extra argument that identified the index of the control triggering the event.

Visual Basic in the .NET world no longer allows control arrays, but you can still share event handlers. To do this, you alter the event method's Handles clause to include all the control events it should handle.

Create a new Windows Forms application, and add three new TextBox controls to Form1. By default, they are named TextBox1, TextBox2, and TextBox3. Add a Label control named ShowInfo. Then add this source code to the form's code template:

```
Private Sub MultipleEvents(ByVal sender As Object, _
    ByVal e As System.EventArgs) Handles _
    TextBox1.Enter, TextBox2.Enter, TextBox3.Enter, _
    TextBox1.TextChanged, TextBox2.TextChanged, _
    TextBox3.TextChanged
    ' ----- Report the current status of this field.
    Dim activeControl As TextBox
```

```
    activeControl = CType(sender, TextBox)
    ShowInfo.Text = "Field #" & _
        Microsoft.VisualBasic.Right(activeControl.Name, 1) & _
        ", " & activeControl.Text.Length & " character(s)"
End Sub
```

Run this program. As you move from text box to text box and type things in, the ShowInfo label updates to show you which text box you are in (based on the number extracted from its control name) and the length of its content. Figure 4-3 shows the form in use.

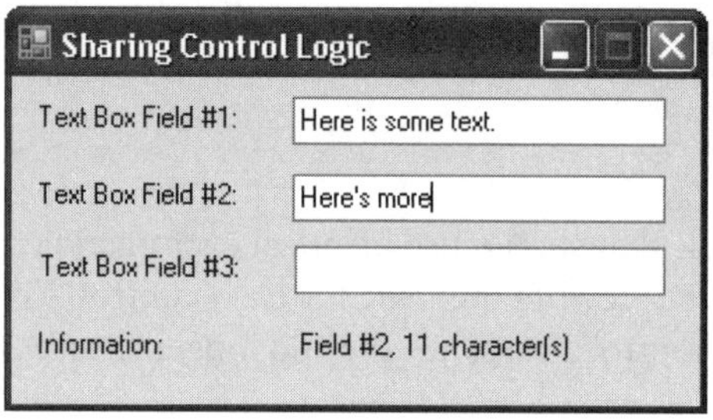

Figure 4-3. A single event handler dealing with multiple events

See Also

Recipes 4.1 and 4.2 also discuss features that are replacements for Visual Basic 6.0 control arrays.

4.4 Working with Timers

Problem

You need to have some action occur on a regular basis in your form.

Solution

Sample code folder: Chapter 04\ClockTimer

Use a Timer control, and set it for the desired interval. Create a new Windows Forms application, and add a Label control named CurrentTime to the form. Also add a Timer control to the form, and name it ClockTimer. Set its Interval property to 1000, and set its Enabled property to True. Then add the following source code to the form's code template:

```
Private Sub ClockTimer_Tick(ByVal sender As System.Object, _
    ByVal e As System.EventArgs) Handles ClockTimer.Tick
    CurrentTime.Text = Now.ToLongTimeString
End Sub
```

When you run the program, that label updates once each second with the current time.

Discussion

The Timer control's Interval property sets the time between Tick events in milliseconds (1,000 per second). Although you can set the Interval as low as one millisecond, the timer's resolution is limited by your system's hardware and operating-system-level factors.

The Tick event fires at *approximately* the interval you specify, if nothing more important is going on. If the code within your Tick event handler is still running when the next Tick event should occur, that subsequent Tick event is disposed without a call to the event handler.

See Also

Recipe 14.8 shows how to have a section of code sleep, or take a small break. Some older Visual Basic code used timers for this purpose, although a timer is not the best solution in this case.

4.5   Determining If a Control Can Take the Focus

Problem

You need to move the current focus to a specific control, but you want to avoid conditions where the focus-setting action would fail.

Solution

Use the control's CanFocus( ) method to determine whether the application can take the focus or not:

```
If (SomeControl.CanFocus( ) = True) Then _
    SomeControl.Focus( )
```

Discussion

Event-driven programming can lead to many runtime surprises based on timing. Depending on how you write your code, it's possible that an event handler will be temporarily interrupted so that another event handler can run instead. Or, more commonly, unrelated event handlers may fire in an order you did not anticipate because of some interesting input action by the user.

If you have an event handler that disables and enables a specific control, and another handler that sets the focus to that control, some situations may arise in which the focus action faisl because the control is disabled. While you could check the Enabled flag before setting the focus, there are other conditions (such as the presence of a separate modal dialog) that can also stop a control from receiving the focus, even when the Enabled flag is True. Using the CanFocus( ) method provides a more accurate method of determining when it is safe to call the Focus( ) method.

4.6   Programmatically Clicking a Button

Problem

You want the Click event handler for a button to run, but you want to initiate this action from code instead of waiting for the user to click the button.

Solution

Call the button's PerformClick( ) method:

```
Button1.PerformClick( )
```

Discussion

While it's nice that the Button control has a PerformClick( ) method to run its Click event handler in an object-oriented manner, most controls and most control events have no such related method. If you wish to call an event handler immediately through code, you have to call it like any other method, passing the correct arguments:

```
' ---- Call the text box control's GotFocus handler.
TextBox1_GotFocus(TextBox1, New System.EventArgs)
```

In this case, calling the TextBox1 control's GotFocus( ) event handler will run that handler's code, but it will not cause the focus to move to the text box. An even better solution would be to write a shared routine that the GotFocus( ) event handler and your other code both call.

4.7   Drawing a Control

Problem

You want to provide custom drawing code for a control.

Solution

Sample code folder: Chapter 04\ControlDrawing

For most controls, provide an event handler for the Paint event, and add your drawing code there. This event's second argument includes a Graphics property representing the canvas on which you can issue your drawing commands. Some controls also provide separate DrawItem events that let you draw specific portions of the control, such as distinct items in a ListBox control. You can also draw directly on the form's surface. This recipe's code includes samples for all these activities.

Create a new Windows Forms application, and add two controls: a Button control named XButton and a ComboBox control named ColorList. Change the ColorList control's DrawMode property to OwnerDrawFixed and its DropDownStyle property to DropDownList. Then add the following source code to the form's code template:

```
Private Sub Form1_Load(ByVal sender As Object, _
      ByVal e As System.EventArgs) Handles Me.Load
   ' ----- Add some basic colors to the color list.
   ColorList.Items.Add("Red")
   ColorList.Items.Add("Orange")
   ColorList.Items.Add("Yellow")
   ColorList.Items.Add("Green")
   ColorList.Items.Add("Blue")
   ColorList.Items.Add("Indigo")
   ColorList.Items.Add("Violet")
End Sub

Private Sub Form1_Paint(ByVal sender As Object, _
      ByVal e As System.Windows.Forms.PaintEventArgs) _
      Handles Me.Paint
   ' ----- Draw an ellipse on the form.
   e.Graphics.DrawEllipse(Pens.Black, 10, 10, _
      Me.ClientRectangle.Width - 20, _
      Me.ClientRectangle.Height - 20)
End Sub

Private Sub XButton_Paint(ByVal sender As Object, _
      ByVal e As System.Windows.Forms.PaintEventArgs) _
      Handles XButton.Paint
   ' ----- Draw a big x in a rectangle on the button surface.
   Dim usePen As Pen

   ' ----- Provide a neutral background.
   e.Graphics.Clear(SystemColors.Control)

   ' ----- Draw the outline box.
   usePen = New Pen(SystemColors.ControlText, 3)
   e.Graphics.DrawRectangle(usePen, XButton.ClientRectangle)

   ' ----- Draw the x.
   e.Graphics.DrawLine(usePen, 0, 0, _
      XButton.Width, XButton.Height)
   e.Graphics.DrawLine(usePen, 0, _
      XButton.Height, XButton.Width, 0)
   usePen.Dispose( )
End Sub

Private Sub ColorList_DrawItem(ByVal sender As Object, _
      ByVal e As System.Windows.Forms.DrawItemEventArgs) _
      Handles ColorList.DrawItem
   ' ----- Draw the color instead of the text.
   Dim useBrush As Brush
```

```
    ' ----- Check for a nonselected item.
    If (e.Index = -1) Then Return

    ' ----- Set the neutral background.
    e.DrawBackground()

    ' ----- Fill in the color.
    useBrush = New SolidBrush(Color.FromName(CStr( _
        ColorList.Items(e.Index))))
    e.Graphics.FillRectangle(useBrush, _
        e.Bounds.Left + 2, e.Bounds.Top + 2, _
        e.Bounds.Width - 4, e.Bounds.Height - 4)
    useBrush.Dispose()

    ' ----- Surround the color with a black rectangle.
    e.Graphics.DrawRectangle(Pens.Black, _
        e.Bounds.Left + 2, e.Bounds.Top + 2, _
        e.Bounds.Width - 4, e.Bounds.Height - 4)

    ' ----- Show the item selected if needed.
    e.DrawFocusRectangle()
End Sub

Private Sub XButton_Click(ByVal sender As System.Object, _
    ByVal e As System.EventArgs) Handles XButton.Click
    MsgBox("Button clicked.")
End Sub
```

Run the program. The XButton control no longer looks like a button; it instead looks like a custom-drawn "X." Although the button looks strange, it still works. The ellipse we drew directly on the form's surface is there. Also, the ComboBox control now displays actual colors instead of just the names of colors. This all appears in Figure 4-4.

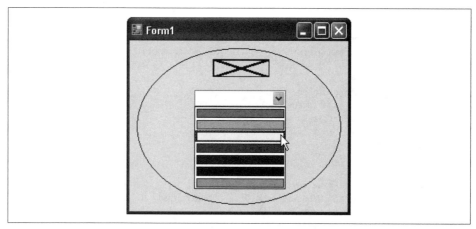

Figure 4-4. Controls drawn with custom code

Discussion

Some of the controls that support item-level drawing, such as the ListBox and ComboBox controls, include an e.State property in the data passed to the event handler. This value indicates the current state of the item being drawn: selected, not selected, or a half dozen other relevant states. You do not need to take that property into account if your implementation doesn't require it, but it is generally a good idea to provide feedback to the user in a way the user expects. Adjusting the display based on this property helps achieve that purpose.

As shown in the sample code, the DrawItem event handler includes e.DrawBackground() and e.DrawFocusRectangle() methods that help you properly draw the item. Availability of these methods varies by control type.

See Also

See the recipes in Chapter 9 for examples that use the various GDI+ drawing commands.

4.8   Making a Form the Top-Most Form

Problem

You want a specific form to appear on top of all other forms in your application, no matter which form is selected.

Solution

If you wish to have a Toolbox-type form that is accessible at the same time as other forms but always remains on top, set the form's TopMost property to True.

Discussion

If you also want to disable access to all other forms, open the important form of the moment using its ShowDialog() method:

```
Form1.ShowDialog()
```

No other forms already displayed by the application will be available until the ShowDialog() form closes.

4.9   Indicating the Accept and Cancel Buttons on a Form

Problem

On a form, you want to have the Enter key trigger a specific button (such as an "OK" button) and have the Escape key trigger another button (such as a "Cancel" button).

Solution

Use the form's `AcceptButton` and `CancelButton` properties to assign the appropriate buttons. In the Visual Studio Form Designer, setting these form properties to the names of buttons on the form will enable the keyboard shortcuts for those buttons.

Discussion

Setting a button to be a form's `CancelButton` object has the side effect of changing that button's `DialogResult` property to `Cancel`.

Even if you set an accept button, the Enter key doesn't always trigger it. For instance, if another button on the form has the focus, that button, and not the form's accept button, is triggered when the user presses the Enter key.

4.10 Remembering a Form's Position Between Uses

Problem

You would like the position of a form to be retained between exiting the application (or closing that form) and the next time you access that same form.

Solution

Sample code folder: Chapter 04\RememberFormPosition

Tie the form's `Location` property to a member of the `My.Settings` object. You do this using the form's application-setting property bindings.

Create a new Windows Forms application. Access the Project Properties window through the Project → WindowsApplication1 Properties (or similar) menu command. Select the Settings tab in this window, as shown in Figure 4-5.

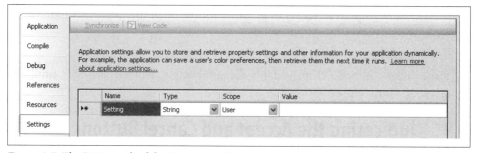

Figure 4-5. The Settings tab of the Properties window

In the first row of the Settings grid, set the Name field to `MainFormLocation`, and select `System.Drawing.Point` in the Type field (Figure 4-6). Close the Project Properties window.

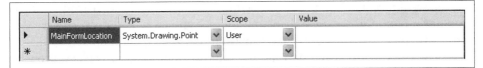

	Name	Type	Scope	Value
▶	MainFormLocation	System.Drawing.Point	User	
✳				

Figure 4-6. The added MainFormLocation property

Back on `Form1`, expand its (`ApplicationSettings`) property. One of the subproperties should be `Location`. Change its value to `MainFormLocation`.

The program is ready to use. Run it, and move the form to a conspicuous location. Then exit the program. When you run the program again, the form will be where you moved it.

Discussion

If, when you expand the (`ApplicationSettings`) property, you don't see the `Location` subproperty, use the (`PropertyBinding`) subproperty instead. Click on the "..." button in its value area to display the "Application Settings for 'Form1'" dialog. Locate the `Location` entry in the form's settings list, and set its value to `MainFormLocation`, as shown in Figure 4-7.

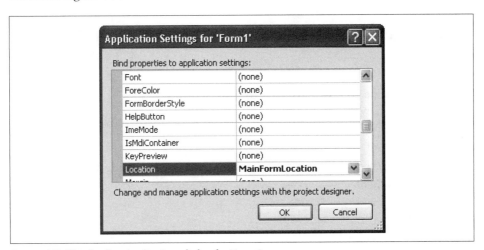

Figure 4-7. The Application Settings dialog for Form1

Any settings added to the Settings tab in the Project Properties window appear as members of the `My.Settings` object. In this recipe's case, you get a new property of type `System.Drawing.Point` with the name `My.Settings.MainFormLocation`. You can access this property as needed in your code.

Another way to add a control-linked setting is to skip the trip to the Project Properties' window's Settings panel, and add the new setting directly from the control's list of properties. When you select the (`ApplicationSettings`) property for the form or control and bring up the Application Settings dialog (Figure 4-7), if you click the drop-down button in the second column for any property, one of the choices that appears is "(new)." Clicking this link brings up the New Application Setting dialog, where you can enter the name and starting value of a new setting. The new property automatically obtains the right data type for the linked field. Figure 4-8 shows this method in action.

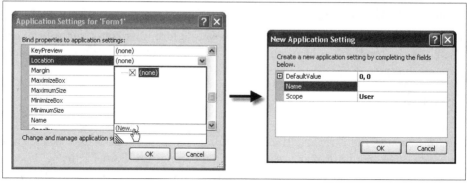

Figure 4-8. Adding a new setting for the form's Location property

4.11   Attaching a Control to the Edge of a Form

Problem

You want a specific control, such as a toolbar, to always "stick" to one edge of the form, no matter how it is resized.

Solution

Use the control's Dock property to permanently affix the control to the selected side or other "dock region."

Discussion

Dock has six possible values:

None
> The control performs no docking.

Top
> The control attaches itself to the top of the form's client area and fills the entire width of the client area, if the control supports such resizing.

Bottom
> The control attaches itself to the bottom of the form's client area and fills the entire width of the client area, if the control supports such resizing.

Left

    The control attaches itself to the left edge of the form's client area and fills the entire height of the client area, if the control supports such resizing.

Right

    The control attaches itself to the right edge of the form's client area and fills the entire height of the client area, if the control supports such resizing.

Fill

    The control fills the entire client area of the form, if the control supports such resizing.

If multiple controls have Dock settings other than None, they are attached to the form edges according to their z-order settings, starting from the back-most control. To alter the z-order of a control, right-click on the control in the Form Designer and select either "Bring to Front" or "Send to Back" from the shortcut menu. Figures 4-9 and 4-10 show a form with two controls with different z-orders docked to its bottom edge: a MonthCalendar control (notice how it automatically fills the width of the form by adding months) and a StatusStrip control.

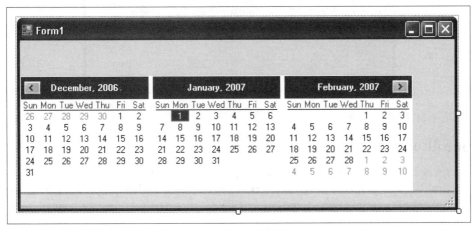

Figure 4-9. The form when the calendar's z-order is in front

Some controls are designed to dock along a specific edge of the form's client area. The most obvious example is the StatusStrip control, shown in this recipe's figures, which is designed to dock along the bottom edge of the form. Other controls, such as the CheckBox control, really aren't designed for docking. While you can still dock them, they may not look very nice.

Docking also applies to panels and other containers that can include subordinate controls. Figure 4-11 displays a Panel control with an included ComboBox control that is docked along the top edge of the panel.

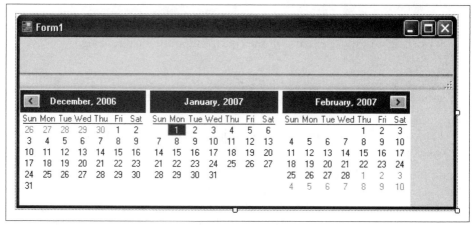

Figure 4-10. The form when the calendar's z-order is in back

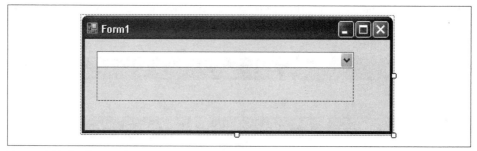

Figure 4-11. Docking within a container

See Also

Recipe 4.12 discusses the Anchor property, which can be used to attach a control to one, two, three, or four sides of the form. The Dock and Anchor properties cannot be used at the same time on the same control. The last one you set on that control is the one used.

4.12   Moving or Resizing Controls as a Form Resizes

Problem

You want a control to move or stretch in proportion to how the form is resized.

Solution

Use the control's Anchor property to attach it to one or more sides of the form.

Discussion

Setting the Anchor property of a control tells that control to permanently maintain a consistent distance relationship with one or more sides of the form or container. You can anchor a control to any or all of the four sides of a form. By default, controls are anchored to the left and top sides of the form. This means that as the form resizes, the controls remain the same distance from the form's left and top edges (i.e., they do not appear to move).

The available Anchor property choices include Left, Top, Right, and Bottom, and you can use them in any combination. The following list shows the types of combinations you can use with the Anchor property:

Anchored to one side
> As the form is resized, the center point of the control along the anchored edge is matched to a position on that form edge relative to the changing size of the form. The size of the control does not change. For instance, if a control is anchored to the top of a form and the form is made wider, the control moves to the right in proportion to the size of the form, as shown in Figure 4-12.

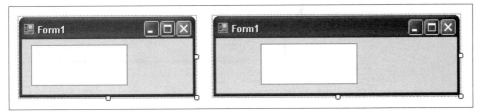

Figure 4-12. The top-anchored control moves when the form is resized

Anchored to two adjacent sides
> As the form is resized, the control maintains its distance from both anchor sides. In other words, it seems to be joined to the corner that is shared by the two anchor sides. By default, most controls anchor to the left and top sides of the form and do not appear to move when the right and bottom borders of the form are moved in a resize operation.

Anchored to two opposite sides
> The anchor sides of the control remain a fixed distance from the anchor borders. For instance, if a control is anchored on the left and right, the control grows by the same number of pixels as the form is widened (see Figure 4-13). When the unanchored direction is resized, the control is moved to keep the portion of space between the unanchored sides and the control the same, but the control is not resized in that direction.

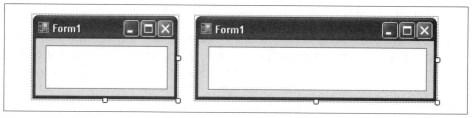

Figure 4-13. The left-and-right-anchored control stretches as the form widens

Anchored to three sides

The control resizes between the two anchor sides that are opposite to each other and remains the same distance from the single anchor border, as shown in Figure 4-14.

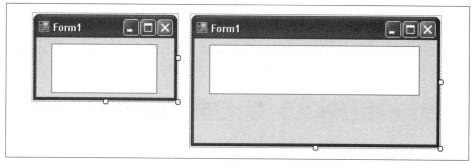

Figure 4-14. Anchored to top, left, and right, the edges of the control remain a fixed distance from all but the bottom edge of the form

Anchored to all four sides

The control is continually resized with the form. All its sides stay the same distance from all anchored form borders, as shown in Figure 4-15.

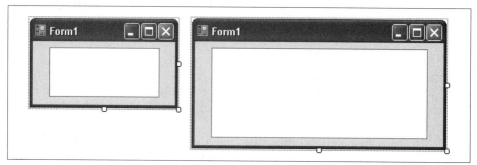

Figure 4-15. Anchored to top, left, bottom, and right, the proportions of the control change in concert with the form's proportions

Anchoring also applies to panels and other containers that can include subordinate controls.

See Also

See Recipe 4.11 for details on the Dock property, which you can use to attach a control to one side of a form's client area. The Dock and Anchor properties cannot be used at the same time on the same control. The last one you set on that control is the one used.

4.13 Limiting the Sizing of a Form

Problem

You want the user to be able to resize a form, but within limits.

Solution

Use the MinimumSize and MaximumSize properties of the form to limit the user's adjustments of the form's size. As with the standard Size property, these two properties encapsulate separate width and height values. Figure 4-16 shows these settings in use in the Properties panel.

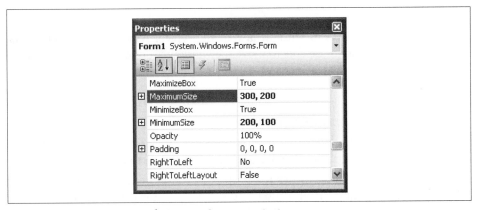

Figure 4-16. MaximumSize and MinimumSize properties in use

Discussion

These properties do limit the size of the form, whether the user is resizing the form directly or your code sets the Size property. You will usually want to set the form's FormBorderStyle property to Sizable, and you must set the MaximizeBox property to False (or in some other way hide the maximize box, such as by setting the ControlBox property to False).

4.14   Centering a Form

Problem

You want a form to be in the center of the display when it first appears.

Solution

Set the form's StartPosition property to CenterScreen.

Discussion

That was easy, but there may be cases where you need to set this property to Manual, but you still want the form to appear centered *sometimes*. To accomplish this, add the following code to the Load event handler for your form:

```
Me.Location = New Point(( _
    Screen.PrimaryScreen.Bounds.Width - Me.Width) / 2, _
    (Screen.PrimaryScreen.Bounds.Height - Me.Height) / 2)
```

4.15   Creating and Moving a Borderless Form

Problem

You want to display a form without any of the typical window border elements. Also, you want the user to be able to move the window around by clicking and dragging a PictureBox control.

Solution

Sample code folder: Chapter 04\MoveBorderlessForm

Turning off the border elements is easy: set the form's FormBorderStyle property to None. Then you can manage the drawing of the form elements yourself.

Creating a fake titlebar that moves the form is a little more involved. Create a new Windows Forms application, and add two controls: a Button control named ActClose and a PictureBox control named DragBar. Change the button's Text property to Close. Change the picture box's BackColor property to ActiveCaption, one of the system colors. Also, change the form's FormBorderStyle property to None. The form should look something like Figure 4-17.

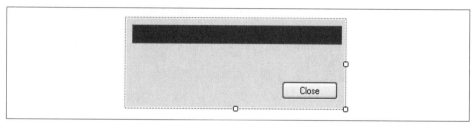

Figure 4-17. A borderless form with a pretend titlebar

Now, add the following source code to the form's code template:

```
Const HT_CAPTION As Integer = &H2
Const WM_NCLBUTTONDOWN As Integer = &HA1

Private Sub DragBar_MouseDown(ByVal sender As Object, _
        ByVal e As System.Windows.Forms.MouseEventArgs) _
        Handles DragBar.MouseDown
    ' ----- When the user clicks the left mouse button, act
    '          as if the user actually clicked on the form's
    '          title bar.
    If (e.Button = Windows.Forms.MouseButtons.Left) Then
        ' ----- Don't hold on to the mouse locally.
        DragBar.Capture = False

        ' ----- Trick the form into thinking it received a
        '          title click.
        Me.WndProc(Message.Create(Me.Handle, WM_NCLBUTTONDOWN, _
            CType(HT_CAPTION, IntPtr), IntPtr.Zero))
    End If
End Sub

Private Sub ActClose_Click(ByVal sender As System.Object, _
        ByVal e As System.EventArgs) Handles ActClose.Click
    Me.Close()
End Sub
```

Run the program, and drag the colored picture box control to move the form around the display.

Discussion

All of the activity within a Windows form happens through messages being processed through a *Windows procedure*, or WndProc. This method has existed since the introduction of Windows. The .NET Framework put a bunch of pretty classes around the messy parts of this messaging system, but it's still there, and you can interact with it to suit your needs.

Normally, when you left-click on a form window (or a control, which is just a different type of window), a WM_LBUTTONDOWN message is passed to the relevant Windows procedure. That message ultimately triggers a call to one of your form's MouseDown event handlers.

Your application includes a "message pump" that makes calls to each form's WndProc procedure for message processing. But there is nothing to stop you from calling that procedure yourself. In fact, it's exposed as a form class member.

When the DragBar picture box control receives the mouse down event, it says, "Hey, I'll just send a fake message to my window's WndProc routine so that it thinks the user clicked on the titlebar." And that's what the code does. It sends a WM_NCLBUTTONDOWN message to the form. The "NCL" part of that code means "Non-Client," the area that contains the titlebar and borders. The HT_CAPTION flag tells the message that the click occurred in the caption area (the titlebar). This is all that's needed to trick the form.

4.16   Creating a Fading Form

Problem

You want a form to fade out and disappear.

Solution

Sample code folder: Chapter 04\FadingForm

Use the form's Opacity property to slowly fade it out. Create a new Windows Forms application, and add a Button control named ActClose to the form. Change the button's Text property to Close. Then add the following source code to the form's code template:

```
Private Sub ActClose_Click(ByVal sender As Object, _
      ByVal e As System.EventArgs) Handles ActClose.Click
   ' ----- Fade out the form.
   Dim counter As Integer

   For counter = 90 To 10 Step -20
      Me.Opacity = counter / 100
      Me.Refresh( )
      Threading.Thread.Sleep(50)
   Next counter

   Me.Close( )
End Sub
```

Run the program, and click on the Close button to see the form fade away.

Discussion

You'll find that on some systems, the form momentarily blinks to black right when it makes the transition from an opacity of 1.0 to any other opacity value. On such systems, setting the Opacity property to a non-1.0 value during the Load event handler still causes a blink, but it does so when the form first opens, not during the cool fadeout.

```
Private Sub AboutProgram_Load(ByVal sender As Object, _
      ByVal e As System.EventArgs) Handles Me.Load
   ' ----- Prepare the form for later fade-out.
   Me.Opacity = 0.99
End Sub
```

4.17 Creating a Nonrectangular Form

Problem

You want to display a form that is nonrectangular; that is, you want some of the form to be invisible.

Solution

Sample code folder: Chapter 04\PartialInvisibility

Use the form's TransparencyKey property to identify a color that will be invisible. The sample code in this recipe uses fuchsia for its "invisible color," but you can choose any color that meets your display requirements.

Create a new Windows Forms application. Change Form1's FormBorderStyle property to None, its StartPosition property to CenterScreen, and its TransparencyKey property to Fuchsia. Then add the following source code to the form's code template:

```
Private Sub Form1_Click(ByVal sender As Object, _
      ByVal e As System.EventArgs) Handles Me.Click
   ' ----- Any click closes the form.
   Me.Close()
End Sub

Private Sub Form1_Paint(ByVal sender As Object, _
      ByVal e As System.Windows.Forms.PaintEventArgs) _
      Handles Me.Paint
   ' ----- Draw a nice logo form.
   e.Graphics.Clear(Color.Fuchsia)
   e.Graphics.FillRectangle(Brushes.Gold, 0.0F, _
      Me.ClientRectangle.Height / 3.0F, _
      CSng(Me.ClientRectangle.Width), _
      Me.ClientRectangle.Height / 3.0F)
   e.Graphics.FillPolygon(Brushes.Gold, New PointF() { _
      New Point(Me.ClientRectangle.Width / 4, 0), _
      New Point(Me.ClientRectangle.Width / 2, _
      Me.ClientRectangle.Height / 2), _
      New Point(Me.ClientRectangle.Width / 4, _
      Me.ClientRectangle.Height), _
      New Point(0, Me.ClientRectangle.Height / 2)})
   Dim largerFont = New Font(Me.Font.Name, 20)
   e.Graphics.DrawString("My Nice Program", _
      largerFont, Brushes.Black, 20, _
      (Me.ClientRectangle.Height / 2) - _
      (largerFont.Height / 2))
End Sub
```

When you run the program, it appears similar to the display in Figure 4-18. (We left the development environment behind the form so that you could see the invisibility.)

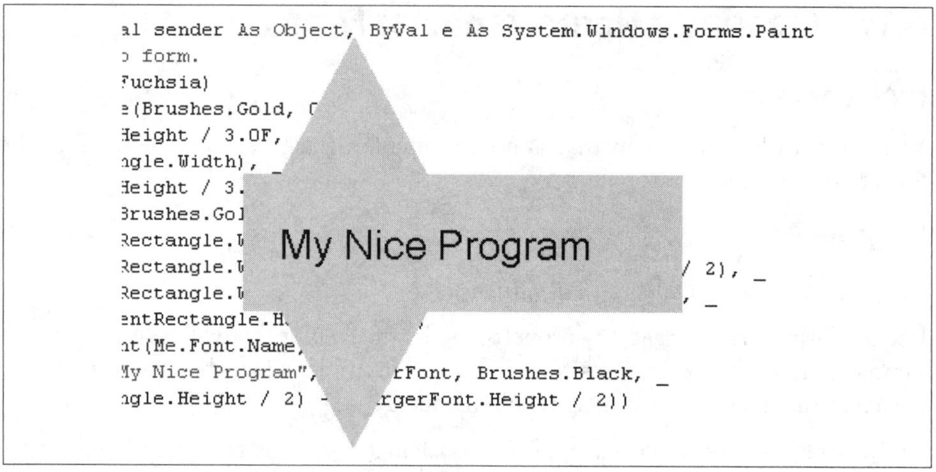

```
al sender As Object, ByVal e As System.Windows.Forms.Paint
 form.
Fuchsia)
e(Brushes.Gold, (
Height / 3.OF,
ngle.Width),  _
Height / 3.
Brushes.Gol
Rectangle.W
Rectangle.W                                    / 2), _
Rectangle.W
entRectangle.H                                 , _
nt(Me.Font.Name,
My Nice Program",          rFont, Brushes.Black, _
ngle.Height / 2) -       rgerFont.Height / 2))
```

My Nice Program

Figure 4-18. A form with transparent portions

Discussion

The initial release of Visual Basic 2005 included a bug that prevented the transparency color from properly appearing as transparent in some cases. Specifically, if your form included an image that contained the transparency color, and the workstation was using more than 24 bits of color for its display, the image appeared as opaque. To get around this problem, you need to set transparency on the image manually before you draw it:

```
Private Sub Form1_Paint(ByVal sender As Object, _
     ByVal e As System.Windows.Forms.PaintEventArgs) _
     Handles Me.Paint
   ' ----- This code assumes that the form's
   '       TransparencyKey property is "Fuchsia".
   Dim logoImage As Bitmap = Bitmap.FromFile( _
      "C:\MyLogo.bmp")
   logoImage.MakeTransparent(Color.Fuchsia)
   e.Graphics.DrawImage(logoImage, 0, 0)
End Sub
```

The Microsoft Knowledge Base number for this article is 822495.

See Also

Recipe 9.10 discusses invisibility colors and the TransparencyKey property in more detail.

4.18 Changing Menus at Runtime

Problem

You want to customize the menu structure in your main form at runtime. The structure should be based on settings made available by some user-configurable method.

Solution

Sample code folder: Chapter 04\RuntimeMenus

The menu-specific classes included in the Windows Forms library can be created at either design time or runtime. This recipe's code adds a basic menu to a form at design time and enhances it at runtime by adding the user's Internet Explorer "Favorites" to one of the menus.

Create a new Windows Forms application, and add a MenuStrip control named MainMenu to the form. Perform the following actions on this menu:

- Add a top-level menu named MenuFile, using &File for its Text property.
- Add a top-level menu named MenuFavorites, using Fa&vorites for its Text property.
- Add a menu item named MenuExitProgram that is subordinate to MenuFile, using E&xit for its Text property. Set its ShortcutKeys property to Alt+F4.
- Add a menu item named MenuNoFavorites that is subordinate to MenuFavorites, using (empty) for its Text property. Set its Enabled property to False.

Figure 4-19 shows a partial look at this form's menu structure in design mode.

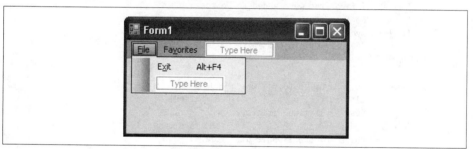

Figure 4-19. The initial menus for the runtime menu sample

Next, replace the form's code template with the following code. I've highlighted the lines that do the actual adding of menu items:

```
Imports MVB = Microsoft.VisualBasic

Public Class Form1
   Private Declare Auto Function GetPrivateProfileString _
      Lib "kernel32" _
      (ByVal AppName As String, _
```

```vb
        ByVal KeyName As String, _
        ByVal DefaultValue As String, _
        ByVal ReturnedString As System.Text.StringBuilder, _
        ByVal BufferSize As Integer, _
        ByVal FileName As String) As Integer

Private Sub MenuExitProgram_Click( _
        ByVal sender As System.Object, _
        ByVal e As System.EventArgs) _
        Handles MenuExitProgram.Click
    ' ----- Exit the program.
    Me.Close()
End Sub

Private Sub Form1_Load(ByVal sender As Object, _
        ByVal e As System.EventArgs) Handles Me.Load
    ' ----- Scan through the user's "Favorites" and
    '       add them as menu items.
    Dim favoritesPath As String

    ' ----- Determine the location of the "Favorites"
    '       folder.
    favoritesPath = Environment.GetFolderPath( _
        Environment.SpecialFolder.Favorites)
    If (favoritesPath = "") Then Return
    If (My.Computer.FileSystem.DirectoryExists( _
        favoritesPath) = False) Then Return

    ' ----- Call the recursive routine that builds the menu.
    BuildFavorites(MenuFavorites, favoritesPath)

    ' ----- If favorites were added, hide the
    '       "no favorites" item.
    If (MenuFavorites.DropDownItems.Count > 1) Then _
        MenuNoFavorites.Visible = False
End Sub

Private Sub BuildFavorites(ByVal whichMenu As _
        ToolStripMenuItem, ByVal fromPath As String)
    ' ----- Given a starting directory, add all files
    '       and directories in it to the specified menu.
    '       Recurse for suborindate directories.
    Dim oneEntry As String
    Dim menuEntry As ToolStripMenuItem
    Dim linkPath As String
    Dim displayName As String

    ' ----- Start with any directories.
    For Each oneEntry In My.Computer.FileSystem. _
        GetDirectories(fromPath)
        ' ----- Create the parent menu, but don't
        '       attach it yet.
        menuEntry = New ToolStripMenuItem( _
            My.Computer.FileSystem.GetName(oneEntry))
```

```vb
      ' ----- Recurse to build the sub-directory branch.
      BuildFavorites(menuEntry, oneEntry)

      ' ----- If that folder contained items,
      '       then attach it.
      If (menuEntry.DropDownItems.Count > 0) Then _
         whichMenu.DropDownItems.Add(menuEntry)
   Next oneEntry

   ' ---- Next, build the actual file links. Only
   '      look at ".url" files.
   For Each oneEntry In My.Computer.FileSystem. _
         GetFiles(fromPath, FileIO.SearchOption. _
         SearchTopLevelOnly, "*.url")
      ' ----- Build a link based on this file. These
      '       files are old-style INI files.
      linkPath = GetINIEntry("InternetShortcut", _
         "URL", oneEntry)
      If (linkPath <> "") Then
         ' ----- Found the link. Add it to the menu.
         displayName = My.Computer.FileSystem. _
            GetName(oneEntry)
         displayName = MVB.Left(displayName, _
            displayName.Length - 4)
         menuEntry = New ToolStripMenuItem(displayName)
         menuEntry.Tag = linkPath
         whichMenu.DropDownItems.Add(menuEntry)

         ' ----- Connect this entry to the event handler.
         AddHandler menuEntry.Click, _
            AddressOf RunFavoritesLink
      End If
   Next oneEntry
End Sub

Private Sub RunFavoritesLink( _
      ByVal sender As System.Object, _
      ByVal e As System.EventArgs)
   ' ----- Run the link.
   Dim whichMenu As ToolStripMenuItem

   whichMenu = CType(sender, ToolStripMenuItem)
   Process.Start(whichMenu.Tag)
End Sub

Private Function GetINIEntry(ByVal sectionName As String, _
      ByVal keyName As String, _
      ByVal whichFile As String) As String
   ' ----- Extract a value from an INI-style file.
   Dim resultLength As Integer
   Dim targetBuffer As New System.Text.StringBuilder(500)

   resultLength = GetPrivateProfileString(sectionName, _
      keyName, "", targetBuffer, targetBuffer.Capacity, _
```

```
            whichFile)
        Return targetBuffer.ToString( )
    End Function
End Class
```

Run the program, and access its Favorites menu to browse and open the current user's Internet Explorer favorites.

Discussion

The bulk of this recipe's code deals with scanning through a directory structure and examining each file and subdirectory. Most of the files in the "Favorites" folder have a *.url* extension and contain data in an "INI file" format.

Here's a sample link to a popular search engine:

```
[DEFAULT]
BASEURL=http://www.google.com/
[InternetShortcut]
URL=http://www.google.com/
```

The last "URL=" line provides the link we need to enable favorites support in our program.

The important part of the program is the building of the menu structure. Each menu item attached to the form's main menu MenuStrip control is a related ToolStripMenuItem class instance. These can be attached to the menu at any time through its DropDownItems collection. Each menu item in turn has its own DropDownItems collection that manages subordinate menu items.

To make each new menu item do something, as you add them, connect them to the previously written RunFavoritesLink method:

```
AddHandler menuEntry.Click, AddressOf RunFavoritesLink
```

4.19   Creating Shortcut Menus

Problem

You want to display a custom shortcut menu to users when they right-click on a form or one of its controls.

Solution

Sample code folder: Chapter 04\ShortcutMenus

Use the ContextMenuStrip control to design a shortcut menu (also called a *context* or *pop-up* menu) that you can attach to the controls (or form) of your choice.

Create a new Windows Forms application, and add a ContextMenuStrip control named MainShortcutMenu to the form. When you select that control, it adds a temporary standard menu to the control that you can use to add new menu items (see Figure 4-20).

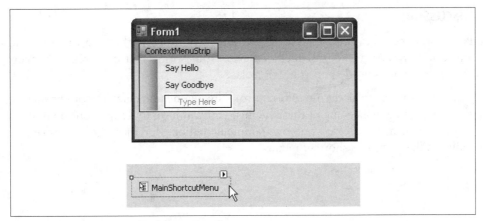

Figure 4-20. Shortcut menus in design mode

Add two menu items to this shortcut menu:

- A menu item named MenuHello, using Say Hello for its Text property
- A menu item named MenuGoodbye, using Say Goodbye for its Text property

Select the form itself, and then change its ContextMenuStrip property to MainShortcutMenu.

Now, add the following source code to the form's code template:

```
Private Sub MenuHello_Click(ByVal sender As System.Object, _
        ByVal e As System.EventArgs) Handles MenuHello.Click
    MsgBox("Hello")
End Sub

Private Sub MenuGoodbye_Click(ByVal sender As System.Object, _
        ByVal e As System.EventArgs) Handles MenuGoodbye.Click
    MsgBox("Goodbye")
End Sub
```

Run the program, and right-click on the form. The shortcut menu will present itself, as shown in Figure 4-21. Clicking on the items puts up a message box saying "Hello" or "Goodbye."

Figure 4-21. The shortcut menu in use

Discussion

Each form and control includes a `ContextMenuStrip` property that you can assign to any `ContextMenuStrip` control included with your form. You can create as many shortcut menus as needed for your controls.

Some controls, such as the `TextBox` control, already include default shortcut menus. If you wish to enhance one of these menus, you will have to design your own menu from scratch and provide your own implementations for menu items previously found in that control's shortcut menu.

Strings

5.0   Introduction

Every Visual Basic developer quickly learns how to manipulate strings, but it's often easy to overlook some of the more powerful techniques available, especially with all the new features in Visual Basic 2005. A good example is the powerful StringBuilder object, which provides an order-of-magnitude improvement for concatenating strings. Visual Basic 6 developers, in particular, will discover lots of exciting new string-processing features. For example, Visual Basic 2005's Substring( ) method provides similar functionality not only to the Mid( ) function, but also to the Left( ) and Right( ) string functions. The regular expression library included with .NET also provides new and powerful ways to analyze and process string data.

5.1   Using a StringBuilder

Problem

You need to process many pieces of string data with more efficiency than is allowed using standard .NET Framework immutable strings.

Solution

The StringBuilder object provides extremely fast and efficient in-place processing of string and character data. The following code demonstrates several of its powerful methods and some of the techniques you can use to speed up your string processing:

```
Dim workText As New System.Text.StringBuilder

' ----- Build a basic text block.
workText.Append("The important")
workText.Append(vbNewLine)
workText.Append("thing is not")
workText.AppendLine()
workText.AppendLine("to stop questioning.")
```

```
workText.Append("--Albert Einstein")
MsgBox(workText.ToString( ))

' ----- Delete the trailing text.
Dim endSize As Integer = "--Albert Einstein".Length
workText.Remove(workText.Length - endSize, endSize)
MsgBox(workText.ToString( ))

' ----- Modify text in the middle.
workText.Insert(4, "very ")
MsgBox(workText.ToString( ))

' ----- Perform a search and replace.
workText.Replace("not", "never")
MsgBox(workText.ToString( ))

' ----- Truncate the existing text.
workText.Length = 3
MsgBox(workText.ToString( ))
```

Discussion

The first line of the previous code creates a new instance of the StringBuilder object. The next half dozen or so lines of code show various common uses of the StringBuilder's Append( ) and AppendLine( ) methods. Each call to Append( ) or AppendLine( ) concatenates another string or character piece into the StringBuilder's buffer. Figure 5-1 shows the result of these first few append actions.

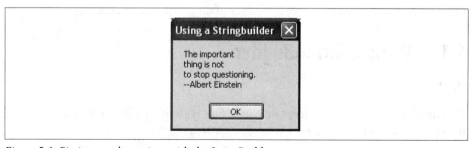

Figure 5-1. Piecing together strings with the StringBuilder

Avoid the temptation to concatenate these string pieces using the & operator as you prepare the various pieces for appending to the StringBuilder. Doing so detracts from the efficiency and speed advantages of the StringBuilder. For example, both of the following lines of code are legal and correct, but the line that uses the & operator does a lot more work behind the scenes:

```
' ----- Don't do this!
workText.Append("This " & "is " & "not advisable!")

' ----- Please do this.
workText.Append("This ").Append("is ").Append("faster!")
```

The first statement (the one using the & operator) must make working copies of the immutable strings to do the concatenations. Timing tests demonstrate that this can slow down your code measurably.

Besides Append( ), the StringBuilder object also provides methods that parallel other functions available for processing true strings. These include Remove( ), Replace( ), and Insert( ) methods, as demonstrated in the sample code presented earlier in this recipe. The Length property shown in the sample is also available as a standard property of strings. The remaining lines of code in the sample demonstrate the use of these methods by modifying parts of the original quote.

A StringBuilder's contents are technically not a string. Rather, the StringBuilder maintains an internal buffer of characters that at any time can easily be converted to a string using the StringBuilder's ToString( ) method. Think of a StringBuilder as a string in the making that's not really a string until you want it to be.

Behind the scenes, the default StringBuilder's buffer starts out with a working space, or *capacity*, of only 16 bytes. The buffer automatically doubles in size whenever it needs more space, jumping to 32 bytes, then 64, and so on. If you have a good idea how much space your string processing may require, you can initialize StringBuilder's buffer to a given capacity during the declaration. For example, this declaration creates a StringBuilder instance with a preallocated buffer size of 1,000 bytes:

```
Dim workText As New System.Text.StringBuilder(1000)
```

The advantage of providing the starting capacity is a potential performance boost. In this case, the buffer's workspace won't need to be doubled until enough strings have been appended to overflow the 1,000-byte limit.

You can access the StringBuilder's capacity at runtime through its Capacity property. It's enlightening to read this property to follow along as the StringBuilder doubles in size during execution. You can set the Capacity to a new value at any time, but if you set the Capacity to less than the StringBuilder's current Length, an exception occurs. If your intent is to shorten, or truncate, the contents of the buffer, set the Length property instead, and leave Capacity alone. The easiest way to empty a StringBuilder of its contents is to set its Length property to zero.

See Also

Recipe 5.26 also discusses building up strings from smaller components.

5.2 Creating a String of N Identical Characters

Problem

You need to create a string comprised of a single character repeated many times. These strings are sometimes useful in the formatting of ASCII text for display or printed output.

Solution

Create a new string of repeated characters using the `String` class itself. One of its overloaded constructors accepts a character to repeat and a repetition count.

Discussion

Most of the time you create string variables using the default constructor, which initializes the variables to `Nothing`. This is why you must assign a string value to a string variable after creating it, but before using its contents. However, you can use overloaded versions of the string constructor to assign string data immediately upon creation. One version of the string constructor takes a character and a count and efficiently builds a string by repeating the character the given number of times. The following statement builds a string of 72 asterisks:

```
Dim lotsOfAsterisks As New String("*"c, 72)
```

Visual Basic 2005 also provides a second way to create strings of duplicated characters. The `StrDup()` function, which is very similar to the original `String()` function found in Visual Basic 6, does the trick:

```
lotsOfAsterisks = StrDup(72, "*")
```

Notice the difference in the order of the parameters between the string constructor syntax and the function call. Fortunately, Visual Studio's IntelliSense means you don't have to memorize the order of the parameters.

VB 6 Users' Update

The VB 6 `String()` function returns a string based on a count and the first character of the string:

```
lotsOfAsterisks = String(72, "*")
```

Most sources mention only the new `String` constructor technique to create strings of duplicate characters in Visual Basic 2005, but after doing a lot of timing tests, we've seen that the `StrDup()` function is very nearly identical in speed and efficiency. Also, its syntax is much more like that of the original VB 6 `String()` function. Use whichever technique suits you better.

See Also

Recipe 5.45 demonstrates another method of creating strings of a common character.

5.3   Creating a String by Repeating a String N Times

Problem

You want a string comprised of a sequence of characters repeated many times. For example, you want to create a fancy separator string comprised of alternating "+" and "~" characters, as shown in Figure 5-2.

Figure 5-2. A string formed by repeating two characters many times

Solution

Use a StringBuilder to append as many copies of the string as desired. Then convert the result to a true string using the StringBuilder's ToString( ) method:

```
Dim fancyString As New System.Text.StringBuilder
For counter As Integer = 1 To 35
    fancyString.Append("+~")
Next counter
MsgBox(fancyString.ToString( ))
```

Discussion

Strings in .NET are immutable, which means that once they've been created, they sit in one spot in memory and can never be modified. All functions that might appear to be changing a string's contents are actually making new copies of the original string, modified en route. In most cases, immutability provides superior string handling and processing capabilities, but when it comes to concatenating strings, the speed and efficiency advantages are nullified.

The StringBuilder object solves the concatenation dilemma nicely. It allows dynamic, in-place modification of a buffer containing a sequence of string characters, without the need to constantly reallocate String objects. If the allocated buffer space runs out, the StringBuilder efficiently and automatically doubles the number of bytes for its character workspace, and it will do so as many times as are required to handle the strings and characters appended to it.

See Also

Recipe 5.27 shows how the StringBuilder alternative really is faster than standard string concatenation.

5.4   Obfuscating a String

Problem

You need to store a string in such a way that a user won't recognize it, but you also want to make sure that the string stays the same length and that it contains only printable ASCII characters.

Solution

Sample code folder: Chapter 05\ObfuscateString

Process each printable character of the string by shifting its ASCII value to that of another character within the same set. The following two functions can be used to obfuscate strings in this way and then return them to their original states:

```
Public Function Obfuscate(ByVal origText As String) As String
   ' ----- Make a string unreadable, but retrievable.
   Dim textBytes As Byte() = _
      System.Text.Encoding.UTF8.GetBytes(origText)
   For counter As Integer = 0 To textBytes.Length - 1
      If (textBytes(counter) > 31) And _
            (textBytes(counter) < 127) Then
         textBytes(counter) += CByte(counter Mod 31 + 1)
         If (textBytes(counter) > 126) Then _
            textBytes(counter) -= CByte(95)
      End If
   Next counter
   Return System.Text.Encoding.UTF8.GetChars(textBytes)
End Function

Public Function DeObfuscate(ByVal origText As String) _
      As String
   ' ----- Restore a previously obfuscated string.
   Dim textBytes As Byte() = _
      System.Text.Encoding.UTF8.GetBytes(origText)
   For counter As Integer = 0 To textBytes.Length - 1
      If (textBytes(counter) > 31) And _
            (textBytes(counter) < 127) Then
         textBytes(counter) -= CByte(counter Mod 31 + 1)
         If (textBytes(counter) < 32) Then _
            textBytes(counter) += CByte(95)
      End If
   Next counter
   Return System.Text.Encoding.UTF8.GetChars(textBytes)
End Function
```

Figure 5-3 shows a string before and after calling Obfuscate( ), and after returning it to its original state by calling DeObfuscate( ).

Figure 5-3. Results of obfuscating a string to make it unreadable, then deobfuscating it

Discussion

The `Obfuscate()` function lets you modify strings to an unreadable state without resorting to full-blown cryptographic techniques. An example of where this might come in handy is for storing string data in the registry in such a manner that the original contents are not easily searched for and that the typical user won't recognize the data.

When modifying individual bytes of a string, it's often best to first convert the string to an array of bytes, as shown in these functions. You can freely modify the byte values in place, unlike the contents of the immutable string they came from, and generate a new string result by converting the entire byte array in one function call.

If you work with international character sets, consider using the Unicode versions of the encoding conversion functions instead of the UTF8 versions. The byte arrays will be twice as large, but you should be able to handle other sets of characters. You'll also need to pay close attention to the numerical shift of the byte values, modifying the above code to keep the results within the desired range of characters.

See Also

Recipe 5.23 discusses additional modifications to strings that can be reversed.

5.5   Converting Binary Data to a Hexadecimal String

Problem

You need to convert a byte array to a hexadecimal string. This is handy for the display or documentation of binary data.

Solution

Use a bit converter to get the hexadecimal representation of each byte within a block of data. The following code generates the hexadecimal string from source data:

```
Dim result As String = Replace(BitConverter.ToString( _
    origBytes), "-", "")
```

Discussion

There are several approaches to solving this problem. A quick review of some of these approaches will demonstrate several different programming techniques available to you in Visual Basic 2005.

The code samples in this recipe assume a byte array named origBytes built using the following code, which creates a byte array of length 256 containing one each of the byte values 0 through 255:

```
Dim origBytes(255) As Byte
For counter As Byte = 0 To 255
    origBytes(counter) = counter
Next counter
```

The first approach is somewhat "brute force" in nature. Each byte of the array is converted to a two-character string using one of the many formatting options of the byte's ToString( ) method. These short strings are concatenated to the result string one at a time:

```
Dim result As String = ""
For counter As Byte = 0 To 255
    result &= origBytes(counter).ToString("X2")
Next counter
```

This is fine for small arrays of bytes, but the string concatenation quickly becomes problematic as the byte count increases. The next approach uses a StringBuilder to make the concatenation more efficient for large data sources:

```
Dim workText As New System.Text.StringBuilder(600)
For counter = 0 To 255
    workText.Append(origBytes(counter).ToString("X2"))
Next counter
Dim result As String = workText.ToString( )
```

This solution runs faster, but it seems to lack the elegance and power we expect of Visual Basic. Fortunately, the .NET Framework is full of surprises, and of useful objects too. The BitConverter object provides a shared method that converts an entire array of bytes to a hexadecimal string in one call. The resulting string has dashes between each pair of hexadecimal characters. This can be nice in some circumstances, but in this case, we're trying to create a compact hexadecimal string comprised of only two characters for each byte. The following two lines of code show how to call the BitConverter.ToString( ) method, and then squeeze out all the dashes using a single call to the Replace( ) function:

```
Dim result As String
result = BitConverter.ToString(origBytes) '00-3F-F7 etc.
result = Replace(result, "-", "")      '003FF7 etc.
```

The solution presented first in this recipe is the result of combining these two function calls into a single line of code. Figure 5-4 shows the resulting hexadecimal string displaying all possible byte values.

Figure 5-4. The hexadecimal string equivalent of a byte array comprised of the values 0 to 255

See Also

Recipes 5.16 and 5.26 show other useful ways of modifying portions of strings.

5.6 Extracting Substrings from Larger Strings

Problem

You want to extract substrings located at the left end, the right end, or somewhere in the middle of a string.

Solution

Visual Basic 2005 strings now have a built-in method named Substring( ) that provides an alternative to the traditional Visual Basic functions Left( ), Mid( ), and Right( ), although the language retains these features if you wish to use them. To emulate each of these functions, set the Substring( ) method's parameters appropriately. The following code shows how to do this:

```
Dim quote As String = "The important thing is not to " & _
    "stop questioning. --Albert Einstein"

' ----- Left(quote, 3) ... "The"
MsgBox(quote.Substring(0, 3))

' ----- Mid(quote, 5, 9) ... "important"
MsgBox(quote.Substring(4, 9))

' ----- Mid(quote, 58) ... "Einstein"
MsgBox(quote.Substring(57))

' ----- Right(quote, 8) ... "Einstein"
MsgBox(quote.Substring(quote.Length - 8))
```

Discussion

Each line of code in the sample is prefaced by a comment line showing the equivalent syntax from VB 6. One of the big differences apparent in these examples is that the first character in the string is now at offset position 0 instead of 1, requiring a change in the offsets supplied to the Substring( ) method. The lengths of the substrings are still the same.

5.7   Converting a String's Case

Problem

You want to convert a string to all uppercase, all lowercase, or mixed case (with only the first letter of each word in uppercase).

Solution

Sample code folder: Chapter 05\MixedCase

The string methods ToUpper( ) and ToLower( ) make it easy to convert strings to upper- and lowercase, and a short special-purpose function can perform the mixed conversion. You can also use the standard Visual Basic UCase( ) and LCase( ) methods. To mix-case a string, use Visual Basic's StrConv( ) function.

Discussion

Changing strings to upper- or lowercase is standard Visual Basic fare:

```
' ----- To upper case.
newString = oldString.ToUpper( )
newString = UCase(oldString)

' ----- To lower case.
newString = oldString.ToLower( )
newString = LCase(oldString)
```

To convert the string to mixed or "proper" case, use one of the conversion methods included in the StrConv( ) function:

```
newString = StrConv(oldString, VbStrConv.ProperCase)
```

This function converts the first letter of each word to uppercase, making every other letter lowercase. Its rules are pretty basic, and it doesn't know about special cases. If you need to correctly capitalize names such as "MacArthur," you have to write a custom routine. The following code provides the start of a routine using an algorithm that works much like the StrConv( ) function. It assumes that space characters separate each word:

```
Public Function MixedCase(ByVal origText As String) As String
    ' ----- Convert a string to "proper" case.
    Dim counter As Integer
    Dim textParts( ) As String = Split(origText, " ")

    For counter = 0 To textParts.Length - 1
        If (textParts(counter).Length > 0) Then _
```

```
        textParts(counter) = _
        UCase(Microsoft.VisualBasic.Left( _
        textParts(counter), 1)) & _
        LCase(Mid(textParts(counter), 2))
    Next counter

    Return Join(textParts, " ")
  End Function
```

The code splits up the original text into an array at space-character boundaries using the Split( ) function. It then processes each word separately and merges them back together with the Join( ) method.

Figure 5-5 shows the results of various conversions on a string, including a conversion using the custom MixedCase( ) function. Notice that "albert" is not capitalized in the mixed-case string. This is because the two leading dashes are considered to be part of this word, based on how the Split( ) function separated the words at space-character locations.

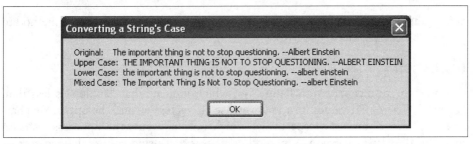

Figure 5-5. The original string before and after various case conversions

VB 6 Users' Update

VB 2005 strings have a built-in Split( ) method, but this example doesn't use it. Instead, we chose to use the Split( ) function, provided for backward compatibility with VB 6. Generally speaking, this function is preferablebecause it makes it easier to split a string using a multicharacter substring at the point of each split. The newer Split( ) method of VB 2005 strings works great for splitting at single-character boundaries.

See Also

Recipe 5.44 discusses the Split( ) function and the Split( ) method.

5.8 Comparing Strings with Case Sensitivity

Problem

You need to compare two strings, taking into account their case.

Solution

Use the shared Compare( ) method provided by the String object to compare two strings:

```
Select Case String.Compare(content1, content2, False)
    Case Is < 0
        MsgBox("Content1 comes before Content2.")
    Case Is > 0
        MsgBox("Content1 comes after Content2.")
    Case Is = 0
        MsgBox("Content1 and Content2 are the same.")
End Select
```

Setting the third parameter of the Compare( ) method to False instructs the method to perform a case-sensitive comparison.

Discussion

Consider the results shown in Figure 5-6, which indicate that "apples" is less than "Apples". The ASCII values for the lowercase character "a" and the uppercase character "A" are 97 and 65, respectively, which normally puts the uppercase version first. But the String.Compare( ) method compares text using culture-defined sorting rules, and by default, English words beginning with lowercase letters are considered "less than" the same words beginning with uppercase letters.

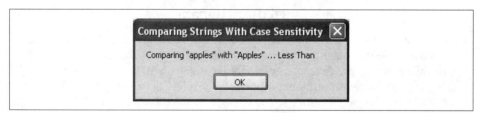

Figure 5-6. Culture-defined rules apply to case-sensitive string comparisons

You can change the comparison rules in several ways to match what you want to accomplish. See the Visual Studio online help for the CompareOptions property for more information on how to make these changes.

See Also

Recipe 5.9 discusses related comparisons.

5.9   Comparing Strings Without Case Sensitivity

Problem

You need to compare two strings without regard to their case.

Solution

Use the shared Compare( ) method provided by the String object to compare two strings:

```
Select Case String.Compare(content1, content2, True)
    Case Is < 0
        MsgBox("Content1 comes before Content2.")
    Case Is > 0
        MsgBox("Content1 comes after Content2.")
    Case Is = 0
        MsgBox("Content1 and Content2 are the same.")
End Select
```

Setting the third parameter of the Compare( ) method to True instructs the method to perform a case-insensitive comparison.

Discussion

This type of string comparison compares all alphabetic characters as though lowercase and uppercase characters were identical. Figure 5-7 shows that "apples" is equal to "Apples" when the strings are compared this way.

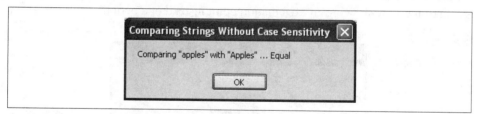

Figure 5-7. When case is ignored, lowercase and uppercase are treated identically

String comparisons are culturally defined by default, so be sure the sort order you get is really what you want. See the Visual Studio online help for the CompareOptions property to find more information on how to make changes to the way strings are sorted.

See Also

Recipe 5.8 discusses related comparisons.

5.10   Converting Strings to and from Character Arrays

Problem

You need to work with individual characters in a string efficiently, changing them in place in memory if possible.

Solution

Sample code folder: Chapter 05\StringsAndCharArrays

Use CType( ) to convert the string to an array of characters, modify characters throughout the array, and then directly convert the character array back to a string:

```
Dim quote As String = "The important thing is not to " & _
    "stop questioning. --Albert Einstein"
Dim charArray() As Char = CType(quote, Char())
charArray(46) = "!"c
Dim result As String = New String(charArray)
MsgBox(result)
```

Discussion

In this example, the string is converted to a character array using the versatile CType( ) type-conversion function. In this form, it's easy to make a change such as replacing the period at index 46 with an exclamation point. The array is then recombined into a string by passing it to the overloaded version of the String constructor that takes an array of characters to initialize the new string. Figure 5-8 shows the displayed string result, now showing an exclamation point instead of a period.

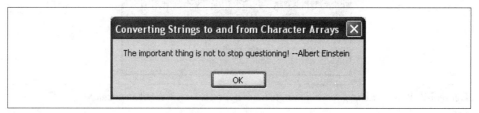

Figure 5-8. Converting a string to an array of characters enables easy modification of individual characters in that string

There is another way to access individual characters in a string, but it's read-only, so you can't use the technique to modify the string:

```
MsgBox(someString.Chars(46))
```

All strings have a Chars( ) property that lets you access an indexed character from the string with minimal overhead. The index is zero-based, so Chars(46) returns the 47th character.

See Also

Recipe 5.12 also examines working with individual characters within a larger string.

5.11   Converting Strings to and from Byte Arrays

Problem

You need to convert a string to bytes, and back to a string from a byte array. This enables you to work with the exact binary data comprising the string.

Solution

Sample code folder: Chapter 05\StringsAndByteArrays

Use shared methods of the System.Text.Encoding object to convert to and from bytes. If you know the string data to be comprised entirely of ASCII characters, use UTF8 encoding to minimize the length of the byte array. Unicode encoding, which results in two bytes per character instead of one, can be used to guarantee no loss of data when making these conversions.

Discussion

The following sample code shows both UTF8 and Unicode encoding methods:

```
Dim quote As String = "The important thing is not to " & _
    "stop questioning. --Albert Einstein"
Dim bytes() As Byte
Dim result As String

' ----- Assumed to be all ASCII character.
bytes = System.Text.Encoding.UTF8.GetBytes(quote)
bytes(46) = 33   ' ASCII exclamation point
result = System.Text.Encoding.UTF8.GetString(bytes)
MsgBox(result)

' ----- Works with all character sets.
bytes = System.Text.Encoding.Unicode.GetBytes(quote)
bytes(92) = 63   ' ASCII question mark
bytes(93) = 0
result = System.Text.Encoding.Unicode.GetString(bytes)
MsgBox(result)
```

When using UTF8 encoding, the number of bytes in the array is the same as the number of characters in the string. The character at indexed position 46 in the string is a period. During the first conversion, this period is changed to an exclamation point, and the resulting string is displayed, a result identical to that previously shown in Figure 5-8.

A Unicode-encoded byte array contains twice as many bytes as the number of characters in the original string. This makes sense when you consider that Unicode characters are 16 bits each (or two bytes) in size. Take a close look at the byte array modifications in the second part of the example code. The byte at position 92 (twice as far into the array as the ASCII variation) is set to the desired ASCII value (63 in this case, for the question mark). But because each character now consumes two bytes in the array, you must set both bytes. Setting the byte at position 93 clears the other half of the two-byte set. Figure 5-9 shows the resulting string, now sporting a question mark at the 46th character position.

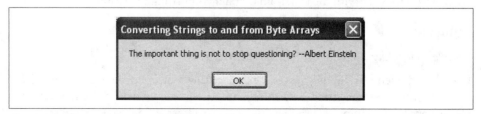

Figure 5-9. Changing the Unicode character at byte locations 92 and 93 to a question mark

5.12   Tallying Characters

Problem

You want to tally, or count the occurrences of, each character value in a string.

Solution

Sample code folder: Chapter 05\TallyCharacters

Convert the string to a byte array, and then tally the 256 possible byte values into an array of integer counts.

Discussion

In the case presented, the string is assumed to be all ASCII, which means conversion using UTF8 encoding is appropriate, and the tally array only needs to be dimensioned to hold 256 counting bins:

```
Dim quote As String = "The important thing is not to " & _
    "stop questioning. --Albert Einstein"
Dim counter As Integer
Dim tally(255) As Integer
```

Convert the string to a byte array, and then loop through each byte of the array to increment the count for each byte value:

```
Dim bytes( ) As Byte = _
    System.Text.Encoding.UTF8.GetBytes(quote)
For counter = 0 To bytes.Length - 1
```

```
        tally(bytes(counter)) += 1
    Next counter
```

The rest of the example prepares the tally for display. For efficiency, the code presents only characters with nonzero counts:

```
Dim result As New System.Text.StringBuilder(quote)
For counter = 0 To 255
    If (tally(counter) > 0) Then
        result.AppendLine( )
        result.Append(Chr(counter))
        result.Append(Space(3))
        result.Append(tally(counter).ToString( ))
    End If
Next counter
MsgBox(result.ToString( ))
```

Figure 5-10 shows the results.

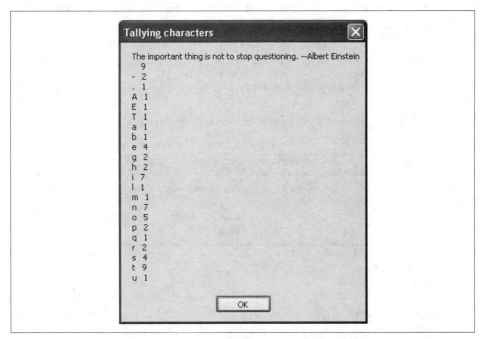

Figure 5-10. A quick tally of the characters in a string

If you want to tally Unicode characters, you need to either dimension a much larger tally array or use a lookup system that constantly adds and counts characters as it finds them.

See Also

Recipe 5.11 provides additional details on encoded conversions.

5.13   Counting Words

Problem

You want to count the words in a string.

Solution

Sample code folder: Chapter 05\CountWords

Use the Split( ) function to split the string at each space character. The length of the resulting array is a good approximation of the number of words in the string.

Discussion

There always seems to be more than one way to get things done in Visual Basic 2005, and counting words is no exception. The following code shows one quick-and-dirty technique that requires very little coding to get the job done:

```
Dim quote As String = "The important thing is not to " & _
    "stop questioning. --Albert Einstein"
Dim wordCount As Integer = Split(quote, Space(1)).Length
MsgBox(quote & vbNewLine & "Number of words: " & _
    wordCount.ToString)
```

Figure 5-11 shows the resulting number of words in the string.

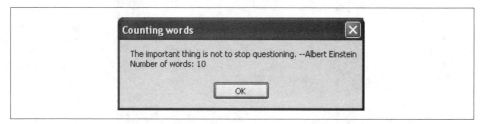

Figure 5-11. Splitting a string to count its words

Inaccuracies can creep in if there are multiple spaces between some words in the string, if extra spaces appear at either or both ends of the string, or if other whitespace characters (such as tabs) are involved. A little preparation of the string can help eliminate some of these problems, but at the expense of added complexity. For example, the following lines of code get rid of runs of two or more space characters, replacing them with single spaces. Adding this code just before the Split( ) function can provide a more accurate word count:

```
Do While (quote.IndexOf(Space(2)) >= 0)
    quote = quote.Replace(Space(2), Space(1))
Loop
```

Similarly, you can use the Replace( ) method to replace all tabs with spaces (probably best done just before converting all multiple spaces to single spaces). As you can probably sense, efforts to guarantee a more accurate count cause the code to grow quickly. The best course is to decide what degree of word-counting accuracy is required, how much value to place on speed of operation, and so on before deciding how much cleanup code to add.

Another solution to this problem involves regular expressions, which are covered in Recipes 5.37 through 5.42.

See Also

Recipe 5.42 shows how to solve this same problem using a different solution.

5.14 Removing Extra Whitespace

Problem

You want to remove all extra whitespace characters from a string, leaving a single space character between each word.

Solution

Sample code folder: Chapter 05\RemoveWhitespace

There are several possible ways to remove extra whitespace from a string. One approach, presented here, is to test each character of the string to see if it is whitespace and to build up the resulting string using a StringBuilder:

```
Dim source As String = _
    Space(17) & "This    string    had " & Chr(12) & _
    StrDup(5, Chr(9)) & "extra whitespace. " & Space(27)
Dim thisIsWhiteSpace As Boolean
Dim prevIsWhiteSpace As Boolean
Dim result As New System.Text.StringBuilder(source.Length)
Dim counter As Integer

For counter = 0 To source.Length - 1
    prevIsWhiteSpace = thisIsWhiteSpace
    thisIsWhiteSpace = _
        Char.IsWhiteSpace(source.Chars(counter))
    If (thisIsWhiteSpace = False) Then
        If (prevIsWhiteSpace = True) AndAlso _
            (result.Length > 0) Then result.Append(Space(1))
        result.Append(source.Chars(counter))
    End If
Next counter
MsgBox("<" & result.ToString() & ">")
```

Discussion

The previous code first builds a test string comprised of words separated by extra spaces, tabs, and other whitespace characters. After processing to replace runs of whitespace characters with single spaces, the resulting string is displayed for inspection, as shown in Figure 5-12.

Figure 5-12. The test string after zapping extra whitespace characters

Another straightforward approach to removing extra whitespace is to use a series of Replace() functions, first to replace tabs and other whitespace characters with spaces, and finally to replace multiple spaces with single ones. This will work fine, but the disadvantage is that many temporary strings are built in memory as the immutable strings are processed. The code presented here moves each character in memory only once, or not at all if the character is an extra whitespace.

Another good approach is to use regular expressions to grab an array of the words and then piece them back together with single spaces using a StringBuilder.

See Also

Recipe 5.42 shows how to use regular expressions to attack the multiwhitespace problem.

5.15   Using the Correct End-of-Line Characters

Problem

You are developing an application that will run on several platforms, so you want to use end-of-line characters that are compatible with all platforms.

Solution

Sample code folder: Chapter 05\EndOfLine

Use the property Environment.NewLine, which returns the end-of-line characters for the current platform. For example, the following code adds a self-describing line of text to a StringBuilder and ends the line with the newline characters for the current platform:

```
Dim result As New System.Text.StringBuilder
result.Append("Environment.NewLine").Append( _
    Environment.NewLine)
MsgBox(result.ToString( ))
```

Discussion

The following code, which simply extends the prevous short snippet, terminates lines in 10 different ways, all with the same result in the Windows environment:

```
Dim result As New System.Text.StringBuilder

result.Append("vbNewLine").Append(vbNewLine)
result.Append("vbCrLf").Append(vbCrLf)
result.Append("vbCr").Append(vbCr)
result.Append("vbLf").Append(vbLf)
result.Append("Chr(13)").Append(Chr(13))
result.Append("Chr(10)").Append(Chr(10))
result.Append("Chr(13) & Chr(10)").Append(Chr(13) & Chr(10))
result.Append("Environment.NewLine").Append( _
    Environment.NewLine)
result.Append("ControlChars.CrLf").Append(ControlChars.CrLf)
result.Append("ControlChars.NewLine").Append( _
    ControlChars.NewLine)

MsgBox(result.ToString())
```

Figure 5-13 shows each of these self-describing lines as displayed by the message box in the last line.

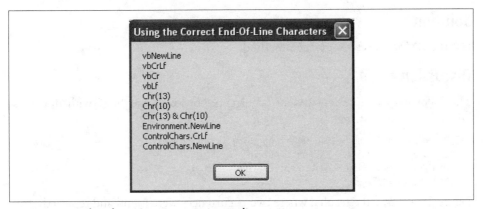

Figure 5-13. No less than 10 ways to terminate a line

Different platforms, such as Linux and Mac OS, expect different combinations of carriage-return and line-feed characters to terminate lines in documents or in displayed text. Visual Basic 2005 defines several constants you can use that explicitly combine these characters in a variety of ways. These named constants are easily identified by their "vb" prefix.

The somewhat generic vbNewLine constant provides a platform-dependent end of line, but only if an application is recompiled on each platform. Feel free to substitute any of the others if you find them more suitable.

The ControlChars.NewLine property is not a constant. Instead, this property polls the current operating system and returns the correct sequence of characters. This is your best choice when you want to compile a .NET application on one platform but run it on another.

 The StreamWriter object has a property named NewLine, which can be altered to change its default end-of-line definition. This lets you change the set of characters inserted into the stream at the end of each call to the StreamWriter's WriteLine( ) method. This can be handy, for example if you wish to automate double spacing of lines.

See Also

Recipe 5.19 makes use of line endings in its adjustment of a string.

5.16   Replacing Substrings

Problem

You need to find and replace all occurrences of a substring in a larger string.

Solution

Use the String object's Replace( ) method.

Discussion

The following example replaces all occurrences of lowercase "ing" with uppercase "ING" in a sample string:

```
Dim quote As String = "The important thing is not to " & _
    "stop questioning. --Albert Einstein"
Dim result As String = quote.Replace("ing", "ING")
MsgBox(result)
```

Figure 5-14 shows the results, where two occurrences were found and replaced.

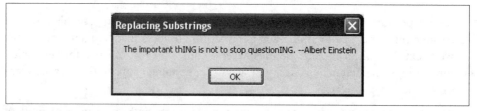

Figure 5-14. Replacing multiple substrings

In this example, the substrings are replaced with a new string of the same length, but the replacement string can be of differing length. In fact, a useful technique is to make a replacement with a zero-length string, effectively deleting all occurrences of a given substring. For example, the following code, applied to the original string, results in the shortened string displayed in Figure 5-15:

```
result = Quote.Replace("not to stop ", "")
```

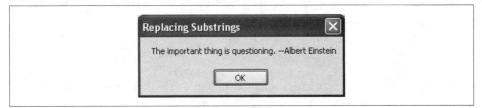

Figure 5-15. Zapping substrings by replacing them with an empty string

See Also

Recipe 5.21 shows how to remove characters from the start and end of a string.

5.17 Inserting a Character or String

Problem

You want to insert a character or string into another string at a given location.

Solution

Use the `String` object's `Insert( )` method.

Discussion

The string method `Insert( )` is overloaded to accept either a character or a string to be inserted at a given location. For example, the following `Insert( )` method adds a comma just after the word "thing" in the sample string:

```
Dim quote As String = "The important thing is not to " & _
    "stop questioning. --Albert Einstein"
Dim result As String = quote.Insert(19, ","c)
MsgBox(result)
```

Figure 5-16 shows the result of inserting the comma character.

Figure 5-16. Sample string with a character inserted

In this case the character is inserted after the 19th character of the string, or just after the "g" in "thing." You can insert a character in the first position of a string by using position 0, and at the end of a string by using the string's Length value.

The following code inserts the word "definitely " into the sample string. The inserted text includes a space at the end to keep the words spaced correctly in the result:

```
Dim quote As String = "The important thing is not to " & _
    "stop questioning. --Albert Einstein"
quote = quote.Insert(23, "definitely ")
MsgBox(quote)
```

The 23rd position in the original string is just after the "s" character in "is not." Figure 5-17 shows the result of this word insertion.

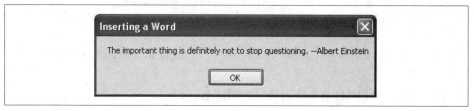

Figure 5-17. Sample string with the word "definitely" (followed by a space) inserted

---

VB 6 Users' Update

The equivalent VB 6 string manipulations to insert one string into another are not nearly as straightforward or as efficient as using Visual Basic 2005's Insert( ) method. The following VB 6 line uses two function calls and concatenates three pieces of strings to get the same result:

```
quote = Left(Quote, 23) & "definitely " & Mid(Quote, 24)
```

See Also

Recipe 5.18 also discusses text insertions.

5.18 Inserting a Line

Problem

You want to insert a complete line of text in a string that contains multiple lines separated by newlines. The desired insertion point is after the *n*th line.

Solution

Sample code folder: Chapter 05\InsertLine

Split the string into a string array using the newlines as the split point, append the line to be inserted to the *n*th string, and use Join( ) to glue the string back together again.

Discussion

Use the string function Split( ), which is not to be confused with the String.Split( ) method, to split the string into a string array. The Split( ) method splits the string at individual-character split points, but the Split( ) function lets you split the string using a multicharacter string for the defined split point. The vbNewLine constant is actually a two-character string, so you must use the Split( ) function to avoid splitting on the carriage-return character only, leaving the line-feed character at the front end of each array string.

Rather than redimensioning the string array to shuffle the lines and create a slot in which to insert the new one, it's easier to just concatenate the new string, accompanied by a newline constant, to the appropriate string in the array. This is a simpler and more efficient procedure that involves less shuffling of string data in memory, and the results after doing a Join( ) are identical.

This insert functionality works well as a standalone function, which is presented in the following lines of code:

```
Public Function InsertLine(ByVal source As String, _
      ByVal lineNum As Integer, _
      ByVal lineToInsert As String) As String
   ' ----- Insert a line in the middle of a set of lines.
   Dim lineSet( ) As String
   Dim atLine As Integer

   ' ----- Break the content into multiple lines.
   lineSet = Split(source, vbNewLine)

   ' ----- Determine the new location, being careful not
   '       to fall off the edge of the line set.
   atLine = lineNum
   If (atLine < 0) Then atLine = 0
   If (atLine >= lineSet.Length) Then
      ' ----- Append to the end of everything.
      lineSet(lineSet.Length - 1) &= vbNewLine & lineToInsert
   Else
      ' ----- Insert before the specified line.
      lineSet(atLine) = _
         lineToInsert & vbNewLine & lineSet(atLine)
   End If

   ' ----- Reconnect and return the parts.
   Return Join(lineSet, vbNewLine)
End Function
```

The string is first split at line boundaries into a string array. LineNum is the number of the line after which the lineToInsert string is inserted. You can pass zero to this parameter to insert the new line before the first one. After appending the new string to the appropriate string in the array, along with a vbNewLine to separate it from the original line, the array is glued back together with the Join() function, using a vbNewLine between each line to restore its original structure. This new string is then returned as the result of the InsertLine() function.

The following lines of code demonstrate the function's use:

```
Dim result As New System.Text.StringBuilder
result.AppendLine("This string")
result.AppendLine("contains")
result.AppendLine("several")
result.AppendLine("lines")
result.Append("of text.")

' ----- Show the original content.
Dim resultAsString As String = result.ToString()
MsgBox(resultAsString)

' ----- Show the modified content.
resultAsString = InsertLine(resultAsString, 3, "(inserted)")
MsgBox(resultAsString)
```

A StringBuilder is used to build the original string containing several lines of text separated by vbNewLines. The first message box (displayed in Figure 5-18) shows the string before the extra line is inserted. The second message box (displayed in Figure 5-19) shows the new string inserted after the third line.

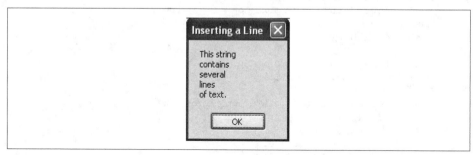

Figure 5-18. The original string containing five lines of text

 The Split() method will accept either a character or a string to define the split points in a string, but only the first character of the string is used. The Split() function, however, uses the entire string parameter, of any length, to split the string. Both the Split() method and the Split() function are very handy, but make sure you understand the difference in the way they work.

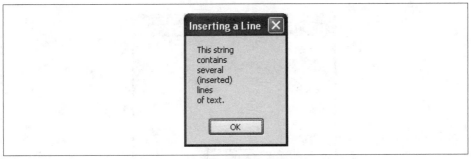

Figure 5-19. The same string after "(inserted)" is inserted after the third line

See Also

Recipe 5.17 also discusses text insertions. The difference between the Split( ) method and the Split( ) function is further discussed in Recipe 5.44.

5.19   Double-Spacing a String

Problem

You want to double-space a string comprised of multiple lines of text separated by newlines.

Solution

Use the String object's Replace( ) method to replace all vbNewLines with two vbNewLines.

Discussion

The Replace( ) method provides an easy solution to this problem. Simply replace each occurrence of a vbNewLine separating the lines of text with a double vbNewLine:

```
content = content.Replace(vbNewLine, vbNewLine & vbNewLine)
```

Figures 5-20 and 5-21 show a multiline example string before and after this replacement.

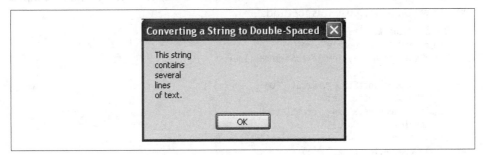

Figure 5-20. A string comprised of five lines of single-spaced text

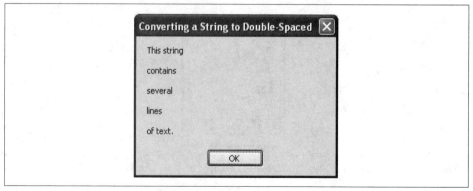

Figure 5-21. The same string, double spaced

See Also

Recipe 5.16 shows how to replace specific substrings within a larger string.

5.20 Formatting Numbers into Strings

Problem

You want to format a number into a string suitable for displaying or printing, something that provides formatting control beyond the defaults.

Solution

Sample code folder: Chapter 05\FormatNumbers

Apply the String object's Format( ) method, and use its custom formatting codes to get the output you desire.

Discussion

There are several ways and places in Visual Basic 2005 to apply formatting to numerical data. One of the best (and possibly the easiest to remember) is the Format( ) method, available as a shared method of the String object. A few simple examples will show you how to use this method:

```
Dim intValue As Integer = 1234567
Dim floatValue As Double = Math.PI
Dim result As New System.Text.StringBuilder

result.AppendLine(String.Format("{0}  ...  {1}", _
    intValue, floatValue))
result.AppendLine(String.Format("{0:N}  ...  {1:E}", _
    intValue, floatValue))
result.AppendLine(intValue.ToString("N5") & "  ...  " & _
    floatValue.ToString("G5"))

MsgBox(result.ToString( ))
```

This example formats an `Integer` and a `Double` in several different ways. Other numerical values, such as `Long`, `Short`, `Single`, `Decimal`, and so on, can be formatted in the same ways. Figure 5-22 shows the result of applying the above formatting.

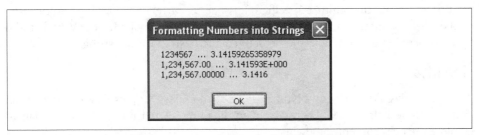

Figure 5-22. A sampling of the many ways numbers can be formatted into strings

The `Format( )` method's first argument is a formatting string that indicates how to use the remaining arguments. It can include zero or more zero-based position specifiers in curly braces. For instance, the text `{1}` says to insert the second data argument at that position. Consider this line of code:

```
result = String.Format( _
    "There are about {0} days in {1} years.", _
    365.25 * 3, 3, 17)
```

The first indexed specifier, `{0}`, inserts the first data argument, the calculated result of 365.25 * 3. The second indexed formatting specifier, `{1}`, inserts the integer value 3 at that spot in the resulting string. The argument list also includes a third data element, 17, but because `{2}` does not appear in the format string, that argument is ignored.

You can use as many indexed formatting specifiers as you want in a single string, but you should always provide a matching indexed argument in the method call following the string, and the first argument is always zero-based. You can use the same argument more than once, you can use them in any order, and you can even skip some arguments. The important thing to remember is to match carefully the index number in the brackets with the argument's position, starting with zero.

When the index appears in the braces by itself, a default format is used. However, there are many formatting options available to customize the formatting. In the previous sample code, the `{0:N}` formatted the number to contain commas between every third digit, and `{1:E}` formatted the number using scientific notation. The Visual Studio online help documentation for the `Format( )` method lists the many formatting options in detail.

You might have noticed that the last formatting line in the example is quite different from the previous ones. If you want to format a number into a string format without directly inserting it into a bigger string, you can use the many formatting options of the `ToString( )` method, a method available to every .NET object (although specially overloaded for the numeric data types). In our example, the first number was formatted using "N5", which inserts commas and formats the digits to five places after the decimal point. The second number was formatted using "G5", causing "general" formatting of the number to five significant digits.

There are other formatting options for creating hexadecimal strings, formatting dates and times, formatting culture-specific data such as currency values, and so on. Several of these formatting options are used throughout this book. See the Visual Studio online documentation for specific predefined and custom format strings.

See Also

See the "String.Format" and "NumberFormatInfo Class" topics listed in the Visual Studio online help index. There are many links to related information, so plan to explore the help content for a while.

5.21 Trimming Sets of Characters from a String

Problem

You need to delete extraneous characters from each end of a string.

Solution

Use the String object's Trim( ) method, passing to it a list of all characters to be deleted.

Discussion

The following example deletes four letters from the head and tail ends of a string. The letters chosen are just for demonstrating how the Trim( ) method works; a real-world example of where this might be handy would be to remove line numbers, colons, or other characters from the beginnings or ends of strings. As shown in Figure 5-23, the following code causes the entire first word ("The") and the last character ("n") to be removed, or trimmed, from the string:

```
Dim quote As String = "The important thing is not to " & _
    "stop questioning. --Albert Einstein"
Dim trimChars( ) As Char = {"T"c, "h"c, "e"c, "n"c}
Dim result As String = quote.Trim(trimChars)
MsgBox(result)
```

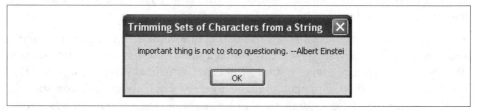

Figure 5-23. Trimming specific characters from the head and tail ends of a string

You do not need to supply the characters in any particular order; all supplied characters will be trimmed. Trimming continues until the first and last characters of the string are something other than those supplied to the Trim( ) method. If you supply no arguments to Trim( ), all whitespace characters are trimmed instead.

If you want to trim certain characters from either the start or end of the string, but not both, use the TrimStart( ) and TrimEnd( ) methods, respectively. They accept the same character-array argument as the Trim( ) method.

See Also

Recipes 5.14 and 5.16 discuss related techniques.

5.22   Identifying and Validating Types of Data in a String

Problem

You want to check a string variable to see whether it has been assigned a value, or if it can be converted to a number, date, or time. This check can prevent an exception, and it can free your code from having to use an exception as part of its testing logic.

Solution

Sample code folder: Chapter 05\StringTypes

Visual Basic 2005 has three string functions that help solve this problem: IsNothing( ), IsNumeric( ), and IsDate( ). Use these to test a string's contents before attempting conversions.

Discussion

The following code demonstrates the use of these three functions with data set to Nothing:

```
Dim theData As String = Nothing
Dim result As New System.Text.StringBuilder

' ----- Format nothing.
result.AppendLine(String.Format( _
   "IsNumeric({0}) ... {1}", theData, IsNumeric(theData)))
result.AppendLine(String.Format( _
   "IsDate({0}) ... {1}", theData, IsDate(theData)))
result.AppendLine(String.Format( _
   "IsNothing({0}) ... {1}", theData, IsNothing(theData)))
result.AppendLine( )
```

String variables are normally undefined, assigned the value of Nothing. We specifically assigned theData the value Nothing in the above code, but if we had left it blank

Visual Studio would have questioned our motives and marked the first use of theData with a warning, as shown in Figure 5-24. As you can see, the unassigned string variable has squiggly lines under it, indicating a problem; hovering the mouse pointer over it causes the displayed explanation to pop up. This is a nonfatal warning, and the program will still run.

```
theData, IsNumeric(theData)))
Variable 'theData' is used before it has been assigned a value. A null reference exception could result at runtime.
```

Figure 5-24. Visual Studio warns you if you attempt to use a string that has no data assigned to it

As shown in the first three lines of output displayed in Figure 5-25 (below), in this case the IsNumeric( ) and IsDate( ) functions verify that the string does not represent a valid number or date, but it does pass the IsNothing( ) test, as expected.

Next, the string is assigned a value that represents a valid number:

```
' ----- Format a number in a string.
theData = "-12.345"
result.AppendLine(String.Format( _
   "IsNumeric({0}) ... {1}", theData, IsNumeric(theData)))
result.AppendLine(String.Format( _
   "IsDate({0}) ... {1}", theData, IsDate(theData)))
result.AppendLine(String.Format( _
   "IsNothing({0}) ... {1}", theData, IsNothing(theData)))
result.AppendLine( )
```

When the three tests are repeated, they match expectations. As shown in the middle three lines of output in Figure 5-25, the IsNumeric( ) test now returns True, and the IsDate( ) and IsNothing( ) tests return False.

Finally, the string is assigned a valid date, and the three tests are repeated for the last time:

```
' ----- Format a date in a string.
theData = "July 17, 2007"
result.AppendLine(String.Format( _
   "IsNumeric({0}) ... {1}", theData, IsNumeric(theData)))
result.AppendLine(String.Format( _
   "IsDate({0}) ... {1}", theData, IsDate(theData)))
result.Append(String.Format( _
   "IsNothing({0}) ... {1}", theData, IsNothing(theData)))

MsgBox(result.ToString( ))
```

In this last case the IsDate( ) function returns True, and the other two tests return False, as shown in the last three lines of output in Figure 5-25.

See Also

Recipes 5.24 and 5.25 show how to examine content for correct processing.

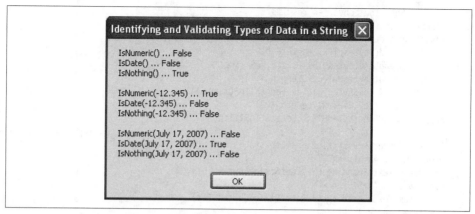

Figure 5-25. Results of testing a string's contents

5.23 Converting Strings Between Encoding Systems

Problem

You need to convert string data to and from byte arrays using an encoding method matched to your data, environment, or culture.

Solution

Sample code folder: Chapter 05\Encoding

Use System.Text.Encoding shared functions to convert between strings and byte arrays, using either UTF7, UTF8, Unicode, or UTF32 encoding, as appropriate.

Discussion

The following code starts with a sample string and then converts it to four byte arrays, one for each type of encoding. The length of each byte array will vary as a function of the encoding (to be explained in more detail later), so the Length property of each array is formatted into a StringBuilder for display at the end of the code. The four byte arrays are then converted back to Strings, using the same encoding in each case, and a quick check is made to verify that the resulting strings match the original:

```
Dim quote As String = "The important thing is not to " & _
    "stop questioning. --Albert Einstein"
Dim result As New System.Text.StringBuilder

' ----- Convert a string to various formats.
Dim bytesUTF7 As Byte() = _
    System.Text.Encoding.UTF7.GetBytes(quote)
Dim bytesUTF8 As Byte() = _
    System.Text.Encoding.UTF8.GetBytes(quote)
Dim bytesUnicode As Byte() = _
    System.Text.Encoding.Unicode.GetBytes(quote)
Dim bytesUTF32 As Byte() = _
    System.Text.Encoding.UTF32.GetBytes(quote)
```

```
' ----- Show the converted results.
result.Append("bytesUTF7.Length = ")
result.AppendLine(bytesUTF7.Length.ToString())
result.Append("bytesUTF8.Length = ")
result.AppendLine(bytesUTF8.Length.ToString())
result.Append("bytesUnicode.Length = ")
result.AppendLine(bytesUnicode.Length.ToString())
result.Append("bytesUTF32.Length = ")
result.AppendLine(bytesUTF32.Length.ToString())

' ----- Convert everything back to standard strings.
Dim fromUTF7 As String = _
    System.Text.Encoding.UTF7.GetString(bytesUTF7)
Dim fromUTF8 As String = _
    System.Text.Encoding.UTF8.GetString(bytesUTF8)
Dim fromUnicode As String = _
    System.Text.Encoding.Unicode.GetString(bytesUnicode)
Dim fromUTF32 As String = _
    System.Text.Encoding.UTF32.GetString(bytesUTF32)

' ----- Check for conversion issues.
If (fromUTF7 <> quote) Then _
    Throw New Exception("UTF7 Conversion Error")
If (fromUTF8 <> quote) Then _
    Throw New Exception("UTF8 Conversion Error")
If (fromUnicode <> quote) Then _
    Throw New Exception("Unicode Conversion Error")
If (fromUTF32 <> quote) Then _
    Throw New Exception("UTF32 Conversion Error")

MsgBox(result.ToString())
```

All strings in .NET are internally stored as two-byte Unicode characters. However, if each character of the string always falls within a known range of characters, the string can be converted to a one-byte-per-character byte array.

UTF7 encoding converts each character of the string to a single byte with the assumption that only the lower seven bits of each byte are used, leaving the highest-order bit as zero in all cases. This is true of ASCII characters with binary values in the range 0 to 127, which covers the normal range of English-language displayable and printable characters.

UTF8 is very similar to UTF7, but it also allows conversion of special characters in the byte value range 128 to 255. This is the extended ASCII character set that is sometimes used for special purposes. UTF8 uses all eight bits of each byte to define each character's value in the range 0 to 255.

Today's computer systems now invariably use the international standard Unicode character set, which requires two bytes per character. Standard ASCII characters still fall within the same 0 to 127 range in Unicode, so the second byte of each Unicode character in this range is set to zero. Other languages and cultures have character sets with Unicode integer values greater than 255, and Visual Basic strings handle them just fine.

UTF32 is not widely used, because it requires four bytes per character. However, even the two-byte Unicode characters occasionally require multiple sequential characters to define the specialized characters defined in some languages. UTF32 covers all possible characters in a simple four-bytes-per-character way, allowing internal processing simplifications. Generally, most worldwide string data is stored on external media in the two-byte Unicode format. Only occasionally is it converted to and processed as four-byte UTF32 bytes, and then only while in memory.

For most ASCII conversions, UTF8 is a good choice, requiring the same number of bytes as UTF7 but handling the full range of character values from 0 to 255. If squeezing bytes down to a minimum is not a mandate, Unicode is the safest bet.

See Also

Recipe 5.11 shows how to store standard string data as byte values.

5.24 Determining a Character's Type

Problem

You want to determine if a character is a letter, a digit, whitespace, or any of several other types before processing it further. This can avoid unexpected exceptions, or prevent having to use an exception on purpose to help determine the type of a character.

Solution

Sample code folder: Chapter 05\CharType

Use one of the many type-testing shared methods of the Char object.

Discussion

The Char object includes several methods that let you determine if a character is part of a larger general category of characters, such as the set of digits. The following code shows many of these in operation while it creates a handy listing of the types of all characters in the ASCII range 0 to 127:

```
Dim result As New System.Text.StringBuilder
Dim counter As Integer
Dim testChar As Char
Dim testHex As String
Dim soFar As Integer

' ----- Scan through the first half of the ASCII chart.
For counter = 0 To 127
    ' ----- What character will we test this time?
    testChar = Chr(counter)
    testHex = "\x" & Hex(counter)

    If Char.IsLetter(testChar) Then _
        result.AppendLine(testHex & "   IsLetter")
    If Char.IsControl(testChar) Then _
        result.AppendLine(testHex & "   IsControl")
```

```
    If Char.IsDigit(testChar) Then _
        result.AppendLine(testHex & "    IsDigit")
    If Char.IsLetterOrDigit(testChar) Then _
        result.AppendLine(testHex & "    IsLetterOrDigit")
    If Char.IsLower(testChar) Then _
        result.AppendLine(testHex & "    IsLower")
    If Char.IsNumber(testChar) Then _
        result.AppendLine(testHex & "    IsNumber")
    If Char.IsPunctuation(testChar) Then _
        result.AppendLine(testHex & "    IsPunctuation")
    If Char.IsSeparator(testChar) Then _
        result.AppendLine(testHex & "    IsSeparator")
    If Char.IsSymbol(testChar) Then _
        result.AppendLine(testHex & "    IsSymbol")
    If Char.IsUpper(testChar) Then _
        result.AppendLine(testHex & "    IsUpper")
    If Char.IsWhiteSpace(testChar) Then _
        result.AppendLine(testHex & "    IsWhiteSpace")

    ' ----- Display results in blocks of 16 characters.
    soFar += 1
    If ((soFar Mod 16) = 0) Then
        MsgBox(result.ToString())
        result.Length = 0
    End If
Next counter
```

The message box displays the results for 16 characters at a time. Figure 5-26 shows the output displayed for the first set of characters, and Figure 5-27 shows the results for characters with hexadecimal values in the range of some of the ASCII digits and letters.

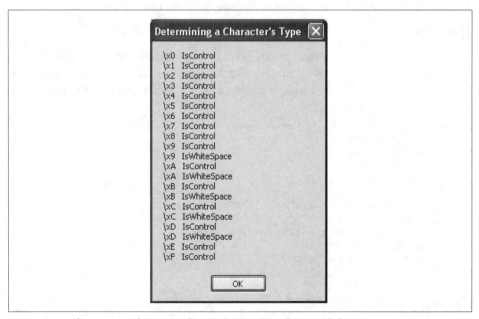

Figure 5-26. Characters with ASCII values 0 to 15 are mostly control characters

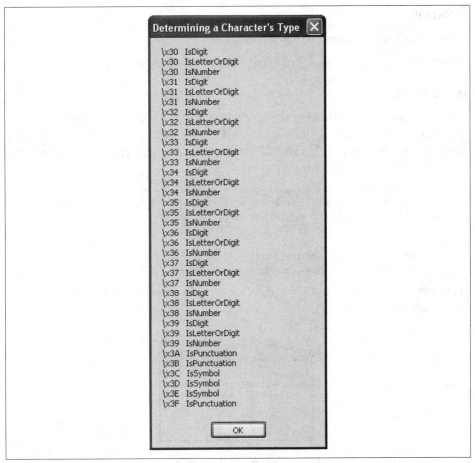

Figure 5-27. Characters in the range hexadecimal 30 to hexadecimal 3F are mostly digits, letters, and numbers

Note that many characters fall into several categories. For example, the "0" (zero) character with hexadecimal value 30 passes the test for IsDigit, IsLetterOrDigit, and IsNumber.

See Also

Recipe 5.22 includes examples of verifying logical data within strings, instead of the individual characters.

5.25 Parsing Strings

Problem

You want to convert string data to several types of numeric or date/time variables in a consistent way.

Solution

Sample code folder: Chapter 05\ParseString

Use the Parse( ) method provided by all types of variables in Visual Basic 2005.

Discussion

The Parse( ) method is the counterpart to each object's ToString( ) method. That is, the string created by calling an object's ToString( ) method will always be in a format suitable for converting back to the same type of object using its Parse( ) method. A few examples can help clarify this:

```
Dim doubleParse As Double = Double.Parse("3.1416")
Dim ushortParse As UShort = UShort.Parse("65533")
Dim dateParse As Date = Date.Parse("December 25, 2007")

MsgBox(String.Format( _
    "doubleParse: {0}{3}ushortParse: {1}{3}dateParse: {2}", _
    doubleParse, ushortParse, dateParse, vbNewLine))
```

As shown in Figure 5-28, the data items are stored in the variables as expected when they are parsed.

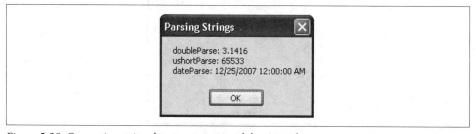

Figure 5-28. Converting string data to numeric and date/time formats

In many cases, you might want to first check the string to make sure it can be parsed to the desired type of variable before making any attempt to do so. For example, use the IsDate( ) function to test a string to make sure it can be converted successfully before calling a Date variable's Parse( ) method to parse the date from the string. If the string is not convertible to the indicated data type, an exception will occur.

See Also

Recipe 5.22 discusses additional content-verification methods.

5.26 Concatenating Strings

Problem

You want to concatenate strings quickly and efficiently.

Solution

Sample code folder: Chapter 05\Concatenate

Use the &= concatenation shortcut, or, even better, use a `StringBuilder`.

Discussion

Visual Basic 2005 offers a few tricks for working with strings more efficiently. The following code presents several helpful techniques, from least to most efficient.

This approach simply concatenates two words and assigns the resulting string to a string variable:

```
Dim quote As String
quote = "The " & "important "
```

This is how additional string data was always concatenated to the end of a string in VB 6 and earlier versions of the BASIC language:

```
quote = quote & "thing "
```

Because .NET strings are immutable, this code copies the current contents of quote to a new location in memory, then copies the short string "thing " to its tail end, and finally assigns the address of the resulting string to the quote variable, marking the previous contents of quote for garbage collection. By the time you've repeat this type of command a few times to concatenate more strings to the tail end of quote, a lot of bytes have gotten shuffled in memory.

This newer technique, available in Visual Basic 2005, provides an improved syntax, although timing tests seem to indicate that a lot of string data is still being shuffled in memory:

```
quote &= "is not to stop questioning. "
quote &= "--Albert Einstein"
```

The `StringBuilder` is by far the better way to proceed when concatenating many strings end to end, and you'll find a lot of examples of its use in this book. As shown here, you can run the `Append( )` method on the results of another `Append( )`, which may or may not make it easier to read the code:

```
Dim result As New _
    System.Text.StringBuilder("The important thing ")
result.Append("is questioning. ")
result.Append("--").Append("Albert ").Append("Einstein")
```

As explained in Recipe 5.1, the `StringBuilder` maintains an internal buffer of characters, not a true string, and the buffer grows by doubling in size whenever room runs out during an `Append( )` operation. String data is concatenated in place in memory, which keeps the total clock cycles for concatenation way down compared to standard string techniques.

Just to round things out, these last few lines show some of the additional commands available when working with a `StringBuilder`:

```
result.Insert(23, "note to stop ")
result.Replace("note", "not")
result.Insert(0, quote & vbNewLine)

MsgBox(result.ToString())
```

These lines complete the building of the string data displayed by the message box shown in Figure 5-29. The two strings demonstrate that identical results are obtained even after we've manipulated the `StringBuilder`'s contents.

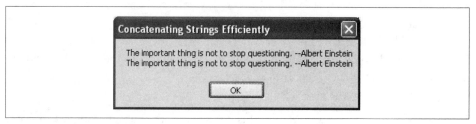

Figure 5-29. The string built up using a StringBuilder

See Also

Recipe 5.1 and Recipe 5.27 discuss the `StringBuilder` class in more detail.

5.27   Speeding Up String Manipulation

Problem

You want to see a timing-test-based example that shows just how much faster a `StringBuilder` can be than standard string concatenation.

Solution

Sample code folder: Chapter 05\StringTime

Create a short routine to concatenate the string values of the numbers 1 to 10,000, first using direct concatenation to a string variable and then using a `StringBuilder`. Use `Date` variables to calculate elapsed time for each loop in milliseconds, and display the results of each for comparison.

Discussion

Here's the code for doing the timing test. The two contestants are ready for the race. content is a conventional immutable string, and result is the highly acclaimed StringBuilder challenger:

```
Dim content As String = ""
Dim result As New System.Text.StringBuilder
```

The supporting cast of characters is ready to rally to the cause. Here, `counter` is a loop counter, `dateTime1` through `dateTime3` are `Date` variables to hold instants in time, and `loopCount` provides the number of laps for the race:

```
Dim counter As Integer
Dim dateTime1 As Date
Dim dateTime2 As Date
Dim dateTime3 As Date
Dim loopCount As Integer = 15000
```

The flag is waved to start the race, and the starting time is noted very accurately:

```
Me.Cursor = Cursors.WaitCursor
dateTime1 = Now
```

The first contestant runs all the loops, concatenating the string representations of the numbers for each lap into one big string named content. The time of completion is carefully noted:

```
For counter = 1 To loopCount
    content &= counter.ToString( )
Next counter
dateTime2 = Now
```

The `StringBuilder` now runs the same laps, appending the same strings in its internal buffer. The time at completion is accurately noted:

```
For counter = 1 To loopCount
    result.Append(counter.ToString( ))
Next counter
dateTime3 = Now
```

The flag drops, signaling the crossing of the finish line for both contestants:

```
Me.Cursor = Cursors.Default
```

In a moment, the results of the race appear:

```
content = String.Format( _
    "First loop took {0:G4} ms, the second took {1:G4} ms.", _
    dateTime2.Subtract(dateTime1).TotalMilliseconds, _
    dateTime3.Subtract(dateTime2).TotalMilliseconds)
MsgBox(content)
```

The results are shown in the message box displayed in Figure 5-30. Due to differences between systems, your results may vary.

Figure 5-30. The StringBuilder is the clear winner of this race

To be fair, this race was highly contrived to help point out the difference in operational speed between string concatenation and StringBuilder appending. If you create a loop in which the same strings are used each time, the timing is much more equal. This is because Visual Basic handles immutable strings very intelligently, reusing existing strings whenever possible and hence speeding up repetitive operations involving the same data. The test shown here creates a unique string for each concatenation by converting the loop index number to a string, forcing a lot of extra string creation and storage in memory during the loops.

When running this test yourself, you might need to adjust the value of loopCount for your system. If the race seems to take too long, stop the program manually and adjust loopCount to a value a few thousand lower; if the race is too fast, resulting in an apparent elapsed time of 0 ms for the StringBuilder, bump up loopCount by a few thousand, and try again.

See Also

Recipe 5.1 and Recipe 5.26 provide additional discussion of strings and StringBuilder instances.

5.28   Counting Occurrences of a Substring

Problem

You need to count occurrences of a specific word or substring in a string.

Solution

Sample code folder: Chapter 05\CountSubstring

There are three standard approaches to this problem:

- Use the regular expression object (System.Text.RegularExpressions.Regex) to provide a count of the number of matches on the string.
- Use the Split( ) function to split the string using the specific substring as a split point, then use the length of the resulting string array to determine the count.
- Loop through the string using the IndexOf( ) method to find all occurrences of the substring.

Discussion

This recipe's sample code presents all three techniques. You can decide, based on your specific programming task, which will work best for you. Here's the setup:

```
Imports System.Text.RegularExpressions

' ...Later, in a method...
```

```
Dim quote As String = "The important thing is not to " & _
    "stop questioning. --Albert Einstein"
Dim count1 As Integer
Dim count2 As Integer
Dim count3 As Integer
```

With the first technique, the Regex.Matches( ) method returns a collection of matches on the searched-for string, and the collection's Count property provides the number we want:

```
count1 = Regex.Matches(quote, "(in)+").Count
```

The second technique splits the string using the searched-for string as the split point. The result of the split is a string array, and its Length is one greater than the number of split points where each substring occurred:

```
count2 = Split(quote, "in").Length - 1
```

The third technique involves a little more coding, but no string data is shuffled in memory during the search, resulting in an efficient way to locate and count each occurrence of the searched-for string. The IndexOf( ) method searches for the next occurrence of a string within another, optionally starting the search at an indexed location within the string:

```
Dim content As String = "in"
Dim position As Integer = -content.Length
Do
    position = quote.IndexOf(content, position + content.Length)
    If (position < 0) Then Exit Do
    count3 += 1
Loop
```

This lets the search proceed from occurrence to occurrence until IndexOf( ) runs out of matches and returns an index of –1. count3 keeps count of the number of times the IndexOf( ) search is successful, providing a count of the occurrences.

The last line of the example code formats and displays the three counts, as shown in Figure 5-31:

```
MsgBox(String.Format( _
    "{0}{3}{1}{3}{2}", count1, count2, count3, vbNewLine))
```

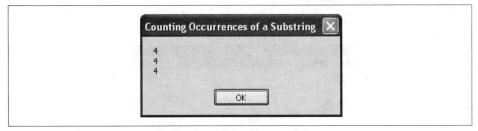

Figure 5-31. The substring "in" occurs four times in the sample string

5.29   Padding a String for Exact Length and Alignment

Problem

You want to pad a string with spaces (or some other character) either on the head end, the tail end, or both ends, such that the resulting string is *n* characters in total length.

Solution

Sample code folder: Chapter 05\PadString

Use the `String.PadLeft()` and `String.PadRight()` methods to pad the head and tail ends of the string, respectively, and use a calculated combination of these two methods to pad the string on both ends.

Discussion

The `PadLeft()` and `PadRight()` methods take a count value that defines the target length of the string after sufficient spaces are concatenated to it. An optional second parameter provides a character to use for the padding if you want something other than spaces to be used. In the first block of code the default space characters are used for the padding:

```
Dim content1 As String
Dim content2 As String
Dim content3 As String
Dim content4 As String
content1 = "Not padded"
content2 = "PadLeft".PadLeft(50)
content3 = "PadRight".PadRight(50)
content4 = "PadCenter"
content4 = content4.PadLeft((50 + _
    content4.Length) \ 2).PadRight(50)
MsgBox(String.Format("{0}{4}{1}{4}{2}{4}{3}", _
    content1, content2, content3, content4, vbNewLine))
```

The `PadCenter()` calculation adds half of the required padding characters to the head end of the string, then pads out the right end to the target length. The `PadLeft()` method is applied to the string first, and the `PadRight()` method is applied to the result, all in a single line. Figure 5-32 shows the strings with the padding causing the text to align to the left, right, and middle, depending on where the padding was applied.

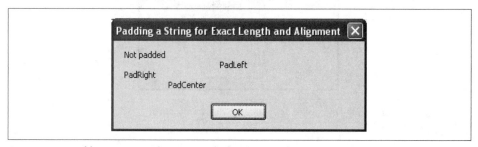

Figure 5-32. Padding strings with spaces at the head, the tail, or both ends

Padding with spaces is often what you want to do in a real-world application, but for display purposes it isn't very helpful. In Figure 5-32, for instance, you can't tell that "PadRight" has 50 spaces at its end. Therefore, let's recode this example, padding the strings with periods instead:

```
content1 = "Not padded"
content2 = "PadLeft".PadLeft(50, "."c)
content3 = "PadRight".PadRight(50, "."c)
content4 = "PadCenter"
content4 = content4.PadLeft((50 + content4.Length) \ 2, _
    "."c).PadRight(50, "."c)
MsgBox(String.Format("{0}{4}{1}{4}{2}{4}{3}", _
    content1, content2, content3, content4, vbNewLine))
```

In this case, the same padding takes place, but with a period for the padding character. Figure 5-33 shows the result, which is more meaningful than Figure 5-32.

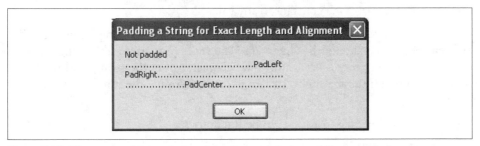

Figure 5-33. The same padding as before, but using periods for padding instead of spaces

5.30   Converting Tabs to Spaces

Problem

You need to convert a string's tab characters to spaces while preserving the string's spacing.

Solution

Sample code folder: Chapter 05\TabsToSpaces

Create a function to convert tabs to spaces in the defined way:

```
Public Function TabsToSpaces(ByVal source As String, _
    ByVal tabSize As Integer) As String
  ' ----- Replace tabs with space characters.
  Dim result As New System.Text.StringBuilder
  Dim counter As Integer

  For counter = 0 To source.Length - 1
    If (source.Chars(counter) = vbTab) Then
      Do
```

```
            result.Append(Space(1))
        Loop Until ((result.Length Mod tabSize) = 0)
      Else
         result.Append(source.Chars(counter))
      End If
   Next counter
   Return result.ToString()
End Function
```

Discussion

The trick to replacing the tabs is to insert just the right number of spaces to preserve the original alignment of the text. Tab characters generally shift the next character to a position that is an exact multiple of the tab spacing. In Visual Studio, this spacing constant is often 4, but in many text editors, and even in the Windows Forms TextBox control, the standard tab spacing is 8. The sample function accepts an argument to set the tab-spacing constant to any value.

The function uses a StringBuilder to rebuild the original string, replacing tabs with enough spaces to maintain the alignment. The Chars property of the string makes it easy to access and process each individual character from the string, and the Mod() function simplifies the math checks required to determine the number of spaces to insert.

This code shows the TabsToSpaces() function in use:

```
Dim tabs As String = _
    "This~is~~a~tabbed~~~string".Replace("~"c, vbTab)
Dim spaces As String = TabsToSpaces(tabs, 8)
Dim periods As String = spaces.Replace(" "c, "."c)
```

The first line builds a string comprised of words separated by multiple tab characters. The tilde (~) characters provide a visual way to see where the tabs will go, and the Replace() method replaces each tilde with a tab.

The second statement calls the new function and places the returned string in spaces. This string contains no tab characters, but it does contain many spaces between the words.

The periods string provides a visual way to see the spaces more clearly. The Replace() method in this case replaces each space with a period.

Figure 5-34 shows these three strings displayed on a form containing three TextBox controls. Setting the Font property to Courier New, a fixed-width font, more clearly shows the alignment of the characters in the strings. The tab-spacing constant in these text boxes is 8, which is the value passed to TabsToSpaces(), correctly replacing the tabs and maintaining the original alignment.

See Also

Recipe 5.16 also discusses replacing substrings.

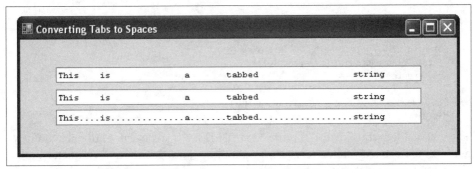

Figure 5-34. The same string with tabs, spaces instead of tabs, and periods instead of spaces

5.31   Reversing a String

Problem

You want to reverse, or mirror image, the order of the characters in a string.

Solution

Use the StrReverse( ) function.

Discussion

The StrReverse( ) function makes reversing a string simple:

```
Dim quote As String = "The important thing is not to " & _
    "stop questioning. --Albert Einstein"
Dim reversed As String = StrReverse(quote)
MsgBox(reversed)
```

Figure 5-35 shows the reversed string as displayed in the message box.

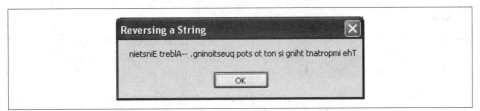

Figure 5-35. The sample string reversed

Another way to reverse a string is to process the characters yourself. This sample code scans through the string in reverse order and appends each found character to a new StringBuilder instance:

```
Dim quote As String = "The important thing is not to " & _
    "stop questioning. --Albert Einstein"
```

```
Dim counter As Integer
Dim result As New System.Text.StringBuilder(quote.Length)

For counter = quote.Length - 1 To 0 Step -1
    result.Append(quote.Chars(counter))
Next counter

Dim reversed As String = result.ToString( )
MsgBox(reversed)
```

The overloaded constructor for the StringBuilder accepts an optional parameter defining the capacity the StringBuilder should use for its internal character buffer. Since we know the reversed string will be the same length as the original, the capacity can be set to exactly the amount needed. This prevents the StringBuilder from having to double its capacity when it runs low on space while appending characters (see Recipe 5.1). Using the Chars property of the string to grab characters and setting the initial capacity of the StringBuilder in this way ensures that the character bytes are transferred in memory just once in a tight, efficient loop.

5.32   Shuffling a String

Problem

You want to shuffle the order of the characters in a string quickly but thoroughly.

Solution

Sample code folder: Chapter 05\StringShuffle

The best technique is to loop through each character location once, swapping the character at that location with a character at a random location anywhere in the string.

Discussion

The basic algorithm for shuffling a string, as presented here, is also good for shuffling arrays or any other ordered data. This algorithm takes a finite amount of time to run, and the results are as random as the random number generator used.

A walk through the code explains the process clearly. These lines declare the variables required and initialize the random number generator to a unique sequence, using the system clock for the random number generator's seed:

```
Dim counter As Integer
Dim position As Integer
Dim holdChar As Char
Dim jumbleMethod As New Random
Dim quote As String = "The important thing is not to " & _
    "stop questioning. --Albert Einstein"
```

To manipulate the individual characters of the string, it's best to convert the string to a character array:

```
Dim chars() As Char = CType(quote, Char())
```

This allows for swapping the characters in memory without having to make multiple copies of immutable strings. You can directly access a string's individual characters using the string's Chars property, but this property is read-only. In this case, we need to store new characters into the string's locations during each swap.

The following loop is the core of the shuffling algorithm:

```
For counter = 0 To chars.Length - 1
    position = jumbleMethod.Next Mod chars.Length
    holdChar = chars(counter)
    chars(counter) = chars(position)
    chars(position) = holdChar
Next counter
```

Each character is sequentially processed by swapping it with another character located randomly at any position in the string. This means that a character might even get swapped with itself occasionally, but that does not reduce the randomness of the results. This loop guarantees that each character gets swapped at least once, but statistically speaking each character gets swapped twice, on average.

The last two lines convert the character array back to a string and then display the result in a message box, as shown in Figure 5-36:

```
Dim result As String = New String(chars)
MsgBox(result)
```

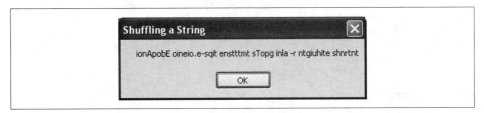

Figure 5-36. The shuffled string

The sample string will be shuffled into a unique random order every time the sample code is run.

See Also

Recipes 6.27 and 8.5 show additional uses of random numbers.

5.33 Using a Simple String Encryption

Problem

You want to encrypt a string using a key. The encrypted result should be a displayable and printable string of standard ASCII characters.

Solution

Sample code folder: Chapter 05\EncryptString

The following short class defines a `SimpleCrypt` object containing shared functions for encrypting and decrypting a string. In addition to the string to be encrypted or decrypted, an integer is passed to each function to serve as the key:

```
Public Class SimpleCrypt
    Public Shared Function Encrypt(ByVal source As String, _
        ByVal theKey As Integer) As String
        ' ----- Encrypt a string.
        Dim counter As Integer
        Dim jumbleMethod As New Random(theKey)
        Dim keySet(source.Length - 1) As Byte
        Dim sourceBytes() As Byte = _
            System.Text.Encoding.UTF8.GetBytes(source)

        jumbleMethod.NextBytes(keySet)
        For counter = 0 To sourceBytes.Length - 1
            sourceBytes(counter) = _
                sourceBytes(counter) Xor keySet(counter)
        Next counter

        Return Convert.ToBase64String(sourceBytes)
    End Function

    Public Shared Function Decrypt(ByVal source As String, _
        ByVal theKey As Integer) As String
        ' ----- Decrypt a previously encrypted string.
        Dim counter As Integer
        Dim jumbleMethod As New Random(theKey)
        Dim sourceBytes() As Byte = _
            Convert.FromBase64String(source)
        Dim keySet(sourceBytes.Length - 1) As Byte

        jumbleMethod.NextBytes(keySet)
        For counter = 0 To sourceBytes.Length - 1
            sourceBytes(counter) = _
                sourceBytes(counter) Xor keySet(counter)
        Next counter

        Return System.Text.Encoding.UTF8.GetString(sourceBytes)
    End Function
End Class
```

Discussion

The following code calls the shared functions of the `SimpleCrypt` class to encrypt a sample string using a key integer value of 123456789, and then decrypts the results using the same key:

```
Dim quote As String = "The important thing is not to " & _
    "stop questioning. --Albert Einstein"
```

```
Dim myKey As Integer = 123456789
Dim encrypted As String = SimpleCrypt.Encrypt(quote, myKey)
Dim decrypted As String = _
    SimpleCrypt.Decrypt(encrypted, myKey)
MsgBox(quote & vbNewLine & encrypted & vbNewLine & decrypted)
```

The encryption function first converts the string to a byte array using UTF8 encoding. Each byte is then Xor'd with a predictable sequence of pseudorandom bytes seeded using the given key integer, and the resulting byte array is converted back to a string. Since this encrypted string likely contains ASCII characters in the range of control and nonprintable characters, the string is then converted to a slightly longer Base64 string comprised of displayable characters.

The decryption function reverses the order of these same steps. First, the Base64 string is converted to a byte array, and the same set of pseudorandom bytes is Xor'd with these bytes to recover the bytes of the original string. Figure 5-37 shows the original string, the encrypted version of this string using a key value of 123456789, and the string that results by decrypting this Base64 string using the same key. As expected, the original string is restored.

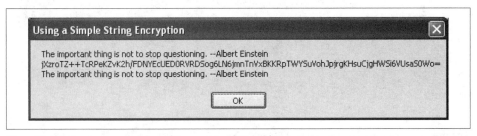

Figure 5-37. Encrypting and decrypting a string using a key integer

The Random object can return an array of pseudorandom bytes with any desired length. This lets the code generate the required number of bytes used in the Xor process with only one call to the Random object.

The supplied key is any integer value from 0 to the maximum value for signed integers, which is 2,147,483,647. You can use a negative integer, but the Random class will automatically take its absolute value as the seed.

With over two billion unique seeds, the average user won't be able to break this simple encryption easily. For quick, simple, relatively secure encryption for typical users, this class can serve you well. However, in cryptographic circles this level of encryption is considered dangerously poor, so be sure to check out Chapter 16 if you need to use something more serious and well tested by the cryptographic community.

See Also

See Chapter 16 for more encryption topics.

5.34   Converting a String to Morse Code

Problem

You want to convert a text string to Morse code characters.

Solution

Sample code folder: Chapter 05\MorseCode

Use the IndexOf( ) string method to look up and cross-reference characters to string array entries representing each Morse code character.

Discussion

The following code converts the string "Hello world!" to a string that displays the Morse code "dahs" and "dits" for each character:

```
Dim source As String = "Hello world!"
Dim characters As String = _
    "~ABCDEFGHIJKLMNOPQRSTUVWXYZ0123456789.,:?'-/"""
Dim morse() As String = { _
"?", ".-", "-...", "-.-.", "-..", ".", "..-.", "--.", "....", _
"..", ".---", "-.-", ".-..", "--", "-.", "---", ".--.", _
"--.-", ".-.", "...", "-", "..-", "...-", ".--", "-..-", _
"-.--", "--..", "-----", ".----", "..---", "...--", _
"....-", ".....", "-....", "--...", "---..", "----.", _
".-.-.-", "--..--", "---...", "..--..", ".----.", _
"-....-", "-..-.", ".-..-."}

Dim result As New System.Text.StringBuilder
Dim counter As Integer
Dim position As Integer

For counter = 0 To source.Length - 1
   position = characters.IndexOf(Char.ToUpper( _
      source.Chars(counter)))
   If (position < 0) Then position = 0
   result.Append(source.Substring(counter, 1))
   result.Append(Space(5))
   result.AppendLine(morse(position))
Next counter

MsgBox(result.ToString( ))
```

For most people this code is not all that useful, but there are some interesting details to be learned from this example. For instance, the second line assigns the standard set of characters covered by Morse code to a string named characters. Notice that at the tail end of this string there are three quote characters in a row. The last one terminates the string, as expected, and the pair just before the last one demonstrates how to enter a single-quote character into a string. By doubling up the quote character, you tell the Visual Basic compiler to enter one double-quote character and not to terminate the string.

At the head of the characters string is a tilde (~) character. This is not a Morse code character, but it provides a way to catch all characters in the string to be converted that aren't found in the set of Morse code characters. For example, in the test string "Hello world!" there's an exclamation point, which is not defined in the table of International Morse code characters. When the IndexOf( ) method attempts to find this exclamation point in characters, a value of −1 is returned. This value is changed to zero, which indexes to the question-mark sequence in the Morse( ) string array. Figure 5-38 shows how the sample string ends up with a question mark instead of the unavailable exclamation point.

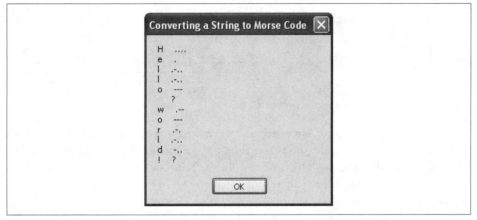

Figure 5-38. The Morse code equivalent of the standard "Hello World!" string

5.35   Adding Strings to an Application's Resources

Problem

You need to store and edit strings in an application's resources. This makes it easy to internationalize the application by changing the strings for each culture.

Solution

To edit the resource strings in the Visual Studio environment, open the project's properties page, and select the Resources tab on the left. Edit the table of string entries, changing the Name, Value, and Comment fields as required.

In the application, refer to each string through the My.Resources object.

Discussion

In Visual Studio, it's very easy to maintain a table of strings in the application's resources. Figure 5-39 shows the project's properties page with the Resources tab selected along the left side.

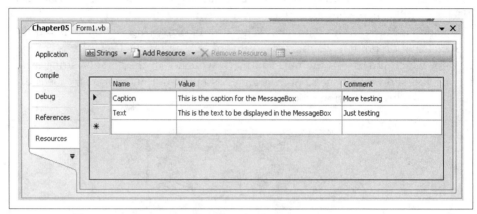

Figure 5-39. Editing resource strings in Visual Studio

The example shows two resource strings, one named Caption and the other named Text. As the following code shows, in the application these two strings are referenced by name through the My.Resources object. This code then displays a message box using the two strings from the resources, as shown in Figure 5-40:

```
Dim stringText As String = My.Resources.Text
Dim stringCaption As String = My.Resources.Caption
MsgBox(stringText, , stringCaption)
```

Figure 5-40. The results of editing the message box's Caption and Text properties

Other types of resources can be added, such as images, sounds, and other files. Each of these resources is accessed in the application through the My.Resources object.

See Also

See Chapter 10 for an example of storing and using media files in your application's resources.

5.36   Converting Any Data to a String

Problem

You have an instance of data and want to convert it to its default string representation.

Solution

Sample code folder: Chapter 05\UseToString

Use the ToString( ) method, which is included in all .NET objects, to return a general string for an object instance. To get you started, the following code demonstrates the default ToString( ) method on several types of variables:

```
Dim someInt As Integer = 123
Dim someDouble As Double = Math.PI
Dim someString As String = "Testing"
Dim someDate As Date = #7/4/1776 9:10:11 AM#
Dim someDecimal As Decimal = 1D / 3D
Dim result As New System.Text.StringBuilder

result.Append("someInt.ToString      ")
result.AppendLine(someInt.ToString( ))

result.Append("someDouble.ToString   ")
result.AppendLine(someDouble.ToString( ))

result.Append("someString.ToString   ")
result.AppendLine(someString.ToString( ))

result.Append("someDate.ToString     ")
result.AppendLine(someDate.ToString( ))

result.Append("someDecimal.ToString ")
result.Append(someDecimal.ToString( ))

MsgBox(result.ToString( ))
```

Discussion

Figure 5-41 shows the results displayed by the sample code. Default formatting is used for all these ToString( ) methods.

The ToString( ) method is often overloaded to support a variety of formatting options, depending on the type of variable. This lets you convert doubles, for instance, to scientific or other formats. Check the Visual Studio online help resources for the ToString( ) method for each type of variable to discover the formatting options available.

All objects sport a ToString( ) method because all objects inherit it from System.Object. An example used repeatedly throughout this chapter is the StringBuilder class, which returns its internal character buffer converted to a string through its ToString( ) method.

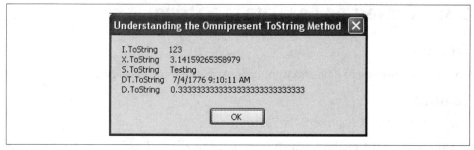

Figure 5-41. Results of converting several variable types by using the ToString() method on each

As you create your own classes, consider adding both a ToString() method and a corresponding Parse() method if the object's state can be represented as a string.

5.37   Using Regular Expressions to Extract All Numbers

Problem

You want to extract all numbers from a string that has extra whitespace, text, and other nonnumeric characters interspersed throughout.

Solution

Sample code folder: Chapter 05\RegexExtractNum

Use a regular expression (Regex) object to identify and parse out a list of all numbers in the string.

Discussion

This is a very tricky problem if the exact format of the string is not known. Identifying exactly which sets of characters are parts of numbers with accuracy in all cases can be difficult. Negative signs, scientific notation, and other complications can arise. Fortunately, the regular expression object greatly simplifies the task. The following code demonstrates how it works:

```
Imports System.Text.RegularExpressions

' ...Later, in a method...

Dim source As String = _
    "This 321.0 string -0.020 contains " & _
    "3.0E-17 several 1 2. 34 numbers"
Dim result As String
Dim parser As New _
    Regex("[-+]?([0-9]*\.)?[0-9]+([eE][-+]?[0-9]+)?")
```

```
Dim sourceMatches As MatchCollection = _
    parser.Matches(source)
Dim counter As Integer

result = "Count: " & _
    sourceMatches.Count.ToString() & vbNewLine
For counter = 0 To sourceMatches.Count - 1
    result &= vbNewLine
    result &= sourceMatches(counter).Value.ToString()
    result &= Space(5)
    result &= CDbl(sourceMatches(counter).Value).ToString()
Next counter
MsgBox(result)
```

The string to be parsed is source, which contains a variety of integer and floating-point numbers, both positive and negative, with words and other nonnumeric characters mixed in. A Regex object named parser is instantiated using a specially crafted regular expression designed to locate all conventionally defined numbers. The Matches() method of the Regex object is applied to the string, and a collection of Matches is returned. This collection's Count property provides a tally of how many numbers were found in the string. Each item in the Matches collection has a Value property with a ToString() method that converts the numeric value to a string.

Figure 5-42 shows the results of parsing the sample string, listing the numbers found using the regular expression. The Matches value displays the string exactly as copied from the original string. That's the first number on lines 2–7 in the message box. The second number shows the string converted to a Double and then back to a string. The reason for this extra step is to verify that the match string does convert to a numeric value.

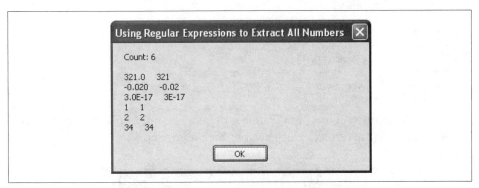

Figure 5-42. Parsing the sample string reveals all the numbers it contains

 The regular expression presented in this example is one of many that can be found on multiple Internet web sites. The Internet provides a great resource for locating regular expressions for any specific purposes.

See Also

Recipe 5.38 also discusses regular expression processing. The following web sites are just some of the many places on the Internet that provide regular expression samples:

http://www.regular-expressions.info/examples.html
http://sitescooper.org/tao_regexps.html
http://en.wikipedia.org/wiki/Regular_expression

5.38   Getting a Count of Regular Expression Matches

Problem

You want a quick count of the number of matches a regular expression finds in a string.

Solution

Sample code folder: Chapter 05\RegexCountMatch

Use the `Count` property of the `Matches()` method of the `Regex` object.

Discussion

The following example code shows how to use regular expressions to count words in a string, as defined by the pattern `\w+`:

```
Imports System.Text.RegularExpressions

' ...Later, in a method...

Dim quote As String = "The important thing is not to " & _
    "stop questioning. --Albert Einstein"
Dim parser As New Regex("\w+")
Dim totalMatches As Integer = parser.Matches(quote).Count
MsgBox(quote & vbNewLine & "Number words: " & _
    totalMatches.ToString)
```

This example returns a count of the number of matches, not a collection of matches. Figure 5-43 shows the results as displayed by the message box.

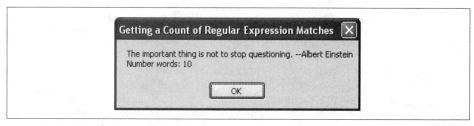

Figure 5-43. Using the Regex object to count words in a string

This technique can be useful for many other types of regular expression searches, too. For example, the regular expression shown in Recipe 5.37 can be used to quickly determine the number of numbers of all types in a string of any size.

See Also

Recipes 5.13 and 5.37 discuss regular expression processing in additional detail.

5.39   Getting the Nth Regular Expression Match

Problem

You want to get the *n*th match of a regular expression search within a string.

Solution

Sample code folder: Chapter 05\RegexMatchN

Use the Regex object to return a MatchCollection based on the regular expression. The *n*th match is accessed by indexing item *n*–1 in the collection.

Discussion

The following code finds all numbers in a sample string, returning all matches as a MatchCollection. In this example, the regular expression accesses the third match in the zero-based collection as item number 2:

```
Imports System.Text.RegularExpressions

' ...Later, in a method...

Dim source As String = "This 7. string -0.02 " & _
    "contains 003.141600 several 0.9 numbers"
Dim parser As New Regex( _
    "[-+]?([0-9]*\.)?[0-9]+([eE][-+]?[0-9]+)?")
Dim sourceMatches As MatchCollection = _
    parser.Matches(source)
Dim result As Double = CDbl(sourceMatches(2).Value)
MsgBox(source & vbNewLine & "The 3rd number: " & _
    result.ToString())
```

Figure 5-44 shows the third number found in the string.

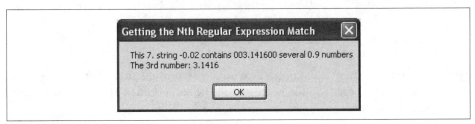

Figure 5-44. Using a regular expression to find the nth match in a string

See Also

Recipe 5.37 discusses the specific regular expression pattern used in this recipe.

5.40   Compiling Regular Expressions for Speed

Problem

You want to compile a regular expression to maximize runtime speed.

Solution

Sample code folder: Chapter 05\RegexDLL

There are two steps to this solution, best described by working through an example. The first step is to run the code to create the compiled DLL file, and the second is to use the new compiled regular expression in one or more applications.

Discussion

First, run the following code one time only to compile and create a DLL file containing a regular expression, in this case using a pattern designed to find all numbers in a string:

```
Imports System.Text.RegularExpressions

' ...Later, in a method...

Dim numPattern As String = _
   "[-+]?([0-9]*\.)?[0-9]+([eE][-+]?[0-9]+)?"
Dim wordPattern As String = "\w+"
Dim whichNamespace As String = "NumbersRegex"
Dim isPublic As Boolean = True

Dim compNumbers As New RegexCompilationInfo(numPattern, _
   RegexOptions.Compiled, "RgxNumbers", _
   whichNamespace, isPublic)
Dim compWords As New RegexCompilationInfo(wordPattern, _
   RegexOptions.Compiled, "RgxWords", whichNamespace, _
   isPublic)
Dim compAll() As RegexCompilationInfo = _
   {compNumbers, compWords}

Dim whichAssembly As New _
   System.Reflection.AssemblyName("RgxNumbersWords")
Regex.CompileToAssembly(compAll, whichAssembly)
```

This code creates a new file named *RgxNumbersWords.dll* that contains the compiled regular expression. The file is created in the same folder in which the executable program is located.

To use the new DLL in an application, you need to add a reference to it. Right-click on References in the Solution Explorer, click the Browse tab, find the DLL file in the folder where the application's EXE file is located, and select it to add the reference. Figure 5-45 shows the new reference in the Solution Explorer.

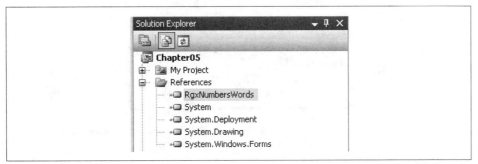

Figure 5-45. The DLL file named RgxNumbersWords added to the References list in the Solution Explorer

You also need to import the namespace defined in this DLL into your application. Either add an `Imports` command at the top of your source code or, in the Project Properties window, select the References tab, and place a checkmark next to the name of the namespace, as shown in Figure 5-46.

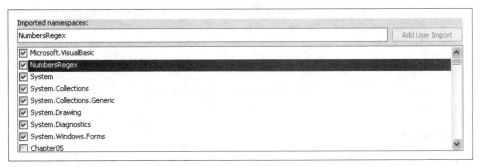

Figure 5-46. Importing a namespace via the Project Properties window

Once the new DLL is referenced and its object's namespace has been imported, you can use the compiled regular expression in an application. The following code uses the new `RgxNumbers` regular expression to count the numbers in a string:

```
Imports System.Text.RegularExpressions

' ...Later, in a method...

Dim source As String = _
    "Making a Pi (3.1415926) is easy as One 1 Two 2 Three 3"
Dim parser As New RgxNumbers
Dim totalMatches As Integer = parser.Matches(source).Count
```

```
MsgBox(source & vbNewLine & "Number count: " & _
    totalMatches.ToString())
```

Figure 5-47 shows the result of running this code to determine how many numbers are in the sample string.

Figure 5-47. Quickly counting numbers in a string using the compiled regular expression

See Also

Recipe 5.37 also discusses regular expression processing.

5.41   Using Regular Expressions to Validate Data

Problem

You need to validate string data entered by a user to ensure it meets defined criteria.

Solution

Sample code folder: Chapter 05\RegexValidate

Use a regular expression to check the string to make sure it matches the type of data expected.

Discussion

The Internet is a good place to find a wide range of regular expressions to validate strings using specific rules, and this recipe won't attempt to list them all. Instead, the following code, which validates a String as an email address, demonstrates a specific example to show you the general technique involved:

```
Imports System.Text.RegularExpressions

' ...Later, in a method...

Dim testString As String
Dim emailPattern As String = _
    "^([0-9a-zA-Z]+[-._+&])*[0-9a-zA-Z]+@" & _
    "([-0-9a-zA-Z]+[.])+[a-zA-Z]{2,6}$"
```

```
testString = "johndoe@nowhere.com"
MsgBox(testString & Space(3) & _
    Regex.IsMatch(testString, emailPattern))

testString = "john@doe@mybad.com"
MsgBox(testString & Space(3) & _
    Regex.IsMatch(testString, emailPattern))
```

This regular expression checks a string to see if it is a valid email address. As shown in Figures 5-48 and 5-49, the first string passes the test, but the second has a problem. In general, the IsMatch( ) method returns True if the string matches the criteria defined in the regular expression and False if it fails the test.

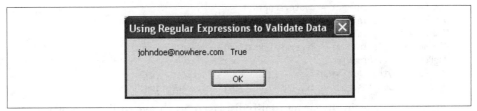

Figure 5-48. A string that passes the regular expression test for valid email addresses

Figure 5-49. A string that fails the regular expression test designed to validate it as a legal email address

See Also

Recipe 5.22 also discusses data validation.

5.42   Using Regular Expressions to Count Characters, Words, or Lines

Problem

You want to count the characters, words, and lines in a string.

Solution

Sample code folder: Chapter 05\RegexCountParts

Use separate regular expressions to count words, characters, and lines in a string of any length.

Discussion

The following code demonstrates three very short regular expressions that provide simple counts of characters, words, and lines in a string of any length:

```
Imports System.Text.RegularExpressions

' ...Later, in a method...

Dim quote As String = _
    "The important thing" & vbNewLine & _
    "is not to stop questioning." & vbNewLine & _
    "--Albert Einstein" & vbNewLine
Dim numBytes As Integer = quote.Length * 2
Dim numChars As Integer = Regex.Matches(quote, ".").Count
Dim numWords As Integer = Regex.Matches(quote, "\w+").Count
Dim numLines As Integer = Regex.Matches(quote, ".+\n*").Count
MsgBox(String.Format( _
    "{0}{5}bytes: {1}{5}Chars: {2}{5}Words: {3}{5}Lines: {4}", _
    quote, numBytes, numChars, numWords, numLines, vbNewLine))
```

The number of bytes in the string is also displayed, as shown in Figure 5-50, but the string's Length property provides this count directly without having to resort to a regular expression.

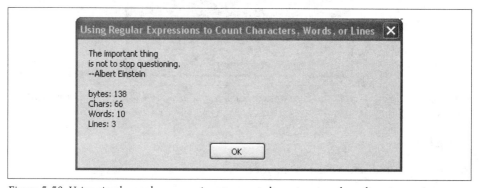

Figure 5-50. Using simple regular expressions to count characters, words, or lines in a string

See Also

Recipe 5.38 also discusses the results of regular expression processing.

5.43 Converting a String to and from Base64

Problem

You want to convert a string to or from Base64 format for predictable transfer across a network.

Solution

Sample code folder: Chapter 05\Base64

To convert a string to Base64, first use `System.Text.Encoding` methods to convert the string to a byte array and then use the `Convert.ToBase64String( )` method to convert the byte array to a Base64 string.

To convert a Base64 string back to the original string, use `Convert.FromBase64String( )` to convert the string to a byte array, and then use the appropriate `System.Text.Encoding` method to convert the byte array to a string.

Discussion

The following code demonstrates these steps as it converts a sample string to Base64 and back again:

```
Dim quote As String = "The important thing is not to " & _
    "stop questioning. --Albert Einstein"
Dim quoteBytes As Byte( ) = _
    System.Text.Encoding.UTF8.GetBytes(quote)
Dim quote64 As String = Convert.ToBase64String(quoteBytes)
Dim byteSet As Byte( ) = Convert.FromBase64String(quote64)
Dim result As String = _
    System.Text.Encoding.UTF8.GetString(byteSet)
MsgBox(quote & vbNewLine & quote64 & vbNewLine & result)
```

UTF8 encoding is used because the sample string's characters all fall within the range of standard ASCII characters. For other character sets, it's best to use Unicode encoding, in which case you should change both occurrences of "UTF8" to "Unicode" in the code sample. The byte array and the Base64 string will each be twice as large when using Unicode, but this eliminates the possibility of any data loss during the conversions.

Figure 5-51 shows the results of the above conversions as displayed by the message box.

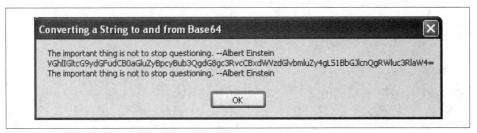

Figure 5-51. A sample string converted to Base64 and back again

See Also

Recipe 5.33 also shows how to convert string data into an alternative format that uses only printable characters.

5.44 Splitting a String

Problem

You want to split a string using a multicharacter string rather than a single character as the split point, but the String object's Split( ) method only splits using one or more individual characters.

Solution

Sample code folder: Chapter 05\SplitString

You can use the Visual Basic Split( ) function instead of the String.Split( ) method, or you can pass an array of strings to String.Split( ).

Discussion

The following code shows the differences between using the Split( ) function and the String.Split( ) method:

```
Dim quote As String = "The important thing is not to " & _
   "stop questioning. --Albert Einstein"
Dim strArray1() As String = Split(quote, "ing")
Dim strArray2() As String = quote.Split(CChar("ing"))
Dim result As New System.Text.StringBuilder
Dim counter As Integer

For counter = 0 To strArray1.Length - 1
   result.AppendLine(strArray1(counter))
Next counter
result.AppendLine(StrDup(30, "-"))

For counter = 0 To strArray2.Length - 1
   result.AppendLine(strArray2(counter))
Next counter
MsgBox(result.ToString())
```

String array strArray1 is created by applying the Split( ) function to the sample string, splitting the string at all occurrences of "ing". strArray2 uses the String.Split( ) method to do the same thing. However, even though the string "ing" is passed to the String.Split( ) method to define the split points, only the first character of this string, the character "i," is used to make the splits. The results of these two splits are quite different, as shown in the output displayed in the message box in Figure 5-52.

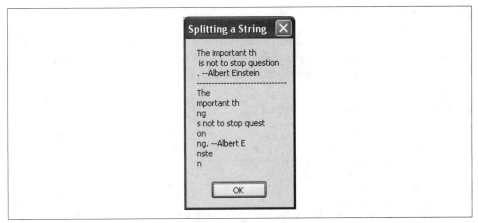

Figure 5-52. Results of passing the Split( ) function and the Split( ) method a multicharacter string as the split point

To confuse the issue even further, it is possible to use the `String.Split( )` method to split a string at whole substring boundaries, but only by passing an array of strings to the method to define the split points (not just a simple string) and passing a required parameter defining split options. The following two lines of code demonstrate this technique, returning the desired results. The first line uses the Visual Basic function, and the second line uses the string array technique just described:

```
Dim strArray1( ) As String = Split(quote, "ing")
Dim strArray1( ) As String = _
    quote.Split(New String( ) {"ing"}, StringSplitOptions.None)
```

Both `String( )` options are very powerful and useful, but you do need to use the correct one, passing appropriate parameters.

See Also

Recipe 5.28 also discusses string parsing using `Split( )`.

5.45   Creating a String of Space Characters

Problem

You want to create a string of *n* space characters.

Solution

Use the `Space(N)` function, which returns a string of *n* space characters.

Discussion

The following sample code actually presents three different ways to create a string of *n* spaces. In most cases the Space( ) function works quite well to create the spaces, but it's informative to compare the three techniques:

```
Dim lotsOfSpaces1 As String = New String(" "c, 500)
Dim lotsOfSpaces2 As String = StrDup(500, " "c)
Dim lotsOfSpaces3 As String = Space(500)
Dim result As String = String.Format( _
    "Length of lotsOfSpaces1: {0}{3}" & _
    "Length of lotsOfSpaces2: {1}{3}" & _
    "Length of lotsOfSpaces3: {2}{3}", _
    lotsOfSpaces1.Length, _
    lotsOfSpaces2.Length, _
    lotsOfSpaces3.Length, vbNewLine)
MsgBox(result)
```

The String constructor is overloaded to initialize strings as they are created in several ways. As shown in the first statement above, you can create a new string comprised of *n* repetitions of any character (in this case, a space character).

The StrDup( ) function is similar in operation in that it also returns a string comprised of *n* occurrences of a given character. Both the String constructor and the StrDup( ) function are useful when the repeated character is something other than a space.

Finally, the Space( ) function returns a string comprised of *n* space characters, without the option to use any other character.

The rest of the code displays the lengths of the three strings of spaces to help verify that they were created as indicated, as shown in Figure 5-53.

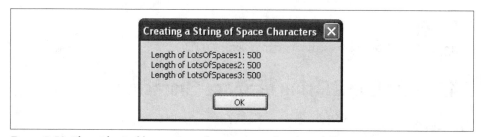

Figure 5-53. Three identical long strings of spaces created in three different ways

See Also

Recipe 5.2 discusses similar functionality.

Numbers and Math

6.0 Introduction

Visual Basic is now completely on a par with C# and other languages in its scientific, engineering, and financial number-crunching capabilities. This chapter demonstrates how easy it is to develop very fast and powerful, yet easy-to-read code for advanced number-crunching applications. Some of the recipes will appeal to almost all developers, such as those demonstrating rounding, the new unsigned integers, and the new Decimal numbers that are suitable for the most demanding financial calculations. Other recipes will appeal to the many scientist and engineer types searching for 21st century updates for FORTRAN, programmable calculators, and Excel.

6.1 Using Compact Operator Notation

Problem

You want to write compact, efficient code using the latest syntax available for assignment operators.

Solution

Sample code folder: Chapter 06\CompactOperators

Visual Basic 2005 now lets you use the same compact assignment notation for some math operations that has been used in the C and C# languages for many years.

There are several compact assignment operators, and they all work the same way. The variable to the left of the operator is used both as a source value and as a destination for the results of the operation. The operators are listed in Table 6-1.

Table 6-1. Compact assignment operators

Operator	Description
^=	Exponentiation
*=	Multiplication
/=	Division
\=	Integer division
+=	Addition
-=	Subtraction
<<=	Shift left
>>=	Shift right
&=	Comparison

Discussion

Consider the following program statement, which increments the variable count:

```
count = count + 1
```

The variable count is repeated twice in this simple line of code, once to retrieve its value and once to assign the results of adding 1 to the value. The new, more efficient compact assignment syntax uses the variable's name just once:

```
count += 1
```

The compact assignment operator += causes the variable to be used both as the source of the value to be operated on and as the destination for the result.

The following sample code demonstrates all of the operators listed in Table 6-1:

```
Dim result As New System.Text.StringBuilder

Dim testDouble As Double = Math.PI
result.Append("Double ").AppendLine(testDouble)
testDouble += Math.PI
result.Append("+= ").AppendLine(testDouble)
testDouble *= Math.PI
result.Append("*= ").AppendLine(testDouble)
testDouble -= Math.PI
result.Append("-= ").AppendLine(testDouble)
testDouble /= Math.PI
result.Append("/= ").AppendLine(testDouble)
testDouble ^= Math.PI
result.Append("^= ").AppendLine(testDouble)
result.AppendLine()

Dim testInteger As Integer = 17
result.Append("Integer ").AppendLine(testInteger)
testInteger \= 2
result.Append("\= 2 ... ").AppendLine(testInteger)
testInteger += 1
```

```
result.Append("+= 1 ... ").AppendLine(testInteger)
testInteger <<= 1
result.Append("<<= 1 ... ").AppendLine(testInteger)
testInteger >>= 3
result.Append(">>= 3 ... ").AppendLine(testInteger)
result.AppendLine()

Dim testString As String = "Abcdef"
result.Append("String ").AppendLine(testString)
testString &= "ghi"
result.Append("&= ghi ... ").AppendLine(testString)
testString += "jkl"
result.Append("+= jkl ... ").AppendLine(testString)

MsgBox(result.ToString())
```

Figure 6-1 shows the results displayed by this block of code. While many of the operators work on double-precision variables, some work only on integers of various sizes, and the concatenation operator works only on strings.

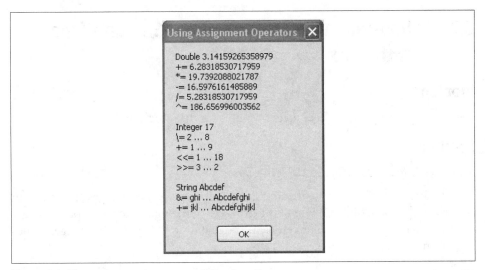

Figure 6-1. The compact assignment operators in action

Although the += (addition) operator is overloaded to operate on either numerical variables or strings, your code will be clearer if you use the addition operator only for mathematical operations. For string concatenation, use the &= operator instead. This rule can also help you avoid hidden errors when working with numbers formatted as strings. For instance, consider the following code, which updates an Integer value with numbers stored in strings:

```
Dim numberFromStrings As Integer
numberFromStrings = "4"
numberFromStrings += "3"
MsgBox(numberFromStrings)
```

When you run this code, it displays "7" in the message box. This works because Visual Basic is "helping you out," automatically converting the strings to Integer values before performing the assignment or addition. If you replace the += operator in that code with the &= operator, the code behaves differently:

```
Dim numberFromStrings As Integer
numberFromStrings = "4"
numberFromStrings &= "3"
MsgBox(numberFromStrings)
```

This time, the message box displays "43," the concatenation of the two strings. Some of the documentation for the += and &= operators claims that the two are functionally equivalent when working with strings, but this example shows that care should be exercised when using them in mixed string/number situations.

See Also

Search for "operator procedures" in Visual Studio Help for more information.

6.2   Choosing Integers of the Right Size and Type for the Job

Problem

You want to use the right-sized integer variable for the job at hand.

Solution

Sample code folder: Chapter 06\UsingIntegers

Visual Basic 2005 now has signed and unsigned integer variable types that range in size from 8 bits to 64 bits (1 byte to 8 bytes). Using the right size and type of integer can save memory, generate more efficient code, and provide ranges of integer values suitable to a variety of needs.

Discussion

Visual Basic 2005 is the first version of Visual Basic to support signed byte values and unsigned integer values in a variety of sizes. Here's a list of all the integer types now supported:

Byte
> Eight-bit (1-byte) values ranging from 0 to 255. Equivalent to System.Byte.

SByte
> A signed type that is 8 bits (1 byte) in size and holds values ranging from –128 to +127. Equivalent to System.SByte.

Short

Sixteen-bit (2-byte) values ranging from −32,768 to +32,767. Equivalent to System.Int16.

UInt16

An unsigned type that is 16 bits (2 bytes) in size and holds values ranging from 0 to 65,535. Equivalent to System.UInt16.

Integer

Thirty-two-bit (4-byte) values ranging from −2,147,483,648 to +2,147,483,647. Equivalent to System.Int32.

UInteger

An unsigned type that is 32 bits (4 bytes) in size and holds values ranging from 0 to 4,294,967,295. Equivalent to System.UInt32.

Long

Sixty-four-bit (8-byte) values ranging from −9,223,372,036,854,775,808 to +9,223,372,036,854,775,807 (−9 to +9 quintillion). Equivalent to System.Int64.

ULong

An unsigned type that is 64 bits (8 bytes) in size and holds values ranging from 0 to 18,446,744,073,709,551,615 (18 quintillion). Equivalent to System.UInt64.

The following code demonstrates each of these integer types by displaying the largest possible value for each:

```
Dim result As New System.Text.StringBuilder()
result.AppendLine("MaxValue...")
result.AppendLine()

Dim maxByte As Byte = Byte.MaxValue
Dim maxSByte As SByte = SByte.MaxValue
Dim maxShort As Short = Short.MaxValue
Dim maxUShort As UShort = UShort.MaxValue
Dim maxInteger As Integer = Integer.MaxValue
Dim maxUInteger As UInteger = UInteger.MaxValue
Dim maxLong As Long = Long.MaxValue
Dim maxULong As ULong = ULong.MaxValue

result.Append("Byte ").AppendLine(maxByte)
result.Append("SByte ").AppendLine(maxSByte)
result.Append("Short ").AppendLine(maxShort)
result.Append("UShort = ").AppendLine(maxUShort)
result.Append("Integer = ").AppendLine(maxInteger)
result.Append("UInteger = ").AppendLine(maxUInteger)
result.Append("Long = ").AppendLine(maxLong)
result.Append("ULong = ").AppendLine(maxULong)

MsgBox(result.ToString())
```

For all unsigned variable types, the minimum possible value is zero. For all signed types, to find the minimum value add one to the maximum value, and change the sign. For example, the maximum value for signed bytes is 127, and the minimum value is –128. As shown above, the MaxValue property of each integer type provides a straightforward way to access the largest possible value. Similarly, you can get the smallest possible value by accessing each type's MinValue property.

Figure 6-2 shows the maximum values for each type of integer, as displayed by the message box in the example code.

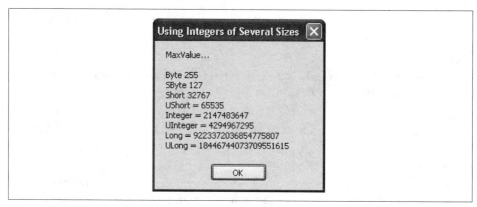

Figure 6-2. Maximum values for the various integer variable types

One other variable type is worth considering for extremely large integer values. Although not true integers, Decimal variables can hold integer values up to 79,228,162,514,264,337,593,543,950,335 (79 octillion). The rule for determining the minimum value for a Decimal-type variable is slightly different than for the true integer types: in this case, just reverse the sign of the maximum value, don't add 1. The MinValue for Decimal variables is thus –79,228,162,514,264,337,593,543,950,335.

Decimal values are signed 128-bit (16-byte) numbers, and they may have a decimal point. If you appropriately round off or truncate values, the Decimal type can accurately hold extremely large integer values. However, even on 64-bit machines, this data type can slow down calculations somewhat because the processor must perform calculations using multiple steps to process each value.

6.3   Using Unsigned Integers

Problem

You want to work with nonnegative integers while minimizing the memory requirements of variables in your code.

Solution

Use the smallest unsigned integer variable types that will hold the desired range of nonnegative values.

Discussion

As mentioned in the previous recipe, the unsigned integer variable types provide many new options for working with nonnegative integers in Visual Basic 2005. The following code provides a specific example to help clarify the concept:

```
Dim testUShort As UShort
Do Until (testUShort > CUShort(33000))
    testUShort += CUShort(1)
Loop
MsgBox("UShort result: " & testUShort.ToString())
```

The standard Visual Basic Short variable type holds signed integers in the range −32,768 to +32,767 and uses only two bytes of memory. If the previous code used signed integers, an exception would be generated during the looping because values up to 33,001 are not allowed. The unsigned testUShort integer stores values up to 65,535, so the program runs successfully, and the variable still requires only two bytes of memory. Figure 6-3 shows a two-byte unsigned variable displaying a number too big for a standard signed two-byte integer.

Figure 6-3. Unsigned integer variables can hold bigger numbers than signed integers, in the same amount of memory

See Also

Search for "UInteger" in Visual Studio Help for more information.

6.4 Swapping Two Integers Without Using a Third

Problem

You want to swap the values of two integer variables without creating a third.

Solution

Sample code folder: Chapter 06\IntegerSwap

Use the exclusive-or bit manipulation function to do the trick.

Discussion

Nowadays efforts to save the space of a single variable in memory seem kind of silly, but this recipe nevertheless demonstrates an interesting technique for swapping two numbers without creating a third variable. More importantly, it demonstrates how bit-manipulation functions can be quite useful in Visual Basic 2005. Here's the sample code:

```
Dim result As String
Dim firstValue As Integer
Dim secondValue As Integer

' ----- Set the initial test values.
firstValue = 17
secondValue = 123
result = String.Format("Before swap: {0}, {1}", _
    firstValue, secondValue)
result &= vbNewLine

' ----- Swap the values at the bit level.
firstValue = firstValue Xor secondValue
secondValue = firstValue Xor secondValue
firstValue = firstValue Xor secondValue
result &= String.Format("After swap: {0}, {1}", _
    firstValue, secondValue)

MsgBox(result)
```

The above code loads values into integers firstValue and secondValue, then swaps their values by applying three successive Xor operators on them. The Xor operator combines the two integers on a bit-by-bit basis, resulting in a 1 bit whenever the original bits are different and a 0 when they are the same. Once these three Xor operations have been performed, the original contents of the two integers will have migrated to the opposite locations in memory. Figure 6-4 shows the results displayed by the sample code.

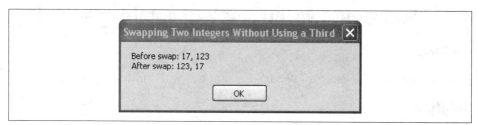

Figure 6-4. Swapping two integers using Xor

See Also

Search for "Xor operator" in Visual Studio Help for more information.

6.5   Using Single- and Double-Precision Variables

Problem

You want to use floating-point numbers but aren't sure if you should use Singles or Doubles.

Solution

Sample code folder: Chapter 06\SingleDouble

Choose the most appropriate variable type based on the range and precision of numbers it can hold and on its memory footprint.

Discussion

To help you understand the capabilities of Single and Double variables, the following sample code uses several useful properties and functions to display information about them:

```
Dim result As New System.Text.StringBuilder
Dim maxSingle As Single = Single.MaxValue
Dim maxDouble As Double = Double.MaxValue
Dim sizeOfSingle As Integer = _
    Runtime.InteropServices.Marshal.SizeOf(maxSingle.GetType)
Dim sizeOfDouble As Integer = _
    Runtime.InteropServices.Marshal.SizeOf(maxDouble.GetType)

result.Append("Memory size of a Single (bytes): ")
result.AppendLine(sizeOfSingle)
result.Append("Maximum value of a Single: ")
result.AppendLine(maxSingle)
result.AppendLine( )

result.Append("Memory size of a Double (bytes): ")
result.AppendLine(sizeOfDouble)
result.Append("Maximum value of a Double: ")
result.AppendLine(maxDouble)

MsgBox(result.ToString( ))
```

The MaxValue constant provided by each type provides the largest possible value for variables of that type. The Marshal.SizeOf( ) function returns the unmanaged size, in bytes, of any class, which in this case is the class returned by the GetType( ) method of our Single and Double variables. Figure 6-5 shows the results.

If you're working with large arrays of numbers and memory issues are of concern, the Single type might be appropriate. If you need greater precision, and using twice the memory per occurrence is not a problem, Doubles might work best.

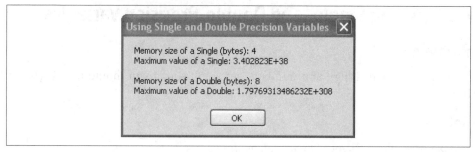

Figure 6-5. Singles and Doubles require a different amount of memory and hold different-sized numbers

Many mathematical functions, such as those provided by the Math class, operate on Doubles only. Generally this is not a problem, as conversion between Single and Double types in memory is efficient. On the other hand, the GDI+ Graphics object operates on Single values, so it's best to work with these where possible when creating graphics. For example, many of the graphics functions and methods accept PointF objects passed as parameters, and a PointF is comprised of a pair of Single numbers, X and Y.

See Also

The "PointF" topic in Visual Studio Help describes how Singles are used for many graphics methods.

The "Math Class" subject lists many useful functions that operate on Doubles.

6.6   Using Decimal Variables for Maximum Precision

Problem

You want to manipulate numbers with many significant digits of accuracy.

Solution

Sample code folder: Chapter 06\SingleDouble

The Decimal number type holds numbers with up to 29 digits of accuracy and is well suited to tasks in which rounding errors are to be kept to a minimum, as in financial calculations.

Discussion

For really big numbers where you want many digits of accuracy, the Decimal number type is ideal. Numbers of this type are stored in 16 bytes (128 bits) of memory each, with up to 29 significant digits. These numbers can be positive or negative, and a decimal point can be included anywhere within the number. The following code demonstrates Decimal variables in action:

```
Dim result As New System.Text.StringBuilder
Dim maxDecimal As Decimal = Decimal.MaxValue
Dim sizeOfDecimal As Integer = _
    Runtime.InteropServices.Marshal.SizeOf(maxDecimal.GetType)

result.Append("Memory size of a Decimal (bytes): ")
result.AppendLine(sizeOfDecimal)
result.Append("Maximum value of a Decimal: ")
result.AppendLine(maxDecimal)
result.Append("Divided by one million: ")
result.AppendLine(maxDecimal / 1000000D)
result.Append("1D / 3D: ")
result.AppendLine(1D / 3D)

MsgBox(result.ToString( ))
```

Figure 6-6 shows the display created by this code. The Marshal.SizeOf( ) function determines the number of bytes of memory the Decimal variable uses, and the MaxValue constant gets the largest possible numerical value it can hold. To demonstrate how the decimal point can be anywhere in the number, the maximum value is divided by one million. The decimal point shifts six digits in from the right as a result. To demonstrate that the math operators are overloaded to accurately take advantage of the Decimal's full precision, the quantity 1/3 is calculated and displayed in the last line of the message box. An uppercase "D" is appended to the constants 1 and 3 in the code to tell the compiler that they are Decimal values.

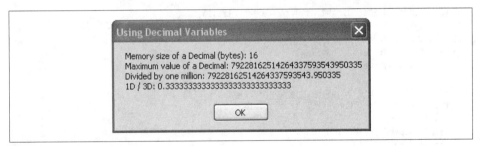

Figure 6-6. Using the Decimal number type

See Also

See "Decimal data type" in Visual Studio Help for more information.

6.7 Converting Between Number Types

Problem

You want to explicitly convert numeric variables and calculation results between the various number types.

Solution

Sample code folder: Chapter 06\ConvertNumber

It's always a good idea to make sure your project's Option Explicit and Option Strict settings are on, but this often forces you to apply explicit conversions when working with more than one type of numeric variable. The solution is to apply one of the many standalone conversion functions provided by Visual Basic or to use one of the many methods of the Convert object.

Discussion

The following code sample demonstrates a simple conversion of Double numeric values to Byte values, using both the standalone CByte( ) function and the Convert.ToByte( ) method. Some people prefer to use the Convert object exclusively, which may be easier to remember because all the conversion methods have names beginning with "To". Others prefer the standalone conversion functions, because many of these have been around in previous versions of Visual Basic for some time now. We look at both approaches here:

```
Dim result As New System.Text.StringBuilder
Dim b1 As Byte = CByte(3.1416) + CByte(314.16 / 2)
Dim b2 As Byte = Convert.ToByte(3.1416) + _
    Convert.ToByte(314.16 / 2)

result.AppendLine("Example conversions to Byte...")
result.AppendLine( )

result.AppendLine("Dim b1 As Byte = CByte(3.1416) + " & _
    "CByte(314.16 / 2)")
result.Append("b1 = ")
result.AppendLine(b1.ToString)
result.AppendLine( )

result.Append("Dim b2 As Byte = Convert.ToByte(3.1416) + ")
result.AppendLine("Convert.ToByte(314.16 / 2)")
result.Append("b2 = ")
result.AppendLine(b2.ToString)
result.AppendLine( )

result.AppendLine("Numeric Conversions...")
result.AppendLine( )
result.AppendLine("CByte(expression)")
result.AppendLine("CSByte(expression)")
result.AppendLine("CShort(expression)")
result.AppendLine("CUShort(expression)")
result.AppendLine("CInt(expression)")
result.AppendLine("CUInt(expression)")
result.AppendLine("CLng(expression)")
result.AppendLine("CULng(expression)")
result.AppendLine("CSng(expression)")
```

```
result.AppendLine("CDbl(expression)")
result.AppendLine("CDec(expression)")

MsgBox(result.ToString())
```

The Double value 314.16 will not convert to a Byte because it is out of range for byte values. Attempting this conversion causes an exception. However, dividing this value by 2 results in a Double value that does convert. The point is that the decimal digits don't cause a problem when converting to a Byte (they are simply rounded to the nearest byte value), but the number must be in the range 0 to 255 to allow the conversion.

Figure 6-7 shows the results of the above demonstration code in action. A sample conversion is shown using both techniques, and a list of the standalone conversion functions is displayed for easy review.

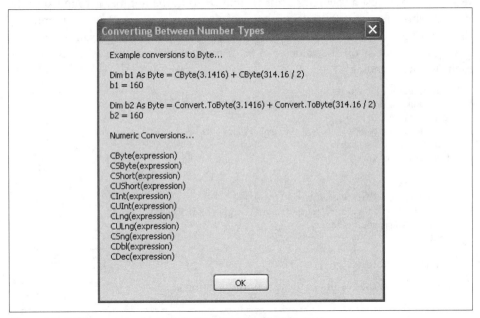

Figure 6-7. Different ways of converting between number types

The signed byte and unsigned integer data types are new with this latest version of Visual Basic, and so are the functions to convert values to them.

See Also

See "conversion functions" in Visual Studio Help for more information on these functions.

6.8   Rounding Numbers Accurately

Problem

You need to round off double-precision numbers in a standard, accurate way.

Solution

Sample code folder: Chapter 06\Rounding

Use the Math.Round( ) function to round numbers to the desired precision.

Discussion

The Math.Round( ) function is overloaded to accept several different sets of parameters. If you pass just a Double or Decimal number to it, the number is rounded to the nearest whole number. By passing a second parameter, you control the number of digits after the decimal point where the rounding is to occur. For example, the following code rounds off the value of pi (π) using zero through five as the number of digits for the rounding:

```
Dim outputFormat As String = _
    "Rounding value: {0} Results: {1}"
Dim oneTry As String
Dim result As New System.Text.StringBuilder
Dim piRounded As Double
Dim digits As Integer

For digits = 0 To 5
    piRounded = Math.Round(Math.PI, digits)
    oneTry = String.Format(outputFormat, digits, piRounded)
    result.AppendLine(oneTry)
Next digits

MsgBox(result.ToString( ))
```

Figure 6-8 shows the results of these rounding actions.

Figure 6-8. Using the Math.Round( ) function to round numbers accurately

A third optional parameter lets you fine-tune the way a number is rounded when the number is exactly halfway between two values at the point where the number is to be rounded. The choices are to have the number rounded to an even digit, or away from zero. The default is to round to an even digit.

See Also

See "Math.Round" in Visual Studio Help for more information.

6.9 Declaring Loop Counters Within Loops

Problem

You want to create a variable to hold the loop counter in a For…Next loop, but you want the variable to exist only within the body of the loop.

Solution

Declare the variable type directly using the optional syntax for doing this in the For…Next loop command.

Discussion

If you include As *Type* immediately after the variable name used in the For…Next statement, Visual Basic 2005 creates this variable on the spot, and its scope is limited to the body of the For…Next loop. If you declare the variable elsewhere, don't add the As *Type* clause in the loop statement; doing so triggers an exception.

This sample code creates nested For…Next loops, with the outer loop counter variable declared outside the loop and the inner loop variable declared just for the body of the loop. Study the lines starting with For to see the difference:

```
Dim formatString As String = "outerLoop: {0} innerLoop: {1}"
Dim result As String = ""
Dim outerLoop As Integer

For outerLoop = 1 To 2
   For innerLoop As Integer = 1 To 2
      result &= String.Format(formatString, _
         outerLoop, innerLoop)
      result &= vbNewLine
   Next innerLoop
Next outerLoop

MsgBox(result)
```

These two loops are nearly the same. Their counter variable values are displayed each time through the inner loop, as shown in Figure 6-9. The variable outerLoop can be referenced past the end of the sample lines of code, but referencing innerLoop will causes an exception. innerLoop exists only within the For...Next loop where it is declared.

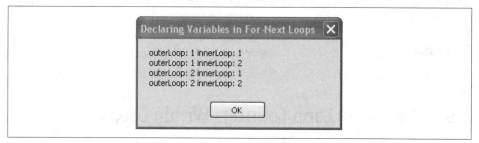

Figure 6-9. The results of our nested loops using two different counter declaration methods

See Also

See "For...Next statements" in Visual Studio Help for more information.

6.10   Converting Between Radians and Degrees

Problem

You want a simple, consistent, easy-to-read, and easy-to-use way to convert angles between radians and degrees.

Solution

Define two constants, RadPerDeg and DegPerRad, and multiply by degrees or radians, respectively, to convert to the other units.

Discussion

You can create standalone functions to perform these conversions, but these constants are straightforward definitions, and your code will compile to inline conversions that are compact and fast. The following code defines the constants and uses them to convert a few sample angular values. It's generally best to define your constants at the top of your source-code files or in a global module, but here they are shown close to the code where they are used for easy reference:

```
Const RadPerDeg As Double = Math.PI / 180#
Const DegPerRad As Double = 180# / Math.PI

Dim radians As Double
Dim degrees As Double

radians = Math.PI / 4#
degrees = radians * DegPerRad
radians = degrees * RadPerDeg
```

```
MsgBox("Radians: " & radians.ToString & _
    vbNewLine & "Degrees: " & degrees.ToString)
```

This code rather redundantly converts radians to degrees and then immediately converts degrees right back to radians. You wouldn't want to do this normally, but it shows both conversions side by side for easy comparison.

Figure 6-10 shows the same angle (45 degrees, or $\pi/4$ radians) expressed in the calculated units after conversion using the constants.

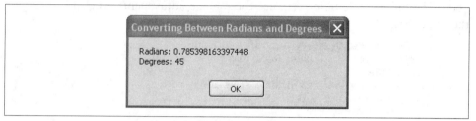

Figure 6-10. Using the RadPerDeg and DegPerRad constants to convert between degrees and radians

Both constants are defined using a division calculation. The Visual Basic 2005 compiler converts this math statement to a single constant by doing the division at compile time rather than at runtime, so there is no inefficiency in expressing the constants this way. The value of π is defined as a constant in the Math object with full double-precision accuracy, so the constants defined here are also accurate with Double values.

See Also

See "Derived Math Functions" in Visual Studio Help for additional derived functions, many of which assume radian units.

6.11   Limiting Angles to a Range

Problem

You want to shift intermediate angular calculation results into a range such as 0° to 360°, −180° to 180°, 0 to 2π radians, or −π to π radians.

Solution

Sample code folder: Chapter 06\AngleRange

Create a function that handles all these range conversions efficiently.

Discussion

Some scientific calculations produce angular results that are beyond normal ranges, requiring adjustment to bring them into the standard range of values. For example, in astronomical calculations a variety of polynomials are used to compute highly accurate positions of the planets and stars, but the polynomials often return angles representing many revolutions of the various orbs. You might say the angles are astronomical in size before they are adjusted into a normalized range such as 0° to 360°. The following function handles these range adjustments efficiently, bringing the values back down to earth:

```
Public Function FixRange(ByVal origValue As Double, _
    ByVal rangeMin As Double, ByVal rangeMax As Double) _
    As Double
  ' ----- Adjust a value to within a specified range.
  '       Use the range size as the adjustment factor.
  Dim shiftedValue As Double
  Dim delta As Double

  shiftedValue = origValue - rangeMin
  delta = rangeMax - rangeMin
  Return (((shiftedValue Mod delta) + delta) Mod delta) + _
    rangeMin
End Function
```

The FixRange( ) function accepts an out-of-range angular value expressed in either degrees or radians (or any range-limited system), followed by the minimum and maximum limits of the desired normalized range. All three parameters must use the same measurement system, such as radians, for the results to make sense.

The function uses a double application of the Mod operator plus some additions and subtractions to bring the value into the desired range. This calculation is more straightforward and efficient than adding or subtracting values in a loop until the value is brought into range, which is the technique sometimes shown in astronomical calculation books.

The following code demonstrates the use of the Range( ) function on a variety of positive and negative angular values as they are brought into a number of desired ranges:

```
Dim result As New System.Text.StringBuilder
Dim formatDegrees As String = _
  "Degrees: {0}  Range: {1},{2}  Value: {3}"
Dim formatRadians As String = _
  "Radians: {0}  Range: {1},{2}  Value: {3}"
Dim degrees As Double
Dim radians As Double
Dim ranged As Double

' ----- Degrees over the range.
degrees = 367.75
ranged = FixRange(degrees, 0, 360)
```

```
result.AppendLine(String.Format(formatDegrees, _
    degrees, 0, 360, ranged))

' ----- Degress under the range.
degrees = -97.5
ranged = FixRange(degrees, 0, 360)
result.AppendLine(String.Format(formatDegrees, _
    degrees, 0, 360, ranged))

' ----- Degrees in range.
degrees = -97.5
ranged = FixRange(degrees, -180, 180)
result.AppendLine(String.Format(formatDegrees, _
    degrees, -180, 180, ranged))

' ----- Radians over the range.
radians = Math.PI * 3.33
ranged = FixRange(radians, -Math.PI, Math.PI)
result.AppendLine(String.Format(formatRadians, _
    radians, -Math.PI, Math.PI, ranged))

MsgBox(result.ToString())
```

Figure 6-11 shows the results produced by this sample code.

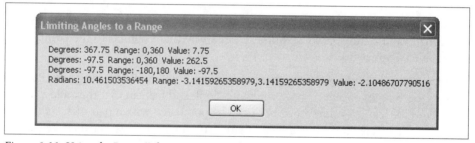

Figure 6-11. Using the Range() function to normalize angles in degrees or radians

See Also

Search for information on the Mod operator in Visual Studio Help.

6.12   Creating Double-Precision Point Variables

Problem

The PointF structure used in many graphics and other methods is defined to hold single-precision X and Y values, but you need greater precision.

Solution

Sample code folder: Chapter 06\DoublePoint

Create your own Point2D class with double-precision X and Y values.

Discussion

The following simple class provides a blueprint for creating Point2D objects containing double-precision X and Y values:

```
Public Class Point2D
    Public X As Double
    Public Y As Double

    Public Sub New(ByVal xPoint As Double, _
        ByVal yPoint As Double)
      Me.X = xPoint
      Me.Y = yPoint
    End Sub

    Public Overrides Function Tostring() As String
        Return "{X=" & X & ",Y=" & Y & "}"
    End Function
End Class
```

As shown in the sample class code, the ToString( ) function overrides the default ToString( ) and returns a string formatted in a way that's similar to the PointF class in the .NET Framework.

The following code demonstrates the creation of both the PointF and new Point2D objects. Both types of objects have the same "look and feel" in that they allow access directly to the X and Y values, they both can be populated with a pair of X, Y values at the moment of creation, and they both return similar strings via their respective ToString( ) functions:

```
Dim result As New System.Text.StringBuilder

' ----- Original PointF version.
Dim singlePoint As New PointF(1 / 17, Math.PI)
result.AppendLine("PointF: " & singlePoint.ToString())
result.AppendLine("X: " & singlePoint.X)
result.AppendLine()

' ----- New Point2D version.
Dim doublePoint As New Point2D(1 / 17, Math.PI)
result.AppendLine("Point2D: " & doublePoint.ToString())
result.AppendLine("X: " & doublePoint.X)
result.AppendLine()

MsgBox(result.ToString())
```

Figure 6-12 shows the results displayed by the message box in this sample code.

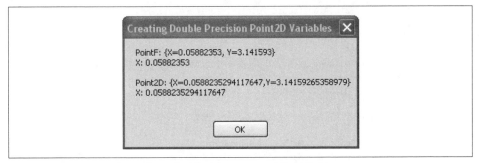

Figure 6-12. Point2D objects have double the precision of PointF objects

See Also

See "Graphics" in Visual Studio Help for more information about the use of two-dimensional points.

6.13 Converting Between Rectangular and Polar Coordinates

Problem

You want to convert between two-dimensional coordinates expressed in either rectangular or polar notation.

Solution

Sample code folder: Chapter 06\ConvertPolar

Create two functions for the two conversions: ToPolar( ) and ToRectangular( ).

Discussion

The PointF structure provides a natural way to handle two-dimensional coordinates because each X, Y pair is handled as a single unit. A straightforward way to handle conversions between coordinates expressed in either rectangular (X, Y) or polar (radius, radians) notation is to simply pass and return PointF objects. This requires you, the programmer, to keep track of the current notation of each PointF object, but this is generally easy to do. Here are the two functions for making the conversions:

```
Public Function ToPolar(ByVal sourcePoint As PointF) _
      As PointF
   ' ----- Convert rectangular coordinates to polar.
   Dim magnitude As Single
   Dim radians As Single

   magnitude = CSng(Math.Sqrt(sourcePoint.X ^ 2 + _
      sourcePoint.Y ^ 2))
```

```
        radians = CSng(Math.Atan2(sourcePoint.Y, sourcePoint.X))
        Return New PointF(magnitude, radians)
    End Function

    Public Function ToRectangular(ByVal sourcePoint As PointF) _
            As PointF
        ' ----- Convert polar coordinates to rectangular.
        Dim X As Single
        Dim Y As Single

        X = CSng(sourcePoint.X * Math.Cos(sourcePoint.Y))
        Y = CSng(sourcePoint.X * Math.Sin(sourcePoint.Y))
        Return New PointF(X, Y)
    End Function
```

Both functions assume angles will be expressed in radians, which is consistent with the way angles are expressed in Visual Basic. You can convert angles to and from degrees using the constants presented in Recipe 6.10.

The following block of code demonstrates the use of the ToPolar( ) and ToRectangular( ) functions:

```
Dim result As New System.Text.StringBuilder
Dim pointA As PointF
Dim pointB As PointF
Dim pointC As PointF

pointA = New PointF(3, 4)
pointB = ToPolar(pointA)
pointC = ToRectangular(pointB)

result.AppendLine("Rectangular: " & pointA.ToString())
result.AppendLine("Polar: " & pointB.ToString())
result.AppendLine("Rectangular: " & pointC.ToString())
MsgBox(result.ToString())
```

The ToString( ) function presents the X and Y values of the PointF data using "X=" and "Y=" labels, which can be misleading when the PointF is holding a coordinate in polar mode. Be sure to keep track of the state of the data as you work with it.

Figure 6-13 shows the formatted string results of the ToRectangular( ) and ToPolar( ) functions in action.

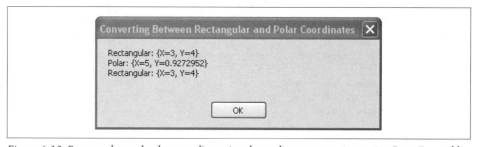

Figure 6-13. Rectangular and polar two-dimensional coordinate conversions using PointF variables

---

See Also

Searching for "polar rectangular" on the Web will lead you to a variety of explanations and learning materials about this subject.

6.14 Creating Three-Dimensional Variables

Problem

You want to work with three-dimensional coordinates as single entities.

Solution

Sample code folder: Chapter 06\ThreePoint

Create a Point3D class that works like the PointF class except that it contains a Z property in addition to X and Y.

Discussion

The following class definition is similar to the Point2D class presented in Recipe 6.12:

```
Public Class Point3D
    Public X As Double
    Public Y As Double
    Public Z As Double

    Public Sub New(ByVal xPoint As Double, _
         ByVal yPoint As Double, ByVal zPoint As Double)
      Me.X = xPoint
      Me.Y = yPoint
      Me.Z = zPoint
    End Sub

    Public Overrides Function Tostring() As String
       Return "{X=" & X & ",Y=" & Y & ",Z=" & Z & "}"
    End Function
End Class
```

The most important modification is the addition of a public Z value for the third dimension. As presented here, the X, Y, and Z properties are all Double precision, but you can easily redefine these to Single if that provides sufficient precision for your calculations, and if you want to save memory when you create large arrays of this data type.

The following code demonstrates the use of some Point3D objects. Notice how the New( ) function lets you create a Point3D variable with nonzero X, Y, and Z values:

```
Dim result As New System.Text.StringBuilder
Dim distance As Double
Dim point1 As Point3D
Dim point2 As Point3D
Dim deltaX As Double
```

```
Dim deltaY As Double
Dim deltaZ As Double

point1 = New Point3D(3, 4, 5)
point2 = New Point3D(7, 2, 3)
deltaX = point1.X - point2.X
deltaY = point1.Y - point2.Y
deltaZ = point1.Z - point2.Z
distance = Math.Sqrt(deltaX ^ 2 + deltaY ^ 2 + deltaZ ^ 2)

result.AppendLine("3D Point 1: " & point1.ToString())
result.AppendLine("3D Point 2: " & point2.ToString())
result.AppendLine("Distance: " & distance.ToString())

MsgBox(result.ToString())
```

Figure 6-14 shows the results of calculating the distance in space between these two coordinates.

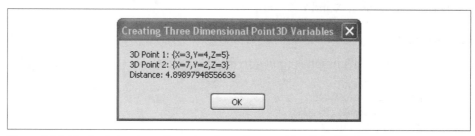

Figure 6-14. Manipulating three-dimensional coordinates with a Point3D class

See Also

Search for "basic 3D math" on the Web for a variety of explanations and further information about this subject.

6.15 Converting Between Rectangular, Spherical, and Cylindrical Coordinates

Problem

You need to convert three-dimensional coordinates between rectangular, spherical, and cylindrical notation.

Solution

Sample code folder: Chapter 06\Convert3D

Create a set of six functions to convert Point3D variables to and from each coordinate notation.

Discussion

The following six functions convert from any one of the three types of three-dimensional coordinates to any of the others. All these functions accept a Point3D argument and return a Point3D value. It is up to you to keep track of the current type of coordinate notation in each Point3D variable. Note that in all cases the Point3D value passed in to any of these functions is not altered; a new Point3D instance is returned instead. Here are the six functions:

```
Public Function RectToCylinder(ByVal pointA As Point3D) _
    As Point3D
  ' ----- Convert rectangular 3D coordinates to
  '       cylindrical coordinates.
  Dim rho As Double
  Dim theta As Double

  rho = Math.Sqrt(pointA.X ^ 2 + pointA.Y ^ 2)
  theta = Math.Atan2(pointA.Y, pointA.X)
  Return New Point3D(rho, theta, pointA.Z)
End Function

Public Function CylinderToRect(ByVal pointA As Point3D) _
    As Point3D
  ' ----- Convert cylindrical coordinates to
  '       rectangular 3D coordinates.
  Dim x As Double
  Dim y As Double

  x = pointA.X * Math.Cos(pointA.Y)
  y = pointA.X * Math.Sin(pointA.Y)
  Return New Point3D(x, y, pointA.Z)
End Function

Public Function RectToSphere(ByVal pointA As Point3D) _
    As Point3D
  ' ----- Convert rectangular 3D coordinates to
  '       spherical coordinates.
  Dim rho As Double
  Dim theta As Double
  Dim phi As Double

  rho = Math.Sqrt(pointA.X ^ 2 + pointA.Y ^ 2 + _
    pointA.Z ^ 2)
  theta = Math.Atan2(pointA.Y, pointA.X)
  phi = Math.Acos(pointA.Z / Math.Sqrt( _
    pointA.X ^ 2 + pointA.Y ^ 2 + pointA.Z ^ 2))
  Return New Point3D(rho, theta, phi)
End Function

Public Function SphereToRect(ByVal pointA As Point3D) _
    As Point3D
  ' ----- Convert spherical coordinates to
  '       rectangular 3D coordinates.
```

```
        Dim x As Double
        Dim y As Double
        Dim z As Double

        x = pointA.X * Math.Cos(pointA.Y) * Math.Sin(pointA.Z)
        y = pointA.X * Math.Sin(pointA.Y) * Math.Sin(pointA.Z)
        z = pointA.X * Math.Cos(pointA.Z)
        Return New Point3D(x, y, z)
    End Function

    Public Function CylinderToSphere(ByVal pointA As Point3D) _
            As Point3D
        ' ----- Convert cylindrical coordinates to
        '           spherical coordinates.
        Dim rho As Double
        Dim theta As Double
        Dim phi As Double

        rho = Math.Sqrt(pointA.X ^ 2 + pointA.Z ^ 2)
        theta = pointA.Y
        phi = Math.Acos(pointA.Z / _
            Math.Sqrt(pointA.X ^ 2 + pointA.Z ^ 2))
        Return New Point3D(rho, theta, phi)
    End Function

    Public Function SphereToCylinder(ByVal pointA As Point3D) _
            As Point3D
        ' ----- Convert spherical coordinates to
        '           cylindrical coordinates.
        Dim rho As Double
        Dim theta As Double
        Dim z As Double

        rho = pointA.X * Math.Sin(pointA.Z)
        theta = pointA.Y
        z = pointA.X * Math.Cos(pointA.Z)
        Return New Point3D(rho, theta, z)
    End Function
```

The following code creates several Point3D variables using names that indicate the types of coordinates they contain. For example, pointCyl is a Point3D variable containing three-dimensional cylindrical coordinates. The various conversion functions are used to populate the variables, and the results are shown in Figure 6-15:

```
Dim result As New System.Text.StringBuilder
Dim pointRec As New Point3D(3, 4, 5)
Dim pointCyl As Point3D = RectToCylinder(pointRec)
Dim pointSph As Point3D = RectToSphere(pointRec)
Dim pointRecToCyl As Point3D = RectToCylinder(pointRec)
Dim pointRecToSph As Point3D = RectToSphere(pointRec)
Dim pointCylToRec As Point3D = CylinderToRect(pointCyl)
Dim pointCylToSph As Point3D = CylinderToSphere(pointCyl)
Dim pointSphToRec As Point3D = SphereToRect(pointSph)
Dim pointSphToCyl As Point3D = SphereToCylinder(pointSph)
```

```
result.AppendLine("Rec: " & pointRec.ToString())
result.AppendLine("Cyl: " & pointCyl.ToString())
result.AppendLine("Sph: " & pointSph.ToString())
result.AppendLine()

result.AppendLine("Rec to Cyl: " & pointRecToCyl.ToString())
result.AppendLine("Rec to Sph: " & pointRecToSph.ToString())
result.AppendLine("Cyl to Rec: " & pointCylToRec.ToString())
result.AppendLine("Cyl to Sph: " & pointCylToSph.ToString())
result.AppendLine("Sph to Rec: " & pointSphToRec.ToString())
result.AppendLine("Sph to Cyl: " & pointSphToCyl.ToString())

MsgBox(result.ToString())
```

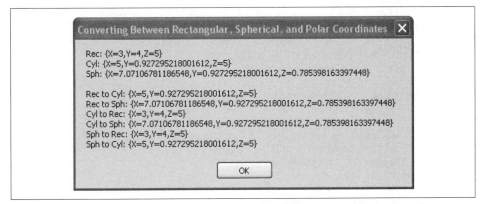

Figure 6-15. Converting Point3D variables between three different types of spatial coordinates

See Also

Search for "rectangular cylindrical spherical" on the Web for a variety of explanations and further information about this subject.

6.16   Working with Complex Numbers

Problem

You want an easy way to calculate with complex numbers.

Solution

Sample code folder: Chapter 06\ComplexNumbers

Create a ComplexNumber structure. Overload the standard mathematical operators so that using complex number variables is easy and natural.

Discussion

This recipe provides a great way to see how overloading standard operators can enhance the usability of your classes and structures. In this case, we've created a ComplexNumber structure. Structures are similar to classes, except that they exist as value types rather than reference types. This allows complex number instances to act the same as other simple variables, such as standard numerical variables.

The following code defines the ComplexNumber number structure. Place this code in its own file named *ComplexNumber.vb* for easy inclusion in any application that requires complex numbers:

```
Structure ComplexNumber
   Public Real As Double
   Public Imaginary As Double

   Public Sub New(ByVal realPart As Double, _
         ByVal imaginaryPart As Double)
      Me.Real = realPart
      Me.Imaginary = imaginaryPart
   End Sub

   Public Sub New(ByVal sourceNumber As ComplexNumber)
      Me.Real = sourceNumber.Real
      Me.Imaginary = sourceNumber.Imaginary
   End Sub

   Public Overrides Function ToString() As String
      Return Real & "+" & Imaginary & "i"
   End Function

   Public Shared Operator +(ByVal a As ComplexNumber, _
         ByVal b As ComplexNumber) As ComplexNumber
      ' ----- Add two complex numbers together.
      Return New ComplexNumber(a.Real + b.Real, _
         a.Imaginary + b.Imaginary)
   End Operator

   Public Shared Operator -(ByVal a As ComplexNumber, _
         ByVal b As ComplexNumber) As ComplexNumber
      ' ----- Subtract one complex number from another.
      Return New ComplexNumber(a.Real - b.Real, _
         a.Imaginary - b.Imaginary)
   End Operator

   Public Shared Operator *(ByVal a As ComplexNumber, _
         ByVal b As ComplexNumber) As ComplexNumber
      ' ----- Multiply two complex numbers together.
      Return New ComplexNumber(a.Real * b.Real - _
         a.Imaginary * b.Imaginary, _
         a.Real * b.Imaginary + a.Imaginary * b.Real)
   End Operator
```

```
      Public Shared Operator /(ByVal a As ComplexNumber, _
            ByVal b As ComplexNumber) As ComplexNumber
         ' ----- Divide one complex number by another.
         Return a * Reciprocal(b)
      End Operator

      Public Shared Function Reciprocal( _
            ByVal a As ComplexNumber) As ComplexNumber
         ' ----- Calculate the reciprocal of a complex number;
         '       that is, the 1/x calculation.
         Dim divisor As Double

         ' ----- Check for divide-by-zero possibility.
         divisor = a.Real * a.Real + a.Imaginary * a.Imaginary
         If (divisor = 0.0#) Then Throw New DivideByZeroException

         ' ----- Perform the operation.
         Return New ComplexNumber(a.Real / divisor, _
            -a.Imaginary / divisor)
      End Function
   End Structure
```

The overloaded New( ) function lets you instantiate a ComplexNumber number using
either a pair of numbers (the real and imaginary parts) or another ComplexNumber
number.

The following code demonstrates how complex numbers are created and how standard operators allow mathematical operations such as addition and subtraction in a natural way. The overloaded + operator also impacts the += assignment operator. The last example in the code demonstrates this by adding complex number b to complex number a using the new assignment-operator syntax:

```
Dim result As New System.Text.StringBuilder
Dim a As ComplexNumber
Dim b As ComplexNumber
Dim c As ComplexNumber

a = New ComplexNumber(3, 4)
b = New ComplexNumber(5, -2)
c = a + b

result.AppendLine("Complex Numbers")
result.AppendLine("a = " & a.ToString( ))
result.AppendLine("b = " & b.ToString( ))

' ----- Addition.
c = a + b
result.AppendLine("a + b = " & c.ToString( ))

' ----- Subtraction.
c = a - b
result.AppendLine("a - b = " & c.ToString( ))
```

```
' ----- Multiplication.
c = a * b
result.AppendLine("a * b = " & c.ToString())

' ----- Division.
c = a / b
result.AppendLine("a / b = " & c.ToString())

' ----- Addition as assignment.
a += b
result.AppendLine("a += b ... a = " & a.ToString())

MsgBox(result.ToString())
```

The ToString() function is overridden in the ComplexNumber structure to format the real and imaginary parts. Figure 6-16 shows the output from the sample code.

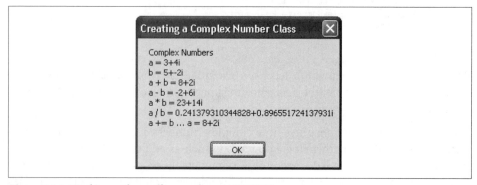

Figure 6-16. Working with complex numbers in VB 2005

See Also

Search for "complex numbers" on the Web for more information on this subject.

6.17   Solving Right Triangles

Problem

You want to calculate all the remaining sides and angles of a right triangle given two known parts of the triangle.

Solution

Sample code folder: Chapter 06\RightTriangle

Create a RightTriangle class that calculates all parts of a right triangle given any two of its parts.

Discussion

The parts of a right triangle we are concerned with are the two sides A and B adjacent to the right angle, the hypotenuse (the side opposite the right angle), and the two angles formed where the hypotenuse meets sides A and B. If you know any two of these values, all the rest can be determined.

There are many ways to set up the RightTriangle class, and the technique chosen here is not the only reasonable approach to the problem. We chose to use the initializing function New( ) to define the triangle by passing in nonzero numbers for the known parts and a value of zero for the unknowns. The IntelliSense pop-up prompt makes it easy to remember what parts of the triangle are passed in at each parameter position. It's as easy as filling in the blanks. The code for the RightTriangle class is as follows:

```
Public Class RightTriangle
    Private StoredSideA As Double
    Private StoredSideB As Double
    Private StoredHypotenuse As Double
    Private StoredAngleA As Double
    Private StoredAngleB As Double

    Public Sub New(ByVal hypotenuse As Double, _
        ByVal sideA As Double, ByVal sideB As Double, _
        ByVal angleA As Double, ByVal angleB As Double)
        Me.StoredHypotenuse = hypotenuse
        Me.StoredSideA = sideA
        Me.StoredSideB = sideB
        Me.StoredAngleA = angleA
        Me.StoredAngleB = angleB
        Me.Resolve( )
    End Sub

    Public ReadOnly Property SideA( ) As Double
        Get
            Return StoredSideA
        End Get
    End Property

    Public ReadOnly Property SideB( ) As Double
        Get
            Return StoredSideB
        End Get
    End Property

    Public ReadOnly Property AngleA( ) As Double
        Get
            Return StoredAngleA
        End Get
    End Property

    Public ReadOnly Property AngleB( ) As Double
        Get
```

```
        Return StoredAngleB
    End Get
End Property

Public ReadOnly Property Hypotenuse() As Double
    Get
        Return StoredHypotenuse
    End Get
End Property

Private Sub Resolve()
    ' ----- Figure out the missing (zero) parts of the
    '       triangle. Start with the angles.
    If (StoredAngleA = 0.0#) And _
        (StoredAngleB <> 0.0#) Then _
        StoredAngleA = Math.PI / 2 - StoredAngleB
    If (StoredAngleB = 0.0#) And _
        (StoredAngleA <> 0.0#) Then _
        StoredAngleB = Math.PI / 2 - StoredAngleA
    If (StoredAngleA <> 0.0#) And _
        (StoredHypotenuse <> 0.0#) Then _
        StoredSideB = StoredHypotenuse * _
        Math.Cos(StoredAngleA)
    If (StoredAngleB <> 0.0#) And _
        (StoredHypotenuse <> 0.0#) Then _
        StoredSideA = StoredHypotenuse * _
        Math.Cos(StoredAngleB)
    If (StoredAngleA <> 0.0#) And _
        (StoredSideA <> 0.0#) Then _
        StoredHypotenuse = StoredSideA / _
        Math.Sin(StoredAngleA)
    If (StoredAngleB <> 0.0#) And _
        (StoredSideB <> 0.0#) Then _
        StoredHypotenuse = StoredSideB / _
        Math.Sin(StoredAngleB)
    If (StoredAngleA <> 0.0#) And _
        (StoredSideB <> 0.0#) Then _
        StoredHypotenuse = StoredSideB / _
        Math.Cos(StoredAngleA)
    If (StoredAngleB <> 0.0#) And _
        (StoredSideA <> 0.0#) Then _
        StoredHypotenuse = StoredSideA / _
        Math.Cos(StoredAngleB)

    ' ----- Now calculate the sides.
    If (StoredSideA <> 0.0#) And _
        (StoredSideB <> 0.0#) Then _
        StoredHypotenuse = Math.Sqrt(StoredSideA ^ 2 + _
        StoredSideB ^ 2)
    If (StoredSideA <> 0.0#) And _
        (StoredHypotenuse <> 0.0#) Then _
        StoredSideB = Math.Sqrt(StoredHypotenuse ^ 2 - _
        StoredSideA ^ 2)
    If (StoredSideB <> 0.0#) And _
```

```
            (StoredHypotenuse <> 0.0#) Then _
                StoredSideA = Math.Sqrt(StoredHypotenuse ^ 2 - _
                StoredSideB ^ 2)
            If (StoredAngleA = 0.0#) Then StoredAngleA = _
                Math.Asin(StoredSideA / StoredHypotenuse)
            If (StoredAngleB = 0.0#) Then StoredAngleB = _
                Math.Asin(StoredSideB / StoredHypotenuse)
        End Sub

        Public Overrides Function Tostring() As String
            ' ----- Display all values of the triangle.
            Dim result As New System.Text.StringBuilder

            result.AppendLine("Right Triangle:")
            result.AppendLine("Hypotenuse=" & _
                StoredHypotenuse.ToString)
            result.AppendLine("Side A=" & StoredSideA.ToString)
            result.AppendLine("Side B=" & StoredSideB.ToString)
            result.AppendLine("Angle A=" & StoredAngleA.ToString)
            result.Append("Angle B=" & StoredAngleB.ToString)
            Return result.ToString()
        End Function
    End Class
```

The core calculations of this class are performed in the private Resolve() function. There, the various triangle parts are tested to see if they are nonzero, and the appropriate calculations are performed to start filling in the blanks for the unknowns. Resolve() is called just once, at the moment when the RightTriangle object is instantiated. All the parts of the right triangle are later returned as required via read-only properties.

Visual Basic internally always assumes angles to be in radians, even though degrees are the most commonly used units for angles among the general population. It's tempting to use degrees in user-defined classes and procedures, but for consistency this book will assume radians throughout.

The following sample code creates an instance of the RightTriangle object and uses it to calculate a typical right triangle. In this example, the lengths of sides A and B are known. All other parts of the triangle are passed as zero when the RightTriangle is instantiated:

```
Dim testTriangle As RightTriangle
Dim area As Double

testTriangle = New RightTriangle(0, 3, 4, 0, 0)
area = (testTriangle.SideA * testTriangle.SideB) / 2
MsgBox(testTriangle.Tostring & vbNewLine & _
    "Area = " & area.ToString)
```

Figure 6-17 shows the results of calculating the missing parts of a right triangle with sides A and B of lengths 3 and 4.

Figure 6-17. Using the RightTriangle class to calculate unknown parts of a right triangle

See Also

Search for "right triangle" on the Web for more information about this subject (see, for example, *http://mathworld.wolfram.com/RightTriangle.html*).

6.18   Solving Any Triangle

Problem

You want to solve any triangle given any three known parts. Examples might include the lengths of any two sides and the measure of the angle between them, or the measures of two angles and the length of the side between them.

Solution

Sample code folder: Chapter 06\AnyTriangle

Create a `Triangle` class to handle the details of calculating all the remaining parts of a triangle given any combination of three of its parts. Also create a separate utility function to calculate any triangle's area given the lengths of its three sides.

Discussion

The `Triangle` class, presented below, allows the remaining elements of any triangle to be calculated given the measures of any three of its sides and angles. The only combination that won't work, of course, is when three angles are given, as these pin down the shape of a triangle but not its size. Here is the code for the `Triangle` class:

```
Imports System.Math

Public Class Triangle
    Private StoredSideA As Double
    Private StoredSideB As Double
    Private StoredSideC As Double
    Private StoredAngleA As Double
```

```vb
Private StoredAngleB As Double
Private StoredAngleC As Double

' ----- The GivenParts variable indicates which parts
'       the user has already supplied. Uppercase letters
'       (A, B, C) indicate sides; lowercase letters
'       (a, b, c) are angles.
Private GivenParts As String = ""

Public Overrides Function ToString() As String
    ' ----- Show the details of the triangle.
    Return String.Format( _
        "SideA={0}, SideB={1}, SideC={2}, " & _
        "AngleA={3}, AngleB={4}, AngleC={5}", _
        StoredSideA, StoredSideB, StoredSideC, _
        StoredAngleA, StoredAngleB, StoredAngleC)
End Function

Public Property SideA() As Double
    Get
        If (GivenParts.Length >= 3) Then _
            Return StoredSideA Else NotYet()
    End Get
    Set(ByVal Value As Double)
        If (Value < 0) Then _
            Throw New ArgumentOutOfRangeException( _
            "Negative side length (A) not allowed.")
        CheckIt("A")
        StoredSideA = Value
        Resolve()
    End Set
End Property

Public Property SideB() As Double
    Get
        If (GivenParts.Length >= 3) Then _
            Return StoredSideB Else NotYet()
    End Get
    Set(ByVal Value As Double)
        If (Value < 0) Then _
            Throw New ArgumentOutOfRangeException( _
            "Negative side length (B) not allowed.")
        CheckIt("B")
        StoredSideB = Value
        Resolve()
    End Set
End Property

Public Property SideC() As Double
    Get
        If (GivenParts.Length >= 3) Then _
            Return StoredSideC Else NotYet()
    End Get
    Set(ByVal Value As Double)
```

```
        If (Value < 0) Then _
            Throw New ArgumentOutOfRangeException( _
            "Negative side length (C) not allowed.")
        CheckIt("C")
        StoredSideC = Value
        Resolve( )
    End Set
End Property

Public Property AngleA( ) As Double
    Get
        If (GivenParts.Length >= 3) Then _
            Return StoredAngleA Else NotYet( )
    End Get
    Set(ByVal Value As Double)
        If (Value < 0) Or (Value > Math.PI) Then _
            Throw New Exception( _
            "Angle (A) must range from 0 to PI.")
        CheckIt("a")
        StoredAngleA = Value
        Resolve( )
    End Set
End Property

Public Property AngleB( ) As Double
    Get
        If (GivenParts.Length >= 3) Then _
            Return StoredAngleB Else NotYet( )
    End Get
    Set(ByVal Value As Double)
        If (Value < 0) Or (Value > Math.PI) Then _
            Throw New Exception( _
            "Angle (B) must range from 0 to PI.")
        CheckIt("b")
        StoredAngleB = Value
        Resolve( )
    End Set
End Property

Public Property AngleC( ) As Double
    Get
        If (GivenParts.Length >= 3) Then _
            Return StoredAngleC Else NotYet( )
    End Get
    Set(ByVal Value As Double)
        If (Value < 0) Or (Value > Math.PI) Then _
            Throw New Exception( _
            "Angle (C) must range from 0 to PI.")
        CheckIt("c")
        StoredAngleC = Value
        Resolve( )
    End Set
End Property
```

```
Private Sub CheckIt(ByVal whatToCheck As String)
    ' ----- Make sure it is OK to adjust a component.
    If (GivenParts.Length >= 3) Then Throw New Exception( _
        "Triangle is immutable once defined by three parts.")
    If (GivenParts.IndexOf(whatToCheck) >= 0) Then _
        Throw New Exception( _
        "Triangle component cannot be modified once set.")

    ' ---- Mark this part as modified.
    GivenParts &= whatToCheck
End Sub

Private Sub NotYet()
    ' ----- The user tried to access components before
    '         anything was calculated.
    Throw New Exception( _
        "Triangle has not yet been completely defined.")
End Sub

Private Sub Resolve()
    ' ----- Calculate the missing angles and sides of
    '         the triangle.
    Dim sinRatio As Double
    Dim inSort() As Char

    ' ----- Wait for the triangle to be completely defined.
    If (GivenParts.Length < 3) Then Return

    ' ----- Sort the known parts list.
    inSort = GivenParts.ToCharArray()
    Array.Sort(inSort)
    GivenParts = New String(inSort)

    ' ----- Time to resolve. In all cases, the goal is to
    '         get three known sides. Then, the ResolveABC()
    '         method can work on getting the missing angles.
    Select Case GivenParts
        Case "ABC"
            ResolveABC()
        Case "ABa"
            sinRatio = Sin(StoredAngleA) / StoredSideA
            StoredAngleB = Asin(StoredSideB * sinRatio)
            StoredAngleC = PI - StoredAngleA - StoredAngleB
            StoredSideC = Sin(StoredAngleC) / sinRatio
        Case "ABb"
            sinRatio = Sin(StoredAngleB) / StoredSideB
            StoredAngleA = Asin(StoredSideA * sinRatio)
            StoredAngleC = PI - StoredAngleA - StoredAngleB
            StoredSideC = Sin(StoredAngleC) / sinRatio
        Case "ABc"
            StoredSideC = Sqrt(StoredSideA ^ 2 + _
                StoredSideB ^ 2 - 2 * StoredSideA * _
                StoredSideB * Cos(StoredAngleC))
        Case "ACa"
```

```
            sinRatio = Sin(StoredAngleA) / StoredSideA
            StoredAngleC = Asin(StoredSideC * sinRatio)
            StoredAngleB = PI - StoredAngleA - StoredAngleC
            StoredSideB = Sin(StoredAngleB) / sinRatio
        Case "ACb"
            StoredSideB = Sqrt(StoredSideA ^ 2 + _
                StoredSideC ^ 2 - 2 * StoredSideA * _
                StoredSideC * Cos(StoredAngleB))
        Case "ACc"
            sinRatio = Sin(StoredAngleC) / StoredSideC
            StoredAngleA = Asin(StoredSideA * sinRatio)
            StoredAngleB = PI - StoredAngleA - StoredAngleC
            StoredSideB = Sin(StoredAngleB) / sinRatio
        Case "Aab"
            sinRatio = Sin(StoredAngleA) / StoredSideA
            StoredSideB = Sin(StoredAngleB) / sinRatio
            StoredAngleC = PI - StoredAngleA - StoredAngleB
            StoredSideC = Sin(StoredAngleC) / sinRatio
        Case "Aac"
            sinRatio = Sin(StoredAngleA) / StoredSideA
            StoredSideC = Sin(StoredAngleC) / sinRatio
            StoredAngleB = PI - StoredAngleA - StoredAngleC
            StoredSideB = Sin(StoredAngleB) / sinRatio
        Case "Abc"
            StoredAngleA = PI - StoredAngleB - StoredAngleC
            sinRatio = Sin(StoredAngleA) / StoredSideA
            StoredSideB = Sin(StoredAngleB) / sinRatio
            StoredSideC = Sin(StoredAngleC) / sinRatio
        Case "BCa"
            StoredSideA = Sqrt(StoredSideB ^ 2 + _
                StoredSideC ^ 2 - 2 * StoredSideB * _
                StoredSideC * Cos(StoredAngleA))
        Case "BCb"
            sinRatio = Sin(StoredAngleB) / StoredSideB
            StoredAngleC = Asin(StoredSideC * sinRatio)
            StoredAngleA = PI - StoredAngleB - StoredAngleC
            StoredSideA = Sin(StoredAngleA) / sinRatio
        Case "BCc"
            sinRatio = Sin(StoredAngleC) / StoredSideC
            StoredAngleB = Asin(StoredSideB * sinRatio)
            StoredAngleA = PI - StoredAngleB - StoredAngleC
            StoredSideA = Sin(StoredAngleA) / sinRatio
        Case "Bab"
            StoredAngleC = PI - StoredAngleA - StoredAngleB
            sinRatio = Sin(StoredAngleB) / StoredSideB
            StoredSideA = Sin(StoredAngleA) / sinRatio
            StoredSideC = Sin(StoredAngleC) / sinRatio
        Case "Bac"
            StoredAngleB = PI - StoredAngleA - StoredAngleC
            sinRatio = Sin(StoredAngleB) / StoredSideB
            StoredSideA = Sin(StoredAngleA) / sinRatio
            StoredSideC = Sin(StoredAngleC) / sinRatio
        Case "Bbc"
            StoredAngleA = PI - StoredAngleB - StoredAngleC
```

```
            sinRatio = Sin(StoredAngleB) / StoredSideB
            StoredSideA = Sin(StoredAngleA) / sinRatio
            StoredSideC = Sin(StoredAngleC) / sinRatio
         Case "Cab"
            StoredAngleC = PI - StoredAngleA - StoredAngleB
            sinRatio = Sin(StoredAngleC) / StoredSideC
            StoredSideA = Sin(StoredAngleA) / sinRatio
            StoredSideB = Sin(StoredAngleB) / sinRatio
         Case "Cac"
            StoredAngleB = PI - StoredAngleA - StoredAngleC
            sinRatio = Sin(StoredAngleC) / StoredSideC
            StoredSideA = Sin(StoredAngleA) / sinRatio
            StoredSideB = Sin(StoredAngleB) / sinRatio
         Case "Cbc"
            StoredAngleA = PI - StoredAngleB - StoredAngleC
            sinRatio = Sin(StoredAngleC) / StoredSideC
            StoredSideA = Sin(StoredAngleA) / sinRatio
            StoredSideB = Sin(StoredAngleB) / sinRatio
         Case "abc"
            Throw New Exception("Cannot resolve " & _
               "triangle with only angles specified.")
         Case Else
            Throw New Exception( _
               "Undefined combination of triangle parts.")
      End Select
      ResolveABC()
   End Sub

   Private Sub ResolveABC()
      ' ----- All three sides are known. Calculate the angles.
      LengthCheck(StoredSideA, StoredSideB, StoredSideC)
      StoredAngleC = Acos((StoredSideA ^ 2 + _
         StoredSideB ^ 2 - StoredSideC ^ 2) / _
         (2 * StoredSideA * StoredSideB))
      StoredAngleB = Acos((StoredSideA ^ 2 + _
         StoredSideC ^ 2 - StoredSideB ^ 2) / _
         (2 * StoredSideA * StoredSideC))
      StoredAngleA = PI - StoredAngleB - StoredAngleC
   End Sub

   Private Sub LengthCheck(ByVal A As Double, _
         ByVal B As Double, ByVal C As Double)
      ' ----- Make sure that one of the sides isn't
      '       too long for the other two.
      If (A >= B) AndAlso (A >= C) AndAlso _
         (A <= (B + C)) Then Return
      If (B >= A) AndAlso (B >= C) AndAlso _
         (B <= (A + C)) Then Return
      If (C >= A) AndAlso (C >= B) AndAlso _
         (C <= (A + B)) Then Return
      Throw New Exception( _
         "One side is too long for the others.")
   End Sub
End Class
```

Exceptions are thrown if the triangle "doesn't make sense." For example, if the sum of two sides is less than the length of the third, or if three angles are given, the triangle is impossible, or at least the data is insufficient to completely define the triangle.

To find the area of any triangle, you could include a shared function within the Triangle class, but for the sake of demonstration (and because it can be useful in a wider variety of computational situations) we've chosen to create a TriangleArea( ) function separate from the class. This makes it easy to find the area of any triangle given the lengths of its three sides, whether or not you're solving triangles using the Triangle class:

```
Public Function TriangleArea(ByVal sideA As Double, _
    ByVal sideB As Double, _
    ByVal sideC As Double) As Double
  ' ----- Calculate the area of a triangle.
  Dim sumHalfSides As Double
  Dim deltaA As Double
  Dim deltaB As Double
  Dim deltaC As Double

  sumHalfSides = (sideA + sideB + sideC) / 2
  deltaA = sumHalfSides - sideA
  deltaB = sumHalfSides - sideB
  deltaC = sumHalfSides - sideC
  Return Math.Sqrt(sumHalfSides * deltaA * deltaB * deltaC)
End Function
```

The following code demonstrates the use of the Triangle class by solving for a triangle that has two sides of length 4 and 5, with a 75°; angle between the two sides. The RadPerDeg constant (see Recipe 6.10) converts 75° to radians at compile time rather than at runtime (to be consistent with all other angular measurements in Visual Basic 2005, radians are always assumed in all the procedures in this book that involve angles):

```
Const RadPerDeg As Double = Math.PI / 180
Dim testTriangle As New Triangle
Dim area As Double

' ----- Build a triangle with sides of 4 and 5, and an
'       angle between them of 75 degrees.
testTriangle.SideA = 4
testTriangle.SideB = 5
testTriangle.AngleC = 75 * RadPerDeg

' ----- The triangle is already resolved. Calculate area.
area = TriangleArea(testTriangle.SideA, _
    testTriangle.SideB, testTriangle.SideC)

MsgBox(testTriangle.ToString & vbNewLine & _
    "Area = " & area.ToString)
```

A ToString( ) function is included in the Triangle class to provide a default format for presenting the triangle's parts in a single string. The solved triangle for our example is shown in Figure 6-18.

Figure 6-18. Solving a triangle with the Triangle class

6.19   Determining if a String Contains a Valid Number

Problem

You want to verify that a user-entered string contains a valid number.

Solution

Use Visual Basic's `IsNumeric( )` function to check the string.

Discussion

Visual Basic 2005 provides a function named `IsNumeric( )` that checks the content of any string, returning a Boolean `True` if the string contains a valid number representation and `False` if it doesn't:

```
Dim result As New System.Text.StringBuilder
Dim testString As String

testString = "2.E3"
result.Append(testString).Append(vbTab)
result.AppendLine(IsNumeric(testString).ToString)

testString = "2.D3"
result.Append(testString).Append(vbTab)
result.AppendLine(IsNumeric(testString).ToString)

testString = "-123"
result.Append(testString).Append(vbTab)
result.AppendLine(IsNumeric(testString).ToString)

testString = "-1 2 3"
result.Append(testString).Append(vbTab)
result.AppendLine(IsNumeric(testString).ToString)

testString = "$54.32"
result.Append(testString).Append(vbTab)
result.AppendLine(IsNumeric(testString).ToString)

MsgBox(result.ToString( ))
```

Currency values are valid numbers, even with the currency symbol included. The IsNumeric( ) function expects a single number in the string, so extra spaces, such as those shown in the next-to-last string in the example, cause IsNumeric( ) to return False. If you want to determine how many valid numbers are in a string, and be able to grab them all, consider using regular expressions instead.

Figure 6-19 shows the strings used in this example and the results returned by IsNumeric( ) for each.

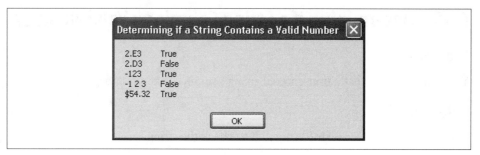

Figure 6-19. Testing whether a string contains a valid number using IsNumeric( )

6.20   Converting Numbers to Integers

Problem

You want to convert numbers to integers, or perhaps truncate or round values to integer values, and you want to understand the various ways to do this.

Solution

As always, use the best tool for the job. If you want to remove decimal parts of a number, consider using Int( ), Floor( ), or the Round( ) function. But if you want to convert a numeric value to an Integer data type, use CInt( ) or Convert.ToInteger( ) instead.

Discussion

The following code demonstrates differences between the CInt( ) and Int( ) functions. Once you gain a good understanding of these two functions, you'll be well on your way to understanding similar functions such as Round( ), Convert.ToInteger( ), and so on.

One important difference between CInt( ) and Int( ) is that Int( ) is overloaded to work with a wide variety of numeric data types. For example, you can pass a Double, such as the value of π, to Int( ), and it will return another Double value that no longer has any post-decimal digits (i.e., it will round to a whole number). This is entirely different from converting a number to an Integer. The Int( ) function works on numbers that are way out of the legal range for an Integer. Using CInt( ) on similar numbers would throw an exception.

The two functions are demonstrated in the following code:

```
Dim result As New System.Text.StringBuilder
Dim number As Double

' ----- Positive decimal value.
number = 3.14
result.Append(number)
result.Append("   CInt( ): ")
result.Append(CInt(number).ToString)
result.Append("   Int( ): ")
result.AppendLine(Int(number).ToString)

' ----- Negative decimal value.
number = -3.14
result.Append(number)
result.Append("   CInt( ): ")
result.Append(CInt(number).ToString)
result.Append("   Int( ): ")
result.AppendLine(Int(number).ToString)

' ----- Number that won't fit in an Integer.
number = 3000000000.0
result.Append(number)
result.Append("   CInt( ): ")
Try
    result.Append(CInt(number).ToString)
Catch
    result.Append("(error)")
End Try
result.Append("   Int( ): ")
result.Append(Int(number).ToString)

MsgBox(result.ToString( ))
```

There are some other functions in the Math object that provide similar functionality to Int( ). For example, the Math.Floor( ) and Math.Ceiling( ) functions also operate on numbers that might be out of the range of Integers. Floor( ) returns the largest whole number less than or equal to a given number, and Ceiling( ) returns the smallest whole number that's greater than or equal to a given number. See Figure 6-20.

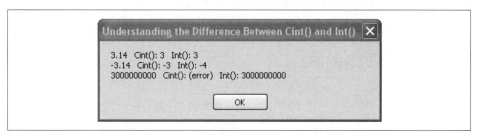

Figure 6-20. The CInt() function converts numbers to Integer data types, while the Int() function returns whole numbers

6.21   Calculating π to Thousands of Digits

Problem

You want to impress people by showing how quickly Visual Basic 2005 can calculate π to a thousand or more decimal places. While you're at it, you might want to discover how to create multidigit mathematical functions using integer arrays of digits.

Solution

Sample code folder: Chapter 06\CalculatePi

Create functions for basic mathematical operations (+, -, *, /) that operate on integer arrays of any reasonable size. Then demonstrate these functions by calculating π to many digits using one of the standard π-calculation algorithms.

Discussion

This recipe includes a module called PiCalculator that contains the functions needed to perform multidigit math, along with one to calculate π to any number of digits. The four main multidigit functions are named ArrayMult( ), ArrayDivide( ), ArrayAdd( ), and ArraySub( ). These are declared as Private to the module because they serve only as support routines to the FindPi( ) function, but you can change them to Public to experiment with them for other purposes. Other supporting functions include ArrayZero( ), which sets all "digits" in an array to zeros, and ArcTangent( ), which calls the other functions to calculate the arctangent of a multidigit number.

The way the basic math functions work is similar to the way math is performed on paper by grade-schoolers: when two digits are added, any overflow is added into the next pair of digits, and so on. Calculating π to 500 decimal places requires a huge number of these small repetitive calculations, but that's what computers are really good at doing.

Here is the code to calculate π. It is based on the following calculation for π:

$$\pi/4 \ = \ \arctan(1/2) + \arctan(1/3)$$

Each part of the algorithm is performed manually, including the arctangent calculation:

```
Module PiCalculator
    Private NumberDigits As Integer

    Public Function FindPi(ByVal digits As Integer) As String
        ' ----- Calculate Pi to the specified number of digits,
        '       based on the formula:
        '             Pi/4 = arctan(1/2) + arctan(1/3)
        Dim result As New System.Text.StringBuilder("PI=3.")
        Dim digitIndex As Integer
        Dim divFactor As Integer
```

```
    ' ----- Build an array that will hold manual calculations.
    NumberDigits = digits + 2
    Dim targetValue(NumberDigits) As Integer
    Dim sourceValue(NumberDigits) As Integer

    ' ---- Perform the calculation.
    divFactor = 2
    ArcTangent(targetValue, sourceValue, divFactor)
    divFactor = 3
    ArcTangent(targetValue, sourceValue, divFactor)
    ArrayMult(targetValue, 4)

    ' ----- Return a string version of the calculation.
    For digitIndex = 1 To NumberDigits - 3
        result.Append(Chr(targetValue(digitIndex) + Asc("0"c)))
    Next digitIndex
    Return result.ToString
End Function

Private Sub ArrayMult(ByRef baseNumber( ) As Integer, _
        ByRef multiplier As Integer)
    ' ----- Multiply an array number by another number by hand.
    '         The product remains in the array number.
    Dim carry As Integer
    Dim position As Integer
    Dim holdDigit As Integer

    ' ----- Multiple each base digit, from right to left.
    For position = NumberDigits To 0 Step -1
        ' ----- If the multiplication went past 9, carry the
        '         tens value to the next column.
        holdDigit = (baseNumber(position) * multiplier) + carry
        carry = holdDigit \ 10
        baseNumber(position) = holdDigit Mod 10
    Next position
End Sub

Private Sub ArrayDivide(ByRef dividend( ) As Integer, ByRef divisor As Integer)
    ' ----- Divide an array number by another number by hand.
    '         The quotient remains in the array number.
    Dim borrow As Integer
    Dim position As Integer
    Dim holdDigit As Integer

    ' ----- Process division for each digit.
    For position = 0 To NumberDigits
        ' ----- If the division can't happen directly, borrow from
        '         the previous position.
        holdDigit = dividend(position) + borrow * 10
        dividend(position) = holdDigit \ divisor
        borrow = holdDigit Mod divisor
    Next position
End Sub
```

```
Private Sub ArrayAdd(ByRef baseNumber() As Integer, ByRef addend() As Integer)
    ' ----- Add two array numbers together.
    '       The sum remains in the first array number.
    Dim carry As Integer
    Dim position As Integer
    Dim holdDigit As Integer

    ' ----- Add each digit from right to left.
    For position = NumberDigits To 0 Step -1
        ' ----- If the sum goes beyond 9, carry the tens
        '       value to the next column.
        holdDigit = baseNumber(position) + addend(position) + carry
        carry = holdDigit \ 10
        baseNumber(position) = holdDigit Mod 10
    Next position
End Sub

Private Sub ArraySub(ByRef minuend() As Integer, ByRef subtrahend() As Integer)
    ' ----- Subtract one array number from another.
    '       The difference remains in the first array number.
    Dim borrow As Integer
    Dim position As Integer
    Dim holdDigit As Integer

    ' ---- Subtract the digits from right to left.
    For position = NumberDigits To 0 Step -1
        ' ----- If the subtraction would give a negative value
        '       for a column, we will have to borrow.
        holdDigit = minuend(position) - subtrahend(position) + 10
        borrow = holdDigit \ 10
        minuend(position) = holdDigit Mod 10
        If (borrow = 0) Then minuend(position - 1) -= 1
    Next position
End Sub

Private Function ArrayZero(ByRef baseNumber() As Integer) As Boolean
    ' ----- Report whether an array number is all zero.
    Dim position As Integer

    ' ----- Examine each digit.
    For position = 0 To NumberDigits
        If (baseNumber(position) <> 0) Then
            ' ----- The number is nonzero.
            Return False
        End If
    Next position

    ' ----- The number is zero.
    Return True
End Function

Private Sub ArcTangent(ByRef targetValue() As Integer, _
        ByRef sourceValue() As Integer, _
        ByVal divFactor As Integer)
```

```
' ----- Calculate an arctangent of a fraction,
'          1/divFactor. This routine performs a modified
'          Maclaurin series to calculate the arctangent.
'          The base formula is:
'              arctan(x) = x - x^3/3 + x^5/5 -
'                            x^7/7 + x^9/9 - ...
'          where -1 < x < 1 (1/divFactor in this case).
Dim workingFactor As Integer
Dim incremental As Integer

' ----- Figure out the "x" part, 1/divFactor.
sourceValue(0) = 1
incremental = 1
workingFactor = divFactor
ArrayDivide(sourceValue, workingFactor)

' ----- Add "x" to the total.
ArrayAdd(targetValue, sourceValue)
Do
    ' ----- Perform the "- (x^y)/y" part.
    ArrayMult(sourceValue, incremental)
    workingFactor = divFactor * divFactor
    ArrayDivide(sourceValue, workingFactor)
    incremental += 2
    workingFactor = incremental
    ArrayDivide(sourceValue, workingFactor)
    ArraySub(targetValue, sourceValue)

    ' ----- Perform the "+ (x^y)/y" part.
    ArrayMult(sourceValue, incremental)
    workingFactor = divFactor * divFactor
    ArrayDivide(sourceValue, workingFactor)
    incremental += 2
    workingFactor = incremental
    ArrayDivide(sourceValue, workingFactor)
    ArrayAdd(targetValue, sourceValue)
Loop Until ArrayZero(sourceValue)
    End Sub
End Module
```

To exercise these procedures, the following statement uses the FindPi( ) function to calculate π to 500 digits:

```
MsgBox(FindPi(500))
```

You can change the 500 argument to obtain a different number of digits. However, even though the time required to calculate π to 500 or even 1,000 digits is fairly negligible, every time you double the count, the FindPi( ) function requires around four times as long to return the results. Try smaller counts first, moving up to larger counts when you have a good feel for just how long the calculation will take on your computer.

Figure 6-21 shows the first 500 digits of π as formatted by the FindPi( ) function. If you prefer to format the digits differently, say in groups of 10 digits or with occasional end-of-line characters, you might want to change FindPi( ) to return an array of digits. The calling code can then format the digits as desired. The "digits" in the array have values in the range 0 to 9, and they need to be converted to ASCII digits by adding the ASCII equivalent of "0" (zero) to their value before applying the Chr( ) conversion function.

Figure 6-21. Pi calculated to 500 decimal places

See Also

There are many places on the Web to see many digits of π and to learn of the different algorithms used for calculating π to even millions of decimal places. See, for example, *http://www.exploratorium.edu/pi/Pi10-6.html*.

6.22   Getting a Number's Prime Factors

Problem

You need to determine all prime factors of a given number, perhaps for demonstrating cryptographic algorithms or for some other purpose.

Solution

Sample code folder: Chapter 06\PrimeFactor

Create a function called PrimeFactors( ) that analyzes any Long integer and returns a string listing all the number's prime factors in a clear format.

Discussion

The algorithm used here is fairly straightforward, suitable for reasonably sized Long integers. The prime factors are found by checking for even divisibility by numbers from 2 to the square root of the number being checked. Whenever a factor is found, it is extracted, and the divisibility check is repeated. Tallies for the factors are converted to string format during this process, and the string is returned when all the checks are completed:

```
Private Function PrimeFactors( _
      ByVal numberToFactor As Long) As String
   ' ----- Calculate the prime factors of a starting number.
```

```
Dim result As New System.Text.StringBuilder
Dim testFactor As Long
Dim workNumber As Long
Dim factorCount As Long

' ----- Scan through all numbers up to
'       Sqrt(numberToFactor).
workNumber = numberToFactor
testFactor = 1
Do While (testFactor < Math.Sqrt(CType(workNumber, _
      Double)))
   testFactor += 1
   factorCount = 0
   Do While (workNumber / testFactor) = _
         (workNumber \ testFactor)
      ' ----- Found a factor.
      factorCount += 1
      workNumber \= testFactor
   Loop
   Select Case factorCount
      Case 1
         ' ----- Show a prime factor.
         result.AppendLine(testFactor)
      Case Is > 1
         ' ----- Show a prime factor as a power.
         result.Append(testFactor)
         result.Append("^")
         result.AppendLine(factorCount)
   End Select
Loop

' ----- Include the final prime factor, if available.
If (workNumber > 1) Then result.Append(workNumber)
Return result.ToString
End Function
```

Here's the code that drives the example, which finds and displays the prime factors for the number 7999848:

```
Dim result As New System.Text.StringBuilder
Dim number As Long = 7999848

result.AppendLine("PrimeFactors(" & number & ")... ")
result.AppendLine( )
result.Append(PrimeFactors(number))

MsgBox(result.ToString( ))
```

Figure 6-22 shows the results of calculating that number's prime factors.

See Also

There are many good resources on the Web for learning about prime numbers and prime factors. See, for example, *http://primes.utm.edu/largest.html*.

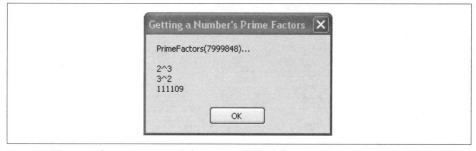

Figure 6-22. Using the PrimeFactors() function to find all the prime factors of a number in one call

6.23 Using Recursion to Calculate Factorials

Problem

You want to study a sample of Visual Basic's ability to define recursive functions, or you need a factorial function for smaller integers.

Solution

Sample code folder: Chapter 06\Factorial

Create a Factorial( ) function that recursively calls itself.

Discussion

The code in this recipe does not represent the most efficient way to calculate factorials for larger integers. You'll want to use a standard For...Next loop or similar process when working with larger numbers, simply because each recursive function call uses up stack space and adds a little overhead. However, recursive functions can be quite useful in some programming situations. A simple recursive function that calculates the factorial of a number is a great way to understand recursion.

The factorial of a number N is the product of all numbers from 1 to N. For example, the factorial of 3 is calculated as $3 \times 2 \times 1$, which results in a value of 6. The Factorial( ) function returns the value 1 if it is passed a value of zero; otherwise, it returns the passed value times the factorial of the next smaller integer. Study the Select Case lines of code in the function to see how this is accomplished:

```
Public Function Factorial(ByVal number As Decimal) As Decimal
    Select Case number
        Case Is < 0
            Throw New Exception("Factorial: Bad argument")
        Case Is = 0
            Return 1
        Case Else
            Return number * Factorial(number - 1)
    End Select
End Function
```

Calling the Factorial( ) function from inside its own code is what recursion is all about. All pending returns are literally stacked up until the value of the passed number finally reaches zero, at which time the pending multiplications all happen in a hurry. As a result of the way this recursion works, if you request the Factorial( ) of a large number, you run the risk of running out of stack memory or of numeric overflow. With Decimal variables, as shown in the previous code, the largest value you can pass to the function without overflow is just 27. Of course, the factorial of 27 is a huge number, and the answer is exact when using Decimal values. You might consider switching the algorithm to use Double values to find approximations of even larger factorials.

The following lines demonstrate the Factorial( ) function by calculating and displaying the factorial of 7:

```
Dim result As New System.Text.StringBuilder
Dim number As Decimal = 7

result.AppendLine("Factorial(" & number & ")... ")
result.AppendLine( )
result.Append(Factorial(number))

MsgBox(result.ToString( ))
```

Figure 6-23 shows the results of calculating the factorial of 7.

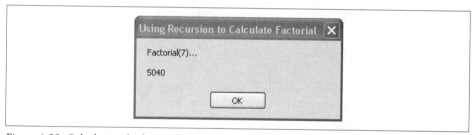

Figure 6-23. Calculating the factorial of a number with the Factorial() function

See Also

Search for "Factorial" on the Web to learn more about factorials (see, for example, *http://mathworld.wolfram.com/Factorial.html*).

6.24   Manipulating Bits with Bitwise Operators

Problem

You need to shift, mask, and perform other bitwise manipulations on integers.

Solution

Visual Basic 2005 has functions for all the major bit-manipulation techniques, and it's easy to combine these to perform more complicated bitwise calculations as required.

Discussion

There are several operators that are most often thought of as Boolean operators, working with and returning True and False (Boolean) values. However, these operators also accept and return integer values of various sizes, and this is where they can be of value for bit manipulations. These bitwise operators include the following:

And
> Bits are combined to 1 only if they are both 1.

Not
> Bits are inverted, 0 to 1 and 1 to 0.

Xor
> Bits are combined to 1 only if the two bits are not the same.

Or
> Bits are combined to 1 if either bit is a 1.

<<
> Bits are all shifted left a given number of bit positions.

>>
> Bits are all shifted right a given number of bit positions.

 The two bit-shift operators can be used as assignment operators. That is, the following two lines of code provide identical results:

```
a = a << 3
a <<= 3
```

In both cases the bits in integer variable a are shifted to the left three positions. The And, Or, Not, and Xor operators don't support assignment notation.

The following code demonstrates a sampling of these bit manipulations. You can change the program to experiment with the various operators:

```
Dim result As New System.Text.StringBuilder
Dim number As Integer = 7

result.Append(number)
result.Append(" <<= 3 ... ")
number <<= 3
result.AppendLine(number)
```

```
result.Append(number)
result.Append(" Xor 17 ... ")
number = number Xor 17
result.AppendLine(number)

MsgBox(result.ToString())
```

Figure 6-24 shows the output displayed by this sample code.

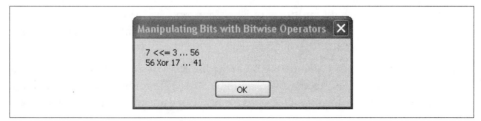

Figure 6-24. Bit manipulations with Visual Basic 2005

See Also

Search for "Logical and Bitwise Operators in Visual Basic" in Visual Studio Help to learn more about this topic.

6.25   Storing and Retrieving Bits in a BitArray

Problem

You want to store and retrieve a lot of bits without wasting memory and without sacrificing speed of operation.

Solution

Sample code folder: Chapter 06\GetPrimes

Use a BitArray to store and access individual bits in memory efficiently.

Discussion

The BitArray object lets you access bits by indexed position, and all the details of decoding which bit position of which byte the bit is stored in are taken care of transparently behind the scenes. A BitArray of 80 bits is actually stored in 10 bytes of memory.

To demonstrate using a BitArray, we've created a module named *Eratosthenes.vb* that contains code to find all prime numbers between 2 and 8,000,000 very quickly. The 8 million bits are stored in 1 million bytes of memory, and the individual bits are accessed using indexes in the range 0 to 8,000,000.

The Sieve of Eratosthenes (*http://en.wikipedia.org/wiki/Sieve_of_Eratosthenes*) works by first setting all bits to 1, or True. The BitArray can be instantiated with a count and an optional second Boolean parameter that presets all bits to True or False. In this case, True sets them all to 1. Starting with 2, each prime number, or bit that is set, clears all bits that are exact multiples of that number. So, for instance, bit 2 is kept at True, but bits 4, 6, 8, and so on, are all set to False. This marks all even numbers except for 2 as nonprime. Similarly, bit 3 is left True, and bits 6, 9, 12, 15, etc., are set to False to mark all multiples of 3 as nonprime. This looping technique very quickly sets all bits in the BitArray that appear in prime number positions to True and all other bits to False.

The Eratosthenes module contains the BitArray itself, a Sieve( ) method to set all the prime number bits as described earlier, and a GetBit( ) function to retrieve the bit at any location, converting the bit's True or False Boolean value to a 1 or 0 integer value:

```
Module Eratosthenes
    Private Const MaxNumber As Integer = 8000000
    Private PrimeStorage As New BitArray(MaxNumber, True)

    Public Sub Sieve( )
       ' ----- Get all the prime numbers from 1 to MaxNumber.
       Dim index As Integer = 1
       Dim counter As Integer

       ' ----- Scan through all primes.
       Do While (index < (MaxNumber - 1))
          index += 1
          If (PrimeStorage(index) = True) Then
             ' ----- Found a prime. Set all of its multiples
             '       to non-prime.
             For counter = index * 2 To MaxNumber - 1 _
                   Step index
                PrimeStorage(counter) = False
             Next counter
          End If
       Loop
    End Sub

    Public Function GetBit(ByVal index As Integer) As Integer
       ' ----- Retrieve the status of a single prime bit.
       If (PrimeStorage(index) = True) Then _
          Return 1 Else Return 0
    End Function
End Module
```

The following block of code demonstrates the BitArray in action, displaying the prime numbers up to the size of the BitArray. To prevent information overload, only the first and last few numbers in the desired range are formatted into a string for display, as there are a lot of prime numbers between 0 and 8,000,000:

```
Dim result As New System.Text.StringBuilder
Dim counter As Integer
Dim needBreak As Boolean = True
```

```
result.AppendLine( _
    "Prime numbers using the ""Sieve of Eratosthenes""")

' ----- Generate the primes.
Sieve()

' ----- Report each prime.
For counter = 2 To 7999999
    If (GetBit(counter) = 1) Then
        If (counter < 50) Or (counter > 7999800) Then
            ' ----- Only show a limited number of primes.
            result.AppendLine(counter)
        ElseIf (needBreak = True) Then
            ' ----- Show that we are leaving something out.
            result.AppendLine("...")
            needBreak = False
        End If
    End If
Next counter
MsgBox(result.ToString())
```

Figure 6-25 shows the partial list of all the prime numbers as determined by the bits in the BitArray. On your system there could be less than a second's delay during the computation and display of these prime numbers!

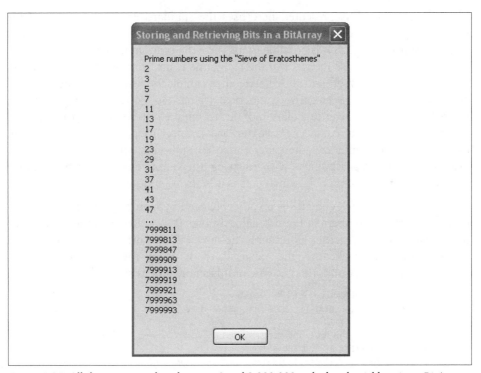

Figure 6-25. All the prime numbers between 0 and 8,000,000, calculated quickly using a BitArray

See Also

Search for "prime numbers" on the Web for more information. See also "Logical and Bitwise Operators in Visual Basic" in the Visual Studio online help.

6.26   Enhancing the Random Number Generator

Problem

You want to greatly extend the cycle length of Visual Basic's pseudorandom number generator.

Solution

Sample code folder: Chapter 06\RepeatRandom

You can use the RNGCryptoServiceProvider class to generate cryptographically strong random numbers, or you can use the technique presented here to greatly extend the cycle length of the standard pseudorandom number generator and make it easier to use.

Discussion

The BetterRandom class presented here uses the standard Rnd( ) function and the Randomize( ) initialization method, but it enhances them in several ways. Contrary to what some people claim, it is possible to initialize the random number generator to a unique but repeatable sequence, but the technique is far from obvious. You have to call the Randomize( ) method immediately after calling the Rnd( ) function, but only after passing Rnd( ) a negative numerical value. So, one advantage of this BetterRandom class is the encapsulation of this technique into something that makes a lot more sense. If you instantiate a BetterRandom object by passing any string to it, each unique string initializes the generator to a unique but repeatable state. If you instantiate a BetterRandom object with no string, the system clock generates a unique sequence for every system tick, which means it is always unique.

The cycle length of the generator is greatly enhanced by maintaining a table of pseudorandom Double numbers in the normalized range 0 to 1. Rolling indexes are used to add table entries together along with the next value returned by Rnd( ), and the result is brought back into the range 0 to 1 using the Mod operator. The GetNextDouble( ) function forms the core of this algorithm, as shown here:

```
Public Function GetNextDouble( ) As Double
    ' ----- Return the next pseudorandom number as a Double.

    ' ----- Move to the next index positions.
    Index1 = (Index1 + 1) Mod TableSize
    Index2 = (Index2 + 1) Mod TableSize
```

```
' ----- Update the random numbers at those positions.
RandomTable(Index1) += RandomTable(Index2) + Rnd()
RandomTable(Index1) = RandomTable(Index1) Mod 1.0

' ----- Return the newest random table value.
Return RandomTable(Index1)
End Function
```

This table keeps the pseudorandom values well mixed while providing a nice flat distribution of the values with excellent statistical results. When the Rnd( ) function cycles back around to its starting point, the table will be in a completely different state, which means the cycle length of the values returned from this table will be some off-the-chart astronomical value. It simply won't repeat in the amount of time there is in this universe to exercise the algorithm.

The table size is set to 32, but feel free to make the table larger or smaller as desired. A larger table will be slightly slower to initialize, but subsequent pseudorandom numbers will be calculated and returned just as fast.

Another advantage of this class is that it can be used to return several types of pseudorandom numbers. The GetNextDouble( ) function, which is demonstrated in this recipe, returns a double-precision value between 0 and 1. The next few recipes in this chapter will demonstrate how the BetterRandom class can be used to return several other types of pseudorandom numbers. The code for the class is presented here in its entirety for easy review:

```
Public Class BetterRandom
    Private Const TableSize As Integer = 32
    Private RandomTable(TableSize - 1) As Double
    Private Index1 As Integer
    Private Index2 As Integer

    Public Sub New( )
        ' ----- Generate truly pseudorandom numbers.
        InitRandom(Now.Ticks.ToString)
    End Sub

    Public Sub New(ByVal Key As String)
        ' ----- Generate a repeatable random sequence.
        InitRandom(Key)
    End Sub

    Private Sub InitRandom(ByVal repeatKey As String)
        ' ----- Prepare the random number generator.
        Dim stringIndex As Integer
        Dim workNumber As Double
        Dim counter As Integer

        ' ----- All sequences start with the same base sequence.
        Randomize(Rnd(-1))
```

```
' ----- Initialize the table using the key string.
For counter = 0 To TableSize - 1
   stringIndex = counter Mod repeatKey.Length
   workNumber = Math.PI / _
      Asc(repeatKey.Substring(stringIndex, 1))
   RandomTable(counter) = (Rnd( ) + workNumber) Mod 1.0
Next counter

' ----- Set the starting state for the table.
Index1 = TableSize \ 2
Index2 = TableSize \ 3

' ----- Cycle through a bunch of values to get a good
'       starting mix.
For counter = 0 To TableSize * 5
   GetNextDouble( )
Next counter

' ----- Reset the random sequence based on our
'       preparations.
Randomize(Rnd(-GetNextSingle( )))
End Sub

Public Function GetNextDouble( ) As Double
   ' ----- Return the next pseudorandom number as
   '       a Double.

   ' ----- Move to the next index positions.
   Index1 = (Index1 + 1) Mod TableSize
   Index2 = (Index2 + 1) Mod TableSize

   ' ----- Update the random numbers at those positions.
   RandomTable(Index1) += RandomTable(Index2) + Rnd( )
   RandomTable(Index1) = RandomTable(Index1) Mod 1.0

   ' ----- Return the newest random table value.
   Return RandomTable(Index1)
End Function

Public Function GetNextSingle( ) As Single
   ' ----- Return the next pseudorandom number as
   '       a Single.
   Return CSng(GetNextDouble( ))
End Function

Public Function GetNextInteger(ByVal minInt As Integer, _
   ByVal maxInt As Integer) As Integer
   ' ----- Return the next pseudorandom number within an
   '       Integer range.
   Return CInt(Int(GetNextDouble( ) * _
      (maxInt - minInt + 1.0) + minInt))
End Function
```

```
    Public Function GetNextReal(ByVal minReal As Double, _
        ByVal maxReal As Double) As Double
        ' ----- Return the next pseudorandom number within a
        '        floating-point range.
        Return GetNextDouble() * (maxReal - minReal) + minReal
    End Function

    Public Function GetNextNormal(ByVal mean As Double, _
        ByVal stdDev As Double) As Double
        ' ----- Return the next pseudorandom number adjusted
        '        to a normal distribution curve.
        Dim x As Double
        Dim y As Double
        Dim factor As Double
        Dim radiusSquared As Double

        Do
            x = GetNextReal(-1, 1)
            y = GetNextReal(-1, 1)
            radiusSquared = x * x + y * y
        Loop Until radiusSquared <= 1.0
        factor = Math.Sqrt(-2.0 * Math.Log(radiusSquared) / _
            radiusSquared)

        Return x * factor * stdDev + mean
    End Function

    Public Function GetNextExp(ByVal mean As Double) As Double
        ' ----- Return the next pseudorandom number adjusted
        '        for exponential distribution.
        Return -Math.Log(GetNextDouble) * mean
    End Function
End Class
```

The following code demonstrates the BetterRandom class by generating two short sequences of pseudorandom Double numbers in the range 0 to 1. The first sequence is generated uniquely each time by not passing a string during initialization of the BetterRandom object. The second sequence uses the same string each time for initialization, and therefore the sequence is always repeated:

```
Dim result As New System.Text.StringBuilder
Dim generator As BetterRandom

result.AppendLine("Never the same sequence:")
generator = New BetterRandom
result.AppendLine(generator.GetNextDouble.ToString)
result.AppendLine(generator.GetNextDouble.ToString)
result.AppendLine(generator.GetNextDouble.ToString)
result.AppendLine()

result.AppendLine("Always the same sequence:")
generator = New BetterRandom( _
    "Every string creates a unique, repeatable sequence")
```

```
result.AppendLine(generator.GetNextDouble.ToString)
result.AppendLine(generator.GetNextDouble.ToString)
result.AppendLine(generator.GetNextDouble.ToString)

MsgBox(result.ToString())
```

Figure 6-26 shows the never- and always-repeating sequences generated by this demonstration code.

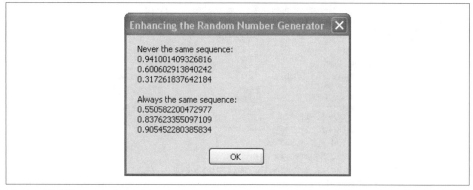

Figure 6-26. Two pseudorandom sequences are generated: one that's always unique and one that always repeats

See Also

Search Visual Studio Help for "Random Class" and "RNGCryptoServiceProvider Class" for information about other ways to generate pseudorandom numbers in Visual Basic.

6.27   Generating Random Integers in a Range

Problem

You need to generate a sequence of pseudorandom integers with a flat distribution over a given range.

Solution

Sample code folder: Chapter 06\RepeatRandom

The BetterRandom class (see Recipe 6.26) sports a GetNextInteger() function. Two parameters define the range limits for the returned pseudorandom integer, as shown here:

```
newRnd.GetNextInteger(minInt, maxInt)
```

The returned integer has a statistically flat distribution across the given range.

Discussion

The following code creates a new instance of the BetterRandom object, which it then uses to generate 200 pseudorandom integers in the range –10 to +10. The results are collected and then displayed for review. As a programming exercise, you might consider changing this code to display the average and perhaps the standard deviation for these returned values.

The generator object is created without passing a string to initialize the generator, so a unique sequence is created every time this program is run:

```
Dim result As New System.Text.StringBuilder
Dim generator As New BetterRandom
Dim minInt As Integer = -10
Dim maxInt As Integer = 10
Dim counter As Integer

result.Append("Random integers in range ")
result.AppendLine(minInt & " to " & maxInt)
For counter = 1 To 200
    ' ----- Add one random number.
    result.Append(generator.GetNextInteger(-10, 10))
    If ((counter Mod 40) = 0) Then
        ' ----- Group on distinct lines periodically.
        result.AppendLine()
    Else
        result.Append(",")
    End If
Next counter

MsgBox(result.ToString())
```

Figure 6-27 shows the results of generating the 200 pseudorandom integers.

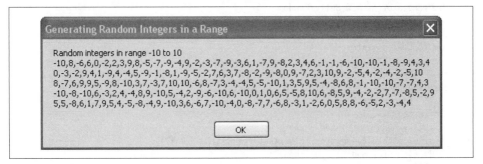

Figure 6-27. Pseudorandom integers in the range –10 to +10 generated by the BetterRandom object

See Also

Recipe 6.26 shows the full code for the BetterRandom class.

Search Visual Studio Help for "Random Class" and "RNGCryptoServiceProvider Class" for information about other ways to generate pseudorandom numbers in Visual Basic.

6.28   Generating Random Real Numbers in a Range

Problem

You need to generate a sequence of pseudorandom real numbers with a flat distribution over a given range.

Solution

Sample code folder: Chapter 06\RepeatRandom

The `BetterRandom` class (see Recipe 6.26) sports a `GetNextReal( )` function. Two parameters define the range limits for the returned pseudorandom real values, and the returned value has a statistically flat distribution across the given range:

```
GetNextReal(minReal, maxReal)
```

Discussion

The following code creates a new instance of the `BetterRandom` object, which it then uses to generate 20 pseudorandom double-precision real numbers in the range –10.0 to +10.0. The results are collected and then displayed for review. As a programming exercise, you might consider changing this code to display the average and perhaps the standard deviation for these returned values.

The generator object is created without passing a string to initialize the generator, so a unique sequence will be created every time this program is run:

```
Dim result As New System.Text.StringBuilder
Dim generator As New BetterRandom
Dim minReal As Integer = -10
Dim maxReal As Integer = 10
Dim counter As Integer

result.Append("Random reals in range ")
result.AppendLine(minReal & " to " & maxReal)
result.AppendLine( )
For counter = 1 To 20
   ' ----- Add one random number.
   result.Append(generator.GetNextReal(minReal, maxReal))
   If ((counter Mod 5) = 0) Then
      ' ----- Group on distinct lines periodically.
      result.AppendLine( )
   Else
      result.Append(",  ")
   End If
Next counter

MsgBox(result.ToString( ))
```

Figure 6-28 shows the results of generating the 20 pseudorandom double-precision real values.

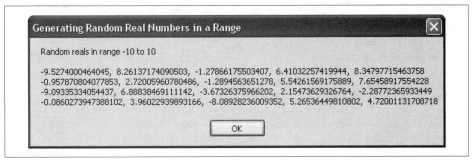

Figure 6-28. Pseudorandom reals in the range −10.0 to +10.0 generated by the BetterRandom object

See Also

Recipe 6.26 shows the full code for the BetterRandom class.

There are many good references on the Web to learn more about random number generation (see, for example, *http://random.mat.sbg.ac.at*).

6.29 Generating Normal-Distribution Random Numbers

Problem

You need to generate a sequence of pseudorandom numbers with a normal distribution, given the distribution's mean and standard deviation.

Solution

Sample code folder: Chapter 06\RepeatRandom

The BetterRandom class (see Recipe 6.26) sports a GetNextNormal( ) function. Two parameters passed to this function define the mean and standard deviation for the distribution of the generated values:

```
GetNextNormal(mean, stdDev)
```

Discussion

The following code creates a new instance of the BetterRandom object, which it then uses to generate 20 pseudorandom double-precision numbers with the desired normal distribution. As a programming exercise you might consider changing this code to display the mean and standard deviation for the returned values, to compare the results with the goal.

The generator object is created without passing a string to initialize the generator, so a unique sequence will be created every time this program is run:

```
Dim result As New System.Text.StringBuilder
Dim generator As New BetterRandom
Dim mean As Double = 100
Dim stdDev As Double = 10
Dim counter As Integer

result.Append("Normal distribution randoms with mean ")
result.AppendLine(mean & " and standard deviation " & stdDev)
result.AppendLine()
For counter = 1 To 20
   ' ----- Add one random number.
   result.Append(generator.GetNextNormal(mean, stdDev))
   If ((counter Mod 3) = 0) Then
      ' ----- Group on distinct lines periodically.
      result.AppendLine()
   Else
      result.Append(",  ")
   End If
Next counter

MsgBox(result.ToString())
```

Figure 6-29 shows the results of generating the 20 pseudorandom double-precision normal-distribution numbers.

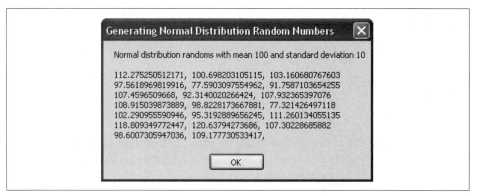

Figure 6-29. Pseudorandom normally distributed numbers generated by the BetterRandom object

See Also

Recipe 6.26 shows the full code for the BetterRandom class.

There are many good references on the Web to learn more about random number generation (see, for example, *http://random.mat.sbg.ac.at*).

6.30 Generating Exponential-Distribution Random Numbers

Problem

You need to generate a sequence of pseudorandom numbers with an exponential distribution given the distribution's mean.

Solution

Sample code folder: Chapter 06\RepeatRandom

The BetterRandom class (see Recipe 6.26) sports a GetNextExp( ) function. One parameter passed to this function defines the mean of the exponentially distributed return values:

```
GetNextExp(mean)
```

Discussion

The following code creates a new instance of the BetterRandom object, which it then uses to generate 20 pseudorandom double-precision numbers with the desired exponential distribution. As a programming exercise you might consider changing this code to display the mean of the returned values, to compare the results with the goal.

The generator object is created without passing a string to initialize the generator, so a unique sequence is created every time this program is run:

```
Dim result As New System.Text.StringBuilder
Dim generator As New BetterRandom
Dim mean As Double = 10
Dim counter As Integer

result.Append("Exponential distribution randoms with mean ")
result.AppendLine(mean)
result.AppendLine( )
For counter = 1 To 20
    ' ----- Add one random number.
    result.Append(generator.GetNextExp(mean))
    If ((counter Mod 3) = 0) Then
        ' ----- Group on distinct lines periodically.
        result.AppendLine( )
    Else
        result.Append(",  ")
    End If
Next counter

MsgBox(result.ToString( ))
```

Figure 6-30 shows the results of generating the 20 pseudorandom double-precision exponential-distribution numbers.

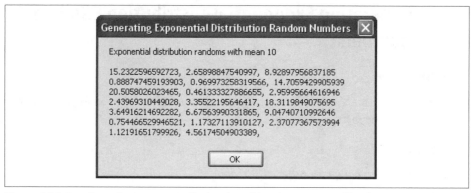

Figure 6-30. Pseudorandom exponentially distributed numbers generated by the BetterRandom object

See Also

Recipe 6.26 shows the full code for the BetterRandom class.

There are many good references on the Web to learn more about random number generation (see, for example, *http://random.mat.sbg.ac.at*).

6.31 Creating a Matrix

Problem

You want to declare a matrix, populate it with nonzero values, and perform several standard matrix calculations on it.

Solution

Sample code folder: Chapter 06\MatrixRecipes

This recipe demonstrates how to declare and populate a matrix in a clear, readable way. A module of matrix functions is also included, although several of the functions it contains will be presented in follow-up recipes.

Discussion

Nested braces containing comma-separated numbers can be used to fill arrays of one or more dimensions. In the case of a two-dimensional matrix, the braces can optionally be separated to show each row of numbers on its own line using the underscore (_) line-continuation character. Feel free to use whatever layout details work for you, but the following sample of a 3×3 matrix can provide a decent, visually appealing layout in your source code:

```
Dim matrixA(,) As Double = { _
    {4, 5, 6}, _
```

```
   {7, 8, 9}, _
   {3, 2, 1}}
MsgBox(MatrixHelper.MakeDisplayable(matrixA))
```

The last line of this code uses a function named MakeDisplayable( ) to return a string representation of a matrix suitable for display, as shown in Figure 6-31. This function is one of several to be presented in the code module named MatrixHelper.

Figure 6-31. The custom output of the matrix

The MatrixHelper module contains several functions to work with matrices, and the recipes that follow will describe them further. A complete listing of *MatrixHelper.vb* can be found at the end of this chapter.

See Also

See the full *MatrixHelper.vb* listing in Recipe 6.35.

6.32 Inverting a Matrix

Problem

You want to invert a matrix.

Solution

Sample code folder: Chapter 06\MatrixRecipes

Use the MatrixHelper.Inverse( ) function presented here and expanded upon in the MatrixHelper module presented in Recipe 6.35.

Discussion

The *inverse* of a matrix is another identically sized matrix that, when multiplied with the original matrix, gives the identity matrix. Only square matrices can be inverted. Matrix inversion is one of the basic matrix operations used for scientific, engineering, and computer graphics work. (A full description of matrices and their operations is beyond the scope of this book.)

Visual Basic 2005 is a good language for developing high-speed .NET Framework–based mathematical collections of number-crunching routines. It allows you to create fast-running classes, structures, and modules containing related functions or methods to meet many requirements. This recipe presents the code required to invert a matrix efficiently:

```
Dim matrixA(,) As Double = { _
    {1, 3, 3}, _
    {2, 4, 3}, _
    {1, 3, 4}}
Dim matrixB(,) As Double = MatrixHelper.Inverse(matrixA)

MsgBox(MatrixHelper.MakeDisplayable(matrixA) & _
    vbNewLine & vbNewLine & "Inverse: " & _
    vbNewLine & MatrixHelper.MakeDisplayable(matrixB))
```

 The MatrixHelper module is listed in its entirety in Recipe 6.35; it includes the Inverse() function and other functions called by Inverse().

Figure 6-32 shows the result of finding the inverse of a 3×3 matrix.

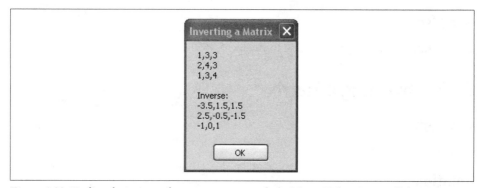

Figure 6-32. Finding the inverse of a square matrix with the MatrixHelper.Inverse() function

To use the MatrixHelper.Inverse() function in your own applications, add the MatrixHelper module to your project and call the function from anywhere within your application.

See Also

See the full *MatrixHelper.vb* listing in Recipe 6.35.

6.33   Calculating the Determinant of a Matrix

Problem

You need to calculate the determinant of a matrix.

Solution

Sample code folder: Chapter 06\MatrixRecipes

Add the `MatrixHelper` module to your application, and pass your matrix to the `MatrixHelper.Determinant()` function.

Discussion

The determinant of a matrix is a single number derived from a matrix. It helps determine if a matrix is invertible, and it also comes into play when using matrices to solve simultaneous equations. (A full description of matrices and their operations is beyond the scope of this book.)

The following sample code creates a square matrix of double-precision numbers and passes it to the `MatrixHelper.Determinant()` function in the `MatrixHelper` module, which returns the determinant of the matrix:

```
Dim matrixA(,) As Double = { _
    {1, 2, 3}, _
    {5, 4, 6}, _
    {9, 7, 8}}
Dim determinant As Double = MatrixHelper.Determinant(matrixA)

MsgBox(MatrixHelper.MakeDisplayable(matrixA) & _
    vbNewLine & vbNewLine & "Determinant: " & _
    determinant.ToString)
```

The complete `MatrixHelper` module is listed in Recipe 6.35. The `Determinant()` function is listed here for easy reference:

```
Public Function Determinant(ByVal sourceMatrix(,) _
        As Double) As Double
    ' ----- Calculate the determinant of a matrix.
    Dim result As Double
    Dim pivots As Integer
    Dim count As Integer

    ' ----- Only calculate the determinants of square matrices.
    If (UBound(sourceMatrix, 1) <> _
            UBound(sourceMatrix, 2)) Then
        Throw New Exception("Determinant only " & _
            "calculated for square matrices.")
    End If
    Dim rank As Integer = UBound(sourceMatrix, 1)
```

```
'----- Make a copy of the matrix so we can work
'      inside of it.
Dim workMatrix(rank, rank) As Double
Array.Copy(sourceMatrix, workMatrix, _
   sourceMatrix.Length)

'----- Use LU decomposition to form a
'      triangular matrix.
Dim rowPivots(rank) As Integer
Dim colPivots(rank) As Integer
workMatrix = FormLU(workMatrix, rowPivots, _
   colPivots, count)

'----- Get the product at each of the pivot points.
result = 1
For pivots = 0 To rank
   result *= workMatrix(rowPivots(pivots), _
      colPivots(pivots))
Next pivots

'----- Determine the sign of the result using
'      LaPlace's formula.
result = (-1) ^ count * result
Return result
End Function
```

A very useful technique for copying one array into another is shown in one of the program lines in the Determinant( ) function. Consider the following line of code:

```
Array.Copy(a, b, a.Length)
```

The Array class sports a shared Copy( ) method that provides a high-speed way to copy the binary data from one array into another. There are several overloaded versions of this method, but as used here, all bytes in array a are copied into array b, starting at the first byte location in each array. The transfer of these bytes from one location in memory to another is highly efficient. You could loop through all of array a's indexed variable locations and copy them one at a time into corresponding locations within array b, but the Array.Copy( ) method copies all the bytes with one function call and no looping.

Figure 6-33 shows the calculated determinant of a 3×3 matrix.

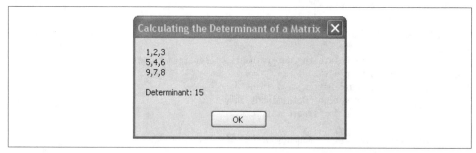

Figure 6-33. Finding the determinant of a square matrix with the MatrixHelper.Determinant() function

See Also

See the full *MatrixHelper.vb* listing in Recipe 6.35.

6.34 Solving Simultaneous Equations

Problem

You want to solve a set of *n* simultaneous equations containing *n* unknowns.

Solution

Sample code folder: Chapter 06\MatrixRecipes

Use the matrix operations presented in the `MatrixHelper` module to solve the equation.

Discussion

Matrices are useful in solving simultaneous equations. The solution is defined in Cramer's Rule, a theorem of linear algebra named after mathematician Gabriel Cramer. (A full description of matrices and their operations is beyond the scope of this book.)

The `MatrixHelper` module contains a special-purpose function that solves simultaneous equations by calling several matrix-analysis functions. You pass a square matrix of size *n* containing the coefficients of the unknowns from the equations, along with a one-dimensional array containing the equation constants. The `MatrixHelper.SimultEq()` function then returns a one-dimensional array containing the solution values for the equation's unknowns. Here is the code listing for the `MatrixHelper.SimultEq()` function:

```
Public Function SimultEq( _
      ByVal sourceEquations(,) As Double, _
      ByVal sourceRHS() As Double) As Double()
   ' ----- Use matrices to solve simultaneous equations.
   Dim rowsAndCols As Integer

   ' ----- The matrix must be square and the array size
   '       must match.
   Dim rank As Integer = UBound(sourceEquations, 1)
   If (UBound(sourceEquations, 2) <> rank) Or _
         (UBound(sourceRHS, 1) <> rank) Then
      Throw New Exception( _
         "Size problem for simultaneous equations.")
   End If

   ' ----- Create some arrays for doing all of the work.
   Dim coefficientMatrix(rank, rank) As Double
   Dim rightHandSide(rank) As Double
   Dim solutions(rank) As Double
```

```
        Dim rowPivots(rank) As Integer
        Dim colPivots(rank) As Integer

        ' ----- Make copies of the original matrices so we don't
        '          mess them up.
        Array.Copy(sourceEquations, coefficientMatrix, _
            sourceEquations.Length)
        Array.Copy(sourceRHS, rightHandSide, sourceRHS.Length)

        ' ----- Use LU decomposition to form a triangular matrix.
        coefficientMatrix = FormLU(coefficientMatrix, _
            rowPivots, colPivots, rowsAndCols)

        ' ----- Find the unique solution for the upper-triangle.
        BackSolve(coefficientMatrix, rightHandSide, solutions, _
            rowPivots, colPivots)

        ' ----- Return the simultaneous equations result in
        '          an array.
        Return solutions
    End Function
```

For example, say you have a pile of 18 coins comprised of pennies, nickels, dimes, and quarters totaling \$2.23. The nickels and dimes total \$.70, and the dimes and quarters total \$2.00. The unknowns are the numbers of each of the four types of coins. The given information provides all you need to solve a set of four equations with four unknowns:

$$P + N + D + Q = 18$$

$$P + 5N + 10D + 25Q = 223$$

$$0P + 5N + 10D + 0Q = 70$$

$$0P + 0N + 10D + 25Q = 200$$

The following code sets up the 4×4 matrix of coefficients and the array of constants, then passes these two arrays to MatrixHelper.SimultEq( ) to solve for the four unknowns:

```
Dim matrixA(,) As Double = { _
    {1, 1, 1, 1}, _
    {1, 5, 10, 25}, _
    {0, 5, 10, 0}, _
    {0, 0, 10, 25}}
Dim arrayB( ) As Double = {18, 223, 70, 200}
Dim arrayC( ) As Double = _
    MatrixHelper.SimultEq(matrixA, arrayB)

MsgBox(MatrixHelper.MakeDisplayable(matrixA) & vbNewLine & _
    vbNewLine & MatrixHelper.MakeDisplayable(arrayB) & _
    vbNewLine & vbNewLine & _
    "Simultaneous Equations Solution:" & _
    vbNewLine & MatrixHelper.MakeDisplayable(arrayC))
```

As shown by the results displayed in Figure 6-34, there are three pennies, four nickels, five dimes, and six quarters in the pile.

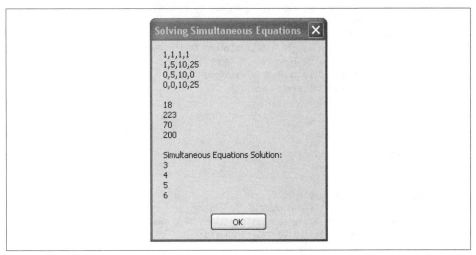

Figure 6-34. Solving a set of four equations with four unknowns

The MatrixHelper.SimultEq() function is listed in the MatrixHelper module code, presented in the next recipe.

See Also

See the full *MatrixHelper.vb* listing in Recipe 6.35.

6.35 Listing of the MatrixHelper Class

Sample code folder: Chapter 06\MatrixRecipes

Following is the full code for the MatrixHelper class described in Recipes 6.31 through 6.34:

```
Module MatrixHelper
   Public Function MakeDisplayable( _
        ByVal sourceMatrix(,) As Double) As String
      ' ----- Prepare a multi-line string that shows the
      '       contents of a matrix, a 2D array.
      Dim rows As Integer
      Dim cols As Integer
      Dim eachRow As Integer
      Dim eachCol As Integer
      Dim result As New System.Text.StringBuilder

      ' ----- Process all rows of the matrix, generating one
      '       output line per row.
      rows = UBound(sourceMatrix, 1) + 1
```

```
      cols = UBound(sourceMatrix, 2) + 1
      For eachRow = 0 To rows - 1
         ' ----- Process each column of the matrix on a
         '       single row, separating values by commas.
         If (eachRow > 0) Then result.AppendLine()
         For eachCol = 0 To cols - 1
            ' ----- Add a single matrix element to the output.
            If (eachCol > 0) Then result.Append(",")
            result.Append(sourceMatrix(eachRow, _
               eachCol).ToString)
         Next eachCol
      Next eachRow

      ' ----- Finished.
      Return result.ToString
   End Function

   Public Function MakeDisplayable( _
         ByVal sourceArray() As Double) As String
      ' ----- Present an array as multiple lines of output.
      Dim result As New System.Text.StringBuilder
      Dim scanValue As Double

      For Each scanValue In sourceArray
         result.AppendLine(scanValue.ToString)
      Next scanValue

      Return result.ToString
   End Function

   Public Function Inverse( _
         ByVal sourceMatrix(,) As Double) As Double(,)
      ' ----- Build a new matrix that is the mathematical
      '       inverse of the supplied matrix. Multiplying
      '       a matrix and its inverse together will give
      '       the identity matrix.
      Dim eachCol As Integer
      Dim eachRow As Integer
      Dim rowsAndCols As Integer

      ' ----- Determine the size of each dimension of the
      '       matrix. Only square matrices can be inverted.
      If (UBound(sourceMatrix, 1) <> _
            UBound(sourceMatrix, 2)) Then
         Throw New Exception("Matrix must be square.")
      End If
      Dim rank As Integer = UBound(sourceMatrix, 1)

      ' ----- Clone a copy of the matrix (not just a
      '       new reference).
      Dim workMatrix(,) As Double = _
         CType(sourceMatrix.Clone, Double(,))
```

```
' ----- Variables used for backsolving.
Dim destMatrix(rank, rank) As Double
Dim rightHandSide(rank) As Double
Dim solutions(rank) As Double
Dim rowPivots(rank) As Integer
Dim colPivots(rank) As Integer

' ----- Use LU decomposition to form a
'       triangular matrix.
workMatrix = FormLU(workMatrix, rowPivots, _
    colPivots, rowsAndCols)

' ----- Backsolve the triangular matrix to get the
'       inverted value for each position in the
'       final matrix.
For eachCol = 0 To rank
    rightHandSide(eachCol) = 1
    BackSolve(workMatrix, rightHandSide, solutions, _
        rowPivots, colPivots)
    For eachRow = 0 To rank
        destMatrix(eachRow, eachCol) = solutions(eachRow)
        rightHandSide(eachRow) = 0
    Next eachRow
Next eachCol

' ----- Return the inverted matrix result.
Return destMatrix
End Function

Public Function Determinant(ByVal sourceMatrix(,) _
    As Double) As Double
    ' ----- Calculate the determinant of a matrix.
    Dim result As Double
    Dim pivots As Integer
    Dim count As Integer

    ' ----- Only calculate the determinants of square
    '       matrices.
    If (UBound(sourceMatrix, 1) <> _
        UBound(sourceMatrix, 2)) Then
        Throw New Exception("Determinant only " & _
            "calculated for square matrices.")
    End If
    Dim rank As Integer = UBound(sourceMatrix, 1)

    ' ----- Make a copy of the matrix so we can work
    '       inside of it.
    Dim workMatrix(rank, rank) As Double
    Array.Copy(sourceMatrix, workMatrix, _
        sourceMatrix.Length)

    ' ----- Use LU decomposition to form a
    '       triangular matrix.
    Dim rowPivots(rank) As Integer
```

```
      Dim colPivots(rank) As Integer
      workMatrix = FormLU(workMatrix, rowPivots, _
         colPivots, count)

      ' ----- Get the product at each of the pivot points.
      result = 1
      For pivots = 0 To rank
         result *= workMatrix(rowPivots(pivots), _
            colPivots(pivots))
      Next pivots

      ' ----- Determine the sign of the result using
      '       LaPlace's formula.
      result = (-1) ^ count * result
      Return result
   End Function

   Public Function SimultEq( _
         ByVal sourceEquations(,) As Double, _
         ByVal sourceRHS() As Double) As Double()
      ' ----- Use matrices to solve simultaneous equations.
      Dim rowsAndCols As Integer

      ' ----- The matrix must be square and the array size
      '       must match.
      Dim rank As Integer = UBound(sourceEquations, 1)
      If (UBound(sourceEquations, 2) <> rank) Or _
            (UBound(sourceRHS, 1) <> rank) Then
         Throw New Exception( _
            "Size problem for simultaneous equations.")
      End If

      ' ----- Create some arrays for doing all of the work.
      Dim coefficientMatrix(rank, rank) As Double
      Dim rightHandSide(rank) As Double
      Dim solutions(rank) As Double
      Dim rowPivots(rank) As Integer
      Dim colPivots(rank) As Integer

      ' ----- Make copies of the original matrices so we don't
      '       mess them up.
      Array.Copy(sourceEquations, coefficientMatrix, _
         sourceEquations.Length)
      Array.Copy(sourceRHS, rightHandSide, sourceRHS.Length)

      ' ----- Use LU decomposition to form a triangular matrix.
      coefficientMatrix = FormLU(coefficientMatrix, _
         rowPivots, colPivots, rowsAndCols)

      ' ----- Find the unique solution for the upper-triangle.
      BackSolve(coefficientMatrix, rightHandSide, solutions, _
         rowPivots, colPivots)
```

```
    ' ----- Return the simultaneous equations result in
    '       an array.
    Return solutions
End Function

Private Function FormLU(ByVal sourceMatrix(,) As Double, _
      ByRef rowPivots() As Integer, _
      ByRef colPivots() As Integer, _
      ByRef rowsAndCols As Integer) As Double(,)
    ' ----- Perform an LU (lower and upper) decomposition
    '       of a matrix, a modified form of Gaussian
    '       elimination.
    Dim eachRow As Integer
    Dim eachCol As Integer
    Dim pivot As Integer
    Dim rowIndex As Integer
    Dim colIndex As Integer
    Dim bestRow As Integer
    Dim bestCol As Integer
    Dim rowToPivot As Integer
    Dim colToPivot As Integer
    Dim maxValue As Double
    Dim testValue As Double
    Dim oldMax As Double
    Const Deps As Double = 0.0000000000000001

    ' ----- Determine the size of the array.
    Dim rank As Integer = UBound(sourceMatrix, 1)
    Dim destMatrix(rank, rank) As Double
    Dim rowNorm(rank) As Double
    ReDim rowPivots(rank)
    ReDim colPivots(rank)

    ' ----- Make a copy of the array so we don't mess it up.
    Array.Copy(sourceMatrix, destMatrix, _
        sourceMatrix.Length)

    ' ----- Initialize row and column pivot arrays.
    For eachRow = 0 To rank
        rowPivots(eachRow) = eachRow
        colPivots(eachRow) = eachRow
        For eachCol = 0 To rank
            rowNorm(eachRow) += _
                Math.Abs(destMatrix(eachRow, eachCol))
        Next eachCol
        If (rowNorm(eachRow) = 0) Then
            Throw New Exception( _
                "Cannot invert a singular matrix.")
        End If
    Next eachRow

    ' ----- Use Gauss-Jordan elimination on the matrix rows.
    For pivot = 0 To rank - 1
        maxValue = 0
```

```
For eachRow = pivot To rank
   rowIndex = rowPivots(eachRow)
   For eachCol = pivot To rank
      colIndex = colPivots(eachCol)
      testValue = Math.Abs(destMatrix(rowIndex, _
         colIndex)) / rowNorm(rowIndex)
      If (testValue > maxValue) Then
         maxValue = testValue
         bestRow = eachRow
         bestCol = eachCol
      End If
   Next eachCol
Next eachRow

' ----- Detect a singular, or very nearly
'       singular, matrix.
If (maxValue = 0) Then
   Throw New Exception( _
      "Singular matrix used for LU.")
ElseIf (pivot > 1) Then
   If (maxValue < (Deps * oldMax)) Then
      Throw New Exception( _
         "Non-invertible matrix used for LU.")
   End If
End If
oldMax = maxValue

' ----- Swap row pivot values for the best row.
If (rowPivots(pivot) <> rowPivots(bestRow)) Then
   rowsAndCols += 1
   Swap(rowPivots(pivot), rowPivots(bestRow))
End If

' ----- Swap column pivot values for the best column.
If (colPivots(pivot) <> colPivots(bestCol)) Then
   rowsAndCols += 1
   Swap(colPivots(pivot), colPivots(bestCol))
End If

' ----- Work with the current pivot points.
rowToPivot = rowPivots(pivot)
colToPivot = colPivots(pivot)

' ----- Modify the remaining rows from the
'       pivot points.
For eachRow = (pivot + 1) To rank
   rowIndex = rowPivots(eachRow)
   destMatrix(rowIndex, colToPivot) = _
      -destMatrix(rowIndex, colToPivot) / _
      destMatrix(rowToPivot, colToPivot)
   For eachCol = (pivot + 1) To rank
      colIndex = colPivots(eachCol)
      destMatrix(rowIndex, colIndex) += _
         destMatrix(rowIndex, colToPivot) * _
```

```
            destMatrix(rowToPivot, colIndex)
          Next eachCol
        Next eachRow
    Next pivot

    ' ----- Detect a non-invertible matrix.
    If (destMatrix(rowPivots(rank), _
        colPivots(rank)) = 0) Then
      Throw New Exception( _
        "Non-invertible matrix used for LU.")
    ElseIf (Math.Abs(destMatrix(rowPivots(rank), _
        colPivots(rank))) / rowNorm(rowPivots(rank))) < _
        (Deps * oldMax) Then
      Throw New Exception( _
        "Non-invertible matrix used for LU.")
    End If

    ' ----- Success. Return the LU triangular matrix.
    Return destMatrix
End Function

Private Sub Swap(ByRef firstValue As Integer, _
      ByRef secondValue As Integer)
    ' ----- Reverse the values of two reference integers.
    Dim holdValue As Integer
    holdValue = firstValue
    firstValue = secondValue
    secondValue = holdValue
End Sub

Private Sub BackSolve(ByVal sourceMatrix(,) As Double, _
      ByVal rightHandSide() As Double, _
      ByVal solutions() As Double, _
      ByRef rowPivots() As Integer, _
      ByRef colPivots() As Integer)
    ' ----- Solve an upper-right-triangle matrix.
    Dim pivot As Integer
    Dim rowToPivot As Integer
    Dim colToPivot As Integer
    Dim eachRow As Integer
    Dim eachCol As Integer
    Dim rank As Integer = UBound(sourceMatrix, 1)

    ' ----- Work through all pivot points. This section
    '       builds the "B" in the AX=B formula.
    For pivot = 0 To (rank - 1)
      colToPivot = colPivots(pivot)
      For eachRow = (pivot + 1) To rank
        rowToPivot = rowPivots(eachRow)
        rightHandSide(rowToPivot) += _
          sourceMatrix(rowToPivot, colToPivot) _
          * rightHandSide(rowPivots(pivot))
      Next eachRow
    Next pivot
```

```
'  ----- Now solve for each X using the general formula
'         x(i) = (b(i) - summation(a(i,j)x(j)))/a(i,i)
For eachRow = rank To 0 Step -1
   colToPivot = colPivots(eachRow)
   rowToPivot = rowPivots(eachRow)
   solutions(colToPivot) = rightHandSide(rowToPivot)
   For eachCol = (eachRow + 1) To rank
      solutions(colToPivot) -= _
         sourceMatrix(rowToPivot, colPivots(eachCol)) _
         * solutions(colPivots(eachCol))
   Next eachCol
   solutions(colToPivot) /= sourceMatrix(rowToPivot, _
      colToPivot)
Next eachRow
   End Sub
End Module
```

Dates and Times

7.0   Introduction

The Date data type holds a compact representation of an exact moment in time, with 100-nanosecond resolution, covering a 10,000-year span of dates starting with day 1 of year 1 AD. Visual Basic 2005 and the .NET Framework provide many powerful functions for working with dates and times, but the syntax and conceptual changes can be daunting, especially if you're updating your skills from VB 6. It can often be tricky to figure out how or what to use to get the job done.

The good news is that once you get up to speed with all the changes, it's now easier than ever to work with dates and times. Is a given year a leap year? How many days are there in a given month? What day of the year is a given date? All of these questions, and many more, can now be answered with single function calls or single lines of code.

The recipes in this chapter provide solutions for many of the common date and time calculations that come up in day-to-day development, and they should get you up to speed in "no time" (pun intended).

7.1   Getting the System Date and Time

Problem

You want to know the current time and date.

Solution

Sample code folder: Chapter 07\SystemDateTime

Use Now, which returns the current moment of time from your system clock as a Date value.

Discussion

The `Now` property returns a `Date`, which you can store in a `Date` variable or process directly. There are many properties and methods available to extract information from `Date`s. The following code demonstrates just a few of them, and the rest of this chapter provides insight into many more:

```
Dim rightNow As Date = Now
Dim result As New System.Text.StringBuilder

result.AppendLine("""Now""...")
result.AppendLine( )
result.Append("Date: ").AppendLine(rightNow.ToShortDateString)
result.Append("Time: ").AppendLine(rightNow.ToShortTimeString)
result.Append("Ticks: ").Append(rightNow.Ticks.ToString)

MsgBox(result.ToString( ))
```

`rightNow` is a `Date` variable used here to grab and store a single value of `Now`. If `Now` were to be used repeatedly in the remainder of this code, it's possible that its value could change in the process. In the code shown, this would not be a problem, but if your application might be affected by having the value of `Now` suddenly change, you should consider assigning its value to a `Date` variable just once, to freeze the moment in time for further processing.

This code uses a `StringBuilder` to piece together several bits of information extracted from `rightNow`. The properties `ToShortDateString` and `ToShortTimeString` extract the date and time in a readable format. Figure 7-1 shows typical output displayed by the message box at the end of the sample code.

Figure 7-1. Basic information about a frozen moment in time

`Ticks` is an interesting property of the `Date` data type. It represents the number of 100-nanosecond intervals of time elapsed since midnight on January 1 of the year 1 AD. This is a value closely tied to how the date and time are stored internally in a `Date` variable. The `Ticks` property is explained in further detail in Recipe 7.3.

7.2   Accessing the System's Time Zone

Problem

You want to programmatically determine the time-zone offset for the local system's time and determine if daylight savings time is currently in effect.

Solution

Sample code folder: Chapter 07\SystemTimeZone

Use the TimeZone object, which provides properties and methods for determining the name of the current time zone, the number of hours offset from Greenwich Mean Time (GMT), and whether daylight savings is currently in effect.

Discussion

The following code shows how the TimeZone information is accessed:

```
Dim theZone As TimeZone = TimeZone.CurrentTimeZone
Dim result As New System.Text.StringBuilder

result.Append("DaylightName: ").AppendLine( _
   theZone.DaylightName)
result.Append("StandardName: ").AppendLine( _
   theZone.StandardName)
result.Append("IsDaylightSavingTime(Now): ").AppendLine( _
   theZone.IsDaylightSavingTime(Now))
result.Append("GetUtcOffset(Now): ").AppendLine( _
   theZone.GetUtcOffset(Now).ToString)
result.Append("System time is Local Time: ")
result.AppendLine(Now.Kind = DateTimeKind.Local)
result.Append("System time is Universal Coordinated Time: ")
result.AppendLine(Now.Kind = DateTimeKind.Utc)
result.Append("System time is Unspecified: ")
result.AppendLine(Now.Kind = DateTimeKind.Unspecified)

MsgBox(result.ToString( ))
```

The TimeZone variable theZone is assigned the current system's time-zone information in the first line of this code. The rest of the lines extract information from this variable and prepare string versions for display by appending to the StringBuilder. The theZone variable lets you determine the name of the time zone, the number of hours that time zone is offset from GMT, and whether daylight savings is currently in effect.

The Kind property determines if a Date represents local time, Coordinated Universal Time (UTC), or is unspecified. This is a property of a Date, not a TimeZone, but the information it provides is closely associated with the TimeZone information.

Figure 7-2 shows the TimeZone information displayed for a computer set to Central Standard Time during the summer.

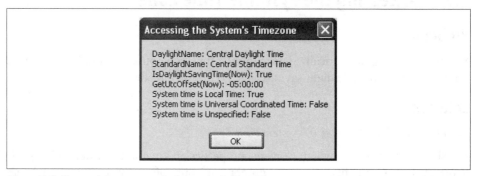

Figure 7-2. Determining a system's time-zone information

7.3   Using System Ticks

Problem

You want to get a simple, sequential number from the system clock for timing purposes, or perhaps you want to get a guaranteed unique bit pattern for seeding a random number generator each time your application starts.

Solution

Sample code folder: Chapter 07\SystemTicks

Use the Now.Ticks property, which returns a long integer containing the number of 100-nanosecond intervals since midnight of January 1 in the year 1 AD.

Discussion

The Ticks property is available on any Date variable, but it's most often used on the ever-changing Now property. Using Now.Ticks means the value returned will always be a unique Long value for every tick of the system clock, providing a good source for unique bit patterns.

Although Ticks appears to be accurate to the nearest 100 nanoseconds, it actually has much less resolution than expected. The following code shows how to access the Ticks property and, more importantly, demonstrates how many times the returned value of Ticks changes per second:

```
Dim lastTicks As Long
Dim numTicks As Long
Dim endTime As Date
Dim results As String

' ----- Count the actual tick changes.
endTime = Now.AddSeconds(1)
Do
    If (Now.Ticks <> lastTicks) Then
        numTicks += 1
        lastTicks = Now.Ticks
    End If
Loop Until (Now > endTime)

' ----- Display the results.
results = "Now.Ticks: " & Now.Ticks.ToString & vbNewLine & _
    "Number of updates per second: " & numTicks.ToString
MsgBox(results)
```

As shown in Figure 7-3, the value of the Ticks property changes only about 65 times per second. At the speed of today's computers, a lot of instructions can be processed in 1/65 of a second, making Ticks a poor choice for high-resolution timing.

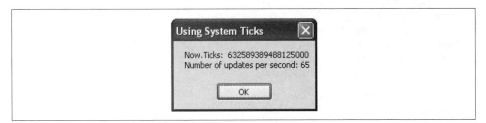

Figure 7-3. Ticks represent short timing units, but they aren't updated very often

Ticks does have some good uses, but for timing that really is accurate to the nearest millisecond, consider using the new Stopwatch object, described later in this chapter.

See Also

Compare the results of this recipe with those of Recipe 7.4, which provides a much greater level of accuracy.

7.4   Timing Application Activities

Problem

You want to time application events with greater accuracy than is provided by the Date type's Ticks property.

Solution

Sample code folder: Chapter 07\Stopwatch

Use the System.Diagnostics.Stopwatch object to accurately determine elapsed time to the nearest millisecond.

Discussion

The new System.Diagnostics.Stopwatch object is easy and intuitive to use. Just like a real stopwatch, you start it when you want and measure elapsed time as needed. The Start() method starts the timing, and the ElapsedMilliseconds property returns the number of elapsed milliseconds. Similarly, there are Stop() and Reset() methods to stop and reset the stopwatch, and these methods behave as you'd expect.

The following code demonstrates how to create an instance of the Stopwatch object and how to measure elapsed time with it. But it also points out an advantage of using this object for fine-grained timing measurements rather than using Ticks. The Do...Loop block of code runs for one second, tallying the number of times the value returned by the ElapsedMilliseconds property changes to a new value:

```
Dim lastMillis As Long
Dim numMillis As Long
Dim testWatch As New System.Diagnostics.Stopwatch
Dim endTime As Date
Dim results As String

' ----- Start the timer.
endTime = Now.AddSeconds(1)
testWatch.Start()
Do
    ' ----- Keep track of each change of the stopwatch.
    If (testWatch.ElapsedMilliseconds <> lastMillis) Then
        numMillis += 1
        lastMillis = testWatch.ElapsedMilliseconds
    End If
Loop Until (Now > endTime)

' ----- Display the results.
results = "Elapsed milliseconds: " & _
    testWatch.ElapsedMilliseconds.ToString & vbNewLine & _
    "Number of updates per second: " & numMillis.ToString
MsgBox(results)
```

As shown in Figure 7-4, the property returns a new number of elapsed milliseconds slightly over 1,000 times during the second, a result to be expected when the loop timing is based on the system clock. Hence, the Stopwatch is accurate to the nearest millisecond.

Figure 7-4. The Stopwatch object accurately maintains a timing resolution of one millisecond

See Also

Compare the results of this recipe with those of Recipe 7.3, which provides a lower level of accuracy.

7.5 Calculating Elapsed Time Using Ticks

Problem

You want a simple way to determine elapsed time when millisecond accuracy is not required.

Solution

Sample code folder: Chapter 07\ElapsedTicks

Use the difference between system ticks returned by Now.Ticks and divide by 10 million to get elapsed decimal seconds.

Discussion

As shown in Recipe 7.1, Ticks returns the number of 100-nanosecond time intervals elapsed since midnight of January 1, 1 AD. Dividing Ticks by 10,000,000 converts the time units to seconds. The following code demonstrates this technique by timing how long the user takes to click an OK button and then displaying the number of decimal seconds elapsed:

```
Dim ticksBefore As Long
Dim ticksAfter As Long
Dim tickSeconds As Double

' ----- Time the user!
ticksBefore = Now.Ticks
```

```
MsgBox("Press OK to see elapsed seconds")
ticksAfter = Now.Ticks

tickSeconds = (ticksAfter - ticksBefore) / 10000000.0
MsgBox("Elapsed seconds: " & tickSeconds.ToString())
```

Figure 7-5 shows the result.

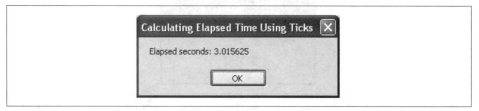

Figure 7-5. Using Ticks to measure elapsed decimal seconds

This is a simple technique for getting decimal seconds for each moment in time, but the real workhorse for determining spans of time is the TimeSpan object, which is demonstrated in Recipe 7.6.

7.6   Calculating Elapsed Time with the Stopwatch

Problem

You want to measure elapsed time accurate to the nearest millisecond.

Solution

Sample code folder: Chapter 07\ElapsedStopwatch

Use the Stopwatch object, which is designed to measure elapsed milliseconds accurately.

Discussion

The new System.Diagnostics.Stopwatch object introduced with Visual Basic 2005 provides better-resolution timing than using system ticks. The ElapsedMilliseconds property accurately returns elapsed time to the nearest millisecond, as demonstrated in Recipe 7.4. This is ideal for timing blocks and loops of code to compare the efficiency of various algorithms or for other high-resolution timing tasks. The following code times how long the user takes to click an OK button when prompted:

```
Dim testWatch As New System.Diagnostics.Stopwatch
Dim results As String

' ----- Start counting.
testWatch.Start()
MsgBox("Press OK to see elapsed seconds")
```

```
' ----- Stop and record.
results = String.Format( _
   "testWatch.Elapsed.Seconds: {0}{3}" & _
   "testWatch.Elapsed.TotalSeconds: {1}{3}" & _
   "testWatch.ElapsedMilliseconds / 1000: {2}", _
   testWatch.Elapsed.Seconds, _
   testWatch.Elapsed.TotalSeconds, _
   testWatch.ElapsedMilliseconds / 1000, vbNewLine)
MsgBox(results)
```

The Elapsed property returns a TimeSpan object, which provides properties useful for extracting time durations. In this example the whole number of seconds is returned by the TimeSpan's Elapsed.Seconds property, and a more exact decimal number of seconds is returned by its Elapsed.TotalSeconds property. Figure 7-6 displays the results.

Figure 7-6. Using the Stopwatch object to accurately measure elapsed time

When using a Stopwatch, be sure to call its Start( ) method before attempting to access elapsed time from it. If Start( ) is not called first, elapsed time is always returned as zero.

You can accumulate elapsed time in pieces by calling the Start( ) and Stop( ) methods repeatedly. The elapsed time freezes when Stop( ) is called; the counting resumes when Start( ) is called. To clear the Stopwatch's count at any time, call the Reset( ) method. These methods simulate the buttons on a real stopwatch, but do so much faster and more accurately than punching buttons by hand!

7.7   Extracting Year, Month, and Day Numbers from a Date Value

Problem

You want to access the year, month, and day numbers from a Date.

Solution

Sample code folder: Chapter 07\DateParts

Use the Year, Month, and Day properties of the Date.

Discussion

These three properties provide a direct route to a Date's date information. Each returns an integer that can be used in further computations. The following code demonstrates these properties in action:

```
Dim rightNow As Date = Now
Dim yearNow As Integer = rightNow.Year
Dim monthNow As Integer = rightNow.Month
Dim dayNow As Integer = rightNow.Day

Dim results As String = String.Format( _
    "Year: {1}{0}Month: {2}{0}Day: {3}{0}", _
    vbNewLine, yearNow, monthNow, dayNow)
MsgBox(results)
```

Figure 7-7 shows the system's current date numbers as displayed by the message box in this sample code.

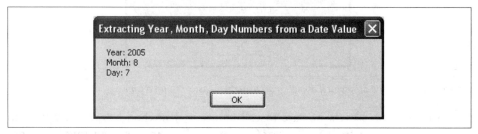

Figure 7-7. Extracting year, month, and day numbers from a Date variable

These properties are read-only, so while they work well for extracting the date values, they are not appropriate for assigning a new date to a Date variable. (As explained in Recipe 7.9, Date variables can be set to specific dates, and they can be modified to new dates by adding amounts of time to them.)

See Also

Recipe 7.8 discusses how to access the hour, minute, and second numbers from a Date.

Assigning a specific date and/or time to a new Date variable is covered in Recipe 7.9, while Recipes 7.12 and 7.13 discuss assigning a new date to an existing Date variable.

7.8 Extracting Hour, Minute, and Second Numbers from a Date Value

Problem

You want to access the hours, minutes, or seconds from a Date.

Solution

Sample code folder: Chapter 07\TimeParts

Use the Hour, Minute, and Second properties of the Date instance.

Discussion

These properties are similar to the Year, Month, and Day properties of the Date object, but they extract and return the time of the day parts of the Date rather than the date parts. Like the date parts, these time parts of the Date are read-only. The following code shows how to access these properties:

```
Dim rightNow As Date = Now
Dim hourNow As Integer = rightNow.Hour
Dim minuteNow As Integer = rightNow.Minute
Dim secondNow As Integer = rightNow.Second
Dim millisecondNow As Integer = rightNow.Millisecond

Dim results As String = String.Format( _
   "Hour: {1}{0}Minute: {2}{0}Second: " & _
   "{3}{0}Millisecond: {4}", vbNewLine, _
   hourNow, minuteNow, secondNow, millisecondNow)
MsgBox(results)
```

The Millisecond property also appears in this code. As of this writing, this property's resolution isn't all that great, although it's possible that in the future the milliseconds value will become more accurate. If you need true millisecond timing, use the Stopwatch object described in Recipe 7.6. Even so, the Millisecond property does provide greater accuracy than just to the nearest second.

Figure 7-8 shows the results of the above sample code as displayed by the message box.

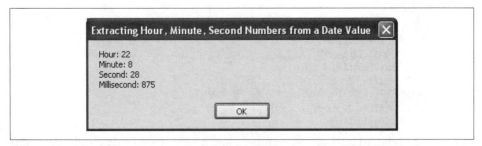

Figure 7-8. Extracting hour, minute, second, and millisecond numbers from a Date

See Also

Recipe 7.7 discusses how to extract the year, month, and day numbers from a Date.

7.9   Creating a Date or Time Value from Its Parts

Problem

You want to create a Date variable and assign it a specific date, a specific time of day, or both, but all you have are the individual components, such as the year, month, and day.

Solution

Sample code folder: Chapter 07\SerialDate

Use one of the overloaded Date constructors to assign date and time numbers as the variable is created.

Discussion

You can hardcode a date and/or a time in your application by delimiting the text representation with a pair of number sign (#) characters. Here's a line of code that assigns a hardcoded date of July 4, 1776 to a date variable named theFourth:

```
theFourth = #7/4/1776#
```

As shown, theFourth is assigned a time value of zero, which occurs during the first second of the day, just after midnight as the date changes from the third to the fourth of July. The sample block of code that follows shows how to assign a specific time in addition to a specific date. The first line sets the date variable thirdOfJuly to the last second of the day:

```
Dim thirdOfJuly As Date = #7/3/1776 11:59:59 PM#
Dim fourthOfJuly As New Date(1776, 7, 4)
Dim inTheMorning As New Date(1776, 7, 4, 9, 45, 30)

MsgBox( _
    "The 3rd and 4th of July, 1776..." & _
    vbNewLine & vbNewLine & _
    "#7/3/1776 11:59:59 PM# ... " & _
    thirdOfJuly.ToString & vbNewLine & _
    "New Date(1776, 7, 4) ... " & _
    fourthOfJuly.ToString & vbNewLine & _
    "New Date(1776, 7, 4, 9, 45, 30) ... " & _
    inTheMorning.ToString)
```

The second and third lines of this example show how to assign a date and a date/time combination to a date variable in a more dynamic way. Rather than a hardcoded date-and-time literal, integer variables containing Year, Month, Day, Hour, Minute, and Second values can be passed to the Date constructor to assign a moment of time to the Date variable as it is created. Figure 7-9 shows the results of these date and time assignments, as displayed by the message box at the end of the sample code.

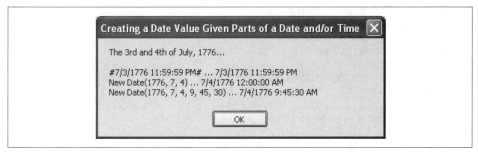

Figure 7-9. Different ways to assign specific dates and times to Date variables

Another approach to adjusting a Date variable's date and time is to add quantities of time to it. For example, a freshly dimensioned but unassigned Date variable contains the default date and time of midnight, January 1, 1 AD. You could add 1,775 years, 6 months, and 3 days to the Date variable to adjust it to July 4, 1776. The various date and time addition methods are explained and demonstrated in Recipe 7.12.

7.10   Formatting Dates and Times

Problem

You want to format a date or time for output using some standard or custom format.

Solution

Sample code folder: Chapter 07\FormatDateTime

Use one of the single-letter format options, or set up a custom format to convert the date or time as desired.

Discussion

The following code displays most of the standard formats available for converting dates and times to strings, plus a sampling of what the custom formatting options can do:

```
Dim rightNow As Date = Now
Dim result As New System.Text.StringBuilder
result.AppendLine("""Now""...")
result.AppendLine()

' ----- Use some of the built-in Date properties to
'       format the date in predefined ways.
result.Append("ToString: ").AppendLine(rightNow.ToString)
result.Append("ToLongDateString: ")
result.AppendLine(rightNow.ToLongDateString)
result.Append("ToShortDateString: ")
result.AppendLine(rightNow.ToShortDateString)
```

```
result.Append("ToLongTimeString: ")
result.AppendLine(rightNow.ToLongTimeString)
result.Append("ToShortTimeString: ")
result.AppendLine(rightNow.ToShortTimeString)
result.Append("ToUniversalTime: ")
result.AppendLine(rightNow.ToUniversalTime)
result.AppendLine( )

' ----- Use format specifiers to control the date display.
result.Append("d: ").AppendLine(rightNow.ToString("d"))
result.Append("D: ").AppendLine(rightNow.ToString("D"))
result.Append("t: ").AppendLine(rightNow.ToString("t"))
result.Append("T: ").AppendLine(rightNow.ToString("T"))
result.Append("f: ").AppendLine(rightNow.ToString("f"))
result.Append("F: ").AppendLine(rightNow.ToString("F"))
result.Append("g: ").AppendLine(rightNow.ToString("g"))
result.Append("G: ").AppendLine(rightNow.ToString("G"))
result.Append("M: ").AppendLine(rightNow.ToString("M"))
result.Append("R: ").AppendLine(rightNow.ToString("R"))
result.Append("s: ").AppendLine(rightNow.ToString("s"))
result.Append("u: ").AppendLine(rightNow.ToString("u"))
result.Append("U: ").AppendLine(rightNow.ToString("U"))
result.Append("y: ").AppendLine(rightNow.ToString("y"))
result.AppendLine().AppendLine( )

' ----- Use custom format specifiers, which provide
'       more flexibility than the single-letter formats.
result.Append("dd: ").AppendLine(rightNow.ToString("dd"))
result.Append("ddd: ").AppendLine(rightNow.ToString("ddd"))
result.Append("dddd: ").AppendLine(rightNow.ToString("dddd"))
result.Append("HH:mm:ss.fff z: ")
result.AppendLine(rightNow.ToString("HH:mm:ss.fff z"))
result.Append("yy/MM/dd g: ")
result.AppendLine(rightNow.ToString("yy/MM/dd g"))

MsgBox(result.ToString)
```

The output of this code appears in Figure 7-10.

The first group of lines shows string conversions provided by specific members of the Date object. You'll probably find these common formats sufficient for most purposes.

The second group of lines shows the single-letter predefined formats, which provide even more options. These letters don't appear in the IntelliSense pop ups, so if you do a lot of formatting along these lines, you might want to make a list for your own reference.

Custom date output is provided by strings of specifically defined characters that format parts of the Date appropriately. A sampling is shown in this code, and the Visual Studio online help documents all available formats.

This recipe's sample code uses the Date's ToString( ) method exclusively to format the dates and times. However, there are other objects that support the IFormattable

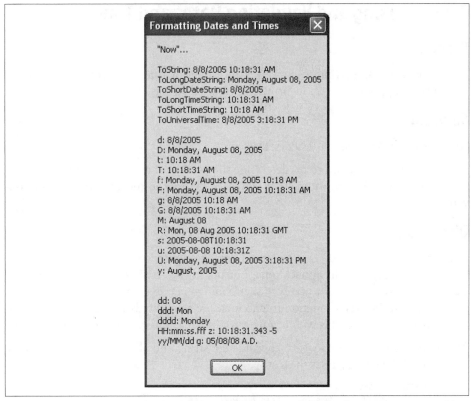

Figure 7-10. A sampling of predefined and custom formats available for formatting Date variables to strings

interface, which provides very similar formatting capabilities. Specifically, the `String.Format( )` shared method provides similar formatting capabilities in its braces-defined format parameters.

For example, here's one of the lines from the previous example code:

```
result.Append("d: ").AppendLine(rightNow.ToString("d"))
```

This same line of output can also be formatted using `String.Format( )`:

```
result.Append(String.Format( _
    "d: {0:d}{1}", rightNow, vbNewLine))
```

In this case, the `{0:d}` format parameter provides the same formatting instruction as the `d` string parameter in the `ToString( )` method. These two lines demonstrate very different syntax, but they produce the same results.

See Also

For details on all predefined and custom format strings available in .NET, access the "formatting types" entry in the Visual Studio online help documentation.

7.11 Parsing and Validating Dates and Times

Problem

You want to parse a string to convert it to a date or time, and you want to avoid using error trapping to detect incorrectly formatted strings.

Solution

Sample code folder: Chapter 07\ParseDate

Use the IsDate( ) function to predetermine the validity of a string's representation of a date or time, and then use the Date.Parse( ) method on the string to reliably convert it to a Date.

Discussion

The new Try...Catch...End Try structured error trapping is a great tool for catching unexpected exceptions in applications, but it's always best to make sure you have clean data before you use it in a way that could generate an error. For example, it's best to use the IsDate( ) function to check a date's validity before trying to use it in your main code's logic; this will turn up errors such as misspelled month names.

The following code uses IsDate( ) to validate a string and allow conversion to a date value only if the string passes the test:

```
Dim testDate As String
Dim results As New System.Text.StringBuilder

' ----- Test an invalid date.
testDate = "Febtember 43, 2007"
If (IsDate(testDate) = True) Then _
    results.AppendLine(Date.Parse(testDate).ToString)

' ----- Test a time.
testDate = "23:57:58"
If (IsDate(testDate) = True) Then _
    results.AppendLine(Date.Parse(testDate).ToString)

' ----- Test a date.
testDate = "December 7, 2007"
If (IsDate(testDate) = True) Then _
    results.AppendLine(Date.Parse(testDate).ToString)

' ----- Test a standardized date and time.
testDate = "2007-07-04T23:59:59"
If (IsDate(testDate) = True) Then _
    results.AppendLine(Date.Parse(testDate).ToString)

' ----- Test another standardized UTC date and time.
testDate = "2007-07-04T23:59:59Z"
```

```
If (IsDate(testDate) = True) Then _
    results.AppendLine(Date.Parse(testDate).ToString)

' ----- Display the results.
MsgBox(results.ToString())
```

As shown in Figure 7-11, the first string is a bad one, so it's not converted. The remaining four strings are correctly parsed to Dates.

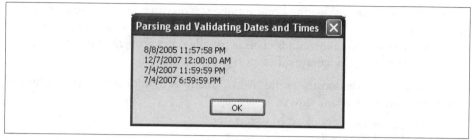

Figure 7-11. Dates parsed from a variety of string representations of dates and times

It's safe to assume that any string that returns True when passed to IsDate( ) will not cause an exception when passed to a Date's Parse( ) method.

> The Visual Basic CDate( ) conversion function also changes a string date to its true Date counterpart:
>
> ```
> Dim realDate As Date = CDate("January 1, 2007")
> ```

7.12 Adding to Dates and Times

Problem

You want to manipulate a Date value by adding an amount of time to it.

Solution

Sample code folder: Chapter 07\AddTime

Use one of the Date functions, such as AddYears( ) or AddMinutes( ), to add specific units of time to a Date's current value.

Discussion

There are seven "Add" functions used to add specific units of time to a Date:

- AddYears( )
- AddMonths( )
- AddDays( )

- AddHours( )
- AddMinutes( )
- AddSeconds( )
- AddMilliseconds( )

Each function adds a given amount of time to the Date. Confusion may arise because the parameters passed to some of these functions must be integers, while others require double-precision floating-point numbers. You can add only integer numbers of years, months, and hours, but you can add values with fractional parts to the days, minutes, seconds, and milliseconds. This is usually not a problem, but be aware that the various functions do require different types of parameters.

The following code demonstrates the "Add" functions by adding various amounts of time to the current date and time:

```
Dim results As New System.Text.StringBuilder
Dim rightNow As Date = Now

' ----- Show the current date and time.
results.AppendLine("RightNow: " & rightNow.ToString)
results.AppendLine( )

' ----- Add date values.
results.AppendLine("RightNow.AddYears(2): " & _
    rightNow.AddYears(2))
results.AppendLine("RightNow.AddMonths(3): " & _
    rightNow.AddMonths(3))
results.AppendLine("RightNow.AddDays(4): " & _
    rightNow.AddDays(4))

' ----- Add time values.
results.AppendLine("RightNow.AddHours(5): " & _
    rightNow.AddHours(5))
results.AppendLine("RightNow.AddMinutes(6): " & _
    rightNow.AddMinutes(6))
results.AppendLine("RightNow.AddSeconds(7): " & _
    rightNow.AddSeconds(7))
results.AppendLine("RightNow.AddMilliseconds(8000): " & _
    rightNow.AddMilliseconds(8000))

' ----- Display the results.
MsgBox(results.ToString( ))
```

Figure 7-12 shows the date and time "right now," and the results of adding the various amounts of time to this value.

Adding a number of years or days accurately can be tricky because the addition can be defined in more than one way. For example, if one month is added to August 31, 2005, you might expect a result of October 1, 2005 because there are only 30 days in September. However, the result of adding one month to either August 30 or August 31 is September 30.

Figure 7-12. Using the "Add" category of Date functions to add various amounts of time to a Date

Similarly, adding one year to February 29, 2004 results in a date of February 28, 2005, instead of March 1, 2005. The variable lengths of months and years are ignored when adding these units of time.

The hard-to-define lengths of years and months could explain why these units are added as integer parameters in the functions described earlier. However, hours are well-defined, invariable units of time, yet AddHours( ) also requires an integer parameter. Go figure (literally)!

7.13   Subtracting from Dates and Times

Problem

You want to subtract some amount of time from a date or time.

Solution

Sample code folder: Chapter 07\SubtractTime

Use the various "Add" functions of the Date object, passing negative values to subtract amounts of time.

Discussion

The Date object does not provide any "Subtract" functions for subtracting specific units of time. You can instead simply "add" negative amounts of time. The following code demonstrates how this works:

```
Dim results As New System.Text.StringBuilder
Dim rightNow As Date = Now

results.AppendLine("RightNow: " & rightNow.ToString)
results.AppendLine( )
```

```
results.AppendLine("One year ago: " & _
    rightNow.AddYears(-1).ToString)

results.AppendLine("365.25 days ago: " & _
    rightNow.AddDays(-365.25).ToString)

MsgBox(results.ToString())
```

Figure 7-13 shows the results of these negative time additions as displayed by the message box in the last line.

Figure 7-13. To subtract years, days, or other amounts of time, add negative quantities

Each Date object does provide a Subtract( ) function, as discussed in Recipe 7.14. However, this function subtracts either another Date value or a TimeSpan. It is possible to create a TimeSpan given an amount of time and its units, but simply adding specific negative units of time is a very straightforward way to get the task accomplished.

See Also

Recipe 7.12 lists the various "Add" date methods.

7.14 Determining the Number of Days Between Two Dates

Problem

You want to calculate the number of days between two dates.

Solution

Sample code folder: Chapter 07\DateDiff

Use the later date's Subtract( ) function to calculate a TimeSpan between the two dates, and then use the Days property of the TimeSpan to get the elapsed number of days.

Discussion

A TimeSpan object is a representation of an elapsed amount of time. As shown in the following code, you can subtract one date from another using its Subtract( ) method, which returns a TimeSpan. To access the units of time from the TimeSpan, access its properties for each type of unit. For example, the following code determines the number of days a person has been on the earth by subtracting his birth date from today's date. The Days property of the resulting TimeSpan provides the desired information:

```
Dim inputString As String
Dim birthDay As Date
Dim lifeTime As TimeSpan
Dim lifeDays As Integer

' ----- Prompt the user for a date.
Do
    inputString = InputBox("Enter the date of your birth")
Loop Until IsDate(inputString) = True

' ----- Perform the amazing calculations.
birthDay = Date.Parse(inputString)
lifeTime = Now.Subtract(birthDay)
lifeDays = lifeTime.Days
MsgBox(String.Format( _
    "There are {0} days between {1:D} and {2:D}", _
    lifeDays, birthDay, Now))
```

Figure 7-14 shows the number of days since Albert Einstein was born (as of August 8, 2005).

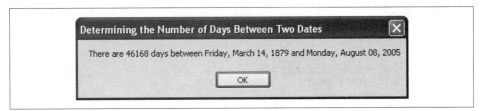

Figure 7-14. Determining the difference between two dates

The five span-generating members are Days, Hours, Minutes, Seconds, and Milliseconds. These each return a whole integer value stating the difference between the two dates or times. Five additional properties (TotalDays, TotalHours, TotalMinutes, TotalSeconds, and TotalMilliseconds) return decimal values that are not rounded to the nearest interval.

7.15   Determining the Day of the Week for a Date

Problem

You want to get a number or a string representing the day of the week for a given date.

Solution

Sample code folder: Chapter 07\DayOfWeek

Use the Date's DayOfWeek property, which returns a number from 0 (Sunday) to 6 (Saturday) for the day of the week, or use its ToString( ) method to return the weekday name. You can also use various string-formatting options of the String.Format( ) method to return either the short or longer string name for the day of the week.

Discussion

If you want a number representation of the day of the week, the Date object's DayOfWeek property provides this directly. By default it returns 0 for Sunday, 1 to 5 for the workdays Monday through Friday, and 6 for Saturday.

To get the name of the weekday, call the DayOfWeek's ToString( ) method:

```
MsgBox(Today.DayOfWeek.ToString( ))
```

To get an abbreviated version of the weekday name, apply the "ddd" formatting as you convert the date to a string. (Use "dddd" for the full weekday name.) The following lines of code demonstrate these techniques:

```
Dim rightNow As Date = Now
Dim weekDay As Integer = rightNow.DayOfWeek
Dim weekDayShort As String = Format(rightNow, "ddd")
Dim weekDayLong As String = String.Format("{0:dddd}", _
   rightNow)

Dim results As String = String.Format( _
   "Today's day of the week: {0}, or {1}, or {2}", _
   weekDay, weekDayShort, weekDayLong)
MsgBox(results)
```

Figure 7-15 shows the results as displayed by the message box in the last line of the example code.

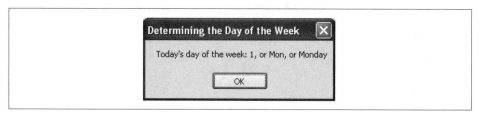

Figure 7-15. Getting the day of the week either as a number from 0 to 6 or as a short or longer string name

7.16   Determining the Day of the Year for a Date

Problem

You want to calculate the day of the year for a date, a number in the range 1 to 366.

Solution

Use the Date object's DayOfYear property to get this number directly, with no calculations required.

Discussion

The following code shows how to determine a date's day of the year:

```
Dim rightNow As Date = Now
Dim yearDay As Integer = rightNow.DayOfYear

Dim results As String = String.Format( _
    "Day of year for {0:D}: {1}", Now, yearDay)
MsgBox(results)
```

Figure 7-16 shows the day of the year for a date, as displayed by the message box in the sample code.

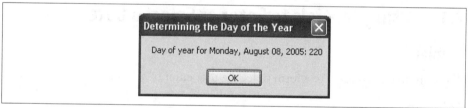

Figure 7-16. Determining the day of year for a specific date with the Date object's DayOfYear property

7.17   Determining the Number of Days in a Month

Problem

You want to calculate the number of days in a given month.

Solution

Use the shared function DaysInMonth provided by the Date object. This function returns the number of days in a month, given the month and year.

Discussion

Unlike the DayOfWeek and DayOfYear properties available on every Date variable, DaysInMonth is a shared function. Instead of prefixing the call with a specific Date, use the generic Date object to access this function. The following code shows the correct syntax as it gets the number of days in the current month:

```
Dim daysInMonth As Integer = _
   Date.DaysInMonth(Now.Year, Now.Month)
MsgBox(String.Format( _
   "Number of days in the current month: {0}", daysInMonth))
```

Figure 7-17 shows the results as displayed by the message box.

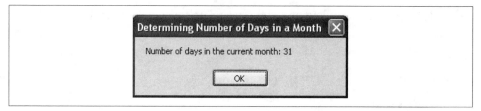

Figure 7-17. Determining the number of days in a given month with the shared function DaysInMonth

7.18   Using Controls to Enter or Select a Date

Problem

You want to add controls to a form to let the user enter or select a date.

Solution

Sample code folder: Chapter 07\DateEntry

Use a text box for easy text entry, a DateTimePicker for a control more tailored to entering a date, or a MonthCalendar control for a more graphical way to allow the user to select a date.

Discussion

The sample code in this recipe presents a form with all three controls, each of which has its uses, advantages, and drawbacks. Experiment with them to determine which will work best for your goals.

Figure 7-18 shows the form during development, with the three date-entry controls and three associated Label controls. As the following code listing shows, changes to the dates in each control are shown in the label control to its right.

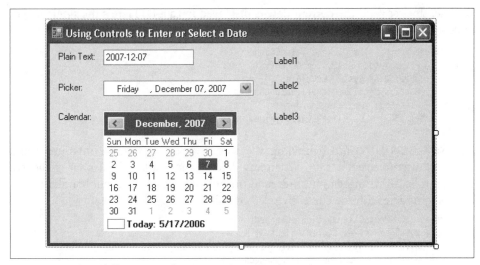

Figure 7-18. Three different ways for a user to enter or select a date

The TextBox control is the simplest in the sense that no special property settings are required to define its behavior as a field for entering dates. Instead, most of the work is done in its TextChanged event:

```
Private Sub TextBox1_TextChanged( _
      ByVal sender As System.Object, _
      ByVal e As System.EventArgs) _
      Handles TextBox1.TextChanged
   ' ----- Check and display only valid dates.
   If (IsDate(TextBox1.Text) = True) Then
      Label1.Text = Date.Parse(TextBox1.Text).ToShortDateString
   Else
      Label1.Text = ""
   End If
End Sub
```

This event activates whenever any change is made to the TextBox's text. During date entry the incomplete string in this text box will probably not represent a valid date, so the IsDate( ) function verifies the entered text before use. If it's not yet a valid date, Label1 displays nothing, but as soon as the text becomes a valid date, the string is parsed, and the date is reformatted for display in Label1.

The DateTimePicker control does have some properties you can use to control the interaction with the user. For example, in this demonstration the control's ShowUpDown property has been set to True to show the little arrows at the end of the field for incrementing and decrementing the displayed date. The control's Format property has also been set to Short to display the date in a simplified format.

At runtime, the DateTimePicker control allows the user to highlight one of the three parts of the date—year, month, or day—and then use the up and down arrows to scroll through possible values for each. The control's ValueChanged event activates as the user does so, and the current date is displayed in Label2. Here's the single line of code added to this event to cause this action:

```
Private Sub DateTimePicker1_ValueChanged( _
    ByVal sender As System.Object, _
    ByVal e As System.EventArgs) _
    Handles DateTimePicker1.ValueChanged
    ' ----- Show the selected date.
    Label2.Text = DateTimePicker1.Value.ToShortDateString
End Sub
```

The MonthCalendar control provides the user with an even more interactive and graphical way to select a date. When any date on the displayed calendar is clicked, the control's DateChanged event fires, and the line of code in this event handler causes Label3 to update with the currently selected date:

```
Private Sub MonthCalendar1_DateChanged( _
    ByVal sender As System.Object, _
    ByVal e As System.Windows.Forms.DateRangeEventArgs) _
    Handles MonthCalendar1.DateChanged
    ' ---- Show the slected date.
    Label3.Text = _
        MonthCalendar1.SelectionStart.ToShortDateString
End Sub
```

The TextBox control's text needs to be parsed to become a Date value, but the DateTimePicker and MonthCalendar controls' Value and SelectionStart properties return Date values directly.

Figure 7-19 shows the form in action as a user is selecting a date using the MonthCalendar control.

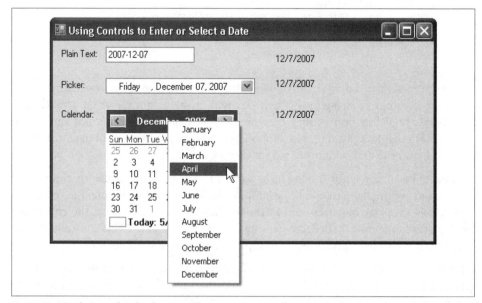

Figure 7-19. The MonthCalendar control sports a variety of interactive features when selecting a date

7.19   Calculating the Phase of the Moon

Problem

You want to calculate the phase of the moon for a given date.

Solution

Sample code folder: Chapter 07\MoonPhase

Use Visual Basic 2005's Date and Math functions to apply a linear-fit equation to calculate the phase of the moon, accurate to within half an hour.

Discussion

The linear curve fit equation presented here was researched and created only recently, using data from the Internet that provided the date and time of all new moons over a period of several centuries. The results are surprisingly accurate, and the equation is easy to use, especially with the helpful math and date functions available in Visual Basic.

Here's the MoonPhase( ) function resulting from the research:

```
Public Function MoonPhase(ByVal dateUtc As Date) As Double
   ' ----- Determine the phase of the moon for any date.
   Dim days As Double = dateUtc.Subtract(#1/1/1600#).TotalDays
   Dim cycles As Double = days * 0.03386319 - 12.5
   Return Math.IEEERemainder(cycles, 1.0) * 29.53059
End Function
```

The date for determining the moon's phase is passed to this function as dateUtc, and it should be an exact date and time value expressed in Coordinated Universal Time. A TimeSpan is calculated by subtracting from the date the literal date constant for midnight, January 1, 1600. The TotalDays property of the resulting TimeSpan provides the total elapsed days, complete with a decimal result for the fraction of the day. The decimal number of days is stored in the Double variable named days.

The heart of this algorithm is in the second line of the function. The number of elapsed days since the start of 1600 is multiplied by 0.03386319, and an offset of 12.5 days is subtracted from the result. This linear equation provides an approximate number of full moons since 1600. The fractional part, which cycles through values from 0 to 1 between successive new moons, is the part that's interesting. Rather than simply extracting the fractional part of cycles, the Math.IEEERemainder( ) function returns a value ranging from -0.5 to $+0.5$, and this value is multiplied by the number of mean days between full moons to get the number of days, plus or minus, to the closest full moon.

The following code reports the closest new moon using the MoonPhase( ) function:

```
Dim phaseDay As Double
Dim result As String
```

```
' ----- Determine the phase of the moon.
phaseDay = MoonPhase(Now.ToUniversalTime)

' ----- Show the nearest new moon.
result = "UTC is now: " & _
    Now.ToUniversalTime.ToString("u") & vbNewLine & vbNewLine
If (phaseDay < 0) Then
    result &= "Approx days until new moon: " & _
        (-phaseDay).ToString("F1")
Else
    result &= "Approx days since new moon: " & _
        phaseDay.ToString("F1")
End If
MsgBox(result)
```

This code converts the current local time to UTC using the ToUniversalTime( ) method before sending that time to the moon-phase calculator. Figure 7-20 shows the sample code in use.

Figure 7-20. The moon is waxing and it's about ¼ lit by the sun

After running a curve fit program to compute the equation used earlier, a second program was written to find the maximum absolute error in time for all new moons in the range of years from 1600 to 2500. Surprisingly, the maximum drift of the time of new moon was less than half an hour. This equation, even though it's a simple one, is good enough to allow you to predict when you'll be able to fish, plant, and dance by the light of the moon.

7.20   Creating a Calendar

Problem

You want to display a full-year calendar on a reasonably sized form.

Solution

Use the MonthCalendar control, dock it to fill its parent form, and size the form large enough that all 12 months appear.

Discussion

The MonthCalendar control normally displays only one month at a time, with buttons and controls to toggle through neighboring months and years as desired. However, if it's docked to the center of the form ("Fill") or other parent control, it attempts to fill the area completely. Instead of displaying larger text, the control displays multiple months either side by side or stacked vertically, depending on which way you stretch the form. Stretch the form a little, and suddenly the one-month calendar changes to display two months. Keep going, and it will display three, four, or more months in a rectangular array. At a form size of about 551 pixels wide by 615 pixels high, a full year of a dozen months displays nicely in a three-across and four-high pattern. Figure 7-21 shows the form at this size.

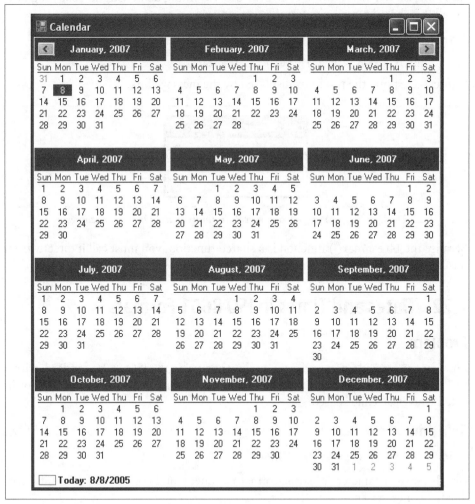

Figure 7-21. A nice one-year calendar displayed with no code at all

7.21   Checking for Leap Years

Problem

You want to check a year to see if it's a leap year.

Solution

Use the shared `IsLeapYear( )` function provided by the `Date` object to test any year.

Discussion

The `IsLeapYear( )` function returns `True` if the year passed to it is a leap year and `False` if it isn't. The following code provides a working demonstration showing how to call this shared function to test the current year:

```
Dim leapYear As Boolean = Date.IsLeapYear(Now.Year)
MsgBox(String.Format( _
    "{0} is a leap year: {1}", Now.Year, leapYear))
```

Figure 7-22 shows the results as displayed by the message box.

Figure 7-22. The Date.IsLeapYear function reveals instantly that 2005 is not a leap year

Because the `IsLeapYear( )` function is a shared function, you must call it directly from the `Date` object, not from an instance of a `Date`.

7.22   Dates and Times in ISO 8601 Formats

Problem

You want to format a date and time into a string using the ISO 8601 standard, with a "T" separating the date and time parts and an optional "Z" at the end if Coordinated Universal Time is used.

Solution

Sample code folder: Chapter 07\ISO8601

Use the single-character "s" string-format parameter and concatenate a "Z" if Coordinated Universal Time is used.

Discussion

String formatting in .NET has much of the ISO 8601 standard built in. The "s" string-format parameter creates a date and time string of the form "yyyy-mm-ddThh:mm:ss," and the "u" format parameter creates the same string minus the "T" that separates the date and time parts and with a "Z" at the tail end to signify Coordinated Universal Time. The standard is actually fairly relaxed about the "T" separator requirement, so these two string-formatting parameters cover most bases. The first two lines of output in Figure 7-23 show the strings created using these formatting parameters.

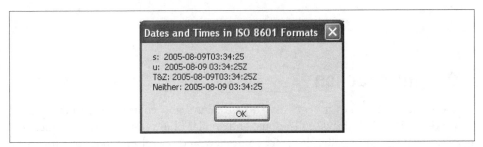

Figure 7-23. Date and time strings that closely conform to the ISO 8601 standard

One scenario not covered is when you want to include both the "T" separator character and the "Z" at the tail end. As shown previously, the "s" and "u" formatting parameters give you one or the other but not both. The other scenario not covered is when you want to drop both the "T" and the "Z" from the string. Fortunately, it's easy to add this functionality.

The following code was used to create the output shown in Figure 7-23:

```
Dim rightNow As Date = Now.ToUniversalTime
Dim format1 As String = rightNow.ToString("s")
Dim format2 As String = rightNow.ToString("u")
Dim format3 As String = rightNow.ToString("s") & "Z"
Dim format4 As String = rightNow.ToString( _
    "u").Substring(0, 19)

MsgBox(String.Format( _
    "s: {1}{0}u: {2}{0}T&Z: {3}{0}Neither: {4}", _
    vbNewLine, format1, format2, format3, format4))
```

To add both the "T" and the "Z" to the formatted string, use the "s" format and concatenate a "Z" to the tail of the result. `format3` in the code and the third line of the output demonstrate this technique.

To eliminate both the "T" and the "Z" from the ISO-formatted string, use the "u" format parameter to create a 20-character string; then use `Substring()` to drop the "Z" from the tail end.

CHAPTER 8

Arrays and Collections

8.0   Introduction

Visual Basic 2005 makes it very easy to pass arrays and collections into and out of methods. This makes arrays, collections, and similar objects very useful for efficiently grouping data. Additionally, there are some new and useful methods for processing arrays that are easy to overlook if you're just moving up from Visual Basic 6.0. Several recipes in this chapter focus on these methods. For example, arrays have a built-in Sort( ) method that will sort some or all of the elements in the array, a feature that had to be coded by hand before .NET.

Generics are also new in Visual Basic 2005, providing a powerful new type-safe way to define collections and other objects such as lists, stacks, and queues. Generics enable compile-time typing of objects without your having to write separate classes for each type you want to support. This chapter demonstrates a simple generic collection. Other chapters provide further examples of generics.

8.1   Filling an Array While Declaring It

Problem

You want to fill an array with starting values without having to explicitly assign each array element individually.

Solution

You can load an array in the Dim statement using empty parentheses after either the array's name or its type designation, followed by braces listing the array elements to be assigned.

Discussion

The following line of code creates a one-dimensional array of integers with three elements (elements 0 through 2):

```
Dim array1D( ) As Integer = {1, 2, 3}
```

A two-dimensional array is only slightly trickier to fill on the spot, requiring nested braces containing the array elements. You can put the nested braces all on one line, or you can use the underscore line-continuation symbol to format the data in a more readable layout, such as in the following example:

```
Dim array2D(,) As Integer = { _
    {1, 2}, _
    {3, 4}}
```

For comparison, the following line of code creates exactly the same array:

```
Dim array2D(,) As Integer = {{1, 2}, {3, 4}}
```

Arrays with three or more dimensions are declared in a similar way, with additional commas and curly braces included as needed:

```
Dim array3D(,,) As Integer = _
    {{{1, 2}, {3, 4}}, {{5, 6}, {7, 8}}}
```

For comparison, the following block of code creates exactly the same three-dimensional array and fills each element with the same values, but does so using a more traditional method of assigning each individual element:

```
Dim array3D(1, 1, 1) As Integer
array3D(0, 0, 0) = 1
array3D(0, 0, 1) = 2
array3D(0, 1, 0) = 3
array3D(0, 1, 1) = 4
array3D(1, 0, 0) = 5
array3D(1, 0, 1) = 6
array3D(1, 1, 0) = 7
array3D(1, 1, 1) = 8
```

8.2   Sorting Array Elements

Problem

You want to sort the elements of an array.

Solution

Sample code folder: Chapter 08\SortingArrays

Use the Sort( ) method of the Array class.

Discussion

The Array class has a shared Sort( ) method that works on arrays of any kind. There are several optional parameters that let you customize the sorting algorithm for different types of objects, but for arrays of strings and numbers, the name of the array is generally all you need to pass. The following example creates a string array containing the names of a few types of fruit, then sorts them into alphabetical order and displays the sorted list of fruit names for review:

```
Dim result As New System.Text.StringBuilder
Dim arrayToSort() As String = { _
   "Oranges", "Apples", "Grapes", "Bananas", "Blueberries"}

' ----- Show the elements before sorting.
result.AppendLine("Before sorting:")
For Each fruit As String In arrayToSort
   result.AppendLine(fruit)
Next fruit

' ----- Show the elements after sorting.
result.AppendLine()
result.AppendLine("After sorting:")
Array.Sort(arrayToSort)
For Each fruit As String In arrayToSort
   result.AppendLine(fruit)
Next fruit

MsgBox(result.ToString())
```

The StringBuilder is first filled with the names of the fruits in the unsorted order used to create the string array. The Array.Sort( ) method is invoked to sort the fruits alphabetically, and the sorted fruits are then added to the StringBuilder to demonstrate the sorted order. Figure 8-1 shows the array before and after the sort.

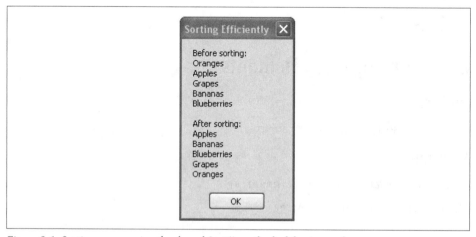

Figure 8-1. Sorting arrays using the shared Sort() method of the Array class

Sorting intrinsic types is simple, but you can also sort custom classes based on any comparison criteria you specify. You do this by implementing the IComparable interface on the custom class. The following class implements a simple comparison interface that merges group and item values into a single string for comparison:

```
Private Class CustomData
    Implements IComparable

    Public GroupName As String
    Public ItemName As String

    Public Sub New(ByVal theGroup As String, _
            ByVal theItem As String)
        GroupName = theGroup
        ItemName = theItem
    End Sub

    Public Overrides Function ToString() As String
        Return GroupName & ": " & ItemName
    End Function

    Public Function CompareTo(ByVal obj As Object) As Integer _
            Implements System.IComparable.CompareTo
        ' ----- Compare two records.
        Dim compareValue As String

        ' ----- Since we're just going to compare the ToString
        '          value, no need to convert to CustomData.
        compareValue = obj.ToString()

        ' ----- Return the relative comparison value.
        Return String.Compare(Me.ToString(), compareValue)
    End Function
End Class
```

The CompareTo() method returns a negative value if the object itself should come before another object supplied for comparison, a positive value if the instance should come after, and zero if they are equal. The String object's comparer was deferred to here, but you can use any complex calculations for comparison.

The following sample sorts an array of CustomData data elements:

```
Dim result As New System.Text.StringBuilder
Dim arrayToSort() As CustomData = { _
    New CustomData("Fruit", "Orange"), _
    New CustomData("Vegetable", "Onion"), _
    New CustomData("Fruit", "Apple"), _
    New CustomData("Vegetable", "Carrot"), _
    New CustomData("Fruit", "Grape")}

' ----- Show the elements before sorting.
result.AppendLine("Before sorting:")
For Each food As CustomData In arrayToSort
```

```
      result.AppendLine(food.ToString())
   Next food

   ' ----- Show the elements after sorting.
   result.AppendLine()
   result.AppendLine("After sorting:")
   Array.Sort(arrayToSort)
   For Each food As CustomData In arrayToSort
      result.AppendLine(food.ToString())
   Next food

   MsgBox(result.ToString())
```

Figure 8-2 shows the output from this code.

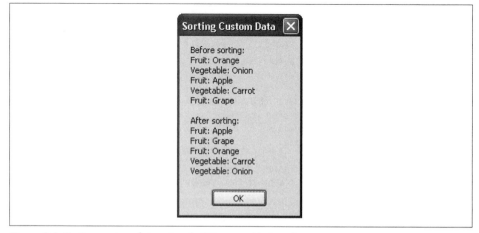

Figure 8-2. Sorting custom data using the IComparable interface

See Also

Recipe 8.3 shows how to reverse the elements of an array, and Recipe 8.5 shows how to randomly rearrange the elements of an array.

8.3   Reversing an Array

Problem

You want to reverse the order of the elements in an array. This might be useful, for instance, immediately after sorting an array to change the sort order from ascending to descending.

Solution

Sample code folder: Chapter 08\ArrayReversal

The Array class provides a shared Reverse() method that reverses the order of its elements.

Discussion

The `Array.Reverse( )` method reverses an array, whether its elements have been sorted first or not. The following code fills a string array with a few fruit names, in no special order. The `Array.Reverse( )` method then reverses the order of the array's elements:

```
Dim result As New System.Text.StringBuilder
Dim arrayReverse( ) As String = { _
    "Oranges", "Apples", "Grapes", "Bananas", "Blueberries"}

' ----- Show the elements before reversal.
result.AppendLine("Before reversing:")
For Each fruit As String In arrayReverse
    result.AppendLine(fruit)
Next fruit

' ----- Show the elements after reversal.
result.AppendLine( )
result.AppendLine("After reversing:")
Array.Reverse(arrayReverse)
For Each fruit As String In arrayReverse
    result.AppendLine(fruit)
Next fruit

MsgBox(result.ToString( ))
```

The `StringBuilder` fills first with the strings from the original array, then with the reversed array's contents for comparison. Figure 8-3 shows the results as displayed by the `StringBuilder` in the message box.

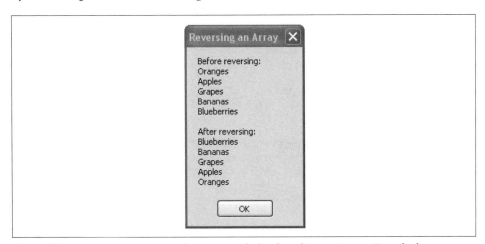

Figure 8-3. Reversing the contents of an array with the shared Array.Reverse() method

See Also

Recipe 8.2 shows another method of arranging the elements of an array.

8.4   Inserting into an Array

Problem

You need to insert a new value at an arbitrary location in the middle of an array.

Solution

Sample code folder: Chapter 08\ArrayInsertion

Unlike some of the collection classes in .NET, arrays do not include a method that lets you insert an element in the middle of an array. Instead, you have to create a new array and copy the elements of the original array into it, reserving space for the new element. The code in this recipe implements such a method.

Discussion

Because arrays can be created using any data type, we will require a generic method capable of handling any data:

```
Public Sub InsertArrayElement(Of T) ( _
      ByRef sourceArray( ) As T, _
      ByVal insertIndex As Integer, _
      ByVal newValue As T)
   ' ----- Insert a value in the middle of an array.
   Dim newPosition As Integer
   Dim counter As Integer

   ' ----- Get a valid positon, checking for boundaries.
   newPosition = insertIndex
   If (newPosition < 0) Then newPosition = 0
   If (newPosition > sourceArray.Length) Then _
      newPosition = sourceArray.Length

   ' ----- Make room in the array.
   Array.Resize(sourceArray, sourceArray.Length + 1)

   ' ----- Move the after-index items.
   For counter = sourceArray.Length - 2 To newPosition Step -1
      sourceArray(counter + 1) = sourceArray(counter)
   Next counter

   ' ----- Store the new element.
   sourceArray(newPosition) = newValue
End Sub
```

The code stretches the initial array, making it one position larger. It then shifts some of the elements one position higher to make room for the new element. Finally, it saves the new element at the desired position.

To use this method, pass it an array of any type, and also indicate the type used for the generic parameter.

You can insert the new value at position 0, just before the very first element, or at a position one greater than the maximum current index of the array. Insert positions outside this range adjust themselves to fit the valid range.

The following example demonstrates calling the InsertArrayElement( ) method by first creating a string array of fruit names and then inserting an element in the middle:

```
Dim result As New System.Text.StringBuilder
Dim arrayInsert( ) As String = { _
   "Oranges", "Apples", "Grapes", "Bananas", "Blueberries"}

' ----- Show the contents before insertion.
result.AppendLine("Before insertion:")
For Each fruit As String In arrayInsert
   result.AppendLine(fruit)
Next fruit

' ----- Insert more fruit.
InsertArrayElement(Of String)(arrayInsert, 2, "Lemons")

' ----- Show the contents after insertion.
result.AppendLine( )
result.AppendLine("After insertion:")
For Each fruit As String In arrayInsert
   result.AppendLine(fruit)
Next fruit

MsgBox(result.ToString( ))
```

The string "Lemons" is inserted at position 2 (counting from zero) in the array. The results are shown in Figure 8-4.

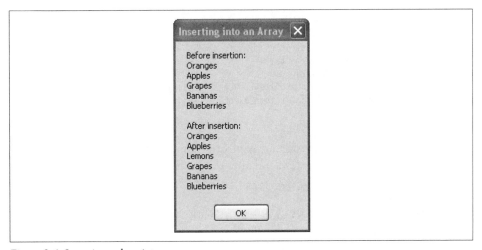

Figure 8-4. Inserting values into an array

See Also

Recipe 8.7 also discusses adding elements to an array.

8.5   Shuffling an Array

Problem

You want to randomize the order of the elements in an array efficiently.

Solution

Sample code folder: Chapter 08\ShuffleArray

Write a routine that randomly rearranges the elements of an array. The code in this recipe does this using an array of any data type.

Discussion

The Shuffle( ) method presented here swaps each element of the array with a randomly selected element from elsewhere in the array. Sometimes this may cause an element to be swapped with itself, but that doesn't make the results any less random. By sequencing through all elements, the algorithm guarantees that each one will be swapped at least once:

```
Public Sub Shuffle(ByRef shuffleArray( ) As Object)
   ' ----- Reorder the elements of an array in a random order.
   Dim counter As Integer
   Dim newPosition As Integer
   Dim shuffleMethod As New Random
   Dim tempObject As Object

   For counter = 0 To shuffleArray.Length - 1
      ' ----- Determine the new position.
      newPosition = shuffleMethod.Next(0, _
         shuffleArray.Length - 1)

      ' ----- Reverse two elements.
      tempObject = shuffleArray(counter)
      shuffleArray(counter) = shuffleArray(newPosition)
      shuffleArray(newPosition) = tempObject
   Next counter
End Sub
```

The following code creates a string array of fruit names, shuffles the array, and displays the array contents both before and after the shuffling:

```
Dim result As New System.Text.StringBuilder
Dim arrayShuffle( ) As String = { _
   "Oranges", "Apples", "Grapes", "Bananas", "Blueberries"}

' ----- Show the pre-random results.
result.AppendLine("Before shuffling:")
For Each fruit As String In arrayShuffle
   result.AppendLine(fruit)
Next fruit
```

```
' ----- Randomize.
Shuffle(arrayShuffle)

' ----- Show the post-random results.
result.AppendLine()
result.AppendLine("After shuffling:")
For Each fruit As String In arrayShuffle
    result.AppendLine(fruit)
Next fruit

MsgBox(result.ToString())
```

Figure 8-5 shows the results from running the sample code, listing the array's contents before and after the shuffling. Your output may vary due to the random nature of the test.

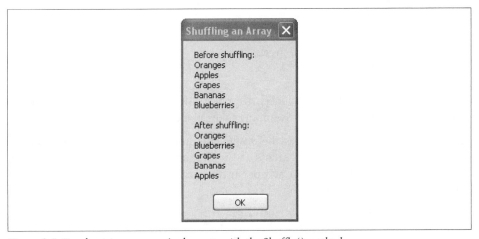

Figure 8-5. Randomizing an array's elements with the Shuffle() method

See Also

Recipe 8.6 uses a portion of this recipe's code to generically reverse two array elements.

8.6 Swapping Two Array Values

Problem

You want to swap the contents of any two elements in an array.

Solution

Sample code folder: Chapter 08\SwapArrayElements

Write a custom method that reverses the positions of two specific array elements. The code in this recipe implements a Swap() method that does just that.

Discussion

The Swap( ) method accepts an array of any data type, plus the positions of two elements to swap. After doing some boundary checking, it reverses the elements:

```
Public Sub Swap(ByRef swapArray() As Object, _
    ByVal first As Integer, ByVal second As Integer)
  ' ----- Reverse two elements of an array.
  Dim tempObject As Object

  ' ----- Check for invalid positions.
  If (first < 0) Then Return
  If (first >= swapArray.Length) Then Return
  If (second < 0) Then Return
  If (second >= swapArray.Length) Then Return
  If (first = second) Then Return

  ' ----- Reverse two elements.
  tempObject = swapArray(first)
  swapArray(first) = swapArray(second)
  swapArray(second) = tempObject
End Sub
```

Several lines of this code simply check to make sure the indexes into the array are valid. If they are out of range, no swapping takes place.

The following code demonstrates the Swap( ) method by creating a string array of fruit names and swapping the contents at the first and third indexes into the array. The ArrayHelper is instanced to accept string parameters, and the string array is passed to its Swap( ) method:

```
Dim result As New System.Text.StringBuilder
Dim arraySwap() As String = { _
  "Oranges", "Apples", "Grapes", "Bananas", "Blueberries"}

' ----- Show the pre-swap data.
result.AppendLine("Before swap:")
For Each fruit As String In arraySwap
    result.AppendLine(fruit)
Next fruit

' ----- Swap two elements.
Swap(arraySwap, 1, 3)

' ----- Show the post-swap data.
result.AppendLine( )
result.AppendLine("After swap:")
For Each fruit As String In arraySwap
    result.AppendLine(fruit)
Next fruit

MsgBox(result.ToString( ))
```

Figure 8-6 shows the array's contents before and after elements 1 and 3 are swapped. Notice that the array elements start at zero, so the swap is between the second and fourth values in the array.

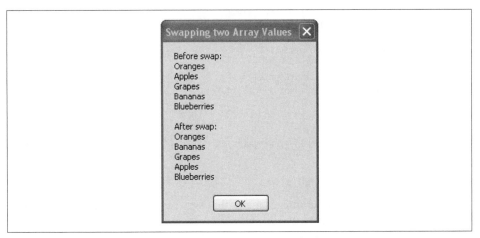

Figure 8-6. Swapping two array elements with the Swap() method

See Also

Recipe 8.5 shows how to randomly rearrange the contents of an entire array.

8.7   Resizing Arrays Without Losing Existing Values

Problem

You want to add an unknown number of elements to an array, resizing the array as needed, but you don't want to lose any data in the process.

Solution

Sample code folder: Chapter 08\SwapArrayElements

Visual Basic 2005 provides the ReDim Preserve command to resize an array without losing any of the array's current contents.

Discussion

Actually, you can lose some contents of an array using ReDim Preserve, but only if you are decreasing the array's size. ReDim Preserve is most often used to grow an array, and it is ideal for adding new elements on the fly, without losing any data already in the array.

For example, the following code creates an integer array and then loops to grow it one element at a time. A number is stored in each new array element as the array grows:

```
Dim result As New System.Text.StringBuilder
Dim growingArray() As String = Nothing

' ----- Add elements to the array.
For counter As Integer = 0 To 2
   ReDim Preserve growingArray(counter)
   growingArray(counter) = (counter + 1).ToString
Next counter

' ----- Display the results.
For Each workText As String In growingArray
   result.AppendLine(workText)
Next workText
MsgBox(result.ToString())
```

Figure 8-7 displays the simple integer array that was resized, one element at a time, to hold the three numbers shown.

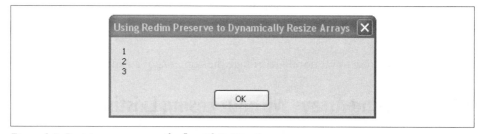

Figure 8-7. Resizing an array on the fly with ReDim Preserve

One nice thing about ReDim Preserve is that it works with arrays that are empty or set to Nothing, as shown in the sample code.

The Array object's Resize() method provides similar functionality.

See Also

Recipe 8.4 shows how to insert elements into the middle of an existing array, instead of just at the end.

8.8   Quickly Copying Part of an Array into Another

Problem

You want to copy elements of one array into another without having to move the items one at a time.

Solution

Sample code folder: Chapter 08\CopyingArrays

Use the `Array.Copy()` method to copy a sequential subset of one array to another array of the same type. Or, if the entire array is to be copied, use the array's `Clone()` method. Assign one array directly to another only if you want both variables to reference the same contents in memory.

Discussion

This recipe explores several ways to copy elements from one array to another, and one way that appears to do a copy but doesn't. It's important to know the difference between these various techniques. The following block of code demonstrates all of them and displays the results in a message box:

```
Dim result As New System.Text.StringBuilder

Dim arrayA() As String = _
   {"One", "Two", "Three", "Four", "Five", "Six"}
result.Append("arrayA: ").AppendLine(Join(arrayA, ","))

Dim arrayB() As String = _
   {"A", "B", "C", "D", "E", "E", "F", "G", "H"}
result.AppendLine()
result.Append("arrayB: ").AppendLine(Join(arrayB, ","))

' ----- Make a reference copy.
Dim arrayC() As String = arrayA
result.AppendLine()
result.AppendLine("Dim arrayC() As String = arrayA")
result.Append("arrayC: ").AppendLine(Join(arrayC, ","))

arrayC(4) = "Was a five here"
result.AppendLine()
result.AppendLine("arrayC(4) = ""Was a five here""")
result.Append("arrayA: ").AppendLine(Join(arrayA, ","))

' ----- Make a full, unique copy of all elements.
Dim arrayD() As String = arrayA.Clone
result.AppendLine()
result.AppendLine("Dim arrayD() As String = arrayA.Clone")
result.Append("arrayD: ").AppendLine(Join(arrayD, ","))

' ----- Copy elements by position.
Array.Copy(arrayB, 0, arrayD, 1, 3)
result.AppendLine()
result.AppendLine("Array.Copy(arrayB, 0, arrayD, 1, 3)")
result.Append("arrayD: ").AppendLine(Join(arrayD, ","))

MsgBox(result.ToString())
```

Let's break down this code into smaller chunks so we can take a closer look. The first three sections create two string arrays, arrayA and arrayB, containing simple strings so we can follow the action later. The first line of the next section is where it gets interesting:

```
Dim arrayC( ) As String = arrayA
```

This appears to be an array copy command, but it isn't. The two array names both reference the same contents in memory. In other words, the reference to the array is copied, not the array itself. The code in the next section demonstrates this clearly:

```
arrayC(4) = "Was a five here"
result.AppendLine( )
result.AppendLine("arrayC(4) = ""Was a five here""")
result.Append("arrayA: ").AppendLine(Join(arrayA, ","))
```

The new string is assigned to arrayC(4), but when the contents of arrayA are formatted for display the new string appears there, too. As Figure 8-8 shows, the new string appears as an element of both arrayA and arrayC.

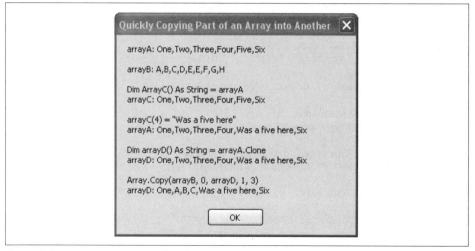

Figure 8-8. Various ways to copy data between arrays

The next-to-last code section demonstrates the proper way to truly copy an entire array to another. The array's Clone( ) method returns a clone, or identical duplicate, of the original array. The result is that the array's contents are copied to a new place in memory. In the example code, the reference to the cloned copy of the array is assigned to arrayD:

```
Dim arrayD( ) As String = arrayA.Clone
result.AppendLine( )
result.AppendLine("Dim arrayD( ) As String = arrayA.Clone")
result.Append("arrayD: ").AppendLine(Join(arrayD, ","))
```

Finally, the last code section demonstrates the use of the `Array` class's `Copy()` method to copy part of one array to another. In this case both arrays must exist before the copy, and the indexes must point to real locations within the arrays. There are several overloaded versions of the `Copy()` method. The version shown here lets you move array elements starting at a given indexed position to any position in the destination array, and the number of elements to copy limits how much data is copied:

```
Array.Copy(arrayB, 0, arrayD, 1, 3)
result.AppendLine()
result.AppendLine("Array.Copy(arrayB, 0, arrayD, 1, 3)")
result.Append("arrayD: ").AppendLine(Join(arrayD, ","))
```

`arrayB`'s contents, starting at index 0, are copied into `arrayD`, starting at index 1, and three items are copied. If you've followed along carefully as these sections of code manipulate the contents of the arrays, you'll see that the result shown in Figure 8-8 does verify this copy action.

8.9   Writing a Comma-Separated-Values File from a String Array

Problem

You need to write data stored in an array to a comma-separated-values (CSV) file. This is often done to provide input to Excel.

Solution

Sample code folder: Chapter 08\CreateCSVFiles

Use the `String` class's `Join()` method to concatenate array contents into strings, using a comma as the character to insert at the join points. Then write the string or strings to a file using the `WriteAllText()` method provided by the `My.Computer.FileSystem` object.

Discussion

In many cases you'll have several data items that you want to appear in each of several rows of a spreadsheet. This is accomplished by separating each data item in each row with a comma, and separating the rows from each other using newline characters. The following code demonstrates various ways to accomplish this. `headings` is a string array containing three words. The `Join()` method concatenates this array into a single string with commas separating each word. To simplify the example, several more similar comma-separated strings are concatenated to the string, each separated with `vbNewLine` characters. The resulting string is written to a file named *Test.csv* in a single command using the `My.Computer.FileSystem.WriteAllText()` method:

```
Dim result As New System.Text.StringBuilder
Dim headings() As String = {"Alpha", "Beta", "Gamma"}
Dim workText As String = String.Join(",", headings)
```

```
' ----- Prepare the raw data.
workText &= vbNewLine
workText &= "1.1, 2.3, 4.5" & vbNewLine
workText &= "4.2, 7.9, 3.1" & vbNewLine
workText &= "3.5, 2.2, 9.8" & vbNewLine

' ----- Convert it to CSV and save it to a file.
Dim filePath As String = _
    My.Computer.FileSystem.CurrentDirectory & "\Test.csv"
My.Computer.FileSystem.WriteAllText(filePath, workText, False)
result.Append("File written: ")
result.AppendLine(filePath)
result.AppendLine()
result.AppendLine("File contents:")
result.Append(workText)

MsgBox(result.ToString())
```

The remaining lines of example code display the new *Test.csv* file contents, as shown in Figure 8-9.

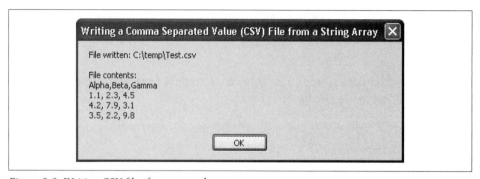

Figure 8-9. Writing CSV files from array data

See Also

Recipe 8.10 is the reverse of this recipe.

8.10   Reading a Comma-Separated-Values File into a String Array

Problem

You need to read a CSV file into an array.

Solution

Sample code folder: Chapter 08\ReadCSVFiles

Use the Split( ) function to parse the file's content to fill an array.

Discussion

Today's computers generally have a lot of memory, which often allows entire files to be read into a single string in one operation. If you have an extremely large CSV file, you might want to read the file one line at a time. In either case, the Split( ) function provides a great tool for parsing the comma-separated values so they can be copied into an array.

The following code reads the entire file created in the previous recipe into a single string, and then splits this string into an array of strings, lineData, using the newline characters as the split point. Each line is then further split at the comma character separating individual words. If the CSV file contains numbers, this is the point where each "word" of the text from the file could be converted to Double, Integer, or whatever type is appropriate. In this example, however, the words are simply reformatted for display and verification in a message box:

```
Dim result As New System.Text.StringBuilder
Dim wholeFile As String
Dim lineData( ) As String
Dim fieldData( ) As String

' ----- Read in the file.
Dim filePath As String = _
   My.Computer.FileSystem.CurrentDirectory & "\Test.csv"
wholeFile = My.Computer.FileSystem.ReadAllText(filePath)

' ----- Process each line.
lineData = Split(wholeFile, vbNewLine)
'OR: lineData = wholeFile.Split(New String( ) {vbNewLine}, _
'        StringSplitOptions.None)
For Each lineOfText As String In lineData
   ' ----- Process each field.
   fieldData = lineOfText.Split(",")
   For Each wordOfText As String In fieldData
      result.Append(wordOfText)
      result.Append(Space(1))
   Next wordOfText
   result.AppendLine( )
Next lineOfText

MsgBox(result.ToString( ))
```

String objects have a Split( ) method, and Visual Basic 2005 also provides a Split( ) function. Notice the commented-out line in the previous code. This line demonstrates how workText can be split using the string's Split( ) method instead of using the Split( ) function, and it's useful to compare that line with the line just above it. In both cases linedata is filled with the lines of the file, but the syntax is different for these two Split( ) variations. With the string Split( ) method, only individual characters or an array of strings can be designated for the split point. In other words, you'll run into trouble if you try to split the lines in the following way:

```
lineData = workText.Split(vbNewLine, StringSplitOptions.None)
```

The special constant vbNewLine is actually two characters in length (carriage return and line feed), and the resulting strings will all still contain one of these two characters. It took considerable time and effort to debug the rather strange results when we first encountered this problem. To avoid it, pass an array of multicharacter strings to the string Split( ) method, as shown in the commented-out line in the code above, or use the Visual Basic 2005 Split( ) function, which has a simpler syntax and does accept multicharacter strings for the split point. Figure 8-10 shows the result of running the example code.

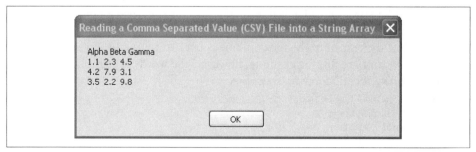

Figure 8-10. Parsing CSV files into arrays using Split( )

See Also

Recipe 8.9 shows the reverse of this recipe.

Recipe 8.12 discusses the differences between the Split( ) function and the Split( ) method in more detail. Also, see Recipe 5.44 for more on the Split( ) function and method.

8.11   Using a Multivalue Array Instead of a Two-Dimensional Array

Problem

You want to store data in a two-dimensional array, but the number of items in each row varies. You don't want to dimension the array for the longest row and waste a lot of space in the array.

Solution

Sample code folder: Chapter 08\MultivalueArray

Instead of creating a two-dimensional array, create an array of arrays, sometimes referred to as a *multivalue array*.

Discussion

A two-dimensional array is identified by its single pair of parentheses containing one comma separating the two indexes. A multivalue array has two sets of parentheses, and the contents are stored as one-dimensional arrays stored in the elements of another one-dimensional array. The following code demonstrates a multivalue array containing three string arrays of varying lengths:

```
Dim result As New System.Text.StringBuilder
Dim multiValue(2)() As String
Dim counter1 As Integer
Dim counter2 As Integer

' ----- Build the multivalue array.
multiValue(0) = New String() {"alpha", "beta", "gamma"}
multiValue(1) = New String() _
    {"A", "B", "C", "D", "E", "F", "G", "H"}
multiValue(2) = New String() {"Yes", "No"}

' ----- Format the array for display.
For counter1 = 0 To multiValue.Length - 1
    For counter2 = 0 To multiValue(counter1).Length - 1
        result.Append(multiValue(counter1)(counter2))
        result.Append(Space(1))
    Next counter2
    result.AppendLine( )
Next counter1

MsgBox(result.ToString( ))
```

Inside the nested For loops is a line where each string from the array of arrays is accessed to form the results displayed in Figure 8-11. Two pairs of parentheses are used to index the specific string stored in the multivalue array:

```
multiValue(counter1)(counter2)
```

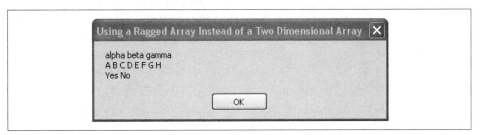

Figure 8-11. Using multivalue arrays to store a variable number of items in each row of a two-dimensional array

A true two-dimensional array element would be accessed with a pair of indexes within one set of parentheses, as in the following:

```
twoDimArray(counter1, counter2)
```

8.12   Converting Between Delimited Strings and Arrays

Problem

You have a string that contains data delimited by one or more characters, and you want to divide the parts into an array. Or you want to reverse the process, moving array elements into a delimited string.

Solution

Sample code folder: Chapter 08\SplitAndJoin

The Split( ) and Join( ) functions provided as part of the Visual Basic 2005 language, and the similar Split( ) and Join( ) methods of the string data type, provide a flexible and powerful way to manipulate string arrays.

Discussion

The Split( ) and Join( ) functions and methods are described in Chapter 5, which deals with strings, but here they are presented in the context of how they add useful functionality when working with string arrays.

Split( ) operates on a single string and returns a string array comprised of pieces of the original string split apart at the designated points. You can split the string at all occurrences of a given single character, at any occurrence of any single character in an array of characters, at any occurrence of any multicharacter string in a string array, or at any occurrence of a single multicharacter string. The overloaded versions of these methods provide considerable flexibility.

You do need to be careful when splitting a string at all occurrences of a single multi-character string. The string Split( ) method accepts a single string as the split parameter, but it uses only the first character of the string to define where to do the split. To use any multicharacter string for the split point, you must pass an array of strings instead of a single string. The string array can have just one string in it, but it must be an array in order to work as expected. (The Visual Basic 2005 Split( ) function doesn't have this limitation.)

To illustrate this, the following code splits a string at all occurrences of "en" and joins it again using Join( ). The string to insert at the join points is "EN". This effectively uppercases all occurrences of "en" in the string. The string array splitArray( ) is the string array created by the split:

```
Dim workText As String
workText = _
    "This sentence will have all ""en"" characters uppercased."
Dim splitArray( ) As String = {"en"}
Dim workArray( ) As String = _
```

```
    workText.Split(splitArray, StringSplitOptions.None)
workText = String.Join("EN", workArray)
MsgBox(workText)
```

Figure 8-12 shows the result.

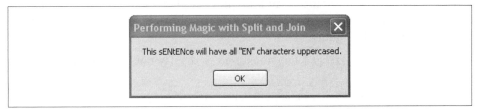

Figure 8-12. Using Split() and Join() to replace all occurrences of a substring

There is a better way to replace all occurrences of a substring with another one: use the Replace( ) function. The following line of code has the same result as the previous code:

```
    workText = Replace(workText, "en", "EN")
```

See Also

See Recipe 5.18 and Recipe 5.44 for more on the Split( ) and Join( ) functions and methods. Recipe 5.16 gives an example of using the Replace( ) function to replace all occurrences of a given substring.

8.13   Formatting an Array as a Single String

Problem

You want to format the contents of an array into a string, but the ToString( ) method returns only a string description of the array reference.

Solution

Sample code folder: Chapter 08\PrintArrays

Build generic helper routines that format the contents of an array nicely.

Discussion

The ToString( ) method all objects inherit from System.Object is ideal in most cases; it gives you a quick and simple string representation of any object's contents. However with arrays, the ToString( ) method returns a description of the array, rather than a listing of its contents. This makes sense in that the array variable name contains a reference, not data, but it makes it tricky to get a listing of the array's contents.

The following code demonstrates how to format the contents of both one- and two-dimensional arrays generically. The two ToBracedString( ) functions accept an appropriately sized array and return a string with braces surrounding the array elements. The braces, data items, and separating commas are formatted in the same way as required when initializing an array in code. For example, output from this function for a two-dimensional array will have nested braces to indicate the layout of the array's rows and columns.

Here are the ToBracedString( ) functions used to display one- and two-dimensional arrays:

```
Public Function ToBracedString(Of T)(ByVal sourceArray( ) _
      As T) As String
   ' ----- Display the contents of a one-dimensional array.
   Dim result As New System.Text.StringBuilder
   Dim counter As Integer

   result.Append("{")
   For counter = 0 To sourceArray.Length - 1
      result.Append(sourceArray(counter).ToString( ))
      If (counter < (sourceArray.Length - 1)) Then _
         result.Append(",")
   Next counter
   result.Append("}")

   Return result.ToString( )
End Function

Public Function ToBracedString(Of T)(ByVal sourceArray(,) _
      As T) As String
   ' ----- Display the contents of a two-dimensional array.
   Dim result As New System.Text.StringBuilder
   Dim counter1 As Integer
   Dim counter2 As Integer
   Dim rank1Size As Integer = sourceArray.GetLength(0)
   Dim rank2Size As Integer = sourceArray.GetLength(1)

   result.Append("{")
   For counter1 = 0 To sourceArray.GetLength(0) - 1
      result.Append("{")
      For counter2 = 0 To rank2Size - 1
         result.Append(sourceArray(counter1, _
            counter2).ToString( ))
         If (counter2 < (rank2Size - 1)) Then _
            result.Append(",")
      Next counter2
      result.Append("}")
      If (counter1 < (rank1Size - 1)) Then result.Append(",")
   Next counter1
   result.Append("}")

   Return result.ToString( )
End Function
```

In the following code, two arrays are created and initialized with sample data, and their contents, as returned by ToBracedString( ), are displayed for review:

```
Dim result As New System.Text.StringBuilder
Dim arrayA( ) As Integer = {1, 2, 3}
Dim arrayB(,) As Integer = {{1, 2, 3}, {4, 5, 6}}

' ----- Show the typical ToString results.
result.AppendLine("arrayA.ToString... ")
result.AppendLine(arrayA.ToString)
result.AppendLine( )

' ----- Format arrayA nicely.
result.AppendLine("ToBracedString(arrayA)... ")
result.AppendLine(ToBracedString(Of Integer)(arrayA))
result.AppendLine( )

' ----- Format arrayB nicely.
result.AppendLine("ToBracedString(arrayB)... ")
result.Append(ToBracedString(Of Integer)(arrayB))

MsgBox(result.ToString( ))
```

Compare the braced initialization strings in the first few lines of the previous code with the output as shown in Figure 8-13. The goal was to duplicate the same simple format.

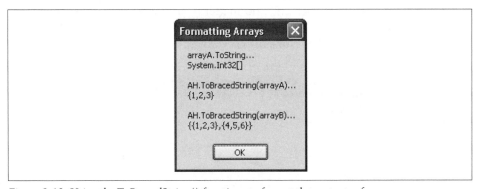

Figure 8-13. Using the ToBracedString( ) functions to format the contents of an array

See Also

Recipe 8.1 shows how to properly format new array content in code.

8.14   Iterating Through Array Elements

Problem

You want to process all the elements of an array without the overhead of creating extra variables, and you'd like to minimize the scope of all working variables.

Solution

Sample code folder: Chapter 08\ForEachLoops

Use the For Each looping construct to process each element of an array.

Discussion

The following code creates a simple string array of fruit names, then processes each string in the array inside a For Each loop:

```
Dim result As New System.Text.StringBuilder
Dim fruitArray( ) As String = { _
    "Oranges", "Apples", "Grapes", "Bananas", "Blueberries"}

For Each fruit As String In fruitArray
    result.AppendLine(fruit)
Next fruit

MsgBox(result.ToString( ))
```

The For Each line declares a temporary variable named fruit that exists only for the duration of the For Each loop. This ties the variable name closely to the processing going on locally and frees up resources as soon as that processing is completed. Also, there is no need to access the length of the array to control the looping because the loop implicitly processes all elements, no matter what the array's size is. (The standard For loop syntax requires a separate counting variable and access to the array's length.) Figure 8-14 shows the results displayed by the example code.

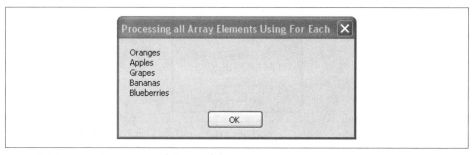

Figure 8-14. Processing arrays with For Each loops

8.15   Passing Arrays to Methods

Problem

You want to pass and return arrays to and from methods as easily as other simple variable types.

Solution

Sample code folder: Chapter 08\ArrayParameters

Unlike Visual Basic 6.0, in Visual Basic 2005 it's easy to pass and return any type of object, including arrays.

Discussion

The following code provides a fun example by passing a string array to a function that returns an even bigger string array. The names of the four card suits are placed in a small string array. This array is passed to `FillDeckOfCards( )`, which creates and returns a string array containing the names of all the cards in a deck:

```
Dim result As New System.Text.StringBuilder
Dim suits( ) As String = {"Spades", "Hearts", "Diamonds", "Clubs"}
Dim cardDeck( ) As String = FillDeckOfCards(suits)

Shuffle(cardDeck)
For counter As Integer = 0 To 6
    result.AppendLine(cardDeck(counter))
Next counter

MsgBox(result.ToString( ))
```

The `Shuffle( )` method (designed in Recipe 8.5) shuffles the returned array, and the first seven cards in the array are displayed for review, as shown in Figure 8-15. Of course, your results will vary based on the state of your random number generator.

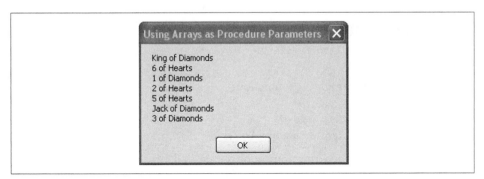

Figure 8-15. Passing and returning arrays

The `FillDeckOfCards( )` function is passed a string array and returns one, too:

```
Public Function FillDeckOfCards(ByVal suit As String()) As String()
    Dim deck(51) As String
    Dim cardNumber As Integer
    Dim suitNumber As Integer

    For counter As Integer = 0 To 51
        cardNumber = counter Mod 13
        suitNumber = counter \ 13
```

```
        Select Case cardNumber
            Case 0
                deck(counter) = "Ace of "
            Case 10
                deck(counter) = "Jack of "
            Case 11
                deck(counter) = "Queen of "
            Case 12
                deck(counter) = "King of "
            Case Else
                deck(counter) = cardNumber.ToString & " of "
        End Select
        deck(counter) &= suit(suitNumber)
    Next counter
    Return deck
End Function
```

You may pass and return objects in Visual Basic 2005, a process similar to using Variants in Visual Basic 6.0. But in general, it is better to pass and return explicitly typed arrays, as in the example presented here. This prevents the runtime overhead required for constantly converting variable types, and it helps the compiler determine at compile time if you're attempting to pass incompatible data. In general, consider overloaded methods and generics as two ways to enhance the flexibility of methods, while optimizing the compile- and runtime operations.

See Also

Recipe 8.16 discusses similar functionality.

8.16   Returning Arrays from Functions

Problem

You want to return an array from a function.

Solution

Sample code folder: Chapter 08\FunctionArrays

Declare the function to return an array of the desired type and do so in the function's Return statement.

Discussion

This recipe is very similar to Recipe 8.15, but the lesson is worth repeating: arrays of any type and size are easily passed to and returned from methods. The following example demonstrates a function that returns an array of 16 hexadecimal characters. The array is joined into a string and displayed for review in a message box, as shown in Figure 8-16:

```
Dim result As New System.Text.StringBuilder
result.Append("Hexadecimal characters: ")
result.Append(String.Join(",", HexadecimalCharacters( )))
MsgBox(result.ToString( ))
```

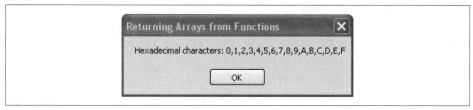

Figure 8-16. Returning an array of hexadecimal characters from a function

The HexadecimalCharacters() function includes a set of parentheses at the very end of the function declaration. This indicates that the function will return a string array and not just an ordinary string. The Return statement near the end of the function returns the string array hexChars():

```
Public Function HexadecimalCharacters() As String()
    ' ----- Return the first 16 hex numbers as an array.
    Dim hexChars(15) As String

    For counter As Integer = 0 To 15
        hexChars(counter) = Hex(counter)
    Next counter
    Return hexChars
End Function
```

See Also

Recipe 8.15 discusses similar functionality.

8.17 Creating a Collection

Problem

You want a simple example of a collection to demonstrate the basics of using the collection object.

Solution

Sample code folder: Chapter 08\Collections

This recipe provides a simple example collection to use as a starting point for further explorations of the topic.

Discussion

Collections provide capabilities similar to those of arrays, but they have some advantages. A collection is inherently more dynamic and allows the insertion and deletion of items, and it can be resized without loss of any current contents. You can do these same tasks with arrays, but collections make the whole process much simpler and more straightforward.

The following example creates a collection of strings. Each string (in this case they are all just simple words) is added to the collection using the collection's Add( ) method. After all words are added to the collection, its entire contents are retrieved for display and review, as shown in Figure 8-17:

```
Dim result As New System.Text.StringBuilder
Dim wordCollection As New Collection

' ----- Build the collection.
wordCollection.Add("This")
wordCollection.Add("is")
wordCollection.Add("a")
wordCollection.Add("collection")
wordCollection.Add("of")
wordCollection.Add("words")

' ----- Display the collection.
For Each word As String In wordCollection
    result.Append(word)
    result.Append(Space(1))
Next word
MsgBox(result.ToString( ))
```

Figure 8-17. A collection of strings

As with arrays, you can retrieve each item from the collection using an index, or you can use the For Each loop, as shown in this example. Unlike with arrays, however, you can optionally pass a key string to the Add( ) method to provide a way to retrieve items from a collection based on their keys.

You can store varying types of data in the same collection. This provides some flexibility, but in most cases you should store only the same type of data in any single collection. Methods you write to process the collection's data will need to handle whatever data type is stored in the collection, so keeping it consistent greatly simplifies the coding requirements.

If data-type issues become a problem with your collections, consider using the new generic collections instead.

See Also

Recipes 8.18 through 8.20 show other features of collections.

8.18   Inserting an Item into a Collection

Problem

You want to insert a new item in the middle of a collection, rather than just adding it to the end of the collection.

Solution

Sample code folder: Chapter 08\Collections

Use the Add( ) method, but include its optional parameters to control the insertion point.

Discussion

The Add( ) method by default appends items to the end of a collection, but optional parameters can modify this behavior. Here's the general syntax of the Add( ) method:

```
variable.Add(content, key, before, after)
```

All parameters other than *content* are optional, and you can't supply values for both *before* and *after* in the same statement. *before* and *after* represent the element positions before or after which the new item should be inserted. In the next code example, the word "slightly" is inserted after position 3 because the *after* parameter passed to the Add( ) method is a 3. The word "longer" is then inserted into the collection before the fifth position, because the *before* parameter of the Add( ) method is a 5:

```
Dim result As New System.Text.StringBuilder
Dim wordCollection As New Collection

' ----- Start with a basic collection.
wordCollection.Add("This")
wordCollection.Add("is")
wordCollection.Add("a")
wordCollection.Add("collection")
wordCollection.Add("of")
wordCollection.Add("words")

' ----- Insert a word after item 3.
wordCollection.Add("slightly", , , 3)

' ----- Insert a word before item 5.
wordCollection.Add("longer", , 5)

' ----- Display the collection.
For Each word As String In wordCollection
   result.Append(word)
   result.Append(Space(1))
Next word
MsgBox(result.ToString( ))
```

The results of these two "before and after" additions into the collection are shown in Figure 8-18.

Figure 8-18. Using a collection's Add( ) method to insert items at a given point

See Also

Recipes 8.17, 8.19, and 8.20 show other features of collections.

8.19 Deleting a Collection Item

Problem

You need to delete an item from a collection.

Solution

Sample code folder: Chapter 08\Collections

Use the collection's Remove( ) method, passing either the position of the item or its key string.

Discussion

The following example fills a collection with several words using "key strings," identifiers that provide an optional way to specify each item. The item at index position 5 is then removed, followed by the item with key "six":

```
Dim result As New System.Text.StringBuilder
Dim wordCollection As New Collection

' ----- Start with a basic collection.
wordCollection.Add("This", "one")
wordCollection.Add("is", "two")
wordCollection.Add("a", "three")
wordCollection.Add("collection", "four")
wordCollection.Add("of", "five")
wordCollection.Add("words", "six")

' ----- Remove an element by position.
wordCollection.Remove(5)

' ----- Remove an element by key.
wordCollection.Remove("six")

' ----- Dipslay the collection.
For Each word As String In wordCollection
    result.Append(word)
```

```
        result.Append(Space(1))
    Next word
    MsgBox(result.ToString( ))
```

Once item number 5 is removed, the item at position 6 moves to position 5. This means that removing items 5 and 6 both by number wouldn't work; you would need to remove the item at position 5 twice in a row. This hints at the usefulness of using key strings to uniquely identify each item, especially when items might be freely added to or removed from the collection over time. Figure 8-19 shows the contents of the collection after the two items are removed.

Figure 8-19. The Remove( ) method removes items from a collection by position or by key

See Also

Recipes 8.17, 8.18, and 8.20 show other features of collections.

8.20   Iterating Through a Collection

Problem

You want to process all the items in a collection one at a time.

Solution

Sample code folder: Chapter 08\Collections

Use a For Each loop, or use the collection's Count property in a For...Next loop.

Discussion

The For Each loop is the recommended way to process items in a collection because you don't need an index variable, you don't have to access the Count property of the collection, and each item in the collection is automatically retrieved (i.e., you don't have to explicitly access each indexed item).

The following code shows both a For...Next loop and a For Each loop used to access the same collection. Each loop creates a single line of the output display, showing the contents of each item in the collection:

```
Dim result As New System.Text.StringBuilder
Dim numberCollection As New Collection

' ----- Start with a basic collection.
numberCollection.Add(14, "C")
numberCollection.Add(25, "D")
```

```
numberCollection.Add(36, "E")
numberCollection.Add(47, "A")
numberCollection.Add(58, "B")

' ----- Scan the collection with a loop counter.
'       Collections are base-1, not base-0.
For counter As Integer = 1 To numberCollection.Count
    result.Append(numberCollection(counter))
    result.Append(",")
Next counter

' ----- Remove the ending comma.
result.Length -= 1
result.AppendLine( )

' ----- Scan the collection by item.
For Each number As Integer In numberCollection
    result.Append(number)
    result.Append(",")
Next number

' ----- Remove the ending comma.
result.Length -= 1
result.AppendLine( )

' ----- Retrieve items by key.
result.Append(numberCollection("A")).Append(",")
result.Append(numberCollection("B")).Append(",")
result.Append(numberCollection("C")).Append(",")
result.Append(numberCollection("D")).Append(",")
result.Append(numberCollection("E"))

' ----- Display the results.
MsgBox(result.ToString( ))
```

The third line of the output is the same collection accessed in the order of the item keys, instead of the default order, which is based on the item positions in the collection. Figure 8-20 shows the collection's items as accessed in each of these three ways.

Figure 8-20. Items in a collection can be accessed with For Next or For Each loops or by the item keys

See Also

Recipes 8.17 through 8.19 show other features of collections.

Graphics

9.0   Introduction

The recipes in this chapter introduce the powerful, fast, and creative graphics capabilities of Visual Basic 2005. They provide working examples of everything from drawing simple lines to creating charts and simple animations. If you're coming from Visual Basic 6.0, you'll be especially pleased with the powerful new capabilities of the GDI+ graphics. Several recipes will help you update your skills by substituting new functionality for the primitive graphics commands provided by Visual Basic 6.0, such as Line, Circle, and so on.

9.1   Creating Graphics Objects

Problem

You're just getting started with GDI+ graphics and want to know where to begin.

Solution

Sample code folder: Chapter 09\GDIObjects

Always start by defining and creating the fundamental graphics objects relied upon by all GDI+ graphics methods. These include colors, pens, fonts, brushes, and of course the Graphics object itself, the drawing surface used by all graphics drawing methods.

Discussion

The sample code in this recipe demonstrates the creation of several graphics-related objects, providing a good starting point for studying some GDI+ fundamentals. We'll look at the code in sections.

The most common place to put drawing code is in the Paint event handler for the form or control on which you will draw:

```
Private Sub Form1_Paint(ByVal sender As Object, _
    ByVal e As System.Windows.Forms.PaintEventArgs) _
    Handles Me.Paint
```

You can draw in other events or methods as well, but you'll run into fewer hassles if you paint when the system tells you to, rather than forcing redrawing of surfaces based on other events.

The Paint event provides a couple of useful parameters to help with the painting. You can create your own Graphics object—a technique handy in some situations—but when drawing in a Paint event, simply use the Graphics object passed to the event. You can reference the e.Graphics object by that nomenclature, or you can create a shorter reference to it (such as, in this example, canvas):

```
' ----- Grab the graphics object for this form.
Dim canvas As Graphics = e.Graphics
```

You typically use the Graphics object a lot in the Paint method, so keeping the reference easy to use can simplify your coding.

Colors can be defined in several ways, some of which are demonstrated in the following group of program lines. You can choose from a long list of enumerated colors with fanciful names like "cornsilk," or you can build your own color by setting each of the red, green, and blue components of the color to a value from 0 to 255. There are also some named system colors you can access to employ the standard colors selected by the user for the entire workstation. The advantage of using these colors is that your graphics will take on the system-described colors, even if the user has changed one of those colors from its default base. A fourth optional parameter (actually passed as the first argument to Color.FromArgb( )), called Alpha, controls the transparency of a color. As shown in the following code, a transparent shade of green is created by setting its Alpha parameter to a middle-of-the-road value of 127:

```
' ----- Create some colors.
Dim colorBackground As Color = Color.Cornsilk
Dim colorRed As Color = Color.FromArgb(255, 0, 0)
Dim colorTransparentGreen As Color = _
    Color.FromArgb(127, 0, 255, 0)
Dim colorControlDark As Color = _
    SystemColors.ControlDark
```

A Pen is used as a parameter for many drawing methods. For example, lines, ellipses, rectangle edges, and polygon edges are all drawn using a designated pen to define the lines used to construct them. A basic Pen object is comprised of a color and an optional width. If not given, the width defaults to 1 unit, and you'll get what you expect if your scaling mode is the default pixels. If a different scaling is used, the thickness of the pen's line will remain at 1 unit, but depending on the scaling this can drastically affect the appearance of the lines you draw (see Recipe 9.8 for more on this topic). The following code block defines pen1 with a width of 1 unit and pen2 with a width of 25:

```
' ----- Create some pens.
Dim pen1 As New Pen(Color.Blue)
Dim pen2 As New Pen(colorRed, 25)
```

Font objects are required whenever text is drawn on a graphics surface. There are several ways to define a new Font object: you can specify its name and a few optional properties such as font size, or you can start with a given font and make changes to it. Both of these techniques are used in the program lines shown here:

```
' ----- Create some fonts.
Dim font1 As New Font("Arial", 24, _
    FontStyle.Bold Or FontStyle.Italic)
Dim font2 As New Font(Me.Font, FontStyle.Regular)
```

Visual Basic 2005 doesn't have a plain old Print command, like the one that was available in the good old days of VB 6. You'll need to become familiar with fonts, brushes, and GDI+ methods such as DrawString( ) to draw even the simplest text content. The upside of this situation is that text can be drawn on any surface in the same way, whether it's a printer page, a form, or the face of a button or other control.

When you draw shapes using lines, you pass the graphics method a pen. When you fill Graphics objects with color, such as when drawing a solid-filled rectangle or ellipse, you pass a brush. Brushes can be solid-filled with a color, as shown here, or they can be created using a repeating fill pattern or image:

```
' ----- Create some brushes.
Dim brush1 As New SolidBrush(Color.DarkBlue)
Dim brush2 As New SolidBrush(colorTransparentGreen)
```

The next lines use several methods of the Graphics object to render ellipses, rectangles, and a string:

```
' ----- Demonstrate a few sample graphics commands.
canvas.Clear(colorBackground)
canvas.DrawEllipse(pen2, 100, 50, 300, 200)
canvas.FillEllipse(brush1, New Rectangle( _
    50, 150, 250, 200))
canvas.FillRectangle(New SolidBrush(colorTransparentGreen), _
    120, 30, 150, 250)
canvas.DrawString("Text is drawn using GDI+", _
    font1, brush1, 120, 70)
```

Figure 9-1 displays the results generated by this code. The biggest ring is a single-line outline of an ellipse, drawn using the pen2 object defined above (it's actually a red pen with a width of 25 units—in this case, the units are the default pixels). The lower ellipse is solid-filled using a blue brush. Clipping takes place automatically, and although the blue ellipse doesn't quite fit on the form's surface, this causes no problems. The rectangle uses the transparent green brush defined earlier, allowing the red and blue ellipses to show through from underneath. Finally, the string of text can be drawn at any location, using any font, any size, any color, and any rotation angle.

Figure 9-1. Creating GDI+ graphics

Proper GDI+ etiquette requires that you properly dispose of all objects you create. Back in the old days before Windows 95, proper cleanup of graphics objects was essential, and the system could crash if it ran out of its few precious graphics resources. Those fears are long gone, but GDI+ objects still consume system resources. The .NET garbage-collection system will eventually dispose of all graphics objects, but it's best if you do it yourself immediately:

```
' ----- Clean up.
brush2.Dispose( )
brush1.Dispose( )
font2.Dispose( )
font1.Dispose( )
pen2.Dispose( )
pen1.Dispose( )
canvas = Nothing
End Sub
```

9.2   Drawing on Controls for Special Effects

Problem

You want to alter the appearance of a control by drawing on it in reaction to mouse or other events.

Solution

Sample code folder: Chapter 09\SpecialEffects

Add code to the control's `Paint` event handler, and if required, call the control's `Refresh( )` method to trigger the `Paint` event.

Discussion

Any visible control has a `Paint` event that lets you patch in code to modify the control's appearance in any way you want. The following code demonstrates this technique by completely changing the appearance and behavior of a standard `Button` control. For the sample, we created a new Windows Forms application, then added a `Panel` control named `Panel1` and two `Button` controls, `Button1` and `Button2`. `Button1` is left untouched for comparison, but `Button2` changes as the mouse is used with it. The button's background color is altered as the mouse moves over its face, and again when the mouse is clicked. The `ButtonBackColor` variable holds the indicated color as set within the various mouse-event procedures, and it is used in the button's `Paint` event to render its background color:

```
Public Class Form1
    Private ButtonBackColor As Color = Color.LightGreen
```

These four events change the background color in response to the mouse cursor entering or leaving the face of the button and to the mouse button being depressed and released when the cursor is over the button:

```
Private Sub Button2_MouseEnter(ByVal sender As Object, _
        ByVal e As System.EventArgs) Handles Button2.MouseEnter
    ' ----- Change the button to show the effect of the mouse.
    ButtonBackColor = Color.FromArgb(32, 192, 32)
End Sub

Private Sub Button2_MouseLeave(ByVal sender As Object, _
        ByVal e As System.EventArgs) Handles Button2.MouseLeave
    ' ----- Return the button to normal mode.
    ButtonBackColor = Color.LightGreen
End Sub

Private Sub Button2_MouseDown(ByVal sender As Object, _
        ByVal e As System.Windows.Forms.MouseEventArgs) _
        Handles Button2.MouseDown
    ' ----- The mouse is clicking the button. Show an effect.
    ButtonBackColor = Color.LightPink
End Sub

Private Sub Button2_MouseUp(ByVal sender As Object, _
        ByVal e As System.Windows.Forms.MouseEventArgs) _
        Handles Button2.MouseUp
    ' ----- The mouse was released. Go back to normal.
    ButtonBackColor = Color.LightGreen
    Button2.Refresh( )
End Sub
```

The Refresh( ) method in the MouseUp event handler tells the control to redraw itself, triggering a Paint event. You would expect the other three event handlers to each need a Refresh( ) call as well, but the Button control issues those calls on our behalf during these events.

The following method repaints Button2's surface whenever Windows fires the Paint event:

```
Private Sub Button2_Paint(ByVal sender As Object, _
    ByVal e As System.Windows.Forms.PaintEventArgs) _
    Handles Button2.Paint
' ----- Draw a fancy button surface.
Dim counter As Integer
Const numberOfLobes As Integer = 5

' ----- Get the graphics object for the button.
Dim canvas As Graphics = e.Graphics

' ----- Set a new background color.
canvas.Clear(ButtonBackColor)
```

The button's Graphics object provides the surface for all graphics commands. The Clear( ) method optionally renders the background in a given color. In this case, the variable ButtonBackColor tells the button what colors to set the background to in response to the various mouse events:

```
' ----- Draw the atomic orbits in blue, two pixels wide.
Dim atomPen As Pen = New Pen(Color.Blue, 2)

' ----- Specify the location and size of the electron orbits.
Dim sizeFactor As Integer = Button2.ClientSize.Width \ 2
Dim lobeLength As Integer = sizeFactor * 8 \ 10
Dim lobeWidth As Integer = lobeLength \ 4

' ----- Shift center of orbits to center of button.
canvas.TranslateTransform(sizeFactor, sizeFactor)
```

The following lines of code repeatedly draw an ellipse in blue, rotated around its center to create an "atom" effect:

```
' ----- Draw orbits rotated around center.
For counter = 1 To numberOfLobes
    canvas.RotateTransform(360 / numberOfLobes)
    canvas.DrawEllipse(atomPen, -lobeLength, -lobeWidth, _
        lobeLength * 2, lobeWidth * 2)
Next counter
End Sub
```

We chose this graphic partly because it was just plain fun to create, but also to show how easy it is to draw some things in Visual Basic 2005 that are cumbersome to draw in VB 6.

The following Paint event handler paints the panel with a background color and some text, as shown in Figure 9-2. This same effect can be accomplished with a standard Label, but this provides another example of how the face of just about any control can be graphically rendered as desired:

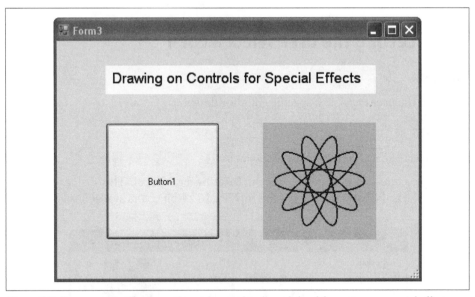

Figure 9-2. Buttons and other controls can be graphically redefined for unique or special effects

```
Private Sub Panel1_Paint(ByVal sender As Object, _
    ByVal e As System.Windows.Forms.PaintEventArgs) _
    Handles Panel1.Paint
  ' ----- Draw a nice title.
  Dim canvas As Graphics = e.Graphics
  canvas.Clear(Color.Azure)
  canvas.DrawString( _
    "Drawing on Controls for Special Effects", _
    New Font("Arial", 14), Brushes.DarkBlue, 5, 5)
End Sub
```

The next two methods, one for Button1 and the other for Button2, are nearly identical. They demonstrate that even though Button2 now appears much different from the more standard Button1 (see Figure 9-2), both buttons behave the same and can be used in a program in the same way:

```
Private Sub Button1_Click(ByVal sender As System.Object, _
    ByVal e As System.EventArgs) Handles Button1.Click
  MsgBox("Button1 clicked!", MsgBoxStyle.Exclamation, _
    "Painting on Controls")
End Sub
```

```
    Private Sub Button2_Click(ByVal sender As System.Object, _
        ByVal e As System.EventArgs) Handles Button2.Click
      MsgBox("Button2 clicked!", MsgBoxStyle.Exclamation, _
        "Painting on Controls")
    End Sub
End Class
```

9.3   Letting the User Select a Color

Problem

You need the user to select a specific color for drawing.

Solution

Sample code folder: Chapter 09\UserColorSelect

For simple color-selection needs, use the ColorDialog control. This dialog, shown in Figure 9-3, lets the user select any of the 16,777,216 24-bit colors available in Windows.

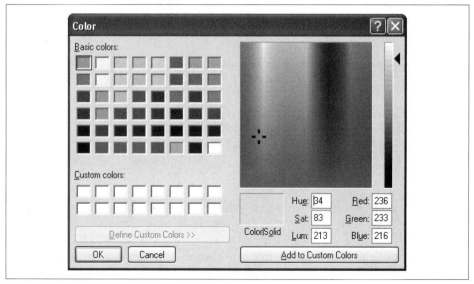

Figure 9-3. The color dialog, in "full open" mode

Discussion

Create a new Windows Forms application, and add the following controls to Form1:

- A Label control named ColorName. Set its Text property to Not Selected.
- A PictureBox control named ColorDisplay. Set its BorderStyle property to FixedSingle.

- A Button control named ActChange. Set its Text property to Change....
- A ColorDialog control named ColorSelector.

Add informational labels if desired. The form should look something like Figure 9-4.

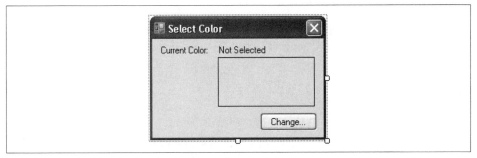

Figure 9-4. The controls on the color selection sample form

Now add the following source code to the form's code template:

```
Private Sub ActChange_Click(ByVal sender As System.Object, _
      ByVal e As System.EventArgs) Handles ActChange.Click
   ' ----- Prompt to change the color.
   ColorSelector.Color = ColorDisplay.BackColor
   If (ColorSelector.ShowDialog() = _
         Windows.Forms.DialogResult.OK) Then
      ' ----- The user selected a color.
      ColorDisplay.BackColor = ColorSelector.Color
      If (ColorSelector.Color.IsNamedColor = True) Then
         ' ----- Windows has a name for this color.
         ColorName.Text = ColorSelector.Color.Name
      Else
         ColorName.Text = "R" & ColorSelector.Color.R & _
            " G" & ColorSelector.Color.G & _
            " B" & ColorSelector.Color.B
      End If
   End If
End Sub
```

Run the program, and click the Change button to access the dialog. The form will show the selected color, and either the name of the color (if known) or its red-green-blue (RGB) value.

The ColorDialog includes a few Boolean properties that let you control the availability of the "color mixer" portion of the form (the right half). The dialog does not include features that let the user indicate transparency or the "alpha" level of a color.

9.4 Working with Coordinate Systems (Pixels, Inches, Centimeters)

Problem

You've been drawing on a graphics canvas (such as the surface of a form or control), and working with pixels. But your program lets the user work in inches or centimeters, and you don't want to do all the conversions yourself.

Solution

Sample code folder: Chapter 09\MeasurementSystems

The Graphics object that you receive in a Paint event handler (or that you create elsewhere) provides a few different ways to scale to different measurement systems. The easiest way is to set its PageUnit property to one of the predefined GraphicsUnit enumeration values. The sample code in this recipe uses GraphicsUnit.Display (the default), .Inch, and .Millimeter.

Discussion

Create a new Windows Forms application, and add the following controls to Form1:

- A RadioButton control named ShowPixels. Set its Text property to Pixel Sample.
- A RadioButton control named ShowInches. Set its Text property to Inches Sample.
- A RadioButton control named ShowCentimeters. Set its Text property to Centimeters Sample.
- A Label control named Comment. Set its AutoSize property to False, and resize it so that it can hold a dozen or so words.
- A PictureBox control named SampleDisplay. Set its BorderStyle property to FixedSingle. Size it at about 250 × 250 pixels.

Your form should look something like Figure 9-5.

Now add the following source code to the form's class template:

```
Private Sub ChangeSystem(ByVal sender As System.Object, _
      ByVal e As System.EventArgs) _
      Handles ShowPixels.CheckedChanged, _
      ShowInches.CheckedChanged, _
      ShowCentimeters.CheckedChanged
   ' ------ Update the example text.
   If (ShowPixels.Checked = True) Then
      Comment.Text = "50x50 rectangle at position " & _
         "(50, 50). Major ruler ticks are at 100 pixels."
   ElseIf (ShowInches.Checked = True) Then
      Comment.Text = "1x1 inch rectangle at position " & _
         "(1, 1). Major ruler ticks are inches."
```

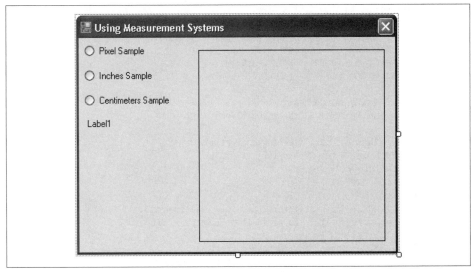

Figure 9-5. The controls in the measurement systems sample

```
    Else
        Comment.Text = "1x1 centimeter rectangle at " & _
            "position (1, 1). Major ruler ticks are centimeters."
    End If

    ' ----- Now update the display.
    SampleDisplay.Invalidate()
End Sub

Private Sub Form1_Load(ByVal sender As Object, _
        ByVal e As System.EventArgs) Handles Me.Load
    ' ----- Show the pixel example by default.
    ShowPixels.Checked = True
End Sub

Private Sub SampleDisplay_Paint(ByVal sender As Object, _
        ByVal e As System.Windows.Forms.PaintEventArgs) _
        Handles SampleDisplay.Paint
    ' ----- Draw the surface based on the user's selection.
    Dim rectangleArea As Rectangle
    Dim thinPen As Pen
    Dim rulerWidth As Single
    Dim tickStep As Single
    Dim tickSize As Single
    Dim counter As Integer
    Dim bigTick As Single
    Const ticks As String = "1424142414241"

    ' ----- Clear any previous content.
    e.Graphics.Clear(Color.White)
```

```
' ----- Adjust to the right system.
If (ShowPixels.Checked = True) Then
    ' ----- Draw a 50-by-50-pixel rectangle at (50,50).
    rectangleArea = New Rectangle(50, 50, 50, 50)
    rulerWidth = e.Graphics.DpiX / 5.0F
    bigTick = 100.0F
ElseIf (ShowInches.Checked = True) Then
    ' ----- Scale for inches.
    e.Graphics.PageUnit = GraphicsUnit.Inch

    ' ----- Draw a 1" x 1" rectangle at (1,1).
    rectangleArea = New Rectangle(1, 1, 1, 1)
    rulerWidth = 0.2F
    bigTick = 1.0F
Else
    ' ----- Scale for centimeters (actually, millimeters).
    e.Graphics.PageUnit = GraphicsUnit.Millimeter

    ' ----- Draw a 1cm x 1cm rectangle at (1,1).
    '       Note: 0.2 inches is 1/5 of 25.4 millimeters.
    rectangleArea = New Rectangle(10, 10, 10, 10)
    rulerWidth = 25.4F / 5.0F
    bigTick = 10.0F
End If

' ----- Create a single-pixel pen.
thinPen = New Pen(Color.Black, 1 / e.Graphics.DpiX)

' ----- Draw a ruler area. The rulerWidth is 0.2 inches
'       wide, no matter what the scale. Make a 3-inch
'       ruler.
e.Graphics.FillRectangle(Brushes.BlanchedAlmond, 0, 0, _
    rulerWidth, rulerWidth * 15)
e.Graphics.FillRectangle(Brushes.BlanchedAlmond, 0, 0, _
    rulerWidth * 15, rulerWidth)
e.Graphics.DrawLine(thinPen, rulerWidth, rulerWidth, _
    rulerWidth, rulerWidth * 15)
e.Graphics.DrawLine(thinPen, rulerWidth, rulerWidth, _
    rulerWidth * 15, rulerWidth)

' ----- Draw the ruler tick marks. Include whole steps,
'       half steps, and quarter steps.
For counter = 1 To ticks.Length
    ' ----- Get the tick measurements. The "ticks" constant
    '       includes a set of "1", "2", and "4" values. "1"
    '       gives a full-size tick mark (for whole units),
    '       "2" gives a half-size tick mark, and "4" gives
    '       a 1/4-size tick mark.
    tickSize = CSng(Mid(ticks, counter, 1))
    tickStep = rulerWidth + ((bigTick / 4.0F) * (counter - 1))

    ' ----- Draw the horizontal ruler ticks.
    e.Graphics.DrawLine(thinPen, tickStep, 0, _
        tickStep, rulerWidth / tickSize)
```

```
'  ----- Draw the vertical ruler ticks.
   e.Graphics.DrawLine(thinPen, 0, tickStep, _
      rulerWidth / tickSize, tickStep)
Next counter

'  ----- Adjust the (0,0) point to the corner of the ruler.
e.Graphics.TranslateTransform(rulerWidth, rulerWidth)

'  ----- Draw the rectangle.
e.Graphics.DrawRectangle(thinPen, rectangleArea)

'  ----- Put things back to normal.
e.Graphics.PageUnit = GraphicsUnit.Display
thinPen.Dispose( )
End Sub
```

Run the program, and click on each of the three radio buttons to see the results. Figure 9-6 shows the application using centimeters.

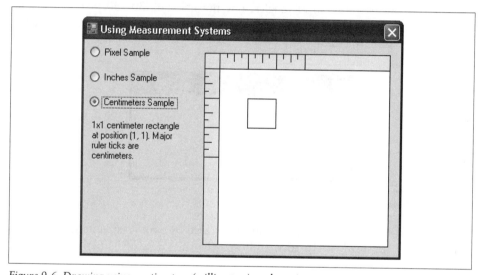

Figure 9-6. Drawing using centimeters (millimeters) as the unit system

The focus of the application is on drawing the black rectangle:

```
e.Graphics.DrawRectangle(thinPen, rectangleArea)
```

The rest of the code is there to make it easy to see the difference between the drawing systems.

The Graphics object defaults to the coordinate system of the display. On a monitor, each unit is a single pixel. When you draw a 10×10 rectangle, you are drawing a rectangle 10 pixels high and 10 pixels wide. To draw a 10×10-*inch* rectangle, you need to change the scaling system so that "1" represents an inch instead of a pixel.

The PageUnit property does just that. It supports a few common measurement systems, including Inches, Millimeters, and even Points.

You can also create your own custom scaling factor in each direction (X and Y) by using the Graphics object's ScaleTransform() method. This lets you set a scaling factor for both the horizontal (X) and vertical (Y) directions. To see scaling in action, create a new Windows Forms application, and add the following source code to the form's code template:

```
Private Sub Form1_Paint(ByVal sender As Object, _
    ByVal e As System.Windows.Forms.PaintEventArgs) _
    Handles Me.Paint
    e.Graphics.Clear(Color.White)
    e.Graphics.DrawRectangle(Pens.Black, 10, 10, 30, 30)
    e.Graphics.ScaleTransform(2, 2)
    e.Graphics.DrawRectangle(Pens.Black, 10, 10, 30, 30)
End Sub
```

This code draws two 30×30 rectangles, one normal (i.e., 30×30 pixels), and one scaled by a factor of two in each direction (resulting in a 60×60 square). Figure 9-7 shows the output of this code.

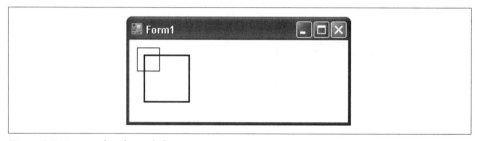

Figure 9-7. A normal and a scaled square

Everything about the second (larger) square is scaled by two: its size, its starting position (at (20,20) instead of (10,10)), and even the thickness of its pen (it's twice as thick).

9.5 Creating a Bitmap

Problem

You want to create off-screen bitmaps to store graphics in memory.

Solution

Sample code folder: Chapter 09\BitmapObject

Create Bitmap objects, and load images into them or draw directly on them.

Discussion

You can create a bitmap in memory, draw graphics onto a Graphics object created for the bitmap, and then draw the bitmap to a form, panel, or other paintable surface. This can provide an increase in speed, and sequentially drawing multiple bitmaps onto a visible surface gives you a simple but effective type of animation.

The code example in this recipe creates a bitmap based on the size of the form and the nature of the Graphics object for the form. A new Graphics object is created based on the new bitmap, so graphics methods will apply to the bitmap. Much of the rest of the code creates radial lines emanating from two points near the center of the bitmap. Finally, once the bitmap graphics are complete, the bitmap is drawn to the form's Graphics object, which paints onto the face of the form:

```
Private Sub Form1_Paint(ByVal sender As Object, _
      ByVal e As System.Windows.Forms.PaintEventArgs) _
      Handles Me.Paint
   ' ----- Draw to the form indirectly through a bitmap.
   Dim x As Single
   Dim y As Single
   Dim xc As Single
   Dim yc As Single
   Dim angle As Single
   Dim radians As Single
   Dim workImage As Bitmap
   Dim canvas As Graphics

   ' ----- Create a bitmap that is the same size and
   '       format as the form surface.
   workImage = New Bitmap(Me.Size.Width, Me.Size.Height, _
      e.Graphics)

   ' ----- Create a canvas for the bitmap. Drawing on the
   '       canvas impacts the bitmap directly.
   canvas = Graphics.FromImage(workImage)

   ' ---- Draw a radial pattern.
   For angle = 0 To 360 Step 2
      radians = angle * Math.PI / 180
      x = 500 * Math.Cos(radians)
      y = 500 * Math.Sin(radians)
      yc = Me.ClientSize.Height / 2
      xc = Me.ClientSize.Width * 10 / 21
      canvas.DrawLine(Pens.Black, xc, yc, xc + x, yc + y)
      xc = Me.ClientSize.Width * 11 / 21
      canvas.DrawLine(Pens.Black, xc, yc, xc + x, yc + y)
   Next angle

   ' ----- Stamp the bitmap on the form surface.
   e.Graphics.DrawImage(workImage, 0, 0)
End Sub
```

The key lines of code here are the ones that create the workImage and canvas objects. They create a bitmap compatible with the form and a graphics surface for the bitmap. All drawing methods require a Graphics object to provide a drawing surface. The last line uses the Graphics.DrawImage( ) method to draw the custom image onto the form, providing a way to get the in-memory bitmap onto a visible surface.

Figure 9-8 shows the new bitmap's contents as drawn onto the face of the form.

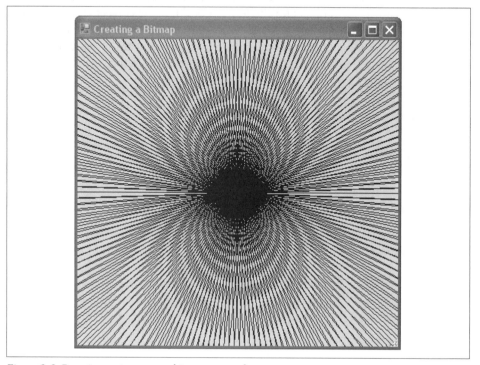

Figure 9-8. Drawing an in-memory bitmap onto a form

As you resize this form, its Paint event fires repeatedly, and the bitmap is recreated on the fly. However, it doesn't redraw the entire surface, because Windows tries to limit screen redraws to only those parts that it thinks have changed. In this case, only the newly exposed areas of the form are redrawn. To circumvent this, add the following code to the form:

```
Private Sub Form1_Resize(ByVal sender As Object, _
      ByVal e As System.EventArgs) Handles Me.Resize
   ' ----- Redraw the surface cleanly.
   Me.Invalidate( )
End Sub
```

Now the entire image is redrawn as the form size changes.

For the smoothest action be sure to set the form's DoubleBuffered property to True. The combination of double buffering and drawing the lines in-memory on a bitmap creates surprisingly smooth graphics updates as the form is resized.

9.6   Setting a Background Color

Problem

You want to customize a form's background color but don't want the controls on the form to look out of place.

Solution

Sample code folder: Chapter 09\BackgroundColor

No problem: most controls automatically take on the same background color as their container.

Discussion

The demonstration of this effect is simple. Add the following code to a button's Click event to change the background color to some random selection. Place any controls of interest on the form to see how the changing background affects them:

```
Private Sub ActBackground_Click( _
      ByVal sender As System.Object, _
      ByVal e As System.EventArgs) _
      Handles ActBackground.Click
   ' ----- Change the background to some random color.
   Dim redPart As Integer
   Dim greenPart As Integer
   Dim bluePart As Integer
   Dim surpriseColor As New Random

   redPart = surpriseColor.Next(0, 255)
   greenPart = surpriseColor.Next(0, 255)
   bluePart = surpriseColor.Next(0, 255)
   Me.BackColor = Color.FromArgb(redPart, _
      greenPart, bluePart)
End Sub
```

As shown in Figure 9-9, the RadioButton, Label, and CheckBox controls all adjust automatically by taking on the same background color as the containing form. The TextBox control's background remains white, by design. Place any other controls you might be using on this form to see how they behave.

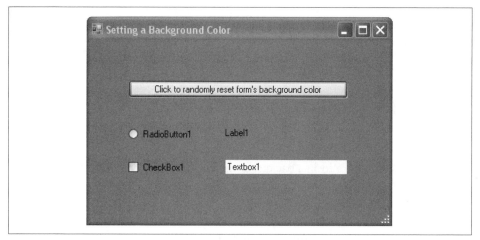

Figure 9-9. Many controls automatically take on the same background color as their container

9.7   Drawing Lines, Ellipses, and Rectangles

Problem

You need to draw some basic shapes on a graphics surface. What choices are available?

Solution

Sample code folder: Chapter 09\DrawingBasicShapes

The System.Drawing.Graphics object includes several methods that draw filled and unfilled shapes, including methods for lines, rectangles, and ellipses. This recipe's code implements a simple drawing program using these basic shapes.

Discussion

Create a new Windows Forms application, and add the following controls to Form1:

- A RadioButton control named DrawLine. Set its Text property to Line and its Checked property to True.
- A RadioButton control named DrawRectangle. Set its Text property to Rectangle.
- A RadioButton control named DrawEllipse. Set its Text property to Ellipse.
- A ComboBox control named LineColor. Set its DropDownStyle property to DropDownList.
- A ComboBox control named FillColor. Set its DropDownStyle property to DropDownList.
- A PictureBox control named DrawingArea. Set its BackColor property to White (or 255, 255, 255) and its BorderStyle property to Fixed3D. Make it somewhat large.

Add informational labels if desired. The form should look like the one in Figure 9-10.

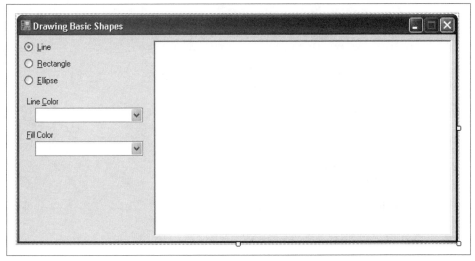

Figure 9-10. The controls on the shape drawing sample

Now add the following source code to the form's code template:

```
Private FirstPoint As Point = New Point(-1, -1)

Private Sub Form1_Load(ByVal sender As System.Object, _
      ByVal e As System.EventArgs) Handles MyBase.Load
   ' ----- Fill in the list of colors.
   For Each colorName As String In New String() _
         {"Black", "Red", "Orange", "Yellow", "Green", _
         "Blue", "Indigo", "Violet", "White"}
      LineColor.Items.Add(colorName)
      FillColor.Items.Add(colorName)
   Next colorName
   LineColor.SelectedIndex = LineColor.Items.IndexOf("Black")
   FillColor.SelectedIndex = LineColor.Items.IndexOf("White")
End Sub

Private Sub DrawingArea_MouseDown(ByVal sender As Object, _
      ByVal e As System.Windows.Forms.MouseEventArgs) _
      Handles DrawingArea.MouseDown
   ' ----- Time to do some drawing.
   Dim useLine As Pen
   Dim useFill As Brush
   Dim canvas As Graphics
   Dim drawBounds As Rectangle

   ' ----- Is this the first or second click?
   If (FirstPoint.Equals(New Point(-1, -1))) Then
      ' ----- This is the first click. Record the location.
      FirstPoint = e.Location
```

```
            ' ----- Draw a marker at this point.
         DrawMarker(FirstPoint)
      Else
         ' ----- Get the two colors to use.
         useLine = New Pen(Color.FromName(LineColor.Text))
         useFill = New SolidBrush(Color.FromName(FillColor.Text))

         ' ----- Get the drawing surface.
         canvas = DrawingArea.CreateGraphics()

         ' ----- Remove the first-point marker.
         DrawMarker(FirstPoint)

         ' ----- For rectangles and ellipses, get the
         '          bounding area.
         drawBounds = New Rectangle( _
            Math.Min(FirstPoint.X, e.Location.X), _
            Math.Min(FirstPoint.Y, e.Location.Y), _
            Math.Abs(FirstPoint.X - e.Location.X), _
            Math.Abs(FirstPoint.Y - e.Location.Y))

         ' ----- Time to draw.
         If (DrawLine.Checked = True) Then
            ' ----- Draw a line.
            canvas.DrawLine(useLine, FirstPoint, e.Location)
         ElseIf (DrawRectangle.Checked = True) Then
            ' ----- Draw a rectangle.
            canvas.FillRectangle(useFill, drawBounds)
            canvas.DrawRectangle(useLine, drawBounds)
         Else
            ' ----- Draw an ellipse.
            canvas.FillEllipse(useFill, drawBounds)
            canvas.DrawEllipse(useLine, drawBounds)
         End If

         ' ----- Clean up.
         canvas.Dispose()
         useFill.Dispose()
         useLine.Dispose()
         FirstPoint = New Point(-1, -1)
      End If
End Sub

Private Sub DrawMarker(ByVal centerPoint As Point)
   ' ----- Given a point, draw a small square at
   '          that location.
   Dim screenPoint As Point
   Dim fillArea As Rectangle

   ' ----- Determine the fill area.
   screenPoint = DrawingArea.PointToScreen(centerPoint)
   fillArea = New Rectangle(screenPoint.X - 2, _
      screenPoint.Y - 2, 5, 5)
```

```
' ----- Draw a red rectangle. Cyan is the RBG
'       inverse of red.
ControlPaint.FillReversibleRectangle(fillArea, Color.Cyan)
End Sub
```

Run the program, and use the `RadioButton` and `ComboBox` controls to select the object style and colors. Click on the `DrawingArea` controls twice to specify the two endpoints of each line, rectangle, or ellipse. Figure 9-11 shows the program in use.

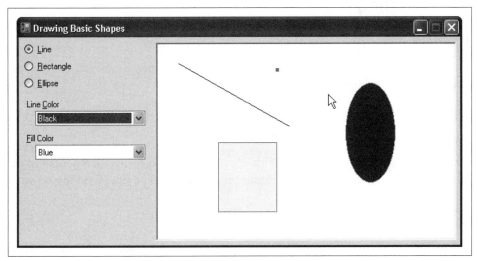

Figure 9-11. Drawing basic shapes

Drawing shapes is so easy in .NET as to make it somewhat humdrum. Back in the early days of computer drawing, drawing a line or circle required a basic understanding of the geometric equations needed to produce such shapes on a Cartesian coordinate system. But no more! The `Graphics` object includes a set of methods designed to make drawing simple. Most of them are used throughout the recipes in this chapter.

This recipe's code spends some time watching for the locations of mouse clicks on the drawing surface. Once it has these locations and the user-selected colors, it draws the basic shapes in just a few quick statements:

```
If (DrawLine.Checked = True) Then
   canvas.DrawLine(useLine, FirstPoint, e.Location)
ElseIf (DrawRectangle.Checked = True) Then
   canvas.FillRectangle(useFill, drawBounds)
   canvas.DrawRectangle(useLine, drawBounds)
Else
   canvas.FillEllipse(useFill, drawBounds)
   canvas.DrawEllipse(useLine, drawBounds)
End If
```

See Also

Recipe 9.26 discusses the `FillReversibleRectangle( )` method used in this recipe's code.

9.8   Drawing Lines One Pixel Wide Regardless of Scaling

Problem

You need to draw a one-pixel-wide line, but this becomes problematic when the graphics scaling mode is changed.

Solution

Sample code folder: Chapter 09\PenWidth

Set the pen's width to –1. Although this approach is not formally documented in the GDI+ references, it does cause the thinnest line possible to be drawn no matter what the scaling is set to.

Discussion

The `Graphics` object's `PageUnit` property allows you to set the scaling to standard units such as inches or millimeters. This can be very handy for some types of graphics-drawing tasks, but it alters the way lines are drawn. The `DrawLine( )` method accepts a pen that defines the color and width of the drawn line. By default the pen's width is always set to 1 unit wide, and as long as the `PageUnit` is left at its default setting of `Pixels`, all is well: a 1-unit-wide line will be drawn as 1 pixel wide. However, when `PageUnit` is set to `Inches`, for example, a 1-unit-wide line is rendered as 1 inch wide, which is likely not what you want at all.

To demonstrate this in action, and to show the workaround, this recipe's code first draws a line diagonally across the form with a red pen set to a width of 1, then draws another line on the other diagonal using a green pen set to a width of –1.

Create a new Windows Forms application, and place three `RadioButton` controls on the form, named `UsePixels`, `UseMillimeters`, and `UseInches`. Set their `Text` properties appropriately. Then add the following code to the form's code template:

```
Private Sub RadioButton_CheckedChanged( _
      ByVal sender As System.Object, _
      ByVal e As System.EventArgs) _
      Handles UsePixels.CheckedChanged, _
      UseMillimeters.CheckedChanged, _
      UseInches.CheckedChanged
```

```
    ' ----- Change the scaling system.
    Me.Refresh( )
End Sub

Private Sub Form1_Paint(ByVal sender As Object, _
        ByVal e As System.Windows.Forms.PaintEventArgs) _
        Handles Me.Paint
    ' ----- Draw contrasting lines.
    Dim xCorner As Single
    Dim yCorner As Single
    Dim canvas As Graphics

    canvas = e.Graphics
    xCorner = Me.ClientSize.Width
    yCorner = Me.ClientSize.Height
    If (UseMillimeters.Checked = True) Then
        canvas.PageUnit = GraphicsUnit.Millimeter
        xCorner /= canvas.DpiX
        yCorner /= canvas.DpiY
        xCorner *= 25.4
        yCorner *= 25.4
    ElseIf (UseInches.Checked = True) Then
        canvas.PageUnit = GraphicsUnit.Inch
        xCorner /= canvas.DpiX
        yCorner /= canvas.DpiY
    Else
        canvas.PageUnit = GraphicsUnit.Pixel
    End If

    ' ----- Clear any previous lines.
    canvas.Clear(Me.BackColor)

    ' ----- Draw a one-unit line.
    canvas.DrawLine(New Pen(Color.Red, 1), 0, 0, _
        xCorner, yCorner)

    ' ----- Draw a one-pixel line.
    canvas.DrawLine(New Pen(Color.Green, -1), xCorner, _
        0, 0, yCorner)
End Sub
```

As this code shows, the graphics PageUnit property is set appropriately for these units, and the red line will show the obvious difference in the line width. Figure 9-12 shows the results when the red line is drawn 1 inch wide (it's black and white here, obviously, but imagine it's red). The green line is drawn 1 pixel wide, no matter which scaling mode is selected.

In addition to the PageUnit mode, the ScaleTransform( ) method can customize the scaling of your graphics. This transform affects all coordinates, and all pen widths too; a pen width of 1 draws a 1-unit-wide line at whatever scale is set. Again, the workaround is to set the pen's width to –1 to get a consistent 1-pixel-wide line.

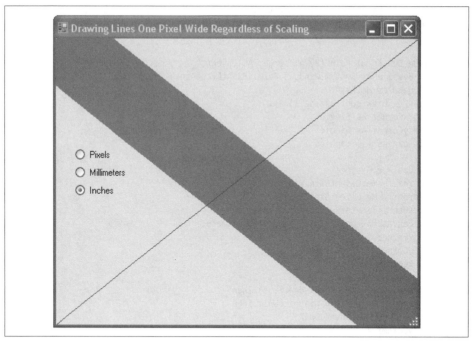

Figure 9-12. A one-inch-wide line and a one-pixel-wide line

9.9   Forcing a Form or Control to Redraw

Problem

You want to activate the Paint event for a form or control to cause its graphics to refresh.

Solution

Sample code folder: Chapter 09\Invalidating

It's best to let the operating system handle exactly when any object should repaint itself. In Visual Basic 2005, this means it's best to draw in an object's Paint event and not to worry about when to activate the painting. However, there are times when you want to control when graphics are redrawn, such as for simple animations, when data values in the program change, or when other events happen that affect the image. In these cases, you can call the Refresh( ) method of the object to be refreshed, or you can call the Invalidate( ) method to do much the same thing. The operating system handles the rest of the details.

Discussion

The demonstration code shown here draws a five-pointed star centered on the mouse cursor. As the mouse moves around on the form, the star moves with it, which means each mouse-move event should trigger a form Paint event. You accomplish this by invalidating the form with each move of the mouse. You can also use the Refresh( ) method.

Create a new Windows Forms application, and add the following code to the form's class template:

```
' ----- Keep track of the mouse position.
Private MouseX As Integer
Private MouseY As Integer

Private Sub Form1_MouseMove(ByVal sender As Object, _
      ByVal e As System.Windows.Forms.MouseEventArgs) _
      Handles Me.MouseMove
   ' ----- Record the mouse position.
   MouseX = e.X
   MouseY = e.Y

   ' ----- Mark the form for redrawing.
   Me.Invalidate( )

   ' ----- If you want to update the form quicker,
   '       call Refresh() instead of Invalidate().
   'Me.Refresh( )
End Sub
```

The form's Paint event grabs the form's Graphics object to provide the surface to draw on, then creates an array of points defining the five points of the star, centered around the current position of the mouse:

```
Private Sub Form1_Paint(ByVal sender As Object, _
      ByVal e As System.Windows.Forms.PaintEventArgs) _
      Handles Me.Paint
   ' ----- Refresh the form display.
   Dim canvas As Graphics = e.Graphics
   Dim starPoints(4) As Point
   Dim angle As Double
   Dim radians As Double
   Dim pointX As Double
   Dim pointY As Double
   Dim counter As Integer
   Const pointDistance As Double = 50
   Const angleStart As Integer = 198
   Const angleRotation As Integer = 144

   ' ----- Calculate each of the star's points.
   angle = angleStart
   For counter = 0 To 4
      angle += angleRotation
```

```
        radians = angle * Math.PI / 180
        pointX = Math.Cos(radians) * pointDistance + MouseX
        pointY = Math.Sin(radians) * pointDistance + MouseY
        starPoints(counter) = New Point(CInt(pointX), _
           CInt(pointY))
    Next counter

    ' ----- Draw the star. I've provided a few alternatives.
    canvas.FillPolygon(Brushes.DarkRed, starPoints, _
       Drawing2D.FillMode.Alternate)
    'canvas.FillPolygon(Brushes.DarkRed, starPoints, _
    '   Drawing2D.FillMode.Winding)
    'canvas.DrawPolygon(Pens.DarkRed, starPoints)
End Sub
```

There are several ways to draw or solid-fill a polygon such as this five-pointed star. The last three statements in the code let you experiment with three different techniques. The algorithm used to fill the center of a polygon can either end up with alternating areas filled, or not. Figure 9-13 shows the results of filling using Drawing2D.FillMode.Alternate. The Drawing2D.FillMode.Winding mode causes the star to be completely filled in, including the center area.

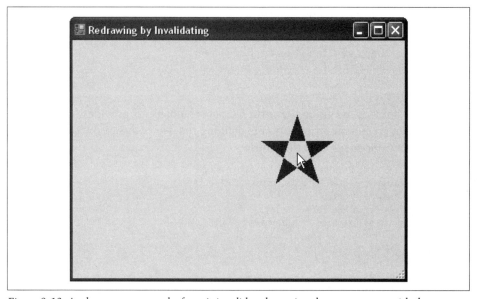

Figure 9-13. As the mouse moves the form is invalidated, causing the star to move with the cursor

The Invalidate( ) method does not force an immediate refresh of the form. Instead, it puts in a request for a redraw the next time the system is not too busy. Windows considers screen updates low-priority tasks, so if your system is busy doing other things, the screen changes will be postponed. If you want the changes to occur immediately, follow the Invalidate( ) method call with a call to the form's (or, if you are drawing on a control, the control's) Update( ) method:

```
Me.Invalidate( )
Me.Update( )
```

The Refresh( ) method combines both lines into one method call. So why would you call Invalidate( ) when the more powerful Refresh( ) method is available? Invalidate( ) accepts arguments that let you narrow down the size of the area to redraw. Redrawing the entire form can be a slow process, especially if you have to do it often. By passing a Rectangle or Region object to Invalidate( ), you can tell Windows, "Redraw only in this limited area."

9.10   Using Transparency

Problem

You know that .NET includes cool new transparency and "alpha blending" features, and you'd like to try them out.

Solution

Windows Forms include a few different transparency features. The simplest are accessible through two properties of each form: Opacity and TransparencyKey. Opacity ranges from 0% to 100% (actually, 0.0 for full transparency and 1.0 for full opacity) and impacts the entire form. Figure 9-14 shows a form set at 50% opacity with this paragraph showing through.

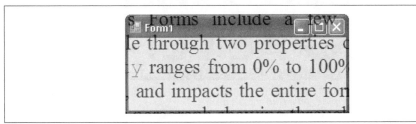

Figure 9-14. A see-through form with 50% opacity

The TransparencyKey property lets you indicate one form color as the "invisibility" color. When used, anything on the form that appears in the indicated color is rendered invisible. Figure 9-15 shows a form with its TransparencyKey property set to Control, the color normally used for the form's background. It appears over this paragraph's text.

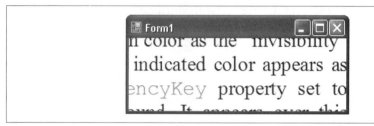

Figure 9-15. A see-through form with surface invisibility

Discussion

A bug in the initial release of Visual Basic 2005 causes some images drawn on a form's surface or on one of its contained controls to ignore the TransparencyKey setting, even if that image contains the invisibility color. There is a workaround that uses a third transparency feature of GDI+, the Bitmap object's MakeTransparent( ) method. The following block of code loads an image from a file, sets the White color as transparent, and draws it on the invisible background from Figure 9-15, producing the results in Figure 9-16:

```
Private Sub Form1_Load(ByVal sender As System.Object, _
    ByVal e As System.EventArgs) Handles MyBase.Load
  Dim backImage As New Bitmap("c:\logo.bmp")
  backImage.MakeTransparent(Color.White)
  Me.BackgroundImage = backImage
End Sub
```

Figure 9-16. A transparent image on a transparent form

A fourth transparency feature involves partially invisible colors. Although the System.Drawing.Color structure includes several predefined colors, you can create your own colors through that structure's FromArgb( ) method. One variation of this method accepts four arguments: red, green, and blue components, and an "alpha" component that sets the transparency of the color. That value ranges from 0 (fully transparent) to 255 (fully opaque). Another variation accepts just an alpha component and a previously defined color:

```
' ----- Make a semi-transparent red color.
Dim semiRed As Integer = New Color(128, Color.Red)

' ----- Here's another way to do the same thing.
Dim semiRed As Integer = New Color(128, 255, 0, 0)
```

You can then use this color to create pens or brushes as you would with any other color.

Some older systems don't support all methods of transparency. If there is any chance your program will run on such older systems, don't depend on transparency as the sole method of communicating something important to the user.

9.11   Scaling with Transforms

Problem

You want to zoom the view of a drawing area so that the user has a wider or narrower view of the content.

Solution

Sample code folder: Chapter 09\ScalingTransform

Add a scaling transform to the drawing surface before outputting the text. The System.Drawing.Graphics object includes a ScaleTransform( ) method that lets you scale the output automatically, with separate scales in the X and Y directions.

Discussion

Create a new Windows Forms application, and add the following controls to Form1:

- A TextBox control named DisplayText. Set its Multiline property to True and its ScrollBars property to Vertical. Size it so that you can see multiple lines of user-entered text.
- A TrackBar control named DisplayScale. Set its Minimum property to 1 and its Maximum property to 5. The TrackBar control appears in the All Windows Forms section of the Toolbox by default.
- A Button control named ActDisplay. Set its Text property to Display.
- A PictureBox control named DrawingArea. Set its BackColor property to White and its BorderStyle property to Fixed3D.

Add informational labels if desired. The form should look like Figure 9-17.

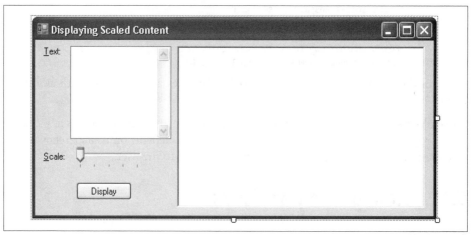

Figure 9-17. The controls on the scaled content sample

Now add the following source code to the form's class template:

```
Private Sub ActDisplay_Click(ByVal sender As System.Object, _
      ByVal e As System.EventArgs) Handles ActDisplay.Click
   ' ----- Force the text to redisplay.
   DrawingArea.Invalidate( )
End Sub

Private Sub DrawingArea_Paint(ByVal sender As Object, _
      ByVal e As System.Windows.Forms.PaintEventArgs) _
      Handles DrawingArea.Paint
   ' ----- Refresh the drawing area.
   Dim titleFont As Font
   Dim mainFont As Font
   Dim titleArea As Rectangle
   Dim textArea As Rectangle
   Dim titleFormat As StringFormat
   Const MainTitle As String = "Important Message"

   ' ----- Clear any existing content.
   e.Graphics.Clear(Color.White)

   ' ----- Build some fonts used for the display text.
   titleFont = New Font("Arial", 16, FontStyle.Bold)
   mainFont = New Font("Arial", 12, FontStyle.Regular)

   ' ----- Determine where the title and main text will go.
   titleArea = New Rectangle(0, 0, _
      DrawingArea.ClientRectangle.Width, titleFont.Height)
   textArea = New Rectangle(0, titleFont.Height * 1.4, _
      DrawingArea.ClientRectangle.Width, _
      DrawingArea.ClientRectangle.Height - _
      (titleFont.Height * 1.4))
```

```
' ----- Scale according to the user's request.
e.Graphics.ScaleTransform(DisplayScale.Value, _
   DisplayScale.Value)

' ----- Add a title to the content.
titleFormat = New StringFormat( )
titleFormat.Alignment = StringAlignment.Center
e.Graphics.DrawString(MainTitle, titleFont, _
   Brushes.Black, titleArea, titleFormat)
titleFormat.Dispose( )

' ----- Draw a nice dividing line.
e.Graphics.DrawLine(Pens.Black, 20, _
   CInt(titleFont.Height * 1.2), _
   DrawingArea.ClientRectangle.Width - 20, _
   CInt(titleFont.Height * 1.2))

' ----- Draw the main text.
e.Graphics.DrawString(DisplayText.Text, mainFont, _
   Brushes.Black, textArea)

' ----- Clean up.
mainFont.Dispose( )
titleFont.Dispose( )
End Sub
```

Run the program, enter some text in the TextBox control, adjust the DisplayScale
control value, and click the ActDisplay button. The drawing area zooms in on the
content as you adjust the scale. Figure 9-18 shows content without scaling
(DisplayScale.Value = 1) and with a 2x scale (DisplayScale.Value = 2).

Figure 9-18. x and 2x scaling of content

The ScaleTransform( ) method scales everything: text and shape sizes, pen thickness,
X and Y positions, rectangular bounding boxes, and so on. The previous sample
code scaled the textArea bounding box used to limit the extent of the main text to
the output display area. When the content was scaled, though, the bounding box

was also scaled, so that the content no longer fits the bounding box. If you still want such bounding boxes to fit, you have to scale them by an inverse factor:

```
textArea = New Rectangle(0, titleFont.Height * 1.4, _
    DrawingArea.ClientRectangle.Width / DisplayScale.Value, _
    DrawingArea.ClientRectangle.Height - _
    (titleFont.Height * 1.4))
```

Figure 9-19 shows the output from this revised block of code.

Figure 9-19. X scaling with boundary adjustments

See Also

Recipe 9.4 discusses scaling based on inches and centimeters.

9.12   Using an Outline Path

Problem

You want to create a complex graphics drawing path that can simplify graphics drawing commands and can be reused repeatedly.

Solution

Sample code folder: Chapter 09\GraphicsPath

The GraphicsPath object lets you create and store a complex sequence of graphics lines, rectangles, ellipses, and polygons as a single object.

Discussion

The GraphicsPath is part of the Drawing2D namespace, so be sure to add the following Imports statement to the top of your code:

```
Imports System.Drawing.Drawing2D
```

In this recipe we'll use a GraphicsPath object to draw a checkerboard. The drawing takes place in the form's Paint event handler:

```
Private Sub Form1_Paint(ByVal sender As Object, _
    ByVal e As System.Windows.Forms.PaintEventArgs) _
    Handles Me.Paint
```

To begin, the graphics surface for the form is referenced, and a static GraphicsPath reference variable (thePath) is created. The path is created the first time the event handler gets called and is used again on successive calls:

```
' ----- Draw a checkerboard.
Dim across As Integer
Dim down As Integer
Dim canvas As Graphics = e.Graphics
Static thePath As GraphicsPath

' ----- Draw the checkerboard the first time only.
If (thePath Is Nothing) Then
    thePath = New GraphicsPath
    For across = 0 To 7
        For down = 0 To 7
            If (((across + down) Mod 2) = 1) Then
                thePath.AddRectangle( _
                    New Rectangle(across, down, 1, 1))
            End If
        Next down
    Next across
End If
```

The scaling needs to take place every time the Paint event is triggered because as the user changes the size of the form (and the graphics surface), the checkerboard stretches to fit it:

```
' ----- Scale the form for the checkerboard.
Dim scaleX As Single
Dim scaleY As Single
scaleX = CSng(Me.ClientSize.Width / 10)
scaleY = CSng(Me.ClientSize.Height / 10)
canvas.ScaleTransform(scaleX, scaleY)
canvas.TranslateTransform(1, 1)
```

Finally, the path is drawn using a blue brush, and its outline is drawn around the edges:

```
' ----- Draw and outline the checkerboard.
canvas.FillPath(Brushes.Blue, thePath)
canvas.DrawRectangle(New Pen(Color.Blue, -1), 0, 0, 8, 8)
End Sub
```

The form's Resize event needs a command to cause the form to refresh as it is resized. This causes the checkerboard to be redrawn on the fly as the form is stretched or shrunk:

```
Private Sub Form1_Resize(ByVal sender As Object, _
    ByVal e As System.EventArgs) Handles Me.Resize
```

```
    ' ----- Redraw the checkerboard.
    Me.Refresh( )
End Sub
```

For maximum smoothness of the action, be sure to set the form's DoubleBuffered property to True.

Figure 9-20 shows the checkerboard when the form has been resized to fairly square dimensions.

Figure 9-20. A checkerboard drawn using a single path

9.13   Using Gradients for Smooth Color Changes

Problem

You want to fill a graphics area with colors that smoothly transition from one shade to another.

Solution

Sample code folder: Chapter 09\SmoothColor

Create a `GraphicsPath` object, use it to create and define a `PathGradientBrush`, set the various colors of the brush, and then use the new gradient brush to fill a graphics area.

Discussion

The `PathGradientBrush` object enables a lot of creative color transitions in your graphics. The code in this recipe provides a good starting point for further experimentation.

Some of these objects require referencing the `Drawing2D` namespace, so be sure to add the following `Imports` statement to the top of your source code:

```
Imports System.Drawing.Drawing2D
```

This example dynamically updates the gradient fill as you move the mouse over the face of the form. To do this, the mouse position is recorded with each `MouseMove` event, and the form repaints itself by calling its `Refresh()` method:

```
' ----- Keep track of the mouse position.
Private MouseX As Integer
Private MouseY As Integer

Private Sub Form1_MouseMove(ByVal sender As Object, _
      ByVal e As System.Windows.Forms.MouseEventArgs) _
      Handles Me.MouseMove
   ' ----- Record the mouse position.
   MouseX = e.X
   MouseY = e.Y

   ' ----- Cause a repaint of the form.
   Me.Refresh()
End Sub
```

The form's `Paint` event handles the important details of the gradient color fill. Let's take this step by step.:

1. The `Paint` event is called with each move of the mouse:

   ```
   Private Sub Form1_Paint(ByVal sender As Object, _
         ByVal e As System.Windows.Forms.PaintEventArgs) _
         Handles Me.Paint
   ```

2. The graphics path can be any shape, even discontinuous rectangles, ellipses, and so on. In this case the path is defined as the rectangle around the edge of the form's client area:

   ```
   ' ----- Create path around edge of form's client area.
   Dim thePath As New GraphicsPath
   thePath.AddRectangle(Me.ClientRectangle)
   ```

3. The `PathGradientBrush` is created using the predefined path. The object uses this geometric information internally to determine smoothly transitioning colors for all pixel locations during drawing:

   ```
   ' ----- Use the path to construct a gradient brush.
   Dim smoothBrush As PathGradientBrush = _
      New PathGradientBrush(thePath)
   ```

4. You can define one point in the center of the brush area to have a specific color. Here, set the point under the mouse cursor to White. Colors will transition away from white based on distance from the mouse cursor to the edges of the path:

```
' ----- Set the color at the mouse point.
smoothBrush.CenterPoint = New PointF(MouseX, MouseY)
smoothBrush.CenterColor = Color.White
```

5. One or more colors can be set along the path using the SurroundColors property of the PathGradientBrush object. Set an array of four colors, so each corner of the form provides a standard color:

```
' ----- Set a color along the entire boundary of the path.
Dim colorArray( ) As Color = _
    {Color.Red, Color.Green, Color.Blue, Color.Yellow}
smoothBrush.SurroundColors = colorArray
```

6. The new PathGradientBrush is used to fill the rectangular area of the form, and all pixels on the form are set to a smoothly transitioned shade depending on the geometry and settings made earlier in the code:

```
' ----- Fill form with gradient path.
e.Graphics.FillRectangle(smoothBrush, Me.ClientRectangle)
End Sub
```

7. To have the effect update smoothly, set the form's DoubleBuffered property to True. Figure 9-21 shows the form's appearance as the mouse is moved around on it.

Figure 9-21. Color gradients open the door to many special color-shading effects

9.14   Drawing Bezier Splines

Problem

You need to draw smooth curves between points, but you'd prefer not to delve into a lot of complex mathematical calculations.

Solution

Sample code folder: Chapter 09\BezierSplines

The DrawBezier( ) graphics method draws a smooth curve between two points, using two other points as *control points*—or points that tug at the curve to change its shape as desired.

Discussion

Bezier splines are defined by two endpoints and two control points. (The mathematical theory behind Bezier splines is beyond the scope of this book. For more information, check out the links in the "See Also" section at the end of this recipe.)

The example program shown here lets you experiment interactively with the DrawBezier( ) graphics method. First, make sure you import the Drawing2D namespace, as follows:

```
Imports System.Drawing.Drawing2D
```

Up to four mouse-click points will be recorded in an array of points. Keep track of the points using a generic list:

```
' ----- Keeps track of the mouse positions.
Dim BendPoints As New Generic.List(Of Point)
```

As the mouse is clicked and new points are added to the array, the form is told to refresh itself by calling its Refresh( ) method:

```
Private Sub Form1_MouseClick(ByVal sender As Object, _
      ByVal e As System.Windows.Forms.MouseEventArgs) _
      Handles Me.MouseClick
   ' ----- Record another mouse position.
   BendPoints.Add(New Point(e.X, e.Y))

   ' ----- Update the display.
   Me.Refresh( )
End Sub
```

The form's Paint event is where the important action takes place:

```
Private Sub Form1_Paint(ByVal sender As Object, _
      ByVal e As System.Windows.Forms.PaintEventArgs) _
      Handles Me.Paint
   ' ----- Get the form's drawing surface.
   Dim canvas As Graphics = e.Graphics
```

Each point is drawn as a small solid-filled ellipse (circle). When there are four points, they are passed to the DrawBezier( ) method to draw the curve using a black pen. The first and fourth clicks are the endpoints. Clicking on the form a fifth time erases all the points, and the curve starts over:

```
Dim scanPoint As Point
Const PointSize As Integer = 7

' ----- Draw available points.
If (BendPoints.Count <= 4) Then
   For Each scanPoint In BendPoints
      canvas.FillEllipse(Brushes.Red, _
      scanPoint.X - PointSize, _
      scanPoint.Y - PointSize, _
      PointSize * 2, PointSize * 2)
   Next scanPoint
End If

' ----- Draw the spline if all points are there.
If (BendPoints.Count >= 4) Then
   canvas.DrawBezier(Pens.Black, BendPoints(0), _
      BendPoints(1), BendPoints(2), BendPoints(3))
   BendPoints.Clear( )
End If
End Sub
```

Figure 9-22 shows the results after four points have been clicked.

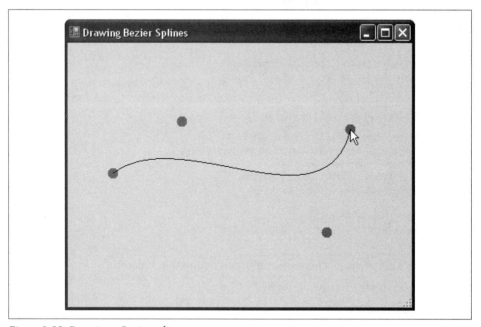

Figure 9-22. Drawing a Bezier spline

See Also

See *http://www.ibiblio.org/e-notes/Splines/Bezier.htm* and *http://mathforum.org/library/drmath/view/54434.html* for more information on Bezier splines.

9.15   Drawing Cardinal Splines

Problem

You need a curve that goes smoothly through two or more points.

Solution

Sample code folder: Chapter 09\CardinalSplines

A Cardinal spline plots a curve through two or more points. Unlike the Bezier spline, the Cardinal spline intersects every point and does not use external control points.

Discussion

The mathematical description of the way the Cardinal spline works is beyond the scope of this book. For a more in-depth discussion and explanation of the math involved, see the links in the "See Also" section at the end of this recipe.

The following code demonstrates the Cardinal spline by collecting points as they are clicked on the face of the form. A list of the points is built up, and with each added point, the Cardinal spline is drawn anew. A button at the top of the form lets you erase all the points to start over, and a TrackBar control lets you set the tension parameter for the spline. The tension is a number ranging from 0 to 1 that is passed to the DrawCurve( ) method to determine the smoothness of the curve as it passes through each point. The easiest way to understand the effect of this parameter is to slide the TrackBar and watch the curve change shape.

Here's the code that lets the form monitor for mouse clicks, builds the set of points, and refreshes the form to activate its Paint event:

```
' ----- Keep track of the mouse positions.
Private BendPoints As New Generic.List(Of Point)

Private Sub Form1_MouseClick(ByVal sender As Object, _
      ByVal e As System.Windows.Forms.MouseEventArgs) _
      Handles Me.MouseClick
   ' ----- Add a mouse position.
   BendPoints.Add(New Point(e.X, e.Y))

   ' ----- Update the display.
   Me.Refresh( )
End Sub
```

The form's Paint event is where the drawing of the selected points and the spline connecting them takes place. The event fires when the form is refreshed, which is caused by calling the Refresh( ) method when the mouse is clicked or the trackbar is adjusted.

This code draws each plotted point in red as the user clicks it. Then, if there are two or more accumulated points, it draws the Cardinal spline using the DrawCurve( ) method:

```
Private Sub Form1_Paint(ByVal sender As Object, _
      ByVal e As System.Windows.Forms.PaintEventArgs) _
      Handles Me.Paint
   ' ----- Draw the spline points and line.
   Dim tension As Single
   Dim canvas As Graphics
   Dim scanPoint As Point
   Const PointSize As Integer = 7

   ' ----- Determine the tension.
   tension = TensionLevel.Value / TensionLevel.Maximum
   LabelTension.Text = "Tension:  " & tension.ToString

   ' ----- Draw the points on the surface.
   canvas = e.Graphics
   For Each scanPoint In BendPoints
      canvas.FillEllipse(Brushes.Red, _
         scanPoint.X - PointSize, _
         scanPoint.Y - PointSize, _
         PointSize * 2, PointSize * 2)
   Next scanPoint

   ' ----- Draw the Cardinal spline.
   If (BendPoints.Count > 1) Then
      canvas.DrawCurve(Pens.Black, _
         BendPoints.ToArray, tension)
   End If
End Sub
```

When the Trackbar's slider is adjusted, the form's Refresh( ) method is called to trigger a repaint:

```
Private Sub TensionLevel_ValueChanged( _
      ByVal sender As Object, ByVal e As System.EventArgs) _
      Handles TensionLevel.ValueChanged
   ' ----- Update the tension and display.
   Me.Refresh( )
End Sub
```

When the Reset button is clicked, the set of points is emptied, and the form is repainted to erase the points and the curve:

```
Private Sub ActReset_Click(ByVal sender As System.Object, _
      ByVal e As System.EventArgs) Handles ActReset.Click
```

```
' ----- Clear all points.
BendPoints.Clear( )
Me.Refresh( )
End Sub
```

Figure 9-23 shows a typical spline curve through six points with the tension set to 0.6.
A lower tension results in sharp angles at the bend points, while higher tension gives
a smoother curve.

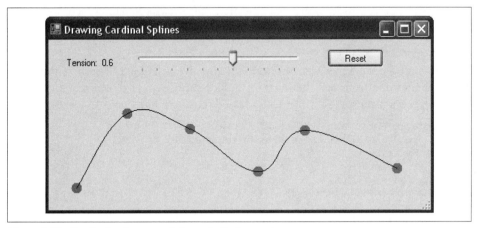

Figure 9-23. Cardinal splines travel through all given points

See Also

See *http://www.ibiblio.org/e-notes/Splines/Cardinal.htm* and *http://en.wikipedia.org/
wiki/Cardinal_spline* for more information on Cardinal splines.

9.16 Limiting Display Updates to Specific Regions

Problem

You want to clip your graphics using some complexly shaped area, without having to
resort to difficult code to compute intersections and other clipping details.

Solution

Sample code folder: Chapter 09\ClippingRegion

Create a Region object defined by a path, set the Graphics object's Clip property to
this region, and draw any standard graphics on the Graphics object surface. Clipping
takes place using the path.

Discussion

A single path can range from a simple sequence of lines to an elaborate mix of connected or disconnected rectangles, ellipses, or polygons. This means that a path can take on a complex outline, and it can involve a lot of independent parts. In the example presented here a large number of tall, thin rectangles are added to a single path, and this path is then used to define a Region object that clips the drawing of a string.

Several of the objects used in this example are in the Drawing2D namespace, so be sure to add the following Imports statement to the top of your source code:

```
Imports System.drawing.Drawing2D
```

The remaining code appears in the form's Paint event handler. The first thing the Paint handler does is access the form's graphics surface, passed as a member of the PaintEventArgs instance (e). The area is cleared to solid white:

```
Private Sub Form11_Paint(ByVal sender As Object, _
    ByVal e As System.Windows.Forms.PaintEventArgs) _
    Handles Me.Paint
  ' ----- Draw using a region to restrict output.
  Dim canvas As Graphics
  Dim fencePath As GraphicsPath
  Dim onePicket As Rectangle
  Dim counter As Integer
  Dim slottedRegion As Region

  ' ----- Clear the background.
  canvas = e.Graphics
  canvas.Clear(Color.White)
```

Next, a GraphicsPath object is created and filled with a lot of tall, thin rectangles, spaced apart somewhat like the pickets on a picket fence. These rectangles don't touch each other, but they are all added to a single complex path object:

```
  ' ----- Create a picket fence path.
  fencePath = New GraphicsPath
  For counter = 0 To 200
    onePicket = New Rectangle(counter * 10, 0, 6, 500)
    fencePath.AddRectangle(onePicket)
  Next counter
```

The path just created is then used to define a new Region object:

```
  ' ----- Create a region from the path.
  slottedRegion = New Region(fencePath)
```

The path itself can't be used to define a clipping region, but a Region object can. Even regions defined by complexly shaped paths provide rapid clipping on the graphics surface. To this end, we'll now assign the slottedRegion to the Graphics object's Clip property:

```
' ----- Set clipping using the region.
canvas.Clip = slottedRegion
```

You can apply any graphics drawing methods you want at this point, and everything drawn will be clipped as defined by the Graphics object's Clip property. In this example we clear the entire surface to a new color (given a white-cyan-white-cyan picket fence image), and then draw a string of text using a large font:

```
' ----- Draw some slotted text.
canvas.Clear(Color.Aqua)
canvas.DrawString("Picket Fence", _
    New Font("Times New Roman", 77), _
    Brushes.Blue, 20, 20)
End Sub
```

Figure 9-24 shows how both graphics methods are clipped.

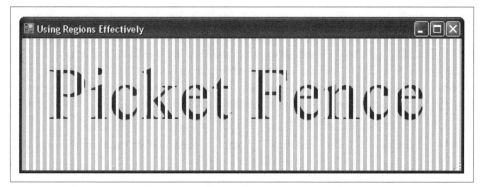

Figure 9-24. Regions can be used to clip graphics in very intricate ways

9.17 Drawing Text

Problem

You want to draw some nicely formatted text on the drawing surface.

Solution

Sample code folder: Chapter 09\DrawingText

The primary tool for drawing text is the Graphics.DrawString() method. To make adjustments to the text, you can alter the font's properties, apply transformations to the canvas itself, or use a StringFormat object. This recipe's sample code uses each of these methods to display a string of text.

Discussion

Create a new Windows Forms application, and add the following controls to Form1:

- A TextBox control named DisplayText. Set its Multiline property to True and its ScrollBars property to Vertical. Size it so that you can see multiple lines of user-entered text.
- A CheckBox control named UseBold. Set its Text property to Bold.
- A CheckBox control named UseItalic. Set its Text property to Italic.
- A CheckBox control named UseUnderline. Set its Text property to Underline.
- A CheckBox control named UseStrikeout. Set its Text property Strikeout.
- A CheckBox control named ShowBoundingBox. Set its Text property to Show Bounding Box.
- A ComboBox control named DisplayAlign. Set its DropDownStyle property to DropDownList.
- A TrackBar control named DisplayRotate. Set its Minimum property to 0, its Maximum property to 360, its TickFrequency property to 15, its SmallChange property to 15, and its LargeChange property to 60. The TrackBar control appears in the All Windows Forms section of the Toolbox by default.
- A Button control named ActDisplay. Set its Text property to Display.
- A PictureBox control named DrawingArea. Set its BackColor property to White and its BorderStyle property to Fixed3D.

Add informational labels if desired. The form should look like Figure 9-25.

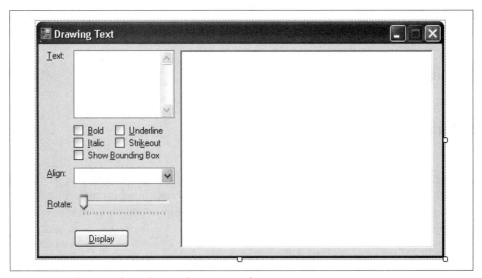

Figure 9-25. The controls on the text drawing sample

Now add the following source code to the form's class template:

```
Private Sub ActDisplay_Click(ByVal sender As System.Object, _
      ByVal e As System.EventArgs) Handles ActDisplay.Click
   ' ----- Force the text to redisplay.
   DrawingArea.Invalidate()
End Sub

Private Sub DrawingArea_Paint(ByVal sender As Object, _
      ByVal e As System.Windows.Forms.PaintEventArgs) _
      Handles DrawingArea.Paint
   ' ----- Refresh the drawing area.
   Dim mainFont As Font
   Dim textArea As Rectangle
   Dim textStyle As New FontStyle
   Dim textFormat As StringFormat
   Dim alignParts() As String

   ' ----- Clear any existing content.
   e.Graphics.Clear(Color.White)

   ' ----- Build the font used for the display text.
   textStyle = FontStyle.Regular
   If (UseBold.Checked = True) Then _
      textStyle = textStyle Or FontStyle.Bold
   If (UseItalic.Checked = True) Then _
      textStyle = textStyle Or FontStyle.Italic
   If (UseUnderline.Checked = True) Then _
      textStyle = textStyle Or FontStyle.Underline
   If (UseStrikeout.Checked = True) Then _
      textStyle = textStyle Or FontStyle.Strikeout
   mainFont = New Font("Arial", 12, textStyle)

   ' ----- Move the (0,0) origin to the center of the
   '       display.
   e.Graphics.TranslateTransform( _
      DrawingArea.ClientRectangle.Width / 2, _
      DrawingArea.ClientRectangle.Height / 2)

   ' ----- Determine where the main text will go. The Offset
   '       method repositions the rectangle's coordinates
   '       by the given X and Y values.
   textArea = New Rectangle(20, 20, _
      DrawingArea.ClientRectangle.Width - 40, _
      DrawingArea.ClientRectangle.Height - 40)
   textArea.Offset( _
      -CInt(DrawingArea.ClientRectangle.Width / 2), _
      -CInt(DrawingArea.ClientRectangle.Height / 2))

   ' ----- Prepare the alignment.
   textFormat = New StringFormat
   alignParts = Split(DisplayAlign.Text, ",")
```

```vbnet
      Select Case alignParts(0)
         Case "Left"
            textFormat.Alignment = StringAlignment.Near
         Case "Center"
            textFormat.Alignment = StringAlignment.Center
         Case "Right"
            textFormat.Alignment = StringAlignment.Far
      End Select
      Select Case alignParts(1)
         Case "Top"
            textFormat.LineAlignment = StringAlignment.Near
         Case "Middle"
            textFormat.LineAlignment = StringAlignment.Center
         Case "Bottom"
            textFormat.LineAlignment = StringAlignment.Far
      End Select

      ' ----- Rotate the world if requested.
      If (DisplayRotate.Value <> 0) Then
         e.Graphics.RotateTransform(DisplayRotate.Value)
      End If

      ' ----- Draw the bounding box if requested.
      If (ShowBoundingBox.Checked = True) Then
         e.Graphics.DrawRectangle(Pens.Gray, textArea)
      End If

      ' ----- Draw the main text.
      e.Graphics.DrawString(DisplayText.Text, mainFont, _
         Brushes.Black, textArea, textFormat)

      ' ----- Clean up.
      mainFont.Dispose()
   End Sub

   Private Sub Form1_Load(ByVal sender As System.Object, _
         ByVal e As System.EventArgs) Handles MyBase.Load
      ' ----- Build the list of alignments.
      DisplayAlign.Items.Add("Left,Top")
      DisplayAlign.Items.Add("Left,Middle")
      DisplayAlign.Items.Add("Left,Bottom")

      DisplayAlign.Items.Add("Center,Top")
      DisplayAlign.Items.Add("Center,Middle")
      DisplayAlign.Items.Add("Center,Bottom")

      DisplayAlign.Items.Add("Right,Top")
      DisplayAlign.Items.Add("Right,Middle")
      DisplayAlign.Items.Add("Right,Bottom")

      DisplayAlign.SelectedIndex = 0
   End Sub
```

To use the program, enter some text in the TextBox field, and adjust the other controls as desired to alter the text. Then click the Display button to refresh the displayed text. Figure 9-26 shows some sample text displayed through the program.

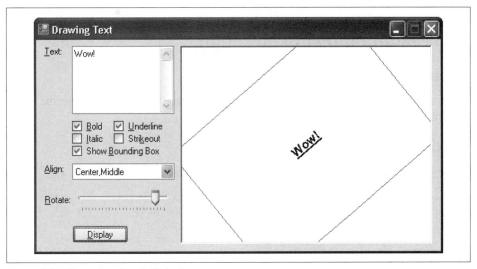

Figure 9-26. Rotated and embellished text

The Graphics.DrawString( ) method is pretty simple to use: you pass it a text string, a position (or bounding rectangle), a font, and a colored or patterned brush, and the text appears on the canvas. Except for how the position and boundaries of the text are specified, there isn't that much flexibility in the method itself. However, there is flexibility in the values passed to the method. Changes to the font or font styles, as demonstrated in this code, clearly have an impact on the results. Similarly, you can create any type of solid, patterned, or image-based brush, and use it to draw the text itself.

Transformations made to the canvas also impact the text output. This recipe's code applies two transformations to the canvas: it repositions the X-Y coordinate system origin from the upper-left corner of the canvas to the center, and it rotates the canvas if requested by the user so that the text appears rotated. Recipe 9.18 discusses the reasons for these two transformations in more detail.

The Drawing.StringFormat class, used in this sample to align the text within its bounding box, provides additional text-drawing options. The StringFormat.FormatFlags property lets you set options that adjust how the text appears in its bounding box. For instance, you can indicate whether the text should automatically wrap or not. The StringFormat.HotkeyPrefix property lets you indicate which character should be used to draw shortcut-key underlines below specific letters of the text, as is done using "&" in Label and other controls.

See Also

Many of the recipes in this chapter show text being formatted and output in a variety of formats and displays.

9.18   Rotating Text to Any Angle

Problem

You want to draw some text onto the output canvas and rotate it by a specific number of degrees.

Solution

Sample code folder: Chapter 09\DrawingText

The code for Recipe 9.17 includes features that let you rotate text in 15-degree increments. The code will not be repeated in full in this recipe, but this recipe's discussion will expand on the text-rotation features in more detail.

Discussion

The sample code in Recipe 9.17 includes two transformations to the canvas. As mentioned in other recipes, transformations impact every drawing command made to the canvas surface, preprocessing all drawing commands for size, position, and rotation before the output appears on the canvas. The sample code performs two transformations: one that repositions the (0,0) origin (or center point) from the upper-left corner of the canvas to the center of the canvas, and one that rotates the canvas by a user-specified amount. Here is the relevant code:

```
' ----- Move the (0,0) origin to the center of the display.
e.Graphics.TranslateTransform( _
   DrawingArea.ClientRectangle.Width / 2, _
   DrawingArea.ClientRectangle.Height / 2)

' ----- Rotate the world if requested.
If (DisplayRotate.Value <> 0) Then
   e.Graphics.RotateTransform(DisplayRotate.Value)
End If
```

Rotating text is a byproduct of canvas rotation; although the user sees the text rotate, your code acts as if the canvas itself is being rotated under the drawing pens. This means that it is not the text that is rotated, but the world of the canvas, and this rotation occurs around the (0,0) origin of the canvas.

In the sample code, the goal is to rotate the text so that the center of the text's bounding box stays in the center of the display. The movement of the origin through the `TranslateTransform( )` method call is required to properly rotate the text about its center point. If the code had left the origin at the upper-left corner of the canvas, the rotation would have occurred around that point, and some rotation angles would have moved the text right off the display. The left half of Figure 9-27 shows the output of text rotated at a 45-degree angle according to the sample code: the text rotates about its own center because the origin of the canvas world was moved to that same position. The right half of the figure shows what would have happened if the origin had remained at the upper-left corner of the `PictureBox` control.

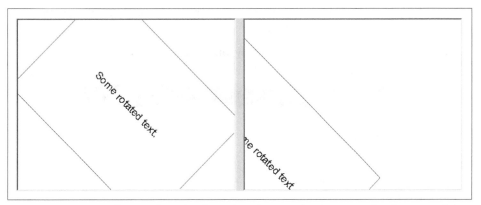

Figure 9-27. Rotating the text's bounding box when the origin has been moved to the center of the canvas (left) and when it remains at the default upper-left corner (right)

Although the sample code allows rotations only in 15-degree increments, you can pass any valid degree value to the `RotateTransform( )` method.

See Also

Recipe 9.17 contains the code discussed in this recipe.

9.19   Mirroring Text on the Canvas

Problem

You want to mirror the text displayed on a graphics canvas.

Solution

Sample code folder: Chapter 09\MirrorText

Use a custom matrix transformation through the `Graphics` object's `Transform` property. This recipe's sample code mirrors text both vertically and horizontally.

Discussion

Create a new Windows Forms application, and add the following controls to Form1:

- A RadioButton control named VerticalMirror. Set its Text property to Vertical and its Checked property to True.

- A RadioButton control named HorizontalMirror. Set its Text property to Horizontal.

- A PictureBox control named MirroredText. Set its BorderStyle property to FixedSingle and its BackColor property to White. Size it so that it can show a sentence or two of text in either direction.

Figure 9-28 shows the layout of the controls on this form.

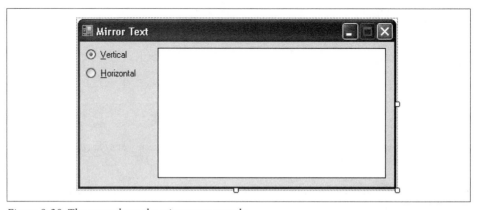

Figure 9-28. The controls on the mirror text sample

Now add the following source code to Form1's class template:

```
Private Const QuoteText As String = _
   "The best car safety device is a rear-view mirror " & _
   "with a cop in it. (Dudley Moore)"

Private Sub VerticalMirror_CheckedChanged( _
      ByVal sender As System.Object, _
      ByVal e As System.EventArgs) _
      Handles VerticalMirror.CheckedChanged
   ' ----- Update the display. This event indirectly
   '       handles both radio buttons.
   MirroredText.Invalidate( )
End Sub

Private Sub MirroredText_Paint(ByVal sender As Object, _
      ByVal e As System.Windows.Forms.PaintEventArgs) _
      Handles MirroredText.Paint
   ' ----- Draw the text and its reverse.
   Dim drawingArea As Rectangle
```

```
Dim saveState As Drawing2D.GraphicsState
Dim mirrorMatrix As Drawing2D.Matrix

' ----- Clear the background.
e.Graphics.Clear(Color.White)

' ----- Deterine the drawing area.
If (VerticalMirror.Checked = True) Then
    ' ----- Put text on the left and right of the mirror.
    drawingArea = New Rectangle(5, 5, _
        (MirroredText.ClientRectangle.Width \ 2) - 10, _
        MirroredText.ClientRectangle.Height - 10)

    ' ----- Draw the mirror line.
    e.Graphics.DrawLine(Pens.Black, _
        MirroredText.ClientRectangle.Width \ 2, _
        5, MirroredText.ClientRectangle.Width \ 2, _
        MirroredText.ClientRectangle.Height - 10)
Else
    ' ----- Put text on the top and bottom of the mirror.
    drawingArea = New Rectangle(5, 5, _
        MirroredText.ClientRectangle.Width - 10, _
        (MirroredText.ClientRectangle.Height \ 2) - 10)

    ' ----- Draw the mirror line.
    e.Graphics.DrawLine(Pens.Black, 5, _
        MirroredText.ClientRectangle.Height \ 2, _
        MirroredText.ClientRectangle.Width - 10, _
        MirroredText.ClientRectangle.Height \ 2)
End If

' ----- Draw the text.
e.Graphics.DrawString(QuoteText, MirroredText.Font, _
    Brushes.Black, drawingArea)

' ----- Mirror the display.
saveState = e.Graphics.Save()
If (VerticalMirror.Checked = True) Then
    mirrorMatrix = New Drawing2D.Matrix(-1, 0, 0, 1, _
        MirroredText.ClientRectangle.Width, 0)
Else
    mirrorMatrix = New Drawing2D.Matrix(1, 0, 0, -1, _
        0, MirroredText.ClientRectangle.Height)
End If
e.Graphics.Transform = mirrorMatrix

' ----- Draw the text, this time, mirrored.
e.Graphics.DrawString(QuoteText, MirroredText.Font, _
    Brushes.Black, drawingArea)

' ----- Undo the mirror.
e.Graphics.Restore(saveState)
End Sub
```

Run the program, and use the RadioButton controls to adjust the direction of the mirror. Figure 9-29 shows the mirror in the vertical orientation.

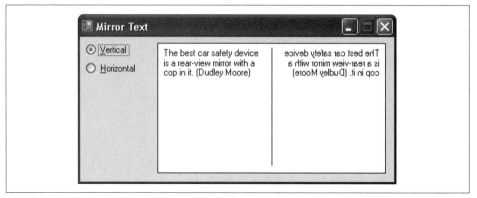

Figure 9-29. Text reversed with a vertical mirror

The Graphics object includes methods that perform basic scaling (ScaleTransform( )), repositioning (TranslateTransform( )), and rotating transformations (RotateTransform( )). While these transformations all seem quite different from each other, they all actually use the same method to accomplish the canvas-level adjustments. Each method sets up a *matrix transformation*, a mathematical construct that maps points in one coordinate system to another through a basic set of operations. In college-level math courses, this system generally appears under the topic of Linear Algebra.

In addition to the predefined transformations, you can define your own matrix calculation to transform the output in any way you need. This recipe's sample code applies a custom matrix that reverses all coordinate system points in either the horizontal or vertical direction. The intricacies of matrix transformations and cross products are beyond the scope of this book. You can find some basic discussions of the math involved by searching for "matrix transformations" in the Visual Studio online help.

9.20   Getting the Height and Width of a Graphic String

Problem

You want to know how many pixels a text string will require in both the horizontal and vertical directions.

Solution

Sample code folder: Chapter 09\MeasuringText

GDI+ includes several features that let you examine the width and height of a string. Graphics.MeasureString( ) is a general-purpose text-measurement method that bases its measurements on a font you pass to it:

```
Dim result As SizeF = _
    e.Graphics.MeasureString("How big am I?", Me.Font, _
    Me.ClientRectangle.Width)
MsgBox("Width = " & result.Width & vbCrLf & _
    "Height = " & result.Height)
```

On our system, using the default form font of Microsoft Sans Serif 8.25 Regular, the message box displays the following response:

```
Width = 75.71989Height = 13.8252
```

Discussion

Font measurement is tricky. Fonts are more than just the width and height of their letters. The height is a combination of the core height, plus the height of ascenders (the part of the letter "d" that sticks up) and descenders (the part of the letter "p" that sticks down). The width of a character string is impacted by *kerning*, the adjustment of two letters that fit together better than others. To get a flavor of some of these measurements, consider the following code:

```
Public Class Form1
    Private Sub PictureBox1_Paint(ByVal sender As Object, _
            ByVal e As System.Windows.Forms.PaintEventArgs) _
            Handles PictureBox1.Paint
        ' ----- Show vertical font measures.
        Dim textArea As SizeF
        Dim linePen As Pen
        Dim largeFont As Font
        Dim fontRatio As Single
        Dim ascentSize As Single
        Dim descentSize As Single
        Dim emSize As Single
        Dim cellHeight As Single
        Dim internalLeading As Single
        Dim externalLeading As Single

        ' ----- Create the font to use for drawing.
        '       Using "AntiAlias" to enable text smoothing
        '       will result in more precise output.
        e.Graphics.TextRenderingHint = _
            Drawing.Text.TextRenderingHint.AntiAlias
        largeFont = New Font("Times New Roman", 96, _
            FontStyle.Regular)

        ' ----- Fonts are measured in design units. We need to
        '       convert to pixels to mix measurement systems.
        '       Determine the ratio between the display line
        '       height and the font design's line height.
        fontRatio = largeFont.Height / _
            largeFont.FontFamily.GetLineSpacing( _
            FontStyle.Regular)
```

```
' ----- Get the measurements.
textArea = e.Graphics.MeasureString("Ag", largeFont)

' ----- Offset everything for simplicity.
e.Graphics.TranslateTransform(20, 20)

' ----- Draw the text.
e.Graphics.DrawString("Ag", largeFont, _
    Brushes.Black, 0, 0)

' ----- Create a line-drawing pen.
linePen = New Pen(Color.Gray, 1)
linePen.DashStyle = Drawing2D.DashStyle.Dash

' ----- Calculate all of the various font measurements.
ascentSize = largeFont.FontFamily.GetCellAscent( _
    FontStyle.Regular) * fontRatio
descentSize = largeFont.FontFamily.GetCellDescent( _
    FontStyle.Regular) * fontRatio
emSize = largeFont.FontFamily.GetEmHeight( _
    FontStyle.Regular) * fontRatio
cellHeight = ascentSize + descentSize
internalLeading = cellHeight - emSize
externalLeading = _
    (largeFont.FontFamily.GetLineSpacing( _
    FontStyle.Regular) * fontRatio) - cellHeight

' ----- Draw the top and bottom lines.
e.Graphics.DrawLine(linePen, 0, 0, textArea.Width, 0)
e.Graphics.DrawLine(linePen, 0, textArea.Height, _
    textArea.Width, textArea.Height)

' ----- Draw the ascender and descender areas.
e.Graphics.DrawLine(linePen, 0, _
    ascentSize, textArea.Width, ascentSize)
e.Graphics.DrawLine(linePen, 0, _
    ascentSize + descentSize, textArea.Width, _
    ascentSize + descentSize)

' ----- Clean up.
linePen.Dispose( )
largeFont.Dispose( )
e.Graphics.ResetTransform( )
End Sub
End Class
```

We added this code to a form with a single PictureBox control. The results appear in Figure 9-30.

The four lines from top to bottom are as follows:

- The top of the "line height" box
- The baseline, based on the ascender height

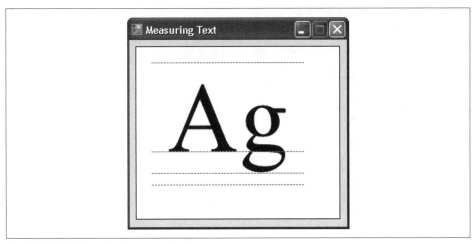

Figure 9-30. Measuring elements of a font

- The bottom of the descender
- The bottom of the "line height" box

The code also includes calculations for other measurements, although they are not used in the output.

9.21 Drawing Text with Outlines and Drop Shadows

Problem

You want to draw some text but display only its outline, and you want the text to have a drop shadow.

Solution

Sample code folder: Chapter 09\OutlineText

Use a GraphicsPath object to record the outside edge of a text string, and then use that outside edge, or *path*, to draw the actual drop shadow and outline elements.

Discussion

Create a new Windows Forms application, and add a PictureBox control named PictureBox1 to the form. Set this control's BackColor property to White and its BorderStyle property to FixedSingle. Give it a size of approximately 400,150. Now add the following source code to the form's class template:

```
Private Sub PictureBox1_Paint(ByVal sender As Object, _
      ByVal e As System.Windows.Forms.PaintEventArgs) _
      Handles PictureBox1.Paint
   ' ----- Draw text using an outline.
```

```
Dim outlinePath As New Drawing2D.GraphicsPath
Dim useFont As Font

' ----- Make some output adjustments to get a better
'       outline.
e.Graphics.TextRenderingHint = _
   Drawing.Text.TextRenderingHint.AntiAlias
e.Graphics.SmoothingMode = _
   Drawing2D.SmoothingMode.AntiAlias

' ----- Draw the text into a path.
useFont = New Font("Times New Roman", _
   96, FontStyle.Regular)
outlinePath.AddString("Outline", useFont.FontFamily, _
   FontStyle.Regular, 96, New Point(0, 0), _
   StringFormat.GenericTypographic)
useFont.Dispose( )

' ----- Replay the path to draw a drop shadow.
e.Graphics.TranslateTransform(25, 25)
e.Graphics.FillPath(Brushes.LightGray, outlinePath)

' ----- Replay the path to the surface.
e.Graphics.TranslateTransform(-5, -5)
e.Graphics.FillPath(Brushes.White, outlinePath)
e.Graphics.DrawPath(Pens.Black, outlinePath)

' ----- Finished.
outlinePath.Dispose( )
End Sub
```

Running this program displays the outline and drop shadow shown in Figure 9-31.

Figure 9-31. Text in an outline form, with a drop shadow

While the Font class includes support for italic, bold, strikeout, and underline formatting, it does not include features that automatically enable outlining or drop shadows. However, you can enable these features yourself using a GraphicsPath object. A *graphics path* is like a tape recording of a set of drawing commands that records the outline of the drawn elements. You use the `GraphicsPath`'s drawing methods to record the outlines of shapes and text strings in the path. You can then later use this path like a macro that can be replayed on the graphics surface.

The `GraphicsPath` object's `AddString()` method adds the outer edge of all characters in the supplied text string to the path. There are additional methods that let you include other shapes, such as `AddLine()`, `AddRectangle()`, and `AddEllipse()`.

See Also

Recipe 9.17 includes some similar alignment and rotation features.

9.22   Calculating a Nice Axis

Problem

You want to create a chart with a "nice" axis; that is, one with reasonable scaling numbers for a given number of tick marks and with a reasonably rounded increment for each tick value. These scale values should be chosen so the range of data points spans most of the length of the axis.

Solution

Sample code folder: Chapter 09\NiceAxis

Use the `NiceAxis()` function presented here to calculate a reasonable axis given the minimum and maximum values of the data and the number of ticks along the axis.

Discussion

This function was created to solve the tricky problem of determining a reasonable plotting axis for a range of numbers. When manually determining a scale, it's easy to accidentally scrunch the data points too closely by choosing a scale with larger than necessary values or a scale with awkward fractional values at each tick mark that make mental interpolation of intermediate values nearly impossible.

This function solves these problems by automatically choosing reasonable values for a chart's axis. In many cases you will want to call this function twice, once for the X-axis and once for the Y-axis.

Pass this function the minimum and maximum data values to be plotted, and the number of divisions or tick marks along the axis. The calculations in the function iterate to find division steps that are reasonable and that still allow all data points to fall within the range of the axis. Here's the code for the `NiceAxis()` function:

```
Public Function NiceAxis(ByVal minimumValue As Double, _
    ByVal maximumValue As Double, _
    ByVal divisions As Double) As Double()
    ' ----- Determine reasonable tick marks along an axis.
```

```
'         Returns an array of three values:
'             0) minimum tick value
'             1) maximum tick value
'             2) tick mark step size
Dim axis(2) As Double
Dim trialDivisionSize As Double
Dim modFourCount As Double = 1
Dim divisionSize As Double

' ----- Get the starting values.
divisionSize = (maximumValue - minimumValue) / divisions
trialDivisionSize = 10 ^ Int(Math.Log10(divisionSize))

' ----- Iterate until we arrive at reasonable values.
Do While (maximumValue > (trialDivisionSize * _
      Int(minimumValue / trialDivisionSize) + _
      divisions * trialDivisionSize))
   modFourCount += 1
   If ((modFourCount Mod 4) > 0) Then
      trialDivisionSize = 8 * trialDivisionSize / 5
   End If
   trialDivisionSize = 5 * trialDivisionSize / 4
Loop

' ----- Return the results.
axis(0) = trialDivisionSize * _
   Int(minimumValue / trialDivisionSize)
axis(1) = axis(0) + divisions * trialDivisionSize
axis(2) = (axis(1) - axis(0)) / divisions
Return axis
End Function
```

This function shows a good example of returning an array. In this case the array returns the minimum and maximum values for the ends of the nice axis, and the step size for the numbers along the tick marks or divisions along the axis.

The following code provides a working example. NiceAxis() is called with minimum and maximum data values of −3.4 and 3.27, and 10 tick marks are requested along the scale of this axis. As shown in Figure 9-32, the function returns the nearest whole-number values for each end of the axis (−4 and 6) and a recommended whole step size of 1 for each tick mark:

```
Dim result As New System.Text.StringBuilder
Dim axis() As Double = NiceAxis(-3.4, 3.27, 10)

result.AppendLine("Minimum Value: -3.4")
result.AppendLine("Maximum Value: 3.27")
result.AppendLine("Divisions: 10")
result.AppendLine()

result.Append("Axis Minimum: ")
result.AppendLine(axis(0).ToString)
result.Append("Axis Maximum: ")
```

```
result.AppendLine(axis(1).ToString)
result.Append("Division Steps: ")
result.AppendLine(axis(2).ToString)

MsgBox(result.ToString())
```

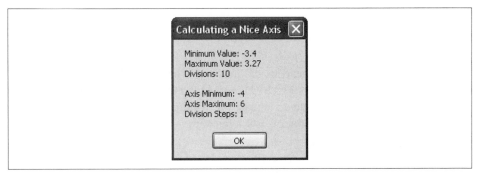

Figure 9-32. The NiceAxis() function returns end points and the division step size for a nicely scaled chart axis

9.23   Drawing a Simple Chart

Problem

You want to create your own data charts, and you would like to have code for a sample chart as a starting point for your own customizations.

Solution

Sample code folder: Chapter 09\DrawingCharts

The simple chart presented in this recipe should provide plenty of creative ideas and useful techniques for designing your own custom charts.

Discussion

The chart presented here provides a good starting point for drawing your own charts, but it shouldn't be used as presented. For one thing, the data values are hard-coded into an array in the form's Paint event, and you'll likely want to pass in your own data for plotting. The goal of this example is to present several graphics techniques in an easy-to-follow way.

As in most of the graphics examples in this chapter, the drawing takes place in the form's Paint event. The graphics drawing surface is referenced for easy use of its drawing methods:

```
Private Sub Form1_Paint(ByVal sender As Object, _
    ByVal e As System.Windows.Forms.PaintEventArgs) _
    Handles Me.Paint
```

```
' ----- Draw a nice chart.
  Dim canvas As Graphics = e.Graphics
```

For demonstration purposes, an array of Y data point values is hardcoded in this routine, and the corresponding X values are assumed to be evenly spaced 10 units apart in the range 0 to 100:

```
' ----- Create an array of data points to plot.
  Dim chartData() As Single = _
     {20, 33, 44, 25, 17, 24, 63, 75, 54, 33}
```

We'll use three pens: a red one, a black one, and a gray one. By setting each pen's widths to -1, we guarantee the sketched lines to be one pixel wide even if the scaling changes, and in this example we do change the scaling to plot the entire chart on the form no matter what size the window is stretched to:

```
' ----- Create some pens.
  Dim penRed As New Pen(Color.Red, -1)
  Dim penBlack As New Pen(Color.Black, -1)
  Dim penShadow As New Pen(Color.Gray, -1)
```

The next lines create the font and brush used to draw the axis numbers along the tick marks. The font size is relative to the chart scaling, which means that as the chart window is resized, the numbers along the axis will grow and shrink proportionately:

```
' ----- Prepare to add labels.
  Dim labelFont As New Font("Arial", 3, FontStyle.Regular)
  Dim labelBrush As New SolidBrush(Color.Blue)
```

Several variables are used during the scaling process and to plot the data points:

```
' ----- Used to plot the various elements.
  Dim x1, y1 As Single 'Lower left corner
  Dim x2, y2 As Single 'Upper right corner
  Dim scaleX, scaleY As Single
  Dim xScan, yScan As Single
  Dim oneBar As RectangleF
```

The chart is drawn in a rectangle from 0 to 100 in both the X and Y directions. By scaling the graphics surface from -10 to 110, a margin is left for the axis labels. By default, the Y scaling of a graphics surface starts at the top-left corner and increases as you move down in the area. A standard X-Y chart assumes an origin in the bottom-left corner, with increasing values going up the graphics surface. This requires the Y scaling factor in the ScaleTransform() method to be a negative value, which inverts the scale. Also, once inverted, the scale origin needs to be shifted, or translated, appropriately to relocate the origin to the bottom left of the graphics surface. This is accomplished using the Graphics object's TranslateTransform() method:

```
' ----- Set the scaling.
  x1 = -10
  y1 = -10
  x2 = 110
  y2 = 110
  scaleX = Me.ClientSize.Width / (x2 - x1)
```

```
scaleY = Me.ClientSize.Height / (y2 - y1)
canvas.ScaleTransform(scaleX, -scaleY)  '(inverted)
canvas.TranslateTransform(-x1, -y2)     '(inverted)
```

The chart's background color, outline, and gridlines are drawn in the following lines of code:

```
' ----- Color the background.
canvas.Clear(Color.Cornsilk)

' ----- Draw chart outline rectangle.
canvas.DrawRectangle(penBlack, New Rectangle(0, 0, 100, 100))

' ----- Draw the chart grid.
For xScan = 10 To 90 Step 10
    canvas.DrawLine(penBlack, xScan, 0, xScan, 100)
Next xScan
For yScan = 10 To 90 Step 10
    canvas.DrawLine(penBlack, 0, yScan, 100, yScan)
Next yScan
```

We'll use a 3D shadowed effect to draw the vertical data bars. First, draw each bar using a transparent shade of gray. To create the transparent gray color, set the alpha component of the solid brush's color to 127. As you can see in Figure 9-33, the gridlines show through the transparent "shadows" created by these rectangles.

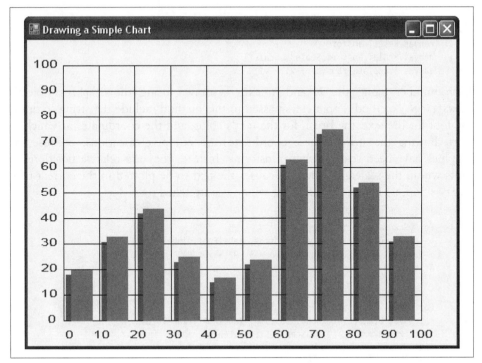

Figure 9-33. A simple chart that can be used as a starting point for customizing your own special-purpose charts

The data bar rectangles (they're actually red) are then drawn on top of and slightly above and to the right of the transparent gray bars. This results in a nice 3D shadowed effect:

```
' ----- Draw some shadowed bars.
For xScan = 0 To 90 Step 10
    ' ----- Draw the shadow first.
    oneBar.X = xScan + 0.6
    oneBar.Y = 0
    oneBar.Width = 6
    oneBar.Height = chartData(xScan \ 10) - 2
    canvas.FillRectangle(New SolidBrush(Color.FromArgb(127, _
        Color.Gray)), oneBar)

    ' ----- Now draw the bars in front.
    oneBar.X = xScan + 2
    oneBar.Y = 0
    oneBar.Height = chartData(xScan \ 10)
    canvas.FillRectangle(New SolidBrush(Color.Red), oneBar)
Next xScan
```

When drawing text, a complication arises if the scaling has been inverted: the text is drawn upside down! This might be useful in some situations, but to get the labels correct on this chart, the Y scaling transform must be reinverted to correctly plot the tick-mark numbers:

```
' ----- Need to un-invert the scaling so text labels are
'           right-side-up.
canvas.ResetTransform( )
canvas.ScaleTransform(ScaleX, ScaleY)
canvas.TranslateTransform(-x1, -y1)
```

Each number along the X and Y axes is drawn using the Graphics object's DrawString( ) method. Parameters passed to this method include the string to draw, the font for the text, the brush for the text's color, and the coordinates at which to start drawing the string. These coordinates are not pixel locations, because the graphics have been scaled using transforms. Instead, they are relative positions or units within the scaled world. This causes the text to be plotted in the correct relative position, no matter what size the window is stretched to:

```
' ----- Label the Y-axis.
For yScan = 0 To 100 Step 10
    canvas.DrawString(yScan.ToString, labelFont, labelBrush, _
        -2 * yScan.ToString.Length - 3, 97 - yScan)
Next yScan

' ----- Label the X-axis.
For xScan = 0 To 100 Step 10
    canvas.DrawString(xScan.ToString, labelFont, labelBrush, _
        xScan + 1.7 - 2 * xScan.ToString.Length, 103)
Next xScan
```

The last step is to clean up all of the graphics objects we've created:

```
' ----- Clean up.
labelFont.Dispose( )
labelBrush.Dispose( )
penRed.Dispose( )
penBlack.Dispose( )
penShadow.Dispose( )
canvas = Nothing
End Sub
```

Figure 9-33 shows the chart drawn on the form as a result of the previous code. Setting the form's `DoubleBuffered` property to `True` ensures that the chart is drawn smoothly and continuously as the form is resized when the following code is included:

```
Private Sub Form1_Resize(ByVal sender As Object, _
    ByVal e As System.EventArgs) Handles Me.Resize
    ' ----- Refresh on resize.
    Me.Refresh( )
End Sub
```

9.24 Creating Odd-Shaped Forms and Controls

Problem

You're tired of the plain rectangular forms and controls. You want to use irregular shapes for your form and the controls included on it.

Solution

Sample code folder: Chapter 09\IrregularShapes

Use a `GraphicsPath` object to define the new drawing and clipping region for the form and controls. This recipe's code uses an ellipse to define the boundaries of a form and a control.

Discussion

Create a new Windows Forms application, and add a `Button` control named `ActClose`. Set its `Text` property to `Close`, and put the button somewhere in the middle of the form. Then add the following source code to the form's class template:

```
Private Sub ActClose_Click(ByVal sender As System.Object, _
    ByVal e As System.EventArgs) Handles ActClose.Click
    ' ----- Close the form.
    Me.Close( )
End Sub

Private Sub Form1_Load(ByVal sender As System.Object, _
    ByVal e As System.EventArgs) Handles MyBase.Load
```

```
' ----- Change the shape of the form and button.
Dim finalShape As Region
Dim shapePath As Drawing2D.GraphicsPath

' ----- Reshape the form.
shapePath = New Drawing2D.GraphicsPath( )
shapePath.AddEllipse(0, 0, Me.Width, Me.Height)
finalShape = New Region(shapePath)
Me.Region = finalShape
shapePath.Dispose( )

' ----- Reshape the button.
shapePath = New Drawing2D.GraphicsPath( )
shapePath.AddEllipse(0, 0, ActClose.Width, ActClose.Height)
finalShape = New Region(shapePath)
ActClose.Region = finalShape
shapePath.Dispose( )
End Sub
```

When you run the program, both the form and the button appear with elliptical shapes. Figure 9-34 shows the form in use. We left the Visual Studio view of the source code in the background so that you can see the nonrectangular shape of the form.

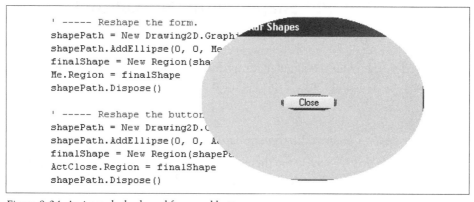

Figure 9-34. An irregularly shaped form and button

So what shapes can you use? If you can build it into a GraphicsPath object, you can use it to define the boundaries of your form or control. Replacing the form or control's Region property results in a new clipping region for the form (the clipping region is the area outside which the form is not drawn; it's not just hidden, it actually doesn't exist).

Since the new region indicates only which portions of the form are drawn or not, you'll find that any normal form or control components that reside only partially within the clipping region will appear cut off. Unfortunately, the result can be somewhat ugly. For example, the elliptical button created by this recipe's sample code doesn't look very good because portions of the original rectangular border still appear. You can also still see small portions of the form border. In addition to providing a custom region, you may want to provide custom drawing code for the control or form in its Paint event handler. For forms, setting the FormBorderStyle to None lets you supply your own form border.

Another way to change the shape of a form is by making a portion of the form invisible. This is done by setting a specific form color to the invisible color using the form's TransparencyKey property.

See Also

Recipe 9.10 shows how to use transparency to make a portion of a form invisible.

9.25 Using the RGB, HSB (HSV), and HSL Color Schemes

Problem

You want to provide the user with options for color selection: RGB (red-green-blue), HSB (hue-saturation-brightness, also known as HSV for hue-saturation-value), and HSL (hue-saturation-luminosity).

Solution

Sample code folder: Chapter 09\RGBandHSV

The easiest way to provide user-based color selection is to use the ColorDialog control to prompt the user to choose a color. This standard Windows dialog includes fields for RGB numeric entry and for HSL entry. Each of the HSL scales ranges from 0 to 240 (239 for hue), and changes to those fields automatically update the displayed RBG values (see Figure 9-35).

The ColorDialog control is described in Recipe 9.3.

In addition to the ColorDialog control, the new .NET System.Drawing.Color structure provides access to many predefined colors, plus methods to specify and obtain color values. Three of its methods let you convert an instance's RBG value to distinct HSB values:

- The GetHue( ) method returns a value from 0 to 360 that indicates the hue of the Color object's current color.
- The GetSaturation( ) method returns a value from 0.0 to 1.0 for the active color, in which 0.0 indicates the neutral grayscale value, and 1.0 is the most saturated value.
- The GetBrightness( ) method returns a value from 0.0 (black) to 1.0 (white).

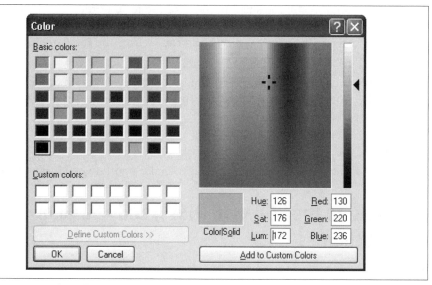

Figure 9-35. Using the ColorDialog control with separate HSL and RBG fields

This recipe's sample code lets the user select a color using either the RBG method or the HSB (a.k.a. HSV) method.

Discussion

Create a new Windows Forms application, and add the following controls to Form1:

- Three HScrollBar controls with the names ValueRed, ValueGreen, and ValueBlue. Set their Maximum properties to 255.
- One HScrollBar control named ValueHue. Set its Maximum property to 360.
- Two HScrollBar controls with the names ValueSaturation and ValueBrightness. Set their Maximum properties to 100.
- A PictureBox control named ShowColor.
- Six Label controls with the names NumberRed, NumberGreen, NumberBlue, NumberHue, NumberSaturation, and NumberBrightness. Set their Text properties to 0.

Add descriptive labels if desired. The form should look like Figure 9-36.

Now add the following source code to the form's class template:

```
Private Sub RBG_Scroll(ByVal sender As System.Object, _
    ByVal e As System.Windows.Forms.ScrollEventArgs) _
    Handles ValueRed.Scroll, ValueGreen.Scroll, _
    ValueBlue.Scroll
    ' ----- Update the HSV values based on RBG.
    Dim rgbColor As Color
```

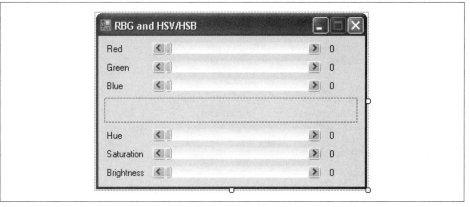

Figure 9-36. The controls on the color model sample

```
    ' ----- The color structure already has the formulas
    '       built in.
    rgbColor = Color.FromArgb(0, ValueRed.Value, _
       ValueGreen.Value, ValueBlue.Value)
    ValueHue.Value = CInt(rgbColor.GetHue())
    ValueSaturation.Value = _
       CInt(rgbColor.GetSaturation() * 100.0F)
    ValueBrightness.Value = _
       CInt(rgbColor.GetBrightness() * 100.0F)

    ' ------ Refresh everything else.
    RefreshDisplay()
End Sub

Private Sub ValueHue_Scroll(ByVal sender As Object, _
       ByVal e As System.Windows.Forms.ScrollEventArgs) _
       Handles ValueHue.Scroll, ValueSaturation.Scroll, _
       ValueBrightness.Scroll
    ' ----- Update the RBG values based on HSV.
    Dim useRed As Integer
    Dim useGreen As Integer
    Dim useBlue As Integer
    Dim useHue As Single
    Dim useSaturation As Single
    Dim useBrightness As Single
    Dim hueSector As Integer
    Dim factor As Single
    Dim target1 As Single
    Dim target2 As Single
    Dim target3 As Single

    ' ----- Convert to relative 0.0 to 1.0 values.
    useHue = CSng(ValueHue.Value)
    useSaturation = CSng(ValueSaturation.Value) / 100.0F
    useBrightness = CSng(ValueBrightness.Value) / 100.0F
```

```
        If (useSaturation = 0.0F) Then
            ' ----- Pure grayscale.
            useRed = CInt(useBrightness * 255)
            useGreen = useRed
            useBlue = useRed
        Else
            hueSector = CInt(useHue / 60.0F)
            factor = Math.Abs((useHue / 60.0F) - CSng(hueSector))
            target1 = useBrightness * (1 - useSaturation)
            target2 = useBrightness * (1 - (factor * useSaturation))
            target3 = useBrightness * (1 - ((1 - factor) * _
                useSaturation))

            Select Case hueSector
                Case 0, 6
                    useRed = CInt(useBrightness * 255.0F)
                    useGreen = CInt(target3 * 255.0F)
                    useBlue = CInt(target1 * 255.0F)
                Case 1
                    useRed = CInt(target2 * 255.0F)
                    useGreen = CInt(useBrightness * 255.0F)
                    useBlue = CInt(target1 * 255.0F)
                Case 2
                    useRed = CInt(target1 * 255.0F)
                    useGreen = CInt(useBrightness * 255.0F)
                    useBlue = CInt(target3 * 255.0F)
                Case 3
                    useRed = CInt(target1 * 255.0F)
                    useGreen = CInt(target2 * 255.0F)
                    useBlue = CInt(useBrightness * 255.0F)
                Case 4
                    useRed = CInt(target3 * 255.0F)
                    useGreen = CInt(target1 * 255.0F)
                    useBlue = CInt(useBrightness * 255.0F)
                Case 5
                    useRed = CInt(useBrightness * 255.0F)
                    useGreen = CInt(target1 * 255.0F)
                    useBlue = CInt(target2 * 255.0F)
            End Select
        End If

        ' ----- Update the RGB values.
        ValueRed.Value = useRed
        ValueGreen.Value = useGreen
        ValueBlue.Value = useBlue

        ' ------ Refresh everything else.
        RefreshDisplay()
    End Sub

    Private Sub RefreshDisplay()
        ' ----- Update the numeric display.
        NumberRed.Text = CStr(ValueRed.Value)
        NumberGreen.Text = CStr(ValueGreen.Value)
```

```
    NumberBlue.Text = CStr(ValueBlue.Value)
    NumberHue.Text = CStr(ValueHue.Value)
    NumberSaturation.Text = _
        Format(CDec(ValueSaturation.Value) / 100@, "0.00")
    NumberBrightness.Text = _
        Format(CDec(ValueBrightness.Value) / 100@, "0.00")

    ' ----- Update the color sample.
    ShowColor.BackColor = Color.FromArgb(255, _
        ValueRed.Value, ValueGreen.Value, ValueBlue.Value)
End Sub

Private Sub Form1_Load(ByVal sender As System.Object, _
        ByVal e As System.EventArgs) Handles MyBase.Load
    ' ----- Set the initial color.
    RBG_Scroll(ValueRed, _
        New Windows.Forms.ScrollEventArgs( _
        ScrollEventType.EndScroll, 0))
End Sub
```

Run the program, and use the six scrollbars to adjust the color selection.

The RGB model for describing colors numerically has become common for use in Microsoft Windows, but it is not always the most convenient method for certain applications or for output to devices other than computer monitors. The HSB/HSV system is more useful in selecting colors for computer-based artwork.

The System.Drawing.Color structure includes methods that let you extract the HSB components of an RGB color, but it doesn't work in the other direction. Therefore, the sample code includes the calculation for HSB-to-RGB conversions.

See Also

A useful web site that discusses color models is EasyRGB, found at *http://www.easyrgb.com*.

See Recipe 9.3 for details on using the ColorDialog control.

9.26 Creating a Rubber-Band Rectangular Selection

Problem

You want to add "rubber-band selection" to your graphics, giving the user the ability to click and drag with the mouse to select a rectangular region of an image.

Solution

Sample code folder: Chapter 09\RubberBand

Use the RubberBand class presented here to use one of three different-appearing rubber-band selection algorithms.

Discussion

You've probably seen rubber-band selection in action when cropping images or working with screen-grabbing programs, paint programs, and so on. The RubberBand class presented here can be included in any project in which you want to let the user select a rectangular area of an image in this way.

The complete code for the class is presented below. The RubberBandStyle enumeration and the public Style property work together to let you set the RubberBand object's appearance while in operation. While the user drags the mouse, the selected area is outlined with either a dashed-line rectangle (as in Figure 9-37, below), a solid line with inverted colors, or a solid-filled box with inverted colors.

There are two overloaded constructors in this class, which let you instantiate a RubberBand object in three different ways. (The plan was to have only one constructor with two optional arguments, but Visual Basic does not permit structure objects—Color, in this case—to be optional.) You can set the RubberBand's Style and BackColor properties when you create the object, or you can set these properties later. You do need to indicate the control on which the RubberBand is to operate, so the painting on the screen can coordinate with the surface of the control. The Start( ), Stretch( ), and Finish( ) methods are called from the program that creates the RubberBand object to update the rectangular selection. Once "rubberbanding" is complete, the Rectangle property returns the results. These methods are demonstrated in the calling code presented later.

Here's the code for the RubberBand class:

```
Public Class RubberBand
   ' ----- The three types of rubber bands.
   Public Enum RubberBandStyle
      DashedLine
      ThickLine
      SolidBox
   End Enum

   ' ----- The current drawing state.
   Public Enum RubberBandState
      Inactive
      FirstTime
      Active
   End Enum

   ' ----- Class-level variables.
   Private BasePoint As Point
   Private ExtentPoint As Point
   Private CurrentState As RubberBandState
   Private BaseControl As Control
   Public Style As RubberBandStyle
   Public BackColor As Color
```

```
Public Sub New(ByVal useControl As Control, _
      Optional ByVal useStyle As RubberBandStyle = _
      RubberBandStyle.DashedLine)
   ' ----- Constructor with one or two parameters.
   BaseControl = useControl
   Style = useStyle
   BackColor = Color.Black
End Sub

Public Sub New(ByVal useControl As Control, _
      ByVal useStyle As RubberBandStyle, _
      ByVal useColor As Color)
   ' ----- Constructor with three parameters.
   BaseControl = useControl
   Style = useStyle
   BackColor = useColor
End Sub

Public ReadOnly Property Rectangle() As Rectangle
   Get
      ' ----- Return the bounds of the rubber-band area.
      Dim result As Rectangle

      ' ----- Ensure the coordinates go left to
      '        right, top to bottom.
      result.X = IIf(BasePoint.X < ExtentPoint.X, _
         BasePoint.X, ExtentPoint.X)
      result.Y = IIf(BasePoint.Y < ExtentPoint.Y, _
         BasePoint.Y, ExtentPoint.Y)
      result.Width = Math.Abs(ExtentPoint.X - BasePoint.X)
      result.Height = Math.Abs(ExtentPoint.Y - BasePoint.Y)
      Return result
   End Get
End Property

Public Sub Start(ByVal x As Integer, ByVal y As Integer)
   ' ----- Start drawing the rubber band. The user must
   '        call Stretch() to actually draw the first
   '        band image.
   BasePoint.X = x
   BasePoint.Y = y
   ExtentPoint.X = x
   ExtentPoint.Y = y
   Normalize(BasePoint)
   CurrentState = RubberBandState.FirstTime
End Sub

Public Sub Stretch(ByVal x As Integer, ByVal y As Integer)
   ' ----- Change the size of the rubber band.
   Dim newPoint As Point

   ' ----- Prepare the new stretch point.
```

```
          newPoint.X = x
          newPoint.Y = y
          Normalize(newPoint)

       Select Case CurrentState
          Case RubberBandState.Inactive
             ' ----- Rubber band not in use.
             Return
          Case RubberBandState.FirstTime
             ' ----- Draw the initial rubber band.
             ExtentPoint = newPoint
             DrawTheRectangle( )
             CurrentState = RubberBandState.Active
          Case RubberBandState.Active
             ' ----- Undraw the previous band, then
             '       draw the new one.
             DrawTheRectangle( )
             ExtentPoint = newPoint
             DrawTheRectangle( )
       End Select
    End Sub

    Public Sub Finish( )
       ' ----- Stop drawing the rubber band.
       DrawTheRectangle( )
       CurrentState = 0
    End Sub

    Private Sub Normalize(ByRef whichPoint As Point)
       ' ----- Don't let the rubber band go outside the view.
       If (whichPoint.X < 0) Then whichPoint.X = 0
       If (whichPoint.X >= BaseControl.ClientSize.Width) _
          Then whichPoint.X = BaseControl.ClientSize.Width - 1

       If (whichPoint.Y < 0) Then whichPoint.Y = 0
       If (whichPoint.Y >= BaseControl.ClientSize.Height) _
          Then whichPoint.Y = BaseControl.ClientSize.Height - 1
    End Sub

    Private Sub DrawTheRectangle( )
       ' ----- Draw the rectangle on the control or
       '       form surface.
       Dim drawArea As Rectangle
       Dim screenStart, screenEnd As Point

       ' ----- Get the square that is the rubber-band area.
       screenStart = BaseControl.PointToScreen(BasePoint)
       screenEnd = BaseControl.PointToScreen(ExtentPoint)
       drawArea.X = screenStart.X
       drawArea.Y = screenStart.Y
       drawArea.Width = (screenEnd.X - screenStart.X)
       drawArea.Height = (screenEnd.Y - screenStart.Y)
```

```
        ' ----- Draw using the user-selected style.
        Select Case Style
            Case RubberBandStyle.DashedLine
                ControlPaint.DrawReversibleFrame( _
                    drawArea, Color.Black, FrameStyle.Dashed)
            Case RubberBandStyle.ThickLine
                ControlPaint.DrawReversibleFrame( _
                    drawArea, Color.Black, FrameStyle.Thick)
            Case RubberBandStyle.SolidBox
                ControlPaint.FillReversibleRectangle( _
                    drawArea, BackColor)
        End Select
    End Sub
End Class
```

To demonstrate the RubberBand class, the following code creates an instance and calls its Start( ), Stretch( ), and Finish( ) methods based on the user's mouse activities. When the mouse button is first depressed, the code calls the Start( ) method. As the mouse is moved, the Stretch( ) method is called to continuously update the visible selection rectangle. When the mouse button is released, the Finish( ) method completes the selection process. At this point, the read-only Rectangle property returns a complete description of the selected area:

```
Public Class Form1
    ' ----- Adust the second and third arguments to
    '        see different methods.
    Dim SelectionArea As RubberBand = New RubberBand(Me, _
        RubberBand.RubberBandStyle.DashedLine, Color.Gray)

    Private Sub Form1_MouseDown(ByVal sender As Object, _
            ByVal e As System.Windows.Forms.MouseEventArgs) _
            Handles MyBase.MouseDown
        ' ----- Start rubber-band tracking.
        SelectionArea.Start(e.X, e.Y)
    End Sub

    Private Sub Form1_MouseMove(ByVal sender As Object, _
            ByVal e As System.Windows.Forms.MouseEventArgs) _
            Handles MyBase.MouseMove
        ' ----- Update the rubber-band display area.
        SelectionArea.Stretch(e.X, e.Y)
    End Sub

    Private Sub Form1_MouseUp(ByVal sender As Object, _
            ByVal e As System.Windows.Forms.MouseEventArgs) _
            Handles MyBase.MouseUp
        ' ----- Finished with the selection.
        SelectionArea.Finish( )
        Me.Refresh( )
    End Sub

    Private Sub Form1_Paint(ByVal sender As Object, _
            ByVal e As System.Windows.Forms.PaintEventArgs) _
```

```
        Handles MyBase.Paint
    ' ----- Add some interest to the form surface.
    Dim canvas As Graphics = e.Graphics
    Dim polygonPoints() As Point = {New Point(300, 150), _
        New Point(200, 300), New Point(400, 300)}

    ' ----- Draw some shapes and text.
    canvas.FillEllipse(New SolidBrush(Color.Red), _
        10, 20, 200, 150)
    canvas.FillRectangle(New SolidBrush(Color.Blue), _
        100, 100, 250, 100)
    canvas.FillPolygon(New SolidBrush(Color.Green), _
        polygonPoints)
    canvas.DrawString(SelectionArea.Rectangle.ToString, _
        New Font("Arial", 12), Brushes.Black, 0, 0)
    End Sub
End Class
```

Figure 9-37 shows the results of running this demonstration code to select a rectangular area on the form. In this case the mouse was dragged down and to the right to select the area, but the code compensates for dragging in any direction and returns a proper rectangle.

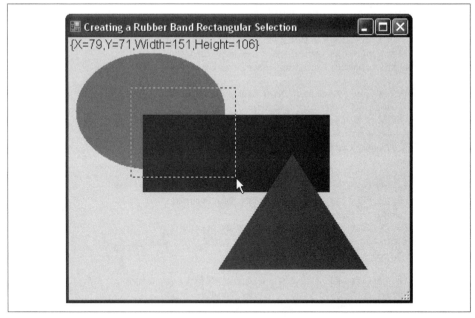

Figure 9-37. The RubberBand class lets you select rectangular areas of any graphics area

9.27 Animating with Transparency

Problem

You want to add some simple animation to a form and make it interesting enough to catch the user's eye without being overbearing or distracting.

Solution

Sample code folder: Chapter 09\TransparentAnimation

One idea is to use a timer to redraw graphics whose transparency varies over time.

Discussion

There are many ways to add simple animation to your graphics, and adjusting the transparency is just one simple trick that can add an interesting and creative effect to your images. This example also demonstrates how the alpha setting of a color changes drawings through the full range of transparency, from completely invisible to completely opaque.

Create a new Windows Forms application, and add a Timer control named Timer1. Set its Interval property to 10 (milliseconds) and its Enabled property to True. Also, set the form's DoubleBuffered property to True.

A good way to drive the animation action is by redrawing with each tick of a timer. Notice that the drawing commands are not done in the timer's Tick event. Instead, you tell the form to refresh itself and add the graphics commands where they really belong—in the form's Paint event. Add the following code to the form's class template to have the timer trigger screen updates:

```
Private Sub Timer1_Tick(ByVal sender As System.Object, _
    ByVal e As System.EventArgs) Handles Timer1.Tick
  ' ----- Update the animated display.
  Me.Refresh()
End Sub
```

The form's Paint event is called at the rate set by the Interval property of the timer. The 10-milliseconds setting provides a fairly smooth and noticeable transparency transition. Use a larger number for slower, more subtle action.

The currentSetting variable increments or decrements each time through the Paint event handler, with the change amount reversing direction when 0 or 255 is reached:

```
Private Sub Form1_Paint(ByVal sender As Object, _
    ByVal e As System.Windows.Forms.PaintEventArgs) _
    Handles Me.Paint
  ' ----- Display the next step in the animation.
  Static currentSetting As Integer = 0
```

```
Static changeFactor As Integer = 1
Dim transparentGreen As Color
Dim canvas As Graphics = e.Graphics
Dim trianglePoints( ) As Point = {New Point(180, 50), _
    New Point(30, 280), New Point(330, 280)}

' ----- Adjust the transparency factor.
currentSetting += changeFactor
If (currentSetting = 0) Or (currentSetting = 255) Then
    ' ----- Change direction.
    changeFactor = -changeFactor
End If
```

The following line is the heart of this example; it shows how to create a color with a controllable degree of transparency. You can pass just red, green, and blue values to Color.FromArgb( ) to create a solid shade, or you can add the fourth parameter, called alpha, to control the color's transparency. The values of all four parameters range from 0 to 255. Anything drawn with the designated color will be drawn with the indicated amount of transparency:

```
' ---- Set the transparent green color.
transparentGreen = Color.FromArgb(currentSetting, 0, 255, 0)
```

These statements draw the solid geometric objects in the background, in preparation for drawing a transparent triangle in front of them:

```
' ----- Draw some geometric figures.
canvas.FillEllipse(New SolidBrush(Color.Red), _
    10, 20, 200, 150)
canvas.FillRectangle(New SolidBrush(Color.Blue), _
    100, 100, 250, 100)
```

There is no GDI+ method to draw a triangle, per se. But a triangle is just a three-sided polygon, so it's easy to use the DrawPolygon( ) or FillPolygon( ) methods to do the trick. In this case we fill a polygon (triangle) using a solid brush comprised of our current shade of transparent green:

```
' ----- Draw a transparent green triangle in front.
canvas.FillPolygon(New SolidBrush(transparentGreen), _
    trianglePoints)
End Sub
```

Figure 9-38 shows the graphics with the triangle drawn using an intermediate transparency.

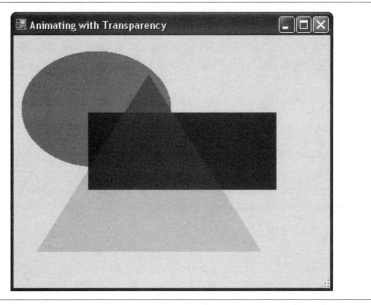

Figure 9-38. The triangle in the foreground fades from complete transparency to complete opacity and back again

9.28   Substitutions for Obsolete Visual Basic 6.0 Features

Problem

You used to use a lot of form-based drawing features in Visual Basic 6.0, but many of them seem to be missing from the .NET versions of Visual Basic.

Solution

Sample code folder: Chapter 09\VB6Replacements

GDI+ is a full-featured drawing package that provides easier access to form-based drawing than Visual Basic 6.0 did. Unfortunately, finding the replacements for some of VB 6's form-based drawing features takes a bit of work. This recipe discusses some of the more significant replacements.

Discussion

Most of the replacement features involve GDI+ drawing, although you can simulate some older features using Label controls. The features discussed in this section focus on those methods and controls that were used directly on a form. In .NET, any of the drawing commands that you use on the form's surface can also be used on any control.

Any discussion that mentions "drawing on the form" refers to drawing through the form's Graphics object. Such drawing is usually done in the form's Paint event handler, which provides you with a Graphics object:

```
Private Sub Form1_Paint(ByVal sender As Object, _
      ByVal e As System.Windows.Forms.PaintEventArgs) _
      Handles Me.Paint
   ' ----- Draw a line.
   e.Graphics.DrawLine(...)
End Sub
```

You can also create a Graphics object at any time in other event handlers and methods using the form's CreateGraphics( ) method:

```
Dim formCanvas As Graphics = Me.CreateGraphics( )
e.Graphics.DrawLine(...)

' ----- Properly dispose of the graphics canvas.
formCanvas.Dispose( )
```

Let's look at some of the specific replacements:

Line *controls*

There are two replacements for Visual Basic 6.0 Line controls. If your line is horizontal or vertical, you can use a Label control with the BackColor property set to the line color you need. Adjust the width or height of the label as needed to increase the thickness of the line. Be sure to clear the Text property and set the AutoSize property to False.

If you need diagonal lines, you can draw them on the form surface in the form's Paint event using the DrawLine( ) method.

Shape *controls*

There is no direct control replacement for the Visual Basic 6.0 Shape controls. Rectangular or elliptical shapes can be drawn directly on the form using the DrawRectangle( ) and DrawEllipse( ) methods. The related FillRectangle( ) and FillEllipse( ) methods draw filled shapes, with no edge lines.

There is no drawing command that can generate a rectangle with rounded corners. You must create it yourself using DrawLine( ) and DrawArc( ) method calls. You can also build this shape as a GraphicsPath object. Here is a method that draws a rounded rectangle directly on a graphics surface. The rounded corner has a radius of five pixels (units, actually):

```
Private Sub DrawRoundedRectangle( _
      ByVal sourceRectangle As Rectangle, _
      ByVal canvas As Graphics, ByVal usePen As Pen)
   ' ----- Draw a rounded rectangle.
   Dim saveState As Drawing2D.GraphicsState
```

```
' ----- Move the origin to the upper-left corner
'       of the rectangle.
saveState = canvas.Save( )
canvas.TranslateTransform(sourceRectangle.Left, _
    sourceRectangle.Top)

With sourceRectangle
    ' ----- Draw the four edges, starting from the top
    '       and moving clockwise.
    canvas.DrawLine(usePen, 5, 0, .Width - 5, 0)
    canvas.DrawLine(usePen, .Width, 5, .Width, .Height - 5)
    canvas.DrawLine(usePen, .Width - 5, .Height, 5, .Height)
    canvas.DrawLine(usePen, 0, .Height - 5, 0, 5)

    ' ----- Draw the four corners, starting from the
    '       upper left and moving clockwise.
    canvas.DrawArc(usePen, 0, 0, 10, 10, 180, 90)
    canvas.DrawArc(usePen, .Width - 10, 0, 10, 10, 270, 90)
    canvas.DrawArc(usePen, .Width - 10, .Height - 10, _
        10, 10, 0, 90)
    canvas.DrawArc(usePen, 0, .Height - 10, 10, 10, 90, 90)
End With

' ----- Restore the original graphics canvas.
canvas.Restore(saveState)
End Sub
```

This code draws a 100-by-100-unit rounded rectangle at position (10,10) on the form's surface:

```
Private Sub Form1_Paint(ByVal sender As Object, _
        ByVal e As System.Windows.Forms.PaintEventArgs) _
        Handles Me.Paint
    DrawRoundedRectangle(New Rectangle(10, 10, 100, 100), _
        e.Graphics, Pens.Black)
End Sub
```

Figure 9-39 shows the output from this code.

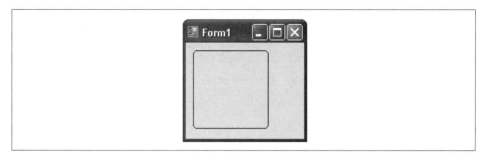

Figure 9-39. A manually rounded rectangle

Cls( ) *method*

To clear the entire graphics surface, use the Clear( ) method. You pass it the color used to clear the surface:

```
e.Graphics.Clear(Color.White)
```

Scale( ) *method*

To change the coordinate system on the form's surface, use the Graphics object's ScaleTransform( ) method. You can also supply a custom matrix transformation by assigning the Graphics object's Transform property.

PSet( ) *method*

There is no method that can draw a single pixel on a graphics surface. You can simulate it using the DrawLine( ), DrawRectangle( ), or FillRectangle( ) methods and providing very precise coordinates. Another way to draw a single point is to create a single-point bitmap and draw the bitmap onto the canvas. The Bitmap class does have a SetPixel method:

```
' ----- Draw a red pixel at (5,5).
Dim tinyBitmap As New Bitmap(1, 1)
tinyBitmap.SetPixel(0, 0, Color.Red)
e.Graphics.DrawImageUnscaled(tinyBitmap, 5, 5)
tinyBitmap.Dispose( )
```

Point( ) *method*

While the Graphics object does not let you query the color of an individual pixel, you can do so with a Bitmap object. This object's GetPixel( ) method returns a Color object for the specified pixel.

Line( ) *method*

Replaced by the DrawLine( ) method.

Circle( ) *method*

Replaced by the DrawEllipse( ) and FillEllipse( ) methods.

PaintPicture( ) *method*

Replaced by the DrawImage( ) method.

Multimedia

10.0 Introduction

The recipes in this chapter provide routines for playing sound files and for displaying video clips and photos. One recipe even demonstrates the "new" functionality of Visual Basic 2005 that commands your computer's internal speaker to emit a system-dependent beep. (That takes us back a few years!) More advanced recipes let you process the JPEG photos from your digital camera. No longer is C++ coding required to manipulate images with respectable speed. Visual Basic programmers now have access to a full set of powerful multimedia-processing features built right into .NET.

10.1 Playing an Audio File

Problem

You want to play a sound clip file, a system sound, or a music file such as an MP3.

Solution

Several different objects and system utilities are available to play sound clips or media files. In this recipe we'll demonstrate the use of:

- `My.Computer.Audio.Play( )` and `SoundPlayer` to play audio clip files such as WAV files
- `My.Computer.Audio.PlaySystemSound( )` to play operating-system-assigned sounds
- `Process.Start( )` to activate Windows Media Player to play MP3 and other media files

Discussion

The code required to play an audio sample is actually quite short. In most cases, a single line of code is all it takes to play a sound. Visual Basic 2005's new My namespace provides a lot of new easy-to-use functionality. The `My.Computer.Audio.Play( )` method is a good example. Simply pass this method the name of an audio file and the play mode that controls how the sound is played:

```
My.Computer.Audio.Play("sample.wav", _
    AudioPlayMode.WaitToComplete)
```

The `AudioPlayMode.WaitToComplete` option causes the program to wait for the sound to complete before proceeding. The two other members of this enumeration are `Background` (plays a sound once in the background) and `BackgroundLoop` (loops the sound repeatedly in the background). To stop a background looping sound, issue this command:

```
My.Computer.Audio.Stop( )
```

Another way to play sounds is with a `SoundPlayer` class instance. This works a lot like the `My.Computer.Audio` features because those features depend on the `SoundPlayer` class:

```
Dim player As New SoundPlayer("sample.wav")
player.Play( )
```

The `SoundPlayer` object provides quite a few properties and methods to control the playing of sound files, and you should check these out if you need special functionality in your application. For example, the `Stop( )` and `Play( )` methods allow you to pause and restart the sound in the middle of the content.

Windows includes several user-configured sounds for various system-level events. For example, when validating user-entered data, you can play the system-assigned sound for Exclamation in coordination with a custom visual message to inform the user of some issue with the input data:

```
My.Computer.Audio.PlaySystemSound(SystemSounds.Exclamation)
```

Some sound formats are beyond the basic capabilities of the `My.Computer.Audio` features. To play these sounds, you can defer to the default applications designated to play sound files with specific extensions. The following lines of code start whatever program is currently assigned to play MP3 files, passing it the name of the MP3 file to be played. Often this will start the Windows Media Player, but the user may have some other program configured to play such files. The `Process.Start( )` method tells the operating system to play the file using its current settings:

```
Dim soundProgram As Process = Process.Start("sample.mp3")
soundProgram.WaitForExit( )
```

10.2   Displaying Image Files

Problem

You want to display pictures, possibly selected by the user, in your Visual Basic 2005 application.

Solution

Sample code folder: Chapter 10\ShowJPG

The OpenFileDialog class provides a standard way to let the user select any file, such as a picture to be displayed, and the PictureBox control gives you a great way to display pictures.

Discussion

It's easy to use an OpenFileDialog control on a form to let the user select a file from anywhere in the system. Create a new Windows Forms application, add a PictureBox control to Form1 named SelectedPicture, and add a Button control named ActLocate. Set the PictureBox's SizeMode property to StretchImage. Add the following code to the button's Click event handler:

```
Private Sub ActLocate_Load(ByVal sender As System.Object, _
    ByVal e As System.EventArgs) Handles ActLocate.Click
    ' ----- Let the user choose a picture.
    Dim locateFile As New OpenFileDialog

    locateFile.Filter = "JPG files (*.jpg)|*.jpg"
    locateFile.Multiselect = False
    If (locateFile.ShowDialog() = _
        Windows.Forms.DialogResult.OK) Then
        ' ----- Show the selected picture.
        SelectedPicture.Load(locateFile.FileName)
    End If
End Sub
```

Figure 10-1 shows the OpenFileDialog during a typical session in which the user is about to select a JPEG picture file.

If a JPEG file is selected, it is loaded into the form's PictureBox for display. It takes only one command to load the picture:

```
SelectedPicture.Load(locateFile.FileName)
```

Figure 10-2 shows the picture as displayed in the PictureBox on the form.

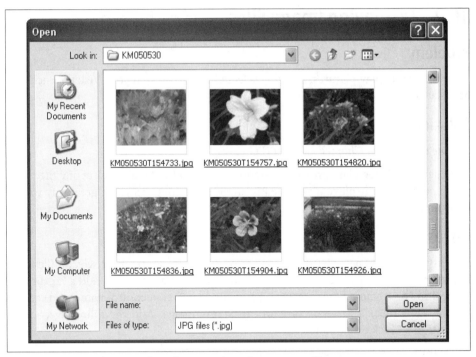

Figure 10-1. Using the OpenFileDialog control to select a picture file

Figure 10-2. Displaying pictures on a form with a PictureBox control

10.3 Playing a Video File

Problem

You want to play video clips from your Visual Basic 2005 application.

Solution

The Process.Start() method lets you automate the playing of video clips in a very reliable and standardized way. Figure 10-3 shows a video run in Windows Media Player using this method.

Figure 10-3. You can launch Windows Media Player from your .NET app to play video clips

Discussion

The Process object lets you run an external application explicitly or implicitly: you can run an application and pass it a specific file to open and run, or you can pass a file and let the operating system implicitly run the associated application based on the file-name's extension. This is a good way to play a video clip—the user's media player of choice is automatically launched to play the clip.

Another advantage of the Process object is its simplicity. The following two lines of code create an instance of the Process class, run a shared method to load and start an AVI file, and wait for the media player to exit:

```
Dim videoProgram As Process = Process.Start("sample.avi")
videoProgram.WaitForExit( )
```

10.4   Making Your Computer Beep

Problem

You want to play a simple sound or sequence of tones based on frequency and duration using the built-in speaker on your computer, rather than relying on the sound board or creating audio files specifically tailored for the purpose.

Solution

Sample code folder: Chapter 10\PlayTones

Visual Basic 2005 now provides a Console.Beep( ) method that plays a tone given frequency and duration parameters.

Discussion

You can use this command to create notification sounds from console applications, but you can also call this method from any Windows application to create specialized effects.

The following PlayTones( ) subroutine plays a sequence of tones passed to it in the form of a Point array. This data structure is ideal for the notes because each note is comprised of integer frequency and duration parameters (similar to the X and Y values of each point):

```
Public Sub PlayTones(ByVal toneArray( ) As Point)
    ' ----- Play a set of tones, one after another.
    Dim frequency As Integer
    Dim duration As Integer
```

```
    For Each tone As Point In toneArray
        frequency = tone.X
        duration = tone.Y
        Console.Beep(frequency, duration)
    Next tone
End Sub
```

The following code creates a Point array to play a simple melody:

```
Dim soundsAlien As Point() = { _
    New Point(932, 500), _
    New Point(1047, 500), _
    New Point(831, 500), _
    New Point(415, 500), _
    New Point(622, 900)}
PlayTones(soundsAlien)
```

This may remind you of something each time you play it; something to do with mashed potatoes, perhaps...

10.5   Creating an Animation Using Multiple Images

Problem

You want to add a simple animation to your application without resorting to complicated video techniques.

Solution

Sample code folder: Chapter 10\ImageListAnim

There are several ways to create simple animations in your Visual Basic 2005 applications, and the next three recipes will show you three different ways to do so. One straightforward and effective technique is to store bitmap images in an ImageList control, and then display them sequentially in a PictureBox with each tick of a timer.

Discussion

An ImageList control holds multiple images in one spot in your application to use with other controls that require multiple images. For example, the ListView, TreeView, Toolbar, and other controls all work hand in hand with an ImageList to display customized images on their surfaces. But you can use an ImageList for other purposes, too, as this recipe shows.

The first step in creating an animation is to create or collect a sequence of images to be displayed. Figure 10-4 displays a collection of wind-tower bitmaps with the turbine blades in rotated positions slightly shifted from one to the next.

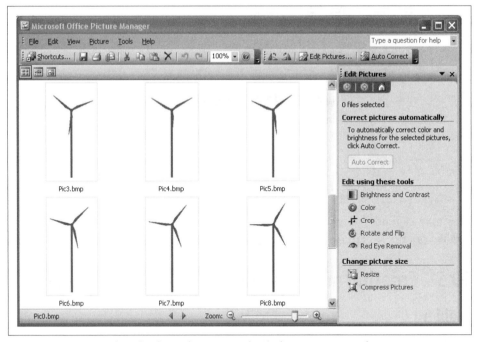

Figure 10-4. A series of nearly identical images can be used to create a smooth-running animation

In the sample application for this recipe, an ImageList has been added to the main form, and its Images collection has been filled with the windmill images (in a specific order). Figure 10-5 shows the image collection.

To display these images sequentially as an animation, add a PictureBox and a Timer control to the form:

```
Private Sub Timer1_Tick(ByVal sender As System.Object, _
    ByVal e As System.EventArgs) Handles Timer1.Tick
  ' ----- Draw the next image on each tick.
  Static imageNumber As Integer
  imageNumber = (imageNumber + 1) Mod ImageList1.Images.Count
  PictureBox1.Image = ImageList1.Images(imageNumber)
End Sub
```

The timer should be enabled, and its Interval property should be set to a number of milliseconds appropriate for the animation. In this case, 40 milliseconds worked well.

As soon as the form loads, the action starts. With each tick of the timer, the static variable imageNumber increments to point to the next image in the ImageList control. The image is loaded, and the program continues until the Timer's next Tick event. Figure 10-6 shows one frame of the animation.

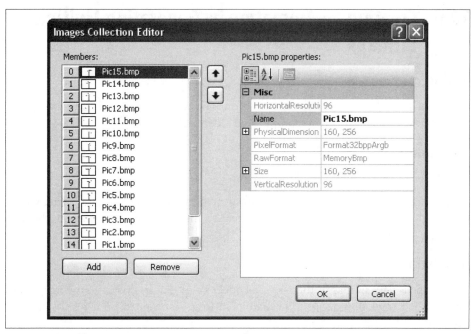

Figure 10-5. Adding images to an ImageList control

Figure 10-6. Displaying images sequentially in a PictureBox to create an animation

10.6   Creating an Animation by Generating Multiple Bitmaps

Problem

You want to add a simple animation to your application based on code-drawn bitmaps, but without resorting to complicated video techniques.

Solution

Sample code folder: Chapter 10\BitmapAnim

This recipe shows how to create an array of bitmaps in memory, fill them with graphic drawings that vary slightly from one to the next, and then display them in sequence to create an animation.

Discussion

This recipe is very similar to the previous one, except that in this case, the images are stored in an array of bitmaps rather than in an ImageList control. The results are very similar.

Create a new Windows Forms application, and add a Timer control named Timer1. Set its Interval property to 50 and its Enabled property to True. Now add the following code to the form's code template:

```
Private StarImages(23) As Bitmap

Private Sub SpinningStar_Resize(ByVal sender As Object, _
      ByVal e As System.EventArgs) Handles Me.Resize
   ' ----- Rebuild the images needed for the animation.
   Dim xCenter As Integer
   Dim yCenter As Integer
   Dim radius As Double
   Dim canvas As Graphics
   Dim counter As Integer
   Dim angle As Double
   Dim x1 As Single
   Dim y1 As Single
   Dim x2 As Single
   Dim y2 As Single
   Const RadPerDeg As Double = Math.PI / 180#

   ' ----- Perform some basic calculations.
   xCenter = Me.ClientSize.Width \ 2
   yCenter = Me.ClientSize.Height \ 2
   radius = IIf(Me.ClientSize.Width < Me.ClientSize.Height, _
      Me.ClientSize.Width, Me.ClientSize.Height) * 0.4

   ' ----- Remove the previous images.
   Array.Clear(StarImages, 0, StarImages.Length)
```

```
      For counter = 0 To StarImages.Length - 1
         StarImages(counter) = New Bitmap( _
            Me.ClientSize.Width, Me.ClientSize.Height)
         canvas   = Graphics.FromImage(StarImages(counter))
         For angle = 0 To 360 Step 72
            x1 = xCenter + radius * _
               Math.Cos(RadPerDeg * (angle + counter * 3))
            y1 = yCenter + radius * _
               Math.Sin(RadPerDeg * (angle + counter * 3))
            x2 = xCenter + radius * _
               Math.Cos(RadPerDeg * (angle + counter * 3 + 144))
            y2 = yCenter + radius * _
               Math.Sin(RadPerDeg * (angle + counter * 3 + 144))
            canvas.DrawLine(SystemPens.ControlText, _
               x1, y1, x2, y2)
         Next angle
         canvas.Dispose( )
      Next counter
   End Sub
```

The code runs every time its form is resized, including once when the form first appears. The 24 bitmap images are recreated nearly instantly, keeping up with the changing form size. Each bitmap is of a five-pointed star, and each star image is rotated slightly from the previous one in the array.

A timer animates the star bitmaps using the 50-millisecond interval set earlier. Add the following code in the timer's Tick event handler to display the next bitmap in the sequence, looping back to the start when the end of the array is reached. The last star is drawn in a position almost rotated to match the first, providing continuously smooth animation:

```
   Private Sub Timer1_Tick(ByVal sender As System.Object, _
         ByVal e As System.EventArgs) Handles Timer1.Tick
      ' ----- Draw one of the star array elements.
      Dim canvas As Graphics
      Static imageNumber As Integer

      On Error Resume Next

      imageNumber = (imageNumber + 1) Mod StarImages.Length
      Try
         canvas = Me.CreateGraphics( )
         canvas.Clear(Me.BackColor)
         canvas.DrawImage(StarImages(imageNumber), 0, 0)
         canvas.Dispose( )
      End Try
   End Sub
```

The DrawImage( ) method of the form's Graphics object copies each bitmap onto the form's surface. For maximum smoothness, check that the form's DoubleBuffered property is set to True.

A couple of frames of the rotating star are shown in Figures 10-7 and 10-8. Try resizing the form while the animation is running; you'll see that the star itself resizes as you resize the form.

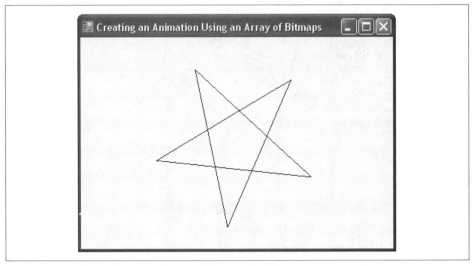

Figure 10-7. Each star bitmap is drawn with a slightly different rotation angle

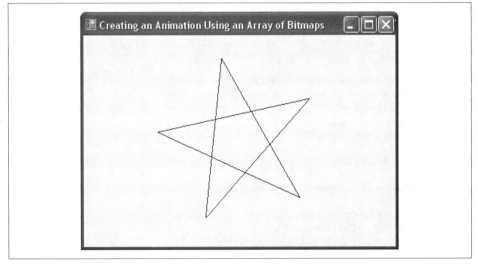

Figure 10-8. Multiple bitmaps stored in an array can provide a smooth animation effect

10.7   Creating an Animation by Drawing at Runtime

Problem

You want to add a simple animation to your application without resorting to complicated video techniques.

Solution

Sample code folder: Chapter 10\DrawAnim

A very direct but often effective technique is to simply draw updated images on a graphics surface with each tick of a timer, as shown in this recipe.

Discussion

The following code handles the Tick event for a timer on a form. It redraws the face of the form at each tick. The current position and direction of a block are maintained in form-level variables. The timer's Tick event handler updates those variables so the block drifts around the form and bounces off the walls; the form's Paint event handler is where the actual drawing of the block takes place. At the end of the timer's Tick event handler is a Refresh( ) command that causes the form to redraw itself. That fires the Paint event, which redraws the block.

Create a new Windows Forms application, and add a Timer control named Timer1. Set its Interval property to 10 and its Enabled property to True. Now add the following code to the form's code template:

```
Private UseX As Integer
Private UseY As Integer
Private MoveX As Integer
Private MoveY As Integer
Private Const BlockSize As Integer = 50

Private Sub Timer1_Tick(ByVal sender As System.Object, _
      ByVal e As System.EventArgs) Handles Timer1.Tick
   ' ----- Draw the next step in the animation.
   UseX += MoveX
   UseY += MoveY

   ' ----- Make adjustments for edge detection.
   If (UseX <= 0) Then MoveX = 1
   If (UseX >= (Me.ClientSize.Width - BlockSize)) Then _
      MoveX = -1
   If (UseY <= 0) Then MoveY = 1
   If (UseY >= (Me.ClientSize.Height - BlockSize)) Then _
      MoveY = -1
```

```
        ' ----- Redraw the image.
        Me.Refresh()
    End Sub

    Private Sub Bounce_Paint(ByVal sender As Object, _
            ByVal e As System.Windows.Forms.PaintEventArgs) _
            Handles Me.Paint
        ' ----- Draw the block.
        e.Graphics.FillRectangle(Brushes.Red, UseX, UseY, _
            BlockSize, BlockSize)
        e.Graphics.DrawRectangle(New Pen(Color.Blue, 5), _
            UseX, UseY, BlockSize, BlockSize)
    End Sub
```

Two rectangles are drawn, one to create a red square and the other to draw a 5-pixel-wide border around the square. The current values for form-level variables UseX and UseY are used for the position at which to draw the squares. Be sure to set the form's DoubleBuffered property to True for the smoothest effect. Figure 10-9 shows the square block as it drifts towards the walls of the form.

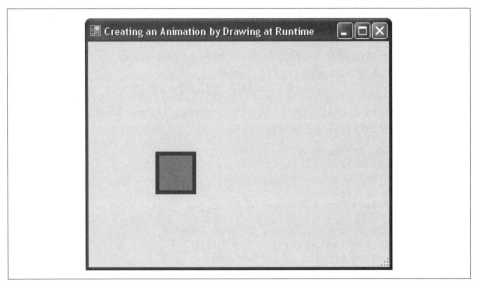

Figure 10-9. The sketched square bounces off the walls smoothly

10.8   Creating Animated Sprites

Problem

You want to create *sprites*, small graphics objects that display in front of a background and can detect collisions with other sprites.

Solution

Sample code folder: Chapter 10\Sprites

The Sprite class presented here provides a very simple but useful starting point for creating sprites as complicated as you desire.

Discussion

The Sprite class exposes public properties for its bitmap, position, and velocity; a method for drawing itself on a graphics surface; and a function that determines if another sprite is currently in collision with this one. This rudimentary sprite class provides a good start at understanding how sprites work. You can add new functionality to enhance your sprites as desired.

This class doesn't define exactly what the sprite will look like or even its size. It provides a public Bitmap property, which the calling program can fill with any desired image. Likewise, the location and velocity properties are very flexible and can take on any signed integer values. The calling program is responsible for setting these properties and for determining when they might change. The Draw( ) method uses the velocity values to update the position values, which minimizes the overhead in the calling program each time the sprite is redrawn.

Create a new Windows Forms application. Add a new class to the project named *Sprite.vb*, and use the following code for its definition:

```
Public Class Sprite
    Public SpriteImage As Bitmap
    Public X As Integer
    Public Y As Integer
    Public VelocityX As Integer
    Public VelocityY As Integer

    Public Sub Draw(ByVal g As Graphics)
        ' ----- Update the location.
        X += VelocityX
        Y += VelocityY

        ' ----- Draw the sprite.
        g.DrawImage(SpriteImage, X, Y)
    End Sub

    Public Function Collision(ByVal targetSprite As Sprite) _
            As Boolean
        ' ----- See if two sprites overlap each other.
        On Error Resume Next

        Dim s1Left As Integer = X
        Dim s1Top As Integer = Y
        Dim s1Right As Integer = s1Left + SpriteImage.Width
        Dim s1Bottom As Integer = s1Top + SpriteImage.Height
        Dim s2Left As Integer = targetSprite.X
```

```
        Dim s2Top As Integer = targetSprite.Y
        Dim s2Right As Integer = s2Left + _
           targetSprite.SpriteImage.Width
        Dim s2Bottom As Integer = s2Top + _
           targetSprite.SpriteImage.Height

        ' ----- Compare the positions.
        If (s1Right < s2Left) Then Return False
        If (s1Bottom < s2Top) Then Return False
        If (s1Left > s2Right) Then Return False
        If (s1Top > s2Bottom) Then Return False

        ' ----- No collision.
        Return True
      End Function
   End Class
```

There are a lot of ways you can enhance this Sprite class. For example, you can add code to the Draw( ) method to create and maintain a bitmap image within the sprite object, perhaps creating a unique Sprite class for each type of sprite image. The collision-detection code shown here simply looks for overlapping rectangular areas; that is, if any parts of the bitmaps for the two sprites are touching, they are in collision. However, you might want to make the collision detection more sophisticated. For example, the code added next uses sprites with transparent corners, yet these transparent corners still count as collision areas. An enhanced version of collision detection might let the sprites overlap in the transparent areas, "bouncing" only when the visible portions touch each other.

To demonstrate the Sprite class, the following code creates two instances, draws colored solid circles with transparent backgrounds to define their bitmaps (that is, everything between the circle and the rectangular border is transparent), and sets them in motion against a background comprised of stripes. This background lets you see clearly how the transparent colors in the rectangular bitmaps make the sprites appear as solid circles only. These sprites and their bitmaps are created just once, as the form loads.

Return to Form1, and set its DoubleBuffered property to True. Add a Timer named Timer1. Now add the following code to the form's code template:

```
Private MySprites(1) As Sprite

Private Sub SpriteDemo_Load(ByVal sender As System.Object, _
     ByVal e As System.EventArgs) Handles MyBase.Load
   ' ----- Prepare the sprites.
   Dim canvas As Graphics

   ' ----- Create the first sprite.
   MySprites(0) = New Sprite
   MySprites(0).X = 37
   MySprites(0).Y = 37
   MySprites(0).VelocityX = 2
   MySprites(0).VelocityY = 1
```

```
MySprites(0).SpriteImage = New Bitmap(30, 30)
canvas = Graphics.FromImage(MySprites(0).SpriteImage)
canvas.Clear(Color.FromArgb(0, 0, 0, 0))
canvas.FillEllipse(Brushes.Red, 0, 0, 30, 30)
canvas.Dispose( )

' ----- Create the second sprite.
MySprites(1) = New Sprite
MySprites(1).X = 97
MySprites(1).Y = 57
MySprites(1).VelocityX = 1
MySprites(1).VelocityY = -2
MySprites(1).SpriteImage = New Bitmap(30, 30)
canvas = Graphics.FromImage(MySprites(1).SpriteImage)
canvas.Clear(Color.FromArgb(0, 0, 0, 0))
canvas.FillEllipse(Brushes.Green, 0, 0, 30, 30)
canvas.Dispose( )

' ----- Start the action.
Timer1.Interval = 10
Timer1.Enabled = True
End Sub
```

With each tick of the timer, the two sprites are each checked to see if they've come in
contact with the walls of the form. If so, their appropriate velocity properties are
reversed to cause them to bounce back into the display area of the form. A quick
check is also made to see if the two sprites are in collision with each other. If they
are, the velocity properties for both sprites are reversed, causing them to bounce
away from each other. This simple action provides a starting point for creating more
complex sprite interaction.

To see the animated sprites in action, add the following code to the form:

```
Private Sub Timer1_Tick(ByVal sender As System.Object, _
      ByVal e As System.EventArgs) Handles Timer1.Tick
   ' ----- Trigger a redraw of the form.
   Me.Refresh( )
End Sub

Private Sub SpriteDemo_Paint(ByVal sender As Object, _
      ByVal e As System.Windows.Forms.PaintEventArgs) _
      Handles Me.Paint
   ' ----- Draw the sprites on a background.
   Dim counter As Integer

   ' ----- Redraw the striped background.
   For counter = 0 To Me.ClientSize.Width * 2 Step 20
      e.Graphics.DrawLine(New Pen(Color.LightBlue, 5), _
         counter, -5, counter - Me.ClientSize.Height - 10, _
         Me.ClientSize.Height + 5)
   Next counter

   ' ----- Draw the sprites.
   MySprites(0).Draw(e.Graphics)
   MySprites(1).Draw(e.Graphics)
```

```
      ' ----- See if the sprites have hit each other.
      If MySprites(0).Collision(MySprites(1)) Then
         MySprites(0).VelocityX = -MySprites(0).VelocityX
         MySprites(0).VelocityY = -MySprites(0).VelocityY
         MySprites(1).VelocityX = -MySprites(1).VelocityX
         MySprites(1).VelocityY = -MySprites(1).VelocityY
      End If

      ' ----- Move the sprites for the next update.
      For counter = 0 To 1
         If (MySprites(counter).X < 0) Then
            MySprites(counter).VelocityX = _
               Math.Abs(MySprites(counter).VelocityX)
         End If
         If (MySprites(counter).Y < 0) Then
            MySprites(counter).VelocityY = _
               Math.Abs(MySprites(counter).VelocityY)
         End If
         If (MySprites(counter).X > _
               (Me.ClientSize.Width - 30)) Then
            MySprites(counter).VelocityX = _
               -Math.Abs(MySprites(counter).VelocityX)
         End If
         If (MySprites(counter).Y > _
               (Me.ClientSize.Height - 30)) Then
            MySprites(counter).VelocityY = _
               -Math.Abs(MySprites(counter).VelocityY)
         End If
      Next counter
   End Sub
```

Figure 10-10 shows the two sprites in action, just after bouncing away from each other. Notice that the bitmaps are created outside each sprite object, so the colors are easily set to something unique. In fact, the bitmaps could easily be made much more unique, with the sprites appearing in different sizes and shapes if desired.

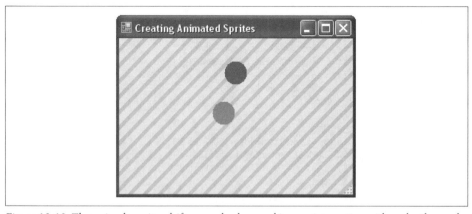

Figure 10-10. These simple sprites drift over a background image, interacting with each other and with the walls of the form

10.9 Resizing and Compressing JPEG Files

Problem

Your digital camera's pictures are great, but they're way too big to send attached to your family emails. You want to shrink them to a manageable size, but you also want to control the compression so there's no compromise in the resulting quality of the images.

Solution

Sample code folder: Chapter 10\CompressImages

The CompressJPEG class presented in this recipe wraps all the code required to compress JPEG pictures to any desired absolute or relative size. It lets you set the compression factor so you get a good balance between file size and quality in the resulting JPEG images.

Discussion

Before presenting the CompressJPEG class itself, let's see how it's called. The following code shows how a large picture named *Family.jpg* is compressed to 25 percent of its starting size using a compression-factor setting of 70 percent. A CompressJPEG object is created, and its SizePercent and QualityPercent properties are set to 25 and 70, respectively. The Load( ) method loads the original JPEG image, and the Save( ) method then saves the compressed and resized image to a new JPEG file:

```
Dim imageConverter As New CompressJPEG
imageConverter.SizePercent = 25
imageConverter.QualityPercent = 70
imageConverter.Load("Family.jpg")
imageConverter.Save("SmallerFamily.jpg")
```

Both the SizePercent and QualityPercent properties affect the final number of bytes in the output file, and it's important to understand the difference between these two settings. SizePercent refers to the physical dimensions of the image; that is, how many pixels wide and high it will be after compression. JPEG compression is not a lossless compression technique, and the QualityPercent setting controls how much of the original information content of the picture is retained. A low setting results in graininess and blockiness in the image, whereas a high value for this setting retains the detail and quality of the original image. Typically, a setting of around 75 to 85 provides good compression with little or no noticeable loss of image quality. If you don't set the QualityPercent property, it defaults to a very reasonable value of 85. If you don't set the SizePercent property, the output image retains the same dimensions as the original.

The following code is for the CompressJPEG class itself. In addition to the properties and methods described so far, there are two more properties you might find handy: instead of setting SizePercent, which resizes the picture to a percentage of its original size, you can set the Width or Height properties to define the compressed file's dimensions. If you set one of these properties, the other is calculated to retain the proportions of the original image. Here's the code for the CompressJPEG class:

```
Imports System.Drawing.Imaging

Public Class CompressJPEG
    Private SourceImage As Image
    Private UseQualityPercent As Double
    Private UseSizePercent As Double
    Private UseWidth As Integer
    Private UseHeight As Integer

    Public Sub Load(ByVal filePath As String)
        ' ----- Assign the user-specified file.
        SourceImage = Image.FromFile(filePath)
    End Sub

    Public Sub Save(ByVal outputFile As String)
        ' ----- Save the file, making adjustments as requested.
        Dim wide As Integer
        Dim tall As Integer
        Dim newImage As Bitmap
        Dim canvas As Graphics
        Dim codecs() As ImageCodecInfo
        Dim jpegCodec As ImageCodecInfo
        Dim scanCodec As ImageCodecInfo
        Dim qualityParam As EncoderParameters

        ' ----- Don't bother if there is no image.
        If IsNothing(SourceImage) = True Then Return

        ' ----- Use default values if needed.
        If UseQualityPercent = 0 Then UseQualityPercent = 85

        ' ----- Calculate the new dimensions.
        If (UseWidth <> 0) And (UseHeight = 0) Then
            ' ----- Proportional to the width.
            wide = UseWidth
            tall = CInt(UseWidth * _
                SourceImage.Height / SourceImage.Width)
        ElseIf (UseWidth = 0) And (UseHeight <> 0) Then
            ' ----- Proportional to the height.
            wide = CInt(UseHeight * _
                SourceImage.Width / SourceImage.Height)
            tall = UseHeight
        ElseIf (UseWidth <> 0) And (UseHeight <> 0) Then
            ' ----- User-specified size.
```

```
         wide = UseWidth
         tall = UseHeight
      ElseIf (UseSizePercent <> 0) Then
         ' ----- Percent scale.
         wide = CInt(SourceImage.Width * _
            UseSizePercent / 100)
         tall = CInt(SourceImage.Height * _
            UseSizePercent / 100)
      Else
         ' ----- Retain the size.
         wide = SourceImage.Width
         tall = SourceImage.Height
      End If

      ' ----- Redraw the image to the new size.
      newImage = New Bitmap(wide, tall)
      canvas = Graphics.FromImage(newImage)
      canvas.DrawImage(SourceImage, 0, 0, wide, tall)
      canvas.Dispose()

      ' ----- Locate the processor for JPEG images.
      codecs = ImageCodecInfo.GetImageEncoders
      jpegCodec = codecs(0)
      qualityParam = New EncoderParameters
      For Each scanCodec In codecs
         If (scanCodec.MimeType = "image/jpeg") Then
            ' ----- Found the one we're looking for.
            jpegCodec = scanCodec
            Exit For
         End If
      Next scanCodec

      ' ----- Prepare the quality reduction.
      qualityParam.Param(0) = New EncoderParameter( _
         Encoder.Quality, CInt(UseQualityPercent))

      ' ----- Adjust and save the new image in one command.
      newImage.Save(outputFile, jpegCodec, qualityParam)
      SourceImage = Nothing
   End Sub

   Public Property QualityPercent() As Double
      Get
         Return UseQualityPercent
      End Get
      Set(ByVal Value As Double)
         Select Case Value
            Case Is < 1
               UseQualityPercent = 1
            Case Is > 100
               UseQualityPercent = 100
            Case Else
               UseQualityPercent = Value
```

```
            End Select
        End Set
    End Property

    Public Property SizePercent() As Double
        Get
            Return UseSizePercent
        End Get
        Set(ByVal Value As Double)
            Select Case Value
                Case Is < 1
                    UseSizePercent = 1
                Case Is > 400
                    UseSizePercent = 400
                Case Else
                    UseSizePercent = Value
            End Select
        End Set
    End Property

    Public Property Width() As Integer
        Get
            If (UseWidth > 0) Then
                Return UseWidth
            Else
                If (SourceImage.Width > 0) Then
                    Return CInt(SourceImage.Width * _
                        UseSizePercent / 100)
                End If
            End If
        End Get
        Set(ByVal Value As Integer)
            UseWidth = Value
        End Set
    End Property

    Public Property Height() As Integer
        Get
            Return UseHeight
        End Get
        Set(ByVal Value As Integer)
            UseHeight = Value
        End Set
    End Property
End Class
```

Figure 10-11 shows an image after compression from the original, much larger file. This compressed file is less than 19 KB in size, reduced from an original of over 1.25 MB!

Figure 10-11. Compressed and reduced images can be made much smaller, without noticeable loss of quality

10.10 Getting JPEG Extended Information

Problem

You want to extract information from within the JPEG pictures your camera creates. You might want to do this, for instance, to rename the pictures based on the date and time they were taken.

Solution

Sample code folder: Chapter 10\JPEGInfo

Use the GetPropertyItem( ) method of the Bitmap class to extract header information from a JPEG file.

Discussion

Each brand of camera seems to create and store different header information in the picture files it creates, so this solution may or may not work for you. This recipe's code is generalized enough so that even though you might not have documentation listing the properties by their access numbers, you can check this program's output to help determine what information is available.

The GetJpgInformation( ) function listed here gets a list of all property IDs from the picture's bitmap, calls GetPropertyItem( ) for each of these, and then formats the results into a string array as best it can, replacing some characters and zero bytes as required to prevent string-handling problems:

```
Public Shared Function GetJpgInformation( _
    ByVal whichFile As String) As String
    ' ----- Retrieve the properties of a JPEG file.
    Dim bytesPropertyID As Byte( )
    Dim stringPropertyID As String
    Dim loadedImage As System.Drawing.Bitmap
    Dim propertyIDs( ) As Integer
    Dim result As New System.Text.StringBuilder
    Dim counter As Integer
    Dim scanProperty As Integer

    ' ----- Retrieve the image and its properties.
    loadedImage = New System.Drawing.Bitmap(whichFile)
    propertyIDs = loadedImage.PropertyIdList

    ' ----- Examine each property.
    For Each scanProperty In propertyIDs
        ' ----- Convert the property to a string format.
        bytesPropertyID = loadedImage.GetPropertyItem( _
            scanProperty).Value
        stringPropertyID = System.Text.Encoding.ASCII. _
            GetString(bytesPropertyID)

        ' ----- Only retain characters in the printable
        '       ASCII range.
        For counter = 0 To 255
            If counter < 32 Or counter > 127 Then
                If (stringPropertyID.IndexOf(Chr(counter)) _
                    <> -1) Then
                    stringPropertyID = Replace(stringPropertyID, _
                        Chr(counter), "")
                End If
            End If
        Next counter

        ' ----- Display the property if it's reasonable.
        If (stringPropertyID.Length > 0) And _
            (stringPropertyID.Length < 70) Then
            result.Append(scanProperty.ToString)
            result.Append(":    ")
            result.AppendLine(stringPropertyID)
        End If
    Next scanProperty
```

```
    ' ----- Display the results.
    Return result.ToString
End Function

Public Shared Function GetString( _
      ByVal sourceBytes As Byte()) As String
    ' ----- Convert a byte array to a string, taking into
    '        account the terminating null character.
    Dim result As String

    result = System.Text.Encoding.ASCII.GetString(sourceBytes)
    If (result.EndsWith(vbNullChar) = True) Then _
      result = result.Substring(0, result.Length - 1)
    Return result
End Function
```

Call the GetJpgInformation( ) function directly with the path to a valid JPEG file to view the properties of the file:

```
MsgBox(ProcessJPEG.GetJpgInformation("sample.jpg"))
```

Figure 10-12 shows a sample of the output produced by this code.

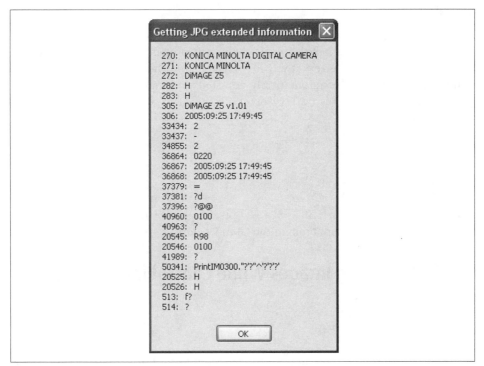

Figure 10-12. The information stored in a JPEG file

As you can see from the output, not all data items are usable, or even recognizable as readable ASCII text. Your output will probably vary depending on the camera or software used to create your image files. For your camera, you can use the date and time stamps as shown to help rename your picture files for easy chronological storage and access.

10.11 Creating Thumbnails

Problem

You want to create good-quality thumbnail JPEG images from larger images. These smaller versions of larger pictures are handy for web pages.

Solution

The CompressJPEG class presented in Recipe 10.9 provides an ideal solution for creating smaller thumbnail versions of large JPEG pictures.

Discussion

Instead of setting the CompressJPEG object's SizePercent property to shrink the pictures to some unknown smaller size, set the Height property to 100 to force the creation of compressed files exactly 100 pixels high. The width of each output thumbnail picture will be automatically adjusted to retain the proportions of the original image. The default QualityPercent value of 85 works just fine for these thumbnails:

```
Dim imageThumb As New CompressJPEG

imageThumb.Height = 100
imageThumb.Load("sample.jpg")
imageThumb.Save("sampleThumb.jpg")
```

The picture shown in Figure 10-13 is a 100-pixel-high copy of an original, and much larger, JPEG picture of a mountain in the Grand Tetons.

10.12 Displaying Images While Controlling Stretching and Sizing

Problem

You want to display a picture in a PictureBox on a form, but you aren't sure which size mode setting to use.

Figure 10-13. Thumbnails are easy to create at any chosen size and quality setting

Solution

Sample code folder: Chapter 10\StretchImage

The sample code in this recipe lets you interactively experiment with the display of a picture on a form to determine which size mode setting will work best for your needs.

Discussion

The PictureBox control is ideal for displaying JPEG and other picture files. However, one of the property settings of the PictureBox changes the way images are displayed in a significant way, and having a clear means of visualizing how it affects the displayed images can help you plan your applications better. The code presented here provides an easy way to see exactly how the SizeMode property works.

Create a new Windows Forms application. Add a PictureBox control to the form, and set its Dock property to Fill. This causes the PictureBox to automatically stretch to fill the client area of the form on which it resides. (The image displayed in the PictureBox won't necessarily stretch to fill the same area—that depends on the SizeMode setting of the PictureBox.) Next, add the following code to the form's code template. The code toggles through the SizeMode settings each time you click on the PictureBox, letting you easily see and experiment with the various settings:

```
Private Sub PictureBox1_Click(ByVal sender As System.Object, _
    ByVal e As System.EventArgs) Handles PictureBox1.Click
    ' ----- Toggle to the next size mode.
    Static displayState As PictureBoxSizeMode = 0

    ' ----- Move to the next state.
    If ([Enum].IsDefined(GetType(PictureBoxSizeMode), _
        CInt(displayState) + 1) = True) Then
        displayState += 1
    Else
        ' ----- Wrap to the first choice.
        displayState = 0
    End If

    ' ----- Update the display.
    PictureBox1.SizeMode = displayState
    Me.Text = "PictureBoxSizeMode." & displayState.ToString( )
End Sub
```

This code toggles through all available values of the PictureBoxSizeMode enumeration, the one used to set the size of a PictureBox control. To select an image when starting the application, add the following code to the form's class:

```
Private Sub Form1_Load(ByVal sender As Object, _
    ByVal e As System.EventArgs) Handles Me.Load
    ' ----- Let the user choose a picture.
    Dim locateFile As New OpenFileDialog

    ' ----- Prompt for the initial file.
    locateFile.Filter = "JPG files (*.jpg)|*.jpg"
    locateFile.Multiselect = False
    If (locateFile.ShowDialog( ) = _
        Windows.Forms.DialogResult.OK) Then
        ' ----- Show the selected picture.
        PictureBox1.Load(locateFile.FileName)
    Else
        ' ----- Exit the program.
        Me.Close( )
    End If

    ' ----- Show the initial state.
    Me.Text = "PictureBoxSizeMode." & _
        PictureBox1.SizeMode.ToString( )
End Sub
```

Figures 10-14 and 10-18 show the display of a picture when SizeMode is set to StretchImage. This setting causes the image to distort horizontally and/or vertically to fit the control, rather than retaining its original proportions.

Figure 10-14. The StretchImage setting distorts images to fit within the dimensions of a PictureBox

As you can see in Figure 10-15, with the Zoom setting, the picture retains its original proportionality. However, this can cause blank areas to appear either on both sides of or above and below the image. The picture appears smaller than when it's stretched to fit the dimensions of the PictureBox, but at least it's not distorted.

Figure 10-15. The Zoom setting reduces an image's width or height to keep it within the PictureBox with no distortion

In Figure 10-16, SizeMode is set to AutoSize, which means the PictureBox automatically resizes itself to show the entire picture at its full resolution. Because the PictureBox is limited to the surface of the form, though, only the upper-left corner of the picture is seen here, and only by expanding the form to great lengths will you begin to see the edge of the mountain in the bottom-right corner of the form. In this figure we only see blue sky and a little bit of the mountain. You may also detect a small blurry bird image in the very corner.

Figure 10-17 shows the picture when SizeMode is set to CenterImage. The picture is once again shown full-scale, as when the mode was set to AutoSize, but in this case you see the very center of the large picture rather than its upper-left corner.

Figure 10-16. The AutoSize setting displays images at full size, even if they don't fit within the area provided

Figure 10-17. CenterImage displays the center of the image in the center of the PictureBox at full size

Figure 10-18 show what happens after the demonstration program cycles through the settings.

Figure 10-18. The demonstration program cycles through the settings, returning to the original StretchImage setting

Each setting has its uses, and you should become familiar with the effects of each when displaying pictures or other graphics.

10.13 Scrolling Images

Problem

You want to display a picture with full resolution, but you want to let the user scroll around to see all parts of the picture.

Solution

Sample code folder: Chapter 10\ScrollImage

Store the picture in a PictureBox with its SizeMode property set to AutoSize, and place it on a form with its AutoScroll property set to True.

Discussion

To see this demonstration in action, add a `PictureBox` to a form, set its `SizeMode` property to `AutoSize`, and set its `Location` property to `0,0`. Don't worry about its size; the `AutoSize` setting will take care of that. Change the form's `AutoScroll` property to `True`. Now add the following code to the form's class, which loads a picture on startup:

```
Private Sub Form1_Load(ByVal sender As Object, _
        ByVal e As System.EventArgs) Handles Me.Load
    ' ----- Let the user choose a picture.
    Dim locateFile As New OpenFileDialog

    ' ----- Prompt for the initial file.
    locateFile.Filter = "JPG files (*.jpg)|*.jpg"
    locateFile.Multiselect = False
    If (locateFile.ShowDialog() = _
            Windows.Forms.DialogResult.OK) Then
        ' ----- Show the selected picture.
        PictureBox1.Load(locateFile.FileName)
        Me.AutoScroll = True
    Else
        ' ----- Exit the program.
        Me.Close()
    End If
End Sub
```

Run the program, and select a large picture. The scrollbars will automatically appear when needed, as shown in Figure 10-19.

Figure 10-19. Implementing scrollbars to enable scrolling around large images

10.14 Merging Two or More Images

Problem

You want to blend two images together, with a variable strength for each, to create a ghost-like effect.

Solution

Sample code folder: Chapter 10\MergeImages

Use the GetPixel( ) method of the Bitmap class to process the pixels from matching locations in each of the original images, and use the SetPixel( ) method to assign the resulting pixels to a third bitmap to create the merged image.

Discussion

This recipe processes the pixels from two identically sized images and creates a third. The action is slow enough that intermediate results are displayed after each row of pixels is processed. To try it out, add the following code to the form's class. The code loads two image files (in Form1_Load( )) and does the actual processing (DoMergeImages( )):

```
Private SourceImages(1) As Bitmap

Private Sub Form1_Load(ByVal sender As System.Object, _
      ByVal e As System.EventArgs) Handles MyBase.Load
   ' ----- Prepare the form.
   Dim counter As Integer
   Dim locateFile As New OpenFileDialog

   ' ----- Display the form immediately.
   Me.Show( )

   ' ----- Prompt for each file.
   locateFile.Filter = "JPG files (*.jpg)|*.jpg"
   For counter = 0 To 1
      ' ----- Prompt for the initial file.
      If (locateFile.ShowDialog( ) <> _
            Windows.Forms.DialogResult.OK) Then
         ' ----- End the program.
         Me.Close( )
         Return
      End If

      ' ----- Load in the picture.
      SourceImages(counter) = New Bitmap(locateFile.FileName)
   Next counter
```

```
    ' ----- Start the processing.
    DoMergeImages()
End Sub

Private Sub Form1_FormClosed(ByVal sender As Object, _
      ByVal e As System.Windows.Forms.FormClosedEventArgs) _
      Handles Me.FormClosed
    ' ----- Exit the program. This is needed just in case the
    '       user closed the form in the middle of the merge.
    End
End Sub

Private Sub DoMergeImages()
    ' ----- Merge two images.
    Dim workBitmap As Bitmap
    Dim across As Integer
    Dim down As Integer
    Dim firstColor As Color
    Dim secondColor As Color
    Dim mixedColor As Color
    Dim redPart As Integer
    Dim greenPart As Integer
    Dim bluePart As Integer
    Dim canvas As Graphics

    ' ----- Use one of the images as the base.
    workBitmap = SourceImages(0)
    canvas = Graphics.FromImage(workBitmap)

    ' ----- Process each row of the image.
    For down = 0 To SourceImages(0).Height - 1
        ' ----- Process each column of the image.
        For across = 0 To SourceImages(0).Width - 1
            Try
                ' ----- Get the colors of a specific pixel.
                firstColor = _
                    SourceImages(0).GetPixel(across, down)
                secondColor = _
                    SourceImages(1).GetPixel(across, down)
            Catch
                ' ----- If an error occurs, the images must have
                '       been mismatched in size.
                Continue For
            End Try

            ' ----- Build a blended color from the parts.
            redPart = (CInt(firstColor.R) + secondColor.R) \ 2
            greenPart = (CInt(firstColor.G) + secondColor.G) \ 2
            bluePart = (CInt(firstColor.B) + secondColor.B) \ 2
            mixedColor = Color.FromArgb(redPart, greenPart, _
                bluePart)
```

```
            ' ----- Update the image.
            workBitmap.SetPixel(across, down, mixedColor)
        Next across

        ' ----- Refresh the display so the user knows
        '        something is happening.
        MergedImage.Image = workBitmap
        Application.DoEvents( )
    Next down
    canvas.Dispose( )
End Sub
```

Figure 10-20 shows the results of blending together images of a goose and the Grand Teton mountains. The code blends the pixels equally by adding together the color values and dividing by two to find their averages. You could easily modify this averaging to place more weight on the pixels from one image or the other. Another creative experiment might be to average together only one or more of the color channels (red, green, or blue).

Figure 10-20. Blending two pictures for a ghostly effect

10.15 Using Resource Images

Problem

You want to manipulate images on your forms at runtime without having to load them from accompanying files shipped with your application.

Solution

Add the images to the application's resources, then load them into controls or process them as needed by accessing them directly from the My.Resources object.

Discussion

Adding pictures, icons, strings, or other items to your application's resources is very straightforward and easy to do in Visual Basic 2005. This recipe shows the steps involved for adding images, but the process easily extends to other types of resources.

Resource items are maintained at design time by double-clicking My Project in the Solution Explorer list and selecting the Resources tab. Figure 10-21 shows an example set of image resources as they appear in the Resources maintenance dialog.

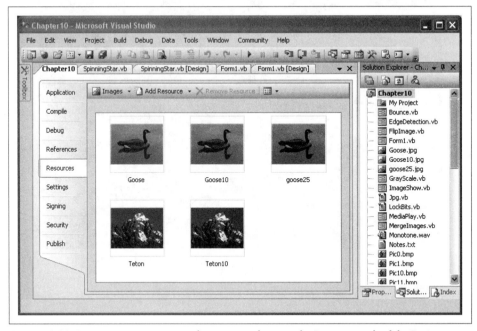

Figure 10-21. Resource-maintenance tasks are carried out on the Resources tab of the Project Properties window

To add a new picture to the collection of images, click the Add Resources pull-down menu, open the New Image submenu, and select JPEG Image, as shown in Figure 10-22.

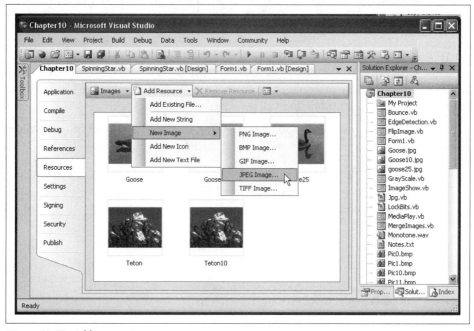

Figure 10-22. Adding new images to your resources

At runtime, the images stored in your application's resources are referenced by name. For example, the following code loads either the Goose or the Teton image into PictureBox1, based on the current state of the static Boolean variable showTheGoose:

```
Private Sub ShowImage(ByVal useTheGoose As Boolean)
    ' ----- Goose or Teton: hard choice!
    If (useTheGoose = True) Then
        PictureBox1.Image = My.Resources.Goose
    Else
        PictureBox1.Image = My.Resources.Teton
    End If
End Sub
```

10.16 Capturing an Image of the Screen

Problem

You want to capture a copy of the screen for processing in your Visual Basic 2005 application as a bitmap image, without resorting to any external applications.

Solution

Sample code folder: Chapter 10\CaptureScreen

Use the GetScreen( ) function in the ScreenGrab module presented in this recipe.

Discussion

There's no straightforward way to grab the contents of the screen using only functionality within the .NET Framework, but it is easy to call the appropriate Windows API functions to get the job done. The ScreenGrab module shown here wraps all the required function declarations and calls in an easy-to-use package.

Create a new Windows Forms application. Add a new module to the project named *ScreenGrab.vb*, and use the following code for its definition:

```
Module ScreenGrab
    Private Declare Function CreateDC _
        Lib "GDI32" Alias "CreateDCA" ( _
        ByVal lpDriverName As String, _
        ByVal lpDeviceName As String, _
        ByVal lpOutput As String, _
        ByVal lpInitData As String _
        ) As IntPtr

    Private Declare Function CreateCompatibleDC _
        Lib "GDI32" (ByVal hDC As IntPtr) As IntPtr

    Private Declare Function CreateCompatibleBitmap _
        Lib "GDI32" ( _
        ByVal hDC As IntPtr, _
        ByVal nWidth As Integer, _
        ByVal nHeight As Integer _
        ) As IntPtr

    Private Declare Function SelectObject _
        Lib "GDI32" ( _
        ByVal hDC As IntPtr, _
        ByVal hObject As IntPtr _
        ) As IntPtr

    Private Declare Function BitBlt _
        Lib "GDI32" ( _
        ByVal srchDC As IntPtr, _
        ByVal srcX As Integer, _
        ByVal srcY As Integer, _
        ByVal srcW As Integer, _
        ByVal srcH As Integer, _
        ByVal desthDC As IntPtr, _
        ByVal destX As Integer, _
        ByVal destY As Integer, _
```

```
      ByVal op As Integer _
      ) As Integer

   Private Declare Function DeleteDC _
      Lib "GDI32" (ByVal hDC As IntPtr) As Integer

   Private Declare Function DeleteObject _
      Lib "GDI32" (ByVal hObj As IntPtr) As Integer

   Const SRCCOPY As Integer = &HCC0020

   Public Function GetScreen() As Bitmap
      ' ----- Take a picture of the screen.
      Dim screenHandle As IntPtr
      Dim canvasHandle As IntPtr
      Dim screenBitmap As IntPtr
      Dim previousObject As IntPtr
      Dim resultCode As Integer
      Dim screenShot As Bitmap

      ' ----- Get a reference to the display.
      screenHandle = CreateDC("DISPLAY", "", "", "")

      ' ----- Make a canvas that is just like the
      '        display's canvas.
      canvasHandle = CreateCompatibleDC(screenHandle)

      ' ----- Create a bitmap that will hold the screen image.
      screenBitmap = CreateCompatibleBitmap(screenHandle, _
         Screen.PrimaryScreen.Bounds.Width, _
         Screen.PrimaryScreen.Bounds.Height)

      ' ----- Copy the screen image to the canvas/bitmap.
      previousObject = SelectObject(canvasHandle, _
         screenBitmap)
      resultCode = BitBlt(canvasHandle, 0, 0, _
         Screen.PrimaryScreen.Bounds.Width, _
         Screen.PrimaryScreen.Bounds.Height, _
         screenHandle, 0, 0, SRCCOPY)
      screenBitmap = SelectObject(canvasHandle, _
         previousObject)

      ' ----- Finished with the canvases.
      resultCode = DeleteDC(screenHandle)
      resultCode = DeleteDC(canvasHandle)

      ' ----- Copy image to a .NET bitmap.
      screenShot = Image.FromHbitmap(screenBitmap)
      DeleteObject(screenBitmap)

      ' ----- Finished.
      Return screenShot
```

```
        End Function
    End Module
```

Now return to Form1, and add a Button control named ActCapture. Set its Text property to Capture Now. Next, add a CheckBox control named IncludeThisForm, set its Checked property to True, and set its Text property to Include This Form. Finally, add a PictureBox control named ScreenSummary, set its SizeMode property to StretchImage, and set its Size property to 200,150. Figure 10-23 shows the form and its controls.

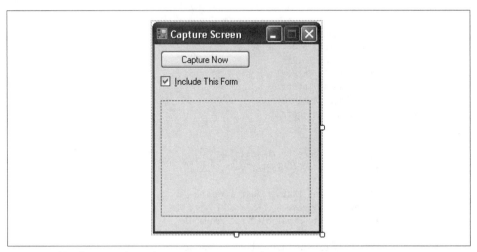

Figure 10-23. The controls on the screen capture sample

Add the following code to Form1's class template:

```
    Private Sub ActCapture_Click(ByVal sender As System.Object, _
        ByVal e As System.EventArgs) Handles ActCapture.Click
        ' ----- Copy the screen.
        ScreenSummary.Image = GetScreen()
    End Sub

    Private Sub IncludeThisForm_CheckedChanged( _
        ByVal sender As System.Object, _
        ByVal e As System.EventArgs) _
        Handles IncludeThisForm.CheckedChanged
        ' ----- Adjust the opacity as needed.
        If (IncludeThisForm.Checked = True) Then
            Me.Opacity = 1.0
        Else
            Me.Opacity = 0.99
        End If
    End Sub
```

It turns out that the standard method of copying the screen ignores semitransparent forms, so setting the form's opacity to anything below 1.0 makes it invisible to the screen capture process.

Run the program, and click the ActCapture button. Figure 10-24 shows the form in use.

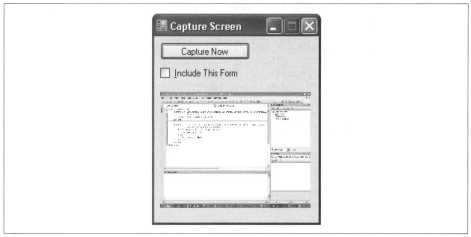

Figure 10-24. A capture of the entire screen with Visual Studio prominently displayed

Details of the API functions included in the ScreenGrab module and their use are beyond the scope of this book, but there are plenty of resources on the Internet if you want to find out how they work.

10.17 Getting Display Dimensions

Problem

You want to determine the dimensions of the user's screen at runtime, including both the entire screen and just the working area that doesn't include the task bar. Also, you want to determine the number of monitors on the user's system, the screen dimensions of each, and which screen is currently active.

Solution

Sample code folder: Chapter 10\ScreenInfo

Access this information from the Screen object, which includes an array of objects, one for each screen on the system.

Discussion

The following code extracts information from each Screen object returned by the Screen.AllScreens property, then formats the various data items returned for easy review:

```
Dim result As New System.Text.StringBuilder
Dim scanScreen As Screen
```

```
' ----- Include some summary data.
result.Append("Number of screens: ")
result.AppendLine(Screen.AllScreens.Length.ToString)
result.AppendLine( )

' ----- Process each installed screen.
For Each scanScreen In Screen.AllScreens
   result.AppendLine("Device Name: " & _
      GetTerminatedString(scanScreen.DeviceName))

   result.AppendLine("Bounds: " & _
      scanScreen.Bounds.ToString)

   result.AppendLine("Working Area: " & _
      scanScreen.WorkingArea.ToString)

   result.AppendLine("Is Primary: " & _
      scanScreen.Primary.ToString)

   result.AppendLine( )
Next scanScreen

MsgBox(result.ToString( ))
```

The device name returned by the scanScreen.DeviceName property may include an old
C-style terminating null character (ASCII 0), so you must to add a custom function
to extract just the part you need:

```
Private Function GetTerminatedString( _
      ByVal sourceString As String) As String
   ' ----- Return all text of a string up to the first
   '       null character.
   Dim index As Integer

   index = sourceString.IndexOf(vbNullChar)
   If (index > -1) Then
      Return sourceString.Substring(0, index)
   Else
      Return sourceString
End If
   End Function
```

As shown in Figure 10-25, the system used for testing this code had only one monitor, with a screen resolution of 1680×1050 pixels and a working area of 1680×990
pixels (the working area is slightly smaller because the task bar was showing along
the bottom edge of the screen).

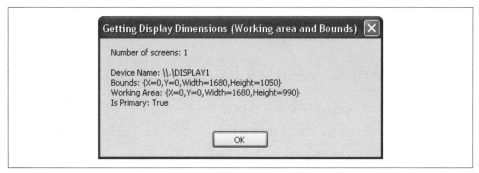

Figure 10-25. The Screen.AllScreens array provides information about any monitors on your system

10.18 Speeding Up Image Processing

Problem

You want to implement some image-processing algorithms, and you want the operations to be reasonably fast.

Solution

Sample code folder: Chapter 10\LockImage

Use the `InteropServices.Marshal.LockBits( )` method to prevent the operating system from moving the bitmap data around in memory. This greatly speeds up the program's access to the pixel data. This recipe presents a `LockImage` class that wraps the `LockBits( )` functionality for easy use.

Discussion

The `LockImage` class presented in this recipe and the remaining recipes in this chapter contains several image-processing methods. (The full `LockImage` class is listed in Recipe 10.21.) The goal is to provide enough examples to enable you to design your own image-processing functionality.

The processing function demonstrated in this recipe is `Mirror( )`, a method of the `LockImage` class that flips an image left and right. To see how it works, create a form with a `PictureBox` on it that has its `Dock` property set to `Fill` and its `SizeMode` property set to `StretchImage`. Load a picture into its `Image` property, and add the following code to its `Click` event:

```
Private Sub PictureBox1_Click(ByVal sender As System.Object, _
    ByVal e As System.EventArgs) Handles PictureBox1.Click
  ' ----- Mirror-image the bitmap.
  Dim mirrorIt As New LockImage
  mirrorIt.Image = PictureBox1.Image
```

```
    mirrorIt.Mirror()
    PictureBox1.Image = mirrorIt.Image
End Sub
```

When you click on the picture, this procedure creates an instance of the LockImage class, copies the PictureBox's image to it, calls the Mirror() method to process the image, and then copies the image back into the PictureBox. This is the pattern for using any of the processing methods of the LockImage class.

Now let's look at the portions of the LockImage class that relate to the mirroring processss.

First, you must import the requisite namespaces. InteropServices.Marshal is required for its LockBits() method. The class defines a few class-level variables:

```
Imports System.Drawing.Imaging
Imports System.Runtime.InteropServices.Marshal

Public Class LockImage
    Private BaseImage As Bitmap
    Private BaseImageWidth As Integer
    Private BaseImageHeight As Integer
    Private TotalPixels As Integer
    Private ImageAddress As IntPtr
    Private ImageContent As BitmapData
    Private ImageBuffer() As Integer
```

The Image property stores or retrieves the bitmap image to be locked and processed:

```
Public Property Image() As Bitmap
    ' ----- User access to the relevant image.
    Get
        Return BaseImage
    End Get
    Set(ByVal Value As Bitmap)
        Dim canvas As Graphics
        BaseImage = New Bitmap(Value.Width, _
            Value.Height, Value.PixelFormat)
        canvas = Graphics.FromImage(BaseImage)
        canvas.DrawImage(Value, 0, 0, _
            Value.Width, Value.Height)
        canvas.Dispose()
    End Set
End Property
```

The LockTheImage() method provides the important core functionality of this class; with it, you can lock down the bits of the bitmap and present the pixel data in an integer array for efficient processing. All pixel processing in the methods you create, such as the Mirror() method presented later, will process in place the integer pixel data stored in ImageBuffer().

Each 32-bit integer in ImageBuffer() represents a single pixel. The most significant byte is alpha, the opacity value. The next most significant byte is for red, then green,

---

and the least significant byte is for blue. Each of these four values ranges from 0 to 255. Two other variables of importance for your image-processing methods are BaseImageWidth and BaseImageHeight. The ImageBuffer( ) array is one-dimensional, so these two values are required to determine the rectangular layout of the pixels:

```
Private Sub LockTheImage( )
    ' ----- Lock the image in memory. How much room
    '       do we need?
    BaseImageWidth = BaseImage.Width
    BaseImageHeight = BaseImage.Height
    TotalPixels = BaseImageWidth * BaseImageHeight

    ' ----- Create a stable (locked) area in memory. It
    '       will store 32-bit color images.
    ReDim ImageBuffer(TotalPixels - 1)
    ImageContent = BaseImage.LockBits( _
        New Rectangle(0, 0, BaseImageWidth, _
        BaseImageHeight), ImageLockMode.ReadWrite, _
        PixelFormat.Format32bppRgb)
    ImageAddress = ImageContent.Scan0

    ' ----- Associate the buffer and the locked memory.
    Copy(ImageAddress, ImageBuffer, 0, TotalPixels)
End Sub
```

The Mirror( ) method works by locating the first and last pixels of each row of the image, then swapping the pixels at those locations. The next and previous pixels in the row are swapped next, and this continues until all pixels in the row have been swapped. Here is the code for the Mirror( ) method:

```
Public Sub Mirror( )
    ' ----- Make a left-to-right mirror image.
    Dim pixelIndex1 As Integer
    Dim pixelIndex2 As Integer
    Dim holdPixel As Integer
    Dim down As Integer

    ' ----- Lock the image for speed.
    LockTheImage( )

    ' ----- Process each row of the image.
    For down = 0 To BaseImageHeight - 1
        ' ----- Process each column, up to halfway across.
        pixelIndex1 = down * BaseImageWidth
        pixelIndex2 = pixelIndex1 + BaseImageWidth - 1
        Do While pixelIndex1 < pixelIndex2
            ' ----- Swap two pixels.
            holdPixel = ImageBuffer(pixelIndex1)
            ImageBuffer(pixelIndex1) = _
                ImageBuffer(pixelIndex2)
            ImageBuffer(pixelIndex2) = holdPixel
            pixelIndex1 += 1
            pixelIndex2 -= 1
```

```
      Loop
   Next down

   ' ----- Finished. Unlock the image.
   UnlockTheImage( )
End Sub
```

The UnlockTheImage( ) method restores the processed pixel data in ImageBuffer( ) to the bitmap, ready to be retrieved by the code that uses the class:

```
Private Sub UnlockTheImage( )
   ' ----- Unlock the memory area.
   Copy(ImageBuffer, 0, ImageAddress, TotalPixels)
   Image.UnlockBits(ImageContent)
   ImageContent = Nothing
   ReDim ImageBuffer(0)
End Sub
```

Figure 10-26 shows a sample picture just before being flipped; Figure 10-27 shows the picture immediately afterwards.

Figure 10-26. An image about to be flipped horizontally

See Also

Recipe 10.21 includes the full source code for the LockImage class.

Figure 10-27. The same image after the Mirror() method has worked its magic

10.19 Converting an Image to Grayscale

Problem

You'd like to convert a picture from color to grayscale from within a Visual Basic 2005 application.

Solution

Sample code folder: Chapter 10\LockImage

Use the MakeGray( ) method of the LockImage class, described in Recipe 10.18.

Discussion

The MakeGray( ) method of the LockImage class (whose full source code is listed in Recipe 10.21) provides a working example that processes the individual color bytes stored in the class's ImageBuffer( ) integer array.

Here's the code for the MakeGray( ) procedure:

```
Public Sub MakeGray( )
    ' ----- Make a grayscale version of the image.
    Dim pixelIndex As Integer
    Dim onePixel As Integer
    Dim alphaPart As Integer
    Dim redPart As Integer
```

```
Dim greenPart As Integer
Dim bluePart As Integer
Dim maxColor As Integer
Dim minColor As Integer
Dim down As Integer
Dim across As Integer

' ----- Lock the image for speed.
LockTheImage()
```

All processing methods added to the LockImage class should call the private method LockTheImage() as the first step and the corresponding UnlockTheImage() method as the last step.

The following two nested loops process all pixels in all rows of the image. pixelIndex walks the pixels across each row and then down the image:

```
' ----- Process each pixel in the grid.
For down = 0 To BaseImageHeight - 1
    For across = 0 To BaseImageWidth - 1
        ' ----- Locate the pixel's color.
        pixelIndex = down * BaseImageWidth + across
```

Each pixel is split up into its parts if the processing requires access to them. The Mirror() method processed the pixels as whole units, but to compute grayscale values, you need to access the individual color components of each pixel:

```
onePixel = ImageBuffer(pixelIndex)

' ----- Extract the color values.
alphaPart = (onePixel >> 24) And &HFF
redPart = (onePixel >> 16) And &HFF
greenPart = (onePixel >> 8) And &HFF
bluePart = onePixel And &HFF
```

The next lines convert the color information to grayscale using an algorithm that averages using the two maximum and minimum values for red, green, and blue. There are other algorithms available for converting to grayscale, and you might want to experiment with others to best meet your requirements. All three colors are assigned the same byte value, which is what forces all pixels to become some shade of gray:

```
' ----- Get the general color intensity.
maxColor = Math.Max(redPart, Math.Max(greenPart, _
    bluePart))
minColor = Math.Min(redPart, Math.Min(greenPart, _
    bluePart))
onePixel = (maxColor + minColor) \ 2

' ----- Use a common intensity for all colors.
bluePart = onePixel
greenPart = onePixel
redPart = onePixel

' ----- Set the pixel to the new color. Retain
'       the original alpha channel.
ImageBuffer(pixelIndex) = (alphaPart << 24) + _
```

```
            (redPart << 16) + (greenPart << 8) + bluePart
        Next across
    Next down
```

As a last step, it's important to call UnlockTheImage( ) when the processing of ImageBuffer( ) is complete:

```
    ' ----- Finished. Unlock the image.
    UnlockTheImage( )
End Sub
```

In this example, 256 shades of gray are created. If you want to convert to 16 shades, or even just 2 (black-and-white monochrome), simply round off onePixel to the nearest shade values desired. For example, for two-level black-and-white images all values of onePixel less than 128 are rounded to zero, and all other byte values are set to 255.

Figure 10-28 shows the results of converting the original color image to grayscale. Although the difference can be hard to discern in the grayscale figures used in this book, it can easily be seen in Figure 10-29, where a two-level grayscale (or monochrome black-and-white) conversion was used. This result was obtained by inserting the following lines to adjust onePixel just before it is assigned to the red, blue, and green variables:

```
If (onePixel < 128) Then
    onePixel = 0
Else
    onePixel = 255
End If
```

Figure 10-28. A color picture converted to grayscale

Figure 10-29. The same image with a 2-level grayscale (black-and-white monochrome) conversion performed instead of a 256-level conversion

See Also

Recipe 10.18 describes the LockImage class used in this recipe. Recipe 10.21 includes the full source code for the LockImage class.

10.20 Performing Edge Detection on an Image

Problem

You want to perform edge detection on a picture.

Solution

Sample code folder: Chapter 10\LockImage

Use the EdgeDetect( ) method of the LockImage class, described in Recipe 10.18.

Discussion

Edge detection is a good example of the complex image-processing routines that can be created within the framework of the LockImage class. The EdgeDetect() method processes the pixels in an image by converting them to grayscale and then using a filter matrix to process neighboring pixels. The matrix processing detects rapid rates of change in the pixels and assigns a darker shade of gray where pixels are changing the fastest. Figure 10-30 shows the edges of the goose after this method has done its work.

Figure 10-30. Edge detection using the LockImage class's EdgeDetect() method

The EdgeDetect() method is a little more involved than the image-processing methods discussed in the previous two recipes. Two 3×3 matrices, edgeX and edgeY, are created to process neighboring pixels for X and Y changes. This processing requires that the pixels be accessed multiple times. It is easier to set up the algorithm by first converting all pixels to shades of gray and storing them in a two-dimensional array. Even with these extra processing steps, the algorithm runs very fast in the .NET Framework.

Here's the code for the EdgeDetect() procedure:

```
Public Sub EdgeDetect()
    ' ----- Enhance the edges within the image.
    Dim onePixel As Integer
    Dim redPart As Integer
```

```
Dim greenPart As Integer
Dim bluePart As Integer
Dim maxColor As Integer
Dim minColor As Integer
Dim down As Integer
Dim across As Integer
Dim pixArray(,) As Integer
Dim target(,) As Integer
Dim sumX As Integer
Dim sumY As Integer
Dim useSum As Integer
Dim squareX As Integer
Dim squareY As Integer

' ----- Define the Sobel Edge Detector gradient
'       matrices.
Dim edgeX(,) = {{-1, 0, 1}, {-2, 0, 2}, {-1, 0, 1}}
Dim edgeY(,) = {{1, 2, 1}, {0, 0, 0}, {-1, -2, -1}}

' ----- Lock the image for speed.
LockTheImage()

' ----- Convert the 1D pixel array to 2D for ease
'       of processing.
ReDim pixArray(BaseImageHeight - 1, BaseImageWidth - 1)
For down = 0 To BaseImageHeight - 1
   For across = 0 To BaseImageWidth - 1
      ' ----- Convert each pixel to a grayscale value.
      onePixel = ImageBuffer(down * BaseImageWidth + _
         across)
      redPart = (onePixel >> 16) And &HFF
      greenPart = (onePixel >> 8) And &HFF
      bluePart = onePixel And &HFF
      maxColor = Math.Max(redPart, Math.Max(greenPart, _
         bluePart))
      minColor = Math.Min(redPart, Math.Min(greenPart, _
         bluePart))
      pixArray(down, across) = (maxColor + minColor) \ 2
   Next across
Next down

' ----- Results will be placed in a second pixel array.
ReDim target(BaseImageHeight - 1, BaseImageWidth - 1)

' ----- Process for edge detection.
For down = 0 To BaseImageHeight - 1
   For across = 0 To BaseImageWidth - 1
      ' ----- Calculate the edge factor.
      sumX = 0
      sumY = 0
```

```
        If (down = 0) Or _
            (down = (BaseImageHeight - 1)) Then
            ' ----- Ignore true edges.
            useSum = 0
        ElseIf (across = 0) Or _
            (across = (BaseImageWidth - 1)) Then
            ' ---- Ignore true edges.
            useSum = 0
        Else
            ' ----- Summarize a small square around
            '       the point.
            For squareX = -1 To 1
                For squareY = -1 To 1
                    sumX += pixArray(down + squareY, _
                        across + squareX) * _
                        edgeX(squareX + 1, squareY + 1)
                    sumY += pixArray(down + squareY, _
                        across + squareX) * _
                        edgeY(squareX + 1, squareY + 1)
                Next squareY
            Next squareX

            ' ----- Force the value into the 0 to 255 range.
            useSum = Math.Abs(sumX) + Math.Abs(sumY)
            If (useSum < 0) Then useSum = 0
            If (useSum > 255) Then useSum = 255
            useSum = 255 - useSum

            ' ----- Save it as a grayscale value in
            '       the pixel.
            target(down, across) = useSum + _
                (useSum << 8) + (useSum << 16)
        End If
    Next across
Next down

' ----- Move results back into the locked pixels array.
For down = 0 To BaseImageHeight - 1
    For across = 0 To BaseImageWidth - 1
        ImageBuffer(down * BaseImageWidth + across) = _
            target(down, across)
    Next across
Next down

' ----- Finished. Unlock the image.
UnlockTheImage( )
End Sub
```

See Also

Recipe 10.18 describes the LockImage class used in this recipe. Recipe 10.21 includes the full source code for the LockImage class.

10.21 Full Listing of the LockImage Class

Sample code folder: Chapter 10\LockImage

This recipe contains the full code for the LockImage class described in Recipes 10.18 through 10.20:

```
Imports System.Drawing.Imaging
Imports System.Runtime.InteropServices.Marshal

Public Class LockImage
    Private BaseImage As Bitmap
    Private BaseImageWidth As Integer
    Private BaseImageHeight As Integer
    Private TotalPixels As Integer
    Private ImageAddress As IntPtr
    Private ImageContent As BitmapData
    Private ImageBuffer() As Integer

    Public Property Image() As Bitmap
        ' ----- User access to the relevant image.
        Get
            Return BaseImage
        End Get
        Set(ByVal Value As Bitmap)
            Dim canvas As Graphics
            BaseImage = New Bitmap(Value.Width, _
                Value.Height, Value.PixelFormat)
            canvas = Graphics.FromImage(BaseImage)
            canvas.DrawImage(Value, 0, 0, _
                Value.Width, Value.Height)
            canvas.Dispose()
        End Set
    End Property

    Private Sub LockTheImage()
        ' ----- Lock the image in memory. How much room
        '       do we need?
        BaseImageWidth = BaseImage.Width
        BaseImageHeight = BaseImage.Height
        TotalPixels = BaseImageWidth * BaseImageHeight

        ' ----- Create a stable (locked) area in memory. It
        '       will store 32-bit color images.
        ReDim ImageBuffer(TotalPixels - 1)
        ImageContent = BaseImage.LockBits( _
            New Rectangle(0, 0, BaseImageWidth, _
            BaseImageHeight), ImageLockMode.ReadWrite, _
            PixelFormat.Format32bppRgb)
        ImageAddress = ImageContent.Scan0

        ' ----- Associate the buffer and the locked memory.
        Copy(ImageAddress, ImageBuffer, 0, TotalPixels)
    End Sub
```

```
Private Sub UnlockTheImage()
    ' ----- Unlock the memory area.
    Copy(ImageBuffer, 0, ImageAddress, TotalPixels)
    Image.UnlockBits(ImageContent)
    ImageContent = Nothing
    ReDim ImageBuffer(0)
End Sub

Public Sub MakeGray()
    ' ----- Make a grayscale version of the image.
    Dim pixelIndex As Integer
    Dim onePixel As Integer
    Dim alphaPart As Integer
    Dim redPart As Integer
    Dim greenPart As Integer
    Dim bluePart As Integer
    Dim maxColor As Integer
    Dim minColor As Integer
    Dim down As Integer
    Dim across As Integer

    ' ----- Lock the image for speed.
    LockTheImage()

    ' ----- Process each pixel in the grid.
    For down = 0 To BaseImageHeight - 1
        For across = 0 To BaseImageWidth - 1
            ' ----- Locate the pixel's color.
            pixelIndex = down * BaseImageWidth + across
            onePixel = ImageBuffer(pixelIndex)

            ' ----- Extract the color values.
            alphaPart = (onePixel >> 24) And &HFF
            redPart = (onePixel >> 16) And &HFF
            greenPart = (onePixel >> 8) And &HFF
            bluePart = onePixel And &HFF

            ' ----- Get the general color intensity.
            maxColor = Math.Max(redPart, Math.Max(greenPart, _
                bluePart))
            minColor = Math.Min(redPart, Math.Min(greenPart, _
                bluePart))
            onePixel = (maxColor + minColor) \ 2

            ' ----- Use a common intensity for all colors.
            bluePart = onePixel
            greenPart = onePixel
            redPart = onePixel

            ' ----- Set the pixel to the new color. Retain
            '       the original alpha channel.
            ImageBuffer(pixelIndex) = (alphaPart << 24) + _
                (redPart << 16) + (greenPart << 8) + bluePart
```

```
        Next across
    Next down

    ' ----- Finished. Unlock the image.
    UnlockTheImage()
End Sub

Public Sub Mirror()
    ' ----- Make a left-to-right mirror image.
    Dim pixelIndex1 As Integer
    Dim pixelIndex2 As Integer
    Dim holdPixel As Integer
    Dim down As Integer

    ' ----- Lock the image for speed.
    LockTheImage()

    ' ----- Process each row of the image.
    For down = 0 To BaseImageHeight - 1
        ' ----- Process each column, up to halfway across.
        pixelIndex1 = down * BaseImageWidth
        pixelIndex2 = pixelIndex1 + BaseImageWidth - 1
        Do While pixelIndex1 < pixelIndex2
            ' ----- Swap two pixels.
            holdPixel = ImageBuffer(pixelIndex1)
            ImageBuffer(pixelIndex1) = _
                ImageBuffer(pixelIndex2)
            ImageBuffer(pixelIndex2) = holdPixel
            pixelIndex1 += 1
            pixelIndex2 -= 1
        Loop
    Next down

    ' ----- Finished. Unlock the image.
    UnlockTheImage()
End Sub

Public Sub EdgeDetect()
    ' ----- Enhance the edges within the image.
    Dim onePixel As Integer
    Dim redPart As Integer
    Dim greenPart As Integer
    Dim bluePart As Integer
    Dim maxColor As Integer
    Dim minColor As Integer
    Dim down As Integer
    Dim across As Integer
    Dim pixArray(,) As Integer
    Dim target(,) As Integer
    Dim sumX As Integer
    Dim sumY As Integer
    Dim useSum As Integer
```

```
Dim squareX As Integer
Dim squareY As Integer

' ----- Define the Sobel Edge Detector gradient
'       matrices.
Dim edgeX(,) = {{-1, 0, 1}, {-2, 0, 2}, {-1, 0, 1}}
Dim edgeY(,) = {{1, 2, 1}, {0, 0, 0}, {-1, -2, -1}}

' ----- Lock the image for speed.
LockTheImage()

' ----- Convert the 1D pixel array to 2D for ease
'       of processing.
ReDim pixArray(BaseImageHeight - 1, BaseImageWidth - 1)
For down = 0 To BaseImageHeight - 1
   For across = 0 To BaseImageWidth - 1
      ' ----- Convert each pixel to a grayscale value.
      onePixel = ImageBuffer(down * BaseImageWidth + _
         across)
      redPart = (onePixel >> 16) And &HFF
      greenPart = (onePixel >> 8) And &HFF
      bluePart = onePixel And &HFF
      maxColor = Math.Max(redPart, Math.Max(greenPart, _
         bluePart))
      minColor = Math.Min(redPart, Math.Min(greenPart, _
         bluePart))
      pixArray(down, across) = (maxColor + minColor) \ 2
   Next across
Next down

' ----- Results will be placed in a second pixel array.
ReDim target(BaseImageHeight - 1, BaseImageWidth - 1)

' ----- Process for edge detection.
For down = 0 To BaseImageHeight - 1
   For across = 0 To BaseImageWidth - 1
      ' ----- Calculate the edge factor.
      sumX = 0
      sumY = 0
      If (down = 0) Or _
            (down = (BaseImageHeight - 1)) Then
         ' ----- Ignore true edges.
         useSum = 0
      ElseIf (across = 0) Or _
            (across = (BaseImageWidth - 1)) Then
         ' ---- Ignore true edges.
         useSum = 0
      Else
         ' ----- Summarize a small square around
         '       the point.
         For squareX = -1 To 1
            For squareY = -1 To 1
```

```
                    sumX += pixArray(down + squareY, _
                        across + squareX) * _
                        edgeX(squareX + 1, squareY + 1)
                    sumY += pixArray(down + squareY, _
                        across + squareX) * _
                        edgeY(squareX + 1, squareY + 1)
                Next squareY
            Next squareX

            ' ----- Force the value into the 0 to 255 range.
            useSum = Math.Abs(sumX) + Math.Abs(sumY)
            If (useSum < 0) Then useSum = 0
            If (useSum > 255) Then useSum = 255
            useSum = 255 - useSum

            ' ----- Save it as a grayscale value in
            '       the pixel.
            target(down, across) = useSum + _
                (useSum << 8) + (useSum << 16)
        End If
      Next across
    Next down

    ' ----- Move results back into the locked pixels array.
    For down = 0 To BaseImageHeight - 1
      For across = 0 To BaseImageWidth - 1
        ImageBuffer(down * BaseImageWidth + across) = _
            target(down, across)
      Next across
    Next down

    ' ----- Finished. Unlock the image.
    UnlockTheImage()
  End Sub
End Class
```

Printing

11.0 Introduction

If there is one thing the typical business computer user needs more than anything else, it's reports. Any readers who have worked in the IS or IT department of a large organization can quickly attest to that. And reports mean printing, and printing means pain. At least, that's what I've always found. Certainly, there are many third-party reporting tools available, such as the version of Crystal Reports included with Visual Studio. But these "banded" reports don't always meet your needs. Sometimes you need to print out some text or graphics formatted in unique and custom ways.

Fortunately, the printing tools included with .NET are powerful, easy to use, and—dare I say it—fun. All of the text and graphics tools you use to update the display with .NET's GDI+ library can be leveraged for printing purposes. The printing commands aren't just similar to those used for screen updates; they're actually the same commands. (Chapter 9 includes many examples that use the graphics tools included with GDI+, so such examples won't be replicated in this chapter.)

11.1 Enumerating Printers

Problem

You want to access a list of the printers available to the current Windows user.

Solution

The "printing" section of GDI+, the .NET drawing system, includes a list of the installed printers. Use the following code to display the names of each:

```
For Each printerName As String In _
        System.Drawing.Printing.PrinterSettings.InstalledPrinters
    MsgBox(printerName)
Next printerName
```

Discussion

An early beta version of Visual Basic 2005 did include a `My.Printers` collection, but it was removed before the final release. But that's okay, because .NET supplies printer information through other .NET classes. The `System.Drawing.Printing.PrinterSettings.InstalledPrinters` collection (of strings) lists the printers attached to the local workstation.

If you need to get a list of all printers available on the local network and not just installed on the local workstation, you can access the information through the Windows Management Instrumentation (WMI) features installed with .NET. By default, the WMI library is not included in new .NET projects, so you must add a reference to the library yourself. In the Project Properties window, select the References tab, and use the Add button to add a reference to *System.Management.dll* to the project. Now use the following code to list all network printers:

```
Dim printerQuery As Management.ManagementObjectSearcher
Dim queryResults As Management.ManagementObjectCollection
Dim onePrinter As Management.ManagementObject

printerQuery = New Management.ManagementObjectSearcher( _
    "SELECT * FROM Win32_Printer")
queryResults = printerQuery.Get( )
For Each onePrinter In queryResults
    MsgBox(onePrinter!Name)
Next onePrinter
```

11.2   Sending "Raw" Data to a Printer

Problem

You need to send unprocessed data directly to a printer or print spooler, without processing by a printer driver.

Solution

Sample code folder: Chapter 11\RawPrinterData

The .NET Framework does not include direct support for this type of "raw" printing, so create your own class that uses various Win32 API calls.

Discussion

The .NET Framework does not include support for "raw" printing, the ability to send your own custom data directly to the printer. Some printers, such as barcode and receipt printers, accept data with embedded "escape sequences" that control the output on the printer. Many of these older printers do not include Windows drivers and can only be used in raw mode.

To print to these printers from .NET, you must use a DLL commonly used in Visual Basic 6.0 development to send raw data and perform other low-level operations on printers. The *winspool.drv* library includes several useful printer-specific functions, including functions that let you open a channel to the printer directly and send raw data. Because this library is not a .NET library, you have to coax .NET through the communication process using the various options to the DllImport attribute that you attach to each library-call definition.

The following code references the relevant public functions in this library and uses them to connect to the printer and send the requested data:

```
Imports System.Runtime.InteropServices

Public Class RawPrinter
    ' ----- Define the data type that supplies basic
    '       print job information to the spooler.
    <StructLayout(LayoutKind.Sequential, _
        CharSet:=CharSet.Unicode)> _
    Public Structure DOCINFO
        <MarshalAs(UnmanagedType.LPWStr)> _
            Public pDocName As String
        <MarshalAs(UnmanagedType.LPWStr)> _
            Public pOutputFile As String
        <MarshalAs(UnmanagedType.LPWStr)> _
            Public pDataType As String
    End Structure

    ' ----- Define interfaces to the functions supplied
    '       in the DLL.
    <DllImport("winspool.drv", EntryPoint:="OpenPrinterW", _
        SetLastError:=True, CharSet:=CharSet.Unicode, _
        ExactSpelling:=True, _
        CallingConvention:=CallingConvention.StdCall)> _
    Public Shared Function OpenPrinter( _
        ByVal printerName As String, ByRef hPrinter As IntPtr, _
        ByVal printerDefaults As Integer) As Boolean
    End Function

    <DllImport("winspool.drv", EntryPoint:="ClosePrinter", _
        SetLastError:=True, CharSet:=CharSet.Unicode, _
        ExactSpelling:=True, _
        CallingConvention:=CallingConvention.StdCall)> _
    Public Shared Function ClosePrinter( _
        ByVal hPrinter As IntPtr) As Boolean
    End Function

    <DllImport("winspool.drv", EntryPoint:="StartDocPrinterW", _
        SetLastError:=True, CharSet:=CharSet.Unicode, _
        ExactSpelling:=True, _
        CallingConvention:=CallingConvention.StdCall)> _
    Public Shared Function StartDocPrinter( _
        ByVal hPrinter As IntPtr, ByVal level As Integer, _
        ByRef documentInfo As DOCINFO) As Boolean
    End Function
```

```vbnet
<DllImport("winspool.drv", EntryPoint:="EndDocPrinter", _
   SetLastError:=True, CharSet:=CharSet.Unicode, _
   ExactSpelling:=True, _
   CallingConvention:=CallingConvention.StdCall)> _
Public Shared Function EndDocPrinter( _
   ByVal hPrinter As IntPtr) As Boolean
End Function

<DllImport("winspool.drv", EntryPoint:="StartPagePrinter", _
   SetLastError:=True, CharSet:=CharSet.Unicode, _
   ExactSpelling:=True, _
   CallingConvention:=CallingConvention.StdCall)> _
Public Shared Function StartPagePrinter( _
   ByVal hPrinter As IntPtr) As Boolean
End Function

<DllImport("winspool.drv", EntryPoint:="EndPagePrinter", _
   SetLastError:=True, CharSet:=CharSet.Unicode, _
   ExactSpelling:=True, _
   CallingConvention:=CallingConvention.StdCall)> _
Public Shared Function EndPagePrinter( _
   ByVal hPrinter As IntPtr) As Boolean
End Function

<DllImport("winspool.drv", EntryPoint:="WritePrinter", _
   SetLastError:=True, CharSet:=CharSet.Unicode, _
   ExactSpelling:=True, _
   CallingConvention:=CallingConvention.StdCall)> _
Public Shared Function WritePrinter( _
   ByVal hPrinter As IntPtr, ByVal buffer As IntPtr, _
   ByVal bufferLength As Integer, _
   ByRef bytesWritten As Integer) As Boolean
End Function

Public Shared Function PrintRaw( _
      ByVal printerName As String, _
      ByVal origString As String) As Boolean
   ' ----- Send a string of raw data to the printer.
   Dim hPrinter As IntPtr
   Dim spoolData As New DOCINFO
   Dim dataToSend As IntPtr
   Dim dataSize As Integer
   Dim bytesWritten As Integer

   ' ----- The internal format of a .NET String is just
   '       different enough from what the printer expects
   '       that there will be a problem if we send it
   '       directly. Convert it to ANSI format before
   '       sending.
   dataSize = origString.Length( )
   dataToSend = Marshal.StringToCoTaskMemAnsi(origString)

   ' ----- Prepare information for the spooler.
   spoolData.pDocName = "My Visual Basic .NET RAW Document"
   spoolData.pDataType = "RAW"
```

```
      Try
          ' ----- Open a channel to the printer or spooler.
          Call OpenPrinter(printerName, hPrinter, 0)

          ' ----- Start a new document and page 1.
          Call StartDocPrinter(hPrinter, 1, spoolData)
          Call StartPagePrinter(hPrinter)

          ' ----- Send the data to the printer.
          Call WritePrinter(hPrinter, dataToSend, _
             dataSize, bytesWritten)

          ' ----- Close everything that we opened.
          EndPagePrinter(hPrinter)
          EndDocPrinter(hPrinter)
          ClosePrinter(hPrinter)
      Catch ex As Exception
          MsgBox("Error occurred: " & ex.ToString)
      Finally
          ' ----- Get rid of the special ANSI version.
          Marshal.FreeCoTaskMem(dataToSend)
      End Try
   End Function
End Class
```

This class includes all shared members, so just call them directly without creating an instance. Use the `PrintRaw` method by passing it a printer name and raw data to send:

```
RawPrinter.PrintRaw("MyPrinter", _
    "Hello, this is a test." & vbCrLf)
```

You can use this to send data to network printers by supplying a printer path in the format \\SystemName\PrinterName.

See Also

The code in this recipe is based on a Microsoft-supplied Knowledge Base article. On the MSDN web site (*http://msdn.microsoft.com*), access article number 322090 for additional details on using the *winspool.drv* file from .NET.

11.3   Get Details About the Default Printer

Problem

You need to know some of the settings for the default printer installed on the local workstation, such as its name and page size.

Solution

Create a `PrintDocument` object, and use it to access the details for the default printer:

```
Dim justChecking As New System.Drawing.Printing.PrintDocument
MsgBox(justChecking.PrinterSettings.PrinterName)
```

Discussion

In .NET, printer settings exist in the context of a document to print. The PrintDocument object includes a PrinterSettings member that fully describes the printer target of the document. When you create a new print document, .NET fills in the settings for the default printer on the local workstation. If you want to examine the settings for another installed printer, modify the PrinterSettings.PrinterName property to indicate the desired printer:

```
With justChecking.PrinterSettings
    .PrinterName = "AnotherPrinter"
    If (.IsValid = True) Then
        ' ----- Look at the other settings.
    End If
End With
```

11.4   Creating a Print Preview

Problem

You want to present a preview of a printed document to the user.

Solution

Sample code folder: Chapter 11\PrintPreview

Use the PrintPreviewDialog class to show the print preview through a form that includes some basic presentation features.

Discussion

The following code displays a basic text string on a print preview document:

```
Imports System.Drawing.Printing

Public Class Form1
    Private WithEvents SampleDoc As Printing.PrintDocument

    Private Sub Button1_Click( _
            ByVal sender As System.Object, _
            ByVal e As System.EventArgs) Handles Button1.Click
        ' ----- Initiate a print preview.
        Dim previewMode As New PrintPreviewDialog

        ' ----- Create the document to preview.
        SampleDoc = New Printing.PrintDocument

        ' ----- Show the preview.
        previewMode.Document = SampleDoc
        previewMode.ShowDialog( )
    End Sub
```

```
Private Sub SampleDoc_PrintPage(ByVal sender As Object, _
        ByVal e As Printing.PrintPageEventArgs) _
        Handles SampleDoc.PrintPage
    ' ----- Generate a fun one-page document.
    e.Graphics.DrawString("Preview is Fun!", _
        New Font("Ariel", 48, FontStyle.Regular), _
        Brushes.Black, 0, 0)
    e.HasMorePages = False
End Sub
End Class
```

Running this sample code (by clicking on a button named Button1) results in the print preview window shown in Figure 11-1.

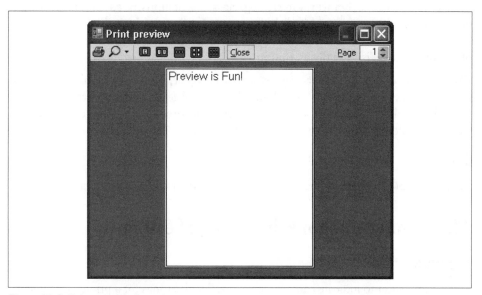

Figure 11-1. Print preview in action

The .NET Framework includes a generalized printing system that allows you to use the same code for both the previewing and the actual printing. All printing is done to a generic graphics surface within a PrintDocument object. .NET uses this surface to print to your printer's paper and to the artificial paper in the print preview form.

The PrintPreviewDialog class also comes in a Windows Forms–based control variation (see Figure 11-2). You can add this control and a related PrintDocument control to your form and generate the print preview that way, but it works just the same. You assign the PrintDocument control to the PrintPreviewDialog's Document property, and then respond to the PrintDocument's PrintPage event. It's the exact same code that appears in this recipe's solution; only the declarations of the PrintPreviewDialog and PrintDocument objects have moved from your source code to the form's surface.

Figure 11-2. The control version of the PrintPreviewDialog class

.NET includes two classes that let you preview your own printed documents. The easiest to use is the PrintPreviewDialog class, as demonstrated in this recipe. It defines a complete form, and it includes some useful controls in the form of a toolbar. But it's a one-size-fits-all solution. Altering the toolbar to include your own set of custom features isn't really an option.

The alternative uses the PrintPreviewControl class, or, more commonly, its equivalent Windows Forms control. By adding this control to an existing form along with any other toolbar-type controls you wish, you can provide an enhanced print preview experience custom-designed for your application.

See Also

Recipe 11.6 provides additional examples of using the PrintDocument class.

11.5   Prompting for Printed Page Settings

Problem

You want the user to indicate some basic paper-related settings for a printed document.

Solution

Use the PageSetupDialog class to prompt the user for these basic settings. The following code displays the Page Setup dialog for a basic print document:

```
Dim pageSetup As New PageSetupDialog
pageSetup.Document = New Printing.PrintDocument
pageSetup.ShowDialog( )
```

Discussion

The PageSetupDialog's ShowDialog( ) method presents the user with the basic Page Setup dialog shown in Figure 11-3. Its initial settings are based on the default printer, or the printer you have specified as the active printer.

The PageSetupDialog class encapsulates a complete form that lets the user set the page size, margins, source, and orientation for an upcoming print job. Normally, you

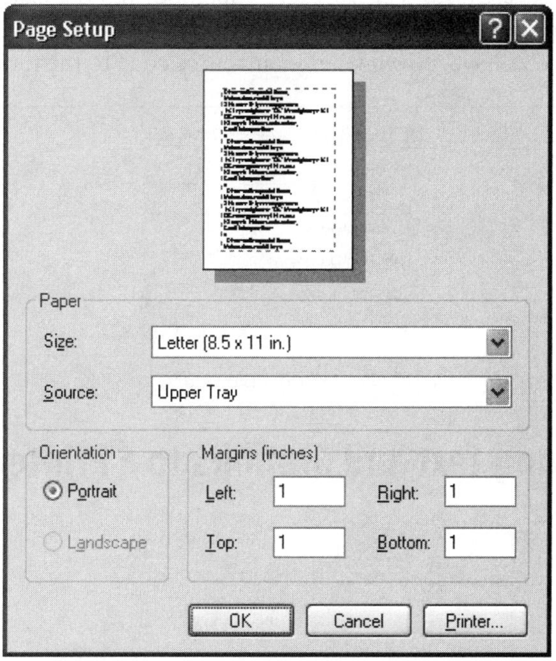

Figure 11-3. The Page Setup dialog

prompt for these settings for a specific document by setting the Document property to a valid PrintDocument object. However, you can also call this form generically by setting its PrinterSettings and PageSettings properties to valid PrinterSettings and PageSettings objects, and setting the printer name to your intended target (if different from the default):

```
Dim pageSetup As New Forms.PageSetupDialog
pageSetup.PageSettings = New Printing.PageSettings
pageSetup.PrinterSettings = New Printing.PrinterSettings

pageSetup.PrinterSettings.PrinterName = "\\MySystem\MyPrinter"
pageSetup.ShowDialog( )
```

Once set, you can assign these PrinterSettings and PageSettings objects to the matching properties in your PrintDocument object:

```
' ----- Assumes a Printing.PrintDocument object named
'       targetDocument.
targetDocument.PrinterSettings = pageSetup.PrinterSettings
targetDocument.DefaultPageSettings = pageSetup.PageSettings
```

The PageSetupDialog class also comes in a Windows Forms–based control variation (see Figure 11-4). You can add this control and a related PrintDocument control to your form and display the page settings that way, but it works just the same. You assign the PrintDocument control to the PageSetupDialog's Document property, and then call the PageSetupDialog's ShowDialog( ) method. It's the exact same code that appears in this recipe's solution; only the declarations of the PageSetupDialog and PrintDocument objects have moved from your source code to the form's surface.

Figure 11-4. The control version of the PageSetupDialog class

11.6   Drawing Text and Graphics to a Printer

Problem

You're ready to print. How do you do it?

Solution

Sample code folder: Chapter 11\TextAndGraphics

Respond to the various events of the PrintDocument object, especially the PrintPage event.

Discussion

The following code sends a two-page document to the default printer when the Button1 button is clicked. Each page includes some simple text and graphics:

```
Imports System.Drawing.Printing

Public Class Form1
    Private WithEvents SampleDoc As Printing.PrintDocument
    Private PageNumber As Integer

    Private Sub Button1_Click( _
            ByVal sender As System.Object, _
            ByVal e As System.EventArgs) Handles Button1.Click
        SampleDoc = New Printing.PrintDocument
        SampleDoc.Print( )
    End Sub

    Private Sub SampleDoc_BeginPrint(ByVal sender As Object, _
            ByVal e As System.Drawing.Printing.PrintEventArgs) _
            Handles SampleDoc.BeginPrint
        ' ----- Start the page counting.
        PageNumber = 0
    End Sub
```

```
Private Sub SampleDoc_PrintPage(ByVal sender As Object, _
    ByVal e As Printing.PrintPageEventArgs) _
    Handles SampleDoc.PrintPage
  ' ----- Keep track of the current page.
  PageNumber += 1
  If (PageNumber >= 2) Then e.HasMorePages = False Else _
    e.HasMorePages = True

  ' ----- Let's use inches, a nice easy measurement system.
  e.Graphics.PageUnit = GraphicsUnit.Inch

  ' ----- Print some text and rectangles.
  e.Graphics.DrawString("This is page " & PageNumber & _
    ".", New Font("Ariel", 48, FontStyle.Regular), _
    Brushes.Black, 2, 2)
  e.Graphics.DrawRectangle(New Pen(Color.Blue, 0.005), _
    3.0!, 3.0!, 3.0!, 0.5!)
  e.Graphics.DrawRectangle(New Pen(Color.Red, 0.005), _
    3.25!, 3.25!, 3.0!, 0.5!)
End Sub
End Class
```

This sample prints two pages similar to the pages in Figure 11-5.

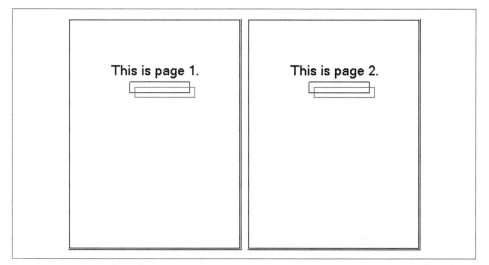

Figure 11-5. Output from the PrintPage event

Make sure that you include the WithEvents keyword in your PrintDocument variable's declaration, or you won't be able to attach an event handler with the Handles keyword.

All printing for a document occurs in the PrintDocument object's PrintPage event. This event includes an e.Graphics property that exposes a full GDI+ graphics drawing surface for a single document page. Use any of the GDI+ drawing methods (such as DrawString( ), FillPie( ), or DrawImage( )) or display transformation features (such as TranslateTransform( )) that you need to organize and print your page.

It's up to you to determine which pages should be included in the print document, and even which page numbers to use. The PrintDocument object does not know which pages should be included, so you need to do those calculations yourself, as was done in this recipe with the PageNumber class member. The PrintDocument. PrinterSettings object's PrintRange, FromPage, and ToPage properties indicate the user-selected pages to include in the output.

Printing will continue until you tell it to stop. The PrintPage event's e.HasMorePages property controls everything. Set it to True if there are more pages to print after the current page or to False when you are printing the last page.

Besides the PrintPage event, the PrintDocument object includes a few other useful events:

BeginPrint

This event fires before the first triggering of the PrintPage event. You can initialize any settings that apply to the entire print process here.

EndPrint

This closing event gives you a chance to free any resources you acquired during the print process. This event always occurs, even if the user aborted the printing early or if an error occurred.

QueryPageSettings

This event allows you to modify the page settings on a page-by-page basis. For instance, you could have all even pages appear in Portrait orientation while all odd pages print using Landscape orientation.

See Also

Chapter 9 includes examples of GDI+ features you can use on the graphics surface.

11.7   Determining the Print Destination

Problem

You want to slightly alter the output to the print surface when the user is printing to either the preview window or the actual printer.

Solution

Access the PrintDocument object's PrintController.IsPreview property during printing to determine if you are in preview mode or not.

Discussion

The following code prints a "preview only" message at the top of each page when printing in preview mode:

```
Private Sub SampleDoc_PrintPage(ByVal sender As Object, _
    ByVal e As Printing.PrintPageEventArgs) _
```

```
      Handles SampleDoc.PrintPage
   ' ----- Print a "preview only" message.
   If (SampleDoc.PrintController.IsPreview = True) Then _
      e.Graphics.DrawString("This is a preview only.", _
      New Font("Ariel", 12, FontStyle.Regular), _
      Brushes.Red, 0, 0)

      ' ----- Add other printing code here.
   End Sub
```

.NET includes two different ways to determine the print-preview status of the current PrintDocument object. The PrintDocument.PrintController.IsPreview property is a simple Boolean value that can be read at any time during the printing process.

During printing, you can also access the e.PrintAction property in the PrintDocument object's QueryPageSettings event to determine the printer-output target. This property uses the three possible values of the System.Drawing.Printing.PrintAction enumeration:

PrintToFile

The print document's output is going to a disk-based file.

PrintToPreview

The print document's output is going to a preview window using the PrintPreviewDialog or PrintPreviewControl classes.

PrintToPrinter

The print document's output is going to a physical printer based on the user's printing choices.

The following code checks the PrintAction flag for a PrintDocument object named SampleDoc and takes action based on its value:

```
   Private Sub SampleDoc_QueryPageSettings( _
      ByVal sender As Object, ByVal e As _
      System.Drawing.Printing.QueryPageSettingsEventArgs) _
      Handles SampleDoc.QueryPageSettings
   If (e.PrintAction = PrintAction.PrintToPreview) Then
      ' ----- Take preview-specific action here.
   End If
   End Sub
```

This property is available only from the QueryPageSettings event. If you want to access its value during the PrintPage event, you will have to save it in a class-level or global variable during the QueryPageSettings event.

The initial release of Version 2.0 of the .NET Framework (part of Visual Studio 2005) included a bug that caused the e.PrintAction flag to indicate the wrong value. Specifically, it never indicates PrintAction.PrintToPreview when in preview mode. Hopefully, by the time you read this recipe, a service pack or update that resolves this issue will be available for the .NET Framework.

11.8   Creating Graph Paper

Problem

You've run out of graph paper, but you need a sheet of it right now. You'd like to brush up on your .NET printing skills at the same time.

Solution

Sample code folder: Chapter 11\GraphPaper

Build a simple application that prints some graph paper for you, using the printing features presented throughout this chapter and various GDI+ methods.

Discussion

Create a new Windows Forms project, and add the following controls to the form:

- A RadioButton control named UseInches. Set its Text property to &Inches and its Checked property to True.
- A RadioButton control named UseCentimeters. Set its Text property to &Centimeters.
- A TextBox control named LinesPerUnit.
- A TextBox control named UnitsWide.
- A TextBox control named UnitsHigh.
- A Button control named ShowPreview. Set its Text property to Preview.
- A Button control named SendToPrinter. Set its Text property to Print.

Add informational labels if desired. The form should look something like the one in Figure 11-6.

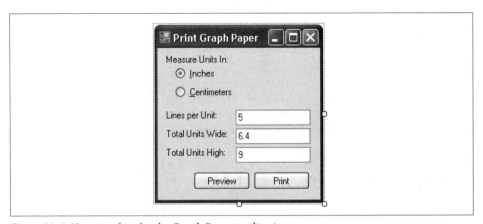

Figure 11-6. User interface for the Graph Paper application

Add the following source code to the form's class template:

```
Imports System.Drawing.Printing

Public Class Form1
    Private WithEvents GraphPaper As Printing.PrintDocument

    Private Sub ShowPreview_Click( _
            ByVal sender As System.Object, _
            ByVal e As System.EventArgs) _
            Handles ShowPreview.Click
        ' ----- Preview the graph paper.
        Dim previewMode As New PrintPreviewDialog

        GraphPaper = New Printing.PrintDocument
        previewMode.Document = GraphPaper
        previewMode.ShowDialog()
        GraphPaper = Nothing
    End Sub

    Private Sub SendToPrinter_Click( _
            ByVal sender As System.Object, _
            ByVal e As System.EventArgs) _
            Handles SendToPrinter.Click
        ' ----- Preview the graph paper.
        Dim pageSetup As New PageSetupDialog

        GraphPaper = New Printing.PrintDocument
        pageSetup.Document = GraphPaper
        If (pageSetup.ShowDialog() = _
            Windows.Forms.DialogResult.OK) Then _
            GraphPaper.Print()
        GraphPaper = Nothing
    End Sub

    Private Sub GraphPaper_PrintPage(ByVal sender As Object, _
            ByVal e As Printing.PrintPageEventArgs) _
            Handles GraphPaper.PrintPage
        ' ----- Printing of the graph paper occurs here.
        Dim unitLines As Single = CSng(LinesPerUnit.Text)
        Dim totalWidth As Single = CSng(UnitsWide.Text)
        Dim totalHeight As Single = CSng(UnitsHigh.Text)
        Dim x1, y1, x2, y2 As Single
        Dim fineBlackPen As New Pen(Color.Black, 0.00001)
        Dim eachLine As Integer
        Dim factor As Single

        ' ----- Set the units.
        If (UseInches.Checked = True) Then
            e.Graphics.PageUnit = GraphicsUnit.Inch
            factor = 1.0!
        Else
            e.Graphics.PageUnit = GraphicsUnit.Millimeter
            factor = 10.0!
        End If
```

```
' ----- Draw the vertical lines.
For eachLine = 0 To CInt(totalWidth * unitLines)
    x1 = factor + (eachLine * factor) / unitLines
    y1 = factor
    x2 = x1
    y2 = y1 + (totalHeight * factor)
    If ((eachLine Mod unitLines) = 0) Then
        ' ----- Each unit marker is thicker.
        fineBlackPen.Width = 0.01 * factor
    Else
        fineBlackPen.Width = 0.000001 * factor
    End If
    e.Graphics.DrawLine(fineBlackPen, x1, y1, x2, y2)
Next eachLine

' ----- Draw the horizontal lines.
For eachLine = 0 To CInt(totalHeight * unitLines)
    x1 = factor
    y1 = factor + (eachLine * factor) / unitLines
    x2 = x1 + (totalWidth * factor)
    y2 = y1
    If ((eachLine Mod unitLines) = 0) Then
        ' ----- Each unit marker is thicker.
        fineBlackPen.Width = 0.01 * factor
    Else
        fineBlackPen.Width = 0.000001 * factor
    End If
    e.Graphics.DrawLine(fineBlackPen, x1, y1, x2, y2)
Next eachLine

' ----- Limit output to a single page.
e.HasMorePages = False
    End Sub
End Class
```

This program builds on the recipes presented throughout this chapter. It creates distinct PrintDocument (with WithEvents specified), PrintPreviewDialog, and PageSetupDialog classes, and it responds to the print document's PrintPage event to perform the actual printing.

The code simply loops through the specified number of vertical and horizontal lines destined for the output based on the user's input, and draws lines at each interval position. The e.Graphics.PageUnit property lets the code easily process both English and metric measurement systems, although the lack of a basic centimeter unit requires the code to combine the millimeter unit with a scaling factor.

Files and File Systems

12.0 Introduction

One of the core features of any operating system is how it interacts with a file system. MS-DOS, the predecessor of Microsoft Windows, even alludes to this importance in its name: the "D" in "MS-DOS" stands for "Disk." With this stress on file systems and files, it's only natural that the .NET Framework includes significant support for manipulating directories, files, and the contents of files.

The recipes in this chapter introduce many of the file-management and -manipulation features found in .NET and Visual Basic. For the Visual Basic programmer, much of the focus is on the My.Computer.FileSystem object, which provides a virtual cornucopia of file-management features.

The Windows file system includes support for security and access limitations, imposed either by the administrator or by standard users. Even if a recipe in this chapter says, "You can do such and such," it may not be true for users who have had file-system limits placed on them or their programs. This is especially true of Click-Once-deployed applications, which can be run in a type of "sandbox" that places harsh limits on file access.

12.1 Enumerating Drives

Problem

You need access to the list of drives available on the local workstation.

Solution

Sample code folder: Chapter 12\EnumerateDrives

Use the My.Computer.FileSystem.Drives collection to enumerate through the logical drives.

Discussion

If you have a form (Form1) with a ListBox control (ListBox1), the following code adds the name of each available drive to the list when the form first opens:

```
Private Sub Form1_Load(ByVal sender As System.Object, _
    ByVal e As System.EventArgs) Handles MyBase.Load
  For Each oneDrive As IO.DriveInfo In _
      My.Computer.FileSystem.Drives
    ListBox1.Items.Add(oneDrive)
  Next oneDrive
End Sub
```

That code adds complete objects of type System.IO.DriveInfo to the list. If you only want to add the drive names, use this code instead:

```
Private Sub Form1_Load(ByVal sender As System.Object, _
    ByVal e As System.EventArgs) Handles MyBase.Load
  For Each oneDrive As IO.DriveInfo In _
      My.Computer.FileSystem.Drives
    ListBox1.Items.Add(oneDrive.Name)
  Next oneDrive
End Sub
```

Each added item appears as X:\, where X is replaced by the drive letter. Figure 12-1 shows the output of this code on a computer with just a "C" drive.

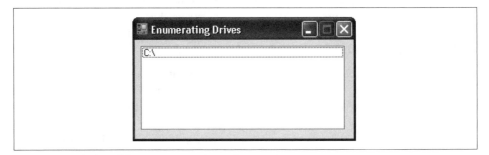

Figure 12-1. The list of drives on a typical one-drive workstation

The My.Computer.FileSystem.Drives collection provides access to details about each local or network drive attached to the workstation. Since it is a collection that exposes the IEnumerable interface, you can use it in a For Each statement, accessing each drive object in the collection.

The System.IO.DriveInfo object includes the following useful properties:

AvailableFreeSpace

> Returns the number of free bytes available to the current user on the drive. If the administrator has instituted disk quotas on the drive, this amount may be considerably less than the total available space on the drive.

DriveFormat

Returns a string indicating the file-system type. Common file systems available in Windows include NTFS, FAT, FAT32, and CDFS.

DriveType

Indicates the type of drive through the System.IO.DriveType enumeration. The most common drive types include Fixed, Removable, and CDRom.

IsReady

Returns a Boolean that indicates whether the drive is ready for use. Typically, this flag is accessed on CD drives to determine whether a CD is in the drive and ready to use.

Name

Gets the name of a drive, in *X*:\ format.

RootDirectory

Returns a System.IO.DirectoryInfo object that refers to the top-most directory of the drive. This property will not be valid if the DriveType property is set to NoRootDirectory.

TotalFreeSpace

Returns the number of free bytes available on the drive. Unlike the AvailableFreeSpace property, this property is not limited by any administrator-defined quotas.

TotalSize

Returns the total number of used and unused bytes on the drive. This property is not limited by any administrator-defined quotas.

VolumeLabel

Indicates the volume label currently assigned to the drive. If the drive supports it, you can modify the volume label by assigning a new String value to this property. Some drives impose length limits on the volume label.

See Also

Recipe 12.8 shows how to iterate directories within a drive.

12.2 Determining if a Directory Exists

Problem

The user has supplied a directory, and you want to confirm that it is valid before accessing it.

Solution

Sample code folder: Chapter 12\DirectoryExists

Use the `My.Computer.FileSystem.DirectoryExists( )` method to determine whether a directory exists or not. Pass the method a `String` containing the directory path to check for validity.

Discussion

To try out this feature, create a new Windows Forms application, and add a `TextBox` control named `TextBox1` and a `Button` control named `Button1` to the form. Now add the following code to the form's class template:

```
Private Sub Button1_Click(ByVal sender As System.Object, _
    ByVal e As System.EventArgs) Handles Button1.Click
  ' ----- Test for a valid directory.
  If (My.Computer.FileSystem.DirectoryExists( _
      TextBox1.Text)) Then
    MsgBox("The directory already exists.")
  Else
    MsgBox("The directory does not exist, " & _
      "or is part of an invalid path.")
  End If
End Sub
```

Figure 12-2 shows this form in use.

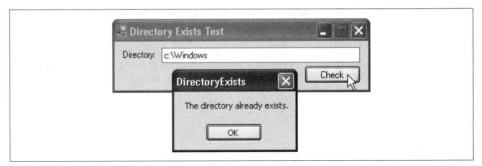

Figure 12-2. Testing a directory to see if it exists

The `DirectoryExists( )` method checks for the actual presence of a directory, not just for a valid directory-name format. It works with three types of drive paths:

- Absolute paths referenced from a drive letter, as in *C:\WINDOWS*.

- Absolute paths referenced through UNC syntax, as in *\\system\share\directory*.

- Relative paths referenced from the current directory as understood by the running application, as in *..\AnotherDirectory*. You can start the path with the current directory (.) or parent directory (..) indicators, or with the name of a directory assumed to be found in the current directory. Use the `My.Computer.FileSystem.CurrentDirectory` property to determine or modify the current directory location.

URL-based directory paths, using the "file://" prefix, cannot be used with this method or with most of the features in `My.Computer.FileSystem`. Security restrictions in effect for the current user may prevent access to certain portions of a file system.

See Also

Recipe 12.10 shows how to determine if a file exists.

12.3   Creating a New Directory

Problem

You need to create a new directory to store user or application data.

Solution

Sample code folder: Chapter 12\NewDirectory

Use the `My.Computer.FileSystem.CreateDirectory( )` method to create the new directory. Pass the method a `String` containing the directory path to create.

Discussion

To try out this feature, create a new Windows Forms application, and add a `TextBox` control named `TextBox1` and a `Button` control named `Button1` to the form. Now add the following code to the form's class template:

```
Private Sub Button1_Click(ByVal sender As System.Object, _
      ByVal e As System.EventArgs) Handles Button1.Click
   ' ----- The user must supply a directory.
   If (Trim(TextBox1.Text) = "") Then
      MsgBox("Please supply a directory.")
      TextBox1.Focus( )
      Exit Sub
   End If

   ' ----- Create the directory requested by the user.
   If (My.Computer.FileSystem.DirectoryExists( _
         TextBox1.Text)) Then
      MsgBox("The directory already exists.")
   Else
      Try
         My.Computer.FileSystem.CreateDirectory(TextBox1.Text)
         MsgBox("Directory created successfully.")
      Catch ex As Exception
```

```
        MsgBox("The directory could not be created due " & _
            "to the following error:" & _
            vbCrLf & vbCrLf & ex.Message)
        End Try
    End If
End Sub
```

The CreateDirectory( ) method accepts either absolute or relative paths in drive-letter or UNC format, but not URL-based "file://" paths. If the directory cannot be created, CreateDirectory( ) generates an exception.

A variation of this method exists through the System.IO.Directory.CreateDirectory( ) function. This function returns a System.IO.DirectoryInfo object for the newly created directory object. It also includes a second overload that accepts security settings for the new directory.

12.4   Copying Directories

Problem

You need to copy the contents of an existing directory to a new location, leaving the original directory intact.

Solution

Use the My.Computer.FileSystem.CopyDirectory( ) method to copy the contents of a directory from one place to another.

Discussion

The basic syntax of the CopyDirectory( ) method is:

```
My.Computer.FileSystem.CopyDirectory( _
    sourceDirectory, destDirectory)
```

The sourceDirectory argument contains an absolute UNC-based or drive-letter-based path, or a relative path based on the current directory from the application's point of view. The destDirectory argument is also an absolute or relative path, although it may not appear hierarchically within the source directory. For example:

```
My.Computer.FileSystem.CopyDirectory( _
    "C:\WorkFiles", "C:\PlayFiles")
```

The duplication of the source directory is complete, creating copies of all subordinate files and directories to any depth.

If the destination directory does not exist, CopyDirectory( ) creates it, including any nonexistent path components between the specified root and the final directory. If the destination directory is already present, any existing files at the destination remain intact, and new files are copied in amongst them, resulting in a merged destination directory. If one of the files to be copied already exists at the destination, CopyDirectory( ) generates an exception. If you want it to overwrite any matching files at the destination silently, use the optional third argument—the overwrite argument—passing a value of True:

```
My.Computer.FileSystem.CopyDirectory( _
    sourceDirectory, destDirectory, True)
```

A variation of CopyDirectory( ) uses a different set of arguments to control the display of on-screen prompts and status notifications during the copy:

```
My.Computer.FileSystem.CopyDirectory( _
    sourceDirectory, destDirectory, _
    showUI [, onUserCancel])
```

The showUI argument accepts one of the following Microsoft.VisualBasic.FileIO. UIOption enumeration values:

UIOption.AllDialogs

> An animated progress dialog appears during the directory copy to indicate the current status as each file is copied. (The dialog might not appear for copies that involve a small amount of content.) Any errors that occur present their own separate error-dialog prompts.

UIOption.OnlyErrorDialogs

> While errors will appear through distinct error-dialog prompts, no animated status display appears, no matter how long the copy takes. This is the default method.

If you include the fourth onUserCancel argument, you provide it one of the following Microsoft.VisualBasic.UICancelOption enumeration values:

UICancelOption.DoNothing

> The on-screen status display during a copy operation includes a Cancel button. If the user clicks the Cancel button when the DoNothing option is in effect, the code calling CopyDirectory( ) will not receive any notification that the copy was aborted early.

UICancelOption.ThrowException

> If the user clicks the Cancel button on the directory copy status dialog when ThrowException is used, the CopyDirectory( ) method generates a System.IOException exception, which can be caught by the initiating code. This is the default method.

See Also

See Recipe 12.19 for details on copying individual files instead of whole directories.

12.5 Moving Directories

Problem

You need to move a directory from one location to another.

Solution

Use the `My.Computer.FileSystem.MoveDirectory( )` method to relocate an existing directory from one place to another.

Discussion

The basic syntax of the `MoveDirectory( )` method is:

```
My.Computer.FileSystem.MoveDirectory( _
    sourceDirectory, destDirectory)
```

The `sourceDirectory` argument contains an absolute UNC-based or drive-letter-based path, or a relative path based on the current directory from the application's point of view. The `destDirectory` argument is also an absolute or relative path, although it may not appear hierarchically within the source directory. For example:

```
My.Computer.FileSystem.MoveDirectory( _
    "C:\WorkFiles", "C:\PlayFiles")
```

If the destination directory does not exist, `MoveDirectory( )` creates it, including any nonexistent path components between the specified root and the final directory.

If all but the final directory component of the source and destination directories are the same, `MoveDirectory( )` acts like a simple directory rename operation. The `My.Computer.FileSystem.RenameDirectory( )` method may provide a clearer method of renaming directories within the same parent directory.

The movement of the source directory is complete, moving all subordinate files and directories to any depth. Also, you can move a directory between different logical disk drives.

The `MoveDirectory( )` method creates the target directory if it does not yet exist. If the destination directory is already present, any existing files at the destination remain intact, and new files are moved in amongst them, resulting in a merged destination directory. If one of the files to be moved already exists at the destination, `MoveDirectory( )` generates an exception. If you want it to overwrite any matching files at the destination silently, use the optional third argument—the `overwrite` argument—passing a value of `True`:

```
My.Computer.FileSystem.MoveDirectory( _
    sourceDirectory, destDirectory, True)
```

A variation of MoveDirectory( ) uses a different set of arguments to control the display of on-screen prompts and status notifications during the directory move:

```
My.Computer.FileSystem.MoveDirectory( _
    sourceDirectory, destDirectory, _
    showUI [, onUserCancel])
```

The showUI argument accepts one of the following Microsoft.VisualBasic.FileIO. UIOption enumeration values:

UIOption.AllDialogs

> An animated progress dialog appears during the directory move to indicate the current status as each file is moved. (The dialog might not appear for moves that involve a small amount of content.) Any errors that occur present their own separate error-dialog prompts.

UIOption.OnlyErrorDialogs

> While errors will appear through distinct error-dialog prompts, no animated status display appears, no matter how long the move takes. This is the default method.

If you include the fourth onUserCancel argument, you provide it one of the following Microsoft.VisualBasic.UICancelOption enumeration values:

UICancelOption.DoNothing

> The on-screen status display during a move operation includes a Cancel button. If the user clicks the Cancel button when the DoNothing option is in effect, the code calling MoveDirectory( ) will not receive any notification that the move was aborted early.

UICancelOption.ThrowException

> If the user clicks the Cancel button on the directory move status dialog when ThrowException is used, the MoveDirectory( ) method generates a System.IOException exception, which can be caught by the initiating code. This is the default method.

See Also

Recipe 12.4 shows how to copy an existing directory instead of moving it. To rename a directory without moving it to another parent directory, see Recipe 12.6.

12.6   Renaming Directories

Problem

You need to rename a directory, but it's not really a directory move because the renamed directory will stay in the same parent directory.

Solution

Use the `My.Computer.FileSystem.RenameDirectory( )` method to change the name of an existing directory.

Discussion

The basic syntax of the RenameDirectory( ) method is:

```
My.Computer.FileSystem.RenameDirectory( _
    sourceDirectory, newName)
```

The sourceDirectory argument contains an absolute UNC-based or drive-letter-based path, or a relative path based on the current directory from the application's point of view. The newName argument includes only the new name of the final directory component; you cannot supply an absolute or relative path for this argument. The following statement is valid:

```
My.Computer.FileSystem.MoveDirectory( _
    "C:\WorkFiles", "PlayFiles")
```

This statement is not:

```
' ----- This statement will fail.
My.Computer.FileSystem.MoveDirectory( _
    "C:\WorkFiles", "C:\PlayFiles")
```

If a directory already exists with the new name, RenameDirectory( ) generates an exception, even if that target directory is empty.

Visual Basic includes an intrinsic function, Rename( ), which can also rename directories. Its syntax is slightly different because its second argument accepts either a new non-path name or any valid path:

```
' ----- Both of these statements will work.
Rename("C:\WorkFiles", "PlayFiles")
Rename("C:\WorkFiles", "C:\PlayFiles")
```

The Rename( ) function also moves a directory to another existing directory tree if requested:

```
Rename("C:\Temp\Important\LogFiles\OldLogs", _
    "C:\Temp\Archive\LogFiles")
```

Generally, the features exposed through the My namespace enhance features already found elsewhere. However, this is one of those times when the older feature provides a more flexible interface. Still, for consistency in new code, you will probably want to use RenameDirectory( ).

See Also

To move a directory to a different parent directory, see Recipe 12.5.

12.7 Parsing File and Directory Paths

Problem

You need to extract a directory name from a full path to a file or get just the file-name portion, and you don't want to mess with all of those backslashes.

Solution

Use the path-parsing methods found in the `My.Computer.FileSystem` object: `CombinePath( )`, `GetName( )`, and `GetParentPath( )`.

Discussion

As a programmer, you spend a lot of time manipulating string data. The .NET Framework has taken on itself some of the burden involved in specific types of string management. XML is a good example: you can use the XML objects included in .NET instead of stringing together the various components yourself. .NET provides similar convenience features for path-string manipulation.

The `My` namespace includes three methods designed to help you manage path strings. None of them compares the supplied paths to existing files or directories on the local or network file system; they are purely string-manipulation methods. Here are the methods:

`My.Computer.FileSystem.CombinePath( )`

The `CombinePath( )` method accepts an absolute path and a relative path to attach to the end of the absolute path. It returns the combined path with the relative part attached to the end of the absolute part, with any necessary "\" characters added where needed. The relative part may be a directory name or a filename. For example:

```
Dim newPath As String = _
    My.Computer.FileSystem.CombinePath( _
    "C:\temp", "WorkFiles\TodaysWork.txt")
MsgBox(newPath)
    ' Displays: "C:\temp\WorkFiles\TodaysWork.txt"
```

If you provide a relative path for the first "absolute" argument, `CombinePath( )` first modifies the argument so that it indicates a directory within the current directory as understood by the application. For instance, if the current directory is *C:\temp*, the statement:

```
MsgBox(My.Computer.FileSystem.CombinePath( _
    "part1", "part2")
```

displays `C:\temp\part1\part2`.

```
My.Computer.FileSystem.GetName( )
```
This method extracts the final component of a supplied path and returns it:

```
' ----- Displays: part2
MsgBox(My.Computer.FileSystem.GetName( _
    "C:\temp\part1\part2"))
```

You can supply absolute or relative paths to the GetName( ) function. The result of the function is always the final path component of whatever string you send.

```
My.Computer.FileSystem.GetParentPath( )
```
The GetParentPath( ) method returns everything except the final component of a supplied path. That is, it returns the directory that contains the final path component. If there is a trailing backslash, it is removed:

```
' ----- Displays: C:\temp\part1
MsgBox(My.Computer.FileSystem.GetParentPath( _
    "C:\temp\part1\part2"))
```

You can supply absolute or relative paths to the GetParentPath( ) function. The result of the function is always the parent-path component of whatever string you send. If you provide a string that contains only a single relative component (such as "MyDirectory" or ".."), this function returns a zero-length string.

Although these three methods deal exclusively with strings and not with actual paths, they do perform some minimal text analysis to ensure you process valid paths. If you attempt to use Unix-style forward slashes ("/") in your paths instead of the Windows-style backslash ("\"), these methods convert all "/" characters to "\" before generating results. Also, these methods raise an exception if you supply a URI-based file path (as in *file://system/directory/file*).

12.8   Searching Iteratively Through Directories and Subdirectories

Problem

You need to recursively traverse a directory tree and identify all subdirectory names.

Solution

Sample code folder: Chapter 12\IterateDirectories

Recursively call the My.Computer.FileSystem.GetDirectories( ) method to scan each subdirectory and its contents in order.

Discussion

This recipe's sample code fills in a TreeView control with all subdirectories and directory descendants of a specified base path.

In a new Windows Forms project, add a TextBox control named StartPath, a Button control named ActTraverse, and a TreeView control named PathTree to Form1. You can add labels and provide meaningful captions if you wish, as is done in Figure 12-3.

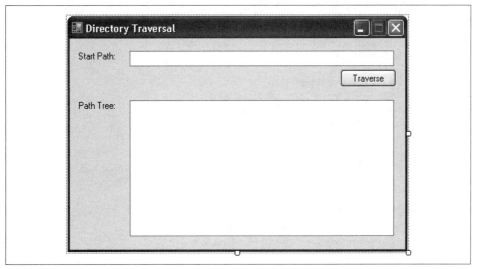

Figure 12-3. Controls for the directory traversal sample

Now add the following source code to the form's class template:

```
Private Sub ActTraverse_Click(ByVal sender As System.Object, _
      ByVal e As System.EventArgs) Handles ActTraverse.Click
   ' ----- Make sure the supplied path is valid.
   If (My.Computer.FileSystem.DirectoryExists( _
         StartPath.Text) = False) Then
      MsgBox("Please supply a valid directory path.", _
         MsgBoxStyle.OkOnly Or MsgBoxStyle.Exclamation, _
         "Invalid Path")
      Exit Sub
   End If

   ' ----- Clear any previous tree.
   PathTree.Nodes.Clear( )

   ' ----- Call the scanning routine, a recursive routine.
   BuildDirectoryTree(Nothing, StartPath.Text)
End Sub

Private Sub BuildDirectoryTree(ByVal fromNode As TreeNode, _
      ByVal basePath As String)
   ' ----- Attach all of the subdirectories found in
   '         basePath to the supplied node. If fromNode is
   '         Nothing, create root entries.
```

```
Dim newDirectory As TreeNode
Dim justTheSubdirectory As String

' ----- Retrieve all directories in this path.
For Each oneDirectory As String In _
        My.Computer.FileSystem.GetDirectories(basePath)
    ' ----- Extract just the final directory name.
    justTheSubdirectory = My.Computer.FileSystem.GetName( _
        oneDirectory)

    If (fromNode Is Nothing) Then
        ' ----- Add a top-level subdirectory.
        newDirectory = PathTree.Nodes.Add( _
            justTheSubdirectory)
    Else
        ' ----- Add a subordinate node.
        newDirectory = fromNode.Nodes.Add( _
            justTheSubdirectory)
    End If

    ' ----- Recurse into the subdirectory.
    BuildDirectoryTree(newDirectory, My.Computer.FileSystem. _
        CombinePath(basePath, justTheSubdirectory))
Next oneDirectory
End Sub
```

To use the program, type a valid directory path into the StartPath field, then click ActTraverse to build the subdirectory tree structure. Figure 12-4 shows this program traversing the Visual Studio installation directory.

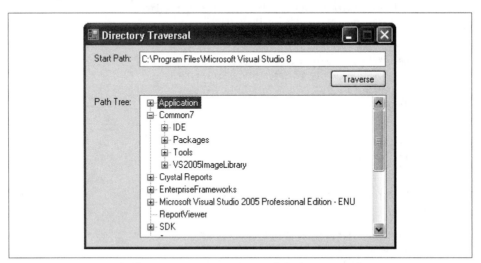

Figure 12-4. Iteration of a directory ("Common7" expanded after traversal)

This code uses several of the path-manipulation features found in the `My.Computer.FileSystem` object, including the `GetDirectories()` method, which returns a list of subdirectory path strings within the supplied parent directory.

Because you cannot know in advance how deep the nesting is for subdirectories, you can't hardcode a specific limit into the routine. By using a *recursive* function—a function that calls itself—you can effectively nest to any depth required. `BuildDirectoryTree()` adds a list of subdirectories in a base parent directory to the `TreeView` control. When it encounters a directory, it first adds it to the `TreeView` control and then calls itself, using the just-added subdirectory as the new base path. That call adds all sub-subdirectories to the just-added subdirectory node. Each of those sub-subdirectories, in turn, calls `BuildDirectoryTree()` yet again to attach its own nested directories. And on it goes, until `BuildDirectoryTree()` reaches a directory with no child directories. At that point, the innermost call to `BuildDirectoryTree()` exits, returning to the previous call. As each level runs out of subdirectories, control is returned up the call stack until the code returns to the initial `ActTraverse_Click` event handler.

See Also

For information on parsing file and directory paths, see Recipe 12.7.

12.9   Finding Directories and Files Using Wildcards

Problem

You need to generate a list of all files and subdirectories in a specific parent directory that have names matching a designated pattern.

Solution

Sample code folder: Chapter 12\UsingWildcards

Use the wildcard features of the `My.Computer.FileSystem.GetFiles()` and `My.Computer.FileSystem.GetDirectories()` methods to retrieve the matching file and directory names.

Discussion

This recipe's sample code fills in a `ListBox` control with all matching directories and files of a specified base path, based on a pattern.

Begin a new Windows Forms project, and add two `TextBox` controls named `StartPath` and `PathPattern`, a `Button` control named `ActMatch`, and a `ListBox` control named `MatchResults` to `Form1`. You can add labels and provide meaningful captions if you wish, as is done in Figure 12-5.

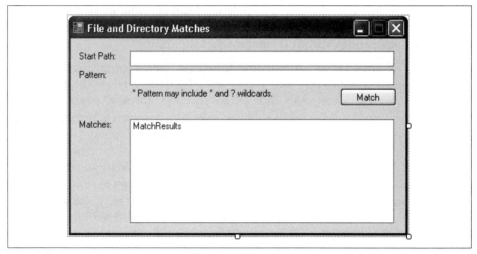

Figure 12-5. Controls for the name-matching sample

Now add the following source code to the form's class template:

```
Private Sub ActMatch_Click(ByVal sender As System.Object, _
      ByVal e As System.EventArgs) Handles ActMatch.Click
   ' ----- Make sure the supplied path is valid.
   If (My.Computer.FileSystem.DirectoryExists( _
         StartPath.Text) = False) Then
      MsgBox("Please supply a valid directory path.", _
         MsgBoxStyle.OkOnly Or MsgBoxStyle.Exclamation, _
         "Invalid Path")
      Exit Sub
   End If

   ' ----- Clear any previous items.
   MatchResults.Items.Clear()

   ' ----- First, add in the subdirectories.
   For Each oneItem As String In _
         My.Computer.FileSystem.GetDirectories( _
         StartPath.Text, _
         FileIO.SearchOption.SearchTopLevelOnly, _
         PathPattern.Text)
      MatchResults.Items.Add("[" & _
         My.Computer.FileSystem.GetName(oneItem) & "]")
   Next oneItem

   ' ----- Second, add in the files.
   For Each oneItem As String In _
         My.Computer.FileSystem.GetFiles(StartPath.Text, _
         FileIO.SearchOption.SearchTopLevelOnly, _
         PathPattern.Text)
      MatchResults.Items.Add( _
```

```
                My.Computer.FileSystem.GetName(oneItem))
        Next oneItem
    End Sub
```

To use the program, type a valid directory path into the StartPath field, type a pattern (such as "*.txt") in the PathPattern field, and then click ActMatch to build the list of matching file and directory names. Figure 12-6 shows this form in use, listing files matching the "*.log" pattern.

Figure 12-6. Displaying files matching a wildcard pattern

The My.Computer.FileSystem.GetFiles() and parallel GetDirectories() methods normally return a list of all files or directories in a specified parent path:

```
' ----- Return all files in C:\Windows
For Each oneFile As String In _
    My.Computer.FileSystem.GetFiles("C:\Windows")
```

However, both methods allow you to pass one or more "wildcard" pattern strings to limit the return list to just those items that match the pattern(s):

```
' ----- Return all "LOG" files in C:\Windows
For Each oneFile As String In _
    My.Computer.FileSystem.GetFiles("C:\Windows", _
    FileIO.SearchOption.SearchTopLevelOnly, _
    "*.LOG")
```

The syntax is identical for GetDirectories(), but it returns a list of matching directories instead of files. The second argument indicates the depth to search for name matches. FileIO.SearchOption.SearchTopLevelOnly returns only matches found directly within the specified parent path. To include all subdirectories, use the FileIO.SearchOption.SearchAllSubDirectories value instead.

The third wildcard argument accepts any string that includes zero or more wildcard characters. The "*" wildcard matches zero or more characters at the position where it appears. The "?" wildcard matches exactly one character at the position where it appears.

If you need to simultaneously match more than one pattern and return all files (or directories) that match any of the patterns, include each pattern as a separate argument:

```
' ----- Return all "LOG" and "TXT" files in C:\Windows
For Each oneFile As String In _
    My.Computer.FileSystem.GetFiles("C:\Windows", _
    FileIO.SearchOption.SearchTopLevelOnly, _
    "*.LOG", "*.TXT")
```

See Also

Recipe 12.8 looks at how to recursively traverse a directory tree and identify all subdirectory names.

12.10 Determining If a File Exists

Problem

You have a file path supplied by the user, but you need to verify that it is valid before using it.

Solution

Use the My.Computer.FileSystem.FileExists( ) method to determine whether a path string is a valid file or not:

```
If (My.Computer.FileSystem.FileExists( _
    userSuppliedPath) = True) Then
  MsgBox("Invalid file specified.")
Else
  ' ----- Process file here.
End If
```

Discussion

If you wish to validate a directory instead of a file, use the equivalent DirectoryExists( ) method:

```
If (My.Computer.FileSystem.DirectoryExists( _
    userSuppliedPath) = True) Then
  MsgBox("Invalid directory specified.")
Else
  ' ----- Process directory here.
End If
```

See Also

Several of the recipes in this chapter use `FileExists( )` before attempting access to a user-specified path.

Recipe 12.2 discusses the `DirectoryExists( )` method.

12.11 Getting and Setting File Attributes

Problem

You want to view and modify some of the file-level attributes for a specific file.

Solution

Sample code folder: Chapter 12\FileAttributes

Use the `Attributes` property of a file's `System.IO.FileInfo` object to interact with the attributes defined for that file. You can get a `FileInfo` object for a specific file through the `My.Computer.FileSystem.GetFileInfo( )` method.

Discussion

This recipe's sample code lets you view and update the Read Only and Hidden attributes for any specific file.

Begin a new Windows Forms project, and add a `TextBox` control named `FilePath`, two `Button` controls named `ActGet` and `ActSet`, and two `CheckBox` controls named `FileReadOnly` and `FileHidden` to `Form1`. You can add labels and provide meaningful captions if you wish, as is done in Figure 12-7.

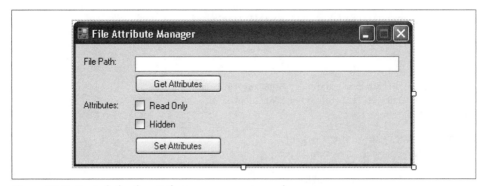

Figure 12-7. Controls for the attribute management sample

Set the `Enabled` properties of the `FileReadOnly`, `FileHidden`, and `ActSet` controls to `False`. Now add the following source code to the form's class template:

```
Private Sub ActGet_Click(ByVal sender As System.Object, _
    ByVal e As System.EventArgs) Handles ActGet.Click
```

```
          ' ----- Locate the file and its attributes.
        If (My.Computer.FileSystem.FileExists(FilePath.Text) _
               = False) Then
           MsgBox("Please supply a valid file.", _
              MsgBoxStyle.OkOnly Or MsgBoxStyle.Exclamation, _
              "Invalid File")
           Exit Sub
        End If

          ' ----- Get the file's attributes.
        Dim fileDetail As IO.FileInfo = _
           My.Computer.FileSystem.GetFileInfo(FilePath.Text)
        FileReadOnly.Checked = fileDetail.IsReadOnly
        FileHidden.Checked = CBool(fileDetail.Attributes _
           And IO.FileAttributes.Hidden)
        FileReadOnly.Enabled = True
        FileHidden.Enabled = True
        ActSet.Enabled = True
     End Sub

     Private Sub ActSet_Click(ByVal sender As System.Object, _
           ByVal e As System.EventArgs) Handles ActSet.Click
        ' ----- Modify the settings of the active file.
        Dim fileDetail As IO.FileInfo = _
           My.Computer.FileSystem.GetFileInfo(FilePath.Text)

          ' ----- Set the read-only flag the easy way.
        fileDetail.IsReadOnly = FileReadOnly.Checked

          ' ----- Set the hidden flag.
        If (FileHidden.Checked = True) Then
           fileDetail.Attributes = fileDetail.Attributes _
              Or IO.FileAttributes.Hidden
        Else
           fileDetail.Attributes = fileDetail.Attributes _
              And Not IO.FileAttributes.Hidden
        End If

          ' ----- Finished.
        MsgBox("Attributes updated.", MsgBoxStyle.OkOnly _
           Or MsgBoxStyle.Information, "Attributes")
     End Sub

     Private Sub FilePath_TextChanged( _
           ByVal sender As System.Object, _
           ByVal e As System.EventArgs) _
           Handles FilePath.TextChanged
        ' ----- Clear the previous file's attributes.
        If (ActSet.Enabled = True) Then
           ActSet.Enabled = False
           FileReadOnly.Enabled = False
           FileHidden.Enabled = False
```

```
        FileReadOnly.Checked = False
        FileHidden.Checked = False
    End If
End Sub
```

To use the program, type a valid directory path into the FilePath field, and click the ActGet button. The FileReadOnly and FileHidden fields will update to show the current attributes for the specified file. Modify these two fields as needed, and then click the ActSet button to modify the file attributes.

The System.IO.FileInfo object abstracts access to all information about a file. Once you have the path to the file, use the following statement to retrieve the FileInfo object:

```
Dim fileDetail As IO.FileInfo = _
    My.Computer.FileSystem.GetFileInfo(theFilePath)
```

The FileInfo object exposes an Attributes property that acts as a *bit field* for the System.IO.FileAttributes enumeration. (Bit fields use the bitwise operators, including And, Or, and Not, to store multiple enumeration values in a single integer variable.) The FileAttributes enumeration includes several members, but here are the four most commonly used when working with files and directories:

- FileAttributes.Archive
- FileAttributes.Directory
- FileAttributes.Hidden
- FileAttributes.ReadOnly

This chapter's sample code examines the bits of the FileInfo.Attributes property to determine whether the file is hidden or not:

```
FileHidden.Checked = CBool(fileDetail.Attributes _
    And IO.FileAttributes.Hidden)
```

Since the FileInfo object also exposes a simple IsReadOnly property, the code uses that to set the Read Only flag, although it could have examined the Attributes property for the FileAttributes.ReadOnly bit instead.

Later, those same IsReadOnly and Attributes properties are set with updated values to modify the attributes assigned to the actual file.

12.12 Accessing Special User and Windows Directories

Problem

You would like to access some of the Windows-defined special directories, such as *My Documents*, but you're not sure where they are.

Solution

Fortunately, you don't have to know where they really are. You need to access only the members of the `My.Computer.FileSystem.SpecialDirectories` object.

Discussion

Microsoft Windows uses several "special" directories to store user and system files. The locations of these directories are generally consistent across workstations of a certain platform (such as Windows XP), but users and administrators can alter some of the paths, and some of the paths differ between operating system releases. (Windows Vista will make several location changes to these paths.)

The `My.Computer.FileSystem.SpecialDirectories` object includes these member properties. Directory components appearing in angle brackets, such as *<user>*, should be substituted by the relevant values, such as the username in the case of *<user>*. The properties listed in the `SpecialDirectories` object include:

AllUsersApplicationData
> The shared application data-storage directory used by all authorized users who log in to the workstation. In Windows XP, this directory is typically found at *C:\ Documents and Settings\All Users\Application Data.*

CurrentUserApplicationData
> The data-storage directory assigned to a specific authorized user and to the currently running .NET application on the workstation. This directory is considered part of the active user's "roaming" profile. In Windows XP, this directory is typically found at *C:\Documents and Settings\<user>\Application Data\ <company>\<application>\<version>.*

Desktop
> The full path to the current authorized user's *Desktop* directory, which defines the items appearing on the Windows desktop. In Windows XP, this directory is typically found at *C:\Documents and Settings\<user>\Desktop.*

MyDocuments
> The *My Documents* directory, used for general file storage by the current authorized user. In Windows XP, this directory is typically found at *C:\Documents and Settings\<user>\My Documents.*

MyMusic
> The *My Music* directory, used to store standard and digital-rights-protected audio data files for the current authorized user. In Windows XP, this directory is typically found at *C:\Documents and Settings\<user>\My Documents\My Music.*

MyPictures
> The *My Pictures* directory, used to store digital images and video content for the current authorized user. In Windows XP, this directory is typically found at *C:\ Documents and Settings\<user>\My Documents\My Pictures.*

ProgramFiles

The default software product installation directory used by all authorized users on the workstation. In Windows XP, this directory is typically found at *C:\ Program Files*.

Programs

The *Programs* directory for the current authorized user's Start menu. In Windows XP, this directory is typically found at *C:\Documents and Settings\<user>\ Start Menu\Programs*.

Temp

The temporary directory used by the current authorized user to store short-lived caching and logging data files. In Windows XP, this directory is typically found at *C:\Documents and Settings\<user>\Local Settings\Temp*.

There are several special Windows directories—directories defined both for the current user and for shared use among all users—that do not have equivalent properties listed in the SpecialDirectories object. The System.Environment object provides access to some of these special directories not made available through the My. Computer.FileSystem.SpecialDirectories object. For instance, to access the *System* directory on the local workstation (defined on my workstation as *C:\WINDOWS\ System32*), use the following property:

```
System.Environment.SystemDirectory
```

You can access other special directory locations with the System.Environment. GetFolderPath( ) method, passing it one of the System.Environment.SpecialFolder enumeration values:

```
' ----- Display the user's "Favorites" directory.
MsgBox(System.Environment.GetFolderPath( _
    Environment.SpecialFolder.Favorites))
```

The System.Environment.SpecialFolder enumeration includes the members listed below. We have listed the typical location for each member as found on a Windows XP Professional workstation. Directory components appearing in angle brackets, such as *<user>*, should be substituted by the relevant values, such as the username in the case of *<user>*.

SpecialFolder.ApplicationData

A directory containing roaming application data for the current user.

C:\Documents and Settings\<user>\Application Data

SpecialFolder.CommonApplicationData

A directory containing shared application data for all users on the local workstation.

C:\Documents and Settings\All Users\Application Data

`SpecialFolder.CommonProgramFiles`

A directory containing shared files used by multiple installed applications.

C:\Program Files\Common Files

`SpecialFolder.Cookies`

A directory containing Internet-based cookies for the current user.

C:\Documents and Settings\<user>\Cookies

`SpecialFolder.Desktop`

The *logical* location of the *Desktop* directory, which is often the same as the physical location, but not always.

C:\Documents and Settings\<user>\Desktop

`SpecialFolder.DesktopDirectory`

The *physical* location of the *Desktop* directory, which is often the same as the logical location, but not always.

C:\Documents and Settings\<user>\Desktop

`SpecialFolder.Favorites`

A directory containing shortcuts to the user's favorite Internet-based and local items.

C:\Documents and Settings\<user>\Favorites

`SpecialFolder.History`

A directory containing a set of web-site shortcuts for recently visited locations.

C:\Documents and Settings\<user>\Local Settings\History

`SpecialFolder.InternetCache`

A directory containing content recently accessed over the Internet.

C:\Documents and Settings\<user>\Local Settings\Temporary Internet Files

`SpecialFolder.LocalApplicationData`

A directory containing nonroaming application data for the current user.

C:\Documents and Settings\<user>\Local Settings\Application Data

`SpecialFolder.MyComputer`

The directory representing the "My Computer" feature on the Windows desktop. On most systems this returns a null or empty string because *My Computer* is an artificial view, not a true directory.

`SpecialFolder.MyDocuments`

The *My Documents* directory for the current user.

C:\Documents and Settings\<user>\My Documents

`SpecialFolder.MyMusic`

 The audio media directory for the current user.

  C:\Documents and Settings\<user>\My Documents\My Music

`SpecialFolder.MyPictures`

 The image and video media directory for the current user.

  C:\Documents and Settings\<user>\My Documents\My Pictures

`SpecialFolder.Personal`

 The personal document directory for the current user. This is typically the *My Documents* directory.

  C:\Documents and Settings\<user>\My Documents

`SpecialFolder.ProgramFiles`

 The shared installation directory for applications on the local workstation.

  C:\Program Files

`SpecialFolder.Programs`

 The current user's "Programs" area within the Start menu.

  C:\Documents and Settings\<user>\Start Menu\Programs

`SpecialFolder.Recent`

 A directory of shortcuts to files recently used by the current user.

  C:\Documents and Settings\<user>\Recent

`SpecialFolder.SendTo`

 A directory of "Send To" target shortcuts for the current user.

  C:\Documents and Settings\<user>\SendTo

`SpecialFolder.StartMenu`

 The top-level Start menu directory for the current user.

  C:\Documents and Settings\<user>\Start Menu

`SpecialFolder.Startup`

 The current user's "Startup" area within the Start menu.

  C:\Documents and Settings\<user>\Start Menu\Programs\Startup

`SpecialFolder.System`

 The *System* directory that stores the primary Windows system components.

  C:\WINDOWS\System32

`SpecialFolder.Templates`

 A directory of new-file templates used when creating new files through Windows Explorer. This is not the same as the directory used to store Microsoft Word templates or other similar application-specific templates.

  C:\Documents and Settings\<user>\Templates

12.13 Determining the Space on a Drive

Problem

You want to report the amount of space available on a drive, including total and remaining space.

Solution

Sample code folder: Chapter 12\DriveSpace

The My namespace provides access to objects representing the logical drives available on the local workstation. My.Computer.FileSystem.Drives exposes a collection of all logical drives, with each drive stored as a System.IO.DriveInfo object. To retrieve a specific drive by name, use the My.Computer.FileSystem.GetDriveInfo( ) method, and pass it the name of a logical drive, such as C:\. The returned DriveInfo object includes properties that report the amount of space on the drive.

Discussion

Create an application that reports the amount of total and free space for any logical drive. Start a new Windows Forms application, and add a ComboBox control named LogicalDrive and three labels for the space totals (FreeSpace, QuotaSpace, and TotalSpace). Set the DropDownStyle property of LogicalDrive to DropDownList, and set the Text properties of the three labels to N/A. You can add some additional field labels if you want, resulting in a form like the one in Figure 12-8.

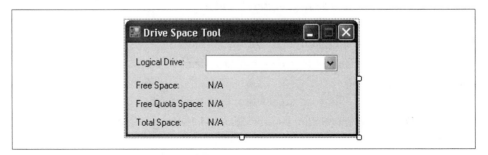

Figure 12-8. Controls for the drive space sample

Add the following source code to the form's class template:

```
Private Const NotADrive As String = "<Not Selected>"

Private Sub Form1_Load(ByVal sender As System.Object, _
      ByVal e As System.EventArgs) Handles MyBase.Load
   ' ----- Fill in the list of logical drives.
   LogicalDrive.Items.Add(NotADrive)
   LogicalDrive.SelectedIndex = 0
```

```
      For Each oneDrive As IO.DriveInfo In _
            My.Computer.FileSystem.Drives
         LogicalDrive.Items.Add(oneDrive.Name)
      Next oneDrive
   End Sub

   Private Sub LogicalDrive_SelectedIndexChanged( _
         ByVal sender As System.Object, _
         ByVal e As System.EventArgs) _
         Handles LogicalDrive.SelectedIndexChanged
      ' ----- Fill in the drive details.
      If (LogicalDrive.Text = NotADrive) Then
         ' ----- <Not Selected>
         FreeSpace.Text = "N/A"
         QuotaSpace.Text = "N/A"
         TotalSpace.Text = "N/A"
      Else
         ' ----- A logical drive is selected.
         Dim oneDrive As IO.DriveInfo = _
            My.Computer.FileSystem.GetDriveInfo( _
            LogicalDrive.Text)
         FreeSpace.Text = Format(oneDrive.TotalFreeSpace, _
            "#,##0") & " bytes"
         QuotaSpace.Text = Format(oneDrive.AvailableFreeSpace, _
            "#,##0") & " bytes"
         TotalSpace.Text = Format(oneDrive.TotalSize, _
            "#,##0") & " bytes"
      End If
   End Sub
```

To use the program, select a valid logical drive from the LogicalDrive drop-down list, and take careful note of the exact byte counts displayed. Figure 12-9 shows this form in use.

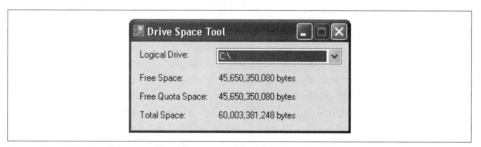

Figure 12-9. Displaying the total and free space on a local hard drive

The DriveInfo object includes three properties that deal with space on a drive:

AvailableFreeSpace

> The amount of free space, in bytes, available to the current user on the logical drive, expressed as a Long value. The system administrator can impose disk-

space quotas for each authorized user on each drive. This property returns only the amount of free space remaining in the current user's quota. It excludes any additional disk space that falls outside the user's quota.

TotalFreeSpace

The amount of total free space, in bytes, on the logical drive, expressed as a Long value. This property ignores all disk quotas and returns the full free space on the drive.

TotalSize

The total space, in bytes, on the logical drive, whether used or not, expressed as a Long value. This property ignores all disk quotas and returns the full space on the drive.

See Also

Recipe 12.1 discusses how to list all the drives on the local system.

12.14 Browsing for a Directory

Problem

The user needs to specify a directory on the file system in which files should be stored or accessed, and you want it to be done graphically, not just through a text-entry field.

Solution

Sample code folder: Chapter 12\DirectoryLocator

Use a FolderBrowserDialog control to display the standard Windows directory-browsing tool.

Discussion

Create a new Windows Forms application, and add a TextBox control named TargetDirectory, a Button control named LookForDirectory, and a FolderBrowserDialog control named DirectoryBrowser. (You'll find the FolderBrowserDialog control in the Dialogs area of the Visual Studio Toolbox.) Change the Text property of the button to Browse.... Adding an informative label gives you the form in Figure 12-10.

Add the following source code to the form's class template:

```
Private Sub LookForDirectory_Click( _
      ByVal sender As System.Object, _
      ByVal e As System.EventArgs) _
      Handles LookForDirectory.Click
   ' ----- Locate a directory graphically.
   DirectoryBrowser.Description = _
```

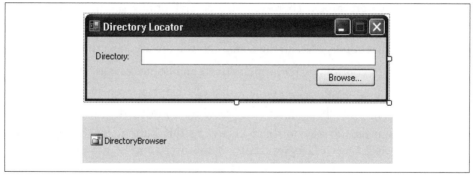

Figure 12-10. Controls for the directory-browsing sample

```
        "Which directory do you want to use?"
    If (DirectoryBrowser.ShowDialog( ) = _
        Windows.Forms.DialogResult.OK) Then
        TargetDirectory.Text = DirectoryBrowser.SelectedPath
    End If
End Sub
```

To use the program, click on the Browse button, and use the resulting dialog (shown in Figure 12-11) to select a directory.

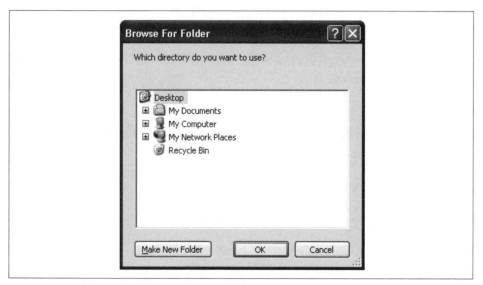

Figure 12-11. The standard directory browser dialog

The FolderBrowserDialog class represents one of several system-supplied dialogs made available to your Visual Basic applications. Other related dialogs let you browse for files (OpenFileDialog and SaveFileDialog), select fonts (FontDialog), and choose colors (ColorDialog). There are also several printer-specific dialogs. (See Chapter 11 for related recipes.)

Despite their different purposes, all the dialog controls are used in a similar way:

1. Add the dialog control to your form, or create an instance of it as a variable.

2. Set any relevant properties, as is done with the Description property in this recipe.

3. Display the dialog to the user with the ShowDialog( ) method.

4. If the user makes a selection and clicks the OK button, the dialog returns System.Windows.Forms.DialogResult.OK. If the user cancels, the dialog returns System.Windows.Forms.DialogResult.Cancel.

5. Examine the properties of the control for user-modified settings.

12.15 Getting File Information

Problem

You need to access a lot of information about a file, such as its size, its last modification time, and its attributes.

Solution

Sample code folder: Chapter 12\FileInformation

Use the My.Computer.FileSystem.GetFileInfo( ) method to retrieve many basic details about a specific file.

Discussion

The following method displays the size, relevant dates, and attributes of a file path:

```
Public Sub ShowFileDetails(ByVal filePath As String)
   ' ----- Given a file path, show some of its details.
   Dim fileDetail As IO.FileInfo

   ' ----- First, make sure the file exists.
   If (My.Computer.FileSystem.FileExists(filePath) _
         = False) Then
     MsgBox("The file '" & filePath & "' does not exist.", _
        MsgBoxStyle.OkOnly Or MsgBoxStyle.Exclamation, _
        "Invalid File")
     Exit Sub
   End If

   ' ----- Retrieve the file details.
   fileDetail = My.Computer.FileSystem.GetFileInfo(filePath)

   ' ----- Show some information.
   MsgBox("Details for '" & filePath & "':" & _
```

```
            vbCrLf & vbCrLf & _
            "Attributes: " & fileDetail.Attributes.ToString( ) & _
            vbCrLf & _
            "Created: " & fileDetail.CreationTime & vbCrLf & _
            "Accessed: " & fileDetail.LastAccessTime & vbCrLf & _
            "Modified: " & fileDetail.LastWriteTime & vbCrLf & _
            "Size: " & fileDetail.Length & " byte(s)", _
            MsgBoxStyle.OkOnly Or MsgBoxStyle.Information, _
            "File Details")
     End Sub
```

Figure 12-12 shows some typical output for this block of code.

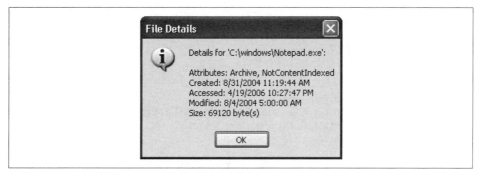

Figure 12-12. File attributes for the Notepad.exe program file

The System.IO.FileInfo object exposes properties that document various features of
a file. It also includes methods that let you create, modify, and delete the file, and
open the file to examine its contents. Features such as these are discussed in other
recipes found throughout this chapter.

A similar detail-laden object exists for directories. Once you have a directory path,
use the My.Computer.FileSystem.GetDirectoryInfo( ) method, which returns an
object of type System.IO.DirectoryInfo.

Some of the properties of the FileInfo object, such as the modification (last write)
time, appear in the Details view of the Windows File Explorer. One part of that view
that isn't directly available through FileInfo is the Type column. This displays a
short name for the type of file based on its extension; for example, the *.bmp* extension equates to a file type of "Bitmap Image." To get this type name, you need to
access values in the system registry. The sample code in this discussion uses the registry features found in the My namespace without much explanation. For additional
information on using these registry features, see Recipe 14.20.

The registry consists of several "hives," one of which is HKEY_CLASSES_ROOT. This hive
contains a key for each file extension recognized by Microsoft Windows. The
"default value" for that key refers to another key in the same hive, and the default
value for that second key will finally give us the name we seek.

The following function extracts the file-type name from the registry. The argument passed must be the valid name of an existing file:

```
Public Function GetFileTypeName( _
      ByVal filepath As String) As String
   ' ----- Given a file path, obtain its file type.
   Dim fileDetail As IO.FileInfo
   Dim oneKey As Microsoft.Win32.RegistryKey
   Dim valueText As String

   ' ----- First, make sure the file exists.
   If (My.Computer.FileSystem.FileExists(filepath) _
         = False) Then
      MsgBox("The file '" & filepath & "' does not exist.", _
         MsgBoxStyle.OkOnly Or MsgBoxStyle.Exclamation, _
         "Invalid File")
      Return ""
   End If

   ' ----- Retrieve the file details.
   fileDetail = My.Computer.FileSystem.GetFileInfo(filepath)
   If (fileDetail.Extension Is Nothing) Then Return ""
   If (fileDetail.Extension = "") Then Return ""

   ' ----- Access the extension's entry in the registry.
   oneKey = My.Computer.Registry.ClassesRoot.OpenSubKey( _
      fileDetail.Extension)
   valueText = oneKey.GetValue("")
   oneKey.Close()
   If (valueText Is Nothing) Then Return ""
   If (valueText = "") Then Return ""

   ' ----- Access the extension type's entry in the registry.
   oneKey = My.Computer.Registry.ClassesRoot.OpenSubKey( _
      valueText)
   valueText = oneKey.GetValue("")
   oneKey.Close()
   If (valueText Is Nothing) Then valueText = ""
   Return valueText
End Function
```

See Also

Recipe 12.10 shows how to determine if a specified file exists.

12.16 Using File-Access Methods

Problem

It seems that there are a million ways to open and edit a file using Visual Basic, and you are unsure of the differences.

Solution

How you edit a file depends on how you first open it. Visual Basic 2005 has some traditional file-editing features that are variations of what it had back in Version 1.0 of the language, and you can use some of the file-editing features provided with the .NET Framework (such as streams). Also, many objects provide options to immediately "serialize" their content to a file in an XML or similar format. This recipe documents some of the common file-editing choices available to you in Visual Basic. It does not provide full source code using each possible option. Instead, it provides an overview of the options available to you.

Discussion

Visual Basic supports two primary methods of file access: handle-based and stream-based.

Handle-based file access

Visual Basic traditionally supports a handle-based method of file management. Each file opened for input or output has a generated numeric ID that is always used to reference that file. The Visual Basic FreeFile( ) method generates this numeric handle, and the handle is assigned before a file is ever accessed. To open an existing file, you first obtain an ID and then open the file:

```
Dim fileHandle As Integer = FreeFile( )
FileOpen(fileHandle, "C:\DataFile.dat", OpenMode.Input, _
   OpenAccess.Read, OpenShare.Shared)
```

There are several other functions in Visual Basic that deal with file manipulation, and all of them use the file handle returned from FreeFile( ). You must continue to use the handle for all interactions with the opened file until you specifically close the file.

Care must be taken when using FreeFile( ). Until you actually use a file handle to open a file, it is considered unused, and FreeFile( ) will keep returning it again and again because it knows it to be unused. Consider the following code:

```
Dim fileHandleIn As Integer = FreeFile( )
Dim fileHandleOut As Integer = FreeFile( )
FileOpen(fileHandleIn, inputFilePath, OpenMode.Input)
FileOpen(fileHandleOut, outputFilePath, OpenMode.Output)
```

The problem with this code is that fileHandleIn and fileHandleOut probably contain the same numeric handle. That handle number will get used by the first FileOpen( ) call, leaving the second one to fail. The following code should be used instead:

```
Dim fileHandleIn As Integer = FreeFile( )
FileOpen(fileHandleIn, inputFilePath, OpenMode.Input)
Dim fileHandleOut As Integer = FreeFile( )
FileOpen(fileHandleOut, outputFilePath, OpenMode.Output)
```

Handle-based files are opened in one of three modes:

Sequential

Sequential files are typically text files, and you add data to or retrieve data from these files in the form of text strings and whole text lines. The FileOpen( ) statement includes three variations of this mode through the OpenMode.Input, OpenMode. Output, and OpenMode.Append arguments, all of which are fairly self-describing. To open a file so that you can append additional data, use this statement:

```
FileOpen(fileHandle, fileName, OpenMode.Append)
```

If the file that you open for Output or Append does not yet exist, FileOpen( ) creates it for you, assuming that the supplied path is valid.

Additional variations of the FileOpen( ) method include additional arguments beyond the three shown above. A fourth argument to FileOpen( ), the OpenAccess argument, indicates your read/write interaction with the file. A fifth argument, OpenShare, declares whether and how you will block other users from the file while you are using it.

Once the file is open, you have a few choices as to the format of the data you will place in the file. Most of the reading and writing features for sequential files appear in pairs. The Write( ) and WriteLine( ) methods send formatted data to the output in a way that is very easy to read back in later. Each value is specifically prepared for output. For instance, date values are surrounded with # characters, and use a consistent format. When you are ready to read such data, the Input( ) method correctly "unformats" the formatted data created using Write( ) and WriteLine( ).

For more free-form management of data, use the Print( ) and PrintLine( ) functions to output character data. Later, you can use the InputString( ) or LineInput( ) functions to retrieve sections of a line or entire text lines.

If you need to line up data columns when outputting data with Print( ) and PrintLine( ), you can use the FileWidth( ), SPC( ), and TAB( ) features that Visual Basic includes to help manage such formatted output.

Binary

Binary files generally store raw binary data, such as image bitmaps, and interaction with these files often occurs through individual bytes or blocks of bytes. The OpenMode.Binary mode marks an open file as binary.

Binary data is generally written using the FilePut( ) and FilePutObject( ) methods and later read back in using the FileGet( ) and FileGetObject( ) methods. There is no concept of "lines" in a binary file; data is written out in chunks, with nothing to delimit the chunks unless you specifically output a delimiter.

Random

Random file access involves records and structures. Positioning within random files is generally done via record number, not by byte or character position. The

`OpenMode.Random` mode marks an open file as random. When using random files, you can add a sixth argument to the `FileOpen()` method that indicates the common length of every record.

As with binary files, random files use the `FilePut()` and `FilePutObject()` methods for output and the `FileGet()` and `FileGetObject()` methods for input. Each object or structure written out to the file is considered to be a unit consistent with the specified record length (if used). When you later read the contents of a random file back in, you must use the same record length to ensure a match between the output and input data boundaries.

Random files allow specific records or sections of the file to be locked and unlocked using the `Lock()` and `Unlock()` methods. You can determine your current position in the file (by record number) using the `Loc()` function.

There are a few functions that work with all file modes. The `FileClose()` and `Reset()` methods let you close a single file and all open files, respectively. The `EOF()` function indicates whether you have reached the end of a file that you are scanning, although it isn't always reliable with random files. Finally, the `Seek()` function and `Seek()` method (two features with the same name) let you determine and move the current position marker within an open file.

Stream-based file access

While Visual Basic continues to support handle-based file access for reasons of compatibility, *streams* are the preferred file access method in .NET. Streams are defined through the `System.IO.Stream` class and through several derived classes that enhance that base class (such as providing a stream focused on network data).

Streams provide three basic operations: `Read()` (and its variations), `Write()` (with variations), and `Seek()`. Not all streams support these basic features. You can use the `CanRead()`, `CanWrite()`, and `CanSeek()` methods to determine their availability.

Streams are useful because they let you manage a file at a granular level, through the individual bytes. However, it isn't always convenient to constantly convert non-Byte data back and forth to Bytes. To make file reads and writes easier, the `System.IO` namespace also includes *stream readers* and *stream writers* as separate classes. These distinct classes get wrapped around a stream and provide start-to-finish reading or writing of a stream's content. The `StreamReader` class wraps a `Stream` object, providing simplified reading of the stream's content. For instance, the `ReadLine()` method returns the next line in the stream as a string:

```
Dim oneLine As String
Dim scanFile As New IO.StreamReader("c:\data.txt")
Do While Not scanFile.EndOfStream
   oneLine = scanFile.ReadLine()
   ' ----- Process the line contents here.
Loop
scanFile.Close()
```

The StreamWriter class provides the opposite features, allowing you to write strings and other basic data types to a stream.

Related stream readers and writers include the StringReader and StringWriter pair (identical to the StreamReader and StreamWriter classes, but using a String as the underlying storage content instead of a Stream) and the BinaryReader and BinaryWriter classes, which provide a simplified method of reading and writing binary and core data-type content.

Some of the objects and features in the My.Computer.FileSystem object provide access to file streams. My.Computer.FileSystem.OpenTextFileReader( ) opens a StreamReader based on an existing file path. You can also create a new file stream using the System.IO.File.Create( ) method or other similar methods.

The My namespace includes a TextFieldParser object that provides simplified access to files with columnar data in either delimited columns (such as tab-delimited fields) or fixed-width fields.

For those objects that support serialization of their content to XML files, the basic transport between the object and the destination file is the Stream. Streams also appear when data needs to pass through some sort of conversion on its way to another destination. The cryptography features in the System.Security.Cryptography namespace frequently use streams during encryption and hashing operations.

See Also

Other recipes in this chapter provide specific examples using the file-processing features available to Visual Basic. Most of the recipes focus on stream-based file access because that is the preferred file-interaction method in .NET.

12.17 Reading and Writing Files as Strings

Problem

You have a rather large string that you need to be able to put into a file and get back later without too much hassle.

Solution

Sample code folder: Chapter 12\SimpleEditor

Use the My.Computer.FileSystem.WriteAllText( ) and related ReadAllText( ) methods to quickly get text data into and out of a file.

Discussion

This recipe's sample code creates a simple Notepad-like text editor. Create a new Windows Forms application, and add two TextBox controls named FilePath and

Editor and two Button controls named ActOpen and ActSave to the form. Set the Editor control's Multiline property to True and its ScrollBars property to Both. Add some informational labels, and arrange the controls to look like Figure 12-13.

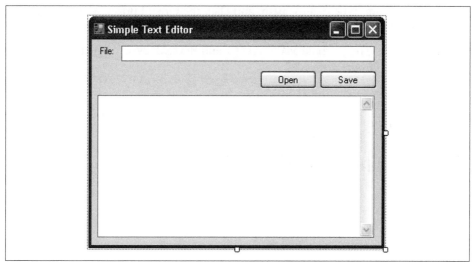

Figure 12-13. Controls for the text editor sample

Add the following source code to the form's class template:

```
Private Sub ActOpen_Click(ByVal sender As System.Object, _
      ByVal e As System.EventArgs) Handles ActOpen.Click
   ' ----- Open an existing file and load its text.
   Try
      Editor.Text = My.Computer.FileSystem.ReadAllText(FilePath.Text)
   Catch ex As Exception
      MsgBox("Could not open the file due to the " & _
         "following error:" & vbCrLf & vbCrLf & ex.Message)
   End Try
End Sub

Private Sub ActSave_Click(ByVal sender As Object, _
      ByVal e As System.EventArgs) Handles ActSave.Click
   ' ----- Save the edited data.
   If (My.Computer.FileSystem.FileExists(FilePath.Text) = _
         True) Then
      If (MsgBox("File exists. Overwrite?", _
         MsgBoxStyle.YesNo Or MsgBoxStyle.Question, _
         "Overwrite") <> MsgBoxResult.Yes) Then Exit Sub
   End If

   ' ----- Save the data.
   Try
      My.Computer.FileSystem.WriteAllText(FilePath.Text, _
         Editor.Text, False)
   Catch ex As Exception
```

```
          MsgBox("Could not save the file due to the " & _
             "following error:" & vbCrLf & vbCrLf & ex.Message)
       End Try
    End Sub
```

To use the program, type in a file path, and click the Open button. Make changes in the Editor field, and then click the Save button to store those changes in the file.

The `My.Computer.FileSystem.ReadAllBytes( )` and `WriteAllBytes( )` methods provide parallel features for byte arrays.

See Also

Recipe 12.18 discusses the processing of binary files.

12.18 Reading and Writing Binary Files

Problem

You need to read or write binary content in a file.

Solution

If you have a block of bytes that you want to push out to a file quickly, use the `My.Computer.FileSystem.WriteAllBytes( )` method:

```
Dim fileData( ) As Byte
' ----- Fill in the array with relevant data, and then...
My.Computer.FileSystem.WriteAllBytes( _
    outputFilePath, fileData, False)
```

The third argument indicates whether the new data should be appended to the end of any existing file data. If you set it to `False`, any existing data is replaced by the new data.

To get the binary data back into a `Byte` array from a file, use the related `ReadAllBytes( )` method:

```
Dim fileData( ) As Byte = _
    My.Computer.FileSystem.ReadAllBytes(inputFilePath)
```

Discussion

If you need to do more than just read and write the file en masse with a `Byte` array, consider using the `BinaryReader` and `BinaryWriter` classes. These classes wrap a basic `Stream` object (such as a `FileStream`), providing convenient methods to read and write content.

The `BinaryWriter` object provides a single massively overridden `Write( )` method that lets you save most of the core Visual Basic data-type values to a stream. This code opens/creates a file and writes out some basic values:

```
Dim value1 As Integer = 5
Dim value2 As Boolean = True
Dim value3 As Char = "A"c
Dim outStream As New IO.FileStream( _
    "c:\data.dat", IO.FileMode.OpenOrCreate)
Dim outFile As New IO.BinaryWriter(outStream)

outFile.Write(value1)
outFile.Write(value2)
outFile.Write(value3)
outFile.Close( )
outStream.Close( )
```

Read back this data using a BinaryReader:

```
Dim value1 As Integer
Dim value2 As Boolean
Dim value3 As Char
Dim inStream As New IO.FileStream( _
    "c:\data.dat", IO.FileMode.Open, IO.FileAccess.Read)
Dim inFile As New IO.BinaryReader(inStream)

value1 = inFile.ReadInt32( )
value2 = inFile.ReadBoolean( )
value3 = inFile.ReadChar( )
inFile.Close( )
inStream.Close( )
```

If you need an even higher level of control, the FileStream object (as derived from the Stream class) also exposes ReadByte( ) and WriteByte( ) methods (and other related methods) that let you read and write individual bytes at any position in the file.

12.19 Copying or Moving a File

Problem

You need to copy or move an existing file from one location to another.

Solution

Use the My.Computer.FileSystem.MoveFile( ) method to move a file from its current location to another place in the file system. Use the related CopyFile( ) method to copy the file instead of moving it. The basic syntax is:

```
' ---- To move the file.
My.Computer.FileSystem.MoveFile( _
    sourceFile, destFile[, overwriteFlag])

' ---- To copy the file.
My.Computer.FileSystem.CopyFile( _
    sourceFile, destFile[, overwriteFlag])
```

Because destFile is a filename and not a directory name, you can effectively rename the file at the same time you move or copy it. When moving the file, you can keep the file in the same directory and just give it a new name, although using the RenameFile( ) method would be clearer. The optional overwriteFlag is a Boolean that indicates whether any existing file at the target should be replaced silently by the source file. It defaults to False.

Discussion

A variation of both MoveFile( ) and CopyFile( ) uses a different set of arguments to control the display of on-screen prompts and status notifications during the move or copy:

```
' ----- MoveFile( ) syntax.
My.Computer.FileSystem.MoveFile( _
    sourceFile, destFile, _
    showUI [, onUserCancel])

' ----- CopyFile( ) syntax.
My.Computer.FileSystem.CopyFile( _
    sourceFile, destFile, _
    showUI [, onUserCancel])
```

The showUI argument accepts one of the following Microsoft.VisualBasic.FileIO. UIOption enumeration values:

UIOption.AllDialogs
    An animated progress dialog appears during the file move or copy to indicate the current status during that operation. (The dialog might not appear for moves or copies that involve a small amount of content.) Any errors that occur present their own separate error-dialog prompts.

UIOption.OnlyErrorDialogs
    While errors will appear through distinct error-dialog prompts, no animated status display appears, no matter how long the move or copy takes. This is the default method.

If you include the fourth onUserCancel argument, you provide it one of the following Microsoft.VisualBasic.UICancelOption enumeration values:

UICancelOption.DoNothing
    The on-screen status display during a move or copy operation includes a Cancel button. If the user clicks the Cancel button when the DoNothing option is in effect, the code calling MoveFile( ) or CopyFile( ) will not receive any notification that the move or copy was aborted early.

UICancelOption.ThrowException
    If the user clicks the Cancel button on the status dialog when ThrowException is used, the MoveFile( ) or CopyFile( ) method generates a System.IOException

exception, which can be caught by the initiating code. This is the default method.

See Also

Recipes 12.4 and 12.5 show you how to move and copy whole directories instead of just files.

12.20 Sending a File to the Recycle Bin

Problem

You need to delete a file or, even better, send it to the Recycle Bin.

Solution

The `My.Computer.FileSystem.DeleteFile()` method allows you to either permanently delete a file or send it to the Recycle Bin. The basic syntax is:

```
My.Computer.FileSystem.DeleteFile(filePath _
   [, showUI [, recycle [, onUserCancel]]] )
```

To send the file to the Recycle Bin, the recycle option needs to be set appropriately:

```
My.Computer.FileSystem.DeleteFile(filePath, _
   UIOption.OnlyErrorDialogs, _
   RecycleOption.SendToRecycleBin)
```

Discussion

The first `DeleteFile()` argument accepts a single file to be deleted, and you can include up to three additional optional arguments: `showUI` (which impacts user presentation during the deletion), `recycle` (which indicates whether or not to use the Recycle Bin), and `onUserCancel` (which sets what happens when the user aborts the deletion).

The `showUI` argument accepts one of the following `Microsoft.VisualBasic.FileIO.UIOption` enumeration values:

UIOption.AllDialogs
   An animated progress dialog appears during the file deletion to indicate the current status during that operation. (The dialog might not appear for deletes that involve a small amount of content.) Any errors that occur present their own separate error-dialog prompts.

UIOption.OnlyErrorDialogs
   While errors will appear through distinct error-dialog prompts, no animated status display appears, no matter how long the delete takes. This is the default method.

The recycle argument accepts one of the following Microsoft.VisualBasic.FileIO. RecycleOption enumeration values:

RecycleOption.DeletePermanently

The file is immediately and permanently removed from the disk.

RecycleOption.SendToRecycleBin

Instead of deleting the file, DeleteFile( ) moves the file to the Recycle Bin pseudodirectory.

If you include the onUserCancel argument, you provide it one of the following Microsoft.VisualBasic.UICancelOption enumeration values:

UICancelOption.DoNothing

The on-screen status display during a delete operation includes a Cancel button. If the user clicks the Cancel button when the DoNothing option is in effect, the code calling DeleteFile( ) will not receive any notification that the deletion was aborted early.

UICancelOption.ThrowException

If the user clicks the Cancel button on the status dialog when ThrowException is used, the DeleteFile( ) method generates a System.IOException exception, which can be caught by the initiating code. This is the default method.

12.21 Creating a Temporary File

Problem

You need to quickly store some data in a file, but the data will just be around for a little while.

Solution

Create a temporary file in the user's "official" temporary file area with the My. Computer.FileSystem.GetTempFileName( ) method:

```
Dim workFile As String = _
    My.Computer.FileSystem.GetTempFileName( )
```

The filename returned represents a brand-new file created by the method that is zero bytes in size. When you are ready to use it, open it with one of the stream-based or file handle-based file-management methods, and make any additions or changes as needed. When you are finished, simply delete the file.

Discussion

The temporary file is added to the user's default temporary file area and always has a *.tmp* extension. The filename is guaranteed to be unique and will not conflict with other temporary filenames stored in that same directory. The typical location for a logged-in Windows user is:

```
C:\Documents and Settings\<user>\Local Settings\Temp\
```

See Also

Recipe 12.16 discusses the editing of files using either stream-based or file handle-based methods.

12.22 Calculating a Checksum for a File

Problem

You want to ensure that the contents of a file have not changed, perhaps after transmitting that file over the Internet.

Solution

Sample code folder: Chapter 12\GenerateChecksum

Generate a checksum for the file. A checksum is a short value or string that is built using the contents of the file. Calculating a checksum on identical content will yield identical results, but different input produces different and varying checksums. A good checksum-generating algorithm is very sensitive to even the smallest change in the source data (a file, in this case).

Discussion

Create a new Windows Forms application, and add two TextBox controls named FileToCheck and HexChecksum and a Button control named GenerateChecksum to the form. Set the HexChecksum.ReadOnly property to True. Add some informational labels and arrange the controls to look like Figure 12-14.

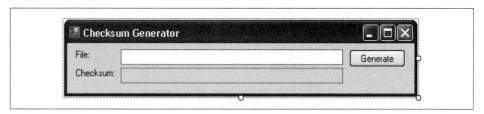

Figure 12-14. Controls for the file checksum sample

Add the following source code to the form's class template. We've also included some needed Imports statements:

```
Imports System.Text
Imports System.Security.Cryptography
```

```vbnet
Public Class Form1
    Private Sub GenerateChecksum_Click( _
            ByVal sender As System.Object, _
            ByVal e As System.EventArgs) _
            Handles GenerateChecksum.Click
        ' ----- The hash value is ready, but I like things in
        '       plain text when possible. Let's convert it to a
        '       long hex string.
        Dim checksum As Byte()
        Dim counter As Integer
        Dim result As String

        ' ----- Generate the checksum for the file.
        Try
            checksum = GenerateFileChecksum(FileToCheck.Text)
        Catch ex As Exception
            MsgBox("An error occurred while trying to " & _
                "calculate the checksum:" & _
                vbCrLf & vbCrLf & ex.Message)
            Exit Sub
        End Try

        ' ----- Prepare the checksum for display.
        If (checksum Is Nothing) Then
            result = "No checksum result."
        Else
            ' ----- Convert the checksum into something readable.
            result = ""
            For counter = 0 To checksum.Length - 1
                result &= String.Format("{0:X2}", _
                    checksum(counter))
            Next counter
        End If

        ' ----- Show the result to the user.
        HexChecksum.Text = result
    End Sub

    Public Function GenerateFileChecksum( _
            ByVal filePath As String) As Byte()
        ' ----- Use the HMACSHA1 hashing function to generate
        '       a checksum for a file.
        Dim hashingFunction As HMACSHA1
        Dim hasingBase() As Byte
        Dim hashValue() As Byte
        Dim inStream As IO.Stream

        ' ----- Make sure the file exists.
        If (My.Computer.FileSystem.FileExists(filePath) _
            = False) Then
            Throw New IO.FileNotFoundException
            Return Nothing
        End If
```

```
' ----- Prepare the hashing key. You have to use
'         the same hashing key every time, or you
'         will get different results.
hasingBase = (New UnicodeEncoding).GetBytes("Cookbook")

' ----- Create the hashing component using the Managed
'         SHA-1 function.
hashingFunction = New HMACSHA1(hasingBase, True)

' ----- Open the file as a stream.
inStream = New IO.FileStream(filePath, _
   IO.FileMode.Open, IO.FileAccess.Read)

' ----- Calculate the checksum value.
hashValue = hashingFunction.ComputeHash(inStream)

' ----- Finished with the file.
inStream.Close( )

' ----- Return the checksum as a byte array.
Return hashValue
   End Function
End Class
```

To use the program, type in a file path, and click the Generate button. The resulting 40-hex-digit checksum will appear in the HexChecksum field. Figure 12-15 shows the results of a checksum calculation.

Figure 12-15. A checksum generated for an executable file

Checksums are especially useful when you want to know if two files, or two sets of data, contain identical content. They are typically generated using a *hashing algorithm*, a processing method that takes some original content and generates a summary value representing the full content. Hashing algorithms process the input data in blocks. As a hash is calculated for each block, the next block is brought in and applied to or overlaid on the existing hash. This constant merging of the data makes the algorithms very sensitive to any changes in the source content.

The .NET Framework includes several hashing algorithms and encryption features in the System.Security.Cryptography namespace. This recipe's code uses the HMACSHA1 class (Hash-based Message Authentication Code, or HMAC, via the SHA-1 hash function) in that namespace to generate the hash. Hash functions such as the SHA-1 function were developed by private organizations and government security agencies to help protect sensitive content. Several similar hash functions and related encryption algorithms are included in System.Security.Cryptography for your use.

12.23 Comparing Two Files for Equality

Problem

You have two files that should contain identical content, and you want to make sure that they do.

Solution

Sample code folder: Chapter 12\CompareFiles

Call the GenerateFileChecksum( ) routine developed in Recipe 12.22 for each of the files, and compare the checksum.

Discussion

The following code uses the GenerateFileChecksum( ) method on two distinct files and compares the resulting checksums:

```
Public Function AreFilesIdentical( _
      ByVal file1 As String, ByVal file2 As String) _
      As Boolean
   ' ----- Return True if two files are identical.
   Dim checksum1 As Byte( )
   Dim checksum2 As Byte( )
   Dim counter As Integer

   On Error GoTo ErrorHandler

   ' ------ Calculate the checksums.
   checksum1 = GenerateFileChecksum(file1)
   checksum2 = GenerateFileChecksum(file2)

   ' ----- See if the results are equal.
   For counter = 0 To UBound(checksum1)
      If (checksum1(counter) <> checksum2(counter)) _
         Then Return False
   Next counter

   ' ----- The checksums are equal.
   Return True

ErrorHandler:
   ' ----- If anything went wrong, assume the
   '       files are unequal.
   Return False
End Function
```

See Also

See Recipe 12.22 for the code needed to complete this recipe.

12.24 Locking a File During Access

Problem

You need to update the content of a file, and you don't want anyone else messing with it while you're in there.

Solution

The System.IO.FileStream object can be used to open a file with various levels of file sharing and locking. When opening a file stream, use the appropriate locking flag to keep other users or processes from accessing the file while you have it open.

Discussion

The System.IO.FileStream constructor includes several arguments that indicate how the file should be opened. One of the basic overloads for this constructor uses a file-sharing flag as its fourth argument:

```
Dim newStream As New IO.Stream(path As String, _
    mode As IO.FileMode, access As IO.FileAccess, _
    share As IO.FileShare)
```

The share argument accepts one of the following System.IO.FileShare enumeration values:

FileShare.None
> The file cannot be opened by any other process, or even by other open requests within this same process.

FileShare.Read
> Other processes can open the file for reading only, not for modification.

FileShare.ReadWrite
> Other processes can open the file for both reading and writing. This is the default setting if you exclude the FileShare option from the opening of the stream.

FileShare.Write
> Other processes can open the file for writing or appending, but they cannot read from it until this process closes the file.

Although the FileShare enumeration indicates whether other processes can open a file while your process is using it, it does not control the authorization of access to this file. The other process must still have security rights to access the file in order to open it, even if you specify FileShare.ReadWrite.

When opening files in random mode using the Visual Basic FileOpen( ) method (see Recipe 12.16), you can lock specific records within the opened file using the Lock( ) method:

```
' ----- Open the file. Each record is 50 bytes.
Dim fileID As Integer = FreeFile( )
FileOpen(fileID, pathToFile, OpenMode.Random, _
    OpenAccess.ReadWrite, OpenShare.LockWrite, 50)

...

' ----- Lock record number five.
Lock(fileID, 5)

...

' ----- Make the needed changes, then unlock the record.
Unlock(fileID, 5)

...

' ----- Finished with the file.
FileClose(fileID)
```

12.25 Reading from a File at a Specific Position

Problem

You need to access content at a specific byte position in a file.

Solution

Use the Seek( ) method of a stream to relocate the current position of the stream:

```
Dim oneByte As Byte
Dim fileData As New IO.FileStream(filePath, _
    IO.FileMode.Open, IO.FileAccess.Read)
' ----- Jump to byte 1000 and read what's there.
fileData.Seek(1000, IO.SeekOrigin.Begin)
oneByte = fileData.ReadByte( )
```

Discussion

The Seek( ) method lets you quickly adjust your position in the file. The second argument specifies how the movement is to occur using one of the System.IO. SeekOrigin enumeration values:

SeekOrigin.Begin
   The offset indicates a forward position from the beginning of the file. The first byte in the file is position 1.

SeekOrigin.Current

> The offset indicates a position relative to the current position in the file. Positive offsets move forward; negative offsets move backward.

SeekOrigin.End

> The offset indicates a position relative to the end of the file. Positive offsets move forward beyond the end of the file; negative offsets move backward from the end of the file.

If you position the current position past the end of the file, the next data you write to the file will fill in all the unwritten space between the current end of the file and your new data. If you attempt to read past the end of the file, an exception occurs. You cannot set the current position to a place before the beginning byte of a file.

To determine the current byte position, access the stream's Position property.

12.26 Reading and Writing Objects in a File

Problem

You've designed a custom class. You want to store instances of that class in a file and load them back into instances later, but you don't want the object to open a stream and do all of the necessary reads and writes by itself.

Solution

Sample code folder: Chapter 12\ReadWriteObjects

Add *serialization* to your class by implementing the ISerializable interface. Serialization is the process of preparing an object's data for transport over a stream (or similar system), and later rebuilding the object from the previously transported content.

Discussion

There are three primary steps needed to make a class serializable:

1. Mark the class with the Serializable attribute, and mark it as implementing the ISerializable interface.
2. Implement the ISerializable.GetObjectData( ) method.
3. Add a custom constructor that uses the same argument signature as ISerializable.GetObjectData( ).

The following code implements a simple employee class. Serialization support is highlighted:

```
Imports System.Runtime.Serialization

' ----- Mark the entire class with the
'       SerializableAttribute attribute.
```

```vb
<Serializable()> _
Public Class Employee
    ' ----- Mark the class as using ISerializable.
    Implements ISerializable

    ' ----- Define the basic members and properties.
    Public FullName As String
    Public HireDate As Date
    Private CurrentSalary As Decimal
    Public Property Salary() As Decimal
        Get
            Return CurrentSalary
        End Get
        Set(ByVal value As Decimal)
            If (value >= 0) Then CurrentSalary = value
        End Set
    End Property

    Public Sub New()
        ' ----- Default constructor. This class should
        '       probably have something more interesting
        '       or data-preparing, but it's just a
        '       serialization sample, so no problem.
    End Sub

    Public Sub New(ByVal info As SerializationInfo, _
            ByVal context As StreamingContext)
        ' ----- Rebuild a previously serialized object by
        '       getting the individual member components
        '       from the serialization store.
        FullName = info.GetString("FullName")
        HireDate = info.GetDateTime("HireDate")
        CurrentSalary = info.GetDecimal("Salary")
    End Sub

    Public Sub GetObjectData( _
            ByVal info As SerializationInfo, _
            ByVal context As StreamingContext) _
            Implements ISerializable.GetObjectData
        ' ----- Serialize the object by adding all the class
        '       members to the serialization store as
        '       name-value pairs.
        info.AddValue("FullName", FullName)
        info.AddValue("HireDate", HireDate)
        info.AddValue("Salary", CurrentSalary)
    End Sub
End Class
```

The SerializationInfo object used in both the serialization and deserialization code includes overloads and parallel methods for all the core Visual Basic data types.

Once you've prepared your class for serialization, you can include it in a stream using one of the formatters included with the serialization system. The

BinaryFormatter class streams out a serializable class in a binary form. The class, located in the `System.Runtime.Serialization.Formatters.Binary` namespace, connects the serializable object to an open stream. The following code serializes and deserializes an Employee object (as defined in this recipe) to a standard file stream:

```
Imports System.Runtime.Serialization

Public Class Form1
    Private Sub Button1_Click(ByVal sender As Object, _
            ByVal e As System.EventArgs) Handles Button1.Click
        SaveToFile()
        GetFromFile()
    End Sub

    Private Sub SaveToFile()
        ' ----- Serialize an employee object to a file.
        Dim newEmp As New Employee
        Dim outFile As IO.FileStream
        Dim formatter As New Formatters.Binary.BinaryFormatter

        ' ----- Build a simple employee record.
        newEmp.FullName = "John Doe"
        newEmp.HireDate = #11/7/2005#
        newEmp.Salary = 10000@

        ' ----- Open the data file for storage.
        outFile = New IO.FileStream("c:\EmpData.dat", _
            IO.FileMode.Create)

        ' ----- Send the employee to the stream through
        '       a binary serialization formatter.
        formatter = New Formatters.Binary.BinaryFormatter
        formatter.Serialize(outFile, newEmp)

        ' ----- Finished.
        outFile.Close()
    End Sub

    Sub GetFromFile()
        ' ----- Build an employee record from storage.
        Dim oldEmp As Employee = Nothing
        Dim inFile As IO.FileStream
        Dim formatter As Formatters.Binary.BinaryFormatter

        ' ----- Open the file with the stored employee.
        inFile = New IO.FileStream("c:\EmpData.dat", _
            IO.FileMode.Open)

        ' ----- Deserialize the employee through the binary
        '       serialization formatter.
        formatter = New Formatters.Binary.BinaryFormatter
        oldEmp = CType(formatter.Deserialize(inFile), Employee)
        inFile.Close()
```

```
'  ----- Prove that the data came back intact.
      MsgBox("Name: " & oldEmp.FullName & vbCrLf & _
        "Hire: " & oldEmp.HireDate.ToString() & vbCrLf & _
        "Salaray: " & oldEmp.Salary.ToString())
   End Sub
End Class
```

The .NET Framework also includes support for nonbinary serialization through distinct XML and SOAP serialization systems. The System.Xml.Serialization. XmlSerializer class provides much of this functionality, although its use differs considerably from the binary formatting presented in this recipe.

12.27 Creating a Comma-Separated-Values File

Problem

You need to output data for use in Excel, without automating Excel directly.

Solution

Sample code folder: Chapter 12\GenerateCSV

Create a CSV file, which is simply a text file with commas separating tabular values. The file will have a *.csv* file extension, which is a format already recognized by Excel.

Discussion

Visual Basic 2005 provides some new, enhanced, easy-to-use shared methods in the My namespace that simplify file reading and writing, among many other things. The sample code presented here uses My.Application.Info.DirectoryPath to get the full path to where the application's EXE file is located and then uses the My.Computer. FileSystem.OpenTextFileWriter() method to create a StreamWriter to write the CSV file at this location:

```
'  ----- Create the new output file.
Dim csvFile As String = My.Application.Info.DirectoryPath & _
   "\Test.csv"
Dim outFile As IO.StreamWriter = _
   My.Computer.FileSystem.OpenTextFileWriter(csvFile, False)

'  ----- Build the output, including a header row.
outFile.WriteLine("Column 1, Column 2, Column 3")
outFile.WriteLine("1.23, 4.56, 7.89")
outFile.WriteLine("3.21, 6.54, 9.87")
outFile.Close()

'  ----- Display the contents as a message.
MsgBox(My.Computer.FileSystem.ReadAllText(csvFile))

'  ----- Display the contents in Excel (if installed).
Process.Start(csvFile)
```

The StreamWriter object's Write( ) and WriteLine( ) methods output lines of text to the file. The Write( ) method does not automatically append a newline with each call, but the WriteLine( ) does, so that's what is used in this code.

The StreamWriter's Close( ) method flushes all lines of text to the file and closes the StreamWriter object. However, when reading a file into a string, you can open, read, and close the file all in one command, as demonstrated by the call to My.Computer. FilesSystem.ReadAllText( ) in the previous sample code. Using this method to load and display the new file results in Figure 12-16.

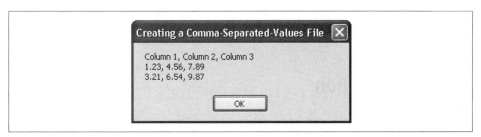

Figure 12-16. The contents of the CSV file loaded into a single string

The last line uses Process.Start( ) to tell the operating system to load the CSV file, using whatever application is registered to process files with a *.csv* extension. If you have Excel installed, this line of code should open the tabular data in a new worksheet, as shown in Figure 12-17.

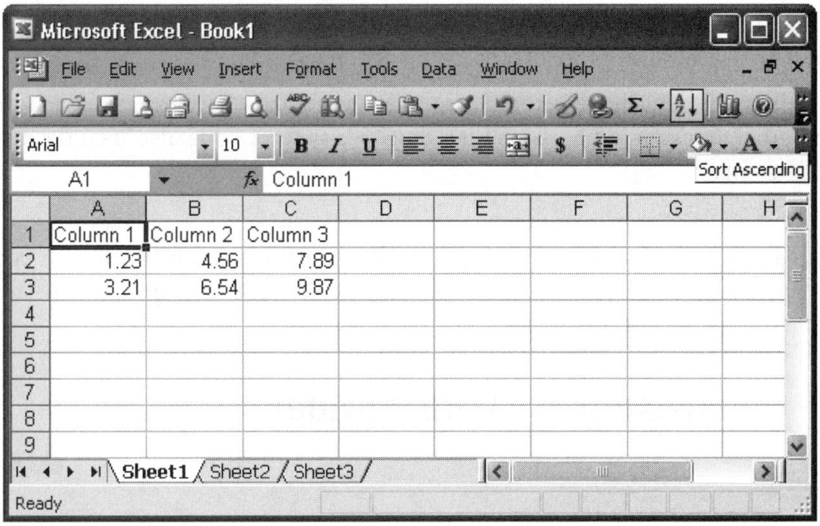

Figure 12-17. The Process.Start() method loads and displays the new CSV file in Excel

Databases

13.0 Introduction

Although Visual Basic 2005 is a flexible programming language that can be used to write a variety of applications, most developers use it to craft database-centric business programs. Interacting with a database is an essential part of Visual Basic development. Fortunately, Visual Basic includes ADO.NET, the primary database-interaction tool for the .NET Framework. ADO.NET is a "disconnected" system; it connects to SQL Server, Oracle, and other databases, but only long enough to transfer the data it needs to manage things in local memory. Older systems, such as ADO and DAO, either allowed both connected and disconnected sessions, or were fully connected. While the new fully disconnected method used in ADO.NET is a change from these older systems, it's turned out to be quite powerful and flexible. ADO.NET also includes new features not available in earlier database-interaction technologies.

The recipes in this chapter often use the System.Data namespace. Each recipe assumes that any source file containing database-specific code also includes the following statement:

```
Imports System.Data
```

Although ADO.NET supports multiple database platforms, all the source code in this chapter targets the SQL Server database. The concepts are the same for all providers, although some class names vary.

13.1 Connecting to a Data Provider

Problem

You are writing an application that interacts with a database, and you need to connect to it to run some queries.

Solution

Use a `Connection` object and a "connection string" to establish the connection you will use for queries and updates.

Discussion

The following set of statements establishes a connection to a SQL Server Express database named `MyDatabase` running on the system named `MySystem`, using the active Microsoft Windows login account for its security access:

```
Dim theDatabase As System.Data.SqlClient.SqlConnection
Dim connectionString As String = _
   "Data Source=MySystem\SQLEXPRESS;" & _
   "Initial Catalog=MyDatabase;Integrated Security=true"

theDatabase = New SqlClient.SqlConnection(connectionString)
theDatabase.Open( )
' ---- Perform database processing here, then...
theDatabase.Close( )
theDatabase.Dispose( )
```

ADO.NET includes several different database libraries. The most generic library, found in the `System.Data` namespace, defines the core classes used to manage database sets in memory. There are distinct classes for tables, columns, and rows of data; classes that let you establish relationships between the tables; and classes that let you bundle tables and relationships in one large "data set." You will probably use these classes quite a bit in your code, but they know nothing of database connections or how to communicate with any external data source (other than specially formatted XML files).

To connect to a database, you must use one of the *providers* included in ADO.NET. Each provider connects to a specific database or data-communication standard. Four providers ship with .NET, each appearing in a specific namespace, as shown in Table 13-1.

Table 13-1. Providers included with .NET

Provider	Namespace	Comments
SQL Server	`System.Data.SqlClient`	Visual Studio 2005 includes various editions of SQL Server 2005, which you can access through ADO.NET. This provider also communicates with older versions of SQL Server, back through Version 7.0.
Oracle	`System.Data.OracleClient`	This is the Microsoft-supplied Oracle provider, and it requires at least Oracle 8.1.7. You must license and install the Oracle Client tools, available directly from Oracle. Oracle also supplies its own ADO.NET provider, which appears through the `Oracle.DataAccess` namespace. You must contact Oracle directly to acquire that provider.

Table 13-1. Providers included with .NET (continued)

Provider	Namespace	Comments
OLE DB	System.Data.OleDb	This OLE DB provider connects to OLE DB data sources, but it is guaranteed to work only with SQL Server, Oracle, and Jet 4.0 data sources. You can try it with other sources, but you may receive incomplete or inadequate results.
ODBC	System.Data.Odbc	This provider is used with ODBC data sources. As with OLE DB, this provider will work with many ODBC data sources, but it may not work with all known sources. If an OLE DB or native provider is available, you should use that instead of the ODBC alternative.

To connect a provider to a data source, you create a connection object using a valid connection string and then use the Open( ) method to establish the connection. ADO.NET connection strings are similar to those used in OLE DB and ADO, and building them can be tricky. Connection strings are semicolon-delimited sets of connection parameters, with each entry taking the form *parameter=value*. The choice of parameters and values varies by connection type and desired features. The connection string used here includes three parameters (Data Source, Initial Catalog, and Integrated Security):

```
Data Source=MySystem\SQLEXPRESS;Initial Catalog=MyDatabase;
Integrated Security=true
```

Setting Integrated Security to True tells SQL Server to use the current Windows user's authentication information to connect to the database. If your database uses SQL Server's built-in authentication system, you can use the following connection string (for user "sa" and password "abc"):

```
Data Source=MySystem\SQLEXPRESS;Initial Catalog=MyDatabase;
User ID=sa;Password=abc
```

Each provider includes a "connection string builder class" (it's found at System.Data.SqlClient.SqlConnectionStringBuilder for the SQL Server provider), and although you can use it, it is simply a string-concatenation tool that attaches the semicolon-delimited parts you provide. You still need to know what each of the parameters and values should be.

The documentation installed with Visual Studio includes an article named "Working with Connection Strings" that includes common parameter names and values. If you look in the online help index for "connection strings [ADO.NET]," the "Working with Connection Strings" article is one of the results. For Oracle connection strings using Oracle's own provider, consult your Oracle documentation or their web site.

Once you have a valid connection string, use it as an argument to the connection object's constructor:

```
Dim theDatabase As System.Data.SqlClient.SqlConnection
Dim connectionString As String = _
    "Data Source=MySystem\SQLEXPRESS;" & _
    "Initial Catalog=MyDatabase;Integrated Security=true"
theDatabase = New SqlClient.SqlConnection(connectionString)
```

Establish the connection by using the Open( ) method:

```
theDatabase.Open( )
```

You don't need to close the connection until you are truly finished interacting with the database. When you use the Open( ) method, ADO.NET opens the connection only long enough to verify the connection. It then closes the connection, waiting for you to issue a SQL statement before it opens the connection again.

When you are really ready to close the connection, use the Close( ) method:

```
theDatabase.Close( )
```

See Also

Although it's not an official Microsoft resource, the *http://www.connectionstrings.com* web site provides many useful examples of ADO.NET connection strings. The site is a little out of date, but it's still the best place we've found so far to locate details on all the various connection-string parameters.

13.2   Issuing SQL Commands

Problem

Now that you've established a connection to a database through a provider, you're ready to issue SQL commands. But how?

Solution

Use a Command object to issue SQL commands directly to your database through the provider connection.

Discussion

The following code updates a SQL Server table named Table1, changing every Column2 field to 25 whenever Column1 has a value of 0:

```
' ----- Connect to the database.
Dim connectionString As String = _
   "Data Source=MySystem\SQLEXPRESS;" & _
   "Initial Catalog=MyDatabase;Integrated Security=true"
Dim theDatabase As New SqlClient.SqlConnection(connectionString)
theDatabase.Open( )

' ----- Prepare the SQL statement for use.
Dim sqlStatement As New SqlClient.SqlCommand( _
   "UPDATE Table1 SET Column2 = 25 WHERE Column1 = 0", _
   theDatabase)
sqlStatement.ExecuteNonQuery( )

' ----- Clean up.
theDatabase.Close( )
theDatabase.Dispose( )
```

Just like connections, command objects are provider-specific. When using the SQL Server provider, the System.Data.SqlClient.SqlCommand class wraps a SQL statement string and prepares it for use by the database. You must supply a valid SQL statement that is recognizable by the database.

The SQL statement you provide to the command can include the standard Data Manipulation Language (DML) SQL statements (SELECT, INSERT, UPDATE, DELETE), or any of the platform-specific Data Definition Language (DDL) statements (such as CREATE TABLE). Do not include a terminating semicolon in the statement.

Instead of including the SQL statement and connection object in the command's constructor, you can assign these values to the command object's CommandText and Connection properties, respectively.

The command object includes several methods that send the command to the database for processing:

ExecuteReader( )
> Issues a command, and returns the data results in the form of a DataReader object. See Recipe 13.3 for additional information on data readers.

ExecuteNonQuery( )
> Issues a command, expecting no results. This method is generally used for INSERT, UPDATE, and DELETE commands.

ExecuteScalar( )
> Issues a command, expecting a single row and column of data in response. The data is returned as a generic System.Object instance, which you can convert to the appropriate data type.

ExecuteXmlReader( )
> Issues a command, and returns the data results as an XmlReader object.

There are also asynchronous versions of these methods (except for ExecuteScalar( )).

See Also

Other recipes in this chapter use additional features of command objects. For instance, Recipe 13.5 uses a command object to access a stored procedure.

13.3   Retrieving Results from a Database Query

Problem

You've issued INSERT, UPDATE, and DELETE statements through a command object, but you need to retrieve some data with a SELECT statement.

Solution

Use a DataReader object to quickly review the results of a SELECT statement.

Discussion

The following code retrieves a set of records from Table1:

```
' ----- Connect to the database.
Dim connectionString As String = _
   "Data Source=MySystem\SQLEXPRESS;" & _
   "Initial Catalog=MyDatabase;Integrated Security=true"
Dim theDatabase As New SqlClient.SqlConnection(connectionString)
theDatabase.Open( )

' ----- Prepare the SQL statement for the reader.
Dim sqlStatement As New SqlClient.SqlCommand( _
   "SELECT * FROM Table1 WHERE Column2 = 25", _
   theDatabase)
Dim dataResults As SqlClient.SqlDataReader = _
   sqlStatement.ExecuteReader( )

' ----- Clean up.
sqlStatement = Nothing
theDatabase.Close( )
theDatabase.Dispose( )
```

Assuming that the query returned records, the dataResults object now makes those records available, one at a time. The Read( ) method retrieves each successive record from the database:

```
Do While dataResults.Read( )
   MsgBox("Column1 = " & CStr(dataResults!Column1))
Loop
dataResults.Close( )
```

Read( ) returns False when there are no more records available.

To check for the presence of any records before using the Read( ) method, use the HasRows property:

```
If (dataResults.HasRows = False) Then MsgBox("No data.")
```

Data readers provide basic and direct access to result sets. They are no-frills objects, but they are quick and simple to use. Their basic and essential features form the basis of other, more complex data-gathering actions in ADO.NET. When you retrieve table results and store them in a DataSet object (described in Recipe 13.7), the DataSet indirectly uses a data reader to transfer the records from the database into the data set.

Records returned by a data reader can be accessed by name or position. For example, if you retrieve data with the columns Column1, Column2, and Column3 (in that order), you can use any of the following statements to access Column2:

```
dataResults!Column2
dataResults("Column2")
dataResults(1)  ' Zero-based array.
```

The fields returned by the reader are stored as System.Object values. You must convert them to their proper data types manually, using the available conversion functions.

Data readers are "forward-only" objects; once you have retrieved a record using Read( ), you cannot return to it without reissuing the SQL command to create a new data reader.

While data readers are most often used to process SELECT statements and stored procedures, there are other statements that return data results. SQL Server 2005 includes a new OUTPUT clause in INSERT statements that you can use to retrieve one or more data fields from the newly inserted record. It's common to create a database table with an automatically generated numeric primary key. After inserting a new record into such a table, you have to use a separate SELECT statement to retrieve the new primary key value. The OUTPUT clause lets you retrieve the new primary key value directly from the INSERT statement:

```
INSERT INTO Table1 (Column2, Column3)
   OUTPUT INSERTED.Column1
   VALUES (10, 20)
```

Sending this INSERT statement to the database using the ExecuteReader( ) method returns a single record with a single field containing the value of the new Column1 field. You can also use the ExecuteScalar( ) method because only a single value is returned:

```
Dim sqlStatement As New SqlClient.SqlCommand( _
   "INSERT INTO Table1 (Column2, Column3) " & _
   "OUTPUT INSERTED.Column1 VALUES (10, 20)", _
   theDatabase)
Dim newID As Integer = CInt(sqlStatement.ExecuteScalar( ))
sqlStatement = Nothing
```

See Also

Recipe 13.7 discusses how to simply replace the new data values in the SQL statement without having to build the SQL statement from scratch each time.

13.4   Using SQL Parameters

Problem

You need to insert a lot of records into a table, and you would like to simply replace the new data values in the SQL statement without having to build the SQL statement from scratch each time.

Solution

Attach one or more Parameter objects to the Command object.

Discussion

The following SQL Server example inserts new records into Table1, setting the Column2 column to a distinct value for each inserted record:

```
' ----- Connect to the database.
Dim connectionString As String = _
   "Data Source=MySystem\SQLEXPRESS;" & _
   "Initial Catalog=MyDatabase;Integrated Security=true"
Dim theDatabase As New SqlClient.SqlConnection(connectionString)
theDatabase.Open()

' ----- Build the generic command text.
Dim theCommand As New SqlClient.SqlCommand()
theCommand.CommandText = _
   "INSERT INTO Table1 (Column1) VALUES (@NewValue)"
theCommand.Connection = theDatabase

' ----- Add the first record.
theCommand.Parameters.AddWithValue("NewValue", "Blue")
theCommand.ExecuteNonQuery()

' ----- Add the second record.
theCommand.Parameters("NewValue").Value = "Red"
theCommand.ExecuteNonQuery()

' ----- Finished.
theCommand = Nothing
theDatabase.Close()
theDatabase.Dispose()
```

Parameters are often used to interact with stored procedures, but you can use them in other, more basic SQL statements to substitute for placeholders included in the SQL statement text. In SQL Server, placeholders begin with an at sign (@) followed by a parameter identifier. These identifiers match the names used when creating SqlParameter objects. These parameters are attached to the SqlCommand object containing the generic SQL text.

Once you've created the command object, adding parameters is simple. The easiest method employs the Parameters collection's AddWithValue() method to add the named parameters. This method accepts a parameter name and a value as any System.Object instance:

```
theCommand.Parameters.AddWithValue("NewValue", "Blue")
```

Once the parameter is in place, you can modify it in later statement reprocessing, accessing it by name:

```
theCommand.Parameters("NewValue").Value = "Red"
```

The exact syntax used to identify parameter placeholders in the SQL statement text may vary between providers.

See Also

Recipe 13.5 uses parameters to interact with stored procedures.

13.5   Using Stored Procedures

Problem

You need to use a stored procedure in your database, and you're not sure how to specify values for its input and output parameters.

Solution

Use the command object's `Parameters` collection to set and retrieve stored procedure argument values.

Discussion

Here's a simple SQL Server stored procedure that does nothing more than retrieve a field from a table given its ID value:

```
CREATE PROCEDURE GetRecordName
   @PriKey int,
   @NameResult varchar(50) OUT
AS
BEGIN
   -- Given an ID value, return the RecordName field.
   SET @NameResult =
      (SELECT RecordName FROM Table1 WHERE ID = @PriKey);
END
```

To use this stored procedure, create a command object that calls it, and add separate input and output parameters:

```
' ----- Connect to the database.
Dim connectionString As String = _
   "Data Source=MySystem\SQLEXPRESS;" & _
   "Initial Catalog=MyDatabase;Integrated Security=true"
Dim theDatabase As New SqlClient.SqlConnection(connectionString)
theDatabase.Open( )

' ----- Build the basic command.
Dim theCommand As New SqlClient.SqlCommand( )
theCommand.CommandType = CommandType.StoredProcedure
theCommand.Connection = theDatabase
theCommand.CommandText = "GetRecordName"

' ----- Add the input parameter. In this case,
'       use a test value of 25.
theCommand.Parameters.AddWithValue("@PriKey", 25)
```

```
' ----- Add the output parameter.
Dim outParam As SqlClient.SqlParameter = _
   theCommand.Parameters.Add( _
   "@NameResult", SqlDbType.VarChar, 50)
outParam.Direction = ParameterDirection.Output

' ----- Run the stored procedure.
theCommand.ExecuteNonQuery( )

' ----- The parameter has been updated for us.
MsgBox(outParam.Value)

' ----- Clean up.
theCommand = Nothing
theDatabase.Close( )
theDatabase.Dispose( )
```

Stored procedures come in a variety of styles. The most basic stored procedure simply returns a set of records, just like a SELECT statement does. Other stored procedures return their results either as return values or as output parameters. ADO.NET supports all these various kinds of stored procedures.

Stored procedures are called using a standard command object, but instead of supplying a SQL statement for the command text, you supply only the name of the stored procedure. Any input and output parameters are added through the command object's Parameters collection. The names given to the parameters in each Parameter object match those included in the stored procedure definition.

Basic input parameters can be added simply with the AddWithValue( ) method:

```
theCommand.Parameters.AddWithValue("@PriKey", 25)
```

Output parameters require a little more configuration:

```
Dim outParam As SqlClient.SqlParameter = _
   theCommand.Parameters.Add( _
   "@NameResult", SqlDbType.VarChar, 50)
outParam.Direction = ParameterDirection.Output
```

The Direction property indicates how this parameter is used by the stored procedure. It can be set to one of the following enumerated values:

- ParameterDirection.Input
- ParameterDirection.Output
- ParameterDirection.InputOutput
- ParameterDirection.ReturnValue

Once the parameters have been added, execute the stored procedure as you would any other command object:

```
theCommand.ExecuteNonQuery( )
```

If the stored procedure returns a set of records, use ExecuteReader( ) instead of ExecuteNonQuery( ) to access those records.

Once processed, ADO.NET automatically updates any output Parameter objects for you. Access the Value properties of these objects to retrieve the stored procedure results.

13.6 Using Transactions

Problem

You need to issue multiple database updates in the context of a single, atomic transaction.

Solution

Use an ADO.NET transaction to envelop the various SQL statements that need to be processed as a unit.

Discussion

The following block of code connects to a database via ADO.NET and makes several database updates within a single transaction:

```
' ----- Connect to the database.
Dim connectionString As String = _
   "Data Source=MySystem\SQLEXPRESS;" & _
   "Initial Catalog=MyDatabase;Integrated Security=true"
Dim theDatabase As New SqlClient.SqlConnection(connectionString)
theDatabase.Open( )

' ----- Create a command object that will hold each
'       processed SQL statement.
Dim sqlStatement As New SqlClient.SqlCommand
sqlStatement.Connection = theDatabase

' ----- Start the transaction.
Dim theTransaction As System.Data.SqlClient.SqlTransaction
theTransaction = theDatabase.BeginTransaction( )
sqlStatement.Transaction = theTransaction

' ----- Issue the first statement.
sqlStatement.CommandText = _
   "UPDATE Table1 SET Column2 = 25 WHERE Column1 = 0"
sqlStatement.ExecuteNonQuery( )

' ----- Issue the second statement.
sqlStatement.CommandText = _
   "UPDATE Table1 SET Column2 = 50 WHERE Column1 = 1"
sqlStatement.ExecuteNonQuery( )
```

```
' ----- Finish the transaction.
theTransaction.Commit( )

' ----- Clean up.
theTransaction = Nothing
sqlStatement = Nothing
theDatabase.Close( )
theDatabase.Dispose( )
```

Transactions allow multiple SQL statements to exhibit all-or-nothing behavior. The ADO.NET transaction object is provider-specific and communicates with the target database to manage the atomic nature of the multi-statement transaction.

The SqlTransaction object establishes a transaction for a set of statements in SQL Server. Instead of creating the object directly, use the connection's BeginTransaction( ) method to create it. This establishes the new transaction at the database level:

```
Dim theTransaction As System.Data.SqlClient.SqlTransaction
theTransaction = theDatabase.BeginTransaction( )
```

All commands issued while the transaction is in effect need to include the transaction object. Assign the object to each command's Transaction property:

```
sqlStatement.Transaction = theTransaction
```

When you have issued all the commands needed for this transaction, use the transaction object's Commit( ) method to permanently write all updates to the database:

```
theTransaction.Commit( )
```

If for any reason you need to cancel the changes in the middle of the transaction, use the Rollback( ) method instead:

```
theTransaction.Rollback( )
```

13.7   Storing the Results of a Query in Memory

Problem

While a data reader is fast and convenient, you would like to keep the retrieved data around for a while, even when you are disconnected from the database or other data source.

Solution

Use the data reader to bring the results into a data set. The DataSet object represents one or more in-memory database tables, each with its records stored in a separate DataTable object.

Discussion

The following code loads all records from the Table1 table into a DataSet object, creating a DataTable object named Table1 within that data set:

```
' ----- Connect to the database.
Dim connectionString As String = _
   "Data Source=MySystem\SQLEXPRESS;" & _
   "Initial Catalog=MyDatabase;Integrated Security=true"
Dim theDatabase As New SqlClient.SqlConnection(connectionString)
theDatabase.Open()

' ----- Prepare the SQL statement for use by the data set.
Dim sqlStatement As New SqlClient.SqlCommand( _
   "SELECT * FROM Table1", theDatabase)

' ----- Create the adapter that links the SQL Server-
'       specific connection and command objects with
'       the database-neutral data set.
Dim theAdapter As New SqlClient.SqlDataAdapter(sqlStatement)

' ----- Create the data set and fill it with the results
'       of the query.
Dim disconnectedSet As New Data.DataSet
theAdapter.Fill(disconnectedSet, "Table1")

' ----- Clean up.
theAdapter = Nothing
sqlStatement = Nothing
theDatabase.Close()
theDatabase.Dispose()
```

Data sets are like miniature in-memory relational databases, complete with tables, relationships, sorting, filters, field data types, and so on. They are a lot more complex than DataReader objects, but their disconnected nature and broader feature set make them useful for the longer-term caching and manipulation of data.

Each data set includes one or more DataTable objects. When you move data from an external data source to a DataSet, there are several objects that make up the connection between the source and the target:

- A Connection object establishes a communication transport between the application and the data source.

- Command objects encapsulate individual SQL statements used to retrieve or update data in the database. Each command may include zero or more Parameter objects that facilitate stored procedure and generic command processing. All Connection processing occurs via Command objects.

- A DataReader provides basic and fast data retrieval from a database via a Command object query.

- A `DataAdapter` builds the individual SQL commands used to retrieve and update data in the database. Working in conjunction with a `CommandBuilder` object, it crafts `SELECT`, `INSERT`, `UPDATE`, and `DELETE` commands that allow a `DataSet` to interact with a provider database, even though it doesn't know that provider's syntax rules. The `DataAdapter` works with a `DataReader` when retrieving results with a `SELECT` statement.
- The `DataSet` object contains the records of table and query data retrieved from the data source. These results are stored in one or more `DataTable` objects.
- The `DataTable` object contains the actual data for a single source table, whether it's a true table or a pseudotable based on a query.
- Data tables are built from distinct `DataRow` and `DataColumn` objects that, when used together, provide access to individual records and fields.

These represent just the most basic objects used in database/DataSet interactions. You can add even more objects and complexity through `DataRelation` and `Constraint` objects.

Once data has been copied from a database into a `DataSet`, you can manipulate it just as though it was still part of an organized data source. For the data retrieved from the `Table1` table in our imaginary database, you can access the first record's `Column1` value using code similar to the following. There are a few different ways to do this, including this statement:

```
disconnectedSet.Tables!Table1.Rows(0)!Column1
```

or the more verbose:

```
disconnectedSet.Tables("Table1").Rows(0).Item("Column1")
```

The `Rows` member of each table is a standard collection, so you can scan it using ordinary collection features in Visual Basic:

```
For Each oneRow As DataRow In disconnectedSet.Tables!Table1.Rows
    MsgBox(oneRow!Column1)
Next oneRow
```

Data sets are great for keeping cached data in memory for ongoing use. But you can also update the fields stored in a data set, and later send those changes back to the database in a batch. You must use a data adapter to help process the individual `INSERT`, `UPDATE`, and `DELETE` statements required to modify the source database. While you can write each command yourself, you can also have a `CommandBuilder` object generate them for you based on the initial `SELECT` statement. The following code modifies this recipe's solution to include updates to the database (we've highlighted the new statements, and to save some space, we left off the database connection and cleanup code):

```
' ----- Prepare the SQL statement for use by the data set.
Dim sqlStatement As New SqlClient.SqlCommand( _
    "SELECT * FROM Table1", theDatabase)
```

```
' ----- Create the adapter that links the SQL Server-
'        specific connection and command objects with
'        the database-neutral data set.
Dim theAdapter As New SqlClient.SqlDataAdapter(sqlStatement)

' ----- Create a command builder that will auto-generate
'        the various UPDATE statements.
Dim theBuilder As New SqlClient.SqlCommandBuilder(theAdapter)

' ----- Create the data set and fill it with the results
'        of the query.
Dim disconnectedSet As New Data.DataSet
theAdapter.Fill(disconnectedSet, "Table1")

' ---- Modify some data.
disconnectedSet.Tables!Table1.Rows(0)!Column1 = 50

' ----- Return the updates to the database.
theAdapter.Update(disconnectedSet, "Table1")
```

If you don't want the "convenience" of the full DataSet object, you can retrieve your results into an individual DataTable object, which has a little less overhead. DataSet objects use DataTable objects anyway to store the records, so there's no reason you can't use them yourself. The following code modifies this recipe's original solution to use a DataTable object instead of a full DataSet object (we've highlighted the lines that are different from the DataSet-specific code):

```
' ----- Connect to the database.
Dim connectionString As String = _
   "Data Source=MySystem\SQLEXPRESS;" & _
   "Initial Catalog=MyDatabase;Integrated Security=true"
Dim theDatabase As New SqlClient.SqlConnection(connectionString)
theDatabase.Open( )

' ----- Prepare the SQL statement for use by the data set.
Dim sqlStatement As New SqlClient.SqlCommand( _
   "SELECT * FROM Table1", theDatabase)

' ----- Create the adapter that links the SQL Server-
'        specific connection and command objects with
'        the database-neutral data set.
Dim theAdapter As New SqlClient.SqlDataAdapter(sqlStatement)

' ----- Create and fill the data table with the results
'        of the query.
Dim singleTable As New Data.DataTable
theAdapter.Fill(singleTable)

' ----- Clean up.
theAdapter = Nothing
sqlStatement = Nothing
theDatabase.Close( )
theDatabase.Dispose( )
```

See Also

Recipe 13.8 demonstrates how to set up manual `DataTable` objects that don't interact with database tables.

13.8   Creating In-Memory Data Tables Manually

Problem

You want to manage some data in a database-table-like fashion, but the source data is not coming from a database, or from anything that looks like a table.

Solution

Build a `DataTable` manually, and fill in all the table details and data yourself.

Discussion

The following code builds a simple table of state information and adds two records:

```
Dim stateTable As DataTable = New DataTable("UnitedStates")

' ----- Use the abbreviation as the primary key.
Dim priKeyCol(0) As Data.DataColumn
priKeyCol(0) = stateTable.Columns.Add("ShortName", GetType(String))
stateTable.PrimaryKey = priKeyCol

' ----- Add other data columns.
stateTable.Columns.Add("FullName", GetType(String))
stateTable.Columns.Add("Admission", GetType(Date))
stateTable.Columns.Add("Population", GetType(Long))

' ----- Add a record.
Dim stateInfo As Data.DataRow = stateTable.NewRow( )
stateInfo!ShortName = "WA"
stateInfo!FullName = "Washington"
stateInfo!Admission = #11/11/1889#
stateInfo!Population = 5894121
stateTable.Rows.Add(stateInfo)

' ----- Add another record.
stateInfo = stateTable.NewRow( )
stateInfo!ShortName = "MT"
stateInfo!FullName = "Montana"
stateInfo!Admission = #11/8/1889#
stateInfo!Population = 902195
stateTable.Rows.Add(stateInfo)

' ----- Prove that the data arrived.
MsgBox(stateTable.Rows.Count)        ' Displays "2"
MsgBox(stateTable.Rows(0)!FullName) ' Displays "Washington"
```

ADO.NET defines the basic structures for tables, columns (fields), and rows (records), and it's pretty easy to use them to build your own tables by hand. To create a table, simply create a DataTable object:

```
Dim stateTable As DataTable = New DataTable("UnitedStates")
```

The table isn't of much use yet because it doesn't have any column definitions, but they are simple to add as well. Columns, at their most basic structure, are composed of a name and a data type. While the columns in your database may be limited to just a few basic data types, ADO.NET table columns can be defined using any data type or class that you can build in .NET. You could even store an entire DataSet object in a column of a DataTable record, although that would be a little strange. To add a column, use the table's Columns.Add( ) method:

```
stateTable.Columns.Add("FullName", GetType(String))
```

To add a record, use the table's NewRow( ) method, which generates a DataRow object. You could create a new DataRow from scratch, but it wouldn't have any of the column definitions already added to the DataTable. Using NewRow( ) takes care of setting up that structure for you. Once you've updated each record field, add it to the table using the table's Rows.Add( ) method:

```
stateTable.Rows.Add(stateInfo)
```

Once your records are in your table, you can manipulate them just like you would in a real database table. For instance, you can sort the records based on one of the fields using the Select( ) method:

```
' ----- Process an array of states sorted by name.
For Each stateInfo In stateTable.Select("", "FullName")
   MsgBox(stateInfo!FullName)
Next stateInfo
```

If you want to go all the way and add your table to a DataSet object, use code similar to the following:

```
Dim fullDataSet As New Data.DataSet
fullDataSet.Tables.Add(stateTable)
```

See Also

Recipe 13.7 shows you how to use DataTable objects in conjunction with a database.

13.9   Writing In-Memory Data Tables to an XML File

Problem

You have some data in a DataSet object, and you would like to export it to an XML file for later reimportation.

Solution

Use the DataSet's WriteXML( ) method to send the DataSet content to the file in a common XML format.

Discussion

Recipe 13.8 builds a DataTable object with two state-specific records. The following code adds that table to a DataSet object and writes its records to an XML file:

```
Dim fullDataSet As New Data.DataSet
fullDataSet.Tables.Add(stateTable)
fullDataSet.WriteXml("C:\StateInfo.xml")
```

These statements generate the following XML content:

```
<?xml version="1.0" standalone="yes"?>
<NewDataSet>
  <UnitedStates>
    <ShortName>WA</ShortName>
    <FullName>Washington</FullName>
    <Admission>1889-11-11T00:00:00-08:00</Admission>
    <Population>5894121</Population>
  </UnitedStates>
  <UnitedStates>
    <ShortName>MT</ShortName>
    <FullName>Montana</FullName>
    <Admission>1889-11-08T00:00:00-08:00</Admission>
    <Population>902195</Population>
  </UnitedStates>
</NewDataSet>
```

You can also output the XML directly from the DataTable object without using a DataSet object:

```
stateTable.WriteXML("C:\StateInfo.xml")
```

ADO.NET was designed with an understanding of data from an XML perspective. Publicly, it exposes this awareness through several XML-specific methods, including the WriteXML( ) method. The schema generated with this XML database is crafted for efficient processing by ADO.NET. When you later import the exported data from the XML file to a DataSet or DataTable object, ADO.NET will complain if the data doesn't match a format it understands.

To access the schema that matches the exported data, use the related WriteXMLSchema( ) method:

```
stateTable.WriteXMLSchema("C:\StateSchema.xml")
```

See Also

Recipe 13.10 shows you how to bring the exported data back into a DataSet object.

13.10 Reading an XML File into In-Memory Data Tables

Problem

You previously exported a DataSet to an XML file, and now you need to get it back.

Solution

Use the DataSet object's ReadXML( ) method to restore data from a previously generated XML export.

Discussion

Recipe 13.9 exports some XML and a related schema for a table with state-specific information. To read it back into a DataSet object, use the following code:

```
Dim stateSet As New Data.DataSet
stateSet.ReadXmlSchema("c:\StateSchema.xml")
stateSet.ReadXml("c:\StateInfo.xml")
```

You do not need to import a previously saved schema into a DataSet before retrieving the related data, but it helps. Without the schema, either you will have to recraft the column definitions in each DataTable object yourself, or you will have to refer to each data column by numeric position and without strong data typing. Reloading a previously saved schema takes care of a lot of the redesigning work for you. If your program will use a consistent schema regularly, you can save it internally in your application source code or in an application resource. You can also import schema and data files directly into a DataTable object, forgoing the larger DataSet object:

```
Dim stateTable As New Data.DataTable
stateTable.ReadXmlSchema("c:\StateSchema.xml")
stateTable.ReadXml("c:\StateInfo.xml")
```

Once you have imported the data, you can use that data just as if you had hand-crafted it using ADO.NET objects or imported it from a standard database:

```
' ----- Process each imported state record.
For Each stateInfo As Data.DataRow In stateTable.Rows( )
   MsgBox(stateInfo!FullName)
Next stateInfo
```

See Also

Recipe 13.9 demonstrates exporting DataSet or DataTable content to an XML file.

Special Programming Techniques

14.0 Introduction

The "A" in BASIC—the predecessor of Visual Basic—stands for "all-purpose." As an heir of that original programming language, Visual Basic has maintained the standard of being an all-purpose language, a language that is generic enough to handle a vast set of different programming needs. That has never been truer than with Visual Basic 2005.

The recipes included in this chapter cover a wide range of topics, from basic application management to credit card verification. The key is that you can do all these varied tasks quite easily in Visual Basic.

14.1 Preventing Multiple Instances of a Running Application

Problem

You don't want the active user to run more than one copy of an application at any one time.

Solution

Sample code folder: Chapter 14\SingleInstanceOnly

Capture attempts to start up secondary instances of an application through an application-wide event handler. This event handler, new to Visual Basic 2005 and available only to Windows Forms applications using the Application Framework, triggers in the primary instance whenever the user tries to start a secondary instance.

Discussion

Create a new Windows Forms application in Visual Studio. The Application Framework is enabled by default; you can confirm this by checking the "Enable application framework" field on the Application tab of the Project Properties window, shown in Figure 14-1.

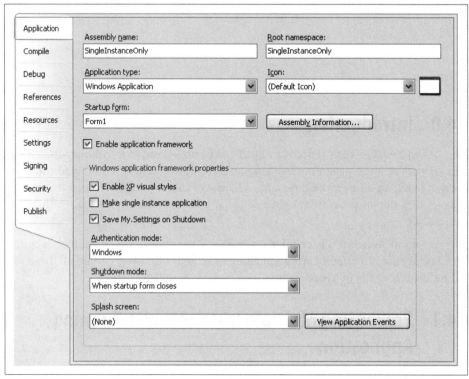

Figure 14-1. Make sure the "Enable application framework" field is checked

Even with the Application Framework enabled, by default the application allows multiple instances to start at once. To prevent this, select the "Make single instance application" field on this same Project Properties panel (Figure 14-1 still shows it as unchecked).

The event to handle is typically called MyApplication_StartupNextInstance, and it appears by default in the project's *ApplicationEvents.vb* file. Since you already have the Application panel of the Project Properties window open, you can access this file quickly by clicking on the View Application Events button. The source code appears, with the start of a partial My.MyApplication class:

```
Namespace My
    Partial Friend Class MyApplication

    End Class
End Namespace
```

To add the event handler, select "(MyApplication Events)" from the Class Name drop-down list, which appears just above and to the left of the source code editor window. Then select "StartupNextInstance" from the Method Name drop-down list that is above and to the right of the code editor. The template for the event handler appears in the MyApplication class:

```
Private Sub MyApplication_StartupNextInstance( _
        ByVal sender As Object, ByVal e As _
        Microsoft.VisualBasic.ApplicationServices. _
        StartupNextInstanceEventArgs) _
        Handles Me.StartupNextInstance

End Sub
```

To complete the program, add the following code to this template:

```
MsgBox("You cannot start a second instance " & _
    "of this program.", _
    MsgBoxStyle.OkOnly Or MsgBoxStyle.Exclamation)
e.BringToForeground = True
```

Even if you limit your application to a single instance, it may be important to capture any command-line arguments supplied with the secondary instance. For example, Microsoft Word works like a single-instance application. It allows you to start up the application, supplying a document to edit as a command-line argument. If you run this command in Microsoft Word:

```
winword.exe C:\Chapter14.doc
```

the *Chapter14.doc* file appears as a new document, but running in the context of the already active single allowable instance of Microsoft Word.

In Visual Basic, you can access command-line arguments through the Command( ) function or through the My.Application.CommandLineArgs collection. However, these methods are valid only for the primary instance. If you examine Command( ) in the MyApplication_StartupNextInstance event handler, you will only see the arguments for the initial instance.

Fortunately, the e argument of the MyApplication_StartupNextInstance handler includes a CommandLine property, which communicates the command-line arguments for the subsequent instance as a String. Use this property as you would the return value of the standard Command( ) function. Once the event handler ends, you won't have access to the second instance's command line, so make sure you examine or save it, if needed, while in the handler.

14.2 Creating a Simple User Control

Problem

You would like to create your own Windows Forms control by building it up from other existing controls.

Solution

Sample code folder: Chapter 14\UserControl

Create a user control, a custom user-interface control built from a drawing surface in which any other existing controls can appear.

Discussion

Visual Basic allows you to build two types of controls: *user controls* and *custom controls*. User controls act somewhat like borderless forms on which you can "draw" other existing controls. Custom controls provide no default user interface; you must manage all custom control drawing yourself through source code. This recipe will focus on the user control, designing a simple control that displays the current time.

Create a new Windows Forms application. For now, we'll just ignore the Form1 form included in the project. To add a new user control to the project, select the Project → Add User Control menu command. Accept the default *UserControl1.vb* name, and then click the Add button on the Add New Item form. A blank user control appears, as shown in Figure 14-2.

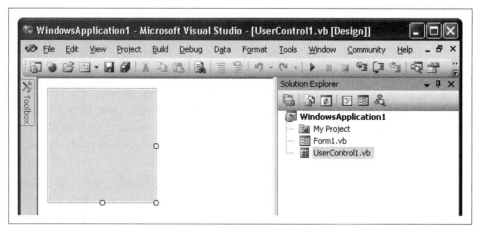

Figure 14-2. A new user control surface

Our simple user control will include two constituent controls: a label to display the time, and a timer that will trigger once a second to update the time. First, resize the user control down to a reasonable size. We used a Size property of 96,24. Add a Label control named Label1, and set the following properties:

- Set AutoSize to False.
- Set Location to 0,0.
- Set Size to 96,24.
- Set Text to 12:00am.
- Set TextAlign to MiddleCenter.

Add a Timer control named Timer1, and set the following properties:

- Set Enabled to True.
- Set Interval to 1000, which sets it to trigger once every second.

Switch to the source code for the user control through the View → Code menu command, and add the following source code:

```
Public Class UserControl1
    Public Event TimeChanged(ByVal sender As UserControl1, _
      ByVal e As System.EventArgs)

    Private Sub Timer1_Tick(ByVal sender As System.Object, _
        ByVal e As System.EventArgs) Handles Timer1.Tick
      ' ----- Update every second.
      Dim newTime As String

      If (Me.DesignMode = False) Then
        newTime = Format(Now, "h:mmtt").ToLower( )
        If (newTime <> Label1.Text) Then
          Label1.Text = newTime
          RaiseEvent TimeChanged(Me, New System.EventArgs)
        End If
      End If
    End Sub

    Private Sub UserControl1_Load(ByVal sender As Object, _
        ByVal e As System.EventArgs) Handles Me.Load
      ' ----- Always reset the time when first started.
      If (Me.DesignMode = False) Then
        Label1.Text = Format(Now, "h:mmtt").ToLower( )
        RaiseEvent TimeChanged(Me, New System.EventArgs)
      End If
    End Sub
End Class
```

That's the whole control. It's just about ready to add to the Form1 surface, but you first have to build the project to allow Visual Studio to create an instance of the control. Build it using the Build → Build WindowsApplication1 menu command.

Switch over to the Form Designer for Form1. If you open the Toolbox, you will see the user control UserControl1 in the magically added WindowsApplication1 Components section, as shown in Figure 14-3. (The section name will vary if you gave your project a different name.)

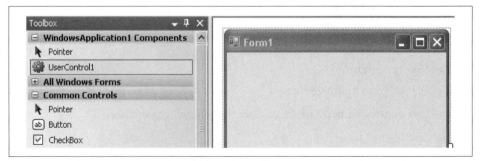

Figure 14-3. The new UserControl1 control in the Toolbox

Double-click the user control in the Toolbox to add it to the form surface. It should display the "12:00am" message we added to the control's label. However, if you run the application, the running form will display the correct time.

Our user control included a public event named `TimeChanged`:

```
Public Event TimeChanged(ByVal sender As UserControl1, _
    ByVal e As System.EventArgs)
```

You can respond to this event from `Form1`. Open the source code for `Form1`, and add the following event handler:

```
Private Sub UserControl11_TimeChanged( _
        ByVal sender As UserControl1, _
        ByVal e As System.EventArgs) _
        Handles UserControl11.TimeChanged
    MsgBox("Changed!")
End Sub
```

Now, when you run the program, a "Changed!" message appears at startup (via the code for the user control's `UserControl1_Load` event handler), and also every time the minute changes (via the user control's `Timer1_Tick` event handler).

Visual Basic 2005 lets you easily design a new user control using mixtures of existing controls. You can also draw on the user control's surface through its `Paint` event handler, but you don't have to. (If you wish to update the surface via `Paint`, and not through subordinate controls, use a custom control instead of a user control.)

All child controls added to the surface of the user control are "owned" by the user control, not by (in this example) `Form1`. This means that your control can monitor any normal control events for its child controls, but the form using your user control will not know about those events. In this recipe, the user control exposes a `Click` event that `Form1` can monitor. An event fires any time the user clicks on the user control surface. However, because we covered the surface with a label, clicks will never reach the user control surface, and the form will never be informed of such click events. If you want clicks on the label to transfer to the user control, you must manage that yourself. Adding this code to the user control's source code will do the trick:

```
Public Shadows Event Click(ByVal sender As Object, _
    ByVal e As System.EventArgs)

Private Sub Label1_Click(ByVal sender As Object, _
      ByVal e As System.EventArgs) Handles Label1.Click
    RaiseEvent Click(Me, e)
End Sub

Private Sub UserControl1_Click(ByVal sender As Object, _
      ByVal e As System.EventArgs) Handles MyBase.Click
    RaiseEvent Click(Me, e)
End Sub
```

Because the UserControl class (from which our UserControl1 class derives) already exposes a Click event, you have to cover it up by declaring a new Click event. The Shadows keyword covers up the event in the base. Now add Click event handlers to capture clicks on both the Label and UserControl surfaces, and pass them on to those who add UserControl1 to their forms. Look carefully at the UserControl1_Click event handler just above. Make sure that it handles MyBase.Click, and not Me.Click. If you use Me.Click, a click on the control surface will repeatedly call itself until you run out of stack space.

After adding this code, resize the label a little smaller so that the user can click on the user control surface. Return to the source code for Form1, and add this code to its class template:

```
Private Sub UserControl11_Click(ByVal sender As Object, _
      ByVal e As System.EventArgs) Handles UserControl11.Click
    MsgBox("Clicked!")
End Sub
```

Now run the program. You will see the "Clicked!" message whether you click on the label or the user control surface.

If you are building a user control for use elsewhere in the same project, any child controls you include on the surface of your user control will, by default, be accessible to the entire application. For instance, in this recipe's code, you can access the caption for the user control's label from the code for Form1. Go back to that UserControl11_TimeChanged event handler you added to Form1. On a new line, type the following:

```
UserControl1.L
```

As you type the letter L, you will see Label1 appear in the IntelliSense pop up. If you don't want this to happen, return to the user control designer, select Label1, and change its Modifers property to Private instead of Friend.

14.3   Describing User Control Properties

Problem

You've added an extra property to your user control, and although it appears in the Properties panel when the control is added to a form, no description appears for that property.

Solution

Sample code folder: Chapter 14\UserControlProperties

Add a <DescriptionAttribute> attribute to the property, and use it to supply any descriptive text you want as metadata attached to the property.

Discussion

Create a new Windows Forms project, and add a new user control to the project through the Project → Add User Control menu command. (See Recipe 14.2 for details on designing new user controls.) Name the new control *SimpleControl.vb*. For this sample, it's not necessary to add any child controls, but you should change the user control's BackColor property to ButtonShadow, just so you will recognize the control when it's added to Form1 later.

Access the source code for the user control and add the following code to the class:

```
Private hiddenData As String

Public Property ExtraData( ) As String
   Get
      Return hiddenData
   End Get
   Set(ByVal value As String)
      hiddenData = value
   End Set
End Property
```

This code adds a simple property, ExtraData, to the control, storing the actual value in the private hiddenData member. The control is complete; build it using the Build → Build WindowsApplication1 menu command.

Return to the form designer for Form1. Locate the new SimpleControl control in the Toolbox and add it to the form. If you look in the Properties panel, you will see the ExtraData property, but it won't have any description (see Figure 14-4).

To add the description, return to the source code for the user control. Add the following line to the top of the *SimpleControl.vb* source-code file:

```
Imports System.ComponentModel
```

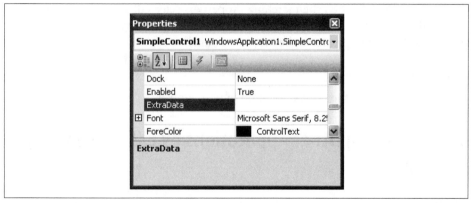

Figure 14-4. The ExtraData property, with no description

Just before the `Public Property ExtraData` line in the `SimpleControl` class, add this new code line:

```
<DescriptionAttribute( _
    "Extra details related to this control.")> _
```

so that the start of the property looks like this:

```
<DescriptionAttribute( _
    "Extra details related to this control.")> _
Public Property ExtraData() As String
```

Rebuild the project, return to `Form1`, and select the user control you added to the form earlier. When selected, the `ExtraData` property should now include a description, as shown in Figure 14-5.

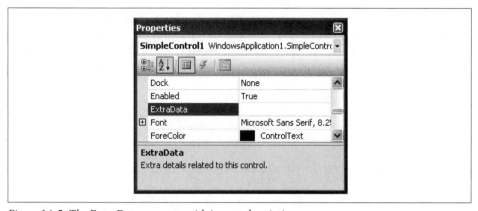

Figure 14-5. The ExtraData property with its new description

The `System.ComponentModel` namespace exposes several attributes that, when used, enhance the elements included in the Properties panel. One of these attributes, `<DescriptionAttribute>`, identifies the text that appears in the description portion of the Properties panel when the matching property is selected. This attribute is stored as metadata attached to the `SimpleControl.ExtraData` property, and it is referenced by the control that implements the Properties panel.

See Also

Recipe 14.2 discusses the implementation of user controls.

14.4   Starting Other Applications by EXE, Document, or URL

Problem

You need to start up a separate application, based on either the path to the executable program file, a document with a registered file extension, or a valid URL for a web page or other resource.

Solution

Use the `System.Diagnostics.Process.Start( )` method to initiate applications external to your own application.

Discussion

The `Start( )` method returns an object of type `System.Diagnostics.Process` that encapsulates the newly started application. `Process.Start( )` works with three types of targets:

- If you know the path to the executable (EXE) file, you can specify it using the first argument to `Process.Start( )`. If you don't supply a full path, Windows will search through the path defined for the current user for the program. Any additional command-line arguments appear in the second argument:

    ```
    ' ----- Start up a new Notepad window.
    Process.Start("C:\Windows\Notepad.exe")

    ' ----- Excluding the path and extension works.
    Process.Start("Notepad")

    ' ----- Open a specific file through Notepad.
    Process.Start("Notepad.exe", "C:\DataFile.txt")
    ```

- You can start an application associated with a registered file extension by specifying a file with that extension as the argument:

    ```
    ' ----- Open Notepad with a specific file.
    Process.Start("C:\DataFile.txt")
    ```

The file must already exist and must have a valid registered file extension, or an exception will occur.

- You can specify any URL, including a web page or email address (in a *mailto://* URL). Any of the accepted URL prefixes, such as `http://`, `mailto://`, or `file://`, can be included in the URL:

```
' ----- Open a specific web page in the default browser.
Process.Start("http://www.microsoft.com")
```

The arguments passed to `Process.Start( )` are similar to those you would enter in the Windows Start → Run menu command prompt, or in the Windows Command Prompt using the `Start` command.

The `Process` object returned by `Process.Start( )` includes several properties and methods that let you monitor and control (somewhat) the new process. To force the new process to exit, use the `Process` object's `Kill( )` method.

Visual Basic also includes another command from its pre-.NET days that starts up external applications. The `Shell( )` function accepts two arguments: the command and the window style. The command is the executable filename of the program to run, with any command-line arguments included. The second argument uses the members of the `Microsoft.VisualBasic.AppWinStyle` enumeration to indicate whether the new program's main window should start as maximized, minimized, or normal, and whether it should immediately receive the input focus. Here are the choices:

- `AppWinStyle.Hide`
- `AppWinStyle.MaximizedFocus`
- `AppWinStyle.MinimizedFocus`
- `AppWinStyle.MinimizedNoFocus`
- `AppWinStyle.NormalFocus`
- `AppWinStyle.NormalNoFocus`

For example, to start up Notepad with a specific file open, use this command:

```
Shell("Notepad.exe C:\DataFile.txt", _
    AppWinStyle.NormalFocus)
```

You can use only executable programs with `Shell( )`. It does not accept URLs or files with registered extensions.

See Also

Recipe 14.5 shows how to wait for the newly started process to complete before continuing with the main program.

14.5 Waiting for Applications to Finish

Problem

You need to start up a separate application. Once it starts, you need to wait until that program completes. Your application can then continue on with its own processing.

Solution

Use the `System.Diagnostics.Process.Start()` method to initiate the program and return an instance of `System.Diagnostics.Process`. Now call that object's `WaitForExit()` method.

Recipe 14.4 discusses how to use the `Start()` method, so we won't repeat all that detail here. The following code starts up Notepad and waits for it to exit before continuing:

```
Dim notepadProcess = Process.Start("Notepad.exe")
notepadProcess.WaitForExit()
MsgBox("Welcome back!")
```

Discussion

The `WaitForExit()` method accepts an optional millisecond count as its only argument. When used, `WaitForExit()` waits up to the number of milliseconds specified and then continues with the program, even if the external process is still running.

Another `Process` class method, `WaitForInputIdle()`, waits until the external process has reached a state where it is waiting for user input before continuing. It also accepts an optional millisecond count.

As discussed in Recipe 14.4, you can also use the Visual Basic `Shell()` function to start applications. This function includes two optional arguments (the third and fourth arguments) that control how long the current program should wait for the external process. The third argument, `wait`, accepts a `Boolean` value that, when set to `True`, causes the current program to wait until the external program completes. The fourth argument, `timeout`, indicates the maximum time, in milliseconds, that the program should wait for the external program to complete before continuing. Its default value is `-1`, which causes `Shell()` to wait forever.

The following statement starts up Notepad and waits up to 10 seconds for it to complete:

```
Shell("Notepad.exe", AppWinStyle.NormalFocus, True, 10000)
```

See Also

Recipe 14.4 discusses the `Shell()` function and the `Process.Start()` method.

14.6   List All Running Processes

Problem

You need to display a list of the processes that are currently running on the local workstation.

Solution

Sample code folder: Chapter 14\RunningProcesses

Use the System.Diagnostics.Process class to access a collection of objects representing all currently running processes.

Discussion

This recipe's sample code displays any process with a window title in a listbox. Create a new Windows Forms application, and add a ListBox control named ListBox1 to Form1. Then add the following event handler to Form1's code:

```
Private Sub Form1_Load(ByVal sender As Object, _
        ByVal e As System.EventArgs) Handles Me.Load
    ' ----- Show all top-level processes.
    For Each oneProcess As Process In Process.GetProcesses()
        If (oneProcess.MainWindowTitle <> "") Then
            ListBox1.Items.Add("Program: " & _
                oneProcess.MainWindowTitle)
        Else
            ListBox1.Items.Add("Process: " & _
                oneProcess.ProcessName)
        End If
    Next oneProcess
End Sub
```

Run the program to display the list of processes. It should generally match the list of processes and applications you see in the Windows Task Manager, although the form itself ("Form1") will probably not appear, since it wasn't yet visible when ListBox1 was populated. Figure 14-6 shows the running program with the listbox populated.

The System.Diagnostics.Process class includes a shared member named GetProcesses() that returns a collection of Process objects, each representing a running process. There are many more processes than just those with window titles; all running Windows services also appear in this collection.

The Process object includes many properties and methods that let you manage each process. However, your level of authorization as configured by the system administrator may prevent you from modifying or even viewing process details.

Figure 14-6. Listing all processes running on a system

14.7   Terminating a Running Process

Problem

You need to stop a running process immediately.

Solution

Sample code folder: Chapter 14\ProcessTerminate

Use the Process object's Kill( ) method to stop the running process.

Discussion

This recipe's code creates a simple program that lets you stop any running application, similar to using the End Task button on the Windows Task Manager. Create a new Windows Forms application, and add to the form a ListBox control named ProcessList and a Button control named KillProcess. Change the Button control's Text property to Kill, and set the ListBox control's Sorted property to True. Now open the source code for the form, and replace the default empty class template with the following code:

```
Public Class Form1
    Private Sub Form1_Load(ByVal sender As Object, _
        ByVal e As System.EventArgs) Handles Me.Load
        ' ----- Display all top-level windows.
        For Each oneProcess As Process In _
            Process.GetProcesses( )
            If (oneProcess.MainWindowTitle <> "") Then
                ProcessList.Items.Add(New SmallProcess( _
```

```
            oneProcess.MainWindowTitle, oneProcess.Id))
        End If
    Next oneProcess
End Sub

Private Sub KillProcess_Click( _
        ByVal sender As System.Object, _
        ByVal e As System.EventArgs) _
        Handles KillProcess.Click
    ' ----- Kill the selected process.
    Dim oneProcess As Process
    Dim selectedProcess As SmallProcess

    On Error Resume Next

    If (ProcessList.SelectedIndex = -1) Then Exit Sub
    selectedProcess = CType(ProcessList.SelectedItem, _
        SmallProcess)

    ' ----- Confirm with the user.
    If (MsgBox("Really kill '" & _
        selectedProcess.ToString() & "'?", _
        MsgBoxStyle.Question Or MsgBoxStyle.YesNo) <> _
        MsgBoxResult.Yes) Then Exit Sub

    ' ----- Locate and kill the process.
    oneProcess = Process.GetProcessById(selectedProcess.ID)
    oneProcess.Kill()

    ' ----- Remove the process from the list.
    ProcessList.Items.Remove(ProcessList.SelectedItem)
    End Sub
End Class

Public Class SmallProcess
    ' ----- A small class that makes it easier to
    '       track processes in the on-screen list.
    Public WindowTitle As String
    Public ID As Integer

    Public Sub New(ByVal processTitle As String, _
        ByVal processID As Integer)
        WindowTitle = processTitle
        ID = processID
    End Sub

    Public Overrides Function ToString() As String
        Return WindowTitle
    End Function
End Class
```

To kill a process, run this program, select a process from the list, and click the Kill button. Be careful: it will stop the indicated program.

By providing the Process.Kill( ) method, .NET endows your application with a lot of power. However, the system administrator may establish limits on the user running your program that will prevent access to or modification of process state.

This recipe's code includes a secondary class, SmallProcess, that helps keep track of items in the ListBox control. The Items collection of a ListBox control can hold any type of object, but how to display its own text is up to the object. You can store an entire Process object in the list, but the output from Process.ToString( ) is not as user-friendly. By storing just the parts you need in a separate class instance that includes its own ToString( ) method, you can get the results you need, both in terms of display and of access to the process IDs.

14.8   Pausing Execution of a Program

Problem

You want to postpone all activities on the current process thread.

Solution

Sample code folder: Chapter 14\PauseExecution

Put the thread to sleep using the System.Threading.Thread.Sleep( ) method. This method accepts an amount of time to "sleep," in milliseconds.

Discussion

Create a new Windows Forms application, and add a Button control named Button1. Now add the following code to the form's class template:

```
Private Sub Button1_Click(ByVal sender As System.Object, _
      ByVal e As System.EventArgs) Handles Button1.Click
   Threading.Thread.Sleep(3000)
   MsgBox("Good Morning")
End Sub
```

When you run the program and click on Button1, the "Good Morning" message appears after a three-second pause.

If your program includes only a single thread (the default behavior), putting the thread to sleep puts the entire application to sleep.

If you pass zero (0) to the Sleep( ) method, the thread pauses temporarily to allow other busy threads to perform some processing.

14.9   Control Applications by Simulating Keystrokes

Problem

You need another application to perform some tasks while your application is running, but it doesn't expose any type of control interface, whether ActiveX or .NET.

Solution

Sample code folder: Chapter 14\UsingSendKeys

Use the `My.Computer.Keyboard.SendKeys()` method to simulate the user controlling the other application from the keyboard.

Discussion

The following method uses `SendKeys()` to control the built-in Windows Paint program, using it to convert an existing image to black and white:

```
Public Sub MakeBitmapBW(ByVal sourceFile As String, _
    ByVal destFile As String)
  ' ----- Use the Paint program built into Windows to
  '       convert an existing bitmap file from color to
  '       black and white.
  Dim paintProcess As Process

  On Error Resume Next

  ' ----- Remove the existing output file.
  Kill(destFile)

  ' ----- Start Paint using the original file.
  paintProcess = Process.Start("mspaint.exe", sourceFile)
  AppActivate(paintProcess.Id)

  ' ----- Wait a bit for the file to open.
  System.Threading.Thread.Sleep(2000)

  ' ----- Convert the image to black and white. First,
  '       display the Attributes form using Control-E.
  My.Computer.Keyboard.SendKeys("^e", True)
  System.Threading.Thread.Sleep(500)

  ' ----- Alt-B sets the "Black and White" field.
  My.Computer.Keyboard.SendKeys("%b", True)
  System.Threading.Thread.Sleep(500)

  ' ----- Use Enter to accept the change. A confirmation
  '       window will appear. Use Enter for that window
  '       as well.
  My.Computer.Keyboard.SendKeys("~", True)
```

```
        System.Threading.Thread.Sleep(500)
        My.Computer.Keyboard.SendKeys("~", True)
        System.Threading.Thread.Sleep(500)

        ' ----- Save the file using the File->Save As... feature.
        My.Computer.Keyboard.SendKeys("%fa", True)
        System.Threading.Thread.Sleep(500)

        ' ----- Add the filename to the Save As window.
        '       Hopefully, the name has no special characters.
        My.Computer.Keyboard.SendKeys(destFile, True)
        My.Computer.Keyboard.SendKeys("~", True)
        System.Threading.Thread.Sleep(1000)

        ' ----- Exit the application.
        My.Computer.Keyboard.SendKeys("%{F4}", True)
    End Sub
```

To use this method, pass it the full path to an existing bitmap file and a path to the desired output location.

The SendKeys( ) method inserts specific keyboard commands into the global keyboard input stream. Those commands appear as if the user had actually typed them from the keyboard. The first argument to SendKeys( ) is a string containing each character to be inserted into the input stream. The second argument, a Boolean, indicates whether SendKeys( ) should wait until the active window acknowledges acceptance of the input.

Normally, each character you include in the character string is sent to the active window, one by one. However, some keys, such as the function keys (F1, F2, etc.) and the arrow keys, don't have single-character equivalents. Instead, there are special sequences you can use for these keys, most enclosed in curly braces. Some normal characters that have special meaning to SendKeys( ) must also appear in curly braces. Table 14-1 lists the text to include in the character string when you wish to use one of these special keyboard keys.

Table 14-1. Special SendKeys( ) key sequences

To include this key...	...use this text
Backspace	{BACKSPACE} or {BS} or {BKSP}
Break	{BREAK}
Caps lock	{CAPSLOCK}
Caret (^)	{^}
Clear	{CLEAR}
Close brace (})	{}}
Close bracket (])	{]}
Close parenthesis ())	{)}

Table 14-1. Special SendKeys( ) key sequences (continued)

To include this key...	...use this text
Delete	`{DELETE}` or `{DEL}`
Down arrow	`{DOWN}`
End	`{END}`
Enter	`~`
Escape	`{ESCAPE}` or `{ESC}`
F1 through F16	`{F1}` through `{F16}`
Help	`{HELP}`
Home	`{HOME}`
Insert	`{INSERT}` or `{INS}`
Keypad add	`{ADD}`
Keypad divide	`{DIVIDE}`
Keypad enter	`{ENTER}`
Keypad multiply	`{MULTIPLY}`
Keypad subtract	`{SUBTRACT}`
Left arrow	`{LEFT}`
Num lock	`{NUMLOCK}`
Open brace ({)	`{{}`
Open bracket ([)	`{[}`
Open parenthesis (()	`{(}`
Page down	`{PGDN}`
Page up	`{PGUP}`
Percent sign (%)	`{%}`
Plus (+)	`{+}`
Print screen	`{PRTSC}`
Return	`{RETURN}`
Right arrow	`{RIGHT}`
Scroll lock	`{SCROLLLOCK}`
Tab	`{TAB}`
Tilde (~)	`{~}`
Up arrow	`{UP}`

For example, if you want to send the number 25, a tab character, and then the number 50 to the input stream, send the following sequence:

```
25{TAB}50
```

You can also simulate the simultaneous use of the Shift, Control, or Alt keys in combination with other keys. Special prefix characters represent these three special modification keys:

- For Shift, use + (the plus sign).
- For Control, use ^ (the caret).
- For Alt, use % (the percent sign).

So, to send the Control-C character, use:

```
^c
```

If you want several characters to be used with one of these three modifiers, surround those keys with parentheses, and put the modifier just before that set. For instance, to send "hello" with the Shift key held down, use:

```
+(hello)
```

The key string provides a shortcut to transmit the same key multiple times, too. To use it, enclose the character to repeat and a count within curly braces. Separate the character and the count with a space. The following text sends 10 question marks:

```
{? 10}
```

There are some caveats when using SendKeys( ). Just because you include characters in the input stream doesn't mean that they will arrive at the program you target. Remember, the user still has access to the real keyboard, and to the mouse. The user could start pressing keys and clicking around the display right in the middle of your SendKeys( ) action, and you would have no control over the destination or sequence of the streaming input.

Similarly, even if you use True for the second argument to have your program wait until the keys are processed, there is no guarantee that the impact of those keys on the destination will complete before the wait is complete. A target program may acknowledge receipt of an input character and start to process it, but it could take several seconds (or longer) for it to complete the associated action. Meanwhile, your call to SendKeys( ) has exited, and your code is continuing on its way, possibly starting another call to SendKeys( ).

If you can control the other application through more direct means, such as through an exposed library or interface, that is preferred. Avoid having an application control itself with SendKeys( ).

Besides the SendKeys( ) command within the My namespace, Visual Basic includes a SendKeys class in the System.Windows.Forms namespace. This class includes shared Send( ) and SendWait( ) methods. Each accepts a string that is identical to the one used with the SendKeys( ) method. Except for slight differences in syntax and location in the .NET hierarchy, there is no essential difference between the My version and the Forms version.

14.10 Watching for File and Directory Changes

Problem

You need to monitor a directory, watching for any files that are added, removed, or changed.

Solution

Sample code folder: Chapter 14\FileWatcher

Use a FileSystemWatcher object and its events notify you of any changes in a specific directory or to specific files. System.IO.FileSystemWatcher includes many properties that let you adjust the types of files or changes to monitor. It also includes distinct events for most types of changes.

Discussion

The code in this recipe implements a simple test program that watches for any change in a selected directory. Create a new Windows Forms application, and add the following controls to Form1:

- A TextBox control named WatchDirectory.
- A TextBox control named WatchFilter.
- A CheckBox control named IncludeSubdirectories. Change its Text property to Include Subdirectories.
- A CheckedListBox control named WatchFor.
- A Button control named StartStop. Change its Text property to Start.
- A ListBox control named DirectoryEvents.

Add additional labels, if desired, and arrange the form to look like the one in Figure 14-7.

Open the source-code file for the form, and add the following code to the Form1 class template:

```
Public WithEvents WatchForChanges As IO.FileSystemWatcher

Private Sub Form1_Load(ByVal sender As System.Object, _
      ByVal e As System.EventArgs) Handles MyBase.Load
   ' ----- Add the types of actions. The Enum class's
   '       GetNames method returns a collection of the
   '       enumeration type's members as strings. Since
   '       "Enum" is a keyword in Visual Basic, the
   '       "Enum" class must be escaped with brackets.
   For Each scanFilters As String In [Enum].GetNames( _
         GetType(IO.NotifyFilters))
      WatchFor.Items.Add(scanFilters)
```

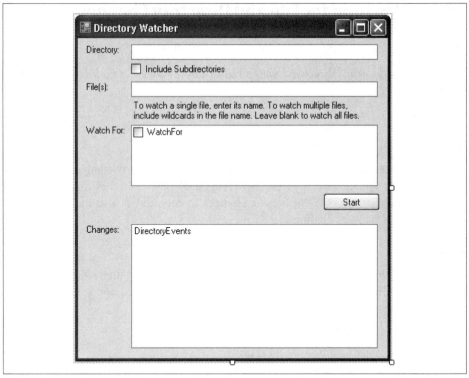

Figure 14-7. Controls for the directory watcher sample

```
      Next scanFilters
   End Sub

   Private Sub StartStop_Click(ByVal sender As System.Object, _
         ByVal e As System.EventArgs) Handles StartStop.Click
      ' ----- Start or stop watching a directory.
      Dim monitorEvents As Integer = 0

      If (StartStop.Text = "Start") Then
         ' ----- Check for valid settings.
         If (My.Computer.FileSystem.DirectoryExists( _
               WatchDirectory.Text) = False) Then
            MsgBox("Please specify a valid directory.")
            Exit Sub
         End If
         If (WatchFor.SelectedItems.Count = 0) Then
            MsgBox("Please specify the events to watch for.")
            Exit Sub
         End If

         ' ----- Build the events setting. The Enum class's
         '       Parse() method converts a string back to its
         '       Integer enumeration value, in this case,
```

```
'          from the IO.NotifyFilters enumeration.
      For Each scanEvents As String In WatchFor.CheckedItems
         monitorEvents = monitorEvents Or _
            CInt([Enum].Parse(GetType(IO.NotifyFilters), _
            scanEvents))
      Next scanEvents

      ' ----- Start the watching process.
      DirectoryEvents.Items.Clear()
      WatchForChanges = New IO.FileSystemWatcher
      WatchForChanges.SynchronizingObject = Me
      WatchForChanges.Path = WatchDirectory.Text
      WatchForChanges.Filter = WatchFilter.Text
      WatchForChanges.NotifyFilter = monitorEvents
      WatchForChanges.IncludeSubdirectories = IncludeSubdirectories.Checked
      WatchForChanges.EnableRaisingEvents = True
      StartStop.Text = "Stop"
   Else
      ' ----- End the watching process.
      WatchForChanges.EnableRaisingEvents = False
      WatchForChanges.Dispose()
      WatchForChanges = Nothing
      StartStop.Text = "Start"
   End If
End Sub

Private Sub WatchForChanges_Changed(ByVal sender As Object, _
      ByVal e As System.IO.FileSystemEventArgs) _
      Handles WatchForChanges.Changed
   DirectoryEvents.Items.Add("Changed: " & e.Name)
End Sub

Private Sub WatchForChanges_Created(ByVal sender As Object, _
      ByVal e As System.IO.FileSystemEventArgs) _
      Handles WatchForChanges.Created
   DirectoryEvents.Items.Add("Created: " & e.Name)
End Sub

Private Sub WatchForChanges_Deleted(ByVal sender As Object, _
      ByVal e As System.IO.FileSystemEventArgs) _
      Handles WatchForChanges.Deleted
   DirectoryEvents.Items.Add("Deleted: " & e.Name)
End Sub

Private Sub WatchForChanges_Renamed(ByVal sender As Object, _
      ByVal e As System.IO.RenamedEventArgs) _
      Handles WatchForChanges.Renamed
   DirectoryEvents.Items.Add("Renamed: " & e.OldName & _
      " to " & e.Name)
End Sub
```

To use the program, enter a valid directory in the WatchDirectory field, optionally enter a filename or wildcard in the WatchFilter field, and select one or more entries in the WatchFor list. Now click the StartStop button, and begin making changes in the target directory.

The FileSystemWatcher class monitors activity in a specific directory and raises events based on changes in that directory. The class often reports any change immediately. This means that if you create a new file in the directory and take several minutes to fill it with data before closing it, FileSystemWatcher will report the creation of the file at the start of its life, not when it was closed. This can lead to interaction issues in your program. When you receive notification of a new file in a monitored directory, you should confirm that the complete file has been written out before processing it.

The FileSystemWatcher class uses a shared memory buffer for part of its processing. This buffer is limited in size, so if you experience a lot of changes in a directory, the buffer may "overflow," and you will lose notifications. The object includes an Error event that will let you know when this happens. Also, you can adjust the InternalBufferSize property to allocate more buffer space.

The Toolbox displayed for a Windows Forms form in Visual Studio includes a FileSystemWatcher control. This control is the same as the class included in this recipe's sample code. If you choose to declare the object through code instead of as a control, make sure you set its SynchronizingObject property to the active form (as is done in the sample code) to prevent intrathread errors.

14.11 Creating an Icon in the System Tray

Problem

You wish to use a System Tray icon to regularly notify the user of the status of your application.

Solution

Sample code folder: Chapter 14\SystemTrayIcon

Add a NotifyIcon control to your application's form. It includes properties that simplify displaying a System Tray icon and its related notification "balloon.". Once you've added the control to your form, assign an icon (*.ico*) file or image to its Icon property, and ensure that its Visible property is set to True. That's it. If you want to enable a tooltip for the icon, set the Text property as needed.

Discussion

The NotifyIcon control also includes support for simple notification balloons. Use the BalloonTipIcon, BalloonTipText, and BalloonTipTitle properties to set the icon, main text, and title of the balloon, respectively.

Create a new Windows Forms application. Add a Button control named Button1 to the form, and set its Text property to Show Warning. Then add a NotifyIcon control named NotifyIcon1 to the form. Set the following properties on that control:

- Set BalloonTipIcon to Warning.
- Set BalloonTipText to Your system is in need of repair.
- Set BalloonTipTitle to Repair Warning.
- Set the Icon property to any valid *.ico* icon file. (See below for a source for icon files.)

Now add the following source code to Form1's class template:

```
Private Sub Button1_Click(ByVal sender As System.Object, _
        ByVal e As System.EventArgs) Handles Button1.Click
    ' ----- Show the balloon for 3 seconds by default.
    NotifyIcon1.ShowBalloonTip(3000)
End Sub
```

Run the program, and click on the Show Warning button to view the notice bubble, as shown in Figure 14-8.

Figure 14-8. A notification icon with a warning balloon

The NotifyIcon control includes many events that can detect various types of clicks or double-clicks on the icon or its balloon.

If you need a notification icon for your application, you can try one of the many icons included with Visual Studio. Depending on how you installed the product, you may find a compressed folder named *VS2005ImageLibrary.zip* in the *Common7\ VS2005ImageLibrary* folder of the main product install folder (usually at *c:\Program Files\Microsoft Visual Studio 8*). This archive includes an *icons* folder with many professionally designed icons in it. You can include them freely in applications for your personal use, but be sure to read the Visual Studio license agreement if you plan to use these icons in your commercial applications.

14.12 Accessing the Clipboard

Problem

You want to store data on the clipboard or retrieve data already found on the clipboard.

Solution

Use the `My.Computer.Clipboard` object to get and set data on the clipboard. This object includes four types of methods:

- `Contains…` methods that indicate whether data of a particular type can be found right now on the clipboard
- `Get…` methods that retrieve data already found on the clipboard in a specific data format
- `Set…` methods that allow you to place data onto the clipboard in one or more predefined or custom formats
- A `Clear( )` method that removes all data from the clipboard

Each `Contains…`, `Get…`, and `Set…` method sets focuses on six types of data:

- Text
- Images
- Sound files
- Sets of files
- Custom data
- Custom data in multiple formats

To retrieve plain text data found on the clipboard, use the following statement:

```
Dim fromClipboard As String = _
   My.Computer.Clipboard.GetText( )
```

Use the `Clear( )` method to remove all data from the clipboard:

```
My.Computer.Clipboard.Clear( )
```

Discussion

The `My.Computer.Clipboard` object includes six distinct `Get…` methods that let you retrieve the contents of the system clipboard, each one based on a different type of data:

GetAudioStream( )

Retrieves audio content from the clipboard as a `System.IO.Stream` object. Any .NET features that support such streams can use the returned data. The following block of code plays a sound file retrieved from the clipboard:

```
My.Computer.Audio.Play( _
   My.Computer.Clipboard.GetAudioStream( ), _
   AudioPlayMode.Background)
```

GetFileDropList( )

Retrieves a list of file paths as a `String` collection. This collection is created by any application that stores compatible file lists on the clipboard. For instance, if you copy files in Windows Explorer, those files (but not their contents) appear on the clipboard as a File Drop List. Use this code to retrieve that list:

```
Dim allFiles As System.Collections.Specialized. _
    StringCollection = _
    My.Computer.Clipboard.GetFileDropList()
Dim oneFile As String

For Each oneFile In allFiles
    ' ----- Process each file here.
Next oneFile
```

GetImage( )

Retrieves any image data stored on the clipboard as a System.Drawing.Image object.

GetText( )

Retrieves text from the clipboard. GetText( ) includes an optional parameter that lets you specify the specific type of text to retrieve, using the values of the System.Windows.Forms.TextDataFormat enumeration. Their names equate to the type of text retrieved:

- TextDataFormat.CommaSeparatedValue

- TextDataFormat.Html

- TextDataFormat.Rtf

- TextDataFormat.UnicodeText

If you don't include the text type argument, GetText( ) retrieves the text in the most basic text format available on the clipboard.

GetData( )

Retrieves data in a custom format from the clipboard. All data stored on the clipboard includes a format name. You must pass a format name to the GetData( ) argument to retrieve data of that type. For example:

```
Dim roundaboutText = _
    CStr(My.Computer.Clipboard.GetData("Text"))
```

The data is returned as a System.Object, and it must be converted to its final data type manually.

GetDataObject( )

The clipboard can store data in multiple formats at once. GetDataObject( ) returns the complete set of all stored data formats, using an interface defined through System.Windows.Forms.IDataObject. Once retrieved, you can query the names of each format using this interface's GetFormats( ) method, check for a specific format using GetDataPresent( ), and retrieve specific data as a System.Object using GetData( ). The following code displays the names of each format included on the clipboard:

```
MsgBox(Join(My.Computer.Clipboard.GetDataObject(). _
    GetFormats(True), ", "))
```

Before attempting to retrieve data in a specific format from the clipboard, it is a good idea to confirm that such data exists. (If the specified data type does not exist, the Get... methods return the value Nothing.) The My.Computer.Clipboard object includes several such confirmation methods that parallel the Get... methods listed above, each of which returns a Boolean value indicating whether or not the specified data is available:

- Clipboard.ContainsAudio( )
- Clipboard.ContainsData(formatName)
- Clipboard.ContainsFileDropList( )
- Clipboard.ContainsImage( )
- Clipboard.ContainsText(formatType)

Since the system clipboard is a resource shared among all running programs, and since the user can modify the clipboard through another program at any time, it is possible that one of these Contains... methods will return True for a particular format, but the related Get... method, even when used immediately, will return nothing.

A group of Set... methods let you store data back to the clipboard in a variety of formats:

SetAudio( )

Stores audio data on the clipboard. The lone argument to this method must be either a Byte array or a Stream containing audio data.

SetFileDropList( )

Stores a list of files on the clipboard. You must pass a collection of strings using the System.Collections.Specialized.StringCollection to this method. For example:

```
Dim filesToInclude As New System.Collections. _
    Specialized.StringCollection
filesToInclude.Add("c:\datafile.txt")
filesToInclude.Add("c:\temp\workfile.txt")
My.Computer.Clipboard.SetFileDropList(filesToInclude)
```

SetImage( )

Stores an image on the clipboard. Pass this method an argument of type System. Drawing.Image.

SetText( )

Stores text in a specific format on the clipboard. The first argument is a String containing the text to add. An optional second argument uses the TextDataFormat enumeration discussed in the earlier GetText( ) entry.

SetData( )

Stores any type of custom data on the clipboard, based on a format name you provide:

```
My.Computer.Clipboard.SetData("MyCustomFormat", dataObject)
```

SetDataObject( )

Lets you append multiple formats at once to the clipboard. You must pass this method an instance of `System.Windows.Forms.DataObject`, populated with data you provide. This object includes each of the `Set...` methods used for the clipboard itself, including `SetText( )` and `SetData( )`:

```
Dim toClipboard As New System.Windows.Forms.DataObject
toClipboard.SetData("MyCustomFormat", dataObject)
toClipboard.SetText(dataObject.ToString( ))
My.Computer.Clipboard.SetDataObject(toClipboard)
```

14.13 Adding Tooltips to Controls

Problem

You want a tooltip to appear when the user hovers the cursor (mouse) over a control.

Solution

Use the `ToolTip` control, included in the Windows Forms Toolbox, on your form. Figure 14-9 shows the `ToolTip` control in the Toolbox and applied to the form.

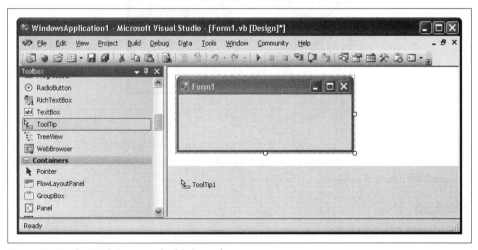

Figure 14-9. The ToolTip control added to a form

Discussion

When applied to a form, the `ToolTip` control enhances all displayable on-form controls, adding a new pseudoproperty to the properties collection *of each control*. If you add a `ToolTip` control named `ToolTip1` to the form, each visible control includes a new "ToolTip on ToolTip1" property. For a specific control, fill this pseudoproperty with the text to display in the tooltip. Figure 14-10 shows a tooltip in use on a running form.

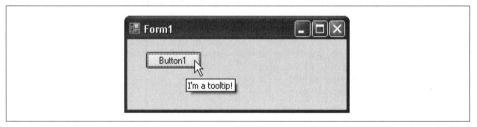

Figure 14-10. A tooltip in use

Normally, adding a single ToolTip control to a form is sufficient for all your tooltip display needs. While each control communicates its own tooltip display text through the added ToolTip pseudoproperty, the ToolTip control itself manages how that text gets displayed, through its own property settings. For instance, the IsBalloon property, when set to True, displays the tooltip in a balloon display instead of a plain square (see Figure 14-11).

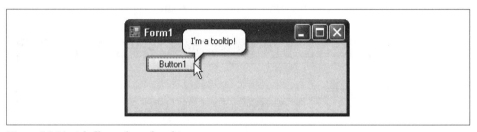

Figure 14-11. A balloon-shaped tooltip

You can also take full control of the drawing of the tooltip by setting its OwnerDraw property to True and responding to the control's Draw event. See Chapter 9 for examples of drawing to a custom graphics surface.

See Also

Recipe 14.11 shows how to add tooltips to notification icons in the System Tray.

14.14 Dragging and Dropping Files to a ListBox

Problem

You want a ListBox control to accept file paths dragged to it from Windows Explorer.

Solution

Sample code folder: Chapter 14\DragDropFiles

Use the control's `DragEnter` and `DragDrop` events to watch for dropped file lists and process them when dropped.

Discussion

Create a new Windows Forms application, and add a `ListBox` control named `ListBox1` to `Form1`. Set this control's `AllowDrop` property to `True`. Now add the following code to the form's source code:

```
Private Sub ListBox1_DragEnter(ByVal sender As Object, _
      ByVal e As System.Windows.Forms.DragEventArgs) _
      Handles ListBox1.DragEnter
   ' ----- Allow the dropping of file lists.
   If (e.Data.GetDataPresent(DataFormats.FileDrop) = _
         True) Then
      e.Effect = DragDropEffects.Copy
   End If
End Sub

Private Sub ListBox1_DragDrop(ByVal sender As Object, _
      ByVal e As System.Windows.Forms.DragEventArgs) _
      Handles ListBox1.DragDrop
   ' ----- Process each dropped file.
   For Each oneFile As String In _
         e.Data.GetData(DataFormats.FileDrop)
      ListBox1.Items.Add(oneFile)
   Next oneFile
End Sub
```

To test the program, run it, and then drag one or more files from Windows Explorer (or any other program that supports the dragging of files). Figure 14-12 shows the result of a multifile drag operation.

Accepting dragged files in a control is a two-step process:

1. Inform the sender of your acceptance criteria through the `DragEnter` event handler.

2. Accept the files through the `DragDrop` event handler.

In this recipe's code, the `DragEnter` event examines the data being dragged into the `ListBox` to determine if it will accept the content. In this case, it looks for a "file drop list" (identified by `DataFormats.FileDrop`). If it finds one, it tells the sender that it will accept the files through a Copy operation, setting the `e.Effect` property. By default, `e.Effect` is set to `DragDropEffects.None`, which indicates that the content is not acceptable.

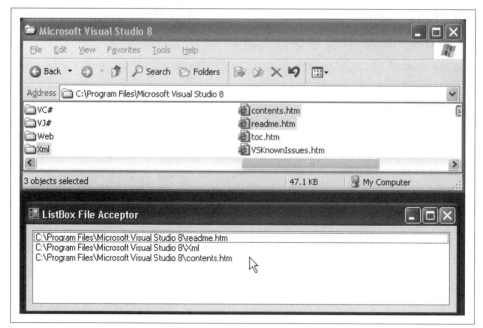

Figure 14-12. Three dragged files accepted by a ListBox control

In the DragDrop event, the dragged content exposed through e.Data is accessed, and its "file drop list" content is extracted as a string array, which is then transferred to the ListBox control.

If you are familiar with the clipboard operations exposed through the My.Computer. Clipboard object, you will recognize the use of the "file drop list" also available through the clipboard.

See Also

Recipe 14.15 shows you how to perform inter-ListBox drag-and-drop operations.

14.15 Dragging and Dropping Between ListBox Controls

Problem

You have two ListBox controls on a form, and you want the user to be able to drag and drop items between the lists.

Solution

Sample code folder: Chapter 14\DragDropLists

Use code similar to that found in Recipe 14.14 in conjunction with the ListBox control's DoDragDrop( ) method to enable dragging and dropping between listboxes.

Discussion

Create a new Windows Forms application, and add two ListBox controls named ListBox1 and ListBox2 to the form. In both controls, set the AllowDrop property to True, and set the SelectionMode property to MultiExtended. In the properties for ListBox1, select the Items property, and click the "..." button in its data value area. In the String Collection Editor window that appears, enter multiple lines of text, separating them by pressing the Enter key. (We entered the words "One" through "Six.") Figure 14-13 shows this process in action.

Figure 14-13. Using the ListBox's String Collection Editor

Close the String Collection Editor; you should have a form that looks like Figure 14-14.

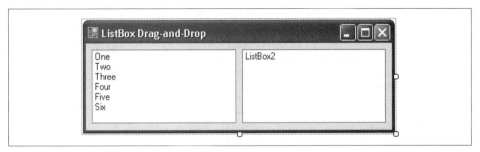

Figure 14-14. Two listboxes with draggable items

Now add the following code to the form:

```
Private dragBounds As Rectangle
Private dragMethod As String

Private Sub ListBox1_DragEnter(ByVal sender As Object, _
      ByVal e As System.Windows.Forms.DragEventArgs) _
      Handles ListBox1.DragEnter
   ' ----- Yes, we accept the items.
   If (e.Data.GetDataPresent(ListBox2.SelectedItems. _
      GetType()) = True) Then _
      e.Effect = DragDropEffects.Move
End Sub

Private Sub ListBox1_DragDrop(ByVal sender As Object, _
      ByVal e As System.Windows.Forms.DragEventArgs) _
      Handles ListBox1.DragDrop
   ' ----- Accept the dropped items.
   For Each oneItem As Object In _
         e.Data.GetData(ListBox2.SelectedItems.GetType())
      ListBox1.Items.Add(oneItem)
   Next oneItem
End Sub

Private Sub ListBox1_MouseDown(ByVal sender As Object, _
      ByVal e As System.Windows.Forms.MouseEventArgs) _
      Handles ListBox1.MouseDown, ListBox2.MouseDown
   ' ----- Prepare the draggable content.
   If (CType(sender, ListBox).SelectedItems.Count = 0) _
      Then Return

   ' ----- Don't start the drag yet. Wait until we move a
   '       certain amount.
   dragBounds = New Rectangle(New Point(e.X - _
      (SystemInformation.DragSize.Width / 2), _
      e.Y - (SystemInformation.DragSize.Height / 2)), _
      SystemInformation.DragSize)
   If (sender Is ListBox1) Then
      dragMethod = "1to2"
   Else
      dragMethod = "2to1"
   End If
End Sub

Private Sub ListBox1_MouseMove(ByVal sender As Object, _
      ByVal e As System.Windows.Forms.MouseEventArgs) _
      Handles ListBox1.MouseMove
   ' ----- Ignore if not dragging from ListBox1.
   If (dragMethod <> "1to2") Then Return

   ' ----- Have we left the drag boundary?
   If (dragBounds.Contains(e.X, e.Y) = False) Then
      ' ----- Start the drag-and-drop operation.
      If (ListBox1.DoDragDrop(ListBox1.SelectedItems, _
```

```
                DragDropEffects.Move) = _
                DragDropEffects.Move) Then
            ' ----- Successful move. Remove the items from
            '       this list.
            Do While ListBox1.SelectedItems.Count > 0
                ListBox1.Items.Remove(ListBox1.SelectedItems(0))
            Loop
        End If
        dragMethod = ""
    End If
End Sub

Private Sub ListBox1_MouseUp(ByVal sender As Object, _
        ByVal e As System.Windows.Forms.MouseEventArgs) _
        Handles ListBox1.MouseUp, ListBox2.MouseUp
    ' ----- End of drag-and-drop.
    dragMethod = ""
End Sub

Private Sub ListBox2_DragEnter(ByVal sender As Object, _
        ByVal e As System.Windows.Forms.DragEventArgs) _
        Handles ListBox2.DragEnter
    ' ----- Yes, we accept the items.
    If (e.Data.GetDataPresent(ListBox1.SelectedItems. _
        GetType()) = True) Then _
        e.Effect = DragDropEffects.Move
End Sub

Private Sub ListBox2_DragDrop(ByVal sender As Object, _
        ByVal e As System.Windows.Forms.DragEventArgs) _
        Handles ListBox2.DragDrop
    ' ----- Accept the dropped items.
    For Each oneItem As Object In _
            e.Data.GetData(ListBox1.SelectedItems.GetType())
        ListBox2.Items.Add(oneItem)
    Next oneItem
End Sub

Private Sub ListBox2_MouseMove(ByVal sender As Object, _
        ByVal e As System.Windows.Forms.MouseEventArgs) _
        Handles ListBox2.MouseMove
    ' ----- Ignore if not dragging from ListBox2.
    If (dragMethod <> "2to1") Then Return

    ' ----- Have we left the drag boundary?
    If (dragBounds.Contains(e.X, e.Y) = False) Then
        ' ----- Start the drag-and-drop operation.
        If (ListBox2.DoDragDrop(ListBox2.SelectedItems, _
            DragDropEffects.Move) = _
            DragDropEffects.Move) Then
            ' ----- Successful move. Remove the items from
            '       this list.
            Do While ListBox2.SelectedItems.Count > 0
                ListBox2.Items.Remove(ListBox2.SelectedItems(0))
```

```
        Loop
      End If
      dragMethod = ""
    End If
  End Sub
```

If you look closely at this code, you will find that much of it is replicated. To support two-way dragging, all code that applies to `ListBox1` appears again for `ListBox2`.

Run this program, and then drag items from one listbox to the other. You can also multiselect and move multiple items at once.

Many controls support the `DoDragDrop( )` method. It accepts data content to send and a set of allowed send methods:

```
If (SomeControl.DoDragDrop(dataContent, _
    DragDropEffects.Move) = DragDropEffects.Move) Then
  ' ----- Successful move.
End If
```

Calling this function is easy, and it can be done at any time. Most of the code in this sample deals with determining what content can be sent and when.

The `DragDropEffects` enumeration, used for the second `DoDragDrop( )` argument, indicates which operations the supplier of the data is permitting with the supplied content. Its `Move`, `Copy`, and `Link` enumeration members can be joined with a bitwise `Or` to indicate multiple allowed features:

```
' ----- Allow copy and move.
Select Case SomeControl.DoDragDrop(dataContent, _
    DragDropEffects.Move Or DragDropEffect.Copy)
  Case DragDropEffects.None
    ' ----- The target did not accept the content.
  Case DragDropEffects.Copy
    ' ----- The target copied the content.
  Case DragDropEffects.Move
    ' ----- The target moved the content.
End Select
```

See Also

Recipe 14.14 shows you how to accept dragged-and-dropped files in a `ListBox`.

14.16 Disposing of Objects Appropriately

Problem

You've created an object that allocates its own resources, and you're ready to get rid of it. What's the correct method?

Solution

Visual Basic provides three primary methods for getting rid of objects that implement the IDisposable interface:

- Call the object's Dispose( ) method, exposed by the IDisposable interface and implemented by the object's type. This is the most direct method of freeing resources. The object should not be used once Dispose( ) has been called.

- Use Visual Basic's Using statement. This block statement automatically calls the object's Dispose( ) method on your behalf when the block ends, or execution jumps out of the block for any reason.

  Many of the GDI+ drawing objects implement IDisposable and should be disposed of properly when no longer in use. The Pen object is one such class. The following code uses the Using statement to declare and properly dispose of a Pen object:

  ```
  Using workPen As New Pen(Color.Red)
      ' ----- Add drawing code here using that red pen.
  End Using
  ' ----- workPen has been released and is unavailable.
  ```

- Let the object go out of scope, or set it to Nothing. This practice is usually undesirable because the garbage-collection process, and not you, will control when the additional resources get released.

Discussion

The constructor for a class may allocate shared resources that need to be properly released as quickly as possible when no longer needed. Some classes implement their own custom method for doing this, such as including a "release all resources" method. You must examine and follow the documented standards for such objects.

Fortunately, most objects that hold such external or shared resources implement the System.IDisposable interface. This interface exposes a standard Dispose( ) method that your code or other standardized generic components can call to free important resources. You can add IDisposable to your own classes, as follows:

```
Class SomeClass
    Implements IDisposable

    Protected Overridable Sub Dispose() _
          Implements IDisposable.Dispose
        ' ----- Add cleanup code here.
    End Sub
End Class
```

For classes that do not allocate shared or external resources, or where holding on to such resources for a long time will not degrade application or system performance, the standard Finalize( ) deconstructor may be used to free held resources. For such classes, no special processing is needed to destroy the object. Simply wait for the object to be released on its own, or set it to Nothing.

If you implement IDisposable on a custom class, you should also override the Finalize() method to ensure that resources are freed even if the user of the class forgets to call Dispose():

```
Protected Overrides Sub Finalize()
   ' ----- Add cleanup guarantee here.
End Sub
```

14.17 Fine-Tuning Garbage Collection

Problem

The .NET garbage-collection process is something of a mystery, a black box that has a mind of its own. Does a programmer have any control over the disposal process?

Solution

The System.GC object exposes several methods that let you "help" the garbage-collection process, either for a specific object or for the entire garbage system.

When you finish using an object by setting it to Nothing or by letting it otherwise become unused (go out of scope), it is added to the garbage-collection system for eventual finalization and disposal. *Finalization* occurs when the object's Finalize() method is called. *Disposal* occurs when the memory allocated to the object is finally reclaimed and made available for use by other managed (or even unmanaged) uses.

Garbage collection occurs in waves, or *generations*. When an object first enters the system, it appears in Generation 0 (zero). If, after a while, the object has not yet been finalized or disposed of, it is moved to the next generation, Generation 1. Not all platforms support this system of aging. Use the System.GC.MaxGeneration property to determine the generation of the longest-lived object. This property always returns zero on platforms that do not use aging.

Discussion

You can use the following members of System.GC to help manage the garbage-collection system in memory-critical applications:

AddMemoryPressure() *and* RemoveMemoryPressure()
   The garbage-collection system concerns itself only with *managed memory*—memory allocated through .NET features. *Unmanaged memory* does not go through the collection process. However, the collection process does take the amount of available memory, both managed and unmanaged, into account when determining how quickly to free resources. The AddMemoryPressure() method accepts a byte count argument and tells the garbage collector, "Act as if this

amount of unmanaged memory has actually been allocated." Depending on the size of the pressure, the collection process will behave differently due to the perceived changes in available memory.

You must later reverse the pressure allocation with the `RemoveMemoryPressure( )` method, using the same byte count supplied with the original pressure request. You can have multiple pressure requests active at once.

Collect( )

This method forces the immediate collection (finalization and disposal) of garbage. By default, this method collects garbage in all generations. You can also pass it a generation number, and it will collect garbage only between Generation 0 and the generation number of the argument.

CollectionCount( )

This method returns a count of the number of times garbage has been collected for a specific generation number. The generation number is passed as an argument.

GetGeneration( )

If you have access to a reference object that has already entered the garbage-collection system, passing it as an argument to GetGeneration( ) returns the generation number in which that object appears.

GetTotalMemory( )

This method returns an estimate of the total allocated managed memory. It accepts a `Boolean` argument that, if `True`, allows garbage collection to occur before the estimate is calculated.

KeepAlive( )

Normally, when an object goes out of scope, you don't care when the garbage-collection process destroys it. However, if you allocate some managed memory that you will share with or pass to an external or unmanaged process (such as an ActiveX DLL function), and that process will use the memory beyond your local use of it, the garbage collector should delay processing of the object until it is truly no longer in use. The KeepAlive( ) method helps you force such a delay.

To use KeepAlive( ), you pass it a reference to the object to retain, and you call this method when you no longer wish to retain it. That is, the call to KeepAlive( ) says, "Keep the object alive, but only until this point; after this call, it can go to garbage collection." For this reason, calls to `GC.KeepAlive( )` generally appear near the end of a method or block of code.

SuppressFinalize( ) *and* ReRegisterForFinalize( )

Passing an object reference to SuppressFinalize( ) tells the garbage collector, "Don't call this object's Finalize( ) method before disposing of the object." This method is most commonly used with objects that implement the `System.IDisposable` interface. If you clean up all allocated resources during the call to `Dispose( )`, such that there is nothing more for the `Finalize( )` method to do, adding a call to SuppressFinalize( ) disables the unneeded call to Finalize( ).

Visual Studio normally adds some template code to your class when you declare it using Implements IDisposable. This template code includes a call to SuppressFinalize( ). You may or may not wish to retain this call, depending on your needs.

If you use the SuppressFinalize( ) method but later find that you need to re-enable the finalization process for an object, call the ReRegisterForFinalize( ) method.

WaitForPendingFinalizers( )

This method suspends execution of the application until all relevant objects in the garbage collector have had their Finalize( ) methods called.

Most of these methods are designed for applications with advanced memory-allocation and processing needs. In most ordinary applications, only the KeepAlive( ) and SuppressFinalize( ) methods will find common use.

14.18 Moving the (Mouse) Cursor

Problem

You want to reposition the cursor (that is, the mouse pointer) programatically.

Solution

Sample code folder: Chapter 14\MoveMouse

Modify the Position property of the System.Windows.Forms.Cursor object with a new System.Drawing.Point containing the new location.

Discussion

Create a new Windows Forms project, and add two Button controls named Button1 and Button2. Now add the following code to the form's class:

```
Private Sub Button1_Click(ByVal sender As System.Object, _
    ByVal e As System.EventArgs) Handles Button1.Click
  Windows.Forms.Cursor.Position = New Point( _
    Me.PointToScreen(Button2.Location).X + _
    Button2.Width / 2, _
    Me.PointToScreen(Button2.Location).Y + _
    Button2.Height / 2)
End Sub
```

When you run the program and click on Button1, the cursor centers itself over Button2.

All controls on a form use the client coordinate system for their positions. Each control's X and Y locations are based on the upper-left corner of the form's client area, the rectangle that is just inside of the form's border. The cursor, however, is a screen-wide resource, and it uses the coordinates for the entire screen, with its X and Y positions offset from the upper-left corner of the screen. To move the cursor based on a screen position, you must translate between the two coordinate systems.

The form includes two methods to perform this translation: PointToScreen( ), which converts a client rectangle location to a matching screen location, and PointToClient( ), which translates in the opposite direction. Actually, every control on the form also includes these two methods. However, all points translated using a control's translation methods are based on the upper-left corner of the control (that is, on its client area), and not on the upper-left corner of the form's client rectangle.

14.19 Intercepting All Key Presses on a Form

Problem

You have a form that needs to watch for certain keys and process them before any control on the form recognizes those keys.

Solution

Sample code folder: Chapter 14\InterceptKeys

Use the form's KeyPreview property to control access to the form's KeyDown, KeyUp, and KeyPress events.

Discussion

Create a new Windows Forms application, and add a single TextBox control named TextBox1. Set the form's KeyPreview property to True. Now add the following code to the form's class:

```
Private Sub Form1_KeyDown(ByVal sender As Object, _
    ByVal e As System.Windows.Forms.KeyEventArgs) _
    Handles Me.KeyDown
  If (e.KeyCode = Keys.F5) Then MessageBox.Show("Form: F5")
  e.Handled = True
End Sub

Private Sub TextBox1_KeyDown(ByVal sender As Object, _
    ByVal e As System.Windows.Forms.KeyEventArgs) _
    Handles TextBox1.KeyDown
  If (e.KeyCode = Keys.F5) Then MessageBox.Show("Text: F5")
End Sub
```

Run the program, and press the F5 key when the input focus is in the text box. You should receive only the "Form: F5" message.

Modify the program by commenting out the e.Handled = True line in the form's KeyDown event handler, and then run the program again. This time, you will receive both messages when you press F5.

Modify the program once again, setting the form's KeyPreview property to False. When you run the program and press F5, only the "Text: F5" message will appear.

Normally, a form ignores all keyboard input whenever a control on that form has the input focus. But you can alter that behavior by setting the KeyPreview property to True. Once set, the program sends all keyboard input first to the form's key-focused event handlers, and after that it sends those same key events to the active control. Stopping processing at the form level is accomplished by setting the e.Handled property to True in any of the form-level keyboard event handlers.

14.20 Accessing the Registry

Problem

You wish to read or write keys and values in one of the registry hives.

Solution

Sample code folder: Chapter 14\RegistryAccess

Use the My.Computer.Registry object and its members to access and update portions of the registry.

Discussion

This recipe's source code implements a read-only (and highly simplified) version of the Windows RegEdit application. Create a new Windows Forms application, and add the following controls to Form1:

- A TreeView control named RegistryTree.

- A ListBox control named RegistryValues.

- A TextBox control named ValueData. Set its Multiline property to True, its ScrollBars property to Vertical, and its ReadOnly property to True.

Add some informational labels if desired, and arrange the controls so the form looks like Figure 14-15.

Now add the following source code to the form's code template:

```
Private Sub Form1_Load(ByVal sender As System.Object, _
    ByVal e As System.EventArgs) Handles MyBase.Load
    ' ----- Load the root objects.
    Dim rootNode As TreeNode
    Dim childNode As TreeNode

    rootNode = RegistryTree.Nodes.Add("My Computer")
```

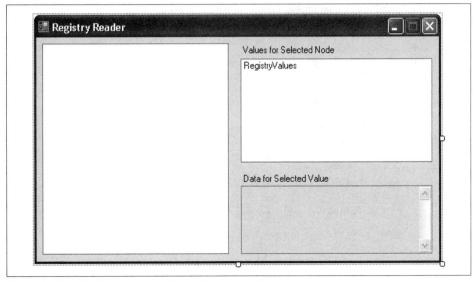

Figure 14-15. The form and controls for the registry viewer

```
    childNode = rootNode.Nodes.Add("HKEY_CLASSES_ROOT")
    childNode.Nodes.Add("")

    childNode = rootNode.Nodes.Add("HKEY_CURRENT_USER")
    childNode.Nodes.Add("")

    childNode = rootNode.Nodes.Add("HKEY_LOCAL_MACHINE")
    childNode.Nodes.Add("")

    childNode = rootNode.Nodes.Add("HKEY_USERS")
    childNode.Nodes.Add("")

    childNode = rootNode.Nodes.Add("HKEY_CURRENT_CONFIG")
    childNode.Nodes.Add("")

    rootNode.Expand( )
End Sub

Private Function BuildRegistryPath( _
        ByVal fromNode As TreeNode) As String
    ' ----- Traverse a tree backward, building the node path.
    If (fromNode.Parent Is Nothing) Then
        ' ----- This is the root node.
        Return "\"
    Else
        ' ----- This is an intermediate node.
        Return BuildRegistryPath(fromNode.Parent) & _
            "\" & fromNode.Text
    End If
End Function
```

```
Private Function GetHiveFromName(ByVal hiveName As String) _
      As Microsoft.Win32.RegistryKey
   ' ----- Given the name of a hive, return its key.
   Select Case hiveName
      Case "HKEY_CLASSES_ROOT"
         Return My.Computer.Registry.ClassesRoot
      Case "HKEY_CURRENT_USER"
         Return My.Computer.Registry.CurrentUser
      Case "HKEY_LOCAL_MACHINE"
         Return My.Computer.Registry.LocalMachine
      Case "HKEY_USERS"
         Return My.Computer.Registry.Users
      Case "HKEY_CURRENT_CONFIG"
         Return My.Computer.Registry.CurrentConfig
      Case Else
         Return Nothing
   End Select
End Function

Private Function GetKeyFromNode(ByVal whichNode As TreeNode) _
      As Microsoft.Win32.RegistryKey
   ' ----- The user is just about to expand a node. If it
   '       includes a blank node, retrieve the actual
   '       child nodes from the registry.
   Dim registryPath As String
   Dim hiveName As String
   Dim registryKey As Microsoft.Win32.RegistryKey

   ' ----- Access this part of the registry.
   registryPath = BuildRegistryPath(whichNode).Substring(2)
   If (registryPath.Contains("\") = True) Then
      ' ----- Extract the hive and path parts.
      hiveName = registryPath.Substring(0, _
         registryPath.IndexOf("\"c))
      registryPath = registryPath.Substring( _
         hiveName.Length + 1)
   Else
      ' ----- The active node is a hive.
      hiveName = registryPath
      registryPath = ""
   End If

   ' ----- Obtain the right hive.
   registryKey = GetHiveFromName(hiveName)
   If (registryKey Is Nothing) Then Return Nothing

   ' ----- Obtain the right subkey, if needed.
   If (registryPath <> "") Then _
      registryKey = registryKey.OpenSubKey(registryPath)

   ' ----- This is the right key.
   Return registryKey
End Function
```

```
Private Sub RegistryTree_AfterSelect( _
      ByVal sender As Object, ByVal e As _
      System.Windows.Forms.TreeViewEventArgs) _
      Handles RegistryTree.AfterSelect
   ' ----- Display the values associated with a node.
   Dim registryKey As Microsoft.Win32.RegistryKey

   ' ----- Clear any existing data.
   RegistryValues.Items.Clear()
   ValueData.Clear()

   ' ----- Ignore if this is the root node.
   If (e.Node.Parent Is Nothing) Then Return

   ' ----- Get the registry key associated with this
   '       tree node.
   registryKey = GetKeyFromNode(e.Node)

   ' ----- There is always a default value.
   RegistryValues.Items.Add("(Default)")

   ' ----- Get all of the values of this key, and add them
   '       to the list.
   Me.Cursor = Cursors.WaitCursor
   Try
      For Each oneValue As String In _
            registryKey.GetValueNames()
         RegistryValues.Items.Add(oneValue)
      Next oneValue
   Finally
      Me.Cursor = Cursors.Arrow
   End Try

   registryKey.Close()
End Sub

Private Sub RegistryTree_BeforeExpand( _
      ByVal sender As Object, ByVal e As _
      System.Windows.Forms.TreeViewCancelEventArgs) _
      Handles RegistryTree.BeforeExpand
   ' ----- The user is just about to expand a node. If it
   '       includes a blank node, retrieve the actual
   '       child nodes from the registry.
   Dim registryKey As Microsoft.Win32.RegistryKey
   Dim keyNode As TreeNode

   ' ----- Ignore if this node was already expanded.
   If (e.Node.FirstNode.Text <> "") Then Return
   e.Node.Nodes.Remove(e.Node.FirstNode)

   ' ----- Get the registry key associated with this tree node.
   registryKey = GetKeyFromNode(e.Node)
```

```
        ' ----- Get all of the child keys of this key, and add them
        '       to the tree.
    Me.Cursor = Cursors.WaitCursor
    Try
        For Each oneKey As String In _
               registryKey.GetSubKeyNames()
            keyNode = e.Node.Nodes.Add(oneKey)
            keyNode.Nodes.Add("")
        Next oneKey
    Finally
        Me.Cursor = Cursors.Arrow
    End Try

    registryKey.Close()
End Sub

Private Sub RegistryValues_SelectedIndexChanged( _
        ByVal sender As System.Object, _
        ByVal e As System.EventArgs) _
        Handles RegistryValues.SelectedIndexChanged
    ' ----- Display the data associated with the selected list item.
    Dim registryKey As Microsoft.Win32.RegistryKey
    Dim actualValue As Object
    Dim valueName As String

    ' ----- Clear any existing data.
    ValueData.Clear()

    ' ----- Ignore if nothing is active.
    If (RegistryValues.SelectedIndex = _
        ListBox.NoMatches) Then Return

    ' ----- Ignore if this is the root node.
    If (RegistryTree.SelectedNode.Parent Is Nothing) _
        Then Return

    ' ----- Get the registry key associated with this
    '       tree node.
    registryKey = GetKeyFromNode(RegistryTree.SelectedNode)

    ' ----- Determine the value to retrieve.
    valueName = RegistryValues.Text
    If (valueName = "(Default)") Then valueName = ""

    ' ----- Display the value.
    actualValue = registryKey.GetValue(valueName)
    If (actualValue IsNot Nothing) Then _
        ValueData.Text = actualValue.ToString()

    registryKey.Close()
End Sub
```

To use the program, expand and select registry keys in the `RegistryTree` control, and select values in the `RegistryValues` control. The `RegistryTree_BeforeExpand` event handler loads only those branches that have been expanded, so the program doesn't have to load the entire registry at once. The program could be greatly enhanced to properly display nonstring and nonnumeric data, and to manage security- and access-related errors.

The system registry is grouped into hives, although most of the hives are simply shortcuts to specific portions of the master `HKEY_CLASSES_ROOT` hive. The `My.Computer.Registry` object provides access to these hives through the following members, each of which is an instance of `Microsoft.Win32.RegistryKey`:

- `ClassesRoot` provides access to the `HKEY_CLASSES_ROOT` hive.
- `CurrentConfig` provides access to the `HKEY_CURRENT_CONFIG` hive.
- `CurrentUser` provides access to the `HKEY_CURRENT_USER` hive.
- `DynData` provides access to the `HKEY_DYNAMIC_DATA` hive.
- `LocalMachine` provides access to the `HKEY_LOCAL_MACHINE` hive.
- `PerformanceData` provides access to the `HKEY_PERFORMANCE_DATA` hive.
- `Users` provides access to the `HKEY_USERS` hive.

The `RegistryKey` class for each hive includes features that let you access the subordinate keys and values associated with that hive or key. Fortunately, any subordinate key you access can also appear as a `RegistryKey` instance, making it easy to traverse the registry from any hive.

This recipe's code uses the `RegistryKey.OpenSubKey()` method to access specific keys below a hive root. For instance, to access the key `\\HKEY_CURRENT_USER\Software\Microsoft`, you would make the following function call:

```
Dim microsoftKey As Microsoft.Win32.RegistryKey = _
    My.Computer.Registry.CurrentUser.OpenSubKey( _
    "Software\Microsoft")
```

Each key includes zero or more values, including a default value (which is actually named default). To retrieve a value for a key, use the key's `GetValue()` method, a feature also used in the sample code. The registry can store data in a variety of formats, so use the related `GetValueKind()` method to determine the type of data stored. To access the default value for a key, use an empty string for the value name.

To add or update a value for a key, use the `RegistryKey.SetValue()` method.

 For both reads and writes of key and value data, the system administrator may impose access limits on certain areas of the registry. Attempting to read or write an inaccessible portion of the registry generates an exception.

14.21 Running Procedures in Threads

Problem

You would like to perform some involved background data processing but keep the user interface for your application responsive to user interaction.

Solution

Sample code folder: Chapter 14\UsingThreads

Use a BackgroundWorker control (or class) to manage the interaction between the main process and a worker thread.

Discussion

This recipe's sample code starts a background worker thread that does some work, reporting its progress back to the main thread on a regular basis. The main thread has the option to cancel the worker thread. Create a new Windows Forms application, and add the following controls to Form1:

- A Button control named StartWork. Change its Text property to Start.
- A Button control named StopWork. Change its Text property to Stop, and set its Enabled property to False.
- A Label control named WorkStatus. Change its Text property to Not started.
- A ProgressBar control named WorkProgress.
- A BackgroundWorker control named BackgroundActivity. Change both the WorkerReportsProgress and WorkerSupportsCancellation properties to True.

Arrange the controls nicely so they look like Figure 14-16.

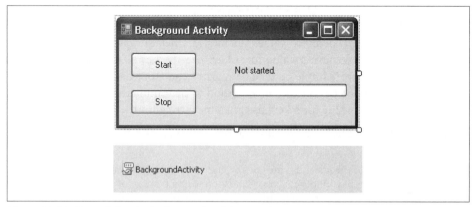

Figure 14-16. Controls for the background activity sample

Add the following Imports statement at the top of the source-code file for Form1:

```
Imports System.ComponentModel
```

Now add the following source code to the Form1 class:

```
Private Sub BackgroundActivity_DoWork( _
    ByVal sender As Object, ByVal e As _
    System.ComponentModel.DoWorkEventArgs) _
    Handles BackgroundActivity.DoWork
  ' ----- The background work starts here.
  Dim theBackground As BackgroundWorker

  ' ----- Call the background thread.
  theBackground = CType(sender, BackgroundWorker)
  TheBusyWork(theBackground)

  ' ----- Check for a cancellation.
  If (theBackground.CancellationPending = True) Then _
    e.Cancel = True
End Sub

Private Sub BackgroundActivity_ProgressChanged( _
    ByVal sender As Object, ByVal e As _
    System.ComponentModel.ProgressChangedEventArgs) _
    Handles BackgroundActivity.ProgressChanged
  ' ----- The background task updated its progress.
  WorkProgress.Value = e.ProgressPercentage
End Sub

Private Sub BackgroundActivity_RunWorkerCompleted( _
    ByVal sender As Object, ByVal e As _
    System.ComponentModel.RunWorkerCompletedEventArgs) _
    Handles BackgroundActivity.RunWorkerCompleted
  ' ----- Finished.
  If (e.Cancelled = True) Then
    WorkStatus.Text = "Cancelled."
  Else
    WorkStatus.Text = "Complete."
  End If
  WorkProgress.Visible = False
  WorkProgress.Value = 0
  StopWork.Enabled = False
  StartWork.Enabled = True
End Sub

Private Sub TheBusyWork(ByVal workerLink As BackgroundWorker)
  ' ----- Perform some work.
  For counter As Integer = 1 To 10
    ' ----- See if we should jump out now.
    If (workerLink.CancellationPending = True) Then _
      Exit For

    ' ----- Take a nap for 2 seconds.
    Threading.Thread.Sleep(2000)
```

```
        ' ----- Inform the primary thread that we've
        '       made significant progress.
        workerLink.ReportProgress(counter * 10)
      Next counter
End Sub

Private Sub StartWork_Click(ByVal sender As System.Object, _
      ByVal e As System.EventArgs) Handles StartWork.Click
   ' ----- Start the background process.
   StartWork.Enabled = False
   StopWork.Enabled = True
   WorkStatus.Text = "Progress..."
   WorkProgress.Value = 0
   WorkProgress.Visible = True
   BackgroundActivity.RunWorkerAsync()
End Sub

Private Sub StopWork_Click(ByVal sender As System.Object, _
      ByVal e As System.EventArgs) Handles StopWork.Click
   ' ----- Tell the worker thread to stop.
   BackgroundActivity.CancelAsync()
End Sub
```

Run the program, and click on the Start button. The progress will update as the background worker proceeds through its activity loop. You can interrupt the background worker by clicking on the Stop button, although it won't actually stop until the end of the current two-second sleep.

Processes running in Windows have the option of dividing their work among separate threads of execution within those processes. By default, Visual Basic processes include only a single thread: the process itself. However, you can start one or more background worker threads to perform some activity apart from the flow of the primary application.

The .NET Framework includes threading support through the System.Threading namespace, and specifically through the Thread class in that namespace. While using the Thread class is relatively simple, you have to develop or enhance the class if you want standardized interactions to occur between your primary and worker threads.

The BackgroundWorker control, part of the System.ComponentModel namespace, implements a lot of these interaction features for you. To use the control, simply add it to your form. You can also use it as a class by declaring it using the WithEvents keyword:

```
Private WithEvents BackgroundActivity _
   As System.ComponentModel.BackgroundWorker
```

When you are ready to initiate the background work, call the BackgroundWorker's RunWorkerAsync() method. This triggers the DoWork event. In this event handler, call the method that will perform the background work. The sample code passes the BackgroundWorker instance to the worker method. You don't have to pass this information, but it makes it easier to communicate back to the primary thread if you do.

For example, if you want the worker thread to report its progress, set the control's WorkerReportsProgress property to True, then monitor the control's ProgressChanged event. Calls to the control's ReportProgress( ) method by the work trigger this event in the primary thread.

This communication works both ways. Setting the control's WorkerSupportsCancellation property to True allows the primary thread to request a cancellation of the work by calling the CancelAsync( ) method. This sets the control's CancellationPending property, as viewed by the worker thread.

Threads make background processing easy, but interactions between threads can be problematic. The issue is that if two threads wish to update the same object instance, there is no guarantee that they will update them in a specific order. Consider a class with three members. Updating these three members occurs over multiple statements:

```
Private SomeInstance As SomeClass
Private Sub UpdateInstance(ByVal scalar As Integer)
    SomeInstance.Member1 = 10 * scalar
    SomeInstance.Member2 = 20 * scalar
    SomeInstance.Member3 = 30 * scalar
End Sub
```

But what happens when two different threads call the UpdateInstance( ) method at the same time (assuming that they are sharing the SomeInstance variable)? Because of the way that threading works, it's possible that the calls could get interleaved in ways that corrupt the data. Suppose thread #1 calls UpdateInstance(2) and thread #2 calls UpdateInstance(3). It's possible the statements within UpdateInstance( ) could be called in this order:

```
SomeInstance.Member1 = 10 * 2  ' From Thread #1
SomeInstance.Member1 = 10 * 3  ' From Thread #2
SomeInstance.Member2 = 20 * 3  ' From Thread #2
SomeInstance.Member2 = 20 * 2  ' From Thread #1
SomeInstance.Member3 = 30 * 2  ' From Thread #1
SomeInstance.Member3 = 30 * 3  ' From Thread #2
```

After this code, Member1 and Member3 is set based on the call from thread #2, but Member2 retains the value from thread #1.

To prevent this from happening, Visual Basic includes a SyncLock statement that acts as a gatekeeper around a block of code. (The .NET Framework also includes other classes and features that perform a similar service.) Using SyncLock to fix the UpdateInstance( ) problem, you must create a common object and use it as a locking mechanism:

```
Private SomeInstance As SomeClass
Private LockObject As New Object
Private Sub UpdateInstance(ByVal scalar As Integer)
    SyncLock LockObject
        SomeInstance.Member1 = 10 * scalar
        SomeInstance.Member2 = 20 * scalar
        SomeInstance.Member3 = 30 * scalar
    End SyncLock
End Sub
```

As each thread enters UpdateInstance( ), SyncLock tries to exclusively lock the LockObject instance. Only when this is successful does the thread proceed through the block of code.

14.22 Reading XML into a TreeView

Problem

You have some XML content in a file. You want to display it using a TreeView control, so that you can expand specific branches.

Solution

Sample code folder: Chapter 14\XMLTreeView

There are many ways to go about this task, but one of the most straightforward is to load the content into an XmlDocument object, then traverse this object's attributes and nodes. This recipe's code loads an XML file into a TreeView control.

Discussion

Create a new Windows Forms application, and add the following controls to Form1:

- A TextBox control named XMLFile.
- A Button control named LoadFile. Set its Text property to Load.
- A TreeView control named XMLTree.

Add informational labels if desired, and arrange the controls so that Form1 looks like the form in Figure 14-17.

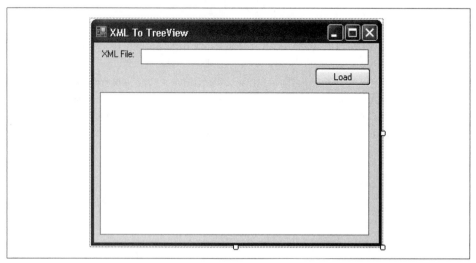

Figure 14-17. Controls on the XML-to-TreeView sample

Now add the following source code to Form1's class template:

```
Private Sub LoadFile_Click(ByVal sender As System.Object, _
        ByVal e As System.EventArgs) Handles LoadFile.Click
    ' ----- Load an XML file into the form's TreeView control.
    Dim fileContent As Xml.XmlDocument

    ' ----- Make sure the file exists.
    If (My.Computer.FileSystem.FileExists(XMLFile.Text) = _
            False) Then
        MsgBox("Please supply a valid file name.")
        Return
    End If

    ' ----- Load the XML content into an XMLDocument object.
    Try
        fileContent = New Xml.XmlDocument
        fileContent.Load(XMLFile.Text)
    Catch ex As Exception
        MsgBox("The XML file could not be loaded due to " & _
            "the following error:" & vbCrLf & vbCrLf & _
            ex.Message)
        fileContent = Nothing
        Return
    End Try

    ' ----- Remove any existing content in the TreeView.
    XMLTree.Nodes.Clear()

    ' ----- Call a recursive method that will scan down
    '          all branches of the XML file.
    For Each oneNode As Xml.XmlNode In fileContent.ChildNodes
        AddNodeToTree(oneNode, Nothing)
    Next oneNode
End Sub

Private Sub AddNodeToTree(ByVal oneNode As Xml.XmlNode, _
        ByVal fromNode As TreeNode)
    ' ----- Add a node and all of its subordinate items.
    Dim baseNode As TreeNode

    ' ----- Ignore plain text nodes, as they are picked up
    '          by the inner-text code below.
    If (oneNode.NodeType = Xml.XmlNodeType.Text) Then Return

    ' ----- Treat the "<?xml..." node specially.
    If (oneNode.NodeType = Xml.XmlNodeType.XmlDeclaration) _
            And (fromNode Is Nothing) Then
        baseNode = XMLTree.Nodes.Add( _
            oneNode.OuterXml.ToString())
        Return
    End If
```

```
' ----- Add the node itself.
If (fromNode Is Nothing) Then
   baseNode = XMLTree.Nodes.Add(oneNode.Name)
Else
   baseNode = fromNode.Nodes.Add(oneNode.Name)
End If

' ----- Add the attributes.
If (oneNode.Attributes IsNot Nothing) Then
   For Each oneAttr As Xml.XmlAttribute In _
         oneNode.Attributes
      baseNode.Nodes.Add("Attribute: " & oneAttr.Name & _
         " = """ & oneAttr.Value & """")
   Next oneAttr
End If

' ----- Add content if available.
If (oneNode.InnerText <> "") Then
   baseNode.Nodes.Add("Content: " & oneNode.InnerText)
End If

' ----- Add the child nodes.
If (oneNode.ChildNodes IsNot Nothing) Then
   For Each subNode As Xml.XmlNode In oneNode.ChildNodes
      AddNodeToTree(subNode, baseNode)
   Next subNode
End If
End Sub
```

To run the program, type a valid XML filename in the XMLFile field, and then click
the Load button. The XML content appears in the TreeView control, with branches
collapsed. This program was run using this recipe's *.vbproj* file for the input (it's an
XML file). Figure 14-18 shows the results.

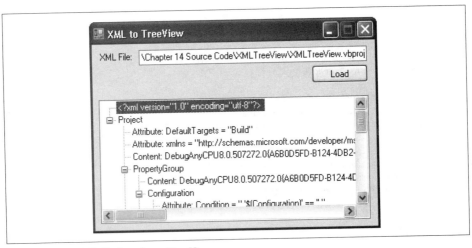

Figure 14-18. XML displayed as a TreeView

The `TreeView` control is designed to present hierarchical data, which is precisely what you find in XML content. The `System.Xml.XmlDocument` object represents the content of XML data by parsing the raw XML text and building distinct `Xml.XmlNode` objects for each element and branch point within the content. Both `XmlDocument` and `XmlNode` include a `ChildNodes` collection that provides access to the XML tags found immediately within the current tag. These objects also include an `Attributes` collection that lists the name and value of each tag attribute.

See Also

Recipes 14.23 and 14.24 discuss other methods of working with XML content.

14.23 Creating an XML Document

Problem

You need to build an XML file that contains important configuration or processing data, and you aren't excited about doing all the string concatenation yourself.

Solution

Sample code folder: Chapter 14\GenerateXMLContent

Use the XML document creation tools in the `System.XML` namespace to generate the XML. This namespace includes a few different ways of building XML content. One of the simplest methods is to fill in a `System.Xml.XmlDocument` object by building it with distinct `System.Xml.XmlElement` objects.

Discussion

This recipe's sample code builds a simple program that outputs a list of email recipients in XML format. It groups recipients by the desired email format, either HTML or plain text. Here is a sample of the generated XML content:

```xml
<?xml version="1.0"?>
<emailData>
  <emailRecipients mailType="HTML">
    <recipient>
      <name>John Smith</name>
      <address>jsmith@fakeemail.com</address>
    </recipient>
    <recipient>
      <name>Jane Jones</name>
      <address>jane.jones@dontmailme.com</address>
    </recipient>
  </emailRecipients>
  <emailRecipients mailType="Text">
    <recipient>
      <name>Brenda Wong</name>
```

```
            <address>puppyfriend@ilikedogs.net</address>
          </recipient>
      </emailRecipients>
  </emailData>
```

Create a new Windows Forms application, and add the following controls to Form1:

- A ComboBox control named EmailType. Set its DropDownStyle property to DropDownList.

- A TextBox control named RecipientName.

- A TextBox control named RecipientAddress.

- A ListBox control named AllRecipients.

- A Button control named AddEmail. Set its Text property to Add.

- A Button control named DeleteEmail. Set its Text property to Delete.

- A TextBox control named XMLFile.

- A Button control named SaveFile. Set its Text property to Save.

Add informational labels if desired, and arrange the controls so that Form1 looks like the form in Figure 14-19.

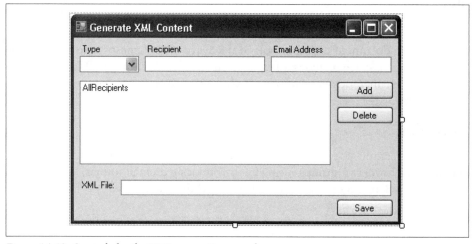

Figure 14-19. Controls for the XML-generation sample

Now add the following source code to Form1's class template:

```
Public Class RecipientData
    ' ----- A simple class to hold the basics of an address.
    Public EmailType As String
    Public EmailName As String
    Public EmailAddress As String

    Public Sub New(ByVal newType As String, _
        ByVal newName As String, ByVal newAddress As String)
```

```
        ' ----- Constructor to build the new record.
        EmailType = newType
        EmailName = newName
        EmailAddress = newAddress
    End Sub

    Public Overrides Function ToString() As String
        ' ----- Display a nicely formatted address.
        Return EmailName & " <" & EmailAddress & ">"
    End Function
End Class

Private Sub Form1_Load(ByVal sender As System.Object, _
        ByVal e As System.EventArgs) Handles MyBase.Load
    ' ----- Add the types of email content.
    EmailType.Items.Add("HTML")
    EmailType.Items.Add("Text")
    EmailType.SelectedIndex = 0
End Sub

Private Sub DeleteEmail_Click(ByVal sender As System.Object, _
        ByVal e As System.EventArgs) Handles DeleteEmail.Click
    ' ----- Remove the selected email address.
    If (AllRecipients.SelectedIndex <> ListBox.NoMatches) Then _
        AllRecipients.Items.Remove(AllRecipients.SelectedItem)
End Sub

Private Sub AddEmail_Click(ByVal sender As System.Object, _
        ByVal e As System.EventArgs) Handles AddEmail.Click
    ' ----- Add an email recipient. Check for missing data.
    If (RecipientName.Text.Trim = "") Then
        MsgBox("Please supply a recipient name.")
        Return
    End If
    If (RecipientAddress.Text.Trim = "") Then
        MsgBox("Please supply a recipient address.")
        Return
    End If

    ' ----- Add this recipient to the list.
    AllRecipients.Items.Add(New RecipientData( _
        EmailType.Text, RecipientName.Text, _
        RecipientAddress.Text))

    ' ----- Get ready for a new entry.
    RecipientName.Clear()
    RecipientAddress.Clear()
    RecipientName.Focus()
End Sub

Private Sub SaveFile_Click(ByVal sender As System.Object, _
        ByVal e As System.EventArgs) Handles SaveFile.Click
    ' ----- Save the XML content.
    Dim emailSet As Xml.XmlDocument
```

```
Dim emailDeclare As Xml.XmlDeclaration
Dim emailRoot As Xml.XmlElement
Dim emailGroup As Xml.XmlElement
Dim emailRecipient As Xml.XmlElement
Dim emailDetail As Xml.XmlElement
Dim counter As Integer
Dim useType As String
Dim scanEmail As Object
Dim oneEmail As RecipientData

' ----- Check for missing data.
If (AllRecipients.Items.Count = 0) Then
   MsgBox("Please enter at least one recipient.")
   Return
End If
If (XMLFile.Text.Trim = "") Then
   MsgBox("Please specify the output file.")
   Return
End If

' ----- Warn if the file exists.
If (My.Computer.FileSystem.FileExists(XMLFile.Text)) Then
   If (MsgBox("The file exists. Overwrite?", _
      MsgBoxStyle.YesNo Or MsgBoxStyle.Question) <> _
      MsgBoxResult.Yes) Then Return
   Try
      Kill(XMLFile.Text)
   Catch ex As Exception
      MsgBox("Could not replace the file. " & ex.Message)
      Return
   End Try
End If

' ----- Start the XML document with an XML declaration.
emailSet = New Xml.XmlDocument
emailDeclare = emailSet.CreateXmlDeclaration("1.0", _
   Nothing, String.Empty)
emailSet.InsertBefore(emailDeclare, _
   emailSet.DocumentElement)

' ----- Add in the root <emailData> element.
emailRoot = emailSet.CreateElement("emailData")
emailSet.InsertAfter(emailRoot, emailDeclare)

' ----- Scan through the recipients, once for each type.
For counter = 0 To EmailType.Items.Count - 1
   ' ----- Prepare for this pass.
   useType = EmailType.Items(counter)
   emailGroup = Nothing

   For Each scanEmail In AllRecipients.Items
      oneEmail = CType(scanEmail, RecipientData)
      If (oneEmail.EmailType = useType) Then
         ' ----- Found a recipient in this group.
```

```
                  '        Add the group if needed.
              If (emailGroup Is Nothing) Then
                 emailGroup = emailSet.CreateElement( _
                    "emailRecipients")
                 emailGroup.SetAttribute("mailType", useType)
                 emailRoot.AppendChild(emailGroup)
              End If

              ' ----- Build the new output entry.
              emailRecipient = emailSet.CreateElement( _
                 "recipient")
              emailGroup.AppendChild(emailRecipient)

              emailDetail = emailSet.CreateElement("name")
              emailDetail.InnerText = oneEmail.EmailName
              emailRecipient.AppendChild(emailDetail)

              emailDetail = emailSet.CreateElement("address")
              emailDetail.InnerText = oneEmail.EmailAddress
              emailRecipient.AppendChild(emailDetail)
           End If
        Next scanEmail
     Next counter

     ' ----- Write out the XML content.
     Try
        emailSet.Save(XMLFile.Text)
        MsgBox("XML content saved.")
     Catch ex As Exception
        MsgBox("Could not write the XML content. " & _
           ex.Message)
     End Try
  End Sub
```

To use the program, select an email type (HTML or Text) from the Type drop-down list, enter in a recipient name and email address in the two text fields next to the drop-down, and then click the Add button to add the recipient to the list. Repeat as needed. When you have added enough recipients, supply an output filename in the XML File field, and then click the Save button.

Most of this recipe's sample code lets you build the list of email recipients in a ListBox control. The embedded RecipientData class helps organize the content stored in each ListBox item.

The real XML work happens in the Click event handler for the SaveFile button. After performing some quick verification, the method creates a new XmlDocument to store the new XML content. For each node in the output, it then creates XmlElement objects using the XmlDocument.CreateElement( ) method. This method generates a generic XML element, representing a standard XML tag. It adds attributes to the element via the XmlElement.SetAttribute( ) method. These completed elements are then inserted into the existing XmlDocument structure relative to other existing nodes.

The various uses of the InsertBefore( ), InsertAfter( ), and AppendChild( ) methods in the sample code show how you can position elements as you need them.

Besides CreateElement( ), XmlDocument includes other Create... methods that generate a variety of XML-specific content entities. For example, the CreateXmlDeclaration( ) method is used in the sample code to generate the <?xml version="1.0"?> tag at the start of the document:

```
emailDeclare = emailSet.CreateXmlDeclaration("1.0", _
    Nothing, String.Empty)
```

Once elements have been added to the XmlDocument, you can traverse them using any of the supported XML tools, such as XPath.

See Also

Recipes 14.22 and 14.24 discuss other methods of working with XML content.

14.24 Validating an XML Document

Problem

You have an XML document that is supposed to adhere to a specific schema. How can you be sure the document is valid?

Solution

There are a variety of XML validation methods, including DTD and both internal and external Schema definitions. If you are going to read the XML content into a System.Xml.XmlDocument object, you can verify it as it is read using any of these validation methods. Normally, an XmlReader reads any valid XML into an XmlDocument object without validation. However, you can indicate the type of validation to perform by setting the various properties of an XmlReaderSettings object and using it when creating the XmlReader. Here is the basic code used to process XML with custom settings:

```
' ----- XML file contained in 'xmlFileName' variable.
Dim readContent As Xml.XmlReader
Dim xmlContent As Xml.XmlDocument
Dim customSettings As New Xml.XmlReaderSettings
' ----- Modify customSettings properties here, then...
readContent = Xml.XmlReader.Create(xmlFileName, customSettings)
xmlContent = New Xml.XmlDocument
xmlContent.Load(readContent)
```

The code you add in the "Modify customSettings" area of the code depends on the type of verification or processing you wish to do. Include the following statements to validate the XML using a known external schema (.xsd) file:

```
customSettings.ValidationType = Xml.ValidationType.Schema
customSettings.Schemas.Add("urn:my-schema", "MySchema.xsd")
```

Discussion

The XmlReaderSettings class includes features that control the processing of XML content during import, including the handling of whitespace and embedded comments. It also determines how to handle validation through its ValidationType property. In Visual Basic 2005, the allowed settings include None (for no validation, the default), DTD (for included DTD content), and Schema (for XSD processing, either internal or external).

Care must be taken when performing DTD validation because malformed DTD entries can cause processing issues. Because of this, DTD processing is disabled by default. To enable it, you must alter two settings:

```
customSettings.ValidationType = Xml.ValidationType.DTD
customSettings.ProhibitDtd = False
```

If your XML content includes an XSD schema within the XML content (i.e., an inline schema), you must enable processing support:

```
customSettings.ValidationType = Xml.ValidationType.Schema
customSettings.ValidationFlags = _
   customSettings.ValidationFlags Or _
   Xml.Schema.XmlSchemaValidationFlags.ProcessInlineSchema
```

When you validate XML, any content that deviates from the schema raises exceptions (System.Xml.XmlException) that emanate from the call to XmlDocument.Load( ). You can also capture problems through a ValidationEventHandler event, exposed by the XmlReaderSettings class.

See Also

Recipes 14.22 and 14.23 discuss other methods of working with XML content.

14.25 Using Generic Collections

Problem

You need to store some objects in a collection, but you want to ensure that the collection allows only objects of a specific type.

Solution

Use one of the generic collections made available in .NET. They are called "generic" because they are data-typed generically, allowing you to replace nonspecific data-type placeholders with your own specific data types. ("Specifics" might have been a better name.) All generic collection classes appear in the System.Collections.Generic namespace.

As an example, the following code creates a stack (represented by the System.Collections.Generic.Stack class) that stores only Date objects. It then adds items to the stack:

```
Dim dateStack As _
    New System.Collections.Generic.Stack(Of Date)
dateStack.Push(Today)
dateStack.Push(DateAdd("d", 28, Today))
```

Discussion

The System.Collections.Generic namespace includes several useful generic collections for your use:

Dictionary(Of TKey, TValue)

 This class implements a basic lookup system, with value objects made available through unique keys. You can indicate the data types of both the key and the value at declaration; they can be different. This class stores items in the dictionary through the related KeyValuePair(Of TKey, TValue) class.

LinkedList(Of T)

 This class implements a doubly linked list, with immediate access to the first and last items in the list. Each list item—implemented through the related LinkedListNode(Of T) class—includes a Previous and Next link to make traversal possible.

List(Of T)

 This class implements a simple list of objects, providing access to items by index number. It includes methods to add, insert, and remove objects. It also includes many methods that locate items already in the list.

Queue(Of T)

 This class represents a generic queue of objects, a "First In, First Out" (FIFO) construct. Items are added to the queue through the Enqueue( ) method and later retrieved and removed from the queue with the Dequeue( ) method. The Peek( ) method retrieves the oldest object from the queue but does not remove it.

SortedDictionary(Of TKey, TValue)

 This class implements a basic lookup system, with value objects made available through unique keys. It also keeps the records sorted using a binary search tree. You can indicate the data types of both the key and the value at declaration; they can be different. If the TKey data type implements the IComparer interface, that type's comparison rules are used for the sort. This class stores items in the dictionary through the related KeyValuePair(Of TKey, TValue) class.

SortedList(Of TKey, TValue)

 This class implements an ordered list. Items in the list are sorted by key as they are added. It is identical to the SortedDictionary(Of TKey, TValue) class, but it is optimized for fast insertion of previously sorted data. If the TKey data type implements the IComparer interface, that type's comparison rules are used for the sort. This class stores items in the dictionary through the related KeyValuePair(Of TKey, TValue) class.

Stack(Of T)

This class represents a generic stack of objects, a "Last In, First Out" (LIFO) construct. Items are added to the stack through the Push( ) method and later retrieved and removed from the stack with the Pop( ) method. The Peek( ) method retrieves the top-most object from the stack, but does not remove it.

14.26 Creating a Screensaver

Problem

You have some down time between projects at work, and you want to implement a simple screensaver in Visual Basic.

Solution

Sample code folder: Chapter 14\SimpleScreenSaver

Use this recipe's sample code as an example of how to develop a screensaver using .NET. The code creates a simple screensaver that displays either the time or the date and time together in the center of the display.

Discussion

Create a new Windows Forms project, and name it SimpleScreenSaver. Change the name of the main form from *Form1.vb* to *ScreenSaver.vb*. Open that form, and set the following properties:

- Set Text to Simple Screen Saver.
- Set FormBorderStyle to None.
- Set TopMost to True.
- Set WindowState to Maximized.

This form will serve as the screensaver view. Maximizing it and setting it as the topmost form forces it to consume the entire display.

Add a Label control named CurrentTime to the form's surface, and set these properties:

- Set AutoSize to False.
- Set Size to 240,120.
- Set Font.Size to 28.
- Set TextAlign to MiddleCenter.

Next, add a Timer control named ClockTimer to the form. Set its Interval property to 1000 (which means 1000 milliseconds), and set its Enabled property to True. The form should be somewhat bland and have the general look of Figure 14-20.

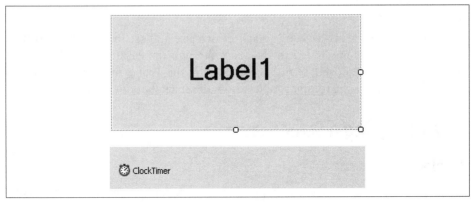

Figure 14-20. The design of the screensaver form

Add the following code to the form's code template:

```
Private LastMousePosition As New Point(-1, -1)

Private Sub ClockTimer_Tick(ByVal sender As System.Object, _
      ByVal e As System.EventArgs) Handles ClockTimer.Tick
   ' ----- Show the time.
   RefreshClock()
End Sub

Private Sub RefreshClock()
   ' ----- Update the display when it changes.
   If (IncludeDateFlag() = True) Then
      CurrentTime.Text = Now.ToLongDateString & vbCrLf & _
         Now.ToLongTimeString
   Else
      CurrentTime.Text = Now.ToLongTimeString
   End If
End Sub

Private Sub ScreenSaver_FormClosing(ByVal sender As Object, _
      ByVal e As System.Windows.Forms.FormClosingEventArgs) _
      Handles Me.FormClosing
   ' ----- Restore the mouse pointer.
   Windows.Forms.Cursor.Show()
End Sub

Private Sub ScreenSaver_KeyDown(ByVal sender As Object, _
      ByVal e As System.Windows.Forms.KeyEventArgs) _
      Handles Me.KeyDown
   ' ----- Pressing any key stops the program.
   Me.Close()
End Sub
```

```
Private Sub ScreenSaver_Load(ByVal sender As Object, _
      ByVal e As System.EventArgs) Handles Me.Load
   ' ----- Hide the mouse cursor.
   Windows.Forms.Cursor.Hide( )
   RefreshClock( )
End Sub

Private Sub ScreenSaver_MouseDown(ByVal sender As Object, _
      ByVal e As System.Windows.Forms.MouseEventArgs) _
      Handles Me.MouseDown
   ' ----- Clicking stops the program.
   Me.Close( )
End Sub

Private Sub ScreenSaver_MouseMove(ByVal sender As Object, _
      ByVal e As System.Windows.Forms.MouseEventArgs) _
      Handles Me.MouseMove
   ' ----- Moving the mouse stops the program.
   If (LastMousePosition <> New Point(-1, -1)) Then
      ' ----- See if the mouse moved since last time.
      If (LastMousePosition <> New Point(e.X, e.Y)) Then
         Me.Close( )
      End If
   End If

   ' ----- Record the current point.
   LastMousePosition = New Point(e.X, e.Y)
End Sub

Private Sub ScreenSaver_Resize(ByVal sender As Object, _
      ByVal e As System.EventArgs) Handles Me.Resize
   ' ----- Center the label on the form.
   CurrentTime.Location = New Point(0, (Me.Height - _
      CurrentTime.Height) / 2)
   CurrentTime.Size = New Size(Me.Width, CurrentTime.Height)
End Sub
```

Add a new module to the project through the Project → Add Module menu command, and name the module file *General.vb*. Add the following two methods to this module's source code:

```
Public Sub Main( )
   ' ----- The screen saver starts here.
   Dim startOption As String = ""

   ' ----- Check the command-line arguments. There are
   '       three that we will look for:
   '          /s = Start the screen saver
   '          /c = Configure the screen saver (default)
   '          /p = Show a preview (not implemented here)
   If (My.Application.CommandLineArgs.Count > 0) Then _
      startOption = My.Application.CommandLineArgs(0). _
      ToUpper( )
   If (startOption = "") Then startOption = "/C"
```

```
        If (startOption.Substring(0, 2) = "/C") Then
            Config.ShowDialog()
            Return
        ElseIf (startOption.Substring(0, 2) <> "/S") Then
            ' ----- Ignore all options besides "startup."
            Return
        End If

        ' ----- Start the screen saver.
        ScreenSaver.ShowDialog()
    End Sub

    Public Function IncludeDateFlag() As Boolean
        ' ----- Get the current configuration value.
        Dim configKey As Microsoft.Win32.RegistryKey
        Dim theValue As Object

        IncludeDateFlag = False
        Try
            ' ----- Load the setting from the registry.
            configKey = My.Computer.Registry.CurrentUser. _
                OpenSubKey("Software\MyCompany\SimpleScreenSaver")
            If (configKey IsNot Nothing) Then
                theValue = configKey.GetValue("IncludeDate")
                If (theValue IsNot Nothing) Then _
                    IncludeDateFlag = CBool(theValue)
                configKey.Close()
            End If
        Catch ex As Exception
            ' ----- Don't show any error.
        Finally
            configKey = Nothing
        End Try
    End Function
```

Finally, add a form that lets the user indicate whether to include the date on the screensaver display. Add the form through the Project → Add Windows Form menu command, and name the form file *Config.vb*. Set the following form properties:

- Set FormBorderStyle to FixedDialog.
- Set Text to Configure Screen Saver.
- Set ControlBox to False.
- Set StartPosition to CenterScreen.

Add a CheckBox control to the form named IncludeDate, and set its Text property to Include Date in Screen Saver Display. Also add two Button controls named ActOK and ActCancel, and set their Text properties to OK and Cancel, respectively.

Select the form again, and set its AcceptButton property to ActOK and its CancelButton property to ActCancel. The form should look like Figure 14-21.

Figure 14-21. The screensaver configuration form

That's it for the main display and code design, but we still need to make a few changes to the project itself to prepare it for screensaver use. Open the Project Properties window. On the Application panel, set "Startup object" to Sub Main, and clear (uncheck) the "Enable application framework" field.

Build the project through the Build → Build SimpleScreenSaver menu command. In Windows Explorer, locate the executable file. It will appear in the *bin\Release* directory within the project source-code directory. Rename the *SimpleScreenSaver.exe* file to *SimpleScreenSaver.scr*. Then, copy that file into your system's *Windows\System32* directory (the exact location will vary by system). The screensaver is ready to use. Open up the Display Properties within your system's Control panel. On the Screen Saver tab, select SimpleScreenSaver from the Screen Saver drop-down list (Figure 14-22).

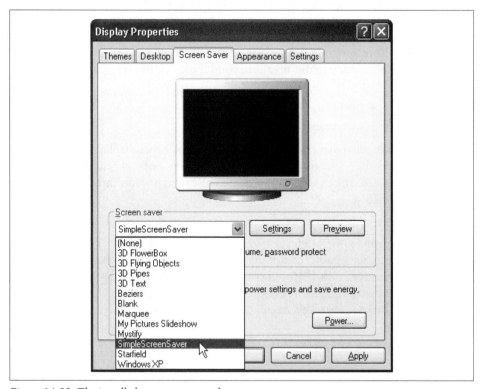

Figure 14-22. The installed screensaver, ready to use

Clicking on the Settings button lets you configure the screensaver through the custom *Config.vb* form. The Preview button runs the screensaver immediately.

Screensavers are regular Windows applications, but they reside only in the *Windows\ System32* directory, and their file extension is *.scr* instead of *.exe*. What the user experiences as a screensaver is simply a maximized borderless form. You can add any controls you want to the form, and you can display any graphics or images you require to make the screen saver interesting.

Screensaver programs perform three distinct functions: main display, preview display, and configuration. (The sample program does not implement the preview display functionality.) The functionality you present depends on the command-line options supplied to the application:

- The /S command-line option tells the program to start the screensaver and continue until the user types a key or uses the mouse. (Actually, there is no firm rule about when to stop the screensaver. These are the traditional methods, but you can require the user to click a button on your main form if you wish.)

- The /C command-line option displays any configuration forms used to alter the behavior of the screensaver. In the sample application, the *Config.vb* form lets the user adjust a single Boolean value, which is stored in a registry value.

- The /P command-line option updates the minipreview display window in the Control Panel Display Properties applet. The second command-line argument is an integer that indicates the Win32 window handle for the preview portion of the applet. Your program can display a preview version of the screensaver in this area if desired. Updating this area is beyond the scope of this recipe.

The recipe's Sub Main routine examines the command-line arguments and takes the appropriate action. In the absence of any command-line arguments, the screensaver should assume the /C argument.

This recipe's code implements a very simple screensaver that displays either the time or the combined date and time, updating the display once per second through a Timer control. It determines whether to display the date portion through a setting in the registry, located at:

```
\\HKEY_CURRENT_USER\Software\MyCompany\SimpleScreenSaver\IncludeDate
```

The screensaver runs until it detects a key press (through the Form.KeyPress event), a mouse click (Form.MouseDown), or a mouse movement (Form.MouseMove). It turns out that each form receives a MouseMove message right when the form first opens, whether the mouse is moving or not. Therefore, the code includes some special code to ensure that the first MouseMove event call does not exit the screensaver.

14.27 Localizing the Controls on a Form

Problem

You want to make your application available to speakers of other languages.

Solution

Sample code folder: Chapter 14\MultiLanguage

Use the features built right into Visual Studio to assist you with the localization process. Windows applications have long supported multiple languages through interchangeable language-specific resource files. When managing the display language for the fields on your application forms, you can have Visual Studio generate the resource files for you automatically.

Discussion

Create a new Windows Forms application, and add two Label controls to Form1, named Label1 and Label2. Set Label1's Text property to The message is:, and set Label2's Text property to Good day!. Arrange the controls as shown in Figure 14-23.

Figure 14-23. The English-language interface

The English-language version of the application is ready to compile and use. (Actually, the default-language version is ready to use, and the default language happens to be English.) To enable support for multiple languages on this form, set its Localizable property to True.

To enable French-language support, change the form's Language property to French. You will see the form blink briefly. Select Label2, and change its Text property to Bon jour!, as shown in Figure 14-24.

Figure 14-24. The French-language interface

To test both language versions, change the language either to the default language or to French when the program first starts. On the Application tab of the Project Properties window, click the View Application Events button to access the *ApplicationEvents.vb* file. Add the following code to the MyApplication class in this file:

```
Private Sub MyApplication_Startup(ByVal sender As Object, _
    ByVal e As Microsoft.VisualBasic.ApplicationServices. _
    StartupEventArgs) Handles Me.Startup
  ' ----- Prompt to change the culture.
  Dim newCulture As String

  newCulture = InputBox("Enter new culture string.")
  If (newCulture <> "") Then
    Threading.Thread.CurrentThread.CurrentUICulture = _
      New Globalization.CultureInfo(newCulture)
  End If
End Sub
```

Run the program. When prompted for a culture, leave the prompt empty to default to English, or enter fr to use French. Then, enjoy the results.

To see what's really going on, build the program through the Build → Build WindowsApplication1 menu command. Then locate the folder with the generated application (the *bin\Release* directory within the project's source-code directory). You will find a subdirectory named *fr*, which contains a "satellite assembly" containing the language-specific resources.

In addition to building language-specific resources when you design your program, you can add them after release by using the *winres.exe* application included with Visual Studio. On our system, the link to this program is found in Start → [All] Programs → Microsoft .NET Framework SDK v2.0 → Tools → Windows Resource Localization Editor (see Figure 14-25). You must have set the form's Localizable property to True to use this tool.

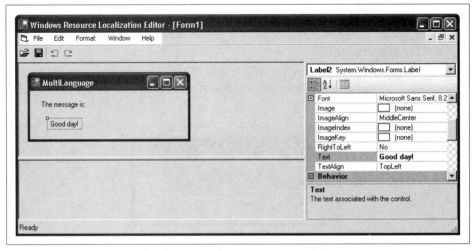

Figure 14-25. The winres.exe localization tool

To use the tool, open the *Form1.resx* resource file associated with the localized form, select each element whose Text property needs to be localized in turn, and enter in the new language-specific settings. When saving the file, you are prompted for an output language. The tool generates a separate language-specific resource file. We chose to create a Japanese-specific resource file; the tool generated *Form1.ja.resx*.

To generate the new resource's satellite assembly, recompile the application. If this is not an option, you can generate the file manually. This is a two-step process, and it must be done on the command line. Open the Visual Studio–specific command line using the Start → [All] Programs → Microsoft Visual Studio 2005 → Visual Studio Tools → Visual Studio 2005 Command Prompt menu command. Change to the source-code directory that contains the new *.resx* resource file:

```
cd sourcedirectory
```

Compile the *.resx* file into a *.resources* file, using the *resgen.exe* application included with Visual Studio:

```
resgen.exe Form1.ja.resx
```

The directory now contains a *Form1.ja.resources* file. Compile it to a satellite assembly using the *al.exe* (Assembly Linker) program. Enter the command on a single line, not on four lines as shown here:

```
al /t:lib /embed:Form1.ja.resources,
   MultiLanguage.Form1.ja.resources /culture:ja
   /out:MultiLanguage.resources.dll
   /template:bin\Release\MultiLanguage.exe
```

Now move the new *MultiLanguage.resources.dll* file to a culture-specific folder within the release directory. You may wish to move the file into a *bin\Release\ja* folder you create within the project directory. On deployment, the file should be installed in a *ja* folder within the release directory.

When you run the program again and enter ja for the culture, you'll see the form in Figure 14-26.

Figure 14-26. The Japanese-language interface

14.28 Adding Pop-up Help to Controls

Problem

Dialog boxes in Windows applications support pop-up help on controls. On such forms, clicking the question-mark button in the upper-right corner of the form and then clicking on a form control displays a tooltip-like message describing the use of the control. (See Figure 14-27 for an example.) You want to add a similar feature to controls on your form.

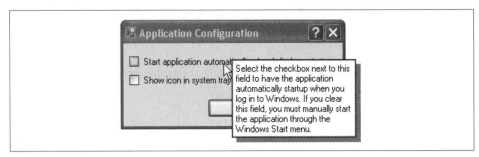

Figure 14-27. Pop-up help for a control

Solution

Sample code folder: Chapter 14\PopupHelp

Include a HelpProvider control on your form, and use it to enable the pop-up help.

Discussion

Create a new Windows Forms application, and add a Button control to the form. We'll add pop-up help to this button. Next, add a HelpProvider control to the form, which you'll find in the Components part of the Windows Forms Toolbox. This control (HelpProvider1) appears in the off-form area of the designer.

Change the form's HelpButton property to True. The button won't appear yet because it only appears when the Minimize and Maximize buttons are hidden. Set both the MinimizeButton and MaximizeButton properties to False to make the help button appear. You'll see the standard Windows question-mark button.

To set the help message for the Button control, select it on the form. One of the control's properties is HelpString on HelpProvider1, which appears indirectly through the HelpProvider1 control. Add some text to this property.

To view the pop-up help, run the program, click on the question-mark button, and then click on the Button control. The pop-up help will appear until you click somewhere else.

The `HelpProvider` control also supports more standard online help methods. It can display help through a web page that appears when the user presses the F1 key from anywhere on the form. It can also display online help through a compiled HTML Help 1.x (*.chm*) file.

To enable web-page-based help, add a `HelpProvider` control to your form, and change its `HelpNamespace` property to any valid web page.

To display help through HTML Help files, set the `HelpProvider` control's `HelpNamespace` property to the help-file path. Change the form's `HelpKeyword` on `HelpProvider1` property (the name may vary based on the name you gave to the help provider control) to the name of the page within the compiled file as defined by your HTML Help editing tool. An example may be `html/EditorPage.htm`. Also change the form's `HelpNavigator` on `HelpProvider1` property to `Topic`.

The `HelpNavigator` on `HelpProvider1` property includes other methods with which you can access compiled help pages. For instance, the `TableOfContents` and `Index` values, when used, bring up the Table of Contents page and the Index page for the online help, respectively.

14.29 Maintaining User-Specific Settings Between Uses of an Application

Problem

The user of your application is allowed to configure certain aspects of the application to suit her preferences. You would like to save these per-user settings so that the application uses them the next time it is run.

Solution

Sample code folder: Chapter 14\UserSettings

Use the `My.Settings` feature of Visual Basic to enable user- and application-specific settings.

Discussion

This recipe's sample code remembers the position of the form on the screen from one use to the next, and it also displays the name of the last user, which it retains in local settings.

Create a new Windows Forms application. Add a `Button` control named `ActPrefs`, and set its `Text` property to `Preferences...` Then add a `Label` control named `UserName`, and set its `Text` property to `Your name is not set.` and its `UseMnemonic` property to `False`. Adjust the form to look like Figure 14-28.

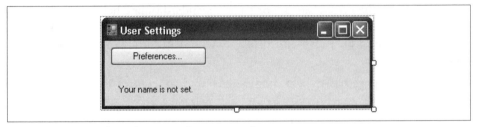

Figure 14-28. Controls on the user preferences sample

Open the Project Properties window, and select the Settings tab. This panel presents a grid of user-specific and application-specific settings. By filling in the grid, you automatically add settings that you can use in your application to retain user-preferred changes. Add two settings rows to this grid:

- Add a setting named PrefsUserName, and leave its Type as String.
- Add a setting named MainFormLocation, and select System.Drawing.Point for its Type.

Leave the Scope for both settings as User, and don't provide any Value column data. Close the Project Properties window and return to the form.

Add the following source code to the form's code template:

```
Private Sub ActPrefs_Click(ByVal sender As System.Object, _
      ByVal e As System.EventArgs) Handles ActPrefs.Click
   ' ----- Prompt the user to change his/her preferred name.
   Dim newName As String

   newName = InputBox("Enter your name.")
   If (newName.Trim() <> "") Then
      ' ----- Save the user's preferences.
      My.Settings.PrefsUserName = newName.Trim
      UserName.Text = "Your name is " & newName.Trim & "."
   End If
End Sub

Private Sub Form1_Load(ByVal sender As System.Object, _
      ByVal e As System.EventArgs) Handles MyBase.Load
   ' ----- Display the user-defined name, if available.
   If (My.Settings.PrefsUserName <> "") Then
      UserName.Text = "Your name is " & _
         My.Settings.PrefsUserName & "."
   End If
End Sub
```

Return to the Form Designer, and select the form. Expand the form's (ApplicationSettings) property, and change the Location subproperty to MainFormLocation.

If Location does not appear as a subproperty, select the (PropertyBinding) subproperty and click its "..." button. On the Application Settings form that appears, locate Location in the list, and set its second column to MainFormLocation. Finally, click OK.

Run the program to test it. Each time you exit and restart the program, it remembers where you moved the form on the display. If you click the Preferences button and enter your name when prompted, it also remembers this setting the next time the program runs.

The My.Settings object is new in Visual Basic 2005. It provides a standard way to manage user- and application-specific settings. Each time the program exits, it saves any settings changes to an XML file, and it reads in that same file the next time the program runs. The exact location of this file varies, but its default location in Windows XP is:

```
C:\Documents and Setting\<username>\Local Settings\
    Application Data\<projectname>\<specialhash>\
    <version>\user.config
```

Application-specific settings, although not used in this sample program, are stored in an *app.config* file in the folder that contains your application assembly. Application-specific settings cannot be modified through the running application; you can only change them by changing the *app.config* file.

14.30 Verifying a Credit Card Number

Problem

You are writing an application that includes credit card processing and verification functionality. While the third-party credit card host will let you know when you have passed an invalid card number, you would like to catch invalid card numbers immediately when users enter them.

Solution

Sample code folder: Chapter 14\LuhnAlgorithm

Use the Luhn Algorithm to determine if a credit card number is valid or not. The Luhn Algorithm (or Luhn Formula) was invented by Hans Peter Luhn of IBM in the 1960s as a method of verifying account numbers of varying lengths. It is also called a "modulus 10" formula because it uses the modulus 10 formula (x Mod 10 in Visual Basic) to confirm the number.

Discussion

Create a new Windows Forms application, and add the following controls to Form1:

- A TextBox control named CreditCard.
- A Button control named ActVerify. Set its Text property to Verify.

Now add the following source code to the form's code template:

```
Private Sub ActVerify_Click(ByVal sender As System.Object, _
      ByVal e As System.EventArgs) Handles ActVerify.Click
   ' ----- Check for a valid credit card number.
   Dim useCard As String = ""
   Dim oneDigit As String
   Dim counter As Integer

   ' ----- Create a string with just the digits of the card,
   '       just in case the user entered spaces or dashes
   '       between digit blocks.
   For counter = 1 To Len(CreditCard.Text)
      oneDigit = Mid(CreditCard.Text, counter, 1)
      If (IsNumeric(oneDigit) = True) Then _
         useCard &= oneDigit
   Next counter
   If (useCard.Length = 0) Then
      MsgBox("Invalid card number.")
   ElseIf (VerifyCreditCard(useCard) = False) Then
      MsgBox("Invalid card number.")
   Else
      MsgBox("Card verified.")
   End If
End Sub

Private Function VerifyCreditCard(ByVal cardNumber _
      As String) As Boolean
   ' ----- Given a card number, make sure it is valid.
   '       This method uses the Luhn algorithm to verify
   '       the number. This routine assumes that cardNumber
   '       contains only digits.
   Dim counter As Integer
   Dim digitTotal As Integer
   Dim holdValue As Integer
   Dim checkDigit As Integer
   Dim calcDigit As Integer
   Dim useCard As String

   ' ----- Perform some initial checks.
   useCard = Trim(cardNumber)
   If (IsNumeric(useCard) = False) Then Return False

   ' ----- Separate out the last digit, the check digit.
   '       For cards with an odd number of digits,
   '       prepend with a zero.
```

```
If ((Len(useCard) Mod 2) <> 0) Then _
    useCard = "0" & useCard
checkDigit = useCard.Substring(Len(useCard) - 1, 1)
useCard = useCard.Substring(0, Len(useCard) - 1)

' ----- Process each digit.
digitTotal = 0
For counter = 1 To Len(useCard)
    If ((counter Mod 2) = 1) Then
        ' ----- This is an odd digit position.
        '       Double the number.
        holdValue = CInt(Mid(useCard, counter, 1)) * 2
        If (holdValue > 9) Then
            ' ----- Process digits (16 becomes 1+6).
            digitTotal += (holdValue \ 10) + _
                (holdValue - 10)
        Else
            digitTotal += holdValue
        End If
    Else
        ' ----- This is an even digit position.
        '       Simply add it.
        digitTotal += CInt(Mid(useCard, counter, 1))
    End If
Next counter

' ----- Calculate the 10's complement of both values.
calcDigit = 10 - (digitTotal Mod 10)
If (calcDigit = 10) Then calcDigit = 0
If (checkDigit = calcDigit) Then Return True Else _
    Return False
End Function
```

Run the program, enter a credit card number, and click the Verify button to see if the card number is valid.

14.31 Capturing a Console Application's Output

Problem

You want to capture and process the output of a console application in your program.

Solution

Sample code folder: Chapter 14\RedirectConsoleOutput

Use the StartInfo portion of a Process object to redirect the output of a console application into your code. The redirected output appears as a standard StreamReader object.

Discussion

This recipe's sample code captures the network data generated by the `ipconfig` command-line tool and displays it in a `ListBox` control.

Create a new Windows Forms application, and add three controls:

- A `ListBox` control named `OutputData`.
- A `CheckBox` control named `IncludeAll`. Change its `Text` property to `Use the '/all' flag to get all details`.
- A `Button` control named `ActProcess`. Set its `Text` property to `Process`.

The controls should appear as in Figure 14-29.

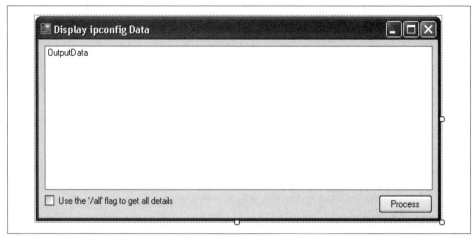

Figure 14-29. The controls for the redirected console output sample

Next, add the following code to the form's class template:

```
Private Sub ActIPConfig_Click( _
      ByVal sender As System.Object, _
      ByVal e As System.EventArgs) _
      Handles ActIPConfig.Click
   ' ----- Load the output of ipconfig.exe into a ListBox.
   Dim ipConfig As Process
   Dim oneLine As String
   Dim lineParts() As String

   ' ----- Remove any existing items.
   OutputData.Items.Clear()

   ' ----- Build and run the command.
   ipConfig = New Process()
   ipConfig.StartInfo.FileName = "ipconfig.exe"
   If (IncludeAll.Checked = True) Then _
      ipConfig.StartInfo.Arguments = "/all"
```

```
ipConfig.StartInfo.UseShellExecute = False
ipConfig.StartInfo.RedirectStandardOutput = True
ipConfig.StartInfo.CreateNoWindow = True
ipConfig.Start( )

' ----- Process each input line.
Do While Not ipConfig.StandardOutput.EndOfStream
    ' ----- Ignore blank lines.
    oneLine = ipConfig.StandardOutput.ReadLine( )
    If (Trim(oneLine) = "") Then Continue Do

    ' ----- Headings have no initial whitespace.
    If (oneLine = oneLine.TrimStart) Or _
        (InStr(oneLine, ":") = 0) Then
        ' ----- A heading line or informational line.
        OutputData.Items.Add(oneLine.Trim)
    Else
        ' ----- A detail line. The format is:
        '          Title . . . : Data
        lineParts = oneLine.Trim.Split(":"c)
        lineParts(0) = Replace(lineParts(0), ". ", "")
        lineParts(1) = lineParts(1).Trim
        OutputData.Items.Add(vbTab & lineParts(0) & _
            ":" & lineParts(1))
    End If
Loop
ipConfig.WaitForExit( )
ipConfig.Dispose( )
End Sub
```

Run the program, alter the IncludeAll field as desired, and click the ActProcess button. The ListBox control will be filled with the data output by the command-line *ipconfig.exe* program. Figure 14-30 shows some sample output for this program.

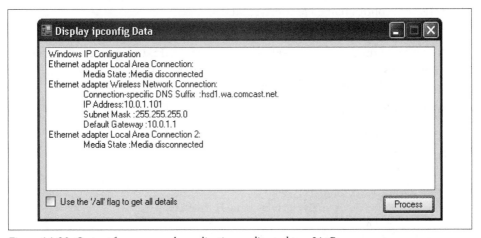

Figure 14-30. Output from a console application, redirected to a ListBox

Some command-line programs, such as *dir.exe*, aren't really programs at all, but rather commands embedded within the command processor. For these programs, you need to use *cmd.exe* for the process *filename* and pass the actual command as an argument of the /c option:

```
ipConfig.StartInfo.FileName = "cmd.exe"
ipConfig.StartInfo.Arguments = "/c dir c:\temp"
```

Unfortunately, you cannot prevent the command window from momentarily appearing when using *cmd.exe* as the process program.

14.32 Reading an Assembly's Details

Problem

You're curious about the contents of an assembly, and it's not because you want to find out its secrets.

Solution

Sample code folder: Chapter 14\AssemblyManifest

Use the classes of the System.Reflection namespace to access the contents of any assembly.

Discussion

This recipe's sample code displays some basic information contained within an assembly. Create a new Windows Forms application, and add the following controls to Form1:

- A TextBox control named AssemblyLocation.
- A Button control named ReadAssembly. Set its Text property to Show.
- A TextBox control named AssemblyDetail. Set its Multiline property to True and its ScrollBars property to Both. Also set its WordWrap property to False. Size this control to fill much of the form, as it will display a lot of content.

The form should look like the one in Figure 14-31.

Now, add the following code to the form's code template:

```
Private Sub ReadAssembly_Click( _
      ByVal sender As System.Object, _
      ByVal e As System.EventArgs) _
      Handles ReadAssembly.Click
   ' ----- Given an assembly, display details from its
   '       manifest.
   Dim useAssembly As System.Reflection.Assembly
   Dim displayContent As New System.Text.StringBuilder
```

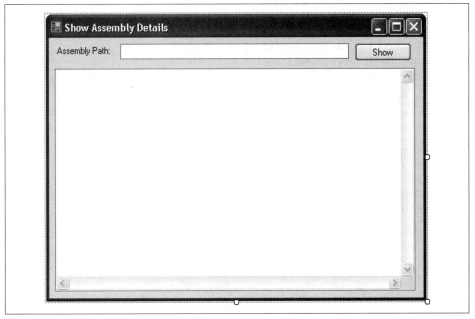

Figure 14-31. The controls on the show assembly details sample

```
' ----- Load this assembly.
If (My.Computer.FileSystem.FileExists( _
      AssemblyLocation.Text) = False) Then
   MsgBox("Please supply a valid assembly file name " & _
      "with a valid path.")
   Return
End If
Try
   useAssembly = Reflection.Assembly.LoadFile( _
      AssemblyLocation.Text)
Catch ex As System.Exception
   MsgBox("Could not access the assembly: " & ex.Message)
   Return
End Try

' ----- Clear the existing content.
AssemblyDetail.Clear( )

' ----- Show its full complex name.
displayContent.AppendLine("Full Name: " & _
   useAssembly.FullName)

' ----- List all of the resources.
displayContent.AppendLine( )
displayContent.AppendLine("Resources")
For Each oneName As String In _
      useAssembly.GetManifestResourceNames( )
```

```
    displayContent.AppendLine("    - " & oneName)
Next oneName

' ----- List all of the exported types.
displayContent.AppendLine()
displayContent.AppendLine("Exported Types")
For Each oneType As System.Type In _
        useAssembly.GetExportedTypes()
    displayContent.AppendLine("    - " & oneType.Name)
Next oneType

' ----- Process each module, and each type within
'       the module.
displayContent.AppendLine()
displayContent.AppendLine("Modules")
For Each oneModule As Reflection.Module In _
        useAssembly.GetLoadedModules()
    displayContent.AppendLine("    - " & oneModule.Name)
    For Each oneType As System.Type In oneModule.GetTypes()
        ' ----- These types will be the primary
        '       classes/forms in the assembly.
        displayContent.AppendLine("      Type: " & _
            oneType.Name)

        ' ----- Show the fields included in each type.
        For Each oneField As Reflection.FieldInfo In _
                oneType.GetFields()
            displayContent.AppendLine("          Field: " & _
                oneField.ToString())
        Next oneField

        ' ----- Show the methods included in each type.
        For Each oneMethod As Reflection.MethodInfo In _
                oneType.GetMethods()
            displayContent.AppendLine("          Method: " & _
                oneMethod.ToString())
        Next oneMethod
    Next oneType
Next oneModule

' ----- Display the results.
AssemblyDetail.Text = displayContent.ToString()
End Sub
```

To use the program, type a valid assembly file path into the `AssemblyLocation` field, and then click the Show button. The `AssemblyDetail` text box will be filled with details from the specified assembly. For Windows Forms assemblies, you will be amazed at the amount of content contained in even the simplest program. Figure 14-32 shows this program used on itself.

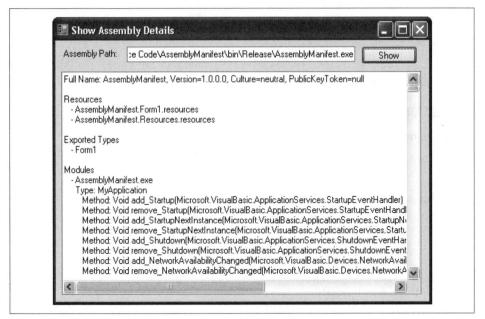

Figure 14-32. The assembly details for an application assembly

The .NET Framework includes a system called *reflection* that lets you examine every aspect of an assembly, if you have the proper security rights. You can view the basic assembly details, such as the version number and copyright name. You can also examine all classes, class methods, method parameters, and even the Intermediate Language (IL) code within a method. It's all available through the System.Reflection namespace.

The code shown here uses only a small portion of the available reflection features. The Reflection.Module class, for example, has many properties and methods that fully describe a module, which is typically an EXE or DLL file.

 This sample code does not take into account nested types. Any class can include subordinate class definitions. To access these from a System.Type instance, use that instance's GetNestedTypes( ) method.

14.33 Performing Serial I/O

Problem

You need to communicate with a device connected to one of the serial ports on the user's workstation.

Solution

Sample code folder: Chapter 14\SerialIO

Use the My.Computer.Ports.OpenSerialPort() method to create a bidirectional System.IO.Ports.SerialPort instance.

Discussion

The following method generically sends data out to the COM1 serial port:

```
Public Sub OutToCOM1(ByVal serialData As String, _
    ByVal useLineTermination As Boolean)
  ' ----- Open COM1 and send the supplied data.
  Dim com1Port As IO.Ports.SerialPort = Nothing

  Try
    ' ----- Access the port.
    com1Port = My.Computer.Ports.OpenSerialPort("COM1")

    ' ----- Write the data.
    If (useLineTermination = True) Then
      com1Port.WriteLine(serialData)
    Else
      com1Port.Write(serialData)
    End If

    ' ----- Finished with the port.
    com1Port.Close()
  Catch ex As Exception
    MsgBox("Error writing data to serial port: " & _
      ex.Message)
  Finally
    If (com1Port IsNot Nothing) Then com1Port.Dispose()
    com1Port = Nothing
  End Try
End Sub
```

The opened serial port is bidirectional, so you can also read pending content:

- For a single byte, use com1Port.ReadByte().
- For multiple bytes, use com1Port.Read().
- For a single character as an Integer, use com1Port.ReadChar().
- For a complete text line, use com1Port.ReadLine().
- For all pending characters, use com1Port.Existing().

When opening the serial port, different constructors allow you to specify the various handshaking options, including baud rate and stop bits. To access the list of available serial ports, use the My.Computer.Ports.SerialPortNames collection.

14.34 Rebooting the System

Problem

You want to programmatically restart the user's workstation.

Solution

Sample code folder: Chapter 14\ShutdownWindows

With all of the convenience features included in .NET, you would think that there would be a ShutdownWindows() method in some convenient class. But alas, there is nothing like that. To shut down Windows, you must depend on some of the Win32 DLL features. This recipe's sample code lets you exit Windows in one of four ways:

- By locking the workstation (although this is not really exiting Windows)
- By logging the current user out of Windows
- By rebooting the system
- By shutting down the system

Discussion

Create a new Windows Forms application. Add four Button controls to Form1, named ActLockWorkstation, ActLogoff, ActReboot, and ActShutdown. Change their Text properties to Lock Workstation, Log off, Reboot, and Shut down, respectively. Then add the following code to the form's code template:

```
Private Sub ActLockWorkstation_Click( _
      ByVal sender As System.Object, _
      ByVal e As System.EventArgs) _
      Handles ActLockWorkstation.Click
   GetOutOfWindows.ExitViaLockWorkstation()
End Sub

Private Sub ActLogoff_Click(ByVal sender As System.Object, _
      ByVal e As System.EventArgs) Handles ActLogoff.Click
   GetOutOfWindows.ExitViaLogoff()
End Sub

Private Sub ActReboot_Click(ByVal sender As System.Object, _
      ByVal e As System.EventArgs) Handles ActReboot.Click
   GetOutOfWindows.ExitViaReboot()
End Sub

Private Sub ActShutdown_Click(ByVal sender As System.Object, _
      ByVal e As System.EventArgs) Handles ActShutdown.Click
   GetOutOfWindows.ExitViaShutdown()
End Sub
```

Add a new class to your project using the Project → Add Class menu command, giving its file the name *GetOutOfWindows.vb*. Use this code for the class body:

```
Public Class GetOutOfWindows
    ' ----- Windows constants used in shutdown permissions.
    Const SE_PRIVILEGE_ENABLED As Integer = &H2
    Const TOKEN_QUERY As Integer = &H8
    Const TOKEN_ADJUST_PRIVILEGES As Integer = &H20
    Const SE_SHUTDOWN_NAME As String = "SeShutdownPrivilege"

    ' ----- Shutdown method flags.
    Private Enum ShutdownMethods As Integer
        Logoff = 0
        Shutdown = 1
        Reboot = 6
    End Enum

    <Runtime.InteropServices.StructLayout( _
    Runtime.InteropServices.LayoutKind.Sequential, Pack:=1)> _
    Private Structure TokenPrivileges
        Public PrivilegeCount As Integer
        Public Luid As Long
        Public Attributes As Integer
    End Structure

    ' ----- External features needed to exit Windows.
    Private Declare Ansi Function AdjustTokenPrivileges _
        Lib "advapi32.dll" _
        (ByVal tokenHandle As IntPtr, _
        ByVal disableAllPrivileges As Boolean, _
        ByRef newState As TokenPrivileges, _
        ByVal bufferLength As Integer, _
        ByVal previousState As IntPtr, _
        ByVal returnLength As IntPtr) As Boolean

    Private Declare Ansi Function ExitWindowsEx _
        Lib "user32.dll" _
        (ByVal flags As Integer, _
        ByVal reason As Integer) As Boolean

    Private Declare Ansi Function GetCurrentProcess _
        Lib "kernel32.dll" ( ) As IntPtr

    Private Declare Ansi Sub LockWorkStation _
        Lib "user32.dll" ( )

    Private Declare Ansi Function LookupPrivilegeValueA _
        Lib "advapi32.dll" _
        (ByVal systemName As String, _
        ByVal privilegeName As String, _
        ByRef lookupID As Long) As Boolean

    Private Declare Ansi Function OpenProcessToken _
        Lib "advapi32.dll" _
```

```
        (ByVal processHandle As IntPtr, _
        ByVal desiredAccess As Integer, _
        ByRef tokenHandle As IntPtr) As Boolean

    Private Shared Sub PerformExit( _
            ByVal usingMethod As Integer)
        ' ----- Log off, reboot, or shut down the system.
        Dim shutdownPrivileges As TokenPrivileges
        Dim processHandle As IntPtr
        Dim tokenHandle As IntPtr = IntPtr.Zero

        ' ----- Give ourselves the privilege of shutting
        '        down the system. First, obtain the token.
        processHandle = GetCurrentProcess()
        OpenProcessToken(processHandle, _
            TOKEN_ADJUST_PRIVILEGES Or TOKEN_QUERY, tokenHandle)

        ' ----- Adjust the token to enable shutdown permissions.
        shutdownPrivileges.PrivilegeCount = 1
        shutdownPrivileges.Luid = 0
        shutdownPrivileges.Attributes = SE_PRIVILEGE_ENABLED
        LookupPrivilegeValueA(Nothing, SE_SHUTDOWN_NAME, _
            shutdownPrivileges.Luid)
        AdjustTokenPrivileges(tokenHandle, False, _
            shutdownPrivileges, 0, IntPtr.Zero, IntPtr.Zero)

        ' ----- Now shut down the system.
        ExitWindowsEx(usingMethod, 0)
    End Sub

    Public Shared Sub ExitViaLockWorkstation()
        ' ----- Lock the workstation.
        LockWorkStation()
    End Sub

    Public Shared Sub ExitViaLogoff()
        ' ----- Log off the current user.
        PerformExit(ShutdownMethods.Logoff)
    End Sub

    Public Shared Sub ExitViaReboot()
        ' ----- Reboot the system.
        PerformExit(ShutdownMethods.Reboot)
    End Sub

    Public Shared Sub ExitViaShutdown()
        ' ----- Shut down the system.
        PerformExit(ShutdownMethods.Shutdown)
    End Sub
End Class
```

Run the program, and click one of the buttons on the form to take the related shut-down action. But be warned: this program will shut down Windows if you choose anything other than "Lock Workstation." Make sure you save your work before running this program.

Most of this code gets into the heart of the Windows system, and how it really works is beyond the scope of this book (and beyond general human comprehension). But here's the gist of it: before you can shut down Windows, you have to give yourself permission to do so. It must be a safety feature, because if you can give yourself permission, it's really not a matter of security.

Still, if your application runs in a security-limited context imposed by the user or the system administrator, the attempt to shut down the system may fail.

Exceptions

15.0 Introduction

Visual Basic has included error handling since its initial release through the On Error statement. Although often derided by developers, this mechanism did effectively catch and process all errors when used properly. Visual Basic 2005 still includes this error-handling methodology, but it also includes *structured error handling*, new with .NET. This chapter considers this new error-processing system, comprised of the Try...Catch...Finally statement and System.Exception-derived error objects.

15.1 Catching an Exception

Problem

Although you've been a Visual Basic 6.0 developer for years, and you've already used On Error statements in your Visual Basic 2005 code, you want to try out the structured error-handling statements you've heard so much about.

Solution

Use the Try...Catch...Finally block statement to locally monitor and handle errors. The statement has three sections:

Try
> The code you need to monitor for errors appears in this first section.

Catch
> When an error occurs, processing jumps immediately from the Try section to a matching Catch block (We'll define "matching" shortly). Any remaining unprocessed statements in the Try block are ignored. You can have any number of Catch entries in your error-handling block.

Finally

Any code you include in this optional section runs whether an exception occurs
or not. It's a useful place to put any cleanup code related to resources you allocated in the Try section.

Here's the syntax of the Try...Catch...Finally statement:

```
Try
   ' ----- Error-prone code here.
Catch ex As System.Exception
   ' ----- Error-processing code here. Multiple
   '       Catch blocks can be included.
Finally
   ' ----- Cleanup code here (optional).
End Try
```

Discussion

Although Visual Basic 2005 still supports the On Error statement and related error-handling logic found way back in Visual Basic 1.0, it also includes a new "structured"
error-handling system that more closely parallels the object-oriented nature of .NET. In
this system, exceptions (errors) exist as objects, inherited from the System.Exception
class. When an error occurs in your code, .NET wraps it up in a System.Exception
object (or one of its more specific derived classes) and triggers it in your code. The
Try...Catch statement watches for any such exceptions and jumps to a Catch block
when an exception occurs.

System.Exception represents the most general type of exception; because all exception objects derive from it, it catches all error types. In this statement:

```
Try
   ' ----- Error-prone code here.
Catch ex As System.Exception
   ' ----- Error-processing code here.
End Try
```

any type of error that occurs in the Try block, no matter what it is, falls into the Catch
block, since that block catches every type of error.

.NET also defines more specific exceptions. For example, the System.
OutOfMemoryException error occurs when any operation lacks sufficient memory to
execute properly:

```
Try
   ' ----- Error-prone code here.
Catch ex As System.OutOfMemoryException
   ' ----- Handle memory errors here.
Catch ex As System.Exception
   ' ----- Handle all other errors here.
End Try
```

Each Catch block handles only the error types specified in its As clause. In the above block of code, the first Catch block handles OutOfMemoryException errors. Any other error that occurs in the Try block skips over that first Catch entry and jumps into the second, more general Catch block. This is what is meant by a "matching" Catch block, as mentioned earlier in this recipe. Exceptions seek the first matching Catch clause, based on an exact class match or a derived match relationship.

When an error occurs, the generated exception is compared to each Catch block's As clause for a match, in order from top to bottom. Therefore, you should place the most restrictive error type first, saving System.Exception for the last Catch block. If no error occurs, all Catch blocks are ignored.

Within a Catch block, the ex variable (included just after the Catch keyword) provides access to the actual exception object. Use its members as you would the members of any other object. A description of the exception appears as ex.Message. You can name the variable anything you want; the name ex has become common in technical documentation, but you are free to change it or even vary it between the different Catch clauses.

If included, the Finally block is always processed, no matter what. It is processed after the relevant Try and Catch blocks complete. Even if you issue an Exit Sub or similar statement from within a Try or Catch block, the Finally section is still processed. All Try statements must include at least one Catch or Finally block.

There are some restrictions on Try...Catch statements. In general, you cannot use GoTo statements to jump into or out of any of the blocks. There is an Exit Try statement that lets you jump out early, but it can't be used in the Finally block.

If an error occurs in a routine but no error handling is in effect (i.e., the code is outside of a Try statement, and no On Error statements appear in the procedure), the error "bubbles up" to the calling procedure, looking for another active error handler to deal with the exception. If no error handlers are available to deal with the error, a message is displayed to the user, and the application exits.

See Also

Recipe 15.3 discusses a global exception handler that catches any exceptions not dealt with in local procedures.

15.2 Throwing an Exception

Problem

An invalid condition has occurred in your custom class code, and you want to generate an exception to inform the calling code of the problem.

Solution

Use the Throw statement to send an exception to the next available error handler. Throw takes an instance of a System.Exception (or derived) object as its only argument:

```
Throw New System.Exception("A great big error occurred.")
```

You can also prepare your exception object in advance and then use its variable in the Throw statement:

```
Dim errorDetail As New System.ArgumentOutOfRangeException( _
    "Year", "The 'Year' must be at least 1995.")
Throw errorDetail
```

Discussion

When .NET detects an error in your program, it also uses the Throw statement to send errors to your code. When you use the Throw statement, your generated errors look just like those issued by the Framework.

You can generate an error at any time using the Throw statement, even within a Try block. The related Catch handler will process the error as if some other system-defined process had generated the error.

Visual Basic also includes an Err.Raise method that generates errors, as was done using pre-.NET versions of Visual Basic. It focuses on error numbers rather than on object-based exceptions. Although .NET will wrap errors issued through Err.Raise in an Exception object, you should use this method only for backward compatibility. Use the Throw statement instead.

15.3   Catching Unhandled Exceptions

Problem

Although you make judicious use of Try...Catch and On Error statements in your code, it's possible that some exceptions will sneak through your structured and unstructured error-handling barriers. You want to keep these errors from crashing the program.

Solution

Sample code folder: Chapter 15\UnhandledException

Handle the application-level UnhandledException event to capture any errors not dealt with elsewhere in your code. This global error handler is part of the Windows Forms Application Framework. In the Project Properties window's Application panel, make sure that "Enable application framework" is selected, and then click on the View

Application Events button on that same panel. Visual Studio opens the *ApplicationEvents.vb* source file, which looks like this:

```
Namespace My
    Partial Friend Class MyApplication

    End Class
End Namespace
```

The global error handler will appear in this `MyApplication` class. Select "(MyApplication Events)" from the Class Name list above and to the left of the code editor window, and then select "UnhandledException" from the Method Name list just to the right of that. Visual Studio will add a template for the `UnhandledException` event handler:

```
Private Sub MyApplication_UnhandledException( _
        ByVal sender As Object, ByVal e As Microsoft. _
        VisualBasic.ApplicationServices. _
        UnhandledExceptionEventArgs) _
        Handles Me.UnhandledException
End Sub
```

Code added to this event handler will run whenever an unhandled error or exception occurs somewhere in your application. Once you have dealt with the error, you can either exit the application immediately (in a more controlled manner than just letting the program crash) or return to a basic waiting-for-input-from-the-user state. Use the e argument's `ExitApplication` property to indicate which choice you want to make. Setting this property to `True`, as shown here, will terminate the program:

```
Private Sub MyApplication_UnhandledException( _
        ByVal sender As Object, ByVal e As Microsoft. _
        VisualBasic.ApplicationServices. _
        UnhandledExceptionEventArgs) _
        Handles Me.UnhandledException
    MsgBox("An unhandled error occurred. That's bad.")
    e.ExitApplication = True
End Sub
```

This code is never called when your application runs in the debugger.

Discussion

The solution listed above is valid only for Windows Forms applications that use the Application Framework. If you choose to disable the Application Framework, or you are writing a non–Windows Forms application, you must manually establish a global error handler for each thread of your application. We'll look at the first case here.

Create a new Windows Forms application, and clear the "Enable application framework" field in the Project Properties window. Open up the source code window for the `Form1` form, and replace the basically empty content with the following code:

```
Public Class Form1
    Private Sub Form1_Click(ByVal sender As Object, _
```

```
            ByVal e As System.EventArgs) Handles Me.Click
        ' ----- Cause a fake unhandled error.
        Throw New System.Exception( )
    End Sub

    Private Sub Form1_FormClosed(ByVal sender As Object, _
            ByVal e As System.Windows.Forms.FormClosedEventArgs) _
            Handles Me.FormClosed
        ' ----- Disable the monitor before exiting.
        RemoveGlobalErrorMonitor( )
    End Sub

    Private Sub Form1_Load(ByVal sender As System.Object, _
            ByVal e As System.EventArgs) Handles MyBase.Load
        ' ----- Enable error monitoring.
        AddGlobalErrorMonitor( )
    End Sub
End Class

Module Module1
    Public Sub AddGlobalErrorMonitor( )
        ' ----- Enable global error monitoring on this thread.
        AddHandler Application.ThreadException, _
            AddressOf GlobalErrorMonitor
    End Sub

    Public Sub RemoveGlobalErrorMonitor( )
        ' ----- Disable global error monitoring on this thread.
        RemoveHandler Application.ThreadException, _
            AddressOf GlobalErrorMonitor
    End Sub

    Public Sub GlobalErrorMonitor(ByVal sender As Object, _
            ByVal e As System.Threading.ThreadExceptionEventArgs)
        ' ----- An unhandled global error occurred in the thread.
        MsgBox("A global error was caught.")
    End Sub
End Module
```

This code uses the AddHandler statement to connect the thread's Application.
ThreadException event to a custom event handler, GlobalErrorMonitor( ). It's added
immediately when the (main) form is first loaded, and it remains until the form
closes. Remember that this code will not work properly within Visual Studio. You
must build the application and run it directly before your global exception handler
can be used.

When writing console applications, monitor the System.AppDomain.CurrentDomain.
UnhandledException event instead of Application.ThreadException:

```
AddHandler System.AppDomain.CurrentDomain. _
    UnhandledException, AddressOf GlobalErrorMonitor
```

15.4   Displaying Exception Information

Problem

An error has occurred, and you want to inform the user in a friendly manner.

Solution

The captured exception object includes all the details concerning the error, with some parts ready for user-friendly presentation. The simplest presentation option uses the exception's ToString( ) method to generate information about the error.

The following code generates the error message in Figure 15-1 when run within Visual Studio:

```
Try
    Throw New System.Exception( )
Catch ex As System.Exception
    MsgBox(ex.ToString( ))
End Try
```

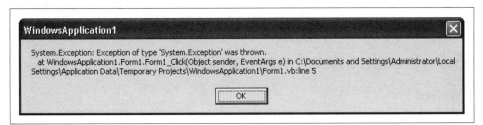

Figure 15-1. A basic error message

Discussion

If you encounter an exception in a block of code where you know errors are likely, you can sometimes compensate for the error through alternate logic without ever informing the user of the problem. In those cases where you cannot continue normally because of the error, your program can inform the user of the situation.

Beyond the basic ToString( ) output, you can handcraft the details of the exception into a form that better communicates the problem to the user. The System.Exception object includes the following useful properties:

Data

> Some errors use the collection exposed by this property to store additional details related to the error. The type of data stored depends on the code that generated the error. It is most often used in custom exceptions.

InnerException

> If this exception is a byproduct of another, earlier exception, this property exposes that previous exception.

Message

This property provides a short yet friendly description of the exception.

Source

This property specifies the name of the application, class, or process ID that generated the error.

StackTrace

This text property provides a semihuman-readable listing of the *stack trace*—the set of called methods that led up to the method generating the error. This stack trace may include internal procedures from the .NET Framework, and its overall length may shock the user.

TargetSite

This property exposes a MethodBase object that fully describes the procedure in which the exception occurred. The properties of this object may or may not be useful in every case, especially when an application has been obfuscated.

Other exception objects further derived from System.Exception may include additional properties with more detailed information. By concatenating the various properties of the captured exception object, you should be able to effectively communicate the problem to the user or store the details in an error log for later analysis.

15.5   Creating New Exception Types

Problem

None of the exception objects supplied with .NET really meets the needs of the error you need to generate.

Solution

Build your own exception object by deriving a new class from System.Exception or another class already derived from it.

Discussion

The following class extends the standard Exception object by adding a place for a SQL statement used in a database query:

```
Public Class ExceptionWithSQL
    Inherits System.Exception

    Public SQLStatement As String

    Public Sub New(ByVal message As String, _
        ByVal sqlText As String, _
        ByVal innerException As System.Exception)
```

```
        ' ----- Store the details of this exception.
        MyBase.New(message, innerException)
        SQLStatement = sqlText
    End Sub
End Class
```

Many business applications that interact with a database use a central procedure to process SQL statements in a consistent manner. While this procedure may have its own error handler, the calling code also wants to know when an error occurred with the SQL statement that it provided. The following ProcessSQL method represents just such a common procedure. If an error occurs in the supplied SQL statement, it uses the ExceptionWithSQL class to communicate the problem:

```
Public Sub ProcessSQL(ByVal sqlText As String)
    Try
        ' ----- Add ADO.NET-specific code here.
    Catch ex As System.Exception
        ' ----- Convert this to a SQL error.
        Throw New WindowsApplication1.ExceptionWithSQL( _
            "A SQL error occurred.", sqlText, ex)
        ' ----- The calling procedure will receive the
        '       modified error.
    End Try
End Sub
```

Since the calling code may issue several different SQL statements within a common Try block, having the errant SQL statement in the exception object provides the additional information a programmer may need to locate the problem:

```
Dim sqlText As String
Try
    sqlText = "DELETE FROM Table1 WHERE RecordType = 5"
    ProcessSQL(sqlText)
    sqlText = "DELETE FROM Table2 WHERE RecordType = 5"
    ProcessSQL(sqlText)
Catch ex As WindowsApplication1.ExceptionWithSQL
    MsgBox("The following SQL statement caused an error:" & _
        vbCrLf & ex.SQLStatement)
End Try
```

You can also create a new ExceptionWithSQL object for any reason on your own and Throw it, even if no underlying database error occurred. With custom errors, the choice of when to use them is yours.

Before .NET, errors in Visual Basic were identified solely by a number, many defined for common use by Microsoft Windows. For instance, error number 7 represents the "Out-of-memory" error condition.

In .NET, all errors are defined by specific classes derived from System.Exception. For example, out-of-memory errors are thrown as instances of System.OutOfMemoryException. You can derive your own exceptions for use in your application code. You will often derive such custom errors directly from System.Exception, but if another derived exception class contains features you don't want to rewrite from scratch, you can derive from that class instead.

The various .NET exceptions derived from System.Exception can also be used directly. For instance, you can throw a System.DivideByZeroException even if you don't actually perform an invalid division, but your code has a zero-value denominator ready to use:

```
Public Function CheckAndDivide(ByVal numerator As Decimal, _
      ByVal denominator As Decimal) As Decimal
   ' ----- Divide numbers, but check for divide-by-zero first.
   If (denominator = 0@) Then
      Throw New System.DivideByZeroException()
   Else
      Return numerator / denominator
   End If
End Function
```

15.6   Ignoring Exceptions in a Block of Code

Problem

You have a block of code that might generate errors, but you don't really care. You want the code to continue on with or without errors and to provide no error report to the user.

Solution

To ignore errors, use the On Error Resume Next statement, or use a Try statement with an empty Catch block.

Discussion

In Visual Basic, the traditional way to ignore errors in a section of code is to use the On Error Resume Next statement. The following code shows both ignored and processed error-handler sections:

```
Public Sub DoSomething()
   On Error Resume Next
   ' ----- Error handling is now disabled. You can do
   '       dangerous things and no errors will occur. The
   '       "Err" object will still be filled in with
   '       error content when an error does occur, so you
   '       can check that if you are concerned.

   On Error GoTo ErrorHandler
   ' ----- Error handling has been turned back on. All
   '       errors will jump down to the labeled section.
   Exit Sub

ErrorHandler:
   ' ----- Do something with the error here, then...
   Resume Next
End Sub
```

If you want to ignore errors but prefer using the structured exception-handling features, add a Try block with an empty Catch block:

```
Public Sub DoSomething()
    Try
        ' ----- As expected, any error that occurs here will
        '          jump to the Catch block.
    Catch
        ' ----- If you don't include any error-handling code
        '          here, the error is just ignored.
    End Try

    ' ----- Errors that occur out here will not be caught by
    '          the Try block, but you knew that already.
End Sub
```

There is a small difference between these two blocks of code. When using the On Error Resume Next statement, any error on a statement causes the code to continue with the next statement. In the Try...Catch example, any error that occurs in the Try block causes the code to continue with the Catch block, and then with the code that follows the entire Try...End Try section. This means that if you have multiple statements in the Try block and an error occurs on the first of those statements, the remaining statements in the Try block are skipped completely.

CHAPTER 16

Cryptography and Compression

16.0   Introduction

In today's world, security is an increasingly important part of development requirements. Visual Basic 2005 and the .NET Framework provide advanced and well-established encryption libraries. This chapter provides recipes for some of the basic tasks you may need to become more familiar with, such as encrypting data files, handling passwords securely, and so on. Closely related to encryption is the science of compression, so some of these recipes also cover this subject.

16.1   Generating a Hash

Problem

You want to hash a string to create a unique, repeatable identifier. This can be used to determine if a string has been altered in any way, to identify a password without revealing the actual password, and to convert a string of any length to a unique fixed-length key for cryptographic algorithms.

Solution

Sample code folder: Chapter 16\Cryptography

Use the .NET Framework's cryptographic services to generate an industry-standard hash of your data.

Discussion

A hash is like a one-way encryption. There's no way to recover an original string given its hash value. In fact, it's technically possible for more than one string to return the exact same hash value, although the odds are against this ever happening in the time allotted for the unfolding of the universe. The MD5 hash used in this recipe returns a 16-byte value, and a quick calculation shows there are over 3×10^{38}

unique combinations of 16 bytes. If you were to check through all the possible hash patterns at the rate of a million combinations each second, you'd still be quite busy after a few trillion centuries.

The advantage of the MD5 hash is that changing the given string in the minutest way results in a completely different and unique hash value. If you hash a string and get the hash value expected for that string, you can feel very confident that the string has not been altered in any way. A password, for example, can be checked against the original password by comparing the hashes for the original password and the new one. If the hashes match, the passwords match, and you don't even have to know what the passwords are.

The following function isolates the code to generate a hash for a string. This function is part of a module named Crypto that's presented in its entirety in Recipe 16.9:

```vb
Public Function GetHash(ByVal plainText As String) As String
    ' ----- Generate a hash. Return an empty string
    '       if there are any problems.
    Dim plainBytes As Byte()
    Dim hashEngine As MD5CryptoServiceProvider
    Dim hashBytes As Byte()
    Dim hashText As String

    Try
        ' ----- Convert the plain text to a byte array.
        plainBytes = Encoding.UTF8.GetBytes(plainText)

        ' ----- Select one of the hash engines.
        hashEngine = New MD5CryptoServiceProvider

        ' ----- Get the hash of the plain text bytes.
        hashBytes = hashEngine.ComputeHash(plainBytes)

        ' ----- Convert the hash bytes to a hexadecimal string.
        hashText = Replace(BitConverter.ToString(hashBytes), "-", "")
        Return hashText
    Catch
        Return ""
    End Try
End Function
```

There are several cryptography service providers in the .NET Framework, including SHA1, Triple DES, Rijndael, and others. The MD5 hashing algorithm is a good standard one to use, but you can change the above code to use a different algorithm if desired.

For convenience, this function returns the 16-byte hash converted to a 32-byte hexadecimal character string. This simplifies tasks such as storing the hash in the registry instead of a password, and it provides a useful way to convert any key string to a 32-byte key for the Rijndael cipher, a technique used in other recipes in this chapter.

The following code demonstrates the GetHash( ) function by hashing a string and displaying the result, shown in Figure 16-1:

```
Dim result As New System.Text.StringBuilder
Dim workText As String = _
    "The important thing is not to stop questioning. " & _
    "--Albert Einstein"
Dim hash As String = GetHash(workText)
result.Append("Plain text: ")
result.AppendLine(workText)
result.Append("Hash value: ")
result.Append(hash)
MsgBox(result.ToString( ))
```

Figure 16-1. Generating an MD5 hash of a string

See Also

Recipe 16.9 includes the full source code for the Crypto module.

16.2   Encrypting and Decrypting a String

Problem

You want to encrypt and later decrypt a string using a private key.

Solution

Sample code folder: Chapter 16\Cryptography

Use the StringEncrypt( ) and StringDecrypt( ) functions, presented in this recipe, which wrap calls to a cryptography services provider in the .NET Framework.

Discussion

The StringEncrypt( ) function processes a plain-text string using a key string and returns a Base64 (MIME) string. This string can be deciphered only by passing it back to the StringDecrypt( ) function, along with the same key string. The returned Base64 string is comprised of viewable and printable ASCII characters and is suitable for printing, emailing, and storing in standard text files. We'll look at the StringEncrypt( ) function first:

```vbnet
Public Function StringEncrypt(ByVal plainText As String, _
      ByVal keyText As String) As String
   ' ----- Encrypt some text. Return an empty string
   '       if there are any problems.
   Try
      ' ----- Remove any possible null characters.
      Dim workText As String = plainText.Replace(vbNullChar, "")

      ' ----- Convert plain text to byte array.
      Dim workBytes() As Byte = Encoding.UTF8.GetBytes(plainText)

      ' ----- Convert key string to 32-byte key array.
      Dim keyBytes() As Byte = _
         Encoding.UTF8.GetBytes(GetHash(keyText))

      ' ----- Create initialization vector.
      Dim IV() As Byte = { _
         50, 199, 10, 159, 132, 55, 236, 189, _
         51, 243, 244, 91, 17, 136, 39, 230}

      ' ----- Create the Rijndael engine.
      Dim rijndael As New RijndaelManaged

      ' ----- Bytes will flow through a memory stream.
      Dim memoryStream As New MemoryStream()

      ' ----- Create the cryptography transform.
      Dim cryptoTransform As ICryptoTransform
      cryptoTransform = _
         rijndael.CreateEncryptor(keyBytes, IV)

      ' ----- Bytes will be processed by CryptoStream.
      Dim cryptoStream As New CryptoStream( _
         memoryStream, cryptoTransform, _
         CryptoStreamMode.Write)

      ' ----- Move the bytes through the processing stream.
      cryptoStream.Write(workBytes, 0, workBytes.Length)
      cryptoStream.FlushFinalBlock()

      ' ----- Convert binary data to a viewable string.
      Dim encrypted As String = _
         Convert.ToBase64String(memoryStream.ToArray)

      ' ----- Close the streams.
      memoryStream.Close()
      cryptoStream.Close()

      ' ----- Return the encrypted string result.
      Return encrypted
   Catch
      Return ""
   End Try
End Function
```

The RijndaelManaged object was chosen for the encryption algorithm, but you may substitute any of the other encryption engines provided in the .NET Framework, such as Triple DES. The Rijndael algorithm was chosen because it is one of the latest and strongest algorithms around. Also known as the Advanced Encryption Algorithm (AES), it survived intense scrutiny by experts in the industry to become the algorithm the government selected to replace the older Data Encryption Standard (DES) algorithm. It's standard, and it's good.

The StringDecrypt() function is similar to StringEncrypt(), except that the encrypted Base64 string is passed to it along with the same key string as used before, and the original plain-text result is returned:

```
Public Function StringDecrypt(ByVal encrypted As String, _
    ByVal keyText As String) As String
  ' ----- Decrypt a previously encrypted string. The key
  '       must match the one used to encrypt the string.
  '       Return an empty string on error.
  Try
    ' ----- Convert encrypted string to a byte array.
    Dim workBytes() As Byte = _
      Convert.FromBase64String(encrypted)

    ' ----- Convert key string to 32-byte key array.
    Dim keyBytes() As Byte = _
      Encoding.UTF8.GetBytes(GetHash(keyText))

    ' ----- Create initialization vector.
    Dim IV() As Byte = { _
      50, 199, 10, 159, 132, 55, 236, 189, _
      51, 243, 244, 91, 17, 136, 39, 230}

    ' ----- Decrypted bytes will be stored in
    '       a temporary array.
    Dim tempBytes(workBytes.Length - 1) As Byte

    ' ----- Create the Rijndael engine.
    Dim rijndael As New RijndaelManaged

    ' ----- Bytes will flow through a memory stream.
    Dim memoryStream As New MemoryStream(workBytes)

    ' ----- Create the cryptography transform.
    Dim cryptoTransform As ICryptoTransform
    cryptoTransform = _
      rijndael.CreateDecryptor(keyBytes, IV)

    ' ----- Bytes will be processed by CryptoStream.
    Dim cryptoStream As New CryptoStream( _
      memoryStream, cryptoTransform, _
      CryptoStreamMode.Read)
```

```
'  ----- Move the bytes through the processing stream.
     cryptoStream.Read(tempBytes, 0, tempBytes.Length)

     '  ----- Close the streams.
     memoryStream.Close()
     cryptoStream.Close()

     '  ----- Convert the decrypted bytes to a string.
     Dim plainText As String = _
        Encoding.UTF8.GetString(tempBytes)

     '  ----- Return the decrypted string result.
     Return plainText.Replace(vbNullChar, "")
   Catch
     Return ""
   End Try
 End Function
```

Notice that the same initialization vector is used in both functions. This is the actual "secret key" you use to encrypt the content. You can use other sets of bytes to initialize the IV( ) array, but both the StringEncrypt( ) and StringDecrypt( ) functions should use exactly the same values.

The Rijndael encryption object expects an array of 32 bytes as the key. The GetHash( ) function presented in Recipe 16.1 makes it easy to convert any key string to a 32-byte key suitable for the encryption. The values of the key bytes in this case vary only over a range of 16 unique values each, but there still are more than 3×10^{38} possible key combinations. Generally, any unique key string always generates a unique 32-byte hash value as a key, and a brute-force attack based on checking all possible keys generated by GetHash( ) is, based on today's technology, out of the question.

The following code demonstrates calling the StringEncrypt( ) and StringDecrypt( ) functions:

```
Dim result As New System.Text.StringBuilder
Dim workText As String = _
   "The important thing is not to stop questioning. " & _
   "--Albert Einstein"
Dim keyString As String = "This string is the key"
Dim encrypted As String = StringEncrypt(workText, keyString)
Dim decrypted As String = StringDecrypt(encrypted, keyString)
result.Append("Plain Text:  ")
result.AppendLine(workText)
result.AppendLine()
result.Append("Encrypted:  ")
result.AppendLine(encrypted)
result.AppendLine()
result.Append("Decrypted:  ")
result.Append(decrypted)
MsgBox(result.ToString())
```

The original plain-text string is encrypted and then decrypted using the same key string. The results of each step are displayed in Figure 16-2.

Figure 16-2. Encrypting a string with the AES algorithm

See Also

Recipe 16.9 includes the full source code for the Crypto module.

16.3   Encrypting and Decrypting a File

Problem

You want an easy-to-use function that encrypts and decrypts any file.

Solution

Sample code folder: Chapter 16\Cryptography

Use the FileEncrypt( ) and FileDecrypt( ) functions presented in this recipe.

Discussion

You can theoretically load an entire file into a string and call the StringEncrypt( ) and StringDecrypt( ) functions presented in Recipe 16.2 to process all its contents in one shot, but there may be problems with this approach. For one thing, larger files require a lot of memory during processing. It's better to process chunks of files a piece at a time until the whole file is processed. In the FileEncrypt( ) and FileDecrypt( ) functions presented here, a buffer of 4,096 bytes processes the streams of data in smaller, manageable chunks. Here are the two functions showing how this buffer is used:

```
Public Sub FileEncrypt(ByVal sourceFile As String, _
    ByVal destinationFile As String, _
    ByVal keyText As String)
  ' ----- Create file streams.
  Dim sourceStream As New FileStream( _
    sourceFile, FileMode.Open, FileAccess.Read)
  Dim destinationStream As New FileStream( _
    destinationFile, FileMode.Create, FileAccess.Write)

  ' ----- Convert key string to 32-byte key array.
  Dim keyBytes() As Byte = _
    Encoding.UTF8.GetBytes(GetHash(keyText))
```

```vb
    ' ----- Create initialization vector.
    Dim IV() As Byte = { _
        50, 199, 10, 159, 132, 55, 236, 189, _
        51, 243, 244, 91, 17, 136, 39, 230}

    ' ----- Create a Rijndael engine.
    Dim rijndael As New RijndaelManaged

    ' ----- Create the cryptography transform.
    Dim cryptoTransform As ICryptoTransform
    cryptoTransform = _
        rijndael.CreateEncryptor(keyBytes, IV)

    ' ----- Bytes will be processed by CryptoStream.
    Dim cryptoStream As New CryptoStream( _
        destinationStream, cryptoTransform, _
        CryptoStreamMode.Write)

    ' ----- Process bytes from one file into the other.
    Const BlockSize As Integer = 4096
    Dim buffer(BlockSize) As Byte
    Dim bytesRead As Integer
    Do
        bytesRead = sourceStream.Read(buffer, 0, BlockSize)
        If (bytesRead = 0) Then Exit Do
        cryptoStream.Write(buffer, 0, bytesRead)
    Loop

' ----- Close the streams.
    cryptoStream.Close()
    sourceStream.Close()
    destinationStream.Close()
End Sub

Public Sub FileDecrypt(ByVal sourceFile As String, _
        ByVal destinationFile As String, _
        ByVal keyText As String)

    ' ----- Create file streams.
    Dim sourceStream As New FileStream( _
        sourceFile, FileMode.Open, FileAccess.Read)
    Dim destinationStream As New FileStream( _
        destinationFile, FileMode.Create, FileAccess.Write)

    ' ----- Convert key string to 32-byte key array.
    Dim keyBytes() As Byte = _
        Encoding.UTF8.GetBytes(GetHash(keyText))

    ' ----- Create initialization vector.
    Dim IV() As Byte = { _
        50, 199, 10, 159, 132, 55, 236, 189, _
        51, 243, 244, 91, 17, 136, 39, 230}

    ' ----- Create a Rijndael engine.
    Dim rijndael As New RijndaelManaged
```

```
' ----- Create the cryptography transform.
Dim cryptoTransform As ICryptoTransform
cryptoTransform = _
    rijndael.CreateDecryptor(keyBytes, IV)

' ----- Bytes will be processed by CryptoStream.
Dim cryptoStream As New CryptoStream( _
    destinationStream, cryptoTransform, _
    CryptoStreamMode.Write)

' ----- Process bytes from one file into the other.
Const BlockSize As Integer = 4096
Dim buffer(BlockSize) As Byte
Dim bytesRead As Integer
Do
    bytesRead = sourceStream.Read(buffer, 0, BlockSize)
    If (bytesRead = 0) Then Exit Do
    cryptoStream.Write(buffer, 0, bytesRead)
Loop

' ----- Close the streams.
cryptoStream.Close( )
sourceStream.Close( )
destinationStream.Close( )
End Sub
```

These two functions are similar to the StringEncrypt( ) and StringDecrypt( ) functions, except for a couple of important features. Instead of the memory stream being used to process the strings, the file contents are processed through file streams. The cryptoStream object is hooked into the file stream to process the bytes as they flow through the streams.

The other difference is the use of a byte-array buffer that holds 4,096 bytes. Chunks of 4,096 bytes are read from the input file, processed by the streams in the process, and then written to the output file. This allows processing of very large files a piece at a time.

The following code demonstrates these two functions by first creating a plain-text file, then encrypting it to a second file, and finally decrypting the result to a third file, always using the same key:

```
Dim result As New System.Text.StringBuilder
Dim file1Text As String = _
    "This is sample content for a text file" & vbNewLine & _
    "to be encrypted and decrypted. File1 and" & vbNewLine & _
    "File3 should show this plain text. File2" & vbNewLine & _
    "is encrypted and will be indecipherable."
Dim file2Text As String
Dim file3Text As String
Dim file1 As String = Application.StartupPath & "\File1.txt"
Dim file2 As String = Application.StartupPath & "\File2.ezz"
Dim file3 As String = Application.StartupPath & "\File3.txt"
```

```
' ----- Create the encrypted and decrypted files.
My.Computer.FileSystem.WriteAllText(file1, file1Text, False)
FileEncrypt(file1, file2, "key")
FileDecrypt(file2, file3, "key")

' ----- Display the results.
file2Text = My.Computer.FileSystem.ReadAllText(file2)
file3Text = My.Computer.FileSystem.ReadAllText(file3)
result.AppendLine("File1:")
result.AppendLine(file1Text)
result.AppendLine()
result.AppendLine("File3:")
result.AppendLine(file3Text)
result.AppendLine()
result.AppendLine("File2:")
result.Append(file2Text)
MsgBox(result.ToString())
```

The original file and the decrypted file are displayed first in the message box, as shown in Figure 16-3, and the encrypted file (File2) is displayed last. The encrypted file consists of binary data unsuitable for normal display, resulting in a truncated list of strange characters.

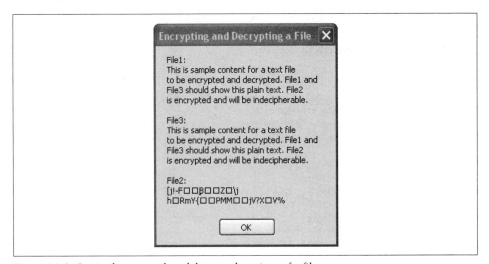

Figure 16-3. Original, encrypted, and decrypted versions of a file

See Also

Recipe 16.9 includes the full source code for the Crypto module.

16.4   Prompting for a Username and Password

Problem

You need to add a password dialog to an application to prevent unauthorized access to the rest of the program.

Solution

Sample code folder: Chapter 16\LoginTest

Use the standard LoginForm dialog provided by Visual Basic 2005.

Discussion

In Visual Studio 2005, you can add new items to your project, selecting from a variety of predefined forms and other objects. If you select the Project → Add Windows Form menu command, one of the form choices you can add is a LoginForm. This form is all set up with User Name and Password text boxes, along with two buttons and a nice graphic. You can modify this dialog to suit your own requirements, perhaps replacing the graphic image with something more appropriate for your business.

The Password text box displays only asterisks as the user enters his password. All TextBox controls have a PasswordChar property, which is normally left blank. Enter an asterisk (or any other character) in this property, and the TextBox displays only the given character. The TextBox.Text property still returns whatever text the user has entered; it's just displayed as all asterisks to mask it from prying eyes.

The following code block shows how hashed values of the User Name and Password text entries can be compared against known hashed values. This code requires the GetHash( ) function defined in Recipe 16.1:

```
Dim result As String

' ----- Store only the hashed values, not the plain text.
Dim hashUserName As String = GetHash("AlbertE")
Dim hashPassword As String = GetHash("E=MC2")

LoginForm1.ShowDialog( )

' ----- Hash the input values.
Dim hashUserInput As String = _
   GetHash(LoginForm1.UsernameTextBox.Text)
Dim hashPassInput As String = _
   GetHash(LoginForm1.PasswordTextBox.Text)

' ----- Test the inputs.
If (hashUserName = hashUserInput) AndAlso _
      (hashPassword = hashPassInput) Then
   result = "Yes, you passed the password test!"
Else
   result = "I'm sorry, please try again."
End If
MsgBox(result)
```

Normally, it's best not to put the user's name and password directly in the code, as shown here, but for demonstration purposes, it works well. In the next recipe we'll store the hashed password in the registry, where the actual password can't be discovered.

Figure 16-4 shows the LoginForm in action, after the user has entered a username and password, but just before the OK button is clicked or the Enter key pressed.

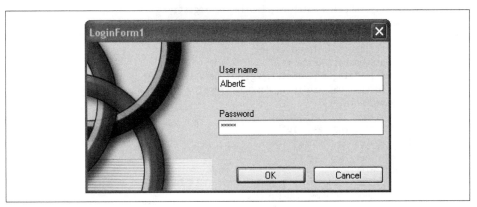

Figure 16-4. Visual Basic 2005's customizable standard LoginForm

16.5   Handling Passwords Securely

Problem

You want to test an entered password against a value stored somewhere, but you don't want anyone to be able to look through the system or through your program to discover what that password is.

Solution

Sample code folder: Chapter 16\SecurePassword

Store the hash of the password in the system registry, and test any user-entered password by comparing its hash against the registry entry.

Discussion

The following demonstration code includes a method that lets you record a username and password (hashed) in the system registry, and another method that compares a newly entered username and password with the previously stored value. This code requires the GetHash( ) function defined in Recipe 16.1:

```
Public Sub StoreUserAndPassword(ByVal userName As String, _
      ByVal passwordText As String)
   ' ----- Save the encrypted password in the registry.
   Dim hashPassword As String = GetHash(passwordText)

   My.Computer.Registry.SetValue _
      ("HKEY_CURRENT_USER\Software\PasswordsTest", _
      userName, hashPassword)
End Sub
```

```
Public Function CheckPassword(ByVal userName As String, _
    ByVal passwordText As String) As Boolean
    ' ----- See if the username and password passed to
    '       this function match entries in the registry.
    Dim hashPassword As String = GetHash(passwordText)

    ' ----- Retrieve any stored value.
    Dim hashPassRead As String = _
        Convert.ToString(My.Computer.Registry.GetValue( _
        "HKEY_CURRENT_USER\Software\PasswordsTest", _
        userName, Nothing))

    ' ----- Compare the passwords.
    If (hashPassRead = Nothing) Then
        ' ----- Invalid username.
        Return False
    ElseIf (hashPassRead = hashPassword) Then
        ' ----- Good username and password.
        Return True
    Else
        ' ----- Good username, bad password.
        Return False
    End If
End Function
```

16.6   Compressing and Decompressing a String

Problem

You want to compress and later decompress a string to save memory or file space.

Solution

Sample code folder: Chapter 16\Compression

Use Gzip stream compression and decompression, new in Version 2.0 of the .NET Framework.

Discussion

The System.IO.Compression namespace contains the GZipStream class, which can compress or decompress bytes as they move through the stream. The compression algorithm is similar to the standard ZIP compression found in many programs, providing decent lossless compression at a high speed.

This compression works best on longer strings. In the following sample code, the contents of the workText string are repeated several times in order to build a redundant string resulting in a lot of compression.

The compression and decompression calls are wrapped in the functions StringCompress() and BytesDecompress(), contained in a module named *Compress.vb*.

The compression function accepts a string and returns a byte array, and the decompression function accepts a byte array and returns a string. The compressed byte array contains just about any and all possible byte values, and keeping this data in the form of a byte array prevents subtle problems from arising when you attempt to convert the array directly to a string:

```
Public Function StringCompress( _
      ByVal originalText As String) As Byte()
   ' ----- Generate a compressed version of a string.
   '       First, convert the string to a byte array.
   Dim workBytes() As Byte = _
      Encoding.UTF8.GetBytes(originalText)

   ' ----- Bytes will flow through a memory stream.
   Dim memoryStream As New MemoryStream()

   ' ----- Use the newly created memory stream for the
   '       compressed data.
   Dim zipStream As New GZipStream(memoryStream, _
      CompressionMode.Compress, True)
   zipStream.Write(workBytes, 0, workBytes.Length)
   zipStream.Flush()

   ' ----- Close the compression stream.
   zipStream.Close()

   ' ----- Return the compressed bytes.
   Return memoryStream.ToArray
End Function

Public Function BytesDecompress( _
      ByVal compressed() As Byte) As String
   ' ----- Uncompress a previously compressed string.
   '       Extract the length for the decompressed string.
   Dim lastFour(3) As Byte
   Array.Copy(compressed, compressed.Length - 4, _
      lastFour, 0, 4)
   Dim bufferLength As Integer = _
      BitConverter.ToInt32(lastFour, 0)

   ' ----- Create an uncompressed bytes buffer.
   Dim buffer(bufferLength - 1) As Byte

   ' ----- Bytes will flow through a memory stream.
   Dim memoryStream As New MemoryStream(compressed)

   ' ----- Create the decompression stream.
   Dim decompressedStream As New GZipStream( _
      memoryStream, CompressionMode.Decompress, True)

   ' ----- Read and decompress the data into the buffer.
   decompressedStream.Read(buffer, 0, bufferLength)
```

```
' ----- Convert the bytes to a string.
    Return Encoding.UTF8.GetString(buffer)
End Function
```

The following code demonstrates these functions by building a moderately long redundant string, passing it to CompressString( ), then passing the compressed byte array back to BytesDecompress( ) to recover the original string:

```
Dim result As New System.Text.StringBuilder
Dim workText As String = ""
For counter As Integer = 1 To 9
    workText &= "This redundant string will be compressed" & _
        vbNewLine
Next counter
Dim compressed( ) As Byte = StringCompress(workText)
Dim uncompressed As String = BytesDecompress(compressed)
result.AppendLine(workText)
result.Append("Original size: ")
result.AppendLine(workText.Length)
result.AppendLine( )
result.Append("Compressed size: ")
result.AppendLine(compressed.Length)
result.AppendLine( )
result.AppendLine(uncompressed)
result.AppendLine( )
result.Append("Uncompressed size: ")
result.Append(uncompressed.Length)
MsgBox(result.ToString( ))
```

Figure 16-5 displays the original string and its length, followed by the length of the compressed byte array, and finally the resulting decompressed string and its length. Longer strings with redundancies, such as this one, compress better than shorter ones.

See Also

Recipe 16.9 includes the full source code for the Compress module.

16.7 Compressing and Decompressing a File

Problem

You want to compress and decompress file data.

Solution

Sample code folder: Chapter 16\Compression

Use Gzip stream compression and decompression, new in Version 2.0 of the .NET Framework.

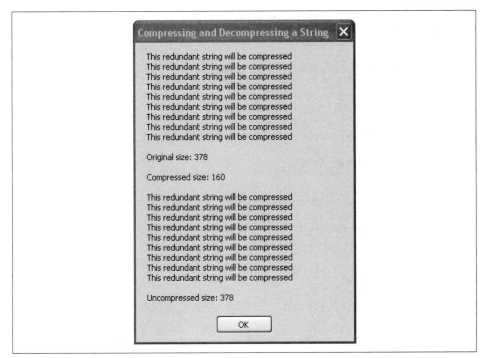

Figure 16-5. Compressing and decompressing a string

Discussion

Because the GZipStream class works on streams, it's easy to point it to file streams as data is read to or written from files. This lets the compression and decompression algorithms intercept the bytes as they move through the file streams.

The FileCompress() and FileDecompress() functions are found in the same *Compress.vb* module that contains the string compression and decompression functions presented in Recipe 16.6. These functions are similar in that they intercept streams to process bytes as they move through them. One important difference is the use of a 4,096-byte buffer to process the file-stream data in chunks, rather than loading the entire file contents into memory. This allows even the largest files to be efficiently processed a piece at a time.

Here are the two file compression and decompression functions:

```
Public Sub FileCompress(ByVal sourceFile As String, _
      ByVal destinationFile As String)
   ' ----- Decompress a previously compressed string.
   '       First, create the input file stream.
   Dim sourceStream As New FileStream( _
      sourceFile, FileMode.Open, FileAccess.Read)
```

```
' ----- Create the output file stream.
Dim destinationStream As New FileStream( _
destinationFile, FileMode.Create, FileAccess.Write)

' ----- Bytes will be processed by a compression
'       stream.
Dim compressedStream As New GZipStream( _
   destinationStream, CompressionMode.Compress, True)

' ----- Process bytes from one file into the other.
Const BlockSize As Integer = 4096
Dim buffer(BlockSize) As Byte
Dim bytesRead As Integer
Do
   bytesRead = sourceStream.Read(buffer, 0, BlockSize)
   If (bytesRead = 0) Then Exit Do
   compressedStream.Write(buffer, 0, bytesRead)
Loop

' ----- Close all the streams.
sourceStream.Close( )
compressedStream.Close( )
destinationStream.Close( )
End Sub

Public Sub FileDecompress(ByVal sourceFile As String, _
      ByVal destinationFile As String)
   ' ----- Compress the entire contents of a file, and
   '       store the result in a new file. First, get
   '       the files as streams.
   Dim sourceStream As New FileStream( _
      sourceFile, FileMode.Open, FileAccess.Read)
   Dim destinationStream As New FileStream( _
      destinationFile, FileMode.Create, FileAccess.Write)

   ' ----- Bytes will be processed through a
   '       decompression stream.
   Dim decompressedStream As New GZipStream( _
      sourceStream, CompressionMode.Decompress, True)

   ' ----- Process bytes from one file into the other.
   Const BlockSize As Integer = 4096
   Dim buffer(BlockSize) As Byte
   Dim bytesRead As Integer
   Do
      bytesRead = decompressedStream.Read(buffer, _
         0, BlockSize)
      If (bytesRead = 0) Then Exit Do
      destinationStream.Write(buffer, 0, bytesRead)
   Loop

   ' ----- Close all the streams.
   sourceStream.Close( )
   decompressedStream.Close( )
```

```
        destinationStream.Close()
    End Sub
```

The entire *Compress.vb* module is listed in Recipe 16.10.

The following code demonstrates file compression and decompression by first filling a file with many repetitions of the same lines of text. Doubling the size of the file several times causes the number of bytes stored in File1 to grow to almost 88K.

FileCompress() is called to compress File1 into File2. Because of the highly redundant nature of the data in this example, the original 88K bytes of data compress down to less than 1K, as stored in File2. Finally, FileDecompress() is called to decompress File2 into File3. This file ends up being exactly the same size and containing exactly the same data as File1, verifying the compression and decompression action:

```
Dim result As New System.Text.StringBuilder
Dim file1Text As String = _
    "This is sample content for a text file to" & vbNewLine & _
    "be compressed and decompressed. File1 and" & vbNewLine & _
    "File3 should show this plain text. File2" & vbNewLine & _
    "is compressed and will be indecipherable." & vbNewLine
For counter As Integer = 1 To 9
    file1Text &= file1Text
Next counter
Dim file2Text As String
Dim file3Text As String
Dim file1 As String = Application.StartupPath & "\File1.txt"
Dim file2 As String = Application.StartupPath & "\File2.gzz"
Dim file3 As String = Application.StartupPath & "\File3.txt"

' ----- Compress and decompress the content files.
My.Computer.FileSystem.WriteAllText(file1, file1Text, False)
FileCompress(file1, file2)
FileDecompress(file2, file3)

' ----- Display the results.
file2Text = My.Computer.FileSystem.ReadAllText(file2)
file3Text = My.Computer.FileSystem.ReadAllText(file3)
result.Append("File1 length (original): ")
result.AppendLine(file1Text.Length)
result.Append("File2 length (compressed): ")
result.AppendLine(file2Text.Length)
result.Append("File3 length (decompressed): ")
result.AppendLine(file3Text.Length)
MsgBox(result.ToString())
```

Figure 16-6 displays the size in bytes of each of the three files after the functions are called.

See Also

Recipe 16.10 includes the full source code for the Compress module.

Figure 16-6. Compressing and decompressing a file

16.8 Generating Cryptographically Secure Random Numbers

Problem

You want to generate reliably unpredictable pseudorandom bytes.

Solution

Sample code folder: Chapter 16\RandomNumbers

Use the RNGCryptoServiceProvider class provided in the System.Security. Cryptography namespace to generate random numbers that are guaranteed to be unpredictable and highly resistant to any pattern analysis.

Discussion

Some random number generators, such as those found in Visual Basic 6.0 and earlier versions of BASIC, were not really that good. They generally were fine for most statistical analysis purposes, but their cycle lengths were comparatively short, and certain types of high-powered random number tests showed them to have subtle patterns in the bits comprising their sequences of bytes. The RNGCryptoServiceProvider class provides a random number generator that's been carefully studied by professional cryptographers and passes all the standard tests for randomness with flying colors. There's no realistic way to analyze or predict the next byte in a sequence generated by this class.

The following code demonstrates the RNGCryptoServiceProvider class by using an instance of it to generate a million random bytes. The mean of these bytes is calculated, as is the time it takes to generate the bytes:

```
Dim result As New System.Text.StringBuilder
Const ProcessSize As Integer = 1000000

' ----- Generate the random content.
Dim randomEngine As New RNGCryptoServiceProvider( )
Dim randomBytes(ProcessSize) As Byte
```

```
Dim timeStart As Date = Now
randomEngine.GetBytes(randomBytes)

' ----- Calculate the mean of all values.
Dim mean As Double
For counter As Integer = 1 To ProcessSize
    mean += randomBytes(counter)
Next counter
mean /= ProcessSize

' ----- How long did this take?
Dim timeElapsed As Double = _
    Now.Subtract(timeStart).TotalSeconds

' ----- Display the results.
result.AppendLine(String.Format( _
    "Generated and found mean of {0} random bytes", _
    ProcessSize))
result.AppendLine(String.Format("in {0} seconds", _
    timeElapsed))
result.Append("Mean: " & mean)
MsgBox(result.ToString())
```

The results for a sample run appear in Figure 16-7. You can call the GetBytes( ) method to fill any size byte array you pass to it with that many random bytes. The previous code generates the million bytes using only one call to the GetBytes( ) method. The loop processes the individual byes to calculate the mean.

Figure 16-7. *Cryptographically secure random bytes generated by the RNGCryptoServiceProvider class*

Because the random bytes have equal probabilities for all values from 0 to 255, the average value should theoretically be very near 127.5. With a million random bytes generated by this sample code, the mean falls very close to this theoretical value almost every time.

16.9   Complete Listing of the Crypto.vb Module

Sample code folder: Chapter 16\Cryptography

This recipe contains the full code for the Crypto module described in Recipes 16.1 through 16.3:

```vb
Imports System.IO
Imports System.Text
Imports System.Security.Cryptography

Module Crypto
    Public Function GetHash(ByVal plainText As String) As String
        ' ----- Generate a hash. Return an empty string
        '       if there are any problems.
        Dim plainBytes As Byte()
        Dim hashEngine As MD5CryptoServiceProvider
        Dim hashBytes As Byte()
        Dim hashText As String

        Try
            ' ----- Convert the plain text to a byte array.
            plainBytes = Encoding.UTF8.GetBytes(plainText)

            ' ----- Select one of the hash engines.
            hashEngine = New MD5CryptoServiceProvider

            ' ----- Get the hash of the plain text bytes.
            hashBytes = hashEngine.ComputeHash(plainBytes)

            ' ----- Convert the hash bytes to a hexadecimal string.
            hashText = Replace(BitConverter.ToString(hashBytes), "-", "")
            Return hashText
        Catch
            Return ""
        End Try
    End Function

    Public Function StringEncrypt(ByVal plainText As String, _
            ByVal keyText As String) As String
        ' ----- Encrypt some text. Return an empty string
        '       if there are any problems.
        Try
            ' ----- Remove any possible null characters.
            Dim workText As String = plainText.Replace(vbNullChar, "")

            ' ----- Convert plain text to byte array.
            Dim workBytes() As Byte = Encoding.UTF8.GetBytes(plainText)

            ' ----- Convert key string to 32-byte key array.
            Dim keyBytes() As Byte = _
                Encoding.UTF8.GetBytes(GetHash(keyText))

            ' ----- Create initialization vector.
            Dim IV() As Byte = { _
                50, 199, 10, 159, 132, 55, 236, 189, _
                51, 243, 244, 91, 17, 136, 39, 230}
```

```vb
    ' ----- Create the Rijndael engine.
    Dim rijndael As New RijndaelManaged

    ' ----- Bytes will flow through a memory stream.
    Dim memoryStream As New MemoryStream()

    ' ----- Create the cryptography transform.
    Dim cryptoTransform As ICryptoTransform
    cryptoTransform = _
        rijndael.CreateEncryptor(keyBytes, IV)

    ' ----- Bytes will be processed by CryptoStream.
    Dim cryptoStream As New CryptoStream( _
        memoryStream, cryptoTransform, _
        CryptoStreamMode.Write)

    ' ----- Move the bytes through the processing stream.
    cryptoStream.Write(workBytes, 0, workBytes.Length)
    cryptoStream.FlushFinalBlock()

    ' ----- Convert binary data to a viewable string.
    Dim encrypted As String = _
        Convert.ToBase64String(memoryStream.ToArray)

    ' ----- Close the streams.
    memoryStream.Close()
    cryptoStream.Close()

    ' ----- Return the encrypted string result.
    Return encrypted
  Catch
    Return ""
  End Try
End Function

Public Function StringDecrypt(ByVal encrypted As String, _
    ByVal keyText As String) As String
  ' ----- Decrypt a previously encrypted string. The key
  '       must match the one used to encrypt the string.
  '       Return an empty string on error.
  Try
    ' ----- Convert encrypted string to a byte array.
    Dim workBytes() As Byte = _
        Convert.FromBase64String(encrypted)

    ' ----- Convert key string to 32-byte key array.
    Dim keyBytes() As Byte = _
        Encoding.UTF8.GetBytes(GetHash(keyText))

    ' ----- Create initialization vector.
    Dim IV() As Byte = { _
        50, 199, 10, 159, 132, 55, 236, 189, _
        51, 243, 244, 91, 17, 136, 39, 230}
```

```vbnet
        ' ----- Decrypted bytes will be stored in
        '       a temporary array.
        Dim tempBytes(workBytes.Length - 1) As Byte

        ' ----- Create the Rijndael engine.
        Dim rijndael As New RijndaelManaged

        ' ----- Bytes will flow through a memory stream.
        Dim memoryStream As New MemoryStream(workBytes)

        ' ----- Create the cryptography transform.
        Dim cryptoTransform As ICryptoTransform
        cryptoTransform = _
            rijndael.CreateDecryptor(keyBytes, IV)

        ' ----- Bytes will be processed by CryptoStream.
        Dim cryptoStream As New CryptoStream( _
            memoryStream, cryptoTransform, _
            CryptoStreamMode.Read)

        ' ----- Move the bytes through the processing stream.
        cryptoStream.Read(tempBytes, 0, tempBytes.Length)

        ' ----- Close the streams.
        memoryStream.Close()
        cryptoStream.Close()

        ' ----- Convert the decrypted bytes to a string.
        Dim plainText As String = _
            Encoding.UTF8.GetString(tempBytes)

        ' ----- Return the decrypted string result.
        Return plainText.Replace(vbNullChar, "")
    Catch
        Return ""
    End Try
End Function

Public Sub FileEncrypt(ByVal sourceFile As String, _
        ByVal destinationFile As String, _
        ByVal keyText As String)
    ' ----- Create file streams.
    Dim sourceStream As New FileStream( _
        sourceFile, FileMode.Open, FileAccess.Read)
    Dim destinationStream As New FileStream( _
        destinationFile, FileMode.Create, FileAccess.Write)

    ' ----- Convert key string to 32-byte key array.
    Dim keyBytes() As Byte = _
        Encoding.UTF8.GetBytes(GetHash(keyText))

    ' ----- Create initialization vector.
    Dim IV() As Byte = { _
        50, 199, 10, 159, 132, 55, 236, 189, _
        51, 243, 244, 91, 17, 136, 39, 230}
```

```
' ----- Create a Rijndael engine.
Dim rijndael As New RijndaelManaged

' ----- Create the cryptography transform.
Dim cryptoTransform As ICryptoTransform
cryptoTransform = _
   rijndael.CreateEncryptor(keyBytes, IV)

' ----- Bytes will be processed by CryptoStream.
Dim cryptoStream As New CryptoStream( _
   destinationStream, cryptoTransform, _
   CryptoStreamMode.Write)

' ----- Process bytes from one file into the other.
Const BlockSize As Integer = 4096
Dim buffer(BlockSize) As Byte
Dim bytesRead As Integer
Do
   bytesRead = sourceStream.Read(buffer, 0, BlockSize)
   If (bytesRead = 0) Then Exit Do
   cryptoStream.Write(buffer, 0, bytesRead)
Loop

' ----- Close the streams.
cryptoStream.Close( )
sourceStream.Close( )
destinationStream.Close( )
End Sub

Public Sub FileDecrypt(ByVal sourceFile As String, _
      ByVal destinationFile As String, _
      ByVal keyText As String)

' ----- Create file streams.
Dim sourceStream As New FileStream( _
   sourceFile, FileMode.Open, FileAccess.Read)
Dim destinationStream As New FileStream( _
   destinationFile, FileMode.Create, FileAccess.Write)

' ----- Convert key string to 32-byte key array.
Dim keyBytes( ) As Byte = _
   Encoding.UTF8.GetBytes(GetHash(keyText))

' ----- Create initialization vector.
Dim IV( ) As Byte = { _
   50, 199, 10, 159, 132, 55, 236, 189, _
   51, 243, 244, 91, 17, 136, 39, 230}

' ----- Create a Rijndael engine.
Dim rijndael As New RijndaelManaged

' ----- Create the cryptography transform.
Dim cryptoTransform As ICryptoTransform
cryptoTransform = _
   rijndael.CreateDecryptor(keyBytes, IV)
```

```
' ----- Bytes will be processed by CryptoStream.
Dim cryptoStream As New CryptoStream( _
   destinationStream, cryptoTransform, _
   CryptoStreamMode.Write)

' ----- Process bytes from one file into the other.
Const BlockSize As Integer = 4096
Dim buffer(BlockSize) As Byte
Dim bytesRead As Integer
Do
   bytesRead = sourceStream.Read(buffer, 0, BlockSize)
   If (bytesRead = 0) Then Exit Do
   cryptoStream.Write(buffer, 0, bytesRead)
Loop

' ----- Close the streams.
cryptoStream.Close( )
sourceStream.Close( )
destinationStream.Close( )
   End Sub
End Module
```

16.10 Complete Listing of the Compress.vb Module

Sample code folder: Chapter 16\Compression

This recipe contains the full code for the Compress module described in Recipes 16.6 and 16.7:

```
Imports System
Imports System.Text
Imports System.IO
Imports System.IO.Compression

Module Compress
   Public Function StringCompress( _
         ByVal originalText As String) As Byte( )
      ' ----- Generate a compressed version of a string.
      '       First, convert the string to a byte array.
      Dim workBytes( ) As Byte = _
         Encoding.UTF8.GetBytes(originalText)

      ' ----- Bytes will flow through a memory stream.
      Dim memoryStream As New MemoryStream( )

      ' ----- Use the newly created memory stream for the
      '       compressed data.
      Dim zipStream As New GZipStream(memoryStream, _
         CompressionMode.Compress, True)
      zipStream.Write(workBytes, 0, workBytes.Length)
      zipStream.Flush( )
```

```vb
    ' ----- Close the compression stream.
    zipStream.Close( )

    ' ----- Return the compressed bytes.
    Return memoryStream.ToArray
End Function

Public Function BytesDecompress( _
        ByVal compressed( ) As Byte) As String
    ' ----- Uncompress a previously compressed string.
    '       Extract the length for the decompressed string.
    Dim lastFour(3) As Byte
    Array.Copy(compressed, compressed.Length - 4, _
        lastFour, 0, 4)
    Dim bufferLength As Integer = _
        BitConverter.ToInt32(lastFour, 0)

    ' ----- Create an uncompressed bytes buffer.
    Dim buffer(bufferLength - 1) As Byte

    ' ----- Bytes will flow through a memory stream.
    Dim memoryStream As New MemoryStream(compressed)

    ' ----- Create the decompression stream.
    Dim decompressedStream As New GZipStream( _
        memoryStream, CompressionMode.Decompress, True)

    ' ----- Read and decompress the data into the buffer.
    decompressedStream.Read(buffer, 0, bufferLength)

    ' ----- Convert the bytes to a string.
    Return Encoding.UTF8.GetString(buffer)
End Function

Public Sub FileCompress(ByVal sourceFile As String, _
        ByVal destinationFile As String)
    ' ----- Decompress a previously compressed string.
    '       First, create the input file stream.
    Dim sourceStream As New FileStream( _
        sourceFile, FileMode.Open, FileAccess.Read)

    ' ----- Create the output file stream.
    Dim destinationStream As New FileStream( _
    destinationFile, FileMode.Create, FileAccess.Write)

    ' ----- Bytes will be processed by a compression
    '       stream.
    Dim compressedStream As New GZipStream( _
        destinationStream, CompressionMode.Compress, True)

    ' ----- Process bytes from one file into the other.
    Const BlockSize As Integer = 4096
    Dim buffer(BlockSize) As Byte
    Dim bytesRead As Integer
```

```
      Do
         bytesRead = sourceStream.Read(buffer, 0, BlockSize)
         If (bytesRead = 0) Then Exit Do
         compressedStream.Write(buffer, 0, bytesRead)
      Loop

      ' ----- Close all the streams.
      sourceStream.Close()
      compressedStream.Close()
      destinationStream.Close()
   End Sub

   Public Sub FileDecompress(ByVal sourceFile As String, _
         ByVal destinationFile As String)
      ' ----- Compress the entire contents of a file, and
      '       store it in a new file. First, get the files
      '       as streams.
      Dim sourceStream As New FileStream( _
         sourceFile, FileMode.Open, FileAccess.Read)
      Dim destinationStream As New FileStream( _
         destinationFile, FileMode.Create, FileAccess.Write)

      ' ----- Bytes will be processed through a
      '       decompression stream.
      Dim decompressedStream As New GZipStream( _
         sourceStream, CompressionMode.Decompress, True)

      ' ----- Process bytes from one file into the other.
      Const BlockSize As Integer = 4096
      Dim buffer(BlockSize) As Byte
      Dim bytesRead As Integer
      Do
         bytesRead = decompressedStream.Read(buffer, _
            0, BlockSize)
         If (bytesRead = 0) Then Exit Do
         destinationStream.Write(buffer, 0, bytesRead)
      Loop

      ' ----- Close all the streams.
      sourceStream.Close()
      decompressedStream.Close()
      destinationStream.Close()
   End Sub
End Module
```

Web Development

17.0 Introduction

Programming for the Web is a vast subject worthy of a whole series of books. While we obviously can't cover everything here, this chapter presents a few web-related recipes for Visual Basic that let you add some useful features to your applications. They will give you some idea of the power of web functionality combined with desktop applications. For a comprehensive collection of Visual Basic web recipes, see *ASP.NET 2.0 Cookbook* by Michael A. Kittel and Geoff T. LeBlond (O'Reilly).

17.1 Displaying Web Pages on a Form

Problem

You want to display a web page on your form, possibly built from custom HTML content.

Solution

Sample code folder: Chapter 17\CustomWebContent

Sample code folder: Chapter 17\WebBrowser

Use the WebBrowser control. It encapsulates the core Microsoft Internet Explorer engine, and it integrates easily into your Windows Forms applications.

Discussion

This recipe's sample code implements a simple web browser. Create a new Windows Forms application, and add the following controls to Form1:

- A Panel control named WebToolbar. Set its Dock property to Top and its Size.Height property to about 40.

- A WebBrowser control named WebContent. Set its Dock property to Fill. It should only fill below the Panel control. If it doesn't, right-click on the Panel control and select "Send to Back" from the shortcut menu.

- A Button control named ActBack. This control should appear on the surface of the Panel control. Set its Text property to &Back.
- A Button control named ActHome. This control should appear on the surface of the Panel control. Set its Text property to &Home.
- A TextBox control named WebAddress. This control should appear on the surface of the Panel control. Set its Anchor property to Top,Left,Right.
- A Button control named ActGo. This control should appear on the surface of the Panel control. Set its Text property to &Go and its Anchor property to Top,Right.

Arrange the controls as presented in Figure 17-1.

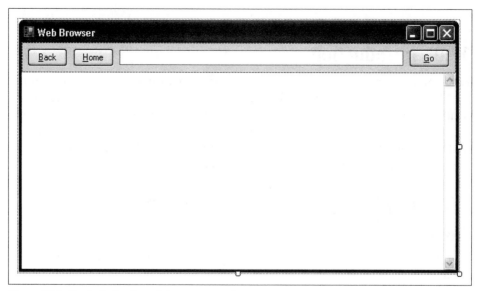

Figure 17-1. Controls for the web browser sample

Now add the following source code to the form's class template:

```
Private Sub ActBack_Click(ByVal sender As System.Object, _
      ByVal e As System.EventArgs) Handles ActBack.Click
   ' ----- Move to the previous web page.
   If (WebContent.CanGoBack() = True) Then _
      WebContent.GoBack()
End Sub

Private Sub ActHome_Click(ByVal sender As Object, _
      ByVal e As System.EventArgs) Handles ActHome.Click
   ' ----- Move to the main web page.
   WebContent.GoHome()
End Sub

Private Sub Form1_Load(ByVal sender As Object, _
      ByVal e As System.EventArgs) Handles Me.Load
```

```
    ' ----- Start from the home page.
    ActHome.PerformClick( )
End Sub

Private Sub ActGo_Click(ByVal sender As Object, _
        ByVal e As System.EventArgs) Handles ActGo.Click
    ' ----- Move to the requested page.
    If (Trim(WebAddress.Text) <> "") Then _
        WebContent.Navigate(WebAddress.Text)
End Sub
```

The previous dozen lines of code are all you need to provide your users with a full
Internet browsing experience (albeit without all of the fancy features). Run the program, and use it like a typical web browser.

You are not limited to Internet-based HTML content in the browser. You can supply your own generated-on-the-fly content as well, by setting the control's
DocumentText property to a string containing the HTML content. We added the following code to a new Form1 that contained only a WebBrowser control:

```
WebBrowser1.DocumentText = "<html><body>" & _
    "<h1>Important</h1><p>This is web content." & _
    "</p></body></html>"
```

Figure 17-2 shows the output.

Figure 17-2. Custom HTML content in a WebBrowser control

Interacting with web-browser links is somewhat indirect. There is no LinkClicked
event that occurs when a user clicks on a link. However, there is a Navigating event
that is pretty close. You can monitor this event to provide support for your own
internal link events. Decorate your custom HTML with a fake URL address, such as
internal://EditCustomer?ID=25 to trigger the editing of the customer with ID number
25. To test this, create a new Windows Forms application, and add a WebBrowser
control named WebBrowser1. Next, add the following source code to the form's code
template:

```
Private Sub Form1_Load(ByVal sender As Object, _
        ByVal e As System.EventArgs) Handles Me.Load
    ' ----- Add some custom content.
    WebBrowser1.DocumentText = "<html><body>" & _
        "<h1>Select an Airport</h1>" & _
```

```
            "<p><a href=""internal://Airport?Code=LAX"">" & _
            "Los Angeles</a></p>" & _
            "<p><a href=""internal://Airport?Code=JFK"">" & _
            "New York</a></p>" & _
            "<p><a href=""internal://Airport?Code=SEA"">" & _
            "Seattle</a></p>" & _
            "</body></html>"
    End Sub

    Private Sub WebBrowser1_Navigating(ByVal sender As Object, _
            ByVal e As System.Windows.Forms. _
            WebBrowserNavigatingEventArgs) _
            Handles WebBrowser1.Navigating
        ' ----- Which link was clicked?
        Dim queryEntries() As String
        Dim oneEntry() As String
        Dim airportCode As String = "Invalid Code"
        Dim scanQuery As String

        ' ----- Look for internal://airport?... links.
        If (e.Url.Scheme = "internal") Then
            If (e.Url.Host = "airport") Then
                If (e.Url.Query.Length > 0) Then
                    ' ----- Found an airport link. Get the
                    '       airport code. The query starts with
                    '       "?". Skip it.
                    queryEntries = _
                        Split(e.Url.Query.Substring(1), "&")
                    For Each scanQuery In queryEntries
                        oneEntry = Split(scanQuery, "=")
                        If (UCase(oneEntry(0)) = "CODE") Then
                            ' ----- Found the airport code.
                            airportCode = UCase(oneEntry(1))
                            Exit For
                        End If
                    Next scanQuery
                End If

                ' ----- Show the code.
                MsgBox(airportCode)
                e.Cancel = True
            End If
        End If
    End Sub
```

Clicking on one of the links gives results similar to Figure 17-3.

Several of the WebBrowser control's properties can be used to limit the allowed actions of the user. For instance, setting the AllowNavigation, WebBrowserShortcutsEnabled, and IsWebBrowserContextMenuEnabled properties to False can effectively shut down all user interaction with the Internet, providing a portal for static web content display only.

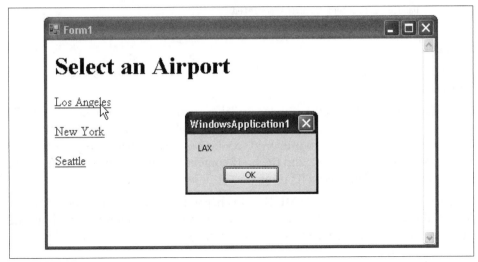

Figure 17-3. An internally processed link

See Also

Recipe 17.12 shows how to add a clickable hyperlink to a Windows form.

17.2 Accessing Content Within an HTML Document

Problem

You need to extract some information from within a web page.

Solution

Sample code folder: Chapter 17\UseHTMLDOM

While you could use standard string-manipulation techniques to scan through a web page, it's a lot of work. If the HTML content you need to parse has a consistent format with identifiable tags and elements, you can use Microsoft's Managed HTML Document Object Model (DOM) to traverse the HTML content as a set of objects.

Discussion

This recipe builds on the code developed in Recipe 17.1. Create a new Windows Forms project following the instructions in that recipe. Now add the following additional code to the form's code template:

```
Private Sub WebContent_DocumentCompleted( _
      ByVal sender As Object, ByVal e As _
      System.Windows.Forms. _
      WebBrowserDocumentCompletedEventArgs) _
```

```
      Handles WebContent.DocumentCompleted
   ' ----- Extract the title and display it.
   MsgBox(WebContent.Document.Title)
  End Sub
```

Run the program, and as you browse from page to page, the title of each page will appear in a message box.

The Managed HTML DOM, made available through the WebBrowser control's Document property, provides object-based access to all elements of an HTML page, including links (via the Links property), cookies associated with the page (via the Cookies string-array property), and the body content (via the Body property). You can search for specific elements by ID using the GetElementByID( ) method.

Specific use of the Managed HTML DOM is beyond the scope of this book. Use the MSDN documentation supplied with Visual Studio to obtain information about the HtmlElement class and other classes used within the DOM.

See Also

Recipe 17.1 includes most of the code used in this recipe. Recipe 17.3 uses the HTML DOM to access links within a web page.

17.3   Getting All Links from a Web Page

Problem

You want to build a list of the hyperlinks included in a specific web page.

Solution

Sample code folder: Chapter 17\ListWebLinks

Use the Managed HTML DOM to traverse the list of web page links as objects.

Discussion

This recipe's sample code builds a list of links from a web page. Create a new Windows Forms application, and add the following controls to Form1:

- A TextBox control named WebAddress.
- A Button control named ActGo. Set its Text property to Go.
- A WebBrowser control named WebContent.
- A ListBox control named WebLinks.

Add informational labels if desired, and arrange the controls to look like Figure 17-4.

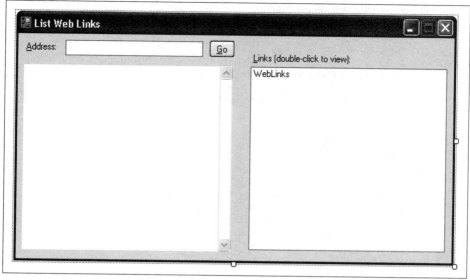

Figure 17-4. Controls for the listing web links sample

Next add the following source code to the form's class template:

```
Private Class LinkDetail
    Public LinkURL As String
    Public LinkText As String

    Public Overrides Function ToString() As String
        Return LinkText
    End Function
End Class

Private Sub ActGo_Click(ByVal sender As System.Object, _
        ByVal e As System.EventArgs) Handles ActGo.Click
    ' ----- Jump to a new web page.
    If (Trim(WebAddress.Text) <> "") Then
        WebLinks.Items.Clear()
        WebContent.Navigate(WebAddress.Text)
    End If
End Sub

Private Sub WebContent_DocumentCompleted( _
        ByVal sender As Object, ByVal e As _
        System.Windows.Forms. _
        WebBrowserDocumentCompletedEventArgs) _
        Handles WebContent.DocumentCompleted
    ' ----- Build the list of links.
    Dim oneLink As HtmlElement
    Dim newLink As LinkDetail

    ' ----- Scan through all the links.
    For Each oneLink In WebContent.Document.Links
```

```
      ' ----- Buld a new link entry.
      newLink = New LinkDetail
      If (oneLink.InnerText = "") Then
         newLink.LinkText = "[Image or Unknown]"
      Else
         newLink.LinkText = oneLink.InnerText
      End If
      newLink.LinkURL = oneLink.GetAttribute("href")

      ' ----- Add the link to the list.
      WebLinks.Items.Add(newLink)
   Next oneLink
End Sub

Private Sub WebLinks_DoubleClick(ByVal sender As Object, _
      ByVal e As System.EventArgs) Handles WebLinks.DoubleClick
   ' ----- Show the detail of a web link.
   Dim linkContent As LinkDetail

   If (WebLinks.SelectedIndex = -1) Then Return
   linkContent = CType(WebLinks.SelectedItem, LinkDetail)
   MsgBox("Display = " & linkContent.LinkText & vbCrLf & _
      "URL = " & linkContent.LinkURL)
   End Sub
```

Run the program, enter an address in the TextBox control, and click the Go button. The web page appears, as does the list of its links. Double-click a link to display its target URL, as shown in Figure 17-5.

Figure 17-5. Displaying the URL for a parsed web link

See Also

Recipe 17.2 discusses the general use of the Managed HTML Document Object Model.

17.4 Get the Local Computer's IP Address

Problem

You want to determine the IP address of the computer on which your program is running.

Solution

Sample code folder: Chapter 17\LocalIPAddresses

Use the features in the System.Net.Dns namespace to obtain the IP address(es) for the local host. A single workstation may have multiple IP addresses; this generally occurs when multiple networking cards are installed and active on that workstation.

Discussion

It may not be possible to determine the *single* IP address for your computer, because a computer may have multiple addresses. What .NET can give you is a list of all current IP addresses for the workstation, and its host name as well.

The following code displays the local host name and all related IP addresses for that host. It uses the System.Net.Dns namespace, which includes features for managing IP addresses and related hosts:

```
Dim hostAddresses() As Net.IPAddress
Dim ipList As String = ""
Dim oneAddress As Net.IPAddress

hostAddresses = Net.Dns.GetHostAddresses( _
   Net.Dns.GetHostName())
For Each oneAddress In hostAddresses
   ipList &= vbCrLf & oneAddress.ToString()
Next oneAddress
MsgBox("The IP address(es) for host '" & _
   Net.Dns.GetHostName() & "' are:" & vbCrLf & ipList)
```

On our system, this code displayed the message box in Figure 17-6.

The GetHostAddresses() method returns IP addresses as they are understood by the local host. These addresses may differ from the IP address of that same workstation as viewed from the Internet. A router that implements Network Address Translation (NAT) can mask the actual (local) IP address of a system.

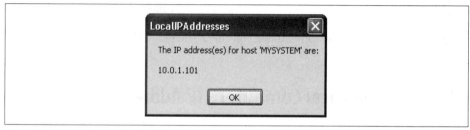

Figure 17-6. Displaying the local host's IP address

See Also

Recipe 17.5 discusses determining IP addresses for systems other than the local workstation.

17.5 Resolving a Host Name or IP Address for Another Computer

Problem

You need to determine the host name for another computer from its IP address, or vice versa.

Solution

Sample code folder: Chapter 17\ResolveHostOrIP

The System.Net.Dns namespace includes methods that let you resolve an IP address to its matching host name or obtain an IP address for a host name.

Discussion

Create a new Windows Forms application, and add the following controls to Form1:

- A TextBox control named IPAddress.
- A Button control named FromIpToHost. Set its Text property to Show Host Name.
- A TextBox control named HostName.
- A Button control named FromHostToIp. Set its Text property to Show IP Address.

Add informational labels if desired. The form should look like the one in Figure 17-7.

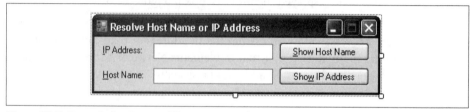

Figure 17-7. Controls for the IP and host name resolution sample

Now add the following source code to the form's code template:

```
Private Sub FromIpToHost_Click( _
      ByVal sender As System.Object, _
      ByVal e As System.EventArgs) _
      Handles FromIpToHost.Click
   ' ----- Convert from IP address to host name.
   If (Trim(IPAddress.Text) <> "") Then _
      MsgBox("Host Name" & vbCrLf & vbCrLf & _
      Net.Dns.GetHostEntry(IPAddress.Text).HostName)
End Sub

Private Sub FromHostToIp_Click( _
      ByVal sender As System.Object, _
      ByVal e As System.EventArgs) _
      Handles FromHostToIp.Click
   ' ----- Convert from host name to IP address.
   Dim hostEntry As Net.IPHostEntry
   Dim scanAddress As Net.IPAddress
   Dim hostAddresses As String = ""

   If (Trim(HostName.Text) <> "") Then
      hostEntry = Net.Dns.GetHostEntry(HostName.Text)
      For Each scanAddress In hostEntry.AddressList
         hostAddresses &= vbCrLf & scanAddress.ToString()
      Next scanAddress
      If (hostAddresses = "") Then _
         hostAddresses = vbCrLf & "None."

      MsgBox("IP Addresses" & vbCrLf & hostAddresses)
   End If
End Sub
```

To use the program, enter an IP address in the IP Address field or a host name in the Host Name field, and click the applicable button to view the resolved name or address.

A bug in some versions of Windows XP prevents the GetHostEntry() method from working correctly. Specifically, if you supply an IP address of a remote system (outside of your local network) to the method, the returned IPHostEntry.HostName property returns the IP address itself instead of the host name. This bug may be resolved in a Windows XP service pack or hotfix; it is resolved in Windows Vista.

See Also

Recipe 17.4 discusses finding the IP address(es) for the local workstation.

17.6 Pinging an IP Address

Problem

You want to perform a "ping" operation on a remote system.

Solution

Use the `My.Computer.Network.Ping( )` method. The general syntax is:

```
My.Computer.Network.Ping(targetSystem[, timeout])
```

targetSystem is a string IP address, a host name, or a `System.Uri` instance. The optional *timeout* argument is supplied in milliseconds and defaults to 500. This method returns `True` if the ping is successful, or `False` on failure or no response.

Discussion

If you receive a ping response from the remote system, it naturally means that the remote system is accessible. However, if you receive no response, this does not mean the remote system is inaccessible. It may have disabled responses to ping requests or a firewall or router between your system, and the remote system may have blocked the request or response.

17.7   Using FTP to Download Files

Problem

You want to add the ability to download a file from a File Transfer Protocol (FTP) server at the click of a button (or at any other point in your application) with completely automatic action.

Solution

Sample code folder: Chapter 17\FTPDownload

Use the `System.Net.FtpWebRequest` class to drive the FTP protocol from within your application.

Discussion

The `FtpWebRequest` class provides a straightforward way to programmatically download files from FTP servers. This works fine either for anonymous FTP, as shown in this recipe's code, or when using a specific user ID and password.

The following code demonstrates downloading a file from an anonymous FTP server on the Internet. Create a new Windows Forms application, and add a `Button` control named `Button1`. Then add the following code to the form's class template:

```
Private Sub Button1_Click(ByVal sender As System.Object, _
      ByVal e As System.EventArgs) Handles Button1.Click
   Dim sourceFile As String

   ' ----- Prompt the user for an FTP path.
   sourceFile = InputBox( _
      "Specify a URL for an FTP file to download.")
   If (sourceFile = "") Then Return
```

```
' ----- Initiate the download.
    DownloadViaFTP(sourceFile, "anonymous", "anony@mous.com")
End Sub
```

The event handler calls the DownloadViaFTP( ) method. That method starts by collecting the information it needs, calculating the target output file. sourceFile is the full path to the file to download, located in a folder on a server specifically set up for FTP access. destinationFile is the full path (including the filename) where you want the file to be downloaded, using the same filename as the source file. userName and password are strings containing the credential information to access the FTP server. For anonymous FTP, use "anonymous" for the username. It's customary to use your email address as the password. Here's the method declaration:

```
Private Sub DownloadViaFTP(ByVal sourceFile As String)
        ByVal userName As String, ByVal password As String)
    ' ----- Download the specified file via FTP and save
    '       it in the application's directory.
    Dim readBuffer(4095) As Byte
    Dim count As Integer
    Dim requestFile As System.Net.FtpWebRequest
    Dim responseFTP As System.Net.FtpWebResponse
    Dim responseStream As IO.Stream
    Dim outFile As IO.FileStream
    Dim destinationFile As String

    ' ----- Get the output location.
    destinationFile = My.Computer.FileSystem.CombinePath( _
        My.Application.Info.DirectoryPath, _
        My.Computer.FileSystem.GetName(sourceFile))
```

The variable requestFile is the instance of the FtpWebRequest that we'll use to drive the FTP protocol. Various properties of requestFile, such as Credentials and Method, provide the control required to define the FTP action:

```
    ' ----- Connect to the file on the FTP site.
    requestFile = CType(System.Net.FtpWebRequest.Create( _
        sourceFile), System.Net.FtpWebRequest)
    requestFile.Credentials = New _
        System.Net.NetworkCredential(userName, password)
    requestFile.KeepAlive = False
    requestFile.UseBinary = True
    requestFile.Method = _
        System.Net.WebRequestMethods.Ftp.DownloadFile
```

The actual flow of the byes comprising the file to be downloaded is handled by the FtpWebResponse object, which provides a Stream to move the bytes:

```
    ' ----- Open a transmission channel for the file content.
    responseFTP = CType(requestFile.GetResponse, _
        System.Net.FtpWebResponse)
    responseStream = responseFTP.GetResponseStream
    outFile = New IO.FileStream(destinationFile, _
        IO.FileMode.Create)
```

The stream of bytes is read into a buffer in chunks of up to 4,096 bytes, and from there it's written to the local file:

```
' ----- Save the content to the output file block by block.
Do
    count = responseStream.Read(readBuffer, 0, _
        readBuffer.Length)
    outFile.Write(readBuffer, 0, count)
Loop Until count = 0
```

Housekeeping wraps up the process:

```
' ----- Clean up.
responseStream.Close( )
outFile.Flush( )
outFile.Close( )
responseFTP.Close( )

MsgBox("File downloaded!" & vbNewLine & sourceFile)
End Sub
```

By this time, the file has been completely downloaded. To verify that the operation was a success, look in the application folder (wherever the executable file for this program resides) to confirm that the file has been created there.

17.8 Calling a Web Service

Problem

You want to access an XML Web Service across the Internet.

Solution

Sample code folder: Chapter 17\WebReference

Add a Web Reference to your project, and use the My.WebServices object to access the service.

Discussion

An XML Web Service is a function located on the Internet that your application can call. But unlike internal functions, calls to XML Web Services communicate via standard HTTP and plain text. They use defined standards, such as SOAP and WSDL, which are beyond the scope of this book.

There are a lot of XML Web Services available on the Internet, some free and some for a fee. For demonstration purposes, the following sample code calls Microsoft's TerraServer engine (*http://terraserver.microsoft.com*) to get a place name for any latitude and longitude around the world.

To call an XML Web Service, you must first add a Web Reference to your project. Create a new Windows Forms project, and select the Project → Add Web Reference menu command. When prompted for a service path URL in the Add Web Reference dialog, enter *http://terraserver.microsoft.com/TerraService.asmx* to access the Terra-Server Web Service. Then click the Add Reference button. Figure 17-8 shows how the Add Web Reference dialog helps you to explore the functionality provided by a service.

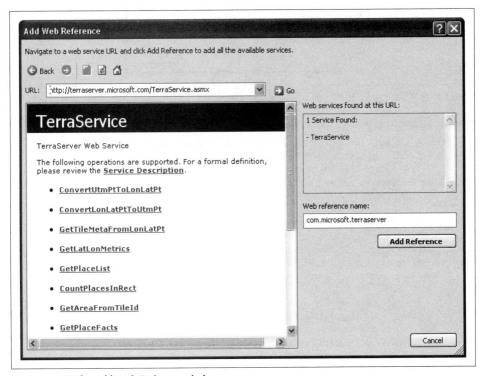

Figure 17-8. The Add Web Reference dialog

To demonstrate one of the functions provided by this service, this recipe's code calls the ConvertPlaceToLonLatPt( ) function to do just what it says: convert a place name to a latitude and longitude location. You can also convert in the other direction, using the service's ConvertLonLatPtToNearestPlace( ) function.

Add two Button controls to your form named ActToPlace and ActToLatLon, and set their Text properties to Locate. Also add five TextBox controls named CityName, StateName, CountryName, Latitude, and Longitude. Add some informational labels if desired. The form should look something like Figure 17-9.

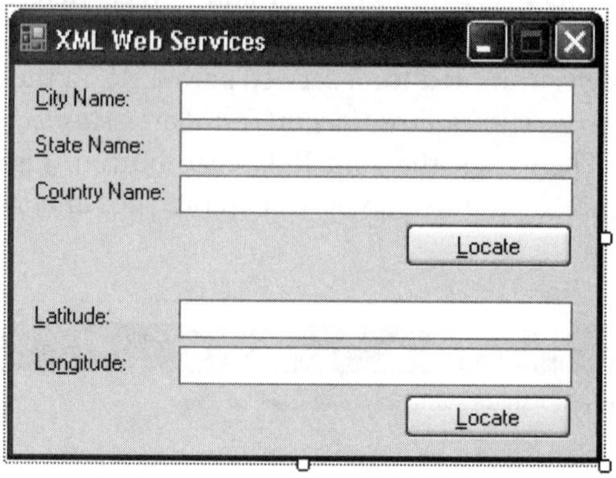

Figure 17-9. Controls for the XML Web Services sample

Now, add the following code to the form's class template:

```
Private Sub ActToLatLon_Click(ByVal sender As System.Object, _
      ByVal e As System.EventArgs) Handles ActToLatLon.Click
   ' ----- Locate the latitude and longitude for a place.
   Dim usePlace As com.microsoft.terraserver.Place
   Dim foundLocation As com.microsoft.terraserver.LonLatPt

   ' ----- Prepare the location details for use.
   usePlace = New com.microsoft.terraserver.Place
   usePlace.City = CityName.Text
   usePlace.State = StateName.Text
   usePlace.Country = CountryName.Text

   ' ----- Call the service with the user-supplied values.
   Me.Cursor = Cursors.WaitCursor
   foundLocation = _
      My.WebServices.TerraService.ConvertPlaceToLonLatPt( _
      usePlace)
   Me.Cursor = Cursors.Default

   ' ----- Inform the user.
   MsgBox("That place is located at:" & vbCrLf & vbCrLf & _
      "Latitude: " & foundLocation.Lat.ToString & vbCrLf & _
      "Longitude: " & foundLocation.Lon.ToString)
End Sub

Private Sub ActToPlace_Click(ByVal sender As System.Object, _
      ByVal e As System.EventArgs) Handles ActToPlace.Click
   ' ----- Locate the place for a latitude and longitude.
   Dim useLatLon As com.microsoft.terraserver.LonLatPt
   Dim foundPlace As String

   ' ----- Prepare the location details for use.
   useLatLon = New com.microsoft.terraserver.LonLatPt
   useLatLon.Lat = CDbl(Latitude.Text)
   useLatLon.Lon = CDbl(Longitude.Text)
```

```
' ----- Call the service with the user-supplied values.
Me.Cursor = Cursors.WaitCursor
foundPlace = My.WebServices.TerraService. _
   ConvertLonLatPtToNearestPlace(useLatLon)
Me.Cursor = Cursors.Default

' ----- Inform the user.
MsgBox("That location is at or near:" & vbCrLf & _
   vbCrLf & vbTab & foundPlace)
End Sub
```

Figure 17-10 shows the form in action. After entering the latitude and longitude for one of our favorite (and certainly one of the most memorably named) airports, a click of the button reveals the server's place name for this location as the airport at Deadhorse, Alaska.

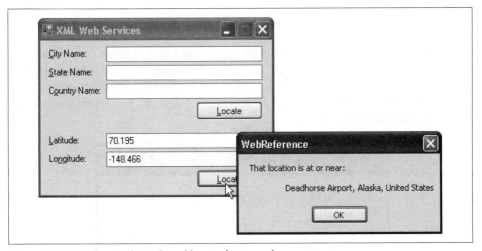

Figure 17-10. Converting latitude and longitude into a place name

This example shows how easy it is to use an Internet-based XML Web Service as if it were a function local to your application's source code. XML is used to make these services hardware- and software-independent, which means this same service can be called from a variety of programming languages using just about any computer and any operating system.

17.9   Sending Email Using SMTP

Problem

You want to send an email automatically from your application without using an external application such as Outlook.

Solution

Sample code folder: Chapter 17\SendEmail

Use the `System.Net.Mail.SmtpClient` class in the .NET Framework, supplying the server name and details specific to the email.

Discussion

The `System.Net.Mail.SmtpClient` class encapsulates an email submission. All you need to do is fill in its properties and call the `Send( )` method, and your mail is delivered to the target recipient.

 To send email, you must have authorized access to an SMTP server.

Create a new Windows Forms application, and add five `TextBox` controls named `ServerHost`, `FromEmail`, `ToEmail`, `SubjectText`, and `BodyText`. Set the `BodyText` control's `Multiline` property to `True`. Also add a `Button` control named `ActSend`, and set its `Text` property to `Send`. Add informational labels if desired. Your form should look something like Figure 17-11.

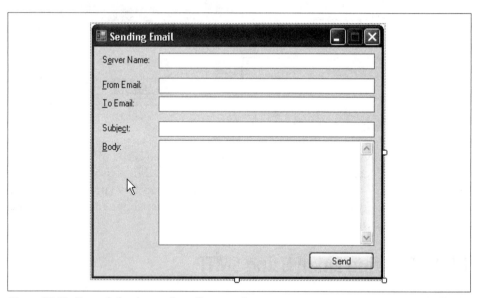

Figure 17-11. Controls for the email-sending sample

Now add the following code to the form's class template:

```
Imports System.Net.Mail

Public Class Form1
    Private Sub ActSend_Click(ByVal sender As System.Object, _
            ByVal e As System.EventArgs) Handles ActSend.Click
        ' ----- Send the requested email.
        Dim emailSender As SmtpClient
        Dim theMessage As MailMessage

        ' ----- Connect to the server. A second optional
        '           argument lets you alter the port number from
        '           the default.
        emailSender = New System.Net.Mail.SmtpClient( _
            ServerHost.Text)

        ' ----- Build the content details.
        theMessage = New MailMessage
        theMessage.From = New MailAddress(FromEmail.Text)
        theMessage.To.Add(ToEmail.Text)
        theMessage.Subject = SubjectText.Text
        theMessage.Body = BodyText.Text

        ' ----- Fill in the details and send.
        emailSender.Send(theMessage)
    End Sub
End Class
```

The `MailMessage` object includes properties that let you add attachments and specify the properties of the email message. Its To property is a collection that lets you add an unlimited number of email recipients. It also includes parallel CC and Bcc collections.

17.10 Getting POP3 Emails

Problem

You want to access emails from an application, perhaps just to get a quick count of available emails or to get the complete contents.

Solution

Sample code folder: Chapter 17\Pop3Email

Use the `TcpClient` class in the `System.Net.Sockets` namespace. The Pop3 class presented here wraps this class with supporting code to make it easier to access your emails.

Discussion

The following class code creates Pop3 objects to simplify accessing emails from a standard POP3 server. Note that some servers require SSL or other authentication, in which case this code will need modification. For standard POP3 servers, it works well as presented.

Create a new Windows Forms application, add a new class named *Pop3.vb*, and use this code for its definition:

```vb
Public Class Pop3
    ' ----- The default TCP/IP port number for POP3 is 110.
    Public Port As Integer = 110
    Public Messages As Integer = 0

    Private Const CommandFailure As String = "-ERR"

    Private Pop3Server As TcpClient
    Private CommandSender As NetworkStream
    Private ContentReceiver As StreamReader

    Public Sub Connect(ByVal serverName As String, _
            ByVal userName As String, ByVal password As String)
        ' ----- Initiate the connection to a POP3 server.
        Dim commandData As String
        Dim contentBuffer() As Byte
        Dim responseString As String
        Dim parts() As String

        ' ----- Connect to the POP3 server.
        Try
            Pop3Server = New TcpClient(serverName, Port)
            CommandSender = Pop3Server.GetStream()
            ContentReceiver = New StreamReader(CommandSender)
        Catch
            Throw
        End Try

        If (userName <> "") Then
            ' ----- Authenticate with the user ID.
            commandData = "USER " & userName & vbCrLf
            contentBuffer = _
                System.Text.Encoding.ASCII.GetBytes( _
                commandData.ToCharArray())
            CommandSender.Write(contentBuffer, 0, _
                contentBuffer.Length)
            responseString = ContentReceiver.ReadLine()
            If (Left(responseString, Len(CommandFailure)) = _
                    CommandFailure) Then
                Throw New Exception("Invalid user name.")
            End If
```

```
        ' ----- Send the authenticating password.
        commandData = "PASS " & password & vbCrLf
        contentBuffer = _
            System.Text.Encoding.ASCII.GetBytes( _
            commandData.ToCharArray())
        CommandSender.Write(contentBuffer, 0, _
            contentBuffer.Length)
        responseString = ContentReceiver.ReadLine()
        If (Left(responseString, Len(CommandFailure)) = _
                CommandFailure) Then
            Throw New Exception("Invalid password.")
        End If
    End If

    ' ----- Logged in. On some servers, the PASS command
    '        is not enough to push the server into a
    '        transaction state. Send a STAT command twice.
    commandData = "STAT" + vbCrLf
    contentBuffer = System.Text.Encoding.ASCII.GetBytes( _
        commandData.ToCharArray())
    CommandSender.Write(contentBuffer, 0, _
        contentBuffer.Length)
    responseString = ContentReceiver.ReadLine()

    ' ----- Get a count of the messages.
    commandData = "STAT" + vbCrLf
    contentBuffer = System.Text.Encoding.ASCII.GetBytes( _
        commandData.ToCharArray())
    CommandSender.Write(contentBuffer, 0, _
        contentBuffer.Length)
    responseString = ContentReceiver.ReadLine()
    If (Left(responseString, Len(CommandFailure)) = _
            CommandFailure) Then
        Throw New Exception( _
            "Could not retrieve message count.")
    End If

    ' ----- The response includes two integers: a count
    '        and a size, separated by a space. Skip over
    '        the "+OK" part also.
    parts = Split(responseString, " ")
    Messages = Val(parts(1))
End Sub

Public Sub Disconnect()
    ' ----- Disconnect from the POP3 server.
    Dim commandData As String
    Dim contentBuffer() As Byte
    Dim responseString As String

    ' ----- Tell the server we're through.
    commandData = "QUIT" & vbCrLf
    contentBuffer = System.Text.Encoding.ASCII.GetBytes( _
        commandData.ToCharArray())
```

```
         CommandSender.Write(contentBuffer, 0, _
            contentBuffer.Length)
         responseString = ContentReceiver.ReadLine()

         ' ----- End the connection.
         ContentReceiver.Close()
         CommandSender.Close()
         Pop3Server.Close()
      End Sub

      Function GetMessage(ByVal whichMessage As Integer) _
            As String
         ' ----- Retrieve a single email message.
         Dim commandData As String
         Dim contentBuffer() As Byte
         Dim responseString As String
         Dim theMessage As New System.Text.StringBuilder
         Dim oneLine As String

         ' ----- Check for an invalid message.
         If (whichMessage < 1) Or (whichMessage > Messages) Then
            Throw New ArgumentOutOfRangeException(whichMessage, _
               "Messages are numbered from 1 to the number " & _
               "identified by the Messages property.")
         End If

         Try
            ' ----- Request the message.
            commandData = "RETR " & whichMessage & vbCrLf
            contentBuffer = _
               System.Text.Encoding.ASCII.GetBytes( _
               commandData.ToCharArray())
            CommandSender.Write(contentBuffer, 0, _
               contentBuffer.Length)
            responseString = ContentReceiver.ReadLine()
            If (Left(responseString, Len(CommandFailure)) = _
                  CommandFailure) Then
               Throw New Exception("Message retrieval failed.")
            End If

            ' ----- The message is all data until a line with
            '        a single dot (.) appears.
            Do While (ContentReceiver.EndOfStream = False)
               oneLine = ContentReceiver.ReadLine()
               If (oneLine = ".") Then Exit Do
               theMessage.AppendLine(oneLine)
            Loop
         Catch ex As InvalidOperationException
            MsgBox("Message retrieval failed: " & ex.Message)
         End Try

         ' ----- Return the constructed message.
         Return theMessage.ToString()
      End Function
   End Class
```

Return to Form1, and add three TextBox controls named ServerName, UserName, and UserPassword. Set the UserPassword control's PasswordChar field to the asterisk character (*). Add a ListBox control named MessageList and two Button controls named ActGet and ActView. Set the Button controls' Text properties to Get Messages and View Message, respectively. Add informational labels if desired. The form should look like the one in Figure 17-12.

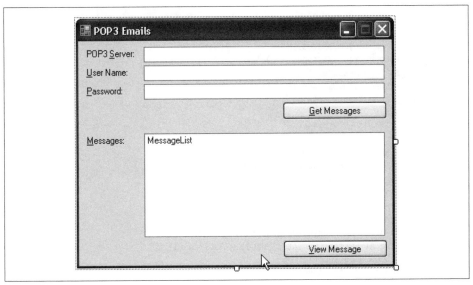

Figure 17-12. Controls for the POP3 sample

Now add the following code to Form1's class template:

```
Private POP3Connection As Pop3 = Nothing

Private Sub ActGet_Click(ByVal sender As System.Object, _
      ByVal e As System.EventArgs) Handles ActGet.Click
   ' ----- Initiate a POP3 connection.
   Dim counter As Integer

   ' ----- First, disconnect any previous connection.
   If (POP3Connection IsNot Nothing) Then
      Try
         POP3Connection.Disconnect()
      Catch ex As Exception
         ' ----- Ignore.
      End Try
   End If
   POP3Connection = Nothing

   ' ----- Clear any previous messages.
   MessageList.Items.Clear()
```

```
    ' ----- Try the new connection.
    Try
        POP3Connection = New Pop3
        POP3Connection.Connect(ServerName.Text, _
            UserName.Text, UserPassword.Text)
    Catch ex As Exception
        MsgBox("Connection failure: " & ex.Message)
        POP3Connection = Nothing
        Return
    End Try

    ' ----- How many messages?
    If (POP3Connection.Messages = 0) Then
        MsgBox("No messages found.")
        POP3Connection.Disconnect()
        POP3Connection = Nothing
        Return
    End If

    ' ----- Show each message.
    For counter = 1 To POP3Connection.Messages
        MessageList.Items.Add("Message Number " & counter)
    Next counter
End Sub

Private Sub ActView_Click(ByVal sender As System.Object, _
        ByVal e As System.EventArgs) Handles ActView.Click
    ' ----- Show a message.
    Dim whichMessage As Integer
    Dim parts As String()
    Dim content As String

    ' ----- Which message? Each item has the format:
    '           Message Number x
    If (MessageList.SelectedIndex = -1) Then Return
    parts = Split(CStr(MessageList.SelectedItem), " ")
    whichMessage = CInt(Val(parts(2)))

    ' ----- Get the content.
    content = POP3Connection.GetMessage(whichMessage)

    ' ----- Show the content.
    MsgBox(content)
End Sub

Private Sub MessageList_DoubleClick(ByVal sender As Object, _
        ByVal e As System.EventArgs) _
        Handles MessageList.DoubleClick
    ' ----- Same as the View button.
    ActView.PerformClick()
End Sub

Private Sub Form1_FormClosing(ByVal sender As Object, _
        ByVal e As System.Windows.Forms.FormClosingEventArgs) _
```

```
      Handles Me.FormClosing
   ' ----- Disconnect before leaving.
   On Error Resume Next

   If (POP3Connection IsNot Nothing) Then
      POP3Connection.Disconnect( )
      POP3Connection = Nothing
   End If
End Sub
```

When you successfully connect to a POP3 server through the ActGet button, it displays a simple list of each message stored on the server. It's not as good as a real email program such as Microsoft Outlook because it hasn't yet read even the sender name or subject text, but it does add one entry for each available message. Clicking on the ActView button retrieves the content for one email message from the server through the Pop3 class's GetMessage( ) method. The connection to the email server is closed when the form closes.

Figure 17-13 shows the content from a test email retrieved from a POP3 server. This rather short sample email arrives with considerable overhead in the header details. The message body is near the end, and it shows the email was sent using HTML content.

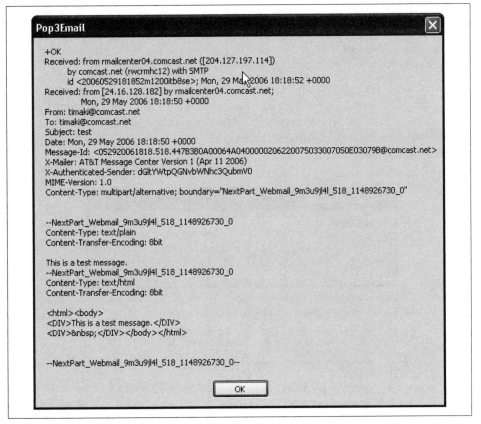

Figure 17-13. An email retrieved from a POP3 server

17.11 Sending a Message to Another Computer

Problem

You want to send a pop-up message to one or more users on your network, something they'll see right away without requiring any special third-party applications to be running on their computers.

Solution

Sample code folder: Chapter 17\SendMessage

Use Windows's *Net.exe* program to send instant messages to named computers on your network.

Discussion

The general syntax of the Net.exe command, when used to send instant messages, is of the form:

```
Net.exe Send ComputerName Message
```

You'll need to know the name of the computer to which you wish to send the message, or you may use "*" as the computer name to send a message to all computers on your network in one shot. If you specify a domain name as the target address, the message is delivered to all computers belonging to that domain.

You can use this command from a Command Prompt window, or you can use a Visual Basic 2005 application as a wrapper for the command. Create a new Windows Forms application, and add two TextBox controls named TargetComputer and MessageText. Also add a Button control named ActSend, and set its Text property to Send. Add informational labels if desired. The form should look something like Figure 17-14.

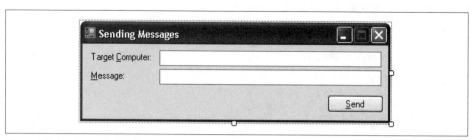

Figure 17-14. Controls for the message-sending sample

Now add the following code to the form's class template:

```
' ----- Send a message to another computer.
Process.Start("net.exe", _
    "send " & TargetComputer.Text & _
    " """ & MessageText.Text & """")
```

The message you send appears in a message box on the other computer, similar to Figure 17-15.

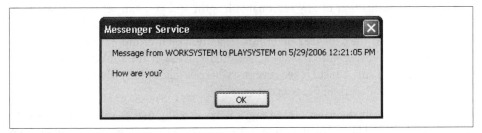

Figure 17-15. A message received by the other computer

Both the sending and the receiving computer(s) must have the Messenger service running, or the message won't be sent. To enable this service under Windows XP, try the following steps:

1. Click Start → Control Panel, and open the Administrative Tools panel.
2. Within the Administrative Tools panel, open Services.
3. Locate Messenger, and double-click its icon to open the Messenger Properties window.
4. Set the Startup Type to Automatic, and click the Start button.
5. Click the OK button, and close all open Control Panel windows.

This starts the Messenger service and causes it to restart each time Windows starts.

17.12 Adding Hyperlinks to a (Desktop) Form

Problem

You want to add a standard hypertext link to text on a Windows form, without resorting to HTML or other browser technology.

Solution

Use the LinkLabel control.

Discussion

The LinkLabel control is similar to a standard Label control, except that it has additional properties and events that provide the behavior expected of a hypertext link as displayed in a browser window. For example, the color of the link before being clicked the first time is determined by the LinkLabel's LinkColor property, and its color after it has been clicked is determined by its VisitedLinkColor property. The defaults for these colors work very well, and the results are much like what you expect after using a browser for any length of time.

The LinkLabel holds text of any reasonable length, and you can set all or just a part of the text as the active, clickable part by setting its LinkArea property. The Start and Length numbers in the LinkArea determine exactly which group of contiguous characters in the label are colored as an active link. Clicks on the LinkLabel within the LinkArea activate its LinkClicked event, whereas clicks anywhere else on the LinkLabel activate the usual Click event.

The code you put in the LinkClicked event is what really makes this control behave like a link should. The following code, for example, sets the LinkArea's LinkVisited property to True, which causes its VisitedLinkColor to show. It also creates a true link to an Internet URL, in this case opening a web site in the default browser:

```
Private Sub LinkLabel1_LinkClicked( _
        ByVal sender As System.Object, _
        ByVal e As System.Windows.Forms. _
        LinkLabelLinkClickedEventArgs) _
        Handles LinkLabel1.LinkClicked
    ' ----- Open that important web site.
    LinkLabel1.LinkVisited = True
    System.Diagnostics.Process.Start( _
        "http://www.oreilly.com/")
End Sub
```

Figure 17-16 shows a small dialog window that displays a single LinkLabel control. The LinkArea is set to the last part of the LinkLabel's text, and the previous code is activated when this area is clicked. Your default browser will then display very interesting O'Reilly Media pages for your enjoyment.

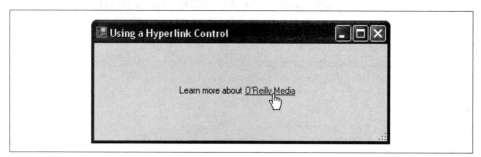

Figure 17-16. Using a LinkLabel to include a hyperlink on your form

Index

Symbols

& (ampersand), 7
&= concatenation shortcut, 145
* (asterisk), 489, 696
<< and >> (bit-shift operators), 226
(hash), 266
{{}} (nested braces), 240, 287
p (pi), calculating to thousands of
  digits, 218–222
? (question mark), 22, 490

A

About boxes, 53
Add New Item dialog, 47, 50
 template choices, 52
Add( ) method, 314, 315
AddHandler statement, 638
AddMemoryPressure( ) method, 582
ADO.NET, 526
 connection strings, 528
 providers, 527
 supported stored procedures, 535
 transactions, 536
AES (Advanced Encryption Algorithm), 648
alpha blending, 345
ampersand (&), 7
And operator, 226
angular calculations, limiting to a
  range, 191–193
animation
 drawing at runtime, 411–412
 from multiple bitmaps, 408
 from multiple images, 405–407

sprites, 412–416
with transparency, 393–395
Append( ) method, 108
application configuration file template, 56
Application.Run( ) method, 31
applications
 basic building blocks, 50
 class instances, initialization with
  data, 57–59
 classes, 47–50
  splitting across files, 63
 code modules, creating, 45–47
 command line, accessing, 31–33
  testing, 33
 Console (see Console applications)
 control via simulated
  keystrokes, 561–564
 instances, release of resources on
  termination, 59–61
 namespaces, 61
 obfuscating, 33–35
 object instances, creating, 56
 pausing execution, 560
 processes, terminating, 558
 running environment, identifying, 36
 running of multiple instances,
  prevention, 545
 running processes, listing, 557
 separate applications, starting by EXE,
  document, or URL, 554
 startup form, setting, 29
 strings, adding to resources, 159
 structures and other objects, passing and
  returning, 65

We'd like to hear your suggestions for improving our indexes. Send email to *index@oreilly.com*.

applications (*continued*)
  structures, creating, 50–52
  timing of application activities, 260
  user-specific settings, maintaining
      between uses, 617
  version numbers, 27
      automatic updating, 28
  Visual Basic-specific template
      choices, 52–56
  waiting for applications to finish, 556
  Web Forms Applications (see ASP.NET
      Web Forms applications)
  Windows Forms applications (see
      Windows Forms)
application-wide event handlers, 545
arctangents, calculating, 218
Array.Copy( ) method, 244
arrays
  converting between delimited strings and
      arrays, 306
  copying part of an array to
      another, 298–301
  CSV files, reading string arrays into, 302
  CSV files, writing from string arrays, 301
  filling during declaration, 286
  functions, returning from, 312
  iterating through elements of, 309
  methods, passing to, 310–312
  multivalue arrays, 304
  ReDim Preserve command, 297
  resizing without losing values, 297–298
  reversing oder of elements, 290
  shuffling, 294–295
  single strings, formatting as, 307–309
  Sort( ) method, 286
  sorting elements, 287–290
  values, inserting into arrays, 292
  values, swapping, 295
As Type clause, 189
ASP.NET button event handler, 18
  Enter key activation, enabling, 19
ASP.NET Web Forms applications, 13–20
  Convert button event handler, 18
  HTML mode, 15
  ListItem Collection Editor, 16
  new web site creation, 14
  RadioButtonList controls, 16
  source code, 18
  Toolbox, 14
assembly details, reading, 624–627
AssemblyInfo.vb file, 28

audio
  audio files, playing, 399
  beeps, playing, 404
authorization, usernames and passwords,
      prompting for, 653
axes, "nice", calculating, 375–377

B

background colors, setting, 335
BackgroundWorker control, 592
.bas file extension, 45
Base64 conversions from strings, 170
beeps, playing, 404
BeginTransaction( ) method, 537
bezier splines, 355–356
binary data, converting to hexadecimal
      strings, 113
binary files, reading and writing, 510
BinaryFormatter class, 523
BinaryReader and BinaryWriter classes, 510
BitArray object, 227
BitConverter object, 114
bitmap file template, 55
bitmaps, 332–335
bitwise operators, 225–227
.bmp file extension, 55
Boolean operators, 226
Byte integer type, 178
byte position access of files, 520

C

calendars, creating, 282
Capacity property, 109
cardinal splines, 357
case conversion on strings, 116
case sensitive string comparisons, 118
CByte( ) function, 186
Char object, 141
character tallies in strings, 122
character types, determining, 141
charts, drawing, 377–381
checksums, calculating on files, 515–518
CInt( ) function, 216
class diagram template, 55
class instances, initializing with data, 57–59
classes, 47–50, 59
  overloaded methods, 58
  splitting across files, 63
ClassesRoot field, 38
Clear( ) method, 324
Click event, 8–9

Clipboard object, 570–573
clipboard, accessing, 569–573
Clone( ) method, 300
code file template, 55
code modules, 45–47
    access keywords, 46
code snippets, 21–27
    Code Snippet Editor, 24
    Code Snippets Manager, 26
    directory locations, 26
    Microsoft XML snippet schema, 24
    new snippets, creating, 23–26
    prewritten, finding and using, 21–23
    sharing, 26
    .snippet files, 26
    snippet picker, accessing, 22
    XML code, 24
Collect( ) method, 583
CollectionCount( ) method, 583
collections, 313
    Count property, 317
    creating, 313
    generic collections, 605
    items, deleting from, 316
    items, inserting into, 315
    iterating through, 317
color gradients, 352
color images, converting to grayscale, 445
color, RGB, HSB, and HSL
        schemes, 383–387
ColorDialog control, 326, 383–387
colors
    background, setting, 335
colors, defining, 320
COM Class template, 53
CombinePath( ) method, 483
Command objects, 538
Command( ) function, 31, 547
comma-separated-values (CSV) files (see CSV
      files)
Commit( ) method, 537
compact operator notation, 175–178
    compact assignment operators, 176
Compare( ) method, 118, 119
CompareTo( ) method, 289
complex numbers, 201–204
compressing JPEG images, 417
    using for thumbnails, 424
compression and decompression
    of files, 658
    of strings, 656
    sample code, 668–670

Connection object, 527, 538
connection string builder class, 528
connection strings, 528
console application output, capturing, 621
Console applications
    output, capturing, 621
Console applications, creating, 10–13
    default code blocks, 10
    module naming and project
        properties, 10
    text and graphics, 13
Console.Beep( ) method, 404
constructors, 57
ControlChars.NewLine property, 128
controls, 4
    tooltips, adding to, 573
    (see also Windows Forms)
Convert.ToByte( ) method, 186
Convert.ToInteger( ) method, 216
coordinates, converting between cylindrical,
        rectangular, and
        spherical, 198–201
Copy( ) method, 301
CopyDirectory( ) method, 478
    showUI argument, 479
CopyFile( ) method, 511
count variable, 176
Cramer's Rule, 245
CreateDirectory( ) method, 477
CreateElement( ) method, 603
credit card verification, 619
cryptography
    crypto module, 664–668
    files, encrypting and decrypting, 650–653
    secure random numbers, generating, 662
    strings, encrypting and
        decrypting, 646–650
    with keys, 155
CryptoStream object, 652
Crystal Reports template, 54
CSV (comma-separated-values) files, 524
    string arrays, reading into, 302
    string arrays, writing from, 301
CType( ) function, 120
CurrentConfig field, 38
CurrentUser field, 38
cursor file template, 55
cursor, programatic repositioning, 584
custom constructors, 58
custom control template, 54
custom controls, 548

D

Data Definition Language (DDL), 530
Data Encryption Standard (DES), 648
Data Manipulation Language (DML), 530
data set template, 53
data, converting to strings, 161
DataAdapter object, 539
databases, 526–544
  ADO.NET, 526
  Command objects, 529
    methods, 530
  connecting to data providers, 526–529
  connection strings, 528
  in-memory data tables, creating
    manually, 541
  in-memory data tables, writing to XML
    files, 542
  queries, retrieving results from, 530
  query results, storing in
    memory, 537–541
  Read( ) method, 531
  SQL commands, issuing, 529
  SQL parameters, 532
  stored procedures, 534
  System.Data namespace, 526
  transactions, 536
  XML files, reading to in-memory data
    tables, 544
DataReader object, 530, 538
DataRow object, 542
DataSet object, 537, 539
  ReadXML( ) method, 544
  WriteXML( ) method, 543
DataTable object, 537, 539, 541
date and time, 255–285
  application activities, timing, 260
  calendars, creating, 282
  Data object, 255
  date and time values
    adding to, 271–273
    creating from parts, 266
    determining the day of week for, 276
    extracting hour, minute, and second
      numbers, 264
    extracting year, month, and day
      numbers, 263
    subtracting from, 273
  Date data type, 255
  Date object
    "Add" functions, 271
    DayOfWeek property, 276

DayOfYear property, 277
DaysInMonth function, 277
IsLeapYear( ) function, 284
Kind property, 258
storage formats, 257
Ticks property, 256, 258, 261
days between two dates,
  determining, 274
days in a month, determining, 277
form controls for date entry or
  selection, 278–280
formatting, 267–269
ISO 8601 formats, 284
leap year checks, 284
moon phases, calculating, 281
parsing and validation, 270
Stopwatch object, 262
system date and time, 255–257
system time zone, accessing, 257
ticks, calculating elapsed time with, 261
Date object
  DaysInMonth function, 278
DateTimePicker control, 278
DayOfWeek property, 276
DayOfYear property, 277
DaysInMonth function, 277, 278
DDL (Data Definition Language), 530
Decimal variables, 180
decimal variables, 184
default constructors, 58
degrees, converting to radians, 190
DeleteFile( ) method, 513
DES (Data Encryption Standard), 648
DescriptionAttribute attribute, 552
destructors, 59–61
development environments
  Code Snippet Editor (see code snippets)
Dialog forms, 52
Dim statement, 56, 286
directories
  browsing, 500
  copying, 478
  creating, 477
  monitoring for changes, 565–568
  moving, 480
  parsing file and directory paths, 483
  renaming, 481
  searching
    iterating through directories and
      subdirectories, 484
    wildcards, using for, 487

special user and Windows directories, accessing, 493–497

URL-based directory paths and My.Computer.Filesystem objects, 477

validating, 475

DirectoryExists( ) method, 476

display dimensions, getting at runtime, 439

display updates, limiting to regions, 359

disposal, 582

Dispose( ) method, 60, 581

DllImport attribute, 459

DML (Data Manipulation Language), 530

DoDragDrop( ) method, 576, 580

DoNotExpandEnvironmentNames flag, 39

Dotfuscator Community Edition, 34

Double numeric value, converting to Byte values, 186

double precision point variables, creating, 193

double precision variables, 183

DrawBezier( ) graphics method, 355

DrawCurve( ) method, 357

DrawImage( ) method, 334

Drawing.StringFormat class, 365

Drawing2D.FillMode.Winding mode, 344

DrawLine( ) method, 340

DrawString( ) method, 361, 365, 380

DriveInfo object, 498

  properties, 499

drives

  available space, determining, 498

  drive paths, 476

  enumerating, 473

DynData field, 38

E

ElapsedMilliseconds property, 260

ellipses, drawing, 336–340

email, sending via SMTP, 687

emails, POP3, accessing, 689–695

"Enable application framework" field, 29

encryption (see cryptography)

end-of-line characters, platform compatibility, 126

Enum statement, 66

enumerations, 66

  string and numeric values, conversions between, 68

Environ( ) function, 37

environment variables, 36

Environment.NewLine property, 126

Err.Raise method, 636

exceptions, 633–643

  catching, 633

    unhandled exceptions, 636

  exception information, displaying, 639

  ignoring in a block of code, 642

  new types, creating, 640

  On Error Resume Next statement, 642

  throwing, 635

exclusive-or bit manipulation, 181

ExecuteReader( ) method, 532

ExecuteScalar( ) method, 532

Explorer forms, 52

F

factorials, calculating with recursion, 224

file checksums, generating, 518

file compression, JPEGs, 417–420

FileExists( ) method, 490

FileInfo object, 503

files and file systems, 473–525

  attributes, getting and setting, 491

  available disk drive space, determining, 498

  binary files, reading and writing, 510

  CSV files, creating, 524

  directories (see directories)

  enumerating drives, 473

  file information, accessing, 502–504

  file-access methods, 504–508

  files, byte position access of, 520

  files, calculating checksums on, 515–518

  files, comparing for equality, 518

  files, compression and decompression, 658

  files, copying or moving, 511

  files, encryption and decryption, 650–653

  files, handle-based, opening modes, 506

  files, locking, 519

  files, reading and writing as strings, 508

  files, reading and writing objects in, 521–524

  files, sending to the Recycle Bin, 513

  files, validating, 490

  monitoring files for changes, 565–568

  parsing file and directory paths, 483

  searching (see searching)

  security, 473

  special user and Windows directories, accessing, 493–497

  stream-based file access, 507

  temporary files, 514

FileSystemWatcher object, 565–568
finalization, 582
Finalize( ) method, 60
floating-point variables, creating in double
    precision, 193
Floor( ) function, 216
FolderBrowserDialog class, 501
FolderBrowserDialog control, 500
Font objects, 321
For Each loops, 310, 317
For...Next loops, nested, 189
forms
    properties, setting, 5
    surface and controls, 4
        tab order, setting, 7
FreeFile( ) method, 505
Friend keyword, 46
FTP (File Transfer Protocol) file
    downloads, 682
FtpWebRequest class, 682

G

garbage collection, 60, 582
GDI+ graphics and methods, 319
GDI+ library printing commands, 457
generator object, 235
generics, 74–76
GetBit( ) function, 228
GetDirectories( ) method, 484, 487
GetDriveInfo( ) method, 498
GetEnvironmentVariable( ) method, 36
GetFileInfo( ) method, 491, 502
GetFiles( ) method, 487
GetGeneration( ) method, 583
GetHostAddresses( ) method, 679
GetHostEntry( ) method, 681
GetName( ) method, 483
GetObjectData( ) method, 521
GetParentPath( ) method, 483
GetPixel( ) method, 431
GetPropertyItem( ) method, 421
GetScreen( ) function, 436
GetTempFileName( ) method, 514
GetTotalMemory( ) method, 583
GetValue( ) method, 38, 39
gradients in color, 352
graph paper, creating and printing, 470–472
graphics
    "nice" axes, calculating, 375–377
    background colors, setting, 335
    bezier splines, 355–356
    bitmaps, creating, 332–335

cardinal splines, 357
charts, drawing, 377–381
color gradients, 352
color schemas (RGB, HSB, and
    HSL), 383–387
colors, defining, 320
controls, drawing on, 322–326
coordinate systems (pixels, inches,
    centimeters), 328–332
display updates, limiting to regions, 359
DrawBezier( ) method, 355
drawing lines, ellipses and
    rectangles, 336–340
enabling color selection by users, 326
forms or controls, forcing redraws
    of, 342–345
Graphics object, 321
graphics strings, height and width,
    measuring, 370–373
line controls, 396
methods replacing obsolete VB 6.0
    methods, 398
odd-shaped forms and controls,
    creating, 381
outline paths, 350
Paint event handler, 360
pixel-wide lines, 340–341
PointF structure, 193
Region object, 359
rubber-band selection, 387–392
scaling with tranforms, 347–350
shape controls, 396
text, drawing, 361–366
    mirroring on the canvas, 367
    rotating, 366
    with outlines and drop shadows, 373
transparency, 345
    animation, 393–395
VB 6.0, obsolete features, substituting
    for, 395–398
zooming the drawing area, 347–350
Graphics object, 319
    creating, 319–322
    drawing methods, 336
    DrawString( ) method, 380
    ScaleTransform( ) method, 332
    scaling, 328
    Transform property, 367
    TranslateTransform( ) method, 378
Graphics.DrawImage( ) method, 334
Graphics.DrawString( ) method, 361, 365
Graphics.MeasureString( ) method, 370

Graphics.PageUnit property, 472
GraphicsPath object, 350
    odd-shaped forms and controls, creating
        with, 381
    PathGradientBrush, 353
grayscale image conversions from color, 445
Gzip stream compression and
        decompression, 656
GZipStream class, 659

H

handle-based files, 506
hash generation, 644
HelpProvider controls, 616
hexadecimal strings, creating from binary
        data, 113
Hidden file attributes, viewing and
        updating, 491
hives, registry, 40
host name of remote computers,
        accessing, 680
HSB (HSV) and HSL color
        schemes, 383–387
HTML content, accessing, 675
HTML mode, 15
HTML page template, 55

I

I/O, serial, 627
icon file template, 55
icons, creating in System Tray, 568
IDisposable interface, 60, 581
ImageList controls, 405
images
    displaying while stretching and
        sizing, 424–428
    edge detection on, 448–451
    files, displaying, 401
    grayscale, converting to, 445
    merging, 431
    screen captures, 435–439
    scrolling, 429
    speeding up processing, 441–444
    using in application resources, 434
    (see also JPEG files)
IndexOf( ) method, 148
Inheritance Picker dialog, 64
inherited form template, 54
inherited user control template, 54
Insert( ) method, 109, 129
installer class template, 56

instances, releasing of resources on
        termination, 59–61
instant messaging, 696
Int( ) function, 216
integer types, 178–181
    conversion of numbers to, 216
    swapping integers, 181
    unsigned integers, 180
Integrated Security, 528
interface template, 53
internationalization, localizing of
        controls, 613–615
InteropServices.Marshal.LockBits( )
        method, 441
Invalidate( ) method, 342, 344
inverse of a matrix, 241
IP addresses
    of local computers, accessing, 679
    of remote computers, accessing, 680
    pinging, 681
IPHostEntry.HostName property, 681
IsAttached flag, 36
IsDate( ) function, 270
ISerializable interface, 521
ISerializable.GetObjectData( ) method, 521
IsLeapYear( ) function, 284
IsMatch( ) method, 169
IsNothing( ), IsNumeric( ), and IsDate( )
        functions, 137
IsNumeric( ) function, 215
ISO 8601 date and time format, 284

J

Join( ) method, 131, 301, 306
JPEG files
    extended information, extracting, 421
    resizing and compressing, 417–420
    thumbnail files, creating, 424

K

KeepAlive( ) method, 583
key press interception, 585
KeyPreview property, 585
keys, 39
Kill( ) method, 555, 558

L

LCase( ) and UCase( ) methods, 116
leap years, checking for, 284
lines, pixel width, drawing regardless of
        scaling, 340–341

LinkLabel control, 697
ListBox controls
    drag and drop addition of files to, 574
    drag and drop between controls, 576–580
listing running processes, 557
ListItem Collection Editor, 16
LocalMachine field, 38
LockBits( ) method, 442
LockImage class, 452–456
locking files, 519
Login forms, 53
LoginForm dialog, 654
Long integer type, 179
loop counters, declaring within loops, 189
Luhn Algorithm, 619

M

Main( ) method, 30
"Make single instance application" field, 32
Managed HTML Document Object Model
        (DOM), 675, 676
managed memory, 582
MatchCollection object, 165
Matches( ) method, 163
math operations (see numerical and math
        operations)
Math.IEEERemainder( ) function, 281
Math.Round( ) function, 188
matrices, 240
    calculating determinants of, 243
    inverse of a matrix, 241
    matrix transformations, 370
MD5 hash, 644
.mdf file extension, 53
MDI (Multi Document Interface) parent
        forms, 53
messaging other computers, 696
method overloading, 69
Microsoft XML snippet schema, 24
Mod operator, 192
module template, 53
modulus 10 formula, 619
MonthCalendar control, 283
Morse code, converting strings to, 158
mouse, programmatic repositioning, 584
MoveDirectory( ) method, 480
    ShowUI argument, 481
MoveFile( ) method, 511
MS-DOS, 473
Multi Document Interface (MDI) parent
        forms, 53

multimedia
    animation (see animation)
    audio files, playing, 399
    beeps, playing, 404
    images and image files (see images)
    JPEG files
        extended information, extracting, 421
        resizing and compressing, 417–420
        thumbnails, creating, 424
    resource images, 434
    user's screen dimensions, getting, 439
    video files, playing, 403
multivalue arrays, 304
My namespace, 41–43
My.Application.CommandLineArgs
        collection, 31
My.Computer.Audio class
    Play( ) method, 400
    PlaySystemSound( ) method, 399
My.Computer.Clipboard object, 570
My.Computer.FileSystem class
    CopyDirectory( ) method, 478
    CreateDirectory( ) method, 477
    DeleteFile( ) method, 513
    DirectoryExists( ) method, 476
    Drives collection, 473
    FileExists( ) method, 490
    GetDirectories( ) method, 484, 487
    GetDriveInfo( ) method, 498
    GetFileInfo( ) method, 491, 502
    GetFiles( ) method, 487
    GetTempFileName( ) method, 514
    MoveDirectory( ) method, 480
    MoveFile( ) method, 511
    OpenTextFileWriter( ) method, 524
    RenameDirectory( ) method, 482
    SpecialDirectories object, 494
    WriteAllBytes( ) method, 510
My.Computer.Keyboard.SendKeys( )
        method, 561
My.Computer.Network.Ping( ) method, 682
My.Computer.Ports.OpenSerialPort( )
        method, 628
My.Computer.Registry object, 586
My.Settings object, 617
My.User.Name property, 44
My.WebServices object, 684
MyApplication_StartupNextInstance event
        handler, 546

N

Namespace statement, 62
namespaces, 61
    .NET library (DLL) namespaces, naming
        of, 62
nested braces, 287
.NET Framework
    cryptography services, 645
    garbage collection, 60, 582
    Gzip stream compression and
        decompression, 656
    hashing and encryption algorithms, 517
    method overloading, 69
    reflection, 627
    System.Exception objects, 634
    Throw statement, 636
    types, 51
    threading support, 594
Net.exe program, 696
New keyword, 56
New Project Dialog, 1
New( ) method, 197, 203
NewRow( ) method, 542
"nice" axes, calculating, 375–377
Not operator, 226
NotifyIcon control, 568
Now property, 255–257
Now.Ticks property, 258
number sign character (#), 266
number types
    conversions, 185–187
        integer conversions, 216
numbers, formatting into strings, 134
numbers, rounding, 188
numerical and math operations
    angular calculations, limiting to a
        range, 191–193
    bits, storage and retrieval in
        BitArrays, 227–230
    bitwise operators, 225–227
    compact operator notation, 175–178
    complex numbers, 201–204
    conversions between radians and
        degrees, 190
    decimal variables, 184
    factorials, calculating with recursion, 224
    integers, swapping, 181
    loop counters, declaring within
        loops, 189
    matrices, calculating determinants of, 243
    matrices, creating, 240
    matrices, inverting, 241

number to integer conversions, 216
number type conversions, 185–187
pi, calculating to thousands of
        digits, 218–222
point variables, creating in double
        precision, 193
prime factors, calculating, 222
random number generation (see random
        number generation)
rectangular and polar coordinates,
        converting between, 195–197
rectangular, spherical, and cylindrical
        coordinates, converting
        between, 198–201
rounding numbers, 188
signed and unsigned variable types, sizing
        of, 178–180
simultaneous equations, 245
single and double precision variables, 183
three-dimensional variables, creating, 197
triangles, solving, 208–215
    right triangles, 204–208
unsigned integers, 180
validating numbers in strings, 215
Xor operators, 181

O

obfuscating an application, 33–35
object disposal, 580
object instances, 56
ODBC, 528
OLE DB, 528
On Error Resume Next statement, 642
Opacity property, 345
OpenFileDialog class, 401
OpenSerialPort( ) method, 628
OpenSubKey( ) method, 591
OpenTextFileWriter( ) method, 524
operator overloading, 70–73
Option Explicit and Option Strict
        settings, 186
Optional keyword, 59
Or operator, 226
Oracle, 527
outline paths, 350
overloading
    of methods, 58
    overloadable operators, 70–73
    overriding, compared to, 70
Overloads keyword, 58, 69
overriding, compared to overloading, 70

P

PadCenter( ) method, 150
PadLeft( ) and PadRight( ) methods, 150
PageSetupDialog class, 464
PageUnit property, 340
Paint event handler, 320, 360
Paint events, 323
Parse( ) method, 68, 144, 271
partial class, 63
Partial keyword, 63
password security, 655
passwords and usernames, prompting
    for, 653
PATH environment variable, retrieving, 37
PathGradientBrush object, 353
Pen objects, 320
Pen, setting pixel width line for, 340
PerformanceData field, 38
pi, calculating to thousands of
    digits, 218–222
PictureBox control
    image display while stretching and
        sizing, 424–428
    scrolling images, 429
    SizeMode setting, 425
Ping( ) method, 682
pinging an IP address, 681
PointF structure, 193, 195
PointToClient( ) method, 585
PointToScreen( ) method, 585
polar coordinates, converting to
    rectangular, 195–197
POP3 emails, accessing, 689–695
prime factors, calculating, 222
Print command, VB 6.0, 321
PrintDocument object, 466
    PrintController.IsPreview property, 468
PrintDocument object, for accessing printer
    default info, 461
printers and printing, 457–472
    bypassing the printer driver, 458–461
    default printer details, accessing, 461
    enumerating printers, 457
    graph paper, creating, 470–472
    installed printers, 457
    print destination, determining, 468
    print previews, creating, 462
    prompting users for page settings, 464
    "raw" data, printing, 458–461
    text and graphics, drawing to
        printers, 466

PrintPage event, 466
PrintPreviewDialog class, 462–464
Private keyword, 47
procedures, running in threads, 592–596
Process.Start( ) method, 400, 403, 554, 556
processes, listing running, 557
processes, terminating, 558
programming techniques
    adding tooltips to controls, 573
    application completion, waiting for, 556
    application control via simulated
        keystrokes, 561–564
    applications, preventing multiple
        instances, 545
    applications, startup within other
        applications, 554
    assembly detail, reading, 624–627
    clipboard, accessing, 569–573
    console application output,
        capturing, 621
    credit card verification, 619
    cursor (mouse), repositioning, 584
    file and directory changes,
        monitoring, 565–568
    garbage disposal, 582
    generic collections, 605
    key presses, interception on a form, 585
    ListBox controls, drag and drop addition
        of files to, 574
    ListBox controls, dragging and dropping
        between, 576–580
    listing running processes, 557
    object disposal, 580
    processes, terminating, 558
    program execution, pausing, 560
    rebooting, 629–632
    registry, accessing, 586–591
    screen savers, 607–612
    serial I/O, 627
    System Tray icons, creating, 568
    threads, running procedures in, 592–596
    user control properties, describing, 552
    user controls, creating, 548–551
    user-specific application settings,
        maintaining between uses, 617
    Windows Forms controls
        localization, 613–615
        pop-up controls, adding, 616
    XML documents, 599–604
        validating, 604
    XML, reading into a tree view, 596–599
programs, pausing execution of, 560

projects, 3
  creating, 1
Properties window, 5
Public keyword, 46

Q

QueryPageSettings event, 469
question mark (?), 22

R

radians, converting to degrees, 190
RadioButtonList controls, 16
random number generation, 662
  algorithms, string shuffling with, 154
  exponential-distribution random
      numbers, 239
  normal-distribution random
      numbers, 237
  random integers, generation within a
      range, 234
  random real numbers, generation within a
      range, 236
  Visual Basic's pseudorandom number
      generator, enhancing, 230–234
Random object, 157
Randomize( ) method, 230
Read Only file attributes, viewing and
      updating, 491
ReadAllText( ) method, 508
ReadXML( ) method, 544
rebooting, 629–632
rectangles, drawing, 336–340
rectangular coordinates, converting to
      polar, 195–197
rectangular, spherical and cylindrical
      coordinates, converting
      between, 198–201
recursion, using to calculate factorials, 224
ReDim Preserve statement, 297
reference types, 51
Refresh( ) method, 324, 342
refreshing graphics, 342–345
Regex object, 163
Regex.Matches( ) method, 149
Region object, 359
registry, 37–40
  accessing, 586–591
  hives, keys and values, 39
  password hashes, storing in, 655
  system registry, 591
Registry object, 38

RegistryKey class, 591
RegistryKey objects and members, 38
RegistryKey.OpenSubKey( ) method, 591
RegistryKey.SetValue( ) method, 591
regular expression object, 148
regular expressions
  compiling for speed, 166
  counting characters, words, or lines, 169
  counting matches of, 164
  data validation using, 168
  extracting numbers from strings, 162
  matches, counting, 164
  matching the Nth regular expression, 165
Remove( ) method, 109, 316
RemoveMemoryPressure( ) method, 583
Rename( ) function, 482
RenameDirectory( ) method, 482
Replace( ) method, 109, 126, 128
  doublespacing, 133
  tabs, converting to spaces, 152
Report template, 54
ReRegisterForFinalize( ) method, 583
Resize( ) method, 298
resource images, 434
resources file template, 55
.resx file extension, 55
RGB color scheme, 383–387
right triangles, solving, 204–208
RijndaelManaged object, 648
Rnd( ) function, 230
Rollback( ) method, 537
RotateTransform( ) method, 367, 370
Round( ) function, 216
rounding numbers, 188
.rpt file extension, 54
rubber-band selection, 387–392
RunWorkerAsync( ) method, 594

S

SByte integer type, 178
ScaleTransform( ) method, 332, 341, 347,
      349, 370
screen captures, 435–439
screen dimensions, getting at runtime, 439
Screen object, 439
screen savers, 607–612
  command-line options, 612
searching
  iterating through directories and
      subdirectories, 484
  wildcards in file and directory
      searches, 487

security
    hashes, generating, 644
    passwords, secure handling, 655
    usernames and passwords, prompting
        for, 653
    (see also cryptography)
Seek( ) method, 520
Send( ) method, 688
SendKeys( ) method, 561–564
    key sequences, 562
serial I/O, 627
serialization, 521
SerializationInfo object, 522
SetPixel( ) method, 431
.settings file template, 55
SetValue( ) method, 38
Shared keyword, 46
Shell( ) function, 555
Short integer type, 179
ShowDialog( ) method, 464
shuffling algorithm for string shuffling, 154
Sieve of Eratosthenes, 228
signed variable types
    size, choosing, 178–180
simultaneous equations, 245
single precision variables, 183
SMTP, using to send email, 687
snippet picker, 22
snippets (see code snippets)
Solution Explorer, 3
Sort( ) method, 286, 287–290
SoundPlayer class, 400
Space( ) function, 173
SpecialDirectories object, 494
SpecialFolder enumeration values and
        members, 495
spherical, rectangular, and cylindrical
        coordinates, converting
        between, 198–201
Splash Screen forms, 53
Split( ) function, 124, 131, 172, 303, 306
sprites, 412–416
SQL commands, issuing, 529
SQL database template, 53
SQL parameters, 532
SQL Server, 527
SqlCommand class, 530
SqlTransaction object, 537
standard operators, using custom classes
        in, 70–73
Start( ) method, 260

startup code, setting to a Sub Main
        procedure, 30
StartupNextInstance, 32
Stopwatch object, 260, 262
stored procedures, 534
StrConv( ) function, 116
StrDup( ) function, 110, 174
streams, 507
StreamWriter object, 524
String( ) function
    VB 6 version, 110
String.Split( ) method, 131, 172
StringBuilder object, 107–109
    Append( ) method, 108
    buffer, 109
    Capacity property, 109
    concatenation using, 145
    methods, 109
    string manipulation, speeding up, 146
    strings, removing whitespace from, 125
    ToString( ) method, 109, 111
StringFormat object, 361
strings
    application resources, adding to, 159
    arrays, formatting as single
        strings, 307–309
    Base64, converting to, 170
    binary data, converting to hexadecimal
        strings, 113
    byte arrays, converting to and from, 121
    case, converting, 116
    character arrays, converting to and
        from, 120
    character types, determining, 141
    characters or strings, inserting into, 129
    characters, counting, 122
    Chars( ) property, 120
    Compare( ) method, 118, 119
    comparison incorporating case
        sensitivity, 118
    comparison without case sensitivity, 119
    compression and decompression, 656
    concatenating, 144
    converting between delimited strings and
        arrays, 306
    creating of N identical characters, 109
    creating through N repetitions of a
        string, 111
    CType( ) function, 120
    data type identification and
        validation, 137
    data, converting to, 161

double spacing, 133
encoding systems, conversion
        between, 139
encrypting with a key, 155
encryption and decryption, 646–650
files, reading and writing as, 508
Insert( ) method, 129
IsNothing( ), IsNumeric( ), and IsDate( )
        functions, 137
Join( ) method, 131
LCase( ) and UCase( ) methods, 116
Morse code, converting to, 158
numbers, formatting into strings, 134
obfuscating, 112
padding for length and alignment, 150
parsing, 143
regular expressions (see regular
        expressions)
Replace( ) method, 126, 128
    doublespacing, 133
reversing, 153
sets of characters, trimming from, 136
shuffling, 154
space character strings of N quantity,
        creating, 173
speeding up manipulation, 146
Split( ) function, 124, 131
splitting, 172
strings, converting to Morse code, 158
Substring( ) method, 107
substrings, counting occurences of, 148
substrings, extracting from, 115
substrings, replacing, 128
tabs, converting to spaces, 151
ToUpper( ) and ToLower( ) methods, 116
Trim( ), TrimStart( ), and TrimEnd( )
        methods, 136
valid numbers in, verifying, 215
whitespace, removing from, 125
words in, counting, 124
(see also StringBuilder object), 107
strong data typing in weakly typed
        collections, 73–76
StrReverse( ) function, 153
structures, 50–52
    passing and returning, 65
Substring( ) method, 107
Subtract( ) method, 274, 275
SuppressFinalize( ) method, 583
surface, 4
SyncLock statements, 595

system date and time, 255–257
system information, accessing, 40–44
system reboots, 629–632
system registry, 591
system ticks, 258
system time zone, accessing, 257
System Tray icons, creating, 568
System.Collections.Generic namespace, 605
System.Data namespace, 526
System.Data.SqlClient class
    SqlCommand class, 530
    SqlConnectionStringBuilder, 528
System.Diagnostics class
    Debugger.IsAttached flag, 36
    Process class, 557
    Process.Start( ) method, 554, 556
    Stopwatch object, 260, 262
System.Drawing class
    Color structure, 387
    Graphics object, 336
    Printing.PrinterSettings.InstalledPrinters
        collection, 458
System.Environment.SpecialFolder
        enumeration values and
        members, 495
System.Exception class, 634
System.GC object, 582
System.GC.MaxGeneration property, 582
System.IO class
    Compression namespace
        GZipStream class, 656
    DriveInfo object, 474, 498
    FileInfo object
        Attributes property, 491
    FileStream object, 519
System.IOclass
    DriveInfo object
        properties, 499
System.Net class
    Dns namespace, 679, 680
    FtpWebRequest class, 682
    Mail.SmtpClient class, 688
    Sockets namespace, 689
System.Reflection namespace, 624
System.Security.Cryptography
        namespace, 662
System.Text class
    Encoding functions, 139
    Encoding object, 121
    RegularExpressions.Regex object, 148
System.Threading.Thread.Sleep( )
        method, 560

System.Windows.Forms class
    Cursor object, 584
    SystemInformation object, 41
System.Xml.XmlDocument object, 599

T

targets, 3
TcpClient class, 689
temperature conversion application
    ASP.NET Web Forms version, 13–20
    Console version, 10–13
    Windows Forms version, 1–9
temporary files, 514
terminating running processes, 558
text file template, 55
text, drawing, 361–366
    mirroring on the canvas, 367
    outlines and drop shadows, 373
    rotating, 366
TextBox control, 279
TextChanged event, 279
Thread.Sleep( ) method, 560
threads, 592–596
three-dimensional variables, creating, 197
Throw statement, 636
thumbnails, creating, 424
Ticks property, 256, 258, 261
time (see date and time)
TimeChanged public event, 550
TimeSpan object, 263, 275
TimeZone object, 257
Toolbox, 4
ToolTip control, 573
tooltips, adding to controls, 573
ToShortDateString andToShortTimeString
    properties, 256
ToString( ) method, 68, 109, 111, 114, 144,
    161, 194, 307
    displaying exception information
        using, 639
    Triangle class, 214
ToUniversalTime( ) method, 282
ToUpper( ) and ToLower( ) methods, 116
TrackBar control, 357
transactional component template, 56
transactions, 536
TranslateTransform( ) method, 370, 378
transparency, 345
    animation, 393–395
TransparencyKey property, 345
TreeView control, 599

triangles, solving, 208–215
    right triangles, 204–208
Trim( ), TrimStart( ), and TrimEnd( )
    methods, 136
Try...Catch...Finally block statement, 633
two-dimensional arrays versus multivalue
    arrays, 304

U

UCase( ) and LCase( ) methods, 116
UInt16 integer type, 179
UInteger integer type, 179
ULong integer type, 179
UnhandledException event handler, 636
Unicode encoding conversions, 139
unmanaged memory, 582
unsigned integers, 180
unsigned variable types
    size, choosing, 178–180
User Control template, 54
user controls, 548
    control properties, describing, 552
user controls, creating, 548–551
user's name, accessing, 44
usernames and passwords, prompting
    for, 653
Users field, 38
Using statement, 61
UTF7, UTF8, and UTF32 encoding
    conversions, 139

V

validation of numbers in strings, 215
value types, 51
values, 39
variables, As Type clause, 189
variables in three dimensions, creating, 197
vbNewLine constant, 127, 131
version numbers, 27
    automatic updating, 28
video files, playing, 403
Visual Basic 2005
    compiler, 21
    versions and cost, xxi
Visual Basic 6.0
    date and time storage formats, 257
    obsolete graphics features, substitutes
        for, 395–398
    string insertion, 130
Visual Studio 2005, 21
    code snippets (see code snippets)

W

WaitForExit( ) method, 556
WaitForInputIdle( ) method, 556
WaitForPendingFinalizers( ) method, 584
Web custom control template, 54
web development, 671–698
    email, sending with SMTP, 687
    FTP downloads, 682
    host name or IP address resolution for
        remote computers, 680
    hyperlinks, adding to forms, 697
    IP addresses, pinging, 681
    links, collecting from web pages, 676
    local computer IP address, getting, 679
    messaging other computers, 696
    POP3 emails, accessing, 689–695
    web pages, displaying on a
        form, 671–675
    web pages, extracting information
        from, 675
    XML Web Services, accessing, 684
WebBrowser control, 671
whitespace, removing from strings, 125
wildcards, 487
Windows file system security, 473
Windows Forms, 52
    basic forms, using to create new ones, 64
    Click event, 8–9
    controls
        date entry or selection, 278–280
        drawing on controls, 322–326
        forcing refreshes, 342–345
        localizing controls, 613–615
        odd-shaped forms and controls, 381
        pop-up controls, adding to, 616
        TextBox control, 279
        TextChanged event, 279
        user control properties,
            describing, 552
        web pages, displaying on a
            form, 671–675
    creating, 1–9
    form properties, setting, 5
    host names or IP addresses of remote
        computers, accessing, 680
    hyperlinks, adding to, 697

key press interception, 585
links, collecting from web pages, 676
New Project Dialog, 1
project creation, 1
Properties Window, 5
Solution Explorer, 3
startup form, setting, 29
tab order, setting, 7
text, drawing, 362
text, drawing with outlines, drop
    shadows, 373
Toolbox, 4
user controls, creating, 548–551
web pages, extracting HTML content
    from, 675
Windows Management Instrumentation
    (WMI), 458
Windows registry (see registry)
Windows service template, 56
winres.exe application, 614
winspool.drv library, 459
WMI (Windows Management
    Instrumentation), 458
words, counting in strings, 124
WriteAllBytes( ) method, 510
WriteAllText( ) method, 301, 508
WriteXML( ) method, 543

X

XML documents, 599–604
    validating, 604
XML file template, 55
XML Schema template, 55
XML snippet schema, 24
XML Web Service, accessing, 684
XML, reading into a tree view, 596–599
XmlDocument.CreateElement( )
    method, 603
XmlReaderSettings class, 605
Xor operators, 181, 226
.xsd file extension, 53
XSLT file template, 55

Z

zooming users' views, 347–350

About the Authors

Tim Patrick is a software architect and developer with over 20 years of experience in designing and building custom solutions. His very first computer program was written in BASIC. While he has used other programming languages over the years, today he spends most of his time using a descendant of that same BASIC language: Visual Basic 2005. He is a Microsoft Certified Solution Developer (MCSD). Tim's recent books include *The Visual Basic .NET Style Guide* (Pearson Education) and the third edition of O'Reilly's *Visual Basic 2005 in a Nutshell*. He has also published many magazine articles on topics related to Visual Basic development.

John Clark Craig has programmed in just about every version of the BASIC language available. He has authored over a dozen books on Visual Basic and other programming topics praised for their utility and ease of use. During his career as a software engineer, John has worked on several fascinating astronomical, energy, and environmental projects, including several of the world's largest solar energy and wind-power production facilities. His current projects combine the power of Visual Basic Express with microcontroller-based robotics inventions, bringing the power of Visual Basic to an exciting new field of applications.

Colophon

The animal on the cover of *Visual Basic 2005 Cookbook* is a bream. "Bream" is the name given to a variety of salt and freshwater fish included in the genera *Abramis*. They are generally tall, narrow fish, between 14–33 inches and 2–13 pounds. There are many species of bream, including the *Abramis ballerus*, or blue bream.

Another type of bream, the carp bream (*Abramis brama*), can be found in northern Europe, from France to the Caspian Sea. They are silvery green with a white belly, and they live in slow-moving or still freshwater. Carp bream spawn between April and June, when the females lay from 100,000 to 300,000 eggs, which hatch after 3 to 12 days. The fish mature in three to four years.

Bream are bottom-feeders, consuming plankton, plants, insects, worms, snails, slugs, and bivalves such as clams, scallops, and oysters. They are considered a popular sport fish, and can be caught year round with a fishing rod using bait such as maggots and chopped worms.

The cover image is from *The Riverside Natural History*. The cover font is Adobe ITC Garamond. The text font is Linotype Birka; the heading font is Adobe Myriad Condensed; and the code font is LucasFont's TheSans Mono Condensed.

Better than e-books

Buy *Visual Basic 2005 Cookbook* and access
the digital edition FREE on Safari for 45 days.

Go to www.oreilly.com/go/safarienabled
and type in coupon code WTHT-1Q1I-WY15-4NI9-ZG5C

Search
thousands of
top tech books

Download
whole chapters

Cut and Paste
code examples

Find
answers fast

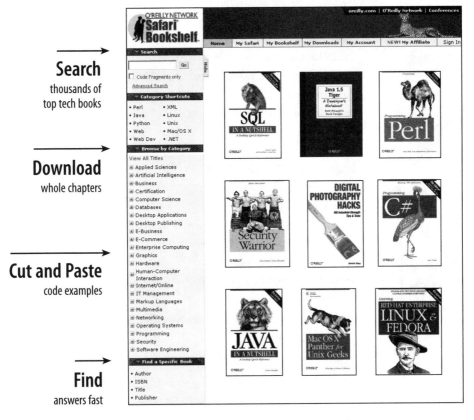

Search Safari! The premier electronic reference
library for programmers and IT professionals.

Related Titles from O'Reilly

.NET

ADO.NET Cookbook

ASP.NET 2.0 Cookbook

ASP.NET 2.0: A Developer's Notebook

C# Cookbook, *2nd Edition*

C# in a Nutshell, *2nd Edition*

C# Language Pocket Guide

Learning C# 2005, *2nd Edition*

.NET and XML

.NET Gotchas

Programming .NET Components, *2nd Edition*

Programming .NET Security

Programming .NET Web Services

Programming ASP.NET, *3rd Edition*

Programming Atlas

Programming C#, *4th Edition*

Programming MapPoint in .NET

Programming Visual Basic 2005

Programming Windows Presentation Foundation

Visual Basic 2005: A Developer's Notebook

Visual Basic 2005 Cookbook

Visual Basic 2005 in a Nutshell, *3rd Edition*

Visual Basic 2005 Jumpstart

Visual C# 2005: A Developer's Notebook

Visual Studio Hacks

Windows Developer Power Tools

XAML in a Nutshell

Our books are available at most retail and online bookstores.

To order direct: 1-800-998-9938 • *order@oreilly.com* • *www.oreilly.com*

Online editions of most O'Reilly titles are available by subscription at *safari.oreilly.com*